KEY SEQUENCE	COMMAND
F7	**Exit Key** Save and clear screen; save and exit; clear screen without saving; exit WordPerfect.
Alt-F7	**Math/Columns Key** With Math on: (1) Math on/off toggle, (2) calculate, (3) Column on/off toggle, (4) define newspaper or parallel columns, (5) display columns side by side. With Math off, option 2 becomes define math columns.
Ctrl-F7	**Footnote Key** (1) Create footnote, (2) edit footnote, (3) renumber footnotes, (4) options, (5) create endnote, (6) edit endnote.
Shift-F7	**Print Key** (1) Print full text, (2) print page, (3) change print options temporarily, (4) printer control screen, (5) Type-thru (typewriter mode), (6) preview document.
F8	**Underline Key** Underline on/off toggle; with Block on, underline defined block.
Alt-F8	**Page Format Key** (1) Page-number position, (2) new page number, (3) center page top to bottom, (4) page length, (5) top margin, (6) headers or footers, (7) page-number column position, (8) suppress for current page only, (9) conditional end of page, (A) widow/orphan protection. With Block on, prevents block from being split by a page break.
Ctrl-F8	**Print formatting** (1) Pitch, font, (2) lines per inch, (3) right justification off, (4) right justification on; (5–8) underline style; (9) sheet feeder bin number; (A) insert printer command; (B) line numbering on/off.
Shift-F8	**Line Format Key** (1), (2) Tabs, (3) margins, (4) line spacing, (5) hyphenation, (6) alignment character.
F9	**Merge Return Key** Designate end of a field in a secondary merge file; end of text input for a field in a merge operation from the keyboard.
Alt-F9	**Merge Codes Key** Display menu of 12 merge codes.
Ctrl-F9	**Merge/Sort Key** (1) Merge, (2) sort and select, (3) sorting sequences.
Shift-F9	**Merge End Key** Designate the end of a record in a secondary merge file.
F10	**Save Key** Save document on screen to disk.
Shift-F10	**Retrieve Key** Retrieve file from disk and copy it to the screen.
Ctrl-F10	**Macro Define Key** Record all keystrokes in a macro file.
Alt-F10	**Invoke Macro Key** Start a previously defined macro.

CURSOR MOVEMENT

KEY SEQUENCE	COMMAND	KEY SEQUENCE	COMMAND
↓	Move one line down.	↑	Move one line up.
←	Move one position left.	→	Move one position right.
Ctrl-←	Move one word left.	Ctrl-→	Move one word right.
PgDn	Move one page down (top of next page).	PgUp	Move one page up (top of previous page).
+ (numeric keypad)	Move one screen down.	− (numeric keypad)	Move one screen up.
Home-↓	Move one screen down.	Home-↑	Move one screen up.
Home Home ↑	Move to beginning of file.	Home Home ↓	Move to end of file.
Home Home Home ←	Move to left edge of screen before codes.	Home Home Home →	Move to right edge of screen before codes.
Home-←	Move to left edge of screen.	Home-→	Move to right edge of screen.
Ctrl-Home ↑	Move to top of current page.	Ctrl-Home ↓	Move to bottom of current page.
Ctrl-Home *n*	Go to page *n*.	Ctrl-Home <*character*>	Go to next occurrence of *character*.
Esc <*n*> ↑ (*or* ↓)	Move up or down *n* lines.	Esc <*n*> → (*or* ←)	Move right or left *n* spaces.
Esc *n* <*command*>	Repeat *command n* times.		

WORDPERFECT
DESKTOP COMPANION

WORDPERFECT™
DESKTOP COMPANION

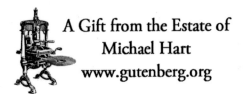

A Gift from the Estate of
Michael Hart
www.gutenberg.org

Greg Harvey
Kay Yarborough Nelson

SYBEX®

SAN FRANCISCO · PARIS · DÜSSELDORF · LONDON

SYBEX Ready Reference Series
Editor in Chief: Dr. Rudolph S. Langer
Managing Editor: Karl Ray
Series Editor: Barbara Gordon
Project Editor: David Kolodney
Editor: Judy Ziajka

Screen printing in this book was produced with XenoFont from XenoSoft, Berkeley, CA.

Canon is a trademark of Canon, Inc.
Centronics is a trademark of Centronics Inc.
dBASE III, dBASE III PLUS and MultiMate are trademarks of Ashton-Tate, Inc.
DIF is a trademark of Software Arts, Inc.
Epson is a trademark of Epson America, Inc.
Hyperion is a trademark of Bytec-Comterm, Inc.
IBM PC, AT, 3270 PC, IBM Graphics Printer, and DisplayWrite III are trademarks of International Business Machines Corporation.
LaserJet, LaserJet 500 +, and LaserJet Plus are trademarks of Hewlett-Packard Corporation.
MS-DOS is a trademark of Microsoft Corporation.
Paradox is a trademark of Ansa Software.
R:BASE 5000, R:BASE System V, and Microrim are trademarks of Microrim.
WordPerfect is a trademark of WordPerfect Corporation.
WordStar is a trademark of MicroPro International Corporation.

SYBEX is a registered trademark of SYBEX, Inc.

SYBEX is not affiliated with any manufacturer.

Library of Congress Card Number: 87-60802
ISBN 0-89588-402-X
Printed by Haddon Craftsmen
Manufactured in the United States of America
10 9 8 7 6 5 4 3 2 1

In memory of Joshua, much loved and sorely missed

—G.H. & K.Y.N.

TABLE OF CONTENTS

APPENDIXES:

LIST OF TABLES

FOREWORD

Greg Harvey is one of my favorite people. Not only is he brilliant, witty, and sensitive, I think he knows more about computers than anyone else I know. He also loves teaching and being around people, which makes me wonder why he lives like a hermit, working fifteen hours a day, seven days a week to produce this series....

Luckily for us, Greg and his coauthor Kay Nelson also love to write, and it shows in this wonderful book, The *WordPerfect Desktop Companion.* As a complement to my book, *Mastering WordPerfect,* it is ideal. Although it is not intended as a tutorial, the book offers a solid introduction and grounding in the basics of the program's many features. For the user with more experience, the book provides a wealth of information, tips, advice, and assistance that you won't find anywhere else, not even in the WordPerfect manual. For those who simply need a quick but thorough reference when they are stuck, this is it.

The *WordPerfect Desktop Companion* is, in fact, the most complete collection of information about WordPerfect I have ever seen. I can't wait to get my hands on the published edition, at which point I plan to go into total seclusion and read it from cover to cover (dream on). If you really want to know everything there is to know about this fabulous program, you'll do the same.

Susan Baake Kelly
Author, *Mastering WordPerfect*

PREFACE

The *WordPerfect Desktop Companion* was designed to meet an unfulfilled need. Although a great number of excellent basic and advanced books about WordPerfect can take you through the necessary learning steps, none is specifically designed to help you while you are actually using the program and also to assist you in applying the specialized tasks that WordPerfect can perform to a practical work environment. In addition, few books currently available provide you with a library of word processing macros that can be adapted to your work habits and preferences.

The idea behind this book is simple: When you are stymied by a function that does not work as you intended, a command that produces unpredicted results, or a macro that refuses to give up its bugs, you need a single source of information that can help you quickly solve the problem at hand so that you can get on with your work.

When this book was in its planning stages, we looked carefully at alternative ways of organizing its material. At first, the alternatives appeared straightforward: This book could be either a dictionary reference, alphabetically listing all of the commands and functions, or a topical reference, presenting the commands and functions in general discussions.

However, we finally settled on a third structure: We made this book a topical reference with particular WordPerfect features organized according to their functions—such as editing documents or formatting pages—but it also includes specific, structured reference entries that summarize the program's functions and present the key sequences to follow.

USING THE APPLICATION SECTIONS AND REFERENCE ENTRIES

To distinguish between the application and discussion sections and the reference entries, we use two conventions. First, because WordPerfect supports keystroke macros, we provide exact key sequences, indicated by a bold vertical bar, at the beginning of each reference entry to which a key sequence applies. You can use these keystroke sequences as building blocks for the macros you create in WordPerfect. Second, in the index we show reference-entry page numbers in boldface type. If you are simply looking for a step-by-step technique, you can turn directly to the bold-faced page numbers. If you want additional information about ways to apply the technique in your work or tips on how to use it with other techniques, you can refer to the page numbers shown in regular type in the index.

You can use the reference entries to refresh your memory about a certain key sequence or review a basic technique. You do not need to read the more detailed discussion to obtain the information you need to use a particular command or function included in the chapter. The technique and application discussions have been added primarily as enrichment material that places the commands and functions in context and gives you some additional information that may be of use from time to time.

Interpreting Key Sequences

The key sequences themselves are the keystrokes you enter at the keyboard. Each keystroke is separated by a space, although you do not press the space bar. If you must press two keys simultaneously, they are connected by a hyphen. For example,

Shift-F7 1

indicates that you should press the Shift and F7 keys simultaneously and then type **1**. Variable information that you enter is presented in bold italics within angle brackets. For example,

Alt-F6 <*text*> Return

indicates that to align text flush right, you press Alt-F6, enter the text you wish to align, and press Return. If you need to perform an operation other than keyboard entry, that operation is indicated in parentheses. For example,

Alt-F4 (highlight text) Shift-F6 Y

indicates that you must highlight a block of text before proceeding with the command sequence, which in this case centers the highlighted text.

We have followed the convention of presenting text entries you make from the keyboard in **boldface** type.

Using Consistent Terminology

Because the topics in this book are organized according to the functions they perform rather than by the program's commands, you can quickly find the section that contains the information you are looking for. If, for example, you want to find out about setting tabs, look for "Setting Tabs," not for "Using the Alt-F8 Key." Also, in addition, to using WordPerfect's terminology, we have attempted to define program functions in terms used by other popular word processing programs, such as WordStar and Microsoft Word, to help you if you have worked with any of these other programs.

Scope of the Book

This book is a complete reference to all aspects of WordPerfect through Version 4.2. Where there are differences between commands used in earlier versions they are mentioned, but the illustrations assume that you have upgraded to the most recent release of WordPerfect.

If you have not, we urge you to do so: You will have a great many more features available to you, and you will discover that many of the more unwieldy command sequences have been modified. WordPerfect Corporation is continuously upgrading its well-designed product, and it has evolved into a very sophisticated word processor that is at the same time easy to learn and use.

Organization

Part 1, "Fundamental Word Processing Features," consists of six chapters presenting the program's basic functions. These chapters explain basic text entry, formatting, and editing and include full discussions of printing and file management techniques. If you are only a casual word processing user, you will probably find all the information you need in these first six chapters.

Part 2, "Specialized Word Processing Features," presents techniques used to accomplish specific tasks that not all users will require. For example, Chapter 7 discusses techniques for creating indexes and tables of contents as well as tables of authorities, which are widely used within the legal profession. Chapter 8 describes methods for creating multicolumn documents such as newsletters and brochures. Chapters 9 and 10 discuss merge operations and sorting, features that offer you a variety of techniques that can save you a great deal of time if you need to merge or sort information. If your work does not require such specialized techniques, you can safely skip these chapters and return to them when you do need to use them. Likewise, Chapter 11, "Mathematics, Equations, and Special Symbols," presents techniques that will be of interest only if you need to make calculations in your documents, write equations, or use special symbols.

Part 3, "Supplemental Word Processing Features," like Part 2, contains chapters that present specialized topics. Chapter 12, "Using the Speller and Thesaurus," will probably be of interest to all but the most casual word processing users; it contains techniques you can use to produce almost error-free documents with WordPerfect. Chapter 13 discusses WordPerfect's graphics capabilities, which will be of interest if you create forms or generate other documents that require line drawings. Chapter 14, "Creating and Using Macros," describes in detail how you can put this powerful feature to work for you. If you've never used WordPerfect macros before, this chapter will show you how to make the most of all the macros that are presented throughout this book.

Part 4 is a technical reference. Chapter 15 is for those who import and export documents to and from other word processing programs and spreadsheet or database management programs, such as Lotus 1-2-3 and dBASE III. Chapter 16, however, contains material that will be of interest to all readers: It describes how to set up WordPerfect to suit your own working habits and needs. For example, you can set an automatic timed backup feature to make backup copies of your work as often as you specify.

The appendixes also contain valuable information. Appendix A lists the ASCII codes used to enter special characters into your documents from the keyboard. Appendix B lists the formatting codes used within WordPerfect; if you ever have difficulty interpreting a code, turn to Appendix B to see what the code represents. Appendix C will be invaluable if you use any of the Hewlett-Packard LaserJet printers. This appendix contains information about how to configure your LaserJet to work with WordPerfect and about how to use different fonts, both cartridge and soft fonts, in your WordPerfect documents.

If you use WordPerfect with an IBM keyboard other than the standard PC keyboard—if, for example, you work on an AT at work and an XT at home—you may find the keyboard diagrams in Appendix D of use. This appendix contains diagrams of the IBM PC AT and the IBM PC-3270 keyboards as well as the new IBM enhanced keyboard.

MACROS

WordPerfect has often been described as a feature-laden program. It contains many levels of command options, some of which are relatively undocumented. We have attempted to describe these techniques and put them into a context so you can easily use them in your work without having to go through a long learning sequence. In many cases, these techniques require creating a macro that carries out a sequence of instructions. You will find such macros throughout this book, near the applications to which they are related. If you are already familiar with WordPerfect macros, you can simply incorporate them into your work without referring to the chapter about macros.

If you are unfamiliar with WordPerfect macros, you should review Chapter 14, "Creating and Using Macros," before attempting to use any of the macros in this book. Using macros in WordPerfect is a simple and straightforward process, but you should be sure that you understand it before you create macros that may inadvertently damage work you have already completed. As you learn to use macros, be sure to save your documents before you try to use your macros in them. That way, if the macro produces unexpected results, you will still have a saved, correct version of your document.

We have suggested a name for each macro, but you can choose other names if you prefer. For example, you may want to name a macro that deletes a block of text Alt-D (for Delete), Alt-E (for Erase), or Alt-C (for Cut). Also, because you can have only 26 letter macros (A-Z) in any one directory, you are restricted to using each letter only once. However, you can assign macros a name consisting of up to eight letters—for example, INDEX or CONTENTS—which allows you to have more than 26 macros in a directory and to assign more descriptive names.

In this book, we use the following conventions to describe macros creation: The key sequence used to indicate that a macro is being composed is given first, followed by a suggested macro name. If you choose to use that name, enter it and press Return; then continue entering the keystrokes necessary to build the macro, which are listed in the next column. To complete the macro, enter the key sequence in the final column. Consider the following example:

Begin macro	*Macro name*	*Keystrokes*	*End macro*
Ctrl-F10	**Alt-L**	**Shift-F7 6 2**	**Ctrl-F10**

The sequence Ctrl-F10 indicates to WordPerfect that you are beginning to create a macro. To name this macro Alt-L (it does not matter whether you use uppercase or lowercase letters), press the Alt key and the L key simultaneously. Next, enter the key sequence in the Keystrokes column. To end the macro, press Ctrl-F10 again. From then on, whenever you press Alt-L, WordPerfect will implement this key sequence for you—which in this case gives you a preview of how the current page will look when it is printed.

HOW TO USE THIS BOOK

How you use this book depends upon your need at the time. If you are attempting to solve a specific problem, you will probably want to go directly to the reference entry describing the technique you are trying to use. The pages that contain reference entries are shown in boldface type in the index. All of the other pages listed are secondary citations—pages where you can find additional explanatory material, usually in the discussion sections earlier in the same chapter.

Usually you will be able to get sufficient information from the reference entry alone to solve your problem. If, however, your problem is still unresolved, or if you wish to obtain more information and see more examples of how the particular feature can be used, you should refer to the appropriate technique and application discussions that precede the reference entries. You can do this in one of two ways:

- You can refer once again to the index and use it to locate the page numbers for other citations.

- You can turn to the beginning of the chapter you are in and use its table of contents (which lists all of the section headings) to locate the appropriate discussions.

Because of its nature, this book does not require you to use it in any specified order or to read completely any one chapter or section. We have endeavored whenever possible to make all discussions self-contained and to minimize cross references that would require you to continually jump from one section to another to obtain the information you need.

It is our sincere hope that this book provides you with a truly usable reference to which you can turn time and time again to answer the questions and solve the problems that arise as you use WordPerfect.

ACKNOWLEDGMENTS

A project of this magnitude would not have been possible without the expertise and cooperation of a great many people. We were fortunate throughout in having top-quality people to support and guide us at every turn. Our thanks is heartfelt and only begins to repay those involved.

Many thanks to the SYBEX staff, including editor in chief Dr. R. S. Langer, managing editor Karl Ray, series editor Barbara Gordon, project editor David Kolodney, word processor Olivia Shinomoto, typesetter Cheryl Vega, production artist Amparo del Rio, graphics technician Michelle Hoffman, proofreader Aidan Wylde, technical editor Marianne Morgan, indexer Anne Leach, aquisitions editor Dianne King, marketing manager Hannah Robinson, and Judy Ziajka for her manuscript edit.

Also, we want to thank Susan Kelly, whose keen support for this project and deep understanding of WordPerfect helped us in so many particular ways, and whose outstanding work, *Mastering WordPerfect,* provided an excellent base on which to build our reference.

We thank the people at WordPerfect Corporation for supplying us with copies of Version 4.2 and the WordPerfect Library. Special thanks to Jeff Acerson, Denise Wood, and Wendy Bressler for their help with all sorts of issues and details, which has improved the final quality of our work.

Finally, thanks to our families and friends, without whose patience and support this work would not have come into being.

Greg Harvey
Kay Yarborough Nelson
March 6, 1987

PART

1

FUNDAMENTAL WORD
PROCESSING FEATURES

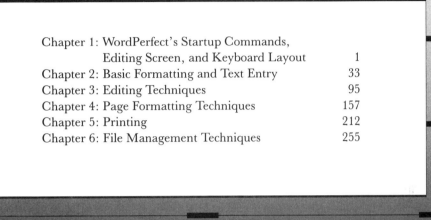

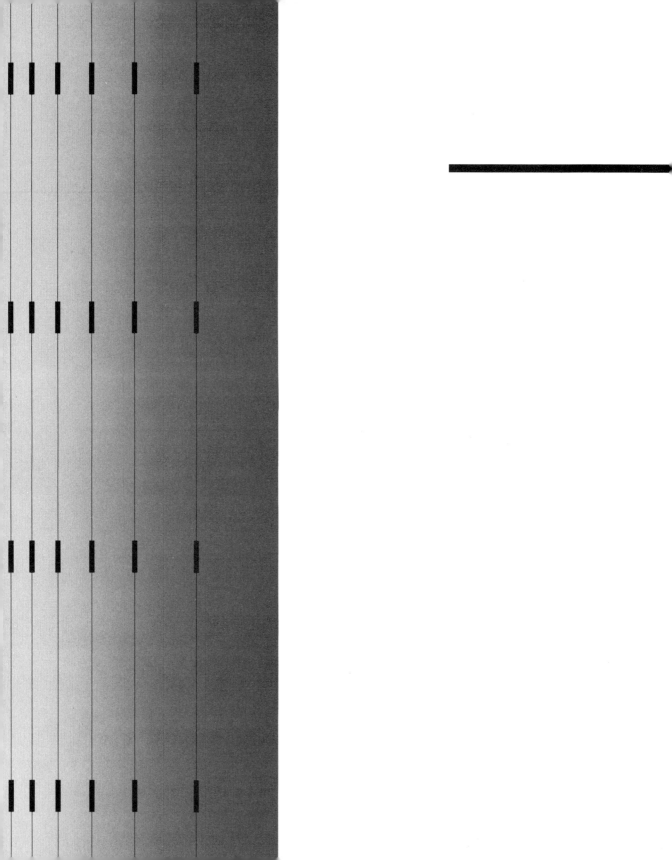

CHAPTER 1

WORDPERFECT'S STARTUP COMMANDS, EDITING SCREEN, AND KEYBOARD LAYOUT

WORDPERFECT'S STARTUP COMMANDS, EDITING SCREEN, AND KEYBOARD LAYOUT

This chapter presents an overview of WordPerfect and how it works, and it acquaints you with the basics of how to start the program (how Word-Perfect is started depends upon the type of computer system you are using). These discussions assume that you have already installed WordPerfect (by making backup copies and configuring your printer to work with it). If this is not the case, you can turn to Chapter 16 for complete installation instructions. There you will also find detailed information about using the various startup options available in the program.

This chapter also orients you to WordPerfect's editing screen and use of the IBM PC keyboard. These discussions introduce you to WordPerfect's appearance on the screen after you start the program and give you a sense of how you will use the keyboard to create documents. The chapter ends with a discussion of how you exit the program. All of the options for saving the documents that you have created and edited during your work session are presented, as well as how to retrieve a document that has been saved when you want to edit it further.

OVERVIEW OF WORDPERFECT

WordPerfect is a screen-oriented word processor, which means that as you create and edit your document, it appears on your screen pretty much as it will when it is printed: What you see is what you get. Thus, the program displays special printing attributes such as underlining (which appears in reverse video or a different color if your computer has a color card) and boldfacing on the screen. It also shows formatting effects such as indentations, centering, newspaper columns, and double-spacing as they will appear in printed form.

However, WordPerfect cannot display all of its editing features on your screen as they will be printed. There are several features it cannot display.

- Right justification
- Proportional spacing, including microspacing and differences in the widths of various letters
- The use of a pitch other than pica type (10 characters per inch)
- The use of special print fonts such as italics and Times Roman
- Headers, footers, footnotes, and endnotes
- Page numbers assigned with the Page Format command (Alt-F8)
- Subscripts and superscripts

Version 4.2 of WordPerfect includes a Print Preview feature (Shift-F7 6) that allows you to view your document in a form much closer to the way in which it will print. In the preview, right-justified text appears flush right; and headers, footers, footnotes, and page numbers appear in their appropriate positions. The only limitations not overcome in this preview are those related to spacing, such as pitch, proportional spacing, and sub- and superscripts. (See Chapter 4 for more information about the Print Preview feature.)

WordPerfect's Reveal Codes Screen

To keep the screen view of your document as similar as possible to the printed versions, WordPerfect does not display any of the special codes it uses to format the text. Unlike such programs as WordStar and MultiMate, which show all of their formatting codes on the screen as part of the document, WordPerfect keeps all of its codes hidden.

WordPerfect also differs from such word processors as WordStar 2000, which allow you to turn on and off the display of formatting codes normally kept invisible in the text. To view the formatting codes in WordPerfect, you must use a special key combination, Alt-F3, referred to as the Reveal Codes key sequence. When you use this key combination, WordPerfect splits the display screen into two windows, as shown in Figure 1.1. The lower window it creates contains a

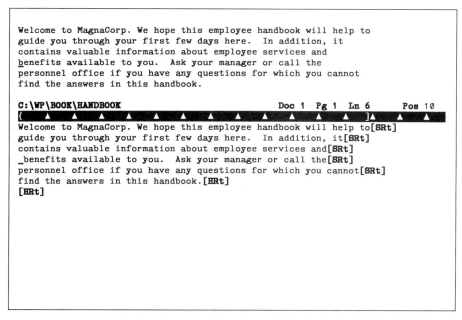

FIGURE 1.1: Viewing WordPerfect's hidden formatting codes. You can see WordPerfect's hidden formatting codes at any time while working in the editing screen by pressing Alt-F3. In many cases you will need to view these codes in order to delete them.

copy of the same text visible in the upper window, except that it displays all of the formatting codes used.

You will often need to use the Reveal Codes key sequence (Alt-F3) to change the formatting of your document. Though WordPerfect's system of codes may appear somewhat intimidating at first, these codes are really quite easy to read (they all use English abbreviations rather than special graphics characters such as MultiMate uses) and to manipulate. As you look up various word processing commands and seek out particular information about WordPerfect's more advanced features, you will find that this book devotes a great deal of attention to the formatting codes used by the various features. It also provides clear, concise information about what changes, if any, you should make to these formatting codes using Alt-F3 (the Reveal Codes key sequence).

Naming and Saving Documents in WordPerfect

In WordPerfect you do not name a new document until you wish to save it. Also, your work is at risk until you issue the Save command. If a power interruption or computer failure occurs and you have not saved the document you are creating, your work will be lost, and you will have to manually reenter it.

To guard against this type of loss, the program provides an automatic timed backup feature. The timed backup feature allows you to set the number of minutes between each automatic save operation. When you save the document when you exit the program at the end of your work session, the special file, {WP}BACK.1, in which your edits are saved is automatically erased. On the other hand, if you should experience some kind of problem that prevents you from exiting WordPerfect normally, this special file is retained. You can then rename it and use it as your working copy of the document. With this feature in effect, the only edits you can possibly lose are those made between the time the last automatic save operation occurred and the time you experienced the power interruption or computer failure.

In addition, WordPerfect provides an original backup feature. This feature is used to automatically save two copies of an edited document: one showing the document's previously saved form and the other containing your most recently saved editing changes. If you use this feature, you must have sufficient storage space on your data disk to accommodate both versions of the document.

> *Note:* Both the automatic timed backup and the original backup features are inactive when you first use WordPerfect. To activate them, you must start WordPerfect using the Setup menu (WP/S). For a complete description of how to set these features, refer to Chapter 16.

STARTING WORDPERFECT

How you start WordPerfect depends upon the kind of hardware you have. Many variations of the basic startup command (WP) are available to accommodate the type of machine you have and the way in which you wish to work. These special startup options are included to maximize the use of your hardware; they are discussed at length in Chapter 16. Here, we will look at only the most basic procedures: how you start the program if you have two disk drives (two drives with doors that accept floppy disks), and how you start the program if you have a hard disk and one disk drive.

All of this information presupposes that you have already installed WordPerfect to work with the hardware you have. If you have not yet installed the program, refer to "Installing WordPerfect" in Chapter 16 and follow the instructions that you find there before returning to this section.

Starting WordPerfect on a System with Two Floppy Disk Drives

If your computer has two floppy disk drives, you will want to save the documents you create on a data disk kept in drive B (the right or lower drive) and keep a working copy of your WordPerfect System disk in drive A (the left or upper drive).

Before turning on the computer, place a copy of your DOS System disk in drive A and a formatted disk on which to store your documents in drive B and then turn on the power switch. After entering the date and time in response to the DOS prompts, replace the DOS System disk with your WordPerfect System disk.

To make drive B, which contains your data disk, the current drive, you then type **B:** after the prompt, like this:

A>**B:**

and press Return. The A> prompt will be replaced with B>, indicating that drive B is the current drive. Now you can enter the WordPerfect startup command:

B>**A:WP**

Then press Return. Once the program has been loaded into your computer's memory, you can begin creating a new document or editing one stored on the disk in drive B. If you create a new document, it will automatically be saved on the data disk in drive B by virtue of the way you started the program.

When you have finished your work session with WordPerfect and exit the program, drive B will still be current. If you wish to use another program, remember to make drive A current by typing **A:** and pressing Return.

Starting WordPerfect with a Batch File

You can automate the startup procedure on a system with two floppy disk drives by creating a batch file that you save on the working copy of your Word-Perfect System disk. To do this, start your computer with the DOS System disk and then replace this disk with the WordPerfect System disk, leaving A as the current drive (you will still see the A> prompt on your screen). You can name this batch file START.BAT. To create this file and save it on your WordPerfect System disk, perform the following steps:

1. Type **COPY CON START.BAT** and press Return.
2. On the next line, type **B:** and press Return.
3. On the next line, type **A:WP** and press Return.
4. On the next line, press the F6 function key and then Return. You will see ^Z displayed on this line. This marks the end of the batch file and instructs the operating system to save the file START.BAT on your Word-Perfect System disk.

From now on, you can start WordPerfect merely by typing **START** (you do not have to type .BAT) after you have replaced the DOS System disk with the Word-Perfect System disk. Always make sure that a data disk on which to save your documents is placed in drive B before you start the program with this batch file.

Starting WordPerfect on a Hard Disk System

If you are using WordPerfect with a hard disk, all of the program files will be kept in their own directory. Because a hard disk offers a very large storage area, it is partitioned into divisions, called *directories*. You can think of these directories as analogous to the file drawers in a filing cabinet. Within each drawer, you store many file folders. Likewise, each directory can contain many files, each with a unique file name and usually grouped by type.

If you did not install WordPerfect yourself, you must find out the name of the directory that contains the WordPerfect program files. Most often, it is given the name WP, which corresponds to the WordPerfect startup command.

When you turn on your computer with drive A empty or unlatched, the system automatically goes to drive C (the letter designation given to the first hard disk in an IBM or compatible personal computer) to find the DOS files that it needs to load into memory. This means that you do not have to use a copy of the DOS System disk when you start the program. (In fact, you must leave drive A empty when powering up the computer or, at least, keep its door open or unlatched if it contains a disk, or you will impede this process.)

Once you supply the date and time (unless this is done automatically for you with a clock/calendar card), the most fundamental, or *root,* directory is current. Before you can start WordPerfect, you must change this to make the directory containing the WordPerfect program files current. The DOS operating system provides a Change Directory (CD) command that allows you to do this.

Assuming that the name of the directory containing your WordPerfect program files is WP, you make the program directory current by typing

    C>**CD\WP**

and pressing Return. (If the directory that contains these files is named something else, you substitute its name for WP in the preceding command.) After making the proper directory current, you start WordPerfect by typing

    C>**WP**

and pressing Return.

STARTING WORDPERFECT WITH A BATCH FILE

You can automate the startup procedure on a hard disk system by creating a batch file command that you save in the root directory of your hard disk. To do this, start your computer and enter the date and time (if required). You can name this batch file WP.BAT. To create this file, perform the following steps:

1. Type **COPY CON WP.BAT** and press Return.
2. On the next line, type **CD\WP** and press Return.

3. On the next line, type **WP** and press Return.

4. On the next line, type **CD** and press Return.

5. On the next line, press the F6 function key and then Return. You will see ^Z displayed on this line. This marks the end of the batch file and instructs the operating system to save the file WP.BAT in the root directory.

From now on, you can start WordPerfect merely by typing **WP** (you don't have to type .BAT) after you have turned on the computer and entered the date and time at the C> prompt. (If the name of the directory that contains the program files is something other than WP, substitute its name wherever WP appears in the preceding steps.) When you exit WordPerfect, this batch file automatically returns you to the root directory on drive C. From there, you can change to directories that contain other software programs or terminate your work session by turning off the computer.

CHANGING DATA DIRECTORIES

When you start WordPerfect, all of the documents you create are automatically saved in the current directory, C:\WP. Most often, you will want to save your documents in separate directories. These are usually attached as subdirectories to the directory that contains the WordPerfect program files. In fact, you can set up many directories in which to keep related documents. For example, if you perform word processing for many people in your office, you can have a directory for each person. Whenever you type a letter or memo for a person, you would then make his or her directory current before creating the document. You could also set up directories based on document type. For instance, you could have one directory for proposals, another for letters, and so on.

WordPerfect makes it easy to create a new subdirectory or make a different subdirectory current. The techniques involved are explained in Chapter 6.

THE WORDPERFECT SCREEN

As soon as you issue the appropriate startup command and press Return, an initial startup screen appears very briefly. This screen lists the current WordPerfect directory, although you may not always be able to read this information as it passes. Directly after the initial startup screen, you will be presented with the editing screen. This screen is shown in Figure 1.2.

The Status Line

The status line in the lower-right corner of the screen tells you the number of the document you are working with (you can work with two documents at once).

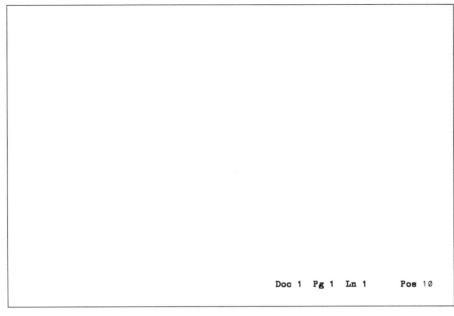

Doc 1 Pg 1 Ln 1   Pos 10

FIGURE 1.2: WordPerfect's editing screen. The program gives you a full screen to work with. Normally the only indications you see are the document number, page number, line number, and cursor position in the lower-right corner. With single spacing (the program default), the screen displays 24 lines; with double spacing, the screen displays 12 lines.

It also indicates which page of the document you are working on as well as the line number and the cursor position. You can specify the number of lines per page (see "Changing Page Length" in Chapter 2), or you can accept the program's default setting of 54 lines (for single-spaced 8½ × 11-inch paper).

Being able to work with two documents at once gives you a great deal of flexibility. For example, you can store text that you use frequently, such as standard paragraphs, product descriptions, and form letters, and switch and copy between the document you are creating and the document that holds the "boilerplate" text (see "Working with Two Documents" in Chapter 3). You can also use the second document as a work space to hold notes or text that you plan to use later.

The Page Indicator

The page indicator on the status line shows you the page number of the document you are working with. It corresponds to the number of the page that will be printed (if you specify page numbering) when you print your document. You can use the program's Go To feature (by pressing Ctrl-Home) to move directly to any page in your document (see "Cursor Movement" later in this chapter).

Page breaks in WordPerfect are shown on the screen. A page break is indicated by a line of hyphens that extends across the entire width of the screen. You can also add your own page breaks (sometimes referred to as *user-defined page breaks* or *forced page breaks*) by pressing Ctrl-Return. In Version 4.2, this type of page break appears as a line of equal signs across the width of the screen (earlier releases did not differentiate page break types).

A user-defined page break can be deleted by using the Reveal Code key combination (Alt-F3) to locate the code [HPg] and then deleting the code. You can also delete a user-defined page break by positioning the cursor at the end of the last line of text above the page break and pressing Del. If there is a blank line above the page-break display, position the cursor at the leftmost position of this blank line and press Del. You can also move to the line after the page break and press Backspace.

The Line Indicator

The line indicator on the status line shows the number of the line on which the cursor is located. As you type, you will notice this number change whenever the cursor moves to a new line. When you use the Next Page or Previous Page function (PgDn or PgUp) or the Go To Page function (Ctrl-Home followed by the page number), the cursor will move to line 1 (Ln 1) of the page indicated.

The Position Indicator

The last number on the status line indicates the column position of the cursor. When the cursor is located in the leftmost column of the screen, the Pos indicator will read "Pos 10," unless you have changed the left margin setting (see "Setting Margins" in Chapter 2). This indicates that your document will be printed with a left margin of 1 inch (assuming that you use the default pitch of 10 characters per inch or pica type). The right margin default setting is position (or column) 74.

In previous versions of WordPerfect, the left margin position of 10 was displayed 10 spaces from the left edge of the screen (mimicking the white space of the left margin on the printed page). In Version 4.2 the default left margin corresponds to the left edge of the screen. This means that the program can display longer lines without horizontal scrolling than in previous versions.

As a result of this change, if you reduce the left margin setting to less than 10, your document will appear to be missing some characters along the left edge when you first retrieve it. This situation is rectified by pressing the → key or vertically scrolling the screen (by pressing the ↓ or PgDn key or pressing Ctrl-Home and typing a page number to go to a specific page). Once you scroll the screen vertically, the display automatically shifts to the right so that all of the hidden characters in columns before 10 are visible on the editing screen.

The default values result in 1-inch margins on both the left and the right of the printed page. You can accept the program's default setting of 74 characters per line, or you can change the margin settings. Lines can be up to 250 characters wide (see ''Setting Margins'' in Chapter 2).

THE KEYBOARD

The WordPerfect program is based on the use of special-function keys to carry out your commands. Because the program has no visible menu bars or ruler lines unless you call them up, you have a full screen to work with. However, you also have few reminders of the special-function keys and their purposes. The template that is supplied with the program explains the use of these function keys, but if you are working without a template or have forgotten some of the command keystroke sequences, you can consult this section. The keyboard referred to in this book is the standard IBM PC and PC/XT keyboard. For other keyboard diagrams, see Appendix D.

The Special-Function Keys

Commands are issued to WordPerfect by pressing the function keys at the left of your keyboard (Figure 1.3) alone or in combination with the Ctrl, Shift, and Alt keys (Figure 1.4).

Each of the function keys (F1 through F10) performs a special function within WordPerfect. For example, pressing F4, the Indent key, indents text according to the tab settings you specify. In combination with the Ctrl, Shift, and Alt keys, these function keys take on different meanings, as summarized in Table 1.1.

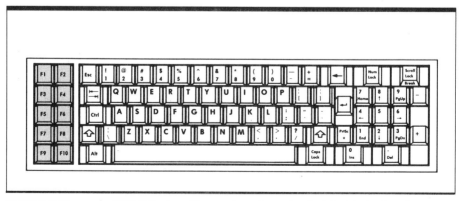

FIGURE 1.3: The standard IBM PC keyboard function keys, located at the left of the keyboard. Word-Perfect's commands are issued by pressing one of these keys alone or in combination with the Ctrl, Shift, or Alt key.

The functions of each of these keys alone and in combination with the Ctrl, Shift, and Alt keys will be discussed in the context of their use in subsequent chapters of this book. These discussions are grouped and arranged according to the word processing function performed by the key or key combination and can be located by referring either to the index or the table of contents located at the beginning of each chapter.

FUNCTION KEY	COMMAND	WITH CTRL	WITH SHIFT	WITH ALT
F1	Cancel or undelete	Shell (exit to DOS)	Superscript, subscript	Use Thesaurus
F2	Forward search	Use Speller	Reverse search	Replace
F3	Help	Change screen	Switch documents	Reveal codes
F4	Indent	Move	L/R indent	Mark block
F5	List files	Text in/out	Insert date	Mark text
F6	Boldface	Align tabs	Center	Flush right
F7	Exit	Footnotes	Print	Use math/ columns
F8	Underline	Print formatting	Line formatting	Page formatting
F9	Merge return	Merge sort	Merge end	Merge codes
F10	Save	Define macro	Retrieve file	Use macro

TABLE 1.1: WordPerfect's Special-Function Key Combinations

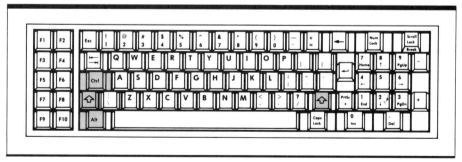

FIGURE 1.4: The Ctrl, Shift, and Alt keys. Used in conjunction with the function keys, these keys give you 40 basic commands. Most of these commands bring up menus on the screen from which you can make additional selections.

On the template that came with your program, a command issued through a combination of a function key and the Shift key is indicated by green, a combination with the Ctrl key is indicated by red, and a combination with the Alt key is indicated by blue. The function key used alone is indicated by black.

If you no longer have the function key template, you can always bring it up on your screen by pressing F3 (the Help key) twice. To obtain a hard copy for reference, turn on your printer and press the Shift-PrtSc key combination.

The Return Key

The Return key, often marked ← on the keyboard, is sometimes called the *Enter* key (Figure 1.5). It is used to indicate the end of a paragraph, to insert blank lines into your document, or in certain cases, to confirm a menu choice, in which case it functions as an Enter key.

WordPerfect automatically wraps words from the end of one line to the beginning of the next line, so you don't have to press Return at the end of each line. If you do, you will insert a hard return, which you may not want in your document at that point (for more information about formatting codes, see Appendix B).

MAKING HARD RETURNS VISIBLE ON THE SCREEN

WordPerfect does not display any visible character to let you know where you have entered a hard return to mark the end of a paragraph. However, Version 4.2 allows you to assign a character of your own choice that will indicate the location of hard returns in a document.

To do this, you must access the WordPerfect Setup menu by starting the program using the WP/S startup command. From the Setup menu, choose option

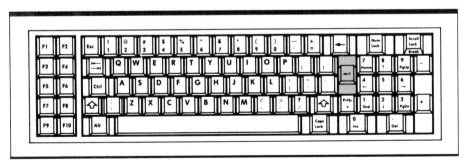

FIGURE 1.5: The Return key. Return functions both as a carriage return key and as an Enter key in WordPerfect, depending on whether you are indicating a hard return to end a paragraph or insert blank lines or selecting from a menu.

3, Set Screen Size and Beep Options. Under the heading Set Screen Options you will see the option

Hard return displayed as ascii value: 32

The default character for a hard return is ASCII code 32, which is the code for a blank space. (That is why the hard return is invisible on the editing screen.)

To reassign the hard return to a character that will be visible on your screen, you must replace the value 32 with the appropriate code for the character you wish to use. Appendix A provides a chart of ASCII codes, showing all of the characters supported by the IBM PC and compatible computers and their ASCII values. You can use this chart to find the value for the character you want to use for the hard return.

For instance, if you decide that you want to use the < (less than) symbol to mark the use of all hard returns in a document, you can use the chart in Appendix A to find its ASCII value (which is 060). To make < the symbol for hard returns, you press Return until the cursor is positioned on the current value of 32. Then you type **60** (you may omit the leading zeros shown in the ASCII chart) over the 32 and press F7 (Exit) to return to the Setup menu options. Another appropriate symbol that you might use to show hard returns is the paragraph symbol, ASCII code 020 (see Appendix A).

The Escape Key

The Escape key, marked *Esc* and located near the upper-left corner of the keyboard (see Figure 1.6), serves several purposes in WordPerfect. Its basic function is to repeat a command (or character) a specified number of times, although pressing it twice cancels a command. The specified number of times that Esc repeats a command is preset to eight, but you can change this simply by typing another number. For example, pressing Esc, typing **5,** and pressing the ↑ key moves the cursor up five lines. (See "Cursor Movement" later in this chapter for a full discussion of techniques for moving the cursor.)

The repeat function of the Esc key is also quite useful for drawing boxes and lines with WordPerfect, because it lets you draw solid lines by repeating a single graphics character (see Chapter 13). The Esc key can also be used to repeat a macro (see Chapter 14) or to delete several lines or characters (see "Deleting Text" in Chapter 2).

> *Note:* The F1 function key is used primarily as a cancel key (although it also works as an undo key), a function often assigned to the Esc key in other software programs. These other programs commonly assign the help function to F1, a function WordPerfect assigns to F3.

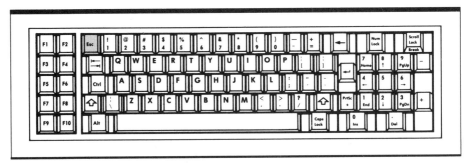

FIGURE 1.6: The Escape (Esc) key. Esc has a variety of uses in WordPerfect, but you will probably use it most often to cancel a command. It allows you to repeat a command any number of times that you specify. The Tab key is located below the Esc key.

The Tab Key

The Tab key, indicated by ⇆ on the left side of the keyboard (Figure 1.6), moves the cursor to the tab settings you have specified. The program's default values are tabs every five spaces, but you can change these settings (see "Setting Tabs" in Chapter 2).

You should not confuse the Tab key with the Indent key (F4) in WordPerfect. Using the Tab key moves the cursor to tab settings, but the Indent key inserts an indent code into your document that tells WordPerfect to indent an entire paragraph. (See "Indenting Paragraphs" in Chapter 2.)

The Backspace and Delete Keys

The Backspace key, represented by ← on the upper-right side of the keyboard, and the Delete key, marked *Del* on the lower-right side of the keyboard (Figure 1.7), are both used to delete characters. You can also use both keys to delete WordPerfect's hidden formatting codes (discussed in Chapter 2).

Note: You cannot change the Backspace key to make it "nondestructive" in WordPerfect as you can with some other word processing programs. This means that you must always use the ← key on the 10-key number pad to move the cursor character by character to the left without deleting existing text.

The "Lock" Keys

Three keys on the standard IBM PC keyboard—Caps Lock, Num Lock, and Ins—lock the keyboard into certain modes. (Scroll Lock is not used in WordPerfect.) You may sometimes press these keys inadvertently and see unexpected results on the screen. The positions of these keys are shown in Figure 1.8.

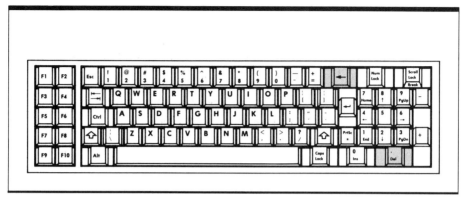

FIGURE 1.7: The Backspace and Delete (Del) keys. Backspace and Del delete characters from your document in different ways. The Del key deletes the character (or space) the cursor is on, and the Backspace key deletes characters to the left of the cursor.

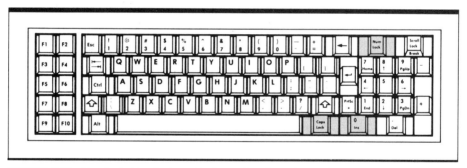

FIGURE 1.8: The Caps Lock, Num Lock, and Ins keys. These keys change the mode of operation of your keyboard. With Caps Lock on, all characters you type are in UPPERCASE. With Num Lock on, the keys on the numeric keypad enter numbers instead of moving the cursor. Pressing Ins toggles you between Insert and Typeover modes.

CAPS LOCK

The Caps Lock key, as its name implies, shifts your typing mode to uppercase letters (when the Shift key is pressed while in Caps Lock mode, letters appear in lowercase). Pressing this key a second time returns you to normal typing mode. The position indicator on the status line changes to uppercase (for example, POS 44) when Caps Lock is on.

Note: When the Caps Lock key is activated (indicated by POS on the status line), only letters are shifted to uppercase. You still have to press one of the Shift keys to use the punctuation and special symbols that share their keys, as with the number keys in the top row. For example, even when Caps Lock is on, you must press Shift and 1 to enter the ! (exclamation point).

NUM LOCK

The Num Lock key changes the keys on the numeric keypad from cursor movement keys to numeric entry keys. The position indicator on the status line flashes when Num Lock is on.

> *Note:* When the word *Pos* in the lower-right corner is flashing, pressing any of the arrow keys, Home, End, PgUp, or PgDn on the numeric pad will cause numbers to be inserted into your text. Press the Num Lock key one more time to reenable the cursor functions.

INSERT

The Insert key (marked *Ins*) changes the mode of operation from Insert mode, in which characters you type are inserted at the position of the cursor and do not replace existing characters, to Typeover mode, in which characters you type replace existing characters. When Typeover mode is on, the word *Typeover* appears in the lower-left corner of the screen.

> *Note:* The default setting when you start WordPerfect is Insert mode. You cannot make Typeover mode the default setting as you can with other word processing programs.

The Numeric Keypad

The numeric keypad, located at the right of your keyboard (Figure 1.9), contains the cursor movement keys and, when Num Lock is on, functions as a numeric entry keypad, as discussed earlier. Each of the cursor movement keys is discussed in detail in the section "Cursor Movement" later in this chapter.

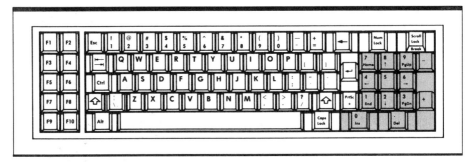

FIGURE 1.9: The numeric keypad on the IBM PC keyboard contains cursor movement keys that, used in combination with other keys, allow you to move quickly through your document as well as execute certain commands. This keypad functions as a numeric entry pad when the Num Lock key is pressed. To reenable cursor movement functions, press Num Lock a second time.

CURSOR MOVEMENT

WordPerfect has many key combinations that allow you to move the cursor through your document. These techniques, which are summarized in Table 1.2 for easy reference, are discussed in the following sections. You will probably not use all of these techniques, but a few you will use over and over. You may want to write macros for some of the cursor movement sequences in combination with commands that you use frequently.

Note: Useful macros will be presented throughout this book where appropriate. For a discussion of macros and how they are used, see Chapter 14, "Creating and Using Macros."

TO MOVE:	KEY SEQUENCE
Character by character	← or →
Word by word	Ctrl-← or Ctrl-→
To the beginning of a line	Home ←
To the end of a line	Home →
To the end of the sentence	Ctrl-Home .
To the next occurrence of a character	Ctrl-Home <*character*>
To the top of the screen	Home ↑ or − (minus)
To the bottom of the screen	Home ↓ or + (plus)
To previous screens	Home ↑ or − (minus) repeatedly
To subsequent screens	Home ↓ or + (plus) repeatedly
To the previous page	PgUp
To the next page	PgDn
To the top of the page	Ctrl-Home ↑
To the bottom of the page	Ctrl-Home ↓
To a specified page	Ctrl-Home <*page number*> Return
To the last cursor position before the cursor-movement command	Ctrl-Home Ctrl-Home
To the beginning of the last-defined block	Ctrl-Home Alt-F4
To the beginning of the document	Home Home ↑
To the end of the document	Home Home ↓

TABLE 1.2: WordPerfect's Cursor Movement Techniques

Moving Character by Character

> **KEY SEQUENCE**
>
> To move one character to right:
> →
>
> To move one character to left:
> ←

The ← and → keys on the numeric keypad move the cursor left one character and right one character, respectively. To move the cursor a specified number of characters to the left or right, press Esc, enter the number, and press either the ← or → key.

Moving Word by Word

> **KEY SEQUENCE**
>
> To move one word right:
> **Ctrl-→**
> To move one word left:
> **Ctrl-←**

To move the cursor word by word through a line, hold down the Ctrl key and press the arrow key corresponding to the direction in which you wish to go. The cursor will jump to the first letter of the word in either direction.

To move a specified number of words to the right or left of the current cursor position, press Esc, enter the number, and press Ctrl and the right or left arrow key simultaneously. For example, to move five words to the right, press Esc, type **5**, and press Ctrl-→.

Moving to the Beginning of a Line

> **KEY SEQUENCE**
>
> **Home ←**

To move to the beginning of the current line, press Home and then press the ← key.

Moving to the End of a Line

KEY SEQUENCE

End or **Home** →

To move to the end of the current line, press the End key (located on the numeric keypad). Alternatively, you can press Home and then the → key.

Moving to the End of a Sentence

KEY SEQUENCE

Ctrl-Home .

To move to the end of a sentence (one that ends with a period), press Ctrl and Home simultaneously; then enter . (a period). You can use the same method to move to the end of a sentence that is terminated by an exclamation point by entering ! instead of a period.

Moving to the Next Occurrence of a Character

KEY SEQUENCE

Ctrl-Home <*character*>

You can use the same method as moving to the end of a sentence to move directly to the next occurrence of any character in your document. Press Ctrl-Home and then type the character. Your cursor will move to the next instance of that character in your document.

Moving Line by Line (Scrolling)

KEY SEQUENCE

To move upward through your document:
  ↑ (hold)
To move downward through your document:
  ↓ (hold)

To move through your document line by line, simply hold down the ↑ or ↓ keys.

Moving to the Top or Bottom of the Screen

KEY SEQUENCE

To top of screen:
   Home ↑ or − (minus)
To bottom of screen:
   Home ↓ or + (plus)

To move to the top of the screen, press Home and then press the ↑ key. To move to the bottom of the screen, press Home and then press the ↓ key. Alternatively, you can press the − (minus) and + (plus) keys located on the right side of the numeric keypad.

Note: If your keyboard has a separate cursor movement pad and 10-key number pad, you will not be able to use the − (minus) and + (plus) on the number pad for entering calculations into your document because WordPerfect uses these keys for scrolling. You will have to use the − (hyphen key) and + (Shift- =) on the top row of the keyboard for mathematical work.

Moving to the Previous or Next Screen

KEY SEQUENCE

To previous screen:
   Home ↑ or − (minus)
To next screen:
   Home ↓ or + (plus)

To move screen by screen, (24 single-spaced lines at a time), press the key or key sequence repeatedly. The plus and minus keys are located on the numeric keypad. Slightly more than two screens of text represent one single-spaced page of printed text.

Moving to the Previous or Next Page

> **KEY SEQUENCE**
>
> To move to previous page:
> **PgUp**
> To move to next page:
> **PgDn**

To move page by page, press the PgUp or PgDn keys on the numeric keypad. PgUp takes you to the beginning of the first line of the previous page; PgDn takes you to the beginning of the next page of your document.

Page breaks are represented in one of two ways on your screen: Hard page breaks (those that you add yourself) are shown by a line of equal signs, and soft page breaks (those that the program adds) are shown by a line of hyphens. If you wish to delete a hard page break, press Alt-F3 (the Reveal Codes key sequence) and delete the code [HPg].

Moving to the Top or Bottom of the Page

> **KEY SEQUENCE**
>
> To top of page:
> **Ctrl-Home ↑**
> To bottom of page:
> **Ctrl-Home ↓**

To move directly to the beginning of the page on which you are working, press Ctrl-Home and then ↑. Likewise, to move directly to the end of the page on which you are working, enter Ctrl-Home ↓.

Moving to a Specific Page

> **KEY SEQUENCE**
>
> **Ctrl-Home** *<page number>* **Return**

To move directly to a specific page in your document, press Ctrl-Home. The prompt "Go to" will appear in the lower-left corner of your screen. Enter the number of the page to which you want to go and press Return. The message "Repositioning" indicates that WordPerfect is repositioning the cursor during this operation. This message appears when you are moving long distances to reassure you that the command is working.

Moving to the Previous Cursor Position

KEY SEQUENCE

Ctrl-Home Ctrl-Home

To move the cursor to the position where it was when you last used a cursor-control command, press Ctrl-Home twice. This technique is useful when you copy and paste text, as it allows you easily to return the cursor to the place where the text came from, or when you want to return to your last position during a search operation or to the first occurrence of the search string after a search and replace operation.

Moving to the Beginning of a Block

KEY SEQUENCE

Ctrl-Home Alt-F4

To move the cursor to the beginning of the last block of text you defined, press Ctrl-Home (the Go To key sequence) followed by Alt-F4 (the Mark Block key sequence). (For information about blocking text in a document, refer to "Marking Blocks of Text" in Chapter 3.)

Moving to the Beginning or End of a Document

KEY SEQUENCE

To move to the beginning of a document:
   Home Home ↑
To move to the end of a document:
   Home Home ↓

To move directly to the beginning or end of your document, press Home twice; then press either the ↑ key (to go to the beginning of your document) or the ↓ key (to go to the end). You will see the message "Repositioning," indicating that WordPerfect is repositioning the cursor.

SAVING A DOCUMENT AND EXITING WORDPERFECT

You should make it a practice to save your work frequently. WordPerfect provides an automatic backup feature that can be extremely valuable if you have a power loss or other computer failure, but you will still have to retrieve the backup file and rename it (see Chapters 6 and 16 for details about how to specify automatic backups and retrieve files). In addition, you will have lost the work you did between the time of the last backup and the power failure. Get into the habit of saving often and regularly.

Save and Continue

KEY SEQUENCE

To save a file for the first time:
  F10 <*file name*> **Return**
To save a previously saved file under the same name:
  F10 Return Y
To save a previously saved file under a new name:
  F10 N <*file name*> **Return**

To save a file while you are working on it and then return to it, press F10. WordPerfect will prompt you for a file name if you have not saved the file before (see "Naming Files" in Chapter 6 for restrictions that apply to file names; Word-Perfect basically follows the same rules as DOS). Enter a name (up to eight characters long and including a directory and drive designation if you want the file saved somewhere other than the current drive and directory) and press Return.

If you have saved the file previously, WordPerfect will provide the file name under which you previously saved the file (see Figure 1.10). To save the file under the same name, press Return and respond **Y** to the prompt

  Replace <*file name*>**? (Y/N) N**

to indicate that you *do* want to replace the existing version of the file with the edited version you are now saving.

```
Recreational Facilities

MagnaCorp participates in the city recreational plan and
therefore its employees have access to the municipal gym located
at First and Brannan Streets.  The jogging track and par course
in Grant park are also nearby.  Showers and lockers for company
employees are located near the south entrance of the main lobby.




Replace C:\WP\HANDBOOK? (Y/N) N
```

FIGURE 1.10: WordPerfect's prompt for saving a previously saved file. You can rename the file at this point or specify a different drive or directory in which to save it. If you accept the previous name by pressing Return and responding yes, the current file will replace the older saved version.

The default setting is N, which allows you to leave the existing file intact and save the new version under another name. If you want to rename the file – for example, if you want to keep two versions of a document – press Return to accept the N setting. WordPerfect will prompt you for a new file name. Enter the new name (including a drive and directory designation, if you do not want to use the current ones) and press Return.

To cancel a save sequence, use the F1 (Cancel) key. Pressing Esc simply cycles you through the screen prompts.

ALT-S: A SAVE-AND-CONTINUE MACRO

You may want to speed up the process of saving your work by writing a simple macro that saves your work and returns you to your document without your having to respond to the on-screen prompts.

Begin macro	Macro name	Keystrokes	End macro
Ctrl-F1	**Alt-S**	**F10 Return Y**	**Ctrl-F10**

See Chapter 14, for details about how to set up and use macros in WordPerfect.

Save and Exit/Clearing the Screen

> **KEY SEQUENCE**
>
> To save a previously saved document and work on another:
> **F7 Y Return Y N**
> To save and exit WordPerfect:
> **F7 Y Return Y Y**

To save your document and exit WordPerfect or to save your document and begin work with another document, use the F7 key. This key is often referred to as the *Exit* key in WordPerfect. If you see an on-screen prompt telling you to press the Exit key, the program.is referring to the F7 function key.

When you press F7 during normal document editing, you will see the prompt

Save Document (Y/N)? Y

at the bottom of your screen. Press Return to accept the default setting, Yes, and WordPerfect will either prompt you for a file name (if you have not saved your document before) or provide the file name you previously gave to your document. If you want to save your document under a different name (for example, if you want to maintain several versions of it), simply type the new name. Word-Perfect will erase the name supplied in the prompt and enter the new name that you type.

If you want to save your document under the same name, simply press Return. WordPerfect will ask you

Replace <*file name*> (Y/N)? N

thus giving you another chance to save your file under a different name. (Remember, when you save your document under the same name, WordPerfect replaces the previously saved version.) Press Return to give the document a different name or type **Y** to replace the previous version of your document with this one.

If you type **Y**, WordPerfect saves the document and then displays the following prompt:

Exit WP (Y/N)? N

Entering **Y** returns you to DOS; pressing Return to accept the No default setting clears the WordPerfect screen and puts you on line 1 of a new, blank document. You can press Shift-F10 to retrieve a previously saved document or begin creating a new document.

To cancel a save sequence, use the F1 (Cancel) key. Pressing Esc simply cycles you through the saving prompts. Table 1.3 summarizes the different methods of exiting WordPerfect.

FUNCTION	KEY SEQUENCE
Save document and clear the screen	F7 Y \<filename\> N
Save document and exit	F7 Y \<filename\> Y
Clear the screen	F7 N N
Exit	F7 N Y

Note: If you are saving a previously saved document, you may simply press Return to accept the existing file name and press Y to replace the earlier version.

TABLE 1.3: Methods for Exiting WordPerfect

Unlike other word processors you may have used, in WordPerfect it is important that you exit the program properly before you turn off your computer. With other software it does not matter if you turn off the computer without using the exit command to return to the DOS operating system, so long as you have saved the document in memory before doing so. This is not the case with WordPerfect. WordPerfect keeps special files, referred to as *Overflow files* (see Chapter 16 for details), that are not emptied and closed until you press F7 (Exit).

If you simply use the save command, F10, and then turn off the power, WordPerfect will detect the presence of these files the next time you start the program and will display this prompt on the initial startup screen:

Are other copies of WordPerfect currently running? (Y/N)

You will then have to type **N** to cause WordPerfect to erase the contents of the Overflow files and move on to the standard editing screen.

Note: Releases of WordPerfect Version 4.1 present three options after displaying the message "Overflow files exist." If you are using one of these releases, type **3** and press Return to erase the contents of these files and to continue to the editing screen.

ALT-Q: A SAVE-AND-EXIT MACRO

As you can see, several keystrokes are required to save and exit. You can reduce the number of keystrokes to two by writing a simple save-and-exit macro to use when you want to end your WordPerfect work session and return to DOS.

Begin macro	Macro name	Keystrokes	End macro
Ctrl-F10	**Alt-Q**	**F7 Y Return Y**	**Ctrl-F10**

Retrieving a Saved Document

> **KEY SEQUENCE**
>
> **Shift-F10** <*file name*> **Return**

The Shift-F10 key combination is used to retrieve a saved document. Press Shift-F10 and enter the name of the document; then press Return.

If you do not enter a document name but instead press Return at the prompt, the last text you used Ctrl-F4 to delete from a document you have been working on in the current session will be inserted at the cursor position.

You can see a list of all the files in your working directory by pressing F5 (the List Files key) at the "Document to be retrieved:" prompt. WordPerfect will respond by displaying the current directory, followed by the wildcard search pattern *.*. The *.* indicates that all files with all extensions will be displayed. (See Chapter 6 for details about directories, subdirectories, and wildcards such as *.*.) Press Return one more time to make the program display a list of all files in the directory. To retrieve a document located in another WordPerfect document directory, edit the directory name displayed and press Return.

To retrieve a file from the alphabetical list displayed on the screen, highlight the file's name and enter **1** (for Retrieve, listed on the menu at the bottom of the screen, as shown in Figure 1.11). To view files in the other directories listed at the top of the screen, highlight the directory name and enter **6** (for Look). You can also retrieve a file directly from these directories by entering **1** when the file is highlighted. See Chapter 6 for details.

If you retrieve a document while you are working on another document, the retrieved document will be inserted at the current cursor position.

SUMMARY

This chapter presented an overview of WordPerfect and how it works. Refer to the subsequent chapters in Part 1 for information about how to use the program's basic editing, formatting, and printing features.

Many of the topics introduced in this chapter are related to others discussed in more detail in other parts of this book. You can use the following guide to locate the information you need.

- If you need more information about creating and using directories; preparing and using data disks on which to store your documents; and renaming,

```
11/20/86  09:04              Directory C:\WP\FILES\*.*
Document Size:      69448                      Free Disk Space:    7065600

 <CURRENT>      <DIR>              .. <PARENT>      <DIR>
MSCHS    .      <DIR>   10/14/86 10:12   0       .CAP      4256   10/02/86 13:05
123SS    .       1010   08/14/86 12:54   123SS   .BK!       943   08/06/86 13:08
A        .CAP    4256   10/02/86 13:05   ADDRESS .PF         12   10/10/86 15:18
ADDRESS  .SF      821   10/10/86 15:29   ALTA    .MAC         9   09/25/86 08:50
ALTB     .MAC       9   09/25/86 08:52   ALTC    .MAC         9   09/25/86 08:53
ALTD     .MAC       2   10/02/86 09:36   ALTE    .MAC        13   09/25/86 08:47
ALTF     .MAC      33   09/30/86 08:15   ALTH    .MAC        28   09/30/86 07:55
ALTL     .MAC      23   09/25/86 10:09   ALTN    .MAC         3   10/09/86 08:39
ALTO     .MAC       5   08/12/86 08:52   ALTR    .MAC        18   10/08/86 09:40
ALTT     .MAC       4   08/12/86 08:56   ALTV    .MAC        13   08/12/86 11:23
ALTW     .MAC       5   08/12/86 08:50   ALTY    .MAC         5   08/12/86 08:51
ALTZ     .MAC      10   10/16/86 10:24   APP     .MAC        12   11/13/86 17:32
APPB     .       2063   11/13/86 17:14
                                         CHAPTER8.ASC      18688   10/29/86 10:40
COPYRITE.        2246   11/13/86 11:30   COPYRITE.ASC       2304   11/13/86 11:30
ESCROW   .        639   10/21/86 20:09   IO      .MAR        853   10/27/86 22:01
IO_ASCII.MAR      896   10/27/86 22:03   KARIN   .          1715   10/09/86 19:58
KARIN    .ASC    1792   10/09/86 19:58   KARIN   .BK!       1792   10/09/86 19:40

1 Retrieve; 2 Delete; 3 Rename; 4 Print; 5 Text In;
6 Look; 7 Change Directory; 8 Copy; 9 Word Search; 0 Exit: 6
```

FIGURE 1.11: Viewing the List Files screen to retrieve a file. You can also look at the contents of other directories and retrieve files directly from them by using this screen.

copying, and deleting files, refer to Chapter 6, "File Management."

- If you need information about how to install WordPerfect and configure it to your computer system, how to permanently change the WordPerfect default settings using the Setup menu, or how to use the various startup options, refer to Chapter 16, "Installation, Setup, and Startup Options."

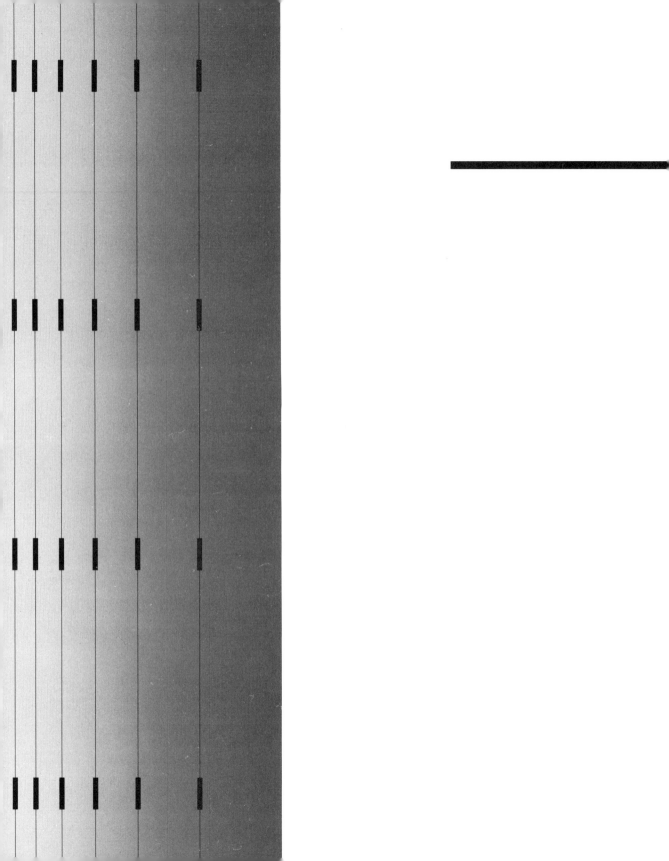

CHAPTER 2

BASIC FORMATTING AND TEXT ENTRY

BASIC FORMATTING
AND TEXT ENTRY

This chapter covers the fundamental entry operations you will perform with WordPerfect: entering text and setting new formats for the documents you create. It also includes information about how to delete text, add simple print enhancements such as boldfacing and underlining, create document-summary screens, and access WordPerfect's on-line help screens.

The formatting operations covered in this chapter include setting new left and right margins, setting tab stops, changing line spacing, indenting text, aligning text within the margin settings, and adding your own page breaks.

For information about other formatting features such as adding headers, footers, and page numbers and keeping blocks of text together on a page (widows and orphans), refer to Chapter 4.

CREATING A NEW DOCUMENT

As soon as you start WordPerfect, after the opening screen has been displayed, you are presented with an editing screen that is completely blank except for the status line in the lower-right corner. This status line keeps you informed at all times of the current position of the cursor in document creation and editing. As soon as you see this screen, you are free to begin work on a new document.

The Document Default Settings

If you immediately begin typing the text of a new document, it will be formatted according to WordPerfect's document default settings. These initial settings are summarized in Table 2.1. As you can see from this table, WordPerfect assumes that your document will be single-spaced and will be printed with 1-inch margins on all sides of an $8^{1}/_{2}$ × 11-inch page.

FORMAT	SETTING	REFERENCE
Paper size	8 ½ by 11	Chapter 2
Page length	54 single-spaced text lines	Chapter 2
Form length	66 single-spaced text lines	Chapter 2
Character spacing (pitch)	10 characters per inch	Chapter 5
Line spacing	Single	Chapter 2
Lines per inch	6	Chapters 2, 5
Line length	65 characters	Chapters 2, 4
Left margin	At 10 characters (approx. 1 inch)	Chapter 2
Right margin	At 74 characters (approx. 1 inch)	Chapter 2
Top margin	6 lines (12 half lines, or 1 inch)	Chapter 2
Bottom margin	6 lines (12 half lines, or 1 inch)	Chapter 2
Tabs	At every 5 spaces; after position 160, at every 10 spaces	Chapters 2, 5
Hyphenation	Off	Chapter 3
Right justification	On	Chapter 4
Page numbers	None	Chapter 4
Headers	None	Chapter 4
Footers	None	Chapter 4

TABLE 2.1: WordPerfect's Document Default Settings

WordPerfect also automatically right justifies all of the text of the new document. Because WordPerfect does not show right justification on the screen as you create a document, it is easy to forget that this setting is in effect until you print your document.

To right align the text on each line of a document, WordPerfect adds spaces between certain words in the line. The placement of these spaces appears somewhat random. As a result of the uneven amount of space between words within a line, a document with right-justified text is sometimes more difficult to read than one with a ragged-right margin. Remember, if you wish your document to have a ragged-right margin, you must change the default setting, turning off right justification (press Ctrl-F8 3).

Whenever you enter text, word wrap is in effect. As soon as you type a word that extends beyond the default right margin of 74, the word is placed at the beginning of the next line. You do not need to press Return when the cursor approaches the end of the line. You should only add a carriage return to mark the end of a paragraph or enter a short line of text whose words are to remain by themselves (as when entering a section heading or table title).

Because WordPerfect's hyphenation feature is off when you first start a new document (in all releases after 4.0), entire words are wrapped to new lines whenever they extend beyond the right margin setting. When you enter a hyphen between words, it will appear in the printed document. If a hyphenated word extends beyond the right margin, it will be split at the hyphen only if the first word will fit within the line's margin setting.

In addition to the default line and margin settings, tab stops are automatically set for you at 5-space intervals. By pressing the Tab key, you can indent the first line of a paragraph. Because the left margin begins at position 10 (letting you know that the left margin will be offset 1 inch from the left edge of the paper), the cursor will jump immediately to position 15 (displayed as Pos 15 on the status line) when you press the Tab key one time. If you press the Tab key a second time, the cursor will jump to position 20, and so on. Tabs beyond position 160 are automatically set at 10-space intervals (remember, however, that your right margin does not extend beyond position 74 unless you increase it).

WordPerfect supports seven different types of tab stop. When you begin a new document, all tabs that have been preset are of one type: left-justify tabs. This type of tab always aligns your text from the left of the tab stop and is the one that you use when you indent a paragraph. In addition to the left-justify tab, you can set right- or center-justify tabs or decimal tabs. Decimal tabs align text on the decimal point (though this character can be changed to something else). They are most often used when you are creating a table that contains columns of figures.

In addition to these kinds of tab, you can create left, right, or decimal tabs that are automatically preceded by dot leaders. The text you enter at these types of tab stop is automatically preceded by strings of periods with spaces between them such as are sometimes used to separate table of contents entries from their page numbers. (Information about how to set all of these types of tab stop can be found later in this chapter in the section "Setting Tabs.")

Changing the Document Default Settings

If the document you are about to create requires different settings from those automatically in effect when you start WordPerfect, you can change them easily. WordPerfect uses the F8 function key in combination with the Shift, Ctrl, and Alt keys to make such changes.

The Shift-F8 combination (referred to as the Line Format key) has six menu options associated with it.

- Change tab stop positions and intervals from 5-space intervals and change the tab type from L, left justify (options 1 and 2).
- Change the left margin from 10 and the right margin from 74 (option 3).

- Change the line spacing from 1 for single-spacing (option 4).
- Turn on and off automatic or program-aided hyphenation (option 5).
- Change the alignment character used by decimal tab stops from the period (option 6).

The Ctrl-F8 combination (referred to as the Print Format key) has 11 menu options associated with it (1–9, A, and B).

- Change the pitch, or horizontal spacing of characters, from 10 characters per inch and the font from font 1 (option 1).
- Change the number of lines per inch, or the vertical spacing of the text, from 6 lines per inch (option 2).
- Turn right justification off and on (options 3 and 4). Choose option 3 to turn right justification off and option 4 to turn it back on.
- Change the style of underlining (options 5–8).
- Change the sheet-feeder bin from bin 1 (option 9).
- Add a special printer command, or control code (option A).
- Turn on the line numbering option that prints line numbers in the left margin (option B).

(For more information about the Print Format options, refer to Chapter 5.)

The Alt-F8 key combination (referred to as the Page Format key) has 10 options associated with it (1–9 and A).

- Add automatic page numbering to a document (option 1). You can also choose the position of the page numbers.
- Renumber pages and choose between Arabic and Roman numerals (option 2).
- Center the text on the page vertically between the top and bottom margins (option 3).
- Change the page length by modifying the form length from 66 lines per page and the number of single-spaced lines per page from 54 (option 4).
- Change the top margin from 12 half lines, or 1 inch (option 5).
- Add headers and footers to a document (option 6).
- Change the column positions used when you add automatic page numbers to the top or bottom of the page from 10 for left-aligned numbers, 42 for centered numbers, and 74 for right-aligned numbers (option 7).
- Suppress a particular page format that you have set up using one or more of the other options on the Page Format menu for the current page only (option 8).

- Keep a certain number of lines of text together on a single page at all times (option 9).
- Turn on widow/orphan protection to avoid having a single line of a paragraph appear alone at the top or bottom of a new page (option A).

(For more information about the Page Format options, refer to Chapter 4.)

All changes made to the document formatting default settings are saved as part of the document. This means that they will be in effect any time you retrieve the document for further editing. However, each time you begin a new document (including beginning a new document in the second window, even if you have modified the default settings in the document in the first window), Word-Perfect will revert to the document defaults settings.

If most of your documents require settings different from the default settings, you can change the default settings permanently from the Setup menu (see Chapter 16). If you find yourself constantly reusing certain formats for many of the documents you create, you can create macros to save yourself time. For instance, you can create a macro that will reset the margins, set all the tabs stops you need, change the line spacing, and place page numbers where you want them—all in one operation. Then whenever you begin a new document that requires the format created by this macro, you can execute the macro before you begin entering your text. This method saves you the time required to issue all of these formatting commands separately.

LEGAL: A MACRO FOR USING 8½ × 14-INCH PAPER

To see how such a macro can work for you, consider the following macro to format a legal document printed on 8½ × 14-inch paper:

Begin macro	Macro name	Keystrokes	End macro
Ctrl-F10	**LEGAL**	**Ctrl-F8 3 Return** **Alt-F8 4 2 Return** **Shift-F8 4 2 Return**	**Ctrl-F10**

In this macro, the Ctrl-F8 3 sequence turns off right justification so that the document will have a ragged right margin. The next key sequence, Alt-F8 4 2, changes the page length to fit legal-size paper. The final key sequence, Shift-F8 4 2, changes the line spacing from single- to double-spacing.

This macro could be further customized to turn on WordPerfect's automatic line numbering feature. You could also add key sequences to change the left, right, top, and bottom margins; add a header and footer or use one of the program's page numbering options; and clear the existing tab stops and set new tabs more like those required for the documents you usually create when you use legal-size paper.

Entering the Text of the Document

After making any necessary changes to the document formatting default settings, you can begin typing the text of your document. As you type, the number of the position indicator in the extreme lower-right corner of the editing screen will increase, keeping you apprised of the cursor's current column position as it advances across the line. When you reach the end of the line, WordPerfect will automatically advance any words that extend beyond the right margin setting to the beginning of the following line.

If you make typing mistakes while entering your text, you can use Backspace or Del to remove them. You use Backspace to delete any unwanted characters to the left of the cursor. Each time you press Backspace, it moves the cursor to the left as it deletes the character. You use Del to delete the character the cursor is on. If you spot a character in the line that needs to be deleted, you can use → or ← to move the cursor to it and use Del to remove it. You can also make cursor movements that cover more distance to place the cursor in the proper position to delete a character. For more information about moving the cursor, refer to "Cursor Movement" in Chapter 1.

WordPerfect offers you many ways to delete large sections of text, including removing words to the left and right of the cursor and deleting everything from the cursor's position to the end of the line or the page. For a complete list of all of the ways you can delete text in a document, refer to Table 2.2 and the individual reference entries under "Deleting Text," later in this chapter.

If you delete some text in error, you can use WordPerfect's undelete function to restore it. To implement this function, you press F1. So long as you have not just issued a WordPerfect command in which F1 acts as a cancel key, the program will display the text last deleted in inverse video at the cursor's position. You will also be presented with two menu options: 1 Restore and 2 Show Previous Deletion. If you type **1**, WordPerfect will reinsert the text displayed in inverse video. If you type **2**, it will display any text removed in a previous deletion operation. You can then type **1** to have this text reinserted. WordPerfect stores the last three text deletions.

To replace mistakes with the correct characters, you can simply type them after deleting unwanted characters. WordPerfect is in Insert mode unless you press the Ins key and see the message "Typeover" in the lower-left of the screen. In Insert mode, new characters are inserted at the cursor's present position, and all characters to its right are shifted right. The program also automatically reformats the text to fit within the left and right margin settings as soon as you move the cursor up or down using either the ↑ or ↓ key or a scrolling key such as PgUp or PgDn or press the + (plus) or − (minus) key.

To indent the first line of a paragraph to the first tab stop (five spaces in at Pos 15 if you have not changed the margin or tab default settings), you press the Tab key. On many keyboards this key is not marked *Tab* but instead is designated by ⇆.

To mark the end of a paragraph, you press the Return key (referred to as the Enter key in your WordPerfect documentation). On many keyboards this key is not marked with the word *Return* or *Enter,* but instead is designated by ←. A carriage return marking the end of a paragraph (referred to as a *hard return* in Word-Perfect) is not normally visible on your screen (if you are using Version 4.2, you can select a visible character to represent the hard return; see "Making Hard Returns Visible on Screen" in Chapter 1).

You can always locate the position of a carriage return by pressing Alt-F3 (Reveal Codes). A hard return exists anywhere you see the code [HRt]. To join two paragraphs separated by a carriage return, you only need delete the [HRt] code by positioning the cursor (indicated in the Reveal Codes window by a double-intensity flashing bar) cithcr immcdiately before or after the code. If the cursor is immediately before the [HRt] code, use Del to delete the code. If the cursor is positioned immediately after the code, use Backspace to remove the code. Then press the space bar or Return to exit the Reveal Codes screen and return to your document.

To split a section of text into separate paragraphs, position the cursor beneath the first character of the word that is to start the new paragraph and press Return. If you are indenting the first line of each paragraph in your document, then press the Tab key to indent the text to the first tab stop.

If you want to center the text of a single line between the left and right margin settings, press Shift-F6 and begin typing. When you press this center key combination, the cursor will move to the center position. As you type, the text will be centered as the cursor moves to the right. Press Return as soon as you are finished typing the title or phrase.

To uncenter text and make it left justified, you must remove one of the centering codes added by WordPerfect when you pressed Shift-F6. To do this, press Alt-F3 (Reveal Codes). You will see two codes, [C] and [c], before and after the centered text. If you delete either of these codes, the text will become left justified.

In addition to centering text, WordPerfect allows you to right justify text so that it is aligned from the right margin. To format text in a line so that it is flush right, press Alt-F6 and then type your text. The cursor will be positioned at the right margin, and the text you enter will appear from right to left until you press Return to signify the end of the line.

To change to flush left text that has been formatted flush right in this manner, you must remove one of the alignment codes added by WordPerfect when you press Alt-F6. To do this, you press Alt-F3 and find the codes [A] and [a] located before and after the right-justified text (note that this text appears left justified in the Reveal Codes window). When you delete either of these codes, the text will become left justified.

To add simple print enhancements such as boldface type or underlining to words or phrases in the text, you press the appropriate function keys before typing the text. For boldface type, this function key is F6. For underlining, this function key is F8. Both of these enhancements must be turned off after you have entered the word or phrase to be enhanced. (You can also add enhancements to text that has already been entered by first marking the text as a block, as will be discussed in Chapter 3.)

The first time you press F6 to turn on boldfacing, WordPerfect adds the format codes [B] and [b]. When you press F6 a second time after entering the words or phrases to be boldfaced, it positions the cursor past the [b] code. (You can also move the cursor manually by pressing the → key once.) This means that if you look at the text in the Reveal Codes window, you will see the codes [B] and [b] placed before and after the phrase displayed in double intensity in the document above. To delete the boldfacing, you need only delete one of these formatting codes.

For underlining, you use the same process except that you turn underlining on and off by pressing F8, and the formatting codes are [U] and [u]. Also, underlining in the document is represented either by underscore characters (if your computer has a monochrome or Hercules Graphics Card) or by inverse video (if your computer has a color graphics card).

After you have finished entering your text, remember to save your document. Press F7, press Return to answer yes (the default selection) when prompted to save the document, and enter a unique file name for your document (see Chapter 5 for details about naming document files). If you wish to exit WordPerfect, type **Y,** and you will be returned to the DOS operating system. (If you have been working on two documents in separate windows, typing **Y** will return you to the other open document rather than the operating system. See Chapter 3.)

If you wish to remain in the word processor (or the current document window) either to begin a new document or edit another one, press Return to answer no (the default selection) to the prompt to exit WordPerfect or the current document window (Doc1 or Doc2).

Automatic Screen Rewrite

KEY SEQUENCE

Ctrl-F3 5 Y

When you enter or delete text that requires words to move down or up a line, WordPerfect automatically reformats the entire screen when you scroll the text up or down or press the ↑ or ↓ key. You can turn this automatic rewrite feature off by pressing Ctrl-F3, typing **5,** and then typing **N** when you see the Auto Rewrite prompt.

When you turn off the automatic rewrite feature, the program reformats each paragraph a line at a time (as opposed to the entire screen) as you move the cursor up or down. With this feature off, you can, however, reformat the entire screen by pressing Ctrl-F3 twice.

The majority of the time you will want to leave the automatic rewrite feature active (this is the program's default setting). However, if you are working with text columns (see Chapter 8) you may want to turn off the screen rewrite feature as you compose the page.

ADDING A DOCUMENT SUMMARY SCREEN TO YOUR DOCUMENT

KEY SEQUENCE

Ctrl-F5 A

REVEAL CODES

[Smry/Cmnt:]

Version 4.2 of WordPerfect allows you to add a Document Summary screen to any document that you create. You can use this screen to record information about the author and typist of a document as well as to enter a block of comments describing either the content or format of the document. The Document Summary screen also automatically includes the name of the document and the date of its creation.

To add a Document Summary screen to the document you are creating or editing, press Ctrl-F5 (Text In/Out) and type **A.** A Document Summary screen similar to the one shown in Figure 2.1 will then appear on your screen. You can type the name of the author (using up to 40 characters), terminating this entry by pressing Return, or you can bypass this entry by just pressing Return. You can then enter the name of the typist in the same way or bypass this entry too if you wish. After you press Return with the cursor on the Typist entry line, the cursor will automatically appear inside the comments box.

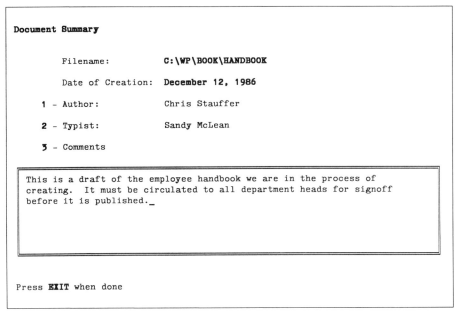

Document Summary

       Filename: **C:\WP\BOOK\HANDBOOK**

       Date of Creation: **December 12, 1986**

 1 - Author: Chris Stauffer

 2 - Typist: Sandy McLean

 3 - Comments

This is a draft of the employee handbook we are in the process of creating. It must be circulated to all department heads for signoff before it is published._

Press **EXIT** when done

FIGURE 2.1: WordPerfect's Document Summary screen, accessed by pressing Ctrl-F5 and typing **A.** You can add a document summary to any document. This summary always displays the file name and date of creation and can include the name of the author and the typist as well as a comments section of up to 880 characters. To display the Document Summary screen at the beginning of a document, you press Ctrl-F5, type **D**, and type **Y** in answer to the prompt, "Display Summary? (Y/N) N." When you use the Look option on the List Files menu (accessed by pressing F5 and Return and typing **6**), the Document Summary screen is displayed above the first part of the text of the document, even if you have suppressed the screen's display in the document itself.

You can add up to 880 characters in the comment box of the Document Summary screen. You can use this area to describe the contents of the document or annotate it in some other manner. Many times, you may find comments regarding any special printing or formatting characteristics for the document, such as special print fonts or paper requirements, beneficial to add.

When you have finished adding your comments, press F7 and Return to return to the document. To have the Document Summary screen displayed at the beginning of the document, press Ctrl-F5 and type **D**. WordPerfect will then display the prompt, "Display Summary? (Y/N) N." After you type **Y**, Word-Perfect will display a second prompt, "Display Comments? (Y/N) N." This refers to the display of nonprinting comments that can be added to annotate the text (see the following section for details). After answering this question **Y** or **N,** you will be returned directly to the document.

To suppress the display of a Document Summary screen, you repeat this same procedure, only this time you just press Return in response to the "Display Summary? (Y/N) N" prompt. Even if the Document Summary screen is displayed at the beginning of the first screen of the document, it will not be printed when you print the page or the entire document. The only way to obtain a printout of the Document Summary screen is press Shift-PrtSc.

When you use the Look option (option 6) on the List Files menu (accessed by pressing F5 and Return), WordPerfect displays the Document Summary screen at the top of the screen. If you press Alt-F3 (Reveal Codes), you will see the first 100 characters in the Document Summary screen, even if its display has been suppressed in the document itself.

The contents of the Document Summary screen can be identified by the Reveal Code [Smry/Cmnt:] followed by the first 100 characters of the summary text. The author and typist are identified by the [HRt] codes that indicate the hard returns separating these lines from the comments. The end of the comments that can be shown is indicated by a right square bracket ( ]). If the contents of the document summary is longer than 100 characters, this will be shown by an ellipsis (...) before the right square bracket, indicating that the screen contains more text than can be displayed in the Reveal Codes window.

To delete a document summary, you must delete its Reveal Code. To do this, position the cursor in the Reveal Codes window immediately before the [Smry/Cmnt:] code and press Del.

You can edit the contents of the Document Summary screen from anywhere in the document by pressing Ctrl-F5 and typing **A.** To change the author's name, you type **1** to place the cursor at the beginning of this entry. To edit the typist's name, you type **2,** and to edit the comments section, you type **3.** After you have finished editing the document summary, press F7 followed by Return. The cursor will automatically return to its original position in the document.

Note: If you wish, you can have WordPerfect automatically prompt you to create a Document Summary screen whenever you exit and save a new document. To do this, you need to start WordPerfect using the /S option to use its Setup menu. Then type **2** to select the Set Initial Settings option. The last option listed on this screen is the Text In/Out option. To activate this option, press Ctrl-F5 (Text In/Out). You will then be prompted with:

Enter Document Summary on Save/Exit? (Y/N) N

Type **Y** to change the default setting from no to yes and press Return to return to the Setup menu. Press Return once more to enter WordPerfect.

ADDING NONPRINTING COMMENTS TO YOUR DOCUMENT

KEY SEQUENCE

Ctrl-F5 B

REVEAL CODES

[Smry/Cmnt:]

WordPerfect Version 4.2 allows you to add nonprinting comments anywhere in your document. This feature is very helpful if you need to insert a comment to remind yourself to add additional text to the document when the information becomes available. You can then use the Search feature to locate the comments that you have added to the document.

To add a comment to your document, press Ctrl-F5 (Text In/Out) and type **B,** the option to create a comment. A Document Comment screen similar to the one shown in Figure 2.2 will be displayed on your screen. The cursor will automatically appear within the comment box bordered by double lines.

The text that you enter in the comment box can consist of up to 1,024 characters. When you have finished entering the text of the comment, press F7 and Return. To have the comment displayed on the screen, you must press Ctrl-F5

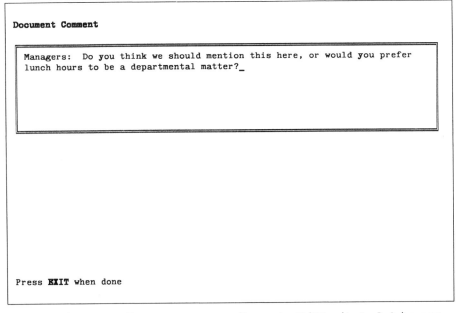

```
Document Comment

  ┌─────────────────────────────────────────────────────────────────┐
  │ Managers:  Do you think we should mention this here, or would you prefer │
  │ lunch hours to be a departmental matter?_                          │
  │                                                                   │
  │                                                                   │
  │                                                                   │
  └─────────────────────────────────────────────────────────────────┘




Press EXIT when done
```

FIGURE 2.2: The Document Comment screen accessed by pressing Ctrl-F5 and typing **B.** A document comment can consist of up to 1,024 characters. Once you have finished entering the comment text, press F7 (Exit). To display the comment you have entered on screen, press Ctrl-F5 and type **D.** Then type **Y** in answer to the prompt, "Display Comments? (Y/N) N" (this prompt appears after you indicate whether you want the Document Summary screen displayed). To display a comment for editing, position the cursor somewhere after the comment display, press Ctrl-F5, and type **C.** After you finish modifying the comment, press F7 to return to the document.

and type **D** to access the Display option. After answering the prompt about displaying the Document Summary screen (see the previous section, "Adding a Document Summary Screen to Your Document"), you will see the prompt

Display Comments? (Y/N) N

Type **Y** if you want all of the comments you add to the document displayed. Later, if you wish to suppress their display, you can execute this same command, this time typing **N** instead of **Y.**

> *Note:* Whether or not you have indicated that comments should be displayed in the document with this command, any comments added at the beginning of the document will be displayed whenever you use the Look option (6) on the List Files screen (accessed by pressing F5). Also, you can always see the first 100 characters of a comment in the Reveal Codes window (accessed by pressing Alt-F3). These are displayed after the code [Sumry/Cmnt:] in the Reveal Codes window.

You can add comments anywhere in the text of your document. If you add a comment between the words in a single line of text, the line will be split apart by the comment box when you have the comment displayed on your screen, but the lines will appear correctly when printed.

A comment added in the middle of a line of text is shown in Figure 2.3. Notice that the comment box has been placed below the line of text that appears cut in half. The continuation of the sentence appears on a separate line below the comment box. Although it appears as if the line has been broken into two by the comment, because the comment does not print, the word processor ignores its presence; the status line (Ln) indicator does not register a change when you move the cursor from one line to the other. When you position the cursor at the end of the last word in the line before the comment and press →, the cursor jumps past the comment box to the first character in the first word in the line below. When the document is printed, these two lines will be printed as one.

If this split display disturbs you when you edit the text, you can suppress the comment display while you are editing and then redisplay the comment when you have finished.

To locate a particular comment in a document, you can use the Search feature to move the cursor to each comment. As with any search procedure, you can search from the cursor's present position to the beginning or to the end of the document (see "Using WordPerfect's Search and Replace Commands" in Chapter 3). To locate a comment that is ahead of the cursor, you press F2 (→ Search) and then press Ctrl-F5. When you do this, you will see the following code in the bottom-left corner of the screen:

– > Srch: [Sumry/Cmnt]

```
Parking_

As parking is limited, please apply to the personnel office for a
parking slot assignment.

Hours

Noon to 1 p.m. has been reserved as lunch hour for all employees.
Some departments have chosen to take lunch
┌─────────────────────────────────────────────────────────────────┐
│ Managers: Do you want to mention this here, or would you prefer lunch │
│ hours to be a departmental matter?                                 │
└─────────────────────────────────────────────────────────────────┘
                                           from 11:30 to 12:30 or
from 12:30 to 1:30; check with your manager.

Cafeteria

The company cafeteria, located on the third floor, is open from 7
a.m. until 2 p.m. daily.  Breakfast is available for your
convenience until 9:00.  After 2 p.m., vending machines with cold
sandwiches and salads are available.

Recreational Facilities
C:\WP2\HANDBOOK                         Doc 1  Pg 1  Ln 15     Pos 17
```

FIGURE 2.3: A comment added in the middle of a line of text. Comments are not printed when you print your document.

When you press F2 again to commence the search, WordPerfect will place the cursor immediately after the first comment it locates *after* the cursor's position. If this is not the comment you wanted to find, press F2 twice to search for the next [Sumry/Cmnt] formatting code. To search for a comment that occurs *before* the cursor's present position, press Shift-F2 (← Search) instead of F2 alone and then proceed as before.

If you wish to delete a comment you have located by using the Search feature, you can press Backspace. So long as you have not moved the cursor from its position after the comment was located by the Search command, you will be prompted as follows:

Delete [Sumry/Cmnt]? (Y/N) N

Type **Y** to delete the comment.

You can also delete a comment box by pressing Alt-F3 (Reveal Codes) and locating the [Sumry/Cmnt:] code. Position the cursor right before this code and press Del to remove the box.

To edit a comment you located by using the Search feature, press Ctrl-F5 and type **C.** This displays the Document Comment screen and places the cursor in the comment box so you can edit its contents. Once you have made your changes, press F7 and Return to return to the document.

If you wish to edit a comment without using the Search feature to locate it, you must place the cursor somewhere in a line below the comment display before pressing Ctrl-F5 and typing **C**. If your cursor is located on a line above the comment box, WordPerfect will display the previous comment on your screen. When you exit this screen, you will find that the cursor is located right after this previous comment (which may be many pages before the comment you wanted to edit). If this happens, press Ctrl-Home twice to move the cursor to its previous position before accessing the comment editing command. Then move the cursor to a line below the comment box and issue the command again.

Obtaining On-line Help as You Work

KEY SEQUENCE

To obtain information about a specific key sequence:
    F3 <*function key combination*> **Return** (to exit help)
To obtain an alphabetical listing of Word Perfect features and the function keys used to access them:
    F3 <*letter*> **Return** (to exit help)
To obtain an on-screen representation of keyboard template
    F3 F3 Return (to exit help)

WordPerfect offers extensive on-line Help screens that you can use whenever you need additional information about a specific feature or command. The F3 function key is WordPerfect's Help key (this key may be hard to remember if you are used to other IBM PC software that uses F1 as the Help key). After you Press F3 (Help), you must then press another key to obtain specific help.

You can use F3 alone to see what version of WordPerfect you are running. This information is always displayed in the upper-right corner of the screen. Right after the version number, you will see a date that further identifies the version. As of this writing, WP 4.2 1/23/87 is the latest version of WordPerfect. If you are using a version prior to this one, you will probably want to contact Word-Perfect Corporation to obtain an update of the program.

When WordPerfect Version 4.1 was the current release, many small changes were added to the word processor under the general heading of Version 4.1. The only way to identify the release was by the release date that appeared on the Help screen. This practice could well be repeated with Version 4.2. In such a case, you will need to note the date of your release as well as its number to determine whether it is still the most recent one.

If you wish to know more about how a particular function key combination operates in WordPerfect, you merely press the function key combination. For example, pressing F3 followed by Ctrl-F5 displays a Help screen that tells you about document conversion, summaries, and comments—the commands associated with Ctrl-F5 (Text In/Out). On this screen you will find numbered options that you can type to obtain other, more specific Help screens. Whenever you wish to return to your document, press Return. Remember not to press F1 (Cancel) or Esc, or you will receive a Help screen describing the functions of these keys instead of being returned to the document.

Instead of pressing a specific function key or key combination after pressing F3, you can also type a letter. For example, if you had forgotten the function keys used to perform the search and replace operation in WordPerfect, you could press F3 and type **S** (for search). WordPerfect would then display an alphabetical list of its features that begin with the letter *s*. This Help screen is shown in Figure 2.4.

As you can see from this figure, the Help screen is arranged in three columns listing the function keys used, the features, and the key names. In this case, you can see that to perform a search and replace operation in WordPerfect, you use Alt-F2. To obtain more information about how the search and replace feature

Function Key	Feature	Key Name
F10	Save Text	Save
+(Num Pad)	Screen Down	Screen Down
-(Num Pad)	Screen Up	Screen Up
Alt -F2	Search & Replace	Replace
Alt -F2	Search & Replace w/Confirm	Replace
F5	Search for Text in File(s)	List Files - 9
Shft-F7	Select Printers	Print - 4 Printer Control
Shft-F7	Send Printer a "GO"	Print - 4 Printer Control
Ctrl-F8	Sheet Feeder Bin #	Print Format
Shft-F7	Sheet Feeder Y/N	Print - 4 then 3 Select Printers
Ctrl-F1	Shell	Shell
Ctrl "-"	Soft Hyphen	Soft Hyphen
Ctrl-F9	Sort	Merge/Sort
Shft-F8	Spacing	Line Format
Ctrl-V	Special Characters	Ctrl-V then decimal ASCII code
Ctrl-F2	Speller	Spell
Ctrl-F3	Split Screen	Screen
Shft-F1	Subscript	Super/Subscript
Shft-F1	Superscript	Super/Subscript
Shft-F3	Switch Documents	Switch_

FIGURE 2.4: The Help screen displayed when you press F3 (Help) and type **S.** When you press F3 (Help) and type a specific letter, WordPerfect displays a Help screen organized by an alphabetical list of features. In this case, the letter **S** was used to obtain the function key combination for search and replace operations. As you can see, the Help screen is arranged in three columns: The first lists the function keys used, the second lists the features, and the third lists WordPerfect's names for the keys. To obtain more help about a specific feature, you need only press the function key combination. In this case, you would press Alt-F2 to access a Help screen describing search and replace operations.

works in the program, you can press Alt-F2 and obtain a Help screen specifically about this command.

Instead of using this method to remind you of the function key assignments, you can obtain an on-screen diagram similar to the keyboard template supplied with the WordPerfect program by pressing F3 after you have accessed the Help screen (in other words, by pressing F3 twice). Figure 2.5 shows this screen.

To obtain a hard copy of this screen, make sure the printer is on and press Shift-PrtSc. To make this printout useful, you will have to mark it in some manner to differentiate the various key combinations. This is because the boldface and underlining used on screen to indicate when the Ctrl and Alt keys are used with function keys do not print when you use the Shift-PrtSc method. One way to distinguish the key combinations is to use different-color highlighters to color code each combination.

All help messages are located on the Learn disk. If you are using WordPerfect on a dual-disk drive system, you must remember to replace the data disk on

```
      WordPerfect 4.2 Template (IBM Layout)

            Shell            Spell
    F1  SUPER/SUBSCRIPT     <-SEARCH      F2
          Thesaurus          Replace
           Cancel           Search->
           Screen            Move                   Legend:
    F3     SWITCH          ->INDENT<-     F4
        Reveal Codes         Block              Ctrl + Function Key
           Help            ->Indent            SHIFT + FUNCTION KEY
        Text In/Out        Tab Align            Alt + Function Key
    F5     DATE             CENTER        F6     Function Key alone
         Mark Text        Flush Right
         List Files          Bold
          Footnote           Print
    F7     PRINT          LINE FORMAT     F8
        Math/Columns      Page Format
           Exit            Underline
         Merge/Sort        Macro Def.
    F9    MERGE E        RETRIEVE TEXT    F10
        Merge Codes          Macro
          Merge R          Save Text
```

FIGURE 2.5: The on-screen function key template accessed by pressing F3 (Help) twice. As you can see from the legend, this screen uses various print enhancements to identify the key combination (if any) used to access a particular group of features. The boldfaced labels identify function keys used with Ctrl. The capitalized labels identify function keys used with Shift. The underlined labels identify function keys used with Alt. Labels in regular text identify function keys used alone.

which you store your documents in drive B with the Learn disk before you press the Help key (also, B:\ must be the current directory when you press F3).

If you are using a hard disk system, you can access help from anywhere in the program without having to switch disks so long as you copied the WPHELP.FIL file from the Learn disk onto the hard disk during installation. To find out whether this file has been copied into your WordPerfect directory, press F5 (List Files) to obtain a list of all of the files in this directory.

If you are in a subdirectory when you press F5 and press Return, move the highlight to ..<PARENT> <DIR> on the right side of the first line of file names and press Return twice. If you do not find the WPHELP.FIL file among the list of file names, refer to the installation instructions in Chapter 16 to find out how to copy this file onto your disk. Press F1 (Cancel) to then return to your document.

If you are inexperienced in using WordPerfect, you should make it a practice to access the Help screen associated with each new feature that you use. Many of these Help screens contain information not included in your WordPerfect documentation.

DELETING TEXT

WordPerfect has several methods for deleting various portions of text. They are summarized in Table 2.2 for easy reference.

TO DELETE:	PRESS:
Character by character	**Backspace** (deletes to left of cursor)
	Del (deletes character or space the cursor is on)
Word by word	**Ctrl-Backspace**
Several words	**Esc _n_** (_n_ = number of words to left of the cursor) **Ctrl-Backspace**
The word to the left of the cursor	**Ctrl-← Ctrl-Backspace**
The word to the right of the cursor	**Ctrl-→ Ctrl-Backspace**
To the end of a line	**Ctrl-End**
To the end of a sentence	**Alt-F4 F2 . F2 Del Y**
To the end of a page	**Ctrl-PgDn Y**
To the end of a block	**Alt-F4 Backspace** or **Del Y**

TABLE 2.2: Methods for Deleting Text in WordPerfect

You may want to combine some of these methods into macros to speed up your work (for a discussion of how to create and use WordPerfect macros, see Chapter 14). In particular, the deletion methods that prompt you for confirmation before making a deletion can be speeded up with macros.

Deleting Character by Character

KEY SEQUENCE

To delete the character to the left of the cursor:
   Backspace
To delete the character the cursor is on:
   Del

To delete character by character, use Backspace or Del. Backspace deletes the character to the left of the cursor, and Del deletes the character or space the cursor is on. To progressively delete to the left of the cursor, hold down Backspace. To progressively delete characters to the right of the cursor, hold down Del.

Deleting Word by Word

KEY SEQUENCE

   Ctrl-Backspace

To delete an entire word, position the cursor anywhere in the word, hold down Ctrl, and press Backspace. If you are deleting in the middle of a line, you can continue to delete words in this way, as the cursor will be positioned on the next word to the right, one after another.

Many times you will need to use Ctrl-→ or Ctrl-← to position the cursor on the first character of a word before using Ctrl-Backspace to remove the word. If you need to delete a phrase located to the left of the cursor in a line, you can press Ctrl-← several times to place the cursor on the first word of the phrase before using Ctrl-Backspace. You can then use the word delete function progressively. Each time you press Ctrl-Backspace, word wrap closes the gap caused by removing the word at the cursor. This brings the next word in the phrase to be removed into position, allowing you to delete each word without having to move the cursor.

You can also use the Esc key's Repeat Command function to delete a specified number of words. To do this, you press Esc, enter the number of words you wish to delete, and then press Ctrl-Backspace. For example, to delete the phrase "for a limited time only," you would position the cursor on the *f* in *for,* press Esc, type **5** (because there are five words in this phrase), and press Ctrl-Backspace. As already discussed, you could also position the cursor on the *f* and manually press Ctrl-Backspace five times to remove the phrase.

Deleting the Word to the Left or Right of the Cursor

KEY SEQUENCE

To delete left of the cursor to the word boundary:
   Home Backspace
To delete right of the cursor to the word boundary:
   Home Del

The current version of WordPerfect (Version 4.2) includes two new delete commands: Home Backspace, which deletes from the cursor's position left to the beginning of the word, and Home Del, which deletes from the cursor's position right to the beginning of the next word.

If the cursor is positioned within the word you wish to delete, Home Backspace will remove only the characters to the left of the cursor, preserving the character the cursor is on as well as any to its right. In this way, this commands differs from Ctrl-Backspace (Delete Word), which deletes all of the characters in a word, regardless of which character the cursor is on when the command is issued. Home Del works in the same way, except that it deletes from the cursor's position to the right. Both of these commands can be used to progressively delete several words in a single phrase.

Deleting to the End of a Line

KEY SEQUENCE

   Ctrl-End

To delete from the current cursor position to the end of the line the cursor is on, hold down Ctrl and press End. To delete several lines in this way, press Esc, specify the number of lines you wish to delete, and then press Ctrl-End. When you use the Ctrl-End combination with the Esc repeat function, include the line containing the cursor as part of the count of lines to be deleted. For example, if you wish to delete to the end of the line containing the cursor as well as the next two entire lines of text, press Esc, type **3,** and then press Ctrl-End.

To delete the entire line that the cursor is on, move the cursor to the beginning of the line by pressing Home followed by ← before pressing Ctrl-End.

Deleting to the End of a Sentence

You can delete to the end of a sentence by using WordPerfect's Search function (see Chapter 3). This method requires several keystrokes, so the following macro is suggested.

DES: A MACRO TO DELETE TO THE END OF A SENTENCE

To write a macro that deletes all characters from the cursor position up to and including the next period that occurs in text, construct the following macro, called *DES* (for Delete to the End of the Sentence).

Begin macro	*Macro name*	*Keystrokes*	*End macro*
Ctrl-F10	**DES**	**Alt-F4 F2**	**Ctrl-F10**
		.F2 Del Y	

When using this macro, remember that your sentences may not all end with periods. Some may end with question marks or exclamation points. If you use the DES macro to try to delete this type of sentence, it will delete all of the text from the cursor position to the first period located by the search function (this may remove several sentences). Also, if your sentence contains a period that occurs before the period signifying the end of the sentence (as in ABC, Inc.), this macro will delete only to the first period, not all the way to the end of the sentence, and you will have to issue the macro a second time.

Note: In general, you should not create Alt macros in WordPerfect that delete sections of text. It is too easy to inadvertently press Alt with the letter associated with macro when you mean to press Shift to capitalize a letter. This is why the macro that deletes to the end of a sentence is named *DES* instead of *Alt-E* or some other combination. If you ever use a deletion macro or a delete command in error, remember that WordPerfect's Undelete function (F1 1) is available to restore your text (see "Undeleting" later in this chapter).

Deleting a Paragraph

KEY SEQUENCE

Alt-F4 Return Backspace (or Del) Y

A quick way to delete an entire paragraph (to the next hard return) is to press Alt-F4 to turn on block marking when the cursor is on the first letter in the paragraph; then press Return to mark the entire paragraph as a block. Delete the paragraph by pressing Backspace or Del and responding **Y** to the delete prompt.

You can also extend or contract block highlighting by pressing any of the arrow keys after you have marked a paragraph in this way.

Deleting to the End of a Page

KEY SEQUENCE

Ctrl-PgDn

To delete to the end of the current page, press Ctrl-PgDn. You will then see the confirmation message

Delete Remainder of Page? (Y/N) N

at the bottom of the screen. To delete the text, you must type **Y.** To abort the command, just press Return. Ctrl-PgDn deletes to the end of a user-defined page (marked with the formatting code [HPg] and displayed as a line of equal signs) or to the end of a system-defined page (marked with the formatting code [SPg] and displayed as a line of hyphens).

Deleting a Block of Text

KEY SEQUENCE

Alt-F4 Backspace (or **Del**) **Y**

To delete a block of text, first mark the block by pressing Alt-F4 and highlighting all of the text to be included with the cursor-movement keys (see Chapter 1). Then press Backspace or Del. WordPerfect then displays the following confirmation prompt:

Delete Block? (Y/N) N

Type **Y** to delete the block that you just marked. To abort the command, just press Return. (For more information about defining and using blocks in Word-Perfect, refer to Chapter 3.)

DELETING FORMATTING CODES

WordPerfect inserts formatting codes into your document each time you issue a formatting command—by pressing Return, for example, to signal the end of a paragraph, or by pressing a function key such as F6 to begin or end boldfacing. You cannot see these codes as you type, but they are there. To delete them, you must press Alt-F3 (Reveal Codes). WordPerfect then splits the screen, as shown in Figure 2.6, and in the lower window, shows you the actual formatting codes that have been inserted in and around your text. As you can see, these formatting codes consist of abbreviations for the command or feature they invoke.

To delete formatting codes, you simply move the cursor to the immediate right of the code and then press Backspace. If the cursor is located to the immediate left of the code, you can press Del to remove the code. For example, in Figure 2.6 the cursor is next to the code [u]. If you were to press Backspace at that point, the

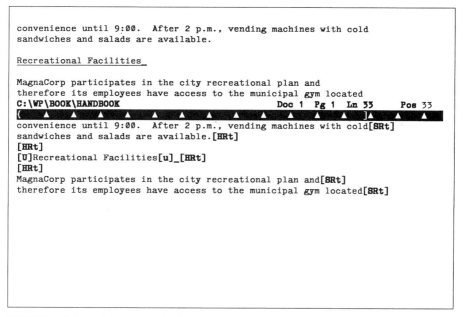

FIGURE 2.6: Deleting formatting codes by pressing Alt-F3 (Reveal Codes) to identify and locate the codes to be removed. Whenever you press Alt-F3, WordPerfect splits the screen into two windows. The lower window shows you the text of the document displayed in the window above bounded by formatting codes. All such codes are enclosed in square brackets. To delete a formatting code, place the cursor (the flashing hyphen shown in double intensity) just before or after one of the brackets. If the cursor is positioned before the left bracket, press Del to remove it. If the cursor is positioned after the right bracket, press Backspace to remove it. In this figure, the cursor is positioned immediately after the right bracket of the [u] that turns off the underlining (begun by the [U] code). To remove the underlining of this phrase, you press Backspace once. Then, to return to editing the document, you press the space bar. This automatically removes the Reveal Codes window from the screen.

[u] code would be deleted from the document, removing the underlining format that had been in effect.

After you delete any unwanted codes, you return to normal document mode by pressing the space bar or Return. The window in the lower part of the screen disappears, and you can continue working on your document.

Some of the more common formatting codes that can be deleted in this manner are listed in Table 2.3. If two codes, such as [B] and [b], are shown, the uppercased code indicates the beginning of a format change—in this case, the beginning of boldfacing—and the lowercased code indicates the end of the formatting change—the end of the section that is to be boldfaced. To delete such formats, which include boldfacing, centering, and underlining, you need only delete one of the codes; the other will disappear as well.

FORMATTING CODE	DESCRIPTION
[HRt]	Hard return (end of paragraph)
[HPg]	Hard page break (forced new page; inserted by user)
[TAB]	Tab
[Tab Set]	Tab setting
[->Indent]	Indent
[->Indent<-]	Left/right indent
[A][a]	Tab align or flush right begin and end
[Align Char:]	Alignment character
[B][b]	Bold begin and end
[C][c]	Center begin and end
[U][u]	Underline begin and end
[Undrl Style:n]	Underlining style (n = style number)
[Rt Just On]	Right justification on
[Rt Just Off]	Right justification off
[Sumry/Cmnt]	Marks the use of a Document Summary or Document Comment screen
[MarginSet:n,n]	Left and right margin settings (n = position)
[<-Mar Rel:n]	Left margin release (n = positions moved)
[Top Mar:n]	Top margin setting (n = number of half lines)
[Pg Lnth:n,n]	Page length setting (n = number of lines)
[Spacing Set:n]	Line spacing setting

TABLE 2.3: Common Formatting Codes That Can Be Deleted

Not all of the formatting codes that appear in the Reveal Codes window can be deleted. For instance, you cannot remove a soft return marked with the code [SRt] or a page break that WordPerfect inserts for you marked with the code [SPg]. If you try to delete a soft-return code (which indicates where Word-Perfect uses word wrap to reformat a line to the margin and tab settings), you will instead delete the space between the last word on the line and the first word of the following line. Likewise, if you try to delete the [SPg] code marking a soft page break, you will delete only the blank space between the last word on one page and the first word on the following page.

Note: If you wish to change the position of a [SPg] code, that is, where the page break occurs, you must do this by using one of the several commands for keeping text together (explained in Chapter 4) or by changing the page length (explained later in this chapter).

Deleting Formatting Codes without Using Reveal Codes

You can also delete formatting codes without using Alt-F3 (Reveal Codes) if the cursor is located on the code when you press the Backspace key. However, this method is often very difficult to use, because you cannot visually locate the code in the text. For this reason, you will need to be familiar with the use of Alt-F3 to display the Reveal Codes window and with how to identify and locate the codes to delete. Whenever there is an easy way to locate a particular formatting code without resorting to Alt-F3 (Reveal Codes), it will be pointed out in this book.

Because formatting codes can be deleted with the Backspace key, you may sometimes be prompted with a Delete message asking you to confirm the removal of a particular format code when your intention is to delete the character to the left of the cursor. If you do not wish to delete the code, just press Return, because in such cases, the No option is always the default.

For example, if you have boldfaced a word and discover that you have mistyped its final letter, you might see the following message when you press Backspace to delete it:

Delete [Bold]? (Y/N) N

To preserve the format code that turns off boldfacing, you would press Return to answer no to the prompt and then press Backspace to delete the final letter of the word.

If the word that you just corrected is at the end of a line and you intend to continue typing, you must also remember to press the → key before pressing the space bar. Using → places the cursor beyond the formatting code that turns off boldfacing (though it does not change the cursor's column position on the screen). If you did not use the → key before pressing the space bar and continuing to type, all of the text that you enter would be boldfaced just like the word you edited.

UNDELETING

> **KEY SEQUENCE**
>
> To restore text removed by last deletion:
>   **F1 1**
> To restore text removed in previous deletion:
>   **F1 2** (until text you wish to restore appears) **1**

You will often want to restore text that you have just deleted. WordPerfect saves your last three deletions (of any length) so that you can restore them whenever you need to. To undelete, simply press F1 (Cancel). The following prompt appears:

Undelete 1 Restore; 2 Show Previous Deletion: 0

Enter **1** to restore the text you most recently deleted. To view the last deletion, enter **2**. To view the next-to-last deletion, enter **2** again. WordPerfect holds the last three deletions in memory.

F1 can also be used as a Cancel key to back out of a menu, to cancel a request, or to turn off block marking (see the next section).

BASIC FORMATTING COMMANDS

This chapter presents only the basic formatting techniques that you will often use as you enter text. For more advanced formatting techniques, see Chapters 4 and 8.

Most of your formatting changes will be made through the Page Format menu (Alt-F8), shown in Figure 2.8. However, changing line spacing, changing margins, and setting tabs are accomplished by using the Line Format menu (Shift-F8) shown in Figure 2.9.

The Page Format menu gives you the following options:

1 Page Number Position specifies the location of page numbers.

2 New Page Number allows you to specify the number on which page numbering starts.

3 Center Page Top to Bottom allows you to center text vertically on a page.

4 Page Length allows you to change the length of the page as well as the number of text lines per page.

5 Top Margin allows you to specify a top margin other than the 1-inch default setting.

```
Page Format

        1 - Page Number Position

        2 - New Page Number

        3 - Center Page Top to Bottom

        4 - Page Length

        5 - Top Margin

        6 - Headers or Footers

        7 - Page Number Column Positions

        8 - Suppress for Current page only

        9 - Conditional End of Page

        A - Widow/Orphan


Selection: 0
```

FIGURE 2.8: The Page Format menu (reached by pressing Alt-F8). This menu allows you to set page length, specify page numbers, add headers and footers, and specify other page formats.

```
            MagnaCorp participates in the city

--------------------------------------------------------------------------------
recreational plan and therefore its employees have

access to the municipal gym located at First and

Brannan Streets.  The jogging track and par course

in Grant park are also nearby.  Showers and lockers

for company employees are located near the south

entrance of the main lobby.



Vacation



Full-time permanent employees are eligible for two
1 2 Tabs; 3 Margins; 4 Spacing; 5 Hyphenation; 6 Align Char: 0
```

FIGURE 2.9: The Line Format menu (reached by pressing Shift-F8). This menu controls tab settings, margins, line spacing, and hyphenation.

6 Headers or Footers allows you to specify text to be printed at the top (header) or bottom (footer) of each page of your document.

7 Page Number Column Positions specifies the column position of the page number.

8 Suppress for Current page only allows you to turn off page numbering, headers, and footers for the current page.

9 Conditional End of Page allows you to specify a condition that must be met to keep lines of text together on one page.

A Widow/Orphan allows you to specify that a single line not appear at the bottom of a page (widow) or the top of a page (orphan).

On the Line Format menu, you can select these options:

1, 2 Tabs allows you to change the placement of tab settings in your document.

3 Margins allows you to set right and left margins.

4 Spacing allows you to set line spacing in half-line increments.

5 Hyphenation allows you to establish a hyphenation zone, after which you will be prompted to specify hyphenation.

6 Align Char allows you to specify a character, such as a decimal point or blank space, on which you want columns of text aligned.

Many of these selections are discussed in detail in Chapter 4. The references in this chapter cover changing line spacing, margins, and page length; setting top and bottom margins; and setting simple tabs.

Most of the formatting options in the WordPerfect program have been preset for your convenience to a standard format. You can change these options by using various key sequences and menus within the program. You can also change the default settings permanently by selecting option 2 on the Setup menu. For information about how to change initial settings using this option, refer to Chapter 16.

These default options are illustrated in Figure 2.10 and summarized in Table 2.1 for ease of reference; methods for changing them are presented throughout this book under the appropriate headings. For example, for information about how to change line spacing, see the next section, "Changing Line Spacing."

Changing Line Spacing

KEY SEQUENCE

Shift-F8 4 <*number* (0.5 increments)>

WELCOME

Welcome to MagnaCorp. We hope this employee handbook will help to guide you through your first few days here. In addition, it contains valuable information about employee services and benefits available to you. Ask your manager or call the personnel office if you have any questions for which you cannot find the answers in this handbook.

Work Day

The official work day at MagnaCorp is 8:30 a.m. to 5:00 p.m. Flexible hours can be arranged with your manager.

Parking

As parking is limited, please apply to the personnel office for a parking slot assignment.

Hours

Noon to 1 p.m. has been reserved as lunch hour for all employees. Some departments have chosen to take lunch from 11:30 to 12:30 or from 12:30 to 1:30; check with your manager.

Cafeteria

The company cafeteria, located on the third floor, is open from 7 a.m. until 2 p.m. daily. Breakfast is available for your convenience until 9:00. After 2 p.m., vending machines with cold sandwiches and salads are available.

Recreational Facilities

MagnaCorp participates in the city recreational plan and therefore its employees have access to the municipal gym located at First and Brannan Streets. The jogging track and par course in Grant Park are also nearby. Showers and lockers for company employees are located near the south entrance of the main lobby.

Vacation

Full-time permanent employees are eligible for two weeks of paid vacation after six months of continuous employment. During the first five years of service, you earn three weeks of vacation per year. After five years of service, you receive four weeks of vacation.

Credit Union

MagnaCorp's credit union is located on the third floor. Hours are 9 to 6 p.m. daily. The credit union observes all national and bank holidays, whereas the company may or may not follow the same schedule.

FIGURE 2.10: A printed 8½ × 11-inch page illustrating the format that results if you do not change WordPerfect's format settings. It contains 54 single-spaced text lines of 65 characters each.

REVEAL CODES

[Spacing Set: <*number*>]

WordPerfect allows you to set line spacing in increments of half lines. The default setting is single-spacing. To change line spacing, press Shift-F8 and enter **4** (for Spacing). Then enter a number indicating the line spacing you want your document to have (**1.5** for a space and a half, **2** for double-spacing, and so forth). When setting spacing that includes half-line increments, always enter the fraction as a decimal (**.5**).

When you set the spacing in whole-number increments such as double, triple, quadruple, and so on, WordPerfect adds the necessary blank lines to show the text of your document properly spaced on your screen.

When you set half-space increments such as one-and-a-half-line spacing or two-and-a-half-line spacing, the half-line increments cannot be properly displayed on the editing screen. Instead, WordPerfect rounds up the fraction and displays the text as it would for spacing specified as the next-highest whole number. For example, if you specify one-and-a-half-line spacing, WordPerfect displays the text as though it were double-spaced. However, the line indicator on the status line will reflect the half-space increments in its count as you move the cursor up and down the lines. For example, if you set the spacing at one and a half at the beginning of your document, the line indicator will change from Ln 1 to Ln 2.5 to Ln 4 and so on as you press ↓ to move down each line of text.

The formatting code used by WordPerfect when you use the Shift-F8, 4 command to change the spacing from its default setting of single-spacing to some other spacing is [Spacing Set]. If you use this command and then enter **2.5** for two-and-a-half-line spacing, you will see this code in the Reveal Codes window:

[Spacing Set:2.5]

WordPerfect follows this format code until it reaches another [Spacing Set] code. This allows you to vary the spacing in one document as often as you need. For instance, you may want to change to single-spacing whenever you enter direct quotations in an otherwise double-spaced document.

To do this, you enter a [Spacing Set:2] code when you begin the document and then enter a [Spacing Set:1] code at the beginning of the first line of the quotation. After you finish typing the quotation, you change the spacing back to double by entering [Spacing Set:2] before entering a hard return to end the paragraph. (You can also enter two Returns—one to end the paragraph and another to enter a blank line—and then enter the [Spacing Set:2] code at the beginning the new line.)

If you have changed the line spacing many times in a document and then wish to make its spacing uniform, you must remove all of the [Spacing Set] codes that you have entered. To do this, you can use the Search feature to locate them. To make sure that you eliminate them all, you should position the cursor at the very beginning of the document by pressing Home Home ↑ (to ensure that you are at the very beginning, press Home ↑ once more or use Alt-F3 and move the cursor with the arrow keys). Then press F2 (Search) followed by Shift-F8 and 4. At the bottom left of the editing screen you will see

– > Search: [Spacing Set]

Press F2 to begin the search. WordPerfect will place the cursor immediately after the first line-spacing formatting code that it locates. To delete the [Spacing Set] code, turn on the Reveal Codes window by pressing Alt-F3 and press Backspace. Then repeat the search by pressing F2 twice and perform the same deletion until you receive the message "Not Found."

> *Note:* You can also accomplish this from the end of the document using the Reverse Search feature. If your cursor is near the end of the document, press Home Home ↓ and then institute a reverse search for the [Spacing Set] codes by pressing Shift-F2 and then following the instructions in the preceding section.

S2 AND **S1**: DOUBLE- AND SINGLE-SPACING MACROS

If you need to vary the line spacing often in the types of documents you create, you can enter your [Spacing Set] formatting codes using macros. The following macros can be used to set double and single line spacing. You can use them to alternate quickly between single- and double-spacing in one document. You can also use these examples as models for creating your own line-spacing macros. Simply choose an appropriate macro name and enter the number of the line spaces you wish to associate with it.

Begin macro	*Macro name*	*Keystrokes*	*End macro*
Ctrl-F10	**S2**	**Shift-F8 4 2 Return**	**Ctrl-F10**
Begin macro	*Macro name*	*Keystrokes*	*End macro*
Ctrl-F10	**S1**	**Shift-F8 4 1 Return**	**Ctrl-F10**

To use these macros, named S2 and S1 respectively, you press Alt-F10, type **S2** or **S1,** and press Return. They will enter the appropriate [Spacing Set] code wherever the cursor is located when you execute them.

Setting Margins (Changing Line Length)

KEY SEQUENCE

Shift-F8 3 Left Margin = *< number of column position >* **Return**
Right Margin = *< number of column position >*

REVEAL CODES

[Margin Set: *< left margin column position >*,
< right margin column position >]

WordPerfect allows you to set margins from 0 to 250. Wide margins are used when you are using an extra-wide printer or printing sideways. When you reset margins, the margins of your document are changed from the cursor position forward, so you must move to the beginning of the document (by pressing Home Home ↑ and Home ↑) before changing margin settings if you want the new margin settings to affect the entire document.

The left margin is preset at 10 spaces, and the right margin is preset at 74 spaces, so the default line length is 65 characters. This line length assumes that you are using pica type, in which the pitch (character spacing) is 10 characters per inch. However, if you change to elite type, which has a pitch of 12 characters per inch, WordPerfect will not automatically change your margin settings, or line length. (Changing the pitch is discussed in Chapter 5.) Because 65 characters in 12 pitch require a shorter line length, you often will need to increase the margin settings when you change to this pitch.

When you press Alt-F3 to see the hidden formatting codes, you can tell from the tab ruler line at the top where your margins have been set (see Figure 2.11). The triangles are tab stops. The bracket (]) on the right indicates the right margin; the left margin is indicated by [, or by { if it coincides with a tab stop setting.

To keep the tab ruler on the screen while creating and editing a document, press Ctrl-F3 (Screen) and type **1** (to choose the Window option). When you see the prompt

 # Lines in this Window: 24

respond by pressing ↑ once. You will then see the tab ruler displayed at the bottom of the screen and the number of lines change from 24 to 23. Press Return to set the ruler in this position. To remove the tab ruler, repeat this command, this time pressing ↓ instead of ↑ before you press Return.

The formatting code that controls the margin settings in this figure is [Margin Set:10,74]. The first value, 10, in the [Margin Set:] code indicates that the left

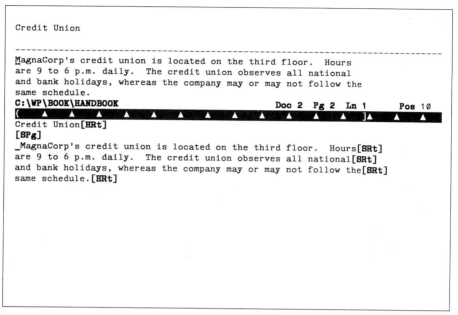

FIGURE 2.11: Viewing current margin settings by looking at the tab ruler line. The left margin ({) is set at character position 10, and the right margin (]) is set at character position 74.

margin is 10 spaces from the first position (0) with the print head at the very edge of the paper. The second value, 74, indicates that the right margin is 74 spaces from position 0.

> *Note:* Unlike many other word processors, WordPerfect calculates both its left and right margin settings from position 0, at the left edge of the paper where the print head begins printing. This represents a very different system from those that use an on-screen left margin of 0 or 1 and, therefore, determines a document's left margin by having you specify a left offset value from the print menu.

To determine the appropriate left and right margin settings in WordPerfect, you must first determine the total number of characters that will fit across the page (that is, 85 with a pitch of 10 characters per inch, and 102 with a pitch of 12 characters per inch for 8½ × 11-inch pages).

Then determine the number of characters needed for each margin. For example, a left margin of an inch and a half requires 15 characters in pica type (10 cpi) and 18 characters in elite type (12 cpi). To determine the right margin, subtract the number of characters required from the total number of characters; then subtract from this value (this last step is necessary because WordPerfect numbers the first position on the ruler 0 instead of 1).

Table 2.4 presents settings commonly used for left and right margins in pica (10 cpi) and elite (12 cpi) type. You can intermix these settings within the same

TYPE	MARGIN SIZE	MARGIN SETTING	
		LEFT	RIGHT
Pica (10 cpi)	1 ″	10	74
	1.5 ″	15	69
	2.0 ″	20	64
Elite (12 cpi)	1 ″	12	89
	1.5 ″	18	83
	2.0 ″	24	77

Note: The right margin setting is calculated by subtracting its size (in characters per inch) from the total number of characters possible on an 8 1/2 × 11-inch page and then subtracting 1 (because WordPerfect numbers margin settings from 0). For pica type (10 cpi), the maximum number of characters is 85 (8.5 × 10); for elite type (12 cpi), it is 102 (8.5 × 12).

TABLE 2.4: Calculating Left and Right Margin Settings for an 8½ × 11-Inch Page

pitch. For example, to use a 1.5-inch left margin and a 1-inch right margin with elite type, the [Margin Set:] code should be [18, 89]. With pica type, it should be [15, 74].

To change the margin settings (line length), press Shift-F8. The following menu appears:

1 2 Tabs; 3 Margins; 4 Spacing; 5 Hyphenation; 6 Align Char: 0

Type **3** for Margins. At the prompt, enter the character positions where you would like the left and right margins to begin. Remember, these are character positions, and they will change if you change type styles (fonts). The default setting of 10, 74 gives you a 65-character line in pica type, which leaves you approximately 1-inch margins on the left and right if you are using 8½ × 11-inch paper. See Chapter 5 for more information about printing and changing fonts.

If you enter a number larger than 250 for the right margin, or if you enter a value for the right margin that is less than the left margin (like 74, 10 instead of 10, 74), or if you enter 0 for both the left and right margins, you will receive the error message "ERROR: Right margin greater than 250 or less than left margin." If this happens, press Return to clear the message and execute the Shift-F8, 3 command again.

> *Note:* It is good practice to change margin settings at the beginning of the document, before you define the header or footer. If you set new margins later in a document, margins for headers or footers that occur before the new margin settings will have the old settings.

To have a header or footer conform to the new margins, you need to edit it. To do this, press Alt-F8 (Page Format) and type **6** (for Headers or Footers). Select the appropriate type and occurrence from the menu options and then press F7 to exit. Repeat this procedure for all of the remaining headers and footers that could be affected. (Refer to Chapter 4 for more information about defining and using headers and footers in a document.)

Changing Page Length (Lines per Page)

KEY SEQUENCE

To set page length for letter-size paper ($8^1/_2$ × 11):

Alt-F8 4 1

To set page length for legal-size paper ($8^1/_2$ × 14):

Alt-F8 4 2

To set page length for nonstandard settings:

Alt-F8 4 3 *<total number single spaced lines on form – 6 × length in inches>* **Return** *<total number of single spaced lines text on page>* **Return**

REVEAL CODES

[**Pg Lnth:** *<lines on form>* , *<lines of text>*]

You often may want to change the number of printed lines that appear on a page. WordPerfect is preset to a form length of 66 lines per page for $8^1/_2$ × 11-inch paper (6 lines per inch × 11 inches = 66 lines). You can set a form length of 84 lines per page for legal-size paper (6 × 14 = 84). Using 1-inch top and bottom margins (the default setting) gives you 54 single-spaced lines per standard-size page and 72 single-spaced lines per legal-size page. These 54 (or 72) lines include the ones used for your headers, footers, and page numbers, if any. (See "Changing Top and Bottom Margins" later in this chapter.)

To change page length, you press Alt-F8 to display the Page Format menu. From this, you select **4,** Page Length. The screen shown in Figure 2.12 appears, showing the currently selected number of lines per page. To change this number, you type **3** for Other and then enter the form length and number of single-spaced text lines you wish to have.

The effect of changing the number of lines per page depends on several variables:

- The size of your top and bottom margins (see "Setting Top and Bottom Margins" later in this chapter).

```
Page Length

    1 - Letter Size Paper: Form Length = 66 lines (11 inches)
        Single Spaced Text lines = 54 (This includes lines
        used for Headers, Footers and/or page numbers.)

    2 - Legal Size Paper: Form Length = 84 lines (14 inches)
        Single Spaced Text Lines = 72 (This includes lines
        used for Headers, Footers and/or page numbers.)

    3 - Other (Maximum page length = 108 lines.)

Current Settings

    Form Length in Lines (6 per inch):  66

    Number of Single Spaced Text Lines: 50




Selection: 0
```

FIGURE 2.12: Changing page length (Alt-F8, 4). Select **3** for Other to change the number of lines per form (page) and number of text lines per page. The maximum number of lines per page is 108 (this number of lines can be attained only with half-line spacing). If you attempt to set the number of lines per page above 108, WordPerfect will automatically set it to 108.

- The number of lines per inch at which you print your document (see Chapter 5).
- The size of the paper on which you print your document (see Chapter 5).

Line spacing is always determined in terms of single-spaced lines per page; WordPerfect automatically adjusts for the spacing you actually select. If you change any of the default settings, you will need to consider how they affect the final number of lines per page. The number of text lines plus the number of lines allowed for top and bottom margins must equal the number of lines per page (form length), which is 66 for standard $8^1/_2 \times 11$-inch paper (54 lines of text plus 12 lines for top and bottom margins of 1 inch) and 84 for legal-size paper (72 lines of text plus 12 lines for top and bottom margins of 1 inch). WordPerfect allows you to set combinations of text lines plus margin allowances without notifying you that the total does not equal your specified form length. You should be sure to calculate the numbers before changing the default settings.

For example, if you want a nonstandard 2-inch top margin (12 lines at 6 lines per inch) and a 1.5-inch bottom margin (9 lines) on legal-size paper, subtract 12 plus 9 (21) from 84 (the total number of lines per page) to determine that you can have 63 text lines per page.

Changing Top and Bottom Margins

KEY SEQUENCE

To change the top margin:
Alt-F8 5 < set half lines (12/inch) from 12 to *number of half lines* > **Return**
Return

REVEAL CODES

[**Top Mar:** < *number of half lines* >]

To change the top and bottom margin settings, you use options 4 (Page Length) and 5 (Top Margin) on the Page Format menu (Alt-F8). Note that to change the bottom margin, you must change the number of lines per printed page using option 4 from the Page Format menu (see the previous reference entry, "Changing Page Length Lines per Page," for details about how to do this).

The top margin is configured in half lines, so you may set top margins in increments of 1/12 of an inch. For example, to set a 1.5-inch top margin, you would change the number of half lines from 12 to 18 ($1.5 \times 12 = 18$). Likewise, to use only an 0.5-inch margin, you would change the setting to 6 half lines ($0.5 \times 12 = 6$).

The bottom margin depends on the number of lines per page that you specify in the Page Length setting (option 4). On a standard $8^1/2 \times 11$-inch page, there are 66 single-spaced lines per page. If you are using a 1-inch top margin, that takes up 6 of those lines (at 6 lines per inch, the default setting). You thus have 60 lines left after your top margin to the absolute bottom of the printed page. The default setting for the bottom margin is also 1 inch (6 lines), which results in a normal page length of 54 lines.

To increase your bottom margin, you must specify fewer than 54 text lines per page. For example, to use 1.5-inch top and bottom margins, you would set the page length at 48 lines (66 − 9 lines, or 18 half lines, for a 1.5-inch top margin − 9 lines for a 1.5-inch bottom margin = 48 lines per page).

Remember that lines per page includes the lines for your headers and footers and for the page number. Your top and bottom margins do not need to have the same value; many people prefer a deeper top or bottom margin. An example showing top and bottom margins that have been altered is shown in Figure 2.13.

                                                        Employee Handbook

Holidays

MagnaCorp designates five official holidays each year. These are
New Year's Day, Memorial Day, Independence Day, Labor Day, and
Thanksgiving Day. In addition, the company closes for Christmas
week. An additional two floating holidays may be taken at your
discretion and with the approval of your manager.

Benefits

Benefits programs include life insurance, health care, dental
services, and travel insurance. They are available to you at no
cost during your employment with MagnaCorp. If you leave the
company for any reason, some of these programs can be continued
at a small monthly charge to you. See the Personnel Department
for details.

Personal Leave

Personal time off with or without pay can be arranged for short
periods with the approval of your manager. In addition, if you
have more than one year of service with MagnaCorp, you may be
granted longer periods of personal leave--to obtain an advanced
degree, for example, or to complete a specialized course of
study. Special types of leave with pay are covered in the
following sections.

Bereavement Leave. Up to three days off with pay are granted in
the event of the death of a member of your immediate family.

Military Leave. Members of armed forces reserve units or the
National Guard may be eligible for two weeks of annual training
leave.

Jury Duty. Paid leave to serve on a jury will be granted for the
term required. MagnaCorp will reimburse you the difference
between juror pay and your regular salary.

Leave for Illness

Sick leave is normally accrued at the rate of one day per month.
In special circumstances, extended leave can be arranged through
your manager. If you are hospitalized, your salary is covered by
disability insurance from the first day of hospitalization.

Performance Appraisals

The key to managing your career at MagnaCorp is to understand the
performance and appraisals process thoroughly. You need to know

FIGURE 2.13: Changing the top and bottom margins. In this figure the top margin has been set to 1.5 inches instead of the default value of 1.0 inch. Note that the effect of the header is to give you greater visual depth. You should always consider the effect of headers and footers when you change top and bottom margin settings.

Setting Tabs

KEY SEQUENCE

To Access the Ruler Line to Change Tab Settings:
   Shift-F8 1 (or **2**)
To Delete Existing Tabs:
Delete all tabs in effect from left margin on:
   Ctrl-End
Delete all tabs in effect:
   Home ← Ctrl-End
Delete all tabs in effect from a specific ruler position on:
   (Move cursor to desired position on the tab ruler line) **Ctrl-End**
To Set Different Types of Tabs and Various Spacing:
   → (or **←**) (to move cursor to desired position on ruler line)
   L (for a left-justified tab)
   C (for a centered tab)
   R (for a right-justified tab)
   D (for a decimal tab)
To set a tab that is automatically preceded by dot leaders (for a left-justified, right-justified, or decimal tab only):
   (Move cursor to the L, R, or C that marks the tab type) **.** (type a period).
   Note: Tabs with dot leaders are indicated on the tab ruler in inverse video.
To Set Uniformly Spaced Tabs:
Make all tabs left justified and spaced at equal increments from a particular position on:
   <start position> , <spacing increment> Return

REVEAL CODES

   [Tab Set <*position and type of tab, position and type of tab,...*>]
   Left-justified tabs: **[TAB]**
   Centered tabs: **[TAB][C][c]**
   Decimal and right-justified tabs: **[A][a]**

   WordPerfect is preset with left-justified tabs every 5 spaces up to column position 160, as shown in Figure 2.14. From column position 160 to 250, left-justified tabs are preset every 10 spaces. To reset these tabs, you use the Line

Format menu (Shift-F8). The Line Format menu gives you six options:

1 2 Tabs; 3 Margins; 4 Spacing; 5 Hyphenation; 6 Align Char: 0

When you select Tabs by typing either **1** or **2,** the screen shown in Figure 2.14 appears. To select a new tab stop, type the number of its position or move the cursor to the position on the ruler line where you want the new tab and type **L** (for a left-justified tab), **R** (for a right-justified tab), **C** (for a centered tab), **D** (for a decimal tab) or **.** (period, for a dot-leader tab). You may use the space bar or → key to position the cursor on the tab ruler line to see where these tabs appear in relation to your text. To delete a tab, move the cursor to it and press Del. To delete all tabs to the end of the line, press Ctrl-End. Most often you will want to use this command to clear all tabs on the tab ruler before attempting to set tab stops that are not uniformly spaced.

> *Note:* Earlier versions of WordPerfect prior to Version 4.2 differentiated between regular tab settings up to column 160 and tabs settings beyond that setting (referred to as *extended tabs*). To set extended tabs, you press Alt-F8 and chose option 2. In Version 4.2, the program does not distinguish between regular and extended tabs, so choosing either option 1 or 2 results in the same

```
MagnaCorp's credit union is located on the third floor.  Hours
are 9 to 6 p.m. daily.  The credit union observes all national
and bank holidays, whereas the company may or may not follow the
same schedule.

Holidays

MagnaCorp designates five official holidays each year.  These are
New Year's Day, Memorial Day, Independence Day, Labor Day, and
Thanksgiving Day. In addition, the company closes for Christmas
week.  An additional two floating holidays may be taken at your
discretion and with the approval of your manager.
=================================================================


Benefits

Benefits programs include life insurance, health care, dental
services, and travel insurance.  They are available to you at no
L....L....L....L....L....L....L....L....L....L....L....L....L....L...
0123456789012345678901234567890123456789012345678901234567890123456789012345678
        20        30        40        50        60        70        80
Delete EOL (clear tabs); Enter number (set tab); Del (clear tab);
Left; Center; Right; Decimal; .= Dot leader; Press EXIT when done.
```

FIGURE 2.14: Selecting tab stops on the tab ruler line. WordPerfect's tabs are preset at five-space intervals. You can set a new tab stop by typing the number of its position or by moving the cursor to it and typing **L** (for a left-justified tab), **R** (for a right-justified tab), **C** (for a centered tab), **D** (for a decimal tab) or **.** (period, for a dot-leader tab).

options and same screen. To set tabs beyond column position 160, you merely move the cursor to the position where you want to set the tab and type the appropriate character.

Version 4.2 of WordPerfect has made significant changes in the types of tabs its supports and the way tabs are defined using the Alt-F8, 1 or 2 command. Table 2.5 lists the various types of tab stops with examples illustrating how they work.

Left-justified tabs are the most commonly used tabs in any document. They work just like regular tabs set on a typewriter. In some other word processing programs, they are referred to as *text* or *textual* tabs to differentiate them from decimal tabs. Whenever you set uniformly spaced tab stops (described in the following paragraphs), WordPerfect automatically creates all left-justified tabs that are indicated by L's on the tab ruler when you access the Page Format menu by pressing Shift-F8 and typing **1** or **2**.

The formatting code for left-justified tabs is [TAB]. To delete a tab indent, you can access the Reveal Codes window by pressing Alt-F3 and then delete the [TAB] code. You can also delete a tab by moving the cursor to the first character

TAB TYPE	HOW SET	EXAMPLE
Left-justified	L	``` First Quarter
..........L..........
5678901234567```
Right-justified	R	```First Quarter
..........R..........
3456789012345```
Centered	C	``` First Quarter
..........C..........
90123456789012```
Decimal	D	``` $1,256.00
..........D..........
901234567```
Dot-leader left	L	```Benefits.............Section 1.11
L...................L..........
789012345678```
Dot-leader right	R	```Benefits...Section 1.11
L...................R..........
678901234567```
Dot-leader decimal	D	```Benefits.....Section 1.11
L...................D..........
890123456789```

TABLE 2.5: Types of Tab Supported by WordPerfect

of the word that is indented and pressing Backspace. WordPerfect will not prompt you before removing a tab as it does when you are about to delete other formatting codes.

Right-justified tabs are used when you want all of the text in a table to appear flush right against a particular tab stop. They are not to be confused with decimal tabs, which are used when you want to align columns of figures on the decimal point. Right-justified tabs are indicated by R's on the tab ruler.

The formatting codes for right-justified tabs are [A] and [a] in the Reveal Codes window (see the following discussion of decimal tabs). If you delete either the [A] or [a] codes, the tab will be removed entirely, and the text will move back to the left margin or be joined with the text that precedes it on the line.

If you set a right-justified tab too close to the left margin and then type more text than can be accommodated in the spaces between it and the left margin, your text will disappear off the screen. If you continue to type text, it will begin to move left of the tab stop as soon the first character is pushed to column position 1. In such a case, you will have to reset the tab stop further left to allow sufficient room for it within the current left-margin setting.

Centered tabs are used when you want to center text on a tab stop. This is especially useful when you are creating a table and want the column headings centered over numbers in the succeeding columns. Centered tabs are indicated by C's on the tab ruler.

The formatting codes for centered tabs are [TAB][C][c] in the Reveal Codes window. If you delete the [C][c], the text will be reformatted as though you had set a left-justified tab. If you delete the [TAB] code as well, the tab will be removed entirely, and the text will move back to the left margin or be joined with the text that precedes it on the line.

Decimal tabs are most often used when you want to align figures in columns. When you use a decimal tab, all punctuation (such as the dollar sign) and numbers are right justified until you type a period. After that, all of the numbers you enter are left justified. When you press the Tab key and the next tab stop is a decimal tab, the message "Align Char = ." will appear at the bottom of the screen.

You can change the alignment character to another character of your choice. For instance, for a table using a European currency such as French francs, you can change the alignment character from the period to a comma. To do this, you press Shift-F8 (Line Format) and type **6** (the Align Char option). You will then see

Align Char = .

and the cursor will be positioned beneath the period. To change the period to a comma, you type , (comma). In response to this format change, WordPerfect enters the format code [Align Char:,] in the document. When you then use a decimal tab, the figures you enter will then align on the comma instead of the period.

Note: The alignment character is also used in WordPerfect with Ctrl-F6 (Tab Align). This key sequence works just like the decimal tab. You will find information about this command later in this chapter in the section "Aligning Text." You will also use decimal tabs when using WordPerfect's math features. For information about how to perform calculations using columns and rows of figures in a table, refer to Chapter 11.

When you set decimal tabs on the tab ruler and use them in a document, their presence is indicated by the formatting codes [A] and [a] (these are the same formatting codes used to indicate text that is formatted flush right; see "Aligning Text" later in this chapter). The second code [a] always immediately precedes the alignment character in effect at that time. For example, if you use a decimal tab to align the number $5,700.50 on the period, the following formatting codes will appear in the Reveal Codes window:

[A]5,700[a].50

To remove the tab, you delete only one of these formatting codes (either [A] or [a]).

In addition to these four basic types of tab, WordPerfect Version 4.2 has three more specialized tabs. These all add dot leaders connecting the text or figures at the previous tab stop to the text or figures that you enter at the current tab. These dot leaders can be added to either left-justified, right-justified, or centered tabs. These types of tabs are set by typing . (period) over the code letter (L, R, or D). They are indicated on the tab ruler by a highlighted rectangle.

The formatting codes for these special tab types are [A] and [a]. These are the same codes used in the Reveal Codes window to indicate the presence of right-justified or decimal tabs. To remove tab stops that use dot leaders, you can delete either the [A] or [a] code.

When you need to set different tabs of the type just discussed, you must manually define them on the ruler by using the → key (or the space bar) to move the cursor to the appropriate column position. To then set a tab stop, you merely type the first letter of the tab type you wish to use. For instance, to specify a right-justified tab at position 25, move the cursor until it is under the 5 after the 20 on the ruler line and type **R.** If you want dot leaders to appear before the text that is right justified at this tab stop, you then also type . (period). Figures 2.15 and 2.16 illustrate the seven different kinds of tab.

Note: When mixing different types of tab on a single ruler line be very careful to ensure that you space them sufficiently so that text placed at one tab stop does not collide with text at the next tab stop. Remember that text entered at a right-justified tab moves toward the left (closer to the previous tab and any text that you have entered there). If you find that text disappears as it collides with an entry made at the previous tab stop, delete the line and reset the tabs, making sure that you space them far enough apart to accommodate all of your text.

```
                              This is a left-justified tab

        This is a right-justified tab
 ━
                      This is a centered tab

    This is a decimal tab using the . as the alignment character
C:\WP\BOOK\CHAP2\FIG2-14                        Doc 1  Pg 1  Ln 4       Pos 10
[                                    ▲                           ]
[Tab Set:L0,L5,L45][TAB]This is a left[-]justified tab[HRt]
[HRt]
[Tab Set:L0,L5,R45][A]This is a right[-]justified tab[a][HRt]
_[HRt]
[Tab Set:L0,L5,C45][TAB][C]This is a centered tab[c][HRt]
[HRt]
[Tab Set:L0,L5,D45][A]This is a decimal tab using the [a]. as the alignment char
acter[HRt]
```

FIGURE 2.15: WordPerfect's left-justified, right-justified, centered, and decimal tabs. The Reveal Codes window shows the tab settings in effect (the [Tab Set] code) and the various formatting codes used by each kind of tab. Notice that the left-justified tab is indicated simply by the [TAB] code. Both the right-justified and decimal tabs are indicated by the [A] and [a] codes. The centered tab is indicated by the [TAB][C][c] code combination. If you delete only the [C] or [c] code of a centered tab, the tab becomes a left-justified tab, and the text is reformatted flush with the left margin.

To make sure that your new tab ruler takes effect, use the Reveal Codes window to place the cursor immediately after the existing [Tab Set] code before pressing Shift-F8 and typing **1** (or **2**) to set your new tabs.

You can also specify that WordPerfect set left-justified tabs in evenly spaced increments. To do this, press Shift-F8, type **1**, press Ctrl-End, and type the number of the character position where you want tabs to start; then type the increment by which you want them to be spaced. Finally, press Return and press F7 (Exit). For example, to set tabs every 10 spaces starting at character position 20, enter

20, 10

If you access the Reveal Codes (by pressing Alt-F3), you will then see the following formatting code on the screen:

**[TabSet:L0,L5,L20,L30,L40,L50,L60,L70,L80,L90,L100,L110,
L120,L130,L140,L150,L160,L170,L180,L190,L200,L210,L220,
L230,L240,L250]**

```
        This is . . . . . . . . . . . . .a dot leader left tab

 _      This is . . .a dot leader right tab

        This is . a  dot leader decimal tab . using the period

C:\WP\BOOK\CHAP2\FIG2-14                    Doc 1  Pg 1  Ln 11      Pos 10
[         ▲                                  ▲                         ]
[HRt]
[Tab Set:L0,L5,L15,L50][TAB]This is[A][a]a dot leader left tab[HRt]
[HRt]
[Tab Set:L0,L5,L15,R50]_[TAB]This is[A]a dot leader right tab[a][HRt]
[HRt]
[Tab Set:L0,L5,L15,D50][TAB]This is[A]a  dot leader decimal tab[a] . using the p
eriod
```

FIGURE 2.16: WordPerfect's dot-leader left-justified, right-justified, and decimal tabs with the Reveal Codes window. Notice that L, R, and D in the [Tab Set] formatting code are shown highlighted. This marks them as dot-leader tabs as opposed to regular left-justified, right-justified, and decimal tabs (illustrated in Figure 2.15). All three types of dot-leader tabs are indicated by the [A] and [a] formatting codes.

Notice that the tab stops at column positions 0 and 5 (L0 and L5 in the Reveal Codes) are not affected by this command. This is because the command for deleting to the end of the line (Ctrl-End) was issued with the cursor at column position 10 (thus eliminating the tab stop there), the default left margin used by WordPerfect. The command 20, 10 only affects the columns from column position 20 on.

If you do not issue the command for deleting to the end of the line (Ctrl-End), the default tab settings (every 5 spaces to position 160 and every 10 spaces thereafter to position 250) will not be overwritten by new tabs set in this manner.

Indenting Paragraphs

KEY SEQUENCE

Left indent:
F4

Left and right indent:
  Shift-F4
Hanging indent:
  F4 Shift-Tab

REVEAL CODES

Left indent:
  [->Indent]
Left and right indent:
  [->Indent<-]
Hanging indent:
  [->Indent][Mar Rel]

In WordPerfect, you can indent paragraphs in three ways.

- Left indent, in which all text of a paragraph is indented a number of spaces from the left margin
- Left and right indent, in which a paragraph is indented an equal number of spaces from the right and left margins
- Hanging indent, in which the first line of a paragraph is not indented, but the following lines are

These three types of indention are illustrated in Figure 2.17.

All three of these types of indention are accomplished by using the F4 (Indent) key. (These examples assume you are using the default tab stops, which are set every 5 spaces.)

- For left indent, press F4 at the beginning of your paragraph. It is then indented 5 spaces from the left margin. If you press F4 at the beginning of an existing paragraph, it will be reformatted. If you press F4 at the beginning of a paragraph you are typing, it will be indented as you type until you press Return again to signal the beginning of a new paragraph. Press F4 a second time to indent the paragraph 10 spaces, a third time to indent it 15 spaces, and so forth.
- For left and right indent, you press Shift-F4. The paragraph will be indented 5 spaces from the left and right margins. Continue to press Shift-F4 to indent the paragraph in increments of 5 spaces. To indent only the first line in a paragraph (as a paragraph indent in a block of quoted text, for example), use the Tab key.

```
        Cafeteria

        The company cafeteria, located on the third floor, is open
        from 7 a.m. until 2 p.m. daily.  Breakfast is available for
        your convenience until 9:00.  After 2 p.m., vending machines
        with cold sandwiches and salads are available.

Recreational Facilities

        MagnaCorp participates in the city recreational plan
        and therefore its employees have access to the
        municipal gym located at First and Brannan Streets.
        The jogging track and par course in Grant park are also
        nearby.  Showers and lockers for company employees are
        located near the south entrance of the main lobby.

Vacation

Full-time permanent employees are eligible for two weeks of paid
        vacation after six months of continuous employment. During
        the first five years of service, you earn three weeks of
        vacation per year. After five years of service, you receive
        four weeks of vacation.

C:\WP\BOOK\HANDBOOK                    Doc 2  Pg 1  Ln 42      Pos 10
```

FIGURE 2.17: WordPerfect's three types of paragraphs indention: left, left and right, and hanging. In this figure, the first paragraph uses left indent, the second text paragraph uses left and right indents, and the third paragraph uses hanging indent.

- For a hanging indent, press F4 to indent the paragraph and then press Shift-Tab to remove the indention for the first line. Shift-Tab is the margin-release key sequence. It removes the indention for the first line only; succeeding lines will be indented (see Figure 2.17). The margin release causes the text to move back the number of spaces between the tab setting used by the left indent and the previous tab setting. If your tabs are uniformally spaced at 10-space intervals, the text will move back 10 spaces, and the formatting code will appear as [Mar Rel:10].

To remove an indention, you backspace over it. You can also delete indentions by using Alt-F3 to identify and locate the formatting codes in the Reveal Codes windows. To delete a left indent code, locate the [->Indent] code and delete it with either Del or Backspace.

To delete a left and right indent, locate the [->Indent<-] code in the window and delete it. If you used F4 to create a left indent before you pressed Shift-F4 to create a left and right indent, the text will be left indented at the previous tab stop.

To delete a hanging indent, locate the [Mar Rel] code and delete it. Once you delete the [Mar Rel] code, the [->Indent] code immediately before it will cause the text to be left indented at the tab stop. However, if you delete the [->Indent] code that precedes the [Mar Rel] and do not also delete the [Mar Rel] code, the text will be reformatted to the left of the left margin setting, and it will move left the number of spaces between the tab stop used by the left indent and the previous tab on the ruler line. This will make the first part of the line of text disappear from the editing screen. To rectify this situation, delete the [Mar Rel] code, and the beginning of the line will be reformatted to the left margin setting in effect.

Beginning a New Page

KEY SEQUENCE

Ctrl-Return

REVEAL CODES

[HPg]

You often may want to begin a new page (force a page break) at a certain point in your document. For example, you may want to keep a quotation on the same page as the text that explains it. To indicate the beginning of a new page, simply press Ctrl-Return. The double dashed line that appears on your screen (see Figure 2.18) indicates where the new page will begin. To remove the page break, move the cursor below the page break line and press Backspace.

You can also specify that a page break occur when certain conditions are met, that a block of lines be kept together, or that widows and orphans (incomplete lines at the bottom or top of a page) do not occur in your documents (see Chapter 4).

ALIGNING TEXT

WordPerfect provides three ways of aligning a short line of text within the current left and right margins: You can center it, align it flush with the right margin, or align it flush with the current alignment character (the period, unless you designate another character).

Note that these alignments are intended for use with short lines of text, such as section headings, or the date, return address, or closing in a letter. Each of these is terminated by a carriage return (the Return key). They are not intended for use with lines of text longer than will fit within the margins (because the lines are affected by word wrap).

You can, however, align a block of several short lines after they have been entered. For instance, if you want the date and the return address to appear flush with the right margin, you can enter each line (terminated by Return), highlight all of the lines as a block, and then press Shift-F6 (Center) to center all of the lines at one time.

```
MagnaCorp's credit union is located on the third floor.  Hours
are 9 to 6 p.m. daily.  The credit union observes all national
and bank holidays, whereas the company may or may not follow the
same schedule.

Holidays

MagnaCorp designates five official holidays each year.  These are
New Year's Day, Memorial Day, Independence Day, Labor Day, and
Thanksgiving Day. In addition, the company closes for Christmas
week.  An additional two floating holidays may be taken at your
discretion and with the approval of your manager.
===============================================================================
-

Benefits

Benefits programs include life insurance, health care, dental
services, and travel insurance.  They are available to you at no
cost during your employment with MagnaCorp.  If you leave the
company for any reason, some of these programs can be continued
at a small monthly charge to you.  See the Personnel Department
for details.
C:\WP\BOOK\HANDBOOK                          Doc 2  Pg 3  Ln 1        Pos 10
```

FIGURE 2.18: Inserting a page break with Ctrl-Return. To remove an unwanted page break that you have inserted, move the cursor directly below the page break line, as shown in the figure, and press Backspace. An alternate method is to press Alt-F3 to see the formatting codes, position the cursor to the right of the page break code [HPg], and press Backspace to delete it. Then press Alt-F3 again to return to your document.

Centering

KEY SEQUENCE

To center text as you enter it:
   Shift-F6 *<text>* **Return**
To center existing text:
   Alt-F4 (highlight text) **Shift-F6 Y**

REVEAL CODES

   [C][c]

To center text as you type it, press Shift-F6. The text will be centered between the left and right margins until you press Return. You can also indicate a block of text to be centered (mark the block with Alt-F4).

To delete the centering code, press Alt-F3 to see the formatting codes. Position the cursor to the right or left of the [C] or [c] code and then press either Backspace or Del to remove it. As soon as you delete either one of the center formatting codes, the text will be reformatted so that it is left justified flush with the current left margin setting.

Flush Right

KEY SEQUENCE

To align text flush right before you enter it:
Alt-F6 *< text >* **Return**
To align existing text flush right:
Alt-F4 (highlight text) **Alt-F6 Y**

REVEAL CODES

[A][a]

WordPerfect provides a command, Alt-F6 (referred to as the Flush Right key), to automatically align your text flush with the current right margin. If you have not yet entered the text to be aligned flush right, the cursor will move to the right margin setting. As you type your text, it will be entered from right to left until you press Return to indicate the end of the line.

If you have already typed a short line of text terminated by Return, you can align it flush with the right margin by pressing Alt-F4 (the Block key), highlighting it with the cursor, and then pressing Alt-F6. You will then see this message displayed:

[Aln/FlshR]? (Y/N) N

Type **Y** to have the text aligned flush with the right margin.

If you press Backspace when the cursor is located on one of the flush-right formatting codes, this message will appear at the bottom of the screen:

Delete [Aln/FlshR]? (Y/N) N

To keep the text flush right, press Return. To return the text to flush left, type **Y.**

You can also return text to flush-left format by deleting its formatting code. To do this, press Alt-F3 (Reveal Codes) to display the Reveal Codes window and locate the formatting codes [A] and [a] that surround the text. You need only delete one of these formatting codes. If the cursor is located before the [A] or the [a], press Del to remove it. If it is located after the [A] or [a], press Backspace to remove it.

The Tab Align Command

KEY SEQUENCE

Ctrl-F6

REVEAL CODES

[TAB][A](text entered before align char)**[a]** < *align char* >

The Tab Align command works just like the decimal tab (see "Setting Tabs" earlier in this chapter). It aligns text on the alignment character in effect. As when using decimal tabs, WordPerfect uses the period as the alignment character unless you specify something else. However, unlike decimal tabs, you can use the Tab Align command with any tab stop that is in effect.

To align text on a character other than the period—for example, the colon— you first press Shift-F8 (Line Format) and type **6** (to choose the Align Char option). You will then see

Align Char = .

and the cursor will be positioned beneath the period. To change the alignment character to a colon, type **:** (colon). In response to this format change, WordPer- fect will enter the format code [Align Char::] in the document.

To then align your text on the colon, you press the Tab key until you are only one tab stop away from where you want the text aligned. Then you press Ctrl- F6. The cursor will advance to the next tab stop, and you will see this message at the bottom of the screen:

Align Char = :

As you type your text, it will be entered from right to left, just as it is when using a right-justified or decimal tab. As soon as you type the alignment character—in this case, the colon—the Align Char = : message disappears, and any text you then type is entered from left to right as though you were using a left-justified tab.

When you use the Tab Align command to justify text on a particular align- ment character, you must make sure that you have left enough space to enter all of the text that precedes the alignment character before WordPerfect reaches the left margin. If you have not and your text is longer than can be accommodated, WordPerfect will activate the margin release when it reaches the left margin, and your text will disappear off the screen. If you continue entering characters after the line has reached column position 0, the text will begin to be entered from the alignment tab position to the right. Figure 2.19 illustrates the Tab Align com- mand using the colon as the alignment character.

```
                Name: _____

   Social Security No: _____  --  _____  --  _____

              Address: _____

                 City: _____
C:\WP\BOOK\CHAP2\FIG2-16                      Doc 1   Pg 1   Ln 6      Pos 10
```

[Align Char::][TAB][TAB][TAB][A]Name[a]: _____[HRt]
[HRt]
[TAB][TAB][TAB][A]Social Security No[a]: _____ [-][-] _____ [-][-] _____[
HRt]
_[HRt]
[TAB][TAB][TAB][A]Address[a]: _____[HRt]
[HRt]
[TAB][TAB][TAB][A]City[a]: _____[HRt]

FIGURE 2.19: Part of an entry form created using the Tab Align command. In this figure, the alignment character was changed from a period to a colon (notice the [Align Char::] code in the first line of the Reveal Codes window). As you can see, all of the items are formatted flush with the colon. In the Reveal Codes window, you can see that the Tab key was pressed twice (indicated by the two [TAB] codes) before Ctrl-F6 was pressed to use the Tab Align command (indicated by the [TAB][A] code). Notice that the final alignment format code [a] always precedes the alignment character, which in this case is the colon.

When you need to edit the text on a line aligned using the Tab Align command, use the Reveal Codes window to place the cursor between alignment codes before inserting or deleting any text. To do this, press Alt-F3 and locate the [A] and [a] codes surrounding the text before the alignment character. Then move the cursor somewhere within these codes, press the space bar to return to the document, and edit the text, being careful not to insert more text than can be accommodated between the tab stop where the alignment character is entered and the left margin. When you insert new text, remember that text is entered from right to left, just the opposite of the way you are used to seeing it appear on the screen as you type.

To return text aligned with the Tab Align command to the previous tab stop, access the Reveal Codes window and delete either the [A] or the [a] formatting code. If you want the text flush with the left margin, also delete the [TAB] code. If you press Backspace when the cursor is located on one of these codes, you will see the following message:

Delete [Aln/FlshR]? (Y/N) N

If you wish to retain the current alignment, press Return. If you do not, type **Y**.

BOLDFACING AND UNDERLINING TEXT

WordPerfect allows you to enhance parts of your documents to make them stand out from the rest of the page or to emphasize certain words or phrases in your text. F6 is the Boldface key, and F8 is the Underline key. Both of these keys are toggles—that is, they alternate between off and on each time you press them.

To remove boldfacing or underlining, you must either delete the text affected, including the pair of formatting codes, or press Alt-F3 (Reveal Codes) and delete just the formatting codes. The codes for boldfacing are [B] to turn the feature on and [b] to turn it off. The codes for underlining are [U] to turn this feature on and [u] to turn it off. Examples of both of these print enhancements are shown in Figure 2.20.

Boldfacing

KEY SEQUENCE

To boldface text as you type it:
F6 < *text* > **F6**
To boldface existing text:
Alt-F4 (highlight text) **F6**

REVEAL CODES

[B][b]

To boldface text as you type it, press F6. The characters you type from that point on will be boldfaced (they will appear in high intensity on your screen) until you press F6 again to turn boldfacing off. You can boldface a block of text by first marking the text as a block (Alt-F4) and then pressing F6 to boldface the entire block. This technique is useful when, for example, you review a document and decide that main headings would stand out better if they were boldfaced.

To delete the boldfacing code, press Alt-F3 to see the formatting codes. Position the cursor to the right of either the [B] or [b] code and then press Backspace to delete it (if the cursor is located to the left of either of these codes, press Del to remove it). You need to delete only one of the pair of boldfacing codes to remove both from the document and return the text to normal.

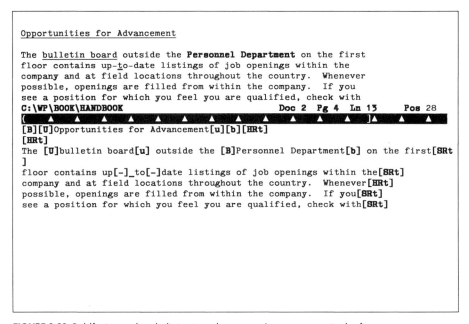

```
Opportunities for Advancement

The bulletin board outside the Personnel Department on the first
floor contains up-to-date listings of job openings within the
company and at field locations throughout the country.  Whenever
possible, openings are filled from within the company.  If you
see a position for which you feel you are qualified, check with
C:\WP\BOOK\HANDBOOK                              Doc 2  Pg 4  Ln 13        Pos 28
▔▔▔▔▔▔▔▔▔▔▔▔▔▔▔▔▔▔▔▔▔▔▔▔▔▔▔▔▔▔▔▔▔▔▔▔▔▔▔▔▔▔▔▔▔▔▔▔▔▔▔▔▔▔▔▔▔
[B][U]Opportunities for Advancement[u][b][HRt]
[HRt]
The [U]bulletin board[u] outside the [B]Personnel Department[b] on the first[SRt]
]
floor contains up[-]_to[-]date listings of job openings within the[SRt]
company and at field locations throughout the country.  Whenever[HRt]
possible, openings are filled from within the company.  If you[SRt]
see a position for which you feel you are qualified, check with[SRt]
```

FIGURE 2.20: Boldfacing and underlining in a document. As you can see in the figure, you can combine both these text attributes or use them separately. The Reveal Codes screen indicates where these formatting codes are in effect.

Underlining

KEY SEQUENCE

To underline text as you enter it:

F8 <*text*> **F8**

To underline existing text:

Alt-F4 (highlight text) **F8**

To change the underlining style to non-continuous (no underlining between tab stops):

Single underlining: **Ctrl-F8 5**

Double underlining: **Ctrl-F8 6**

To change the underlining style to continuous (underlining between tabs):

Single underlining: **Ctrl-F8 7**

Double underlining: **Ctrl-F8 8**

REVEAL CODES

Turn underlining on:
  [U]
Turn underlining off:
  [u]
Non-continuous single underlining:
  [Undrl Style: 5]
Non-continuous double underlining:
  [Undrl Style: 6]
Continuous single underlining:
  [Undrl Style: 7]
Continuous double underlining:
  [Undrl Style: 8]

To underline text, you press F8 before you type. You can also indicate a block of text to be underlined (by pressing Alt-F4 and marking the block). You may want to underline some items, such as book titles, that are usually italicized in print. Most printers are capable of underlining, but many printers are not capable of italics. See Chapter 5 for additional information about using italics and other print enhancements in your documents.

You can also change the style of underlining from the default setting establishing single, non-continuous underlining (one that does not underline spaces between tabs). You can choose double or single underlining that either does or does not continue across tab stops. (Continuing underlining across tab stops is sometimes useful when you are creating tables with tabs, as discussed in Chapter 4.) These different underlining styles are selected using options 5 through 8 of the Print Format menu (Ctrl-F8). You will not see the double underline on the screen, but it will appear in your document when it is printed. See Chapter 5 for details about changing print formats.

Note that in WordPerfect, whether continuous or non-continuous underlining is specified has no impact on whether the spaces between words included between the [U] and [u] formatting codes are underlined. WordPerfect always underlines spaces entered by pressing the space bar so long as they fall between the underlining formatting codes. For example, if you press F8, type the phrase **nolo contendere,** and then press F8 again, the phrase will be printed as follows:

<u>nolo contendere</u>

The only way to underline single words in a phrase and not the spaces between them is to turn off the underline code or move the cursor beyond it when you finish typing the last letter of the word (by pressing F8) before you enter the space. Then, to underline the next word, you must turn underlining on again. To underline only the words in the example just cited, for instance, you would press F8 to turn underlining on, type **nolo,** press F8 to turn the underlining off, press the space bar to enter a space, press F8 to turn underlining on again, type **contendere,** and finally, press F8 to turn underlining off.

Another way to accomplish the same thing is to type the entire phrase and then use Alt-F4 (Block) to mark each word and underline it. Thus, to perform this operation on the example phrase, *nolo contendere,* after typing it, you would move the cursor to the *n* in *nolo,* press Alt-F4, move the cursor to the final *o,* and press F8 to underline the word. Then you would move the cursor to the *c* in *contendere,* press Alt-F4, move the cursor to the final *e,* and press F8. In print, the phrase would then appear as follows:

<u>nolo   contendere</u>

To delete underlining, first press Alt-F3 to see the formatting codes. Position the cursor to the right of either the [U] or [u] code and then press Backspace to remove it (if the cursor is positioned to the left of the [U] or [u] code, press Del to remove it). You need to delete only one of the underlining codes to remove both from the document and return your text to normal.

If you change the underlining style from the default of non-continuous single underlining by choosing one of the other options on the Print Format menu (accessed by Ctrl-F8), WordPerfect will enter its underline style format code in the text. For instance, to change to continuous single underlining, you choose option 7 from this menu, and the program will insert the format code [Undrl Style: 7] in the document. If you turn on underlining and type a word and then press the Tab key and type another word, the words at the tab stops will be connected by underlining, as follows:

<u>Company Name</u>   <u>Address</u>   <u>City</u>   <u>State</u>

If you decide later that you wish to change the underlining style back to option 5 so that only the column headings are underlined and not the spaces between them, you can place the cursor under the initial letter of the first underlined word and enter the formatting code for non-continuous single underlining. So long as the code [Undrl Style: 5], is entered after the code [Undrl Style: 7], the line will change to

<u>Company</u> <u>Name</u>   <u>Address</u>   <u>City</u>   <u>State</u>

If, however, you enter the code [Undrl Style: 5] before [Undrl Style: 7] so that the Reveal Codes window (when you press Alt-F3) shows:

[Undrl Style: 5][Undrl Style: 7][U]Company[Tab]Address [Tab]City [Tab]State[u]

then the spaces between the tabs will continue to be underlined. You can also delete both of the [Undrl Style] codes so that WordPerfect returns to its default setting of non-continuous single underlining.

If you use a special underlining style for a unique item in your text, you might want to add the code to return underlining to the default setting so that the next time you underline some text, you will not inadvertently use the special underlining style. This is especially important when you use double underlining, which cannot be seen on the screen.

Suppose, for instance, that you use double underlining at one place in the text and then do not enter the code to return to single underlining. When you next want to perform single underlining, you may forget that double underlining is in effect, and all of the text you underline in the document will be double underlined, an error you may not catch until the entire document has been printed.

DU AND **SU**: MACROS TO SWITCH FROM SINGLE TO DOUBLE UNDERLINING

If you frequently switch back and forth between single and double underlining in a document, you might want to use macros like those that follow to enter and turn off the appropriate codes.

Begin macro	Macro name	Keystrokes	End macro
Ctrl-F10	**DU**	**Ctrl-F8 6** **Return F8**	**Ctrl-F10**

Begin macro	Macro name	Keystrokes	End macro
Ctrl-F10	**SU**	**Ctrl-F8 5 Return**	**Ctrl-F10**

To use these macros, you press Alt-F10 and type **DU** just before you type the text you want double underlined. When you have finished entering the text, you press F8 to turn off the underlining and press Alt-F10 and type **SU** if you want to return to the single-underlining default setting. If you use these macros together whenever you perform double underlining, you do not have to worry whether text you wanted single underlined will be double underlined by mistake.

Note: The DU macro also includes the keystroke F8 to turn underlining on for you. This allows you to type your text without this extra keystroke. If you want to make this macro more versatile so you can use it with text that you have already entered, you can omit the F8 keystroke. Then you will have to manually press F8 after pressing Alt-F10 and typing **DU** when underlining text that has not yet been entered.

Also, this macro assumes that you do not want either the double or single underlining to be continuous between tab stops. If this is not the case, you will need to change the 6 in the DU macro to 8 and the 5 in the SU macro to 7. You can also create another, similar set of macros using these options.

REPEATING A COMMAND

WordPerfect allows you to repeat a command any number of times. Press Esc and then enter the number of times you want the next command or keyboard entry to be repeated.

This technique can save you time in many situations. For example, you may want to delete 5 (or 50, or any number you like) lines in a list. Instead of marking the lines as a block and deleting them, you can enter

Esc 5 Ctrl-End

You can use this technique to repeat characters. For example, to insert a string of dot leaders before a particular item in a list, you press Esc. The program will respond

n = 8

on the screen (8 is the default number of repetitions). You then specify the number of periods you wish to have inserted followed immediately by the period key; WordPerfect will enter as many periods as you specify in the $n = 8$ prompt. You can also use this command to add a line of underscores to a document. To do this, you would use the same procedure, only this time typing the underscore (Shift-hyphen) instead of a period.

This feature is extremely useful when you use WordPerfect's line and box drawing feature. It allows you to complete your drawing quickly by using the Esc key to repeat the particular graphics character you are using at the time (see Chapter 13 for more information about this technique).

SUMMARY

This chapter presented many of the fundamental formatting commands that you commonly use in WordPerfect, including those for setting tab stops, indenting paragraphs, aligning text within the margins, changing the margin settings, spacing, and adding page breaks. It also covered basic text-entry operations, including how to add print enhancements such as boldfacing and underlining and how to delete various sections of text. It also discussed the use of WordPerfect's Document Summary and Document Comment screens and how to get on-line help while working on your documents.

Chapter 3, "Editing Techniques," will present more advanced techniques for editing the documents you create—block operations, working with two documents at the same time, using search and replace, redlining and striking out text, and working with form letters and standard paragraphs (boilerplate). For page formatting techniques beyond the overview presented in this chapter, see Chapter 4, "Page Formatting Techniques." This chapter contains information about such topics as using headers and footers, specifying page numbers, and creating tables.

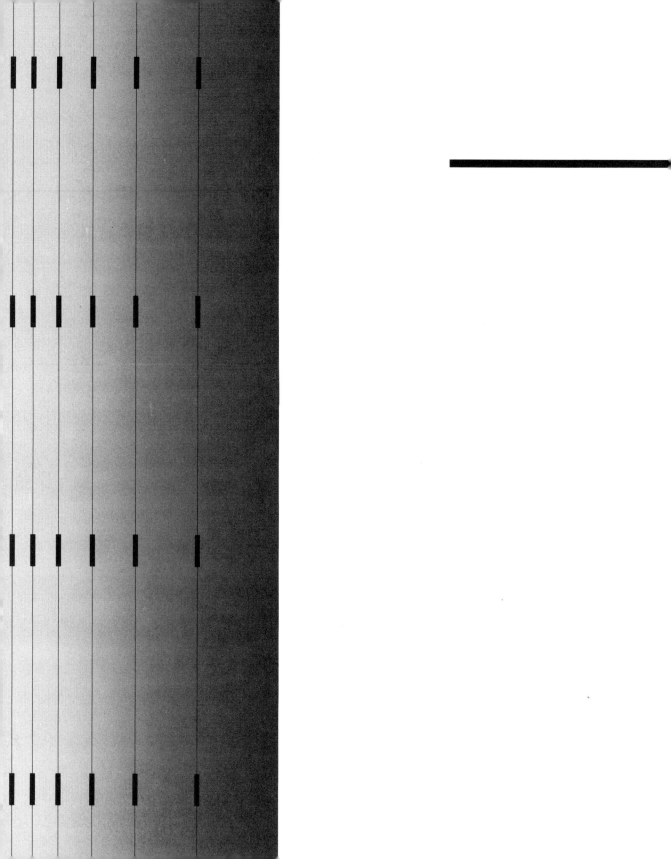

Editing Techniques

EDITING TECHNIQUES

WordPerfect contains many functions for editing the documents you create. Knowing only a few of these basic techniques can save you a great deal of time. This chapter contains techniques that you can use when you create documents as well as when you revise documents you have already created.

For example, you can use WordPerfect's search and replace feature to mark passages in your text that you want to return to and revise later. You can also, with a little imagination, use the search and replace feature as a kind of glossary containing abbreviations for words and phrases that you use often as you type, but do not want to take the time to spell out each time you type them. For example, if you know that your document is not going to contain special symbols such as # and @, you can use such symbols in place of complicated names such as *pharyngoesophageal* and *Taddeuz E. Zamczyk;* when your document is complete, you simply search for the symbols and have WordPerfect replace them with the longer words or phrases.

WordPerfect also allows you to work with two documents at once. You can mark text in one document and transfer it to another or store "boilerplate"— standard text that you use frequently—in one document and copy from it as you build a master document. You can even mark blocks of text and save them in separate files as you work, without having to save and close the document you are working on. In addition, WordPerfect's Window feature lets you view two different portions of your document at once: While you work at the beginning of a document, you can view text that is near the end of the document.

WordPerfect also offers Redlining and Strikeout features. Strikeout lets you indicate text that is to be deleted from your document by placing a dashed line through portions to be removed. Redlining lets you place vertical bars in the margin next to text that you wish to draw attention to. This technique comes in handy when you must submit a revised document for review, but want to indicate to your readers which parts of the document are new or revised.

This chapter explores all of these functions plus a few techniques for performing such operations as transposing words, converting text from lowercase to uppercase and vice versa, using hyphens, alphabetizing lists, editing tables, and creating special symbols.

WordPerfect also contains functions for creating tables of contents, endnotes, footnotes, lists, and citations; these techniques will be discussed in detail in Chapter 7.

RETRIEVING A DOCUMENT FOR EDITING

To edit a document, you must retrieve a copy of it from the disk where it is stored so that you can view it in one of the two document windows. Once you have made all necessary changes, you can then either save it under the same file name or assign it a new name. If you are using the Automatic Backup feature (activated from the Setup menu), WordPerfect will automatically save a copy of the file without your editing changes, even if you do not rename the document when you save it. (See Chapter 16 for information about the Setup program.)

Using the Retrieve Command

WordPerfect provides two ways to retrieve a document for editing. If you know the document's name, you can retrieve it by pressing Shift-F10 (the Retrieve key sequence). When you press this key combination, WordPerfect responds with the prompt

Document to be Retrieved:

Enter the name of the document as you saved it (uppercase and lowercase letters can be used interchangeably). (For information about how to save a document, see Chapter 1. For information about how to name document files, see Chapter 6.) If the name you gave to the document contains a file name extension, be sure to include this. After typing the document's name, press Return. If you typed the document's name correctly and the document is located on the current default directory or drive (if you save your documents on a floppy disk), Word-Perfect will read the document into memory, and the first part of it will appear on your screen.

If you misspelled the file name, if you forgot to include the three-character extension you assigned to the file name, or if the file is not located on the default directory, the following error message will appear:

ERROR: File Not Found

After this message is displayed, it will be replaced by the "Document to be Retrieved" prompt, and the cursor will be placed on the first character of the file name you entered. If you know why WordPerfect could not locate the file you specified, you can edit the file name (as you would any other text in WordPerfect) and then press Return again. If you cannot figure out the problem, press F1 (Cancel) to abort the retrieve command and use the second method for retrieving a document, described in the next section.

If you know that the document you wish to edit is not located in the current default directory (defined by the Startup command you used to load Word-Perfect or by using one of the methods for designating a new default directory), you can still retrieve the file without having to change the directory. To do so, just include the drive letter and path name as part of the file name you type in response to the "Document to be Retrieved" prompt.

For example, if you are using WordPerfect on a hard disk system and the current directory is a subdirectory of WordPerfect (such as C:\WP\JOHN) and the document you wish to edit is located on a floppy disk in drive A, you must include the drive letter as part of the file name when using Shift-F10 (Retrieve). If the name of the document you wish to edit is IBMPROP1, you enter the document name as

A:\IBMPROP1

When you save any editing changes you make to this document using F10 (Save), WordPerfect will suggest the original file name as the name to save the document under. If you press Return without editing the drive specification of the file name, your changes will be saved under the original file name and in the original file on the data disk in drive A. If you wish to save the document in a new directory or in the same directory under a new name, enter the complete new file name, including the directory path, before pressing Return.

Using the List Files Command to Retrieve a Document

To retrieve a document whose name you do not remember or of whose spelling you are unsure, you can use F5, the List Files key. Pressing F5 causes WordPerfect to list the current directory with the search pattern *.* (the two asterisks represent the DOS wildcard search characters that enable it to give a complete list of all files on the default directory). If your document is located on the default directory displayed, press Return to obtain an alphabetical list of the files that directory contains.

If your document is located in another directory, type = (the equal sign) and edit the directory path name when you see the prompt "New Directory:" on the screen. When you press Return after editing the name, WordPerfect will display the new default directory, including the DOS wildcards *.*. Press Return again to obtain a complete list of the files contained in the new directory.

WordPerfect displays a screen containing up to the first 36 files in the directory—less if the directory contains many subdirectory listings. If you cannot locate the file name of the document you wish to edit on this screen, press the PgDn key to scroll the list up. You have reached the last screen when pressing PgDn does not alter the display.

When you locate the file you wish to edit, move the highlight to it with one of the cursor movement keys and type **1** (the Retrieve option) to retrieve it. As soon as you type **1,** you will be returned to the document editing screen, and the first part of the document you chose will appear on your screen. (For information about how to change directories to locate a particular document from the List Files screen using its directory listing, see Chapter 6.)

Working with Two Documents

WordPerfect allows you to work on two documents at one time. To accomplish this, it keeps each document in a separate document window. These windows are identified by Doc 1 and Doc 2 on the status line. To work with two documents, all you have to do is retrieve your first document (using one of the methods indicated in the previous sections), switch to the second document window, and retrieve another document.

SWITCHING BETWEEN FULL-SCREEN WINDOWS CONTAINING DIFFERENT DOCUMENTS

To move to the second document window, you press Shift-F3 (the Switch key sequence). You can keep track of which document you are in by checking the status line. As you press Shift-F3, the Doc indicator will change from 1 to 2. If you press this key combination again, it will change from 2 to 1. You can use Shift-F3 (Switch) at any time to toggle between the two documents open in the windows.

> *Note:* If you do not use Shift-F3 (Switch) to change to a new document window before you give the command to retrieve your second document, the text of the second document will be read into the text of the first document at the cursor's position. If this happens, you can press F7 (Exit), type **N** (to abandon the composite document without saving it), and press Return (to stay in Word-Perfect). Then repeat the retrieval procedure again, this time making sure you press Shift-F3 to change the document window before you retrieve your second document.

The primary reasons for using document windows are to compare the contents of each against one another and to move and copy blocks of text from one to the other. If you need to compare two parts of your text to one another, you probably should split the editing display screen so that you can see both parts in one view (see the following sections for details regarding this procedure). If you are using windows to move or copy text from one document to another, you will need to be familiar with marking blocks of text and using WordPerfect's move and copy commands (see "Copying and Moving Text" and "Block Operations" later in this chapter).

DISPLAYING TWO DOCUMENTS ON THE SCREEN

To display parts of two documents in the same screen display, you need to use WordPerfect's Window feature. You press Ctrl-F3 (the Screen key) and choose option 1 (for Window). When you type **1,** you will see the following prompt:

 # Lines in this Window: 24

The cursor will be positioned under the 2 in 24. The default value is 24 because WordPerfect allows you to use 24 of the 25 lines of text displayed on a typical monitor—it reserves the twenty-fifth line for status line information and the prompts and error messages.

To display two document windows on the same screen, you must change the number of lines to a number between 1 and 22. (If you specify 23, all you will see is the ruler line displayed on the screen, and there will not be any lines below this for displaying the text of a second document.) If you specify 12 as the number of lines, the two document windows will be of equal size. If you specify a number less than or equal to 0 or a number greater than 24, WordPerfect will ignore your entry, and the full-screen window display will not be changed.

To set the size of the windows in the display, you can either enter the number of lines or press the ↑ key. Pressing ↑ gives you visual feedback as you size the windows. This is especially helpful if you have already retrieved the two documents (see the previous section) before you set the sizes for the windows, because it allows you to see what sizes work best with the text you are primarily interested in comparing.

As you press the ↑ key, WordPerfect will continue to display the "# Lines in this Window" prompt, changing the number that follows it as you increase the size of the lower window and decrease the size of the upper window. You can always tell where the bottom of the upper window is by the position of the highlighted tab ruler displayed on the screen. As you increase the size of the lower window, you will be able to see the words *Doc 2* in the window's status line. You will also see the words *Doc 1* in the status line on the last line of the upper window. When the document windows appear as you want them, press Return to set the display.

Once you have set the windows, you press Shift-F3 (Switch) to move the cursor back and forth between the windows. Remember that the cursor must be located in the document window before you can edit the text you see displayed within it.

WordPerfect keeps you informed of which document window is current (contains the cursor) by the direction of the triangles that mark tab stops on the tab ruler. When the triangles point upward, the upper window is current, and any cursor movements or editing commands you use will affect the document this window contains. When these triangles point downward, the lower window is current. As you switch between the document in each window, not only will the direction of the tab triangles change, but so will their position and those of the margin settings (unless both documents use the same margin and tab settings).

When you have finished your work with the two documents, you can return the display to one full-sized window by pressing Ctrl-F3 (Screen), selecting **1** (Window), typing **24** for the number of lines, and pressing Return. Whichever document window is current at the time you give this command will be the one whose document will be shown in the full-sized window that is created. To display the other document, press Shift-F3 (Switch) key.

Returning the screen display to one full-sized window does not exit or save the document that is no longer displayed. When you work with two documents in memory, you must use the F7 (Exit) key to close and save each. After you press Return to indicate that you want the displayed document to be saved and press Return again to save it under the same name, you will be prompted with

Exit Doc 1 (or 2)? (Y/N) N

If you type **Y,** you will be switched immediately to the second document in memory. To exit and save this document as well, you must repeat the exit procedure.

If you exit and save a document in one of the windows when both are displayed on the screen, the window will not be automatically closed, although the cursor will return to the document still left in memory. You will still have to press Ctrl-F3 (Screen) and select **1** (Window) to set the window size to 24 lines to return to single, full-screen display.

ALT-H: A MACRO TO SPLIT THE DISPLAY INTO TWO EQUAL WINDOWS

If you often use two equal-sized windows to copy, move, or compare text between documents, you may want to create the following macro to save keystrokes and speed up the windowing process.

Begin macro	Macro name	Keystrokes	End macro
Ctrl-F10	**Alt-H**	**Ctrl-F3 1 12 Return**	**Ctrl-F10**

To use this macro, press Alt-H. If you have not yet retrieved your documents, retrieve the document for the first document window, press Shift-F3, and then retrieve the second document. If you have already retrieved your two documents, parts of each will be displayed on the screen as soon as you use Alt-H.

ALT-F: A MACRO TO RETURN THE DISPLAY TO ONE FULL- SIZED WINDOW

Once you have split the screen into two equal windows, you can use the following macro to return quickly to a single full-sized window when you have finished your editing.

Begin macro	*Macro name*	*Keystrokes*	*End macro*
Ctrl-F10	**Alt-F**	**Ctrl-F3 1 24 Return**	**Ctrl-F10**

To use this macro, press Alt-F; the document containing the cursor will be displayed on the entire screen.

Inserting One Document into Another

You can insert the complete text of one document into another by positioning the cursor in the place where you want the other document's text to appear and retrieving the document (using one of the methods outlined previously—using either the Shift-F10 (Retrieve) or F5 (List Files) command). The text located after the cursor's position in the original document will be moved down as required to accommodate all of the new text from the incoming document.

If the document you insert contains no changes to WordPerfect's format default settings (margin, spacing, and tab settings), its text will conform to whatever format settings are in effect in the document it is brought into. On the other hand, if the document you bring in contains modifications to the format default settings, these will be retained when the document is retrieved and combined with the original document. This is because the format of a WordPerfect document is always controlled by the set of formatting codes that precede the text. If you have made changes and thus entered formatting codes into a document, these will be copied when you combine the text of the two documents.

This means that if you combine the text of one document into the middle of another (as opposed to adding it at the end of the document), existing text located after the join may be formatted to the settings of the incoming document. In such a case, you will have to position the cursor at the beginning of the original text that has been disturbed and enter the appropriate format commands to return it to its previous settings.

This technique for inserting the entire text of an external document file must not be confused with that for inserting only certain sections of one document file into another. The latter technique requires a copy operation using one of WordPerfect's block features between two document windows. This kind of copy operation is discussed later in this chapter.

EDITING A DOCUMENT

After retrieving a document (or documents) to be edited, you will probably combine several techniques for making the necessary changes. Usually, the first order of business is to locate the appropriate place in the text where the changes are to be made. WordPerfect offers several methods for locating a particular place in the document's text:

- A Go To function (Ctrl-Home) to position the cursor at the beginning of a particular page or at the beginning of a block of text (when Block is on—see the discussion of Block operations that follows).

- A Forward Search function (F2) to position the cursor at the end of particular characters, words, phrases, or formatting codes that follow the cursor's current position.

- A Reverse Search function (Shift-F2) to position the cursor at the end of particular characters, words, phrases, or formatting codes that precede the cursor's current position.

- A Replace function (Alt-F2) to position the cursor at the end of particular groups of characters, words, or phrases that follow the cursor's current position (there is no reverse search and replace feature in WordPerfect) and replace them with new characters, words, or phrases.

Locating Text to Be Edited by Using the Go To Page Command

If you are editing from a marked-up hard copy of a document that contains page numbers (see Chapter 4 for details about how to set page numbers), you can use the Go To function to move the cursor to the beginning of the page you want to revise. To do this, press Ctrl-Home; you will see

Go to

Enter the appropriate page number and press Return. You will see the message ''Repositioning'' on your screen as WordPerfect moves the cursor to the top of the specified page.

You can use the Go To function even if you have not used page numbers in the document because this function uses the document's Pg counter to locate pages rather than the actual page numbers WordPerfect inserts at printing time. Of course, if your printout does not have page numbers on it, you will have to manually calculate the number of the page that contains the text you want to edit.

Once the cursor is positioned on the proper page, you can use one of the cursor movement keys to move it to the specific text to be modified. If you do not see the place in the text displayed on the first screen, you can press the + (plus) key twice to scroll up the second part of the page.

Locating Text to Be Edited by Using the Search Command

You can also use WordPerfect's Search feature to locate the specific text that you want to edit. You can search for a particular place in the text either from the cursor's present position to the end of the document (Forward Search, effected by pressing F2) or from the cursor's position to the beginning of the document (Reverse Search, effected by pressing Shift-F2). If you have just retrieved a document and have not made any changes to it, your cursor will be located at the top of the first page of the document; in this case, you will want to use the Forward Search function.

You can use either Forward or Reverse Search to locate particular characters, words, phrases, or formatting codes that you have entered into a document. The first time you press F2 to begin a forward search, you will see the following prompt on your screen:

-> Srch:

and the cursor will appear to the right of the colon. You then enter the search string that you want WordPerfect to find. This string can consist of any characters, words, or phrases up to 59 characters total.

Unlike other word processors you may have used, WordPerfect does not include special search options such as Ignore Case, Whole Word, and the like that can be used to refine your search and make it more exact. For example, if you enter the search string *ion* to find all occurrences of the word *ion* (as in "a free ion in a solution"), WordPerfect will find the three characters *ion* wherever they appear, even in the many words that end in *tion* (stat*ion*, relat*ion*, and so on).

You can weed out matches in words that contain *ion* as part of them by typing a space before and after the letters *ion* in the search string. WordPerfect will not consider the *ion* in such words as *relation* a match because *relation* lacks one of the required spaces, the one before the *i* in *ion*.

However, entering the search string this way brings up new problems. WordPerfect will not consider the word *ion* a match if it occurs at the end of a sentence. For example, in the sentence,

In this type of solution we seldom see a free ion.

WordPerfect would not consider *ion* a match because it is looking for an occurrence of <space>*ion*<space>, not <space>*ion*<*period*>; in fact, you might have quite a bit of trouble locating *ion.* in the text.

Also, typing a space before and after letters to mark them as a word means that you can only locate the singular form of the word. For our example, WordPerfect would not identify the plural *ions* as a match for the search string.

Sometimes, when you search for a word, you will have to perform two different searches before you find the occurrence of a word that marks the place where you want to begin editing. If you perform a search operation and Word-Perfect only locates occurrences of the word that you are not interested in and then displays the "Not found" message, you can use Shift-F2 (Reverse Search), edit the search string, and try to find the word on a return pass through the document. This problem can be ameliorated if you search for a phrase instead of a single word (especially if the word is embedded in many other words that you have used). For example, if you specified your search string as

─> Srch: free ion

with no space after the *n* in *ion,* WordPerfect would be more likely to find the place you want on its first pass through your document. Because WordPerfect is looking for the phrase *free*<space>*ion,* it will not recognize the *ion* in the ending of a word like *station* as a match. On the other hand, it will see the occurrence of the phrase *free ions* as a match, even if it occurs at the end of a sentence and is, therefore, followed by some type of punctuation. Also, it will find matches in both *free ion* and *free ions,* eliminating the problem that develops when the plural form of the word occurs.

> *Note:* WordPerfect ignores case differences in a search so long as the search string is entered in all lowercase letters. To make a search case sensitive, you must enter it using the appropriate capital letters. For example, the search string *Ion* would match only capitalized forms of the word *ion,* although it would not automatically eliminate all of the problems alluded to in the preceding discussion. For more information about the Search feature, refer to the reference entry "Search and Replace" later in this chapter.

After you have entered the search string, you press F2 to make WordPerfect perform the search operation and locate the first occurrence of the string in the direction specified. After WordPerfect finds the first occurrence of your search string in the document, you must repeat the Search command to make Word-Perfect locate any subsequent occurrences (WordPerfect does not have a key whose function is to locate the next occurrence of the search string). To reissue the command without changing to the search string, just press F2 twice. If you wish to edit the search string before performing the search again, press F2 once, make your changes, and then press F2 again. If you ever want to abort a search operation after entering the search string, press F1 (Cancel).

Performing an Extended Search

When WordPerfect performs a standard search operation, it does not look for matches to your search string in any headers, footers, footnotes, or endnotes that you have added to the document for matches to your search string. However, you can perform such an extended search operation with Version 4.2. To do this, you press

Home before you press F2 (to perform a forward search), Shift-F2 (to perform a reverse search), or Alt-F2 (to perform search and replace operation).

If WordPerfect finds your search string in a header, footer, footnote, or endnote you have assigned, it will position the cursor after the string in the appropriate function screen. To continue the extended search, you merely reenter the Search or Search and Replace command you used before. To abandon the search, you press Exit (F7) to return to the document.

> *Note:* Most of the time you will want to position the cursor at the very beginning of the document (Home Home ↑) before you begin an extended search that is to include the headers and footers that you have defined for a document. If you begin a forward extended search (Home F2) from somewhere in the middle of the document past the place where the header and footer definition codes exist, WordPerfect will not include them in the search operation unless you also perform a reverse extended search (Home Shift-F2).

SEARCHING FOR FORMATTING CODES

In addition to being able to use the Search function to find text in a document, you can use it to find formatting codes that have been added to the document as you made formatting changes during the document's creation. In some cases, you can even use WordPerfect's Search and Replace function (referred to simply as the Replace function) to make the program automatically replace one code with another. However, this facility is quite limited (see Table 3.1 later in this chapter for a list of possibilities). Where you cannot use the Replace function, you can create a macro that uses the Search function to locate the appropriate code, performs any required deletion, and replaces the code with a new one. This technique is discussed in the following section, "Macros to Search and Replace Formatting Codes."

To have WordPerfect locate a particular formatting code, you use the appropriate Search function (Forward or Reverse) and then press the appropriate function key or key combination (including the number of the menu option) instead of typing an alphanumeric search string. For instance, to perform a forward search to find the first occurrence of a hard page break (one that you entered), you press F2 and then press Ctrl-Return (the function keys used to add a hard page break). In response, the program will display the format code as the search string:

–> Srch: [HPg]

You then press F2 to perform the search. WordPerfect will position the cursor right below the first hard page break it finds. To delete this page break, you then press Backspace. To find the next occurrence of a hard page break, you press F2 twice.

You can also use this technique to find format codes that require the use of menu options. For instance, to locate the place in the text where you first used

WordPerfect's Newspaper Column format (see Chapter 8), you can use the Search function to find the [Col On] code required to activate your column definitions. After you press F2 (assuming that a forward search is required), you press Alt-F7 (the Math/Columns key combination you use to define and turn the columns on and off). You will then see the following list of options:

Math: 1 Def 2 On 3 Off 4 + 5 = 6 * 7 t 8 T 9 ! A N Column: B Def C On D Off 0

To search for the [Col On] code, you type **C,** and you then see the following:

– > Srch: [Col On]

Notice that because this menu line contains more than nine options, Word-Perfect uses the letters *A* through *D*. Option A, N Column, is the Newspaper Columns option (see Chapter 11 for discussion of Math Column options 1–9). Choosing option C supplies the formatting code [Col On] that you need to find the beginning of text formatted in Newspaper Column style.

> *Note:* You cannot use option A to make WordPerfect supply the appropriate code. Typing **A** only supplies *N* as the search string. The *A* appears on this menu only to differentiate the Math Column options from the Newspaper Column options.

In Version 4.2 of WordPerfect, you can use the Search function to find just the second formatting code (or lowercase letter) of a code that is part of a pair—for example, [U][u], [A][a], [C][c], and [B][b]. If you perform a regular search for one of these paired codes, WordPerfect positions the cursor after the uppercase code letter.

For instance, to find your first use of underlining in a document, you press F2 and then F8 (Underline):

– > Srch: [Undrline]

If you then perform the search and the first occurrence of underlining in the text is <u>Mastering WordPerfect</u>, WordPerfect will position the cursor under the *M* in *Mastering*. If you press Alt-F3 (Reveal Codes), you will see that the cursor is really positioned right after the [U] in [U]Mastering WordPerfect[u]. If you press Backspace, the underlining will be removed.

To search for the [u] code, you press F2 and then F8 twice. You will then see the following:

– > Srch: [Undrline][u]

To search for just the second code [u], you need to modify the codes after the Search prompt. Press ← twice and Del to remove the [Undrline] code. If you perform the search without deleting this first code, you will receive the message "Not Found," because nowhere in your text do the codes [U][u] occur together (that is, without any text between them).

Now when you press F2 to perform the search, the cursor will be positioned under the *t* in Mastering WordPerfect. If you turn on the Reveal Code window, you will see that the cursor is really located after the [u] code in [U]Mastering Word-Perfect[u].

Although this feature may not appear to be extremely useful (you can delete underlining by locating and removing either code), it can be applied very skill-fully in macros when you need to delete a paired format code and replace it with another set. See the following section for a full discussion of this technique.

MACROS TO SEARCH AND REPLACE FORMATTING CODES

Often you will have to manually delete and replace formatting codes once you have found them using WordPerfect's Search function. This is because Word-Perfect does not always let you use its Replace function to locate an occurrence of a particular formatting code and replace it with another. Table 3.1 gives you a list of the codes you can use as replacement strings. You must replace all other codes manually or with a WordPerfect macro.

Such a macro will use the Search function to find the particular format code that needs to be replaced, press Backspace to delete the code, and then enter the new format code. As discussed in the previous section, WordPerfect Version 4.2 allows you to find the second occurrence of paired format codes, such as [U] and [u], that surround text to be underlined.

Suppose, for instance, that you want to find and replace underlining in the text of a document and replace it with italics. To create a macro to do this, you must first ascertain that your printer can produce italic type and the font number that WordPerfect assigns to italics for your printer (see Chapter 15). The follow-ing steps are required to make the macro work properly:

1. Use Forward Search to find the first underlining code [U].
2. Add the print font code to produce italics (Font 4 in this example).
3. Use Forward Search again to locate the second underlining code [u].
4. Press Backspace to delete the underlining.
5. Add the print font code for regular type.

These five steps translate into the keystrokes listed for the macro ITAL. (This macro assumes that Font 4 will produce italics on your printer—true if you are

FEATURE	KEY SEQUENCE	REPLACE STRING
Advance Up	Shift-F1 4	[Adv]
Advance Down	Shift-F1 5	[Adv]
Center Page	Alt-F8 3	[Center Pg]
Column On	Alt-F7 C	[Col On]
Column Off	Alt-F7 D	[Col Off]
Hard Space	Home Space bar	[ ]
Hyphen	Hyphen key	[-]
Hyphenation On	Shift-F8 8	[Hyph on]
Hyphenation Off	Shift-F8 9	[Hyph off]
Justification On	Ctrl-F8 4	[Rt Just On]
Justification Off	Ctrl-F8 3	[Rt Just Off]
Math On	Alt-F7 2	[Math On]
Math Off	Alt-F7 3	[Math Off]
Math Operators	Alt-F7	
	4	+
	5	=
	6	*
	7	t
	8	T
	9	!
Merge Codes	Alt-F9	
	1	^C
	2	^D
	3	^F
	4	^G
	5	^N
	6	^O
	7	^P
	8	^Q
	9	^S
	A	^T
	B	^U
	C	^V
Merge E	Shift-F9	^E
Merge R	F9	^R
Overstrike	Shift-F1 3	[OvrStrk]
Soft Hyphen	Ctrl-Hyphen key	-m-
Subscript	Shift-F1 2	[SubScript]
Superscript	Shift-F2 1	[SuprScript]
Widow/Orphan On	Shift-F8 A	[W/O On]
Widow/Orphan Off	Shift-F8 B	[W/O Off]

TABLE 3.1: Format Codes That Can Be Used in a Replace String

using an Epson FX or LX printer. You should, if necessary, substitute the appropriate number to activate italics on your printer for the 4's that appear in the Keystrokes section.)

Begin macro	*Macro name*	*Keystrokes*	*End macro*
Ctrl-F10	**ITAL**	**F2 Del F8 F2**	**Ctrl-F10**
		Ctrl-F8 1 ↓	
		4 Return 0	
		F2 F8 F8	
		← ← Del F2	
		Backspace Y	
		Ctrl-F8 1 ↓	
		1 Return 0	

The macro ITAL begins by accessing the Forward Search function (F2) and then deleting any search string (Del). Because WordPerfect will otherwise retain the previously used search string [u], this procedure is necessary if the macro is used a second time. After deleting any string, WordPerfect enters the [Undrline] code (F8) as the search string and then begins the search operation (F2). When the program finds this code, the macro accesses the Print Format menu (Ctrl-F8) and chooses option 1 (1 for the Pitch, Font option). It then uses ↓ to leave the pitch set at 10, enters **4** (the number of the Font that produces italics), presses Return to enter this new value, and types **0** to return to the document.

After the new font is set, the macro accesses the Forward Search function again (F2) and presses the underlining key (F8) twice. The first time, the cursor moves past the [Undrline] code that still remains from the previous search operation and then enters the second underline code [u]. The macro then moves the cursor to the beginning of the first underlining code [Undrline] (by pressing ← twice) and deletes it (Del). This leaves only the code [u] to be searched for, and the macro next executes this search operation (F2). When it finds this code, the macro deletes the underlining (Backspace, Y—you must confirm the deletion). Finally, the macro accesses the Print Format menu again (Ctrl-F8) and sets the Font back to 1 (1 ↓ 1 Return 0) so that only the text that previously was underlined will now be italicized.

To use this macro, all you have to do is press Alt-F10 and type **ITAL**. The macro will very quickly find and change the first occurrence of underlining to italic type. If it does not find any underlining, all you will see is the message "Please Wait" displayed on your screen very briefly. To find and change subsequent occurrences of underlining, all you have to do is execute the macro again. (You could also chain this macro so that it would search the entire document and change all underlining to italics. See Chapter 14 for details about chaining macros.)

As you can see from this example, macros can be very effective in situations where you cannot use WordPerfect's Replace function to find and change formatting codes. With Version 4.2's ability to find just the second code of those that appear in pairs, your control over the process has been made more exact.

Techniques for Making Simple Insertions and Deletions

Once you have found the text to be edited, you must select the best method for changing it. If your changes consist only of simple text insertions or deletions, you can just go ahead and make them. WordPerfect is always in Insert mode unless you specifically press Ins (Insert). If you do, the message "Typeover" will replace the name of the document you are editing. In Typeover mode, all of the characters you enter at the cursor's position will replace existing ones.

Unlike some word processors, such as MultiMate, WordPerfect does not split the text when you insert new characters. All you have to do to add new text in a particular place is position the cursor where the new text is to appear and start typing (assuming that you are not in Typeover mode). WordPerfect will use word wrap to reformat the paragraph as you type.

If you are inserting a lot of text, you may find the constant reformatting distracting. If this is the case, you can temporarily split the paragraph by positioning the cursor under the first character of the text that will remain unchanged after the insertion is made and entering a carriage return (a hard return). This will move the following text down and keep it separate from the lines that you insert. Once you have entered all of the text you need to insert, you can rejoin the paragraph by removing the [HPg] formatting code that you entered earlier. To do this, move the cursor two spaces past the last inserted character (often a period marking the end of the last sentence inserted) and press Del. The paragraph will be combined, and it will be reformatted as soon as you move the cursor down a line.

When deleting text, you need to decide which of the many commands for making deletions is best suited to the task at hand. (Refer to the reference entries for deleting text in Chapter 2 if you are uncertain of the options available to you.) Generally, the delete commands are intended to remove discrete units of text such as individual characters and words or to remove text from the cursor position to the end of the line or the end of the paragraph. If the text you want to delete forms such a unit, you are best advised to mark the text as a block and delete it using the appropriate command.

The next few sections discuss how to delete, copy, and move blocks of text and how to save blocks of text in separate files.

Marking Blocks of Text

WordPerfect allows you to mark any sized block of text—from a single character to the entire document—using its Block key combination, Alt-F4. When you press this key sequence, the flashing message

Block On

replaces the name of the file you are editing at the bottom of the screen. This message indicates that as you press a cursor movement key, WordPerfect will mark the text as the cursor moves by highlighting it. You use the cursor movement keys (see Chapter 1) to mark all of the text you want to delete, move, copy, print, spell check, sort, enhance, save in a separate file, and so on (see "Block Operations" later in this chapter for a complete list of applications). If you mark too much text, use the opposite cursor movement key to reduce the limits of the block before selecting the appropriate command to perform an operation on it.

Which cursor movement key to use in marking a block depends upon the extent of the block. To mark just a few words, you would position the cursor on the first character of the first word to be marked and press Ctrl-→ until all of the words are highlighted.

To mark just a few lines of text, you can press ↓ several times to highlight each line to be included, or you can press Esc, type a number corresponding to the number of lines to be included, and then press ↓. Be aware that if the cursor is not positioned at the very beginning of the first line when you press Alt-F4 to turn on blocking and you use ↓ (or ↑), the highlighting in the next line will extend only to the column position that the cursor occupied when you turned blocking on. For example, if you move the cursor to column position 15 on a line and press Alt-F4 and ↓, the highlighting in the line below will extend only to position 15 on that line. If you want to include entire lines, you must position the cursor at the very beginning of the line.

To block a complete or partial paragraph, you can press Return after turning blocking on. This will extend the highlighting from the cursor's position in the paragraph to the end of the paragraph. To extend the highlighting to a particular character in the paragraph or line, type that character after turning blocking on. For example, you could mark up to the end of a sentence that ends with a question mark by typing **?** after turning on blocking with Alt-F4.

If you ever want to abort marking a block of text after pressing Alt-F4, you can either press F1 (Cancel) or press Alt-F4 again (the Block On key is a toggle switch). Because you can apply so many different commands to a block of text once it has been marked, WordPerfect allows you to use Ctrl-Home (Go To) to rehighlight the same block. To use this technique, you must press Alt-F4 to turn blocking on and then press Ctrl-Home twice. You will then see the same block highlighted as you used in the previous command.

This technique has many useful applications. For instance, you can use it to mark a block of text to be centered and then use it to boldface the same block. To do this, you would press Alt-F4, use the cursor movement keys to mark the lines to be centered, press Shift-F6 and type **Y** to center the marked text, press Alt-F4 again, press Ctrl-Home twice, and then press F6 to boldface it. (For more information about applying print enhancements to blocks, see "Adding Enhancements to Blocks of Text" later in this chapter.)

Copying and Moving Text

Most of the time, you will block text to move or copy it to different locations in the same document or to a document in the second window. After marking the text to be copied or moved as described in the previous section, you access the Move menu by pressing Ctrl-F4 (Move). When you press Ctrl-F4 after you have marked a block, you will see the following menu options:

> **1 Cut Block; 2 Copy Block; 3 Append; 4 Cut/Copy Column;
> 5 Cut/Copy Rectangle: 0**

You then select the appropriate option from this menu.

MOVING A BLOCK OF TEXT

If you wish to move the block to a new location in the document (or to a document in the second window), you type **1** to select the Cut Block option. (Word-Perfect considers a move operation to be a cut and paste operation, although it uses the terminology *cut and retrieve block* instead of *cut and paste block.*) The block will then disappear from the screen—it has not been deleted, but rather is retained in a special memory location referred to as a buffer. You then move the cursor to the position in the document where you want the block of text to appear and press Ctrl-F4 again. You will then see the following menu options:

> **Move 1 Sentence; 2 Paragraph; 3 Page; Retrieve 4 Column; 5 Text;
> 6 Rectangle: 0**

You type **5** to select the Retrieve Text option. WordPerfect will insert the text that you cut in the previous step at the cursor's position.

If you want to move a block of text to a different document currently displayed in the second window, you simply press Shift-F3 (Switch) after cutting the block. Then you position the cursor where you want the text inserted, press Ctrl-F4, and type **5**; the text will be inserted.

The text that you cut by blocking it and pressing Ctrl-F4 and typing **1** remains in the buffer until you repeat this procedure for another block of text. This feature means that if you cut a block when you meant to copy it, you need only press

Ctrl-F4 and type **5** without moving the cursor to bring it back (remember, because the text has not been deleted, pressing F1, the Undelete key, will not bring it back).

This feature also means that you can move a block to a new place in the document and then copy it to other places in the same document or in another document in the other window. Because WordPerfect copies the cut block from the buffer into a document without emptying the buffer, the text the buffer contains can be duplicated and placed anywhere in the document as many times as you wish.

COPYING A BLOCK OF TEXT

To copy a section of text that has been marked with Alt-F4 (Block), you simply vary the second step outlined for moving a block. After you finish marking the block, you press Ctrl-F4 and type **2** to select the Copy Block option. This copies the marked text into the same buffer that WordPerfect uses when you move text (meaning that it deletes any text that has been cut or copied previously). The text that was highlighted is not removed from the screen as it is when the Cut Block option is used, although the highlighting disappears.

To copy the text to a new place in the document, move the cursor to the place in the document where you want the copied text to appear, press Ctrl-F4, and type **5**. If you want to copy the block to a different document currently displayed in the second document window, press Shift-F3 and move the cursor to the position where you want the text to appear before you press Ctrl-F4, and type **5** to insert it.

The block of text that you copy into the buffer will remain there until you perform a new move or copy operation, so you can copy the block to many places in the document without having to block the text again. To make multiple copies of the same block, just keep moving the cursor to the places where you want the block to appear, pressing Ctrl-F4, and typing **5**.

Copying and Moving Entire Sentences, Paragraphs, and Pages

Although you can use the procedures just described to move or copy any size block of text (even columns—see Chapters 8 and 11—or rectangles—see Chapter 13), WordPerfect offers you an alternative method for moving or copying entire sentences, paragraphs, or pages. If you recognize ahead of time that the text you want to move or copy is one of these discrete units of text, you can use the following method.

First you need to position the cursor anywhere in the sentence, paragraph, or page you want to move or copy; then press Ctrl-F4 (Move). (Notice that you do not begin this operation by using Alt-F4. You do not need to block the text when you are working with units of sentences, paragraphs, or pages; WordPerfect will do this for you.) When you press Ctrl-F4 (and have not marked a block previously), you will see these menu options:

Move 1 Sentence; 2 Paragraph; 3 Page; Retrieve 4 Column; 5 Text;
6 Rectangle: 0

To move or copy a sentence, you type **1**. For a paragraph, you type **2**, and for a page, you type **3**. If you choose 1, the entire sentence containing the cursor will automatically be highlighted, regardless of where the cursor is positioned within it. If you choose 2, the entire paragraph will be highlighted. If you choose 3, the entire page will be highlighted. You will then see a new menu containing these options:

1 Cut; 2 Copy; 3 Delete: 0

To move the unit of text that is highlighted, type **1** to cut it and copy it into the buffer. The highlighted text will then disappear from the document. Then, move the cursor to the place you want the text to appear, press Ctrl-F4 a second time, and type **5** to insert the text into its new position in the document. If you want to move the sentence, paragraph, or page to a document in the other document window, press Shift-F3 before you press Ctrl-F4; then type **5** to retrieve the text.

To copy the unit of text you have chosen, you vary this procedure only slightly. After you press Ctrl-F4 and choose either sentence (1), paragraph (2), or page (3), you type **2** to choose the Copy option instead of typing **1** to choose the Cut option. WordPerfect will not remove the highlighted sentence, paragraph, or page, but will copy the text to the buffer and then remove the highlighting. You then move the cursor to the place where you want the copy to appear, press Ctrl-F4, and type **5** to insert the text.

Deleting a Block of Text

If you wish to delete a block of text, you have two methods to choose from:

- If the text to be deleted is an entire sentence, paragraph, or page, you press Ctrl-F4, type **1** for a sentence, **2** for a paragraph, or **3** for a page. Then type **3** to select the Delete option from the Cut/Copy menu options that appear.
- If the text is not one of these discrete units, press Alt-F4 and mark the text to be deleted with the cursor movement keys. Then press Backspace. You will then see the message

Delete Block? (Y/N) N

Type **Y** to delete the highlighted text.

It is important to remember that you can press F1 to undelete any block of text that has been deleted in this manner. In fact, you can use the block delete as another way of moving text in a document. After deleting a block of text using one of the methods just described, you can move the cursor to the place in the document where you want the text to appear and press F1; the highlighted block just deleted will reappear on the screen. Then type **1** to undelete the block and insert it into the document at its new position. You can then copy the block elsewhere in the same document or into a document in the other document window by repeating this procedure.

> *Note:* When you delete a sentence, paragraph, or page of text by pressing Ctrl-F4, typing *1*, *2*, or *3*, and then typing *3* (the Delete option on the Cut/Copy menu), the text is copied into a buffer different from the one WordPerfect uses when you copy or move a sentence, paragraph, or page of text. This means that you could cut a page (Ctrl-F4, 3, 1) and then delete the next page (Ctrl-F4, 3, 3), and both pages would be retained in separate buffers. You could then retrieve and place the first cut page elsewhere in the document by pressing Ctrl-F4 and typing *1* and the second deleted page by pressing F1 and typing *1*.
>
> If you want to move two pages (paragraphs or sentences) located in one place in the document to another place further on, you could use this technique to remove both pages, move the cursor to where you want the pages placed, and then insert both pages, using the appropriate methods, without having to move one page forward and then return to move the second one.

ALT-X: A MACRO TO DELETE BLOCKED TEXT

You can define a macro, Alt-X, that deletes text you have marked as a block using the following keystrokes.

Begin macro	*Macro name*	*Keystrokes*	*End macro*
Ctrl-F10	**Alt-X**	**Backspace** (or **Del**) **Y**	**Ctrl-F10**

This simple macro can be used whenever you need to delete text that you have previously highlighted as a block. It can be combined with the macro Alt-M that marks text as a block (discussed later in this chapter).

Saving a Block of Text in Another Document

In addition to being able to copy blocks of text to a document currently displayed in the second document window, you can mark a block of text and either save it in a new file of its own or add it to the end of an existing document file.

SAVING A BLOCK IN A NEW FILE

To save a block of text in a new file, you mark it by pressing Alt-F4, highlight it with the appropriate cursor movement keys, and press F10 to save it. When you press F10, the flashing "Block on" message changes to

Block name:

You then type the file name under which you wish this block of text to be saved and press Return. If you do not specify the drive letter and directory as part of the file name, WordPerfect will save the file in the current default directory. If you want to remove this blocked text that you just saved in a new file, you just press Del or Backspace and type **Y**.

If you have made formatting changes in the document from which you copy the block, these most likely will no longer affect the text in the new file; unless you included the formatting codes used in the first document as part of the block, the text in the new document will use the program's format default settings just as when you create a new document. In such a case, you will have to make appropriate format changes in the new document after you retrieve its file.

APPENDING A BLOCK TO ANOTHER DOCUMENT

To copy a block of text to the end of another document, you press Alt-F4, highlight the text to be included, and press Ctrl-F4. From the Move menu you then choose the Append option by typing **3**. You will then see the prompt

Append to:

You enter the name of the file to which you wish this block of text added and press Return. If you do not specify the drive letter and directory as part of the file name, WordPerfect will save this file in the current default directory.

When you next retrieve the document to which you appended this block of text, you will find the block at the very end of it. If the last sentence in the document was not terminated with a hard return, the text in the first paragraph of the added block will be joined to the last paragraph of the document. Also, the added block of text will conform to the format settings of the document to which it is appended unless the block is preceded by its own set of formatting codes.

Adding Enhancements to Blocks of Text

You can apply boldfacing, underlining, centering, and uppercase letters to blocks of text after they have been marked as described earlier. (For information about using italics, see Chapter 5.)

UNDERLINING AND BOLDFACING BLOCKS

WordPerfect lets you underline and boldface entire blocks of text at a time. This feature provides a shortcut for enhancing text that you have already typed. For example, if you first mark a heading as a block (using Alt-F4), you can then indicate that the heading is to be boldfaced by pressing only one key (F6) instead of having to retype the text and insert the boldface codes.

The heading in Figure 3.1 was first marked as a block and then marked for boldface. To delete boldfacing and underlining codes from blocks of text, press Alt-F3 to see the format codes; then backspace over one of them. If you backspace over one of these invisible formatting codes in the text, you will see the prompt

Delete [Bold]? (Y/N) N

at the bottom of your screen. You can enter **Y** to delete the code or press Return to leave it in place.

You can also change the style of underlining; for details, see Chapter 2.

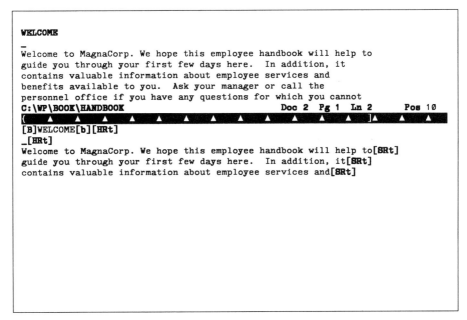

FIGURE 3.1: A block of text marked for boldface. To delete text enhancements such as boldfacing, underlining, and centering, press Alt-F3 to reveal the formatting codes; then backspace over them.

CENTERING BLOCKS OF TEXT

WordPerfect allows you to center entire blocks of text, such as quotations or lists, vertically on the page. Centering text is an effective way of calling the reader's attention to a passage and making it stand out visually on the page.

To center a block of text—a heading, a paragraph, a list, or any other text element—first mark the text as a block (using Alt-F4). Then, with the block highlighted, press Shift-F6. The prompt

[Center]? (Y/N) N

appears at the bottom of your screen. Enter **Y** to center the block. WordPerfect automatically calculates the center position on the text line and centers the block around that position.

To delete centering, press Alt-F3 to see the [C][c] (centering begin and end) codes. Position the cursor at the right of one of these codes and then press Backspace. Press the space bar to return to your document.

CONVERTING BLOCKS TO UPPERCASE FORMAT

You can also convert a block of text that you have marked to uppercase format. This feature is useful when, for example, after entering your entire document you decide that you would like to make the text headings solid capital letters. You can mark all the headings in your document as blocks and then convert them to uppercase format. (While you have them marked as blocks, you can also mark them for your table of contents—see Chapter 7.)

To convert a marked block of text to uppercase format, press Shift-F3 (Switch). The following message will appear in the lower-left corner of the screen:

Block: 1 Upper Case; 2 Lower Case: 0

Enter **1** for uppercase; then press F1 or Alt-F4 to turn off the block.

To convert a block back to lowercase format, follow the same procedure, but enter **2**. When you convert blocks back to lowercase format, you lose whatever capitalization was in that block before. For example, if your heading was

New Hire Requirements

before you converted it to

NEW HIRE REQUIREMENTS

when you convert it back to lowercase format it will appear as

new hire requirements

and you must reinsert the correct capitalization.

ALT-C: A MACRO TO CAPITALIZE LOWERCASE LETTERS

You can write a simple macro that capitalizes the character on which the cursor rests. Such a macro is often useful when you are revising text or correcting typographical errors as well as in the situation just discussed in which you need to correct capitalization in headings that you have lowercased.

Begin macro	*Macro name*	*Keystrokes*	*End macro*
Ctrl-F10	**Alt-C**	**Alt-F4 →** **Shift-F3 1** **Alt-F4 ←**	**Ctrl-F10**

You can write a similar macro to lowercase the character the cursor is on. Simply substitute **2** for **1** in the preceding macro.

Alphabetizing Lines in a Block of Text

One very useful feature of WordPerfect is its ability to alphabetize items in a block of text. This is called a *line sort* in WordPerfect. (For more information about sorting in WordPerfect, see Chapter 10.)

To use this feature, the items to be sorted must be in rows and columns, like names and phone numbers in a phone list. Separate each column with at least one tab. Then highlight the block of items you want to sort by pressing Alt-F4 (Block). When the block of items is highlighted, press Ctrl-F9 (Merge/Sort). The screen shown in Figure 3.2 appears. To accept the default settings, which will sort your list alphabetically using the first word of each item, simply press **1**, Perform Action. Your highlighted list will be alphabetized in ascending order (A to Z).

This technique works for alphabetic entries such as employee lists. You can also specify keys on which to sort, if, for example you want to sort first by last name and then by first name. In addition, you can sort on alphanumeric fields and even specify items to be selected from a list (see Chapter 10 for details about how to perform such sorts in WordPerfect).

ALF: A MACRO THAT ALPHABETIZES LAST AND FIRST NAMES

Rather than having to go through each of the steps just described each time you want to sort a simple list, you can define the following macro, which sorts alphabetically by the second word in each item, which in this case is the last name. (All too often you find that the list you want to sort is not in the order last name, first name—and that is when this macro is handy. If all you want to do is sort by the first word in a list, WordPerfect's default settings will do that for you. Just mark the list as a block, press Ctrl-F9, and type **1**.)

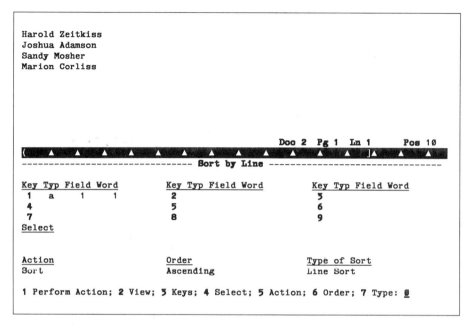

FIGURE 3.2: The Sort by Line screen. As you can see from the screen, you can also specify keys on which to sort so that you could, for example, sort by last name and then by first name within the last name category.

This macro also sorts by first name within last name, which makes it useful for creating phone lists and the like. Note that this particular macro sorts only on the second and first words in a list, which is the type of alphabetizing you will usually have to do. (For additional list-sorting macros, see Chapter 10.)

Remember, you must mark your list as a block (Alt-F4) before you use this macro.

Begin macro	*Macro name*	*Keystrokes*	*End macro*
Ctrl-F10	**ALF**	**Ctrl-F9 3**	**Ctrl-F10**
		→ → 2	
		→ Return	
		F7 1	

This macro instructs WordPerfect to sort a highlighted list (marked with Alt-F4) alphabetically (A–Z) on the second word in the line and then on the first word in the line. To use this macro, mark the list of names, press Alt-F10, type **ALF**, and press Return.

The Sort by Line screen used to create this macro is shown in Figure 3.3. WordPerfect counts words from left to right; spaces separate words. Tabs or indents separate fields, which WordPerfect also counts from left to right. For more information about sorting, refer to Chapter 10.

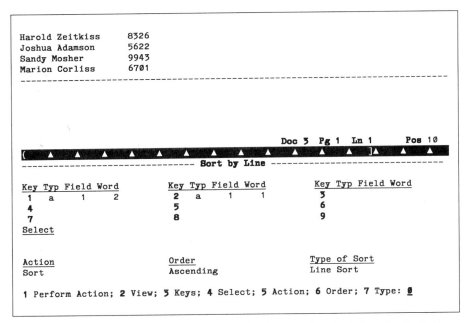

```
Harold Zeitkiss     8326
Joshua Adamson      5622
Sandy Mosher        9943
Marion Corliss      6701
-------------------------------------------------------------------
```

```
                                      Doc 3  Pg 1  Ln 1      Pos 10
(    ▲    ▲    ▲    ▲    ▲    ▲    ▲    ▲    ▲    ▲    ]▲    ▲    ▲
----------------------------- Sort by Line ------------------------
```

```
Key Typ Field Word      Key Typ Field Word      Key Typ Field Word
1    a    1    2         2    a    1    1        3
4                       5                       6
7                       8                       9
Select
```

```
Action                  Order                   Type of Sort
Sort                    Ascending               Line Sort

1 Perform Action; 2 View; 3 Keys; 4 Select; 5 Action; 6 Order; 7 Type: 0
```

FIGURE 3.3: Creating the alphabetizing macro. Note that the second word is indicated as the first key on which to sort and the first word is indicated as the second key. The list appears as it is before it is sorted.

Transposing Characters and Words

Another WordPerfect feature that you can use when editing a document transposes the positions of words or characters—useful when, for example, you correct typographical errors. For instance, to transpose a character, you press Del (to delete the character), → (to move to the right of the deleted character), and F1, 1 (to undelete the character).

Alt-T: A Macro to Transpose Two Characters

The transposition sequence can be incorporated into the following macro to speed up your work.

Begin macro	Macro name	Keystrokes	End macro
Ctrl-F10	**Alt-T**	**Del** → **F1 1**	**Ctrl-F10**

To use this macro, you position the cursor under the character that needs to be transposed and press Alt-T.

TR: A MACRO TO TRANSPOSE TWO WORDS

To transpose the positions of two words that are adjacent, so that

to transpose

is changed to

transpose to

you can create the following macro:

Begin macro	*Macro name*	*Keystrokes*	*End macro*
Ctrl-F10	**TR**	**Alt-F4 Ctrl-→**	**Ctrl-F10**
		Del Y Ctrl-→	
		F1 1	

To use this macro, position the cursor on the first letter in the word to be transposed to the left and press Alt-F10; then type **TR** and press Return. If you ever use this macro in error, just repeat it to return the word order back to the way it was before you used the macro.

Keeping Text Together on a Line

Deleting or inserting text in a document inevitably involves reformatting the paragraph in which you make these changes. Sometimes this causes a phrase to break across a line in a way that you did not anticipate when you entered the text. For instance, if you type the date **02-13-87** and then insert new text before it, you may find that word wrap splits the date across two lines when you press ↓ and the paragraph is reformatted. If this happens, the reader may have difficulty immediately understanding that the numbers represent a date rather than a string of digits.

To keep a hyphenated phrase together on a line no matter how the text that precedes it is changed, you can replace each hyphen with a special nonbreaking hyphen (referred to as a minus sign in the WordPerfect documentation because it is most often used in equations that should not be broken by word wrap—for example, $A - B = C$). A phrase joined together by nonbreaking hyphens is always considered as a single word for purposes of word wrap and paragraph reformatting.

To edit the date 02-13-87 and replace its hyphens with nonbreaking hyphens, you only need to move the cursor to the first hyphen, press Del, and press Home before you type the hyphen again. You then repeat this procedure for the second hyphen in the date. Once you replace the hyphens in this manner and press ↓, WordPerfect will wrap the entire date to a new line instead of breaking it. The numbers in the date will always stay together on a line, regardless of any changes made to the text that precedes it.

Pressing Home and then typing a hyphen always inserts a nonbreaking hyphen. A nonbreaking hyphen is differentiated from a hard hyphen (entered by simply pressing the hyphen key) in the Reveal Codes window (accessed by pressing Alt-F3). A nonbreaking hyphen appears as a dash (—), and a hard (breaking) hyphen appears as a hyphen enclosed in square brackets ([-]). If you do not ever want a hyphenated phrase you are about to type split on different lines, you can enter hard hyphens by pressing Home before you type each hyphen as you enter the phrase.

> *Note:* Do not be confused by the terminology applied to hyphenation. Because WordPerfect offers automatic hyphenation (see the next section), it differentiates between soft hyphens (Ctrl-hyphen) that are not printed if the document is edited so that the word no longer requires hyphenation. A hyphen typed by pressing the hyphen key alone is considered a hard hyphen because it is always printed, whether the hyphenated word or phrase breaks across a line or not. The special type of hyphen being described here (referred to as a nonbreaking hyphen instead of a minus sign) is also a hard hyphen in that it always prints. However, it also binds the hyphenated words together as unit.

WordPerfect allows you to apply the same kind of binding to spaces between words that it does to hyphens. WordPerfect refers to this type of space as a hard space, although you may know it as a nonbreak space if you have used other word processors. You enter this type of space by pressing Home before you press the space bar. In the Reveal Codes window, WordPerfect differentiates a nonbreak space from a regular space by enclosing it in square brackets ([ ]), and it displays a regular space just as it is in the regular document.

> *Note:* The term *hard space* used by the WordPerfect documentation is unfortunate because its function is not equivalent to a hard hyphen (see the previous note). In WordPerfect, a hard space between words will not allow the words to break across lines, whereas a hard hyphen will. To avoid ambiguities, this book refers to what WordPerfect calls a *minus* as a *nonbreaking hyphen* and to a *hard space* as a *nonbreak space* in keeping with these features' fundamental functions and with terminology made common by other word processing packages.

You would use the nonbreak space in situations where a phrase would be less clear if it were broken onto two lines by word wrap. For instance, you might use it when entering the product name *Lotus 1-2-3*—and you might also enter non-breaking hyphens between *1* and *2* and *2* and *3* to ensure that the second word is never split. To do this, you would type **Lotus** and then press Home before pressing the space bar and typing **1-** (Home hyphen) **2-** (Home hyphen) **3.** Now *Lotus* will never be left at the end of one line with *1-2-3* at the beginning of the next line, nor will *1-2-3* ever be broken, regardless of changes made to the text that precedes it.

Hyphenating a Document

WordPerfect gives you a great deal of control over the placement of hyphens. The program uses two kinds of hyphens—hard hyphens and soft hyphens. A hard hyphen is one that you do not want to have the program remove whenever a line is changed—for instance, a hyphen used as a minus sign or a hyphen in a word or phrase that you always want to be hyphenated, such as *self-esteem*.

To insert such a hyphen, simply press the hyphen key. If you do not want the hyphenated word or phrase ever to be broken across lines, press Home before you press the hyphen key (for more information about this special nonbreaking hard hyphen, see the previous section). To insert a soft hyphen, you press Ctrl before you press the - key. A soft hyphen causes WordPerfect to insert a hyphen where you inserted the soft hyphen code if it ever needs to hyphenate that word. If the word does not require hyphenation when you enter it, no hyphen character will appear on the editing screen.

If you check the formatting code (by pressing Alt-F3), you can see the difference between a regular hard hyphen and a soft hyphen: A regular hard hyphen is enclosed in a pair of square brackets [-], and a soft hyphen is just shown as —. A soft hyphen always appears in the Reveal Codes window, even if it is not visible on the editing screen.

You will usually not want to manually enter any hyphens in a document other than hard hyphens, which are required regardless of the word's or phrase's placement on a given line. However, whenever you feel your document requires hyphenation to control the raggedness of the right margin (or the internal spacing when your document is right justified), you can use WordPerfect's hyphenation command.

WordPerfect Version 4.2 allows you to set hyphenation to either automatic or aided. When you use aided hyphenation, WordPerfect alerts you with a beep when it finds a word that should be hyphenated and suggests a place for the hyphen in the word. You can accept this placement for the hyphen by pressing Esc or F1, or you can use ← or → to move the cursor to relocate the hyphen and then press Esc.

If you prefer not to be asked about where to hyphenate words, you can use automatic hyphenation. When you set hyphenation to automatic, WordPerfect hyphenates words that require hyphenation without asking for your approval. All of the hyphens inserted using either automatic or aided hyphenation are soft hyphens (as though you had pressed Ctrl before the hyphen key).

WordPerfect uses a hyphenation zone to determine when the program will stop to hyphenate a word rather than use word wrap to move it to the beginning of the following line when you turn either aided or automatic hyphenation on. This zone is really broken into two areas: a left hyphenation zone and a right hyphenation zone. The left hyphenation zone is determined by counting the number of spaces before the right margin setting, and the right hyphenation zone is determined by counting the number of spaces beyond the right margin setting.

When a word extends beyond the right margin, it will be hyphenated only if it begins at or before the position of the left hyphenation zone and extends beyond the right hyphenation zone. WordPerfect uses a default setting of 7 for the left hyphenation zone (meaning 7 spaces before the right margin, or position 67 if the right margin uses the default setting of 74). The right hyphenation zone has a default setting of 0 (meaning that it corresponds to the right margin setting).

If you reduce the left hyphenation zone, you will be prompted more often to hyphenate words if you are using aided hyphenation, or the program will automatically hyphenate more often if you are using automatic hyphenation. In some cases, you will find that a left setting of 7 is too large to reduce the raggedness of the right margin as much as you would like.

Also, when your document is right justified, you will find that you need a smaller left hyphenation zone than 7 to appreciably reduce the amount of uneven spacing within a line. Remember that with right justification on, WordPerfect right aligns every line by inserting spaces between words. To achieve fairly even spacing, you will have to hyphenate frequently. This is all the more true when you are using several right-justified columns on a page in either newspaper or parallel style (see Chapter 8). For more information about using WordPerfect's hyphenation commands and setting appropriate hyphenation zones, refer to the section "Hyphenation Commands" later in this chapter.

USING DOCUMENT WINDOWS

KEY SEQUENCE

To switch between full-screen windows:
Shift-F3
To split the display into two windows:
Ctrl-F3 1 <*number of lines* or ↑> **Return**

It often is extremely useful to be able to see the contents of one document when you are working on another document—for example, when you are writing a monthly report, you may want to compare the previous month's report. WordPerfect allows you to view two documents at the same time and cut or copy text between them.

In WordPerfect, you can view two separate documents on the screen at the same time by splitting the screen (using Ctrl-F3 1, Window), or you can switch between a full-screen view of each document (using Shift-F3, Switch).

To view another document while you are working on a different document, press Shift-F3. A blank WordPerfect screen appears. Press Ctrl-F10 to retrieve the new file. To return to your original document, press Shift-F3 again. You can always tell which document you are in by looking at the status line in the lower-right corner of the screen.

To split the screen into two windows, you press Ctrl-F3 and select option 1, Window. WordPerfect will prompt you for the number of lines of text you want to see in each window. The screen can display up to 24 lines, and you can enter any combination that adds up to 24. For example, to see 12 lines in each window, you would enter 12; to see 18 lines in one window and 6 in the other, you would enter 18, and so forth.

You can also press Ctrl-F3, enter **1**, use ↑ and ↓ to move the cursor to the position where you want the window split to occur, and then press Return.

To move back and forth between windows, you press Shift-F3 (Switch). The arrows on the tab ruler line that splits the screen change direction to indicate which window the cursor is in, as shown in Figure 3.4.

To remove the split screen and return to full-screen display, press Ctrl-F3 and select option 1. This time enter **0** (or **24**) as the number of lines you want displayed. The second document will still be in memory, and you can return to it at any time by pressing Shift-F3 (Switch). To replace it with another document, switch to it (press Shift-F3) and save and exit from it normally (press F7).

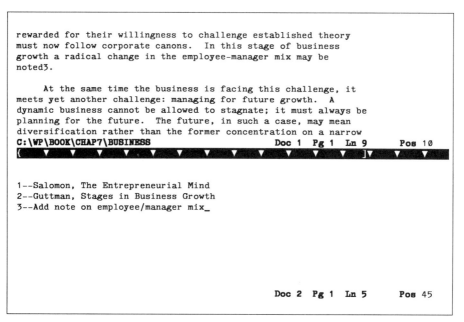

FIGURE 3.4: Working with a split screen. All of WordPerfect's file management features are available to you in each window. You can retrieve another document or transfer text between the documents in each window. In the example in this figure, the second window is being used as a scratch pad to keep track of footnotes that will be expanded to full references later.

If you work with windows frequently, you may want to write a macro that splits the screen and opens the lower window to the number of lines you prefer to work with. For examples of such macros, refer to "Alt-H: A Macro to Split the Display into Two Equal Windows" and "Alt-F: A Macro to Return the Display to One Full-Sized Window" earlier in this chapter.

USING WORDPERFECT'S SEARCH AND REPLACE COMMANDS

One of the most useful techniques for editing text is WordPerfect's Search and Replace function. You can search for any combination of words of up to 59 characters and search either backward or forward in your text, using uppercase, lowercase, and wildcard characters. For example, you can

- Search your document for an error you know has occurred and correct it. For example, if a supplier has moved to a new address, you can search for and change that address each time it occurs in your document.

- Search for specific formatting codes in your document and change them to different codes. For example, you can search for each margin setting to make sure that all margin settings in your document are the same. Or you can search for and remove special symbols and carriage returns from documents you import into WordPerfect (see Chapter 15). Or you can search for any formatting code (but you cannot automatically replace codes that require input from you, such as margin-setting codes).

- Search for a word you think you have misspelled but are not sure how you spelled it each time. Using the wildcard character Ctrl-X in place of the letter you're not sure about can help you find each occurrence of a word. For example, if you have spelled *conceived* as both *conceived* and *concieved,* you can search for conc ^X to find all occurrences of each spelling. To search for a word using Ctrl-X, first enter the beginning of the word. (You cannot use Ctrl-X as the first character in a word.) When you come to the point at which you are unsure of the letter, enter Ctrl-X. In Version 4.2, press Ctrl-V, then press Ctrl-X at the n = prompt to enter the ^X on your screen.

- Search for abbreviations that you have deliberately used in your document so that you do not have to type an entire word or phrase repeatedly. For example, you can use a special symbol such as # or * to stand for up to 59 characters.

- Search for a heading or particular word in a section of text you wish to edit. Using the Search feature in this way allows you to go quickly to the area you want to find without having to scroll through your document or use the PgUp and PgDn keys. You can mark text that you want to revise later with a special symbol such as **#** or **qq** and then search for it to return to it quickly.

WordPerfect's Search and Search and Replace features work through the F2 function key. The following sections describe how to use each Search and Search and Replace feature.

Forward Search

KEY SEQUENCE

Forward search (from cursor to end of document):
   F2 <*search string*> **F2**
To perform an extended search that includes headers, footers, footnotes, and endnotes:
   Home F2 <*search string*> **F2**

The Forward Search key in WordPerfect is F2. When you press F2,

   –> Srch:

appears at the bottom of your screen (Figure 3.5). The direction of the arrow at the right indicates that WordPerfect will search for the string of characters that you enter from the cursor's present position to the end of the document.

You can enter up to 59 characters for the program to search for. If you enter your characters in lowercase style, WordPerfect will ignore capitalization when it searches. For example, if you enter

   file list

WordPerfect will find all occurrences of File List, file list, file List, and File list. If you do not enter a space before *file* and after *list,* WordPerfect will also return any occurrences of the two words together within other words, such as "re*file list*ings." To have WordPerfect search for an entire word by itself, enter a space before and after it. To have WordPerfect search for a string in the headers, footers, footnotes, and endnotes that you have entered in the document, press Home before you press F2 and type the search string.

If you enter characters using uppercase format, WordPerfect will search for those characters only in uppercase format. For example, if you enter

   FILE LIST

WordPerfect will search for FILE LIST or File List.

If WordPerfect does not find a match in the document for your search string, it will display the message "* Not Found *," and the cursor will not move from its

```
WELCOME

Welcome to MagnaCorp. We hope this employee handbook will help to
guide you through your first few days here.  In addition, it
contains valuable information about employee services and
benefits available to you.  Ask your manager or call the
personnel office if you have any questions for which you cannot
find the answers in this handbook.

Work Day

The official work day at MagnaCorp is 8:30 a.m. to 5:00 p.m.
Flexible hours can be arranged with your manager.

Parking

As parking is limited, please apply to the personnel office for a
parking slot assignment.

Hours

Noon to 1 p.m. has been reserved as lunch hour for all employees.
Some departments have chosen to take lunch from 11:30 to 12:30 or
from 12:30 to 1:30; check with your manager.
-> Srch: manage_
```

FIGURE 3.5: Searching for a word in your document. Here the word being searched for is *manage*. WordPerfect will find all occurrences of *manage* as well as *manager, management, mismanage,* and so forth. If you want WordPerfect to locate only the word *manage*, enter a space before and after the search string.

original position. In such a case, you can press F2 again and retype or edit the search string. If you want to edit only part of the search string, press → to move the cursor to the appropriate position and make your changes as you would to any text. Remember not to press Return when you have finished editing the search string. Press F2 instead to initiate the search for your new search string.

Searching in Reverse

KEY SEQUENCE

Reverse search (from cursor to beginning of document):
    Shift-F2 <*search string*> **F2**

To perform an extended search that includes headers, footers, footnotes, and endnotes:
    Home Shift-F2 <*search string*> **F2**

When you initiate a regular search using F2 (Search), WordPerfect searches from the position the cursor is on to the end of your document. You can instruct WordPerfect to search backward through your document to the beginning by pressing Shift-F2 instead of F2. When you press Shift-F2, WordPerfect responds with this prompt:

<– Srch:

The direction of the arrow at the left shows you that WordPerfect will search from the cursor's present position to the beginning of the document. After you enter your search string, you just press F2 alone to initiate the reverse search. To perform the reverse search operation once again to locate a subsequent occurrence, you press Shift-F2. To change directions and perform a forward search using the same search string, you merely press F2 instead of Shift-F2.

You can also have WordPerfect perform an extended reverse search by pressing Home before you press Shift-F2 and enter your search string.

USING WILDCARDS

In WordPerfect, Ctrl-X can be used as a wildcard when searching for words or phrases in your documents. It can be substituted for any character. For example, a search for

no^X

returns *now*, *not*, *nor*, *non*, and so forth. It also returns words that contain *now*, *nor*, *non*, and so forth, such as *nowadays*, *notable*, *nonapplicable*, *enormous*, *denoted*, and *anonymous*. Also note that you cannot use Ctrl-X at the beginning of a search string. In Version 4.2, to enter Ctrl-X in your search string, press Ctrl-V first to let the program know you are inserting a special character. Then press Ctrl-X. Using Ctrl-X as a wildcard is useful if you do not remember the exact spelling of the word you wish to find. If you want to limit WordPerfect's search to complete words, you must enter spaces before and after the search string.

SEARCHING FOR SPECIAL CHARACTERS

With WordPerfect you can enter special characters that cannot be entered directly from the keyboard by entering their ASCII codes in one of two ways: by mapping the character to a particular Alt- or Ctrl-*letter* key combination using the Screen function key (Ctrl-F3) and selecting option 3 (Ctrl or Alt key), or by pressing Alt and typing the ASCII code using the 10-key number pad or pressing Ctrl-V and typing the ASCII code using the regular top-line numbers (see Chapter 11 for details about how to do this).

If you have used such methods to insert special foreign-language and math symbols into your text, you can use WordPerfect's Search function to locate them. To do this, you simply press F2 (or Shift-F2 if you need to perform a reverse search) and enter the character as the search string just as you originally entered it into the text.

If you do not remember the Alt- or Ctrl-*letter* key combination you used or did not map the character to such a key combination, you need to know the character's ASCII code in order to find it in the text. For example, you can find the letter ñ with a tilde above it in the name *Cañada College* in your document by searching for the character ñ. If you look up this character on a list of ASCII codes like the one in Appendix A of this book or the one shown when you press Ctrl-F3 and type **3**, you will see that its ASCII code is 164.

To enter ñ as the search string, you press F2 (or Shift-F2) and then press Alt and type **164** from the 10-key pad. Your screen will display

   –> Srch: ñ

Press F2, and WordPerfect will position the cursor after the first occurrence of ñ in *Cañada College*.

You can also use this method with WordPerfect's Replace feature to search for special characters and replace them with others. See the "Search and Replace" reference entry that follows for information about how to initiate a search and replace operation.

On some keyboards, pressing Alt and typing the ASCII code from the 10-key pad does not work when using WordPerfect. In such a case, you can use Ctrl-V to initiate the sequence. When you press this key combination, WordPerfect displays

   n =

as though you had pressed Esc (though it does not display the 8). When you see this prompt, type the appropriate ASCII code using the numbers on the top line of the keyboard. When you press Return, WordPerfect will convert the numbers you see there to the character associated with them. In the example presented here, for instance, you would press F2, press Ctrl-V, and type **164** from the top line. Your screen would look like this:

   n = 164

when you pressed Return, the screen would change to

   –> Srch: ñ

When you pressed F2 to initiate the search, WordPerfect would find the character's first occurrence just as previously described.

Using the Search Commands to Find Formatting Codes

In addition to using the Search commands to find specific characters, words, or phrases in a document, you can use it to locate format codes that you have used. To do this, you use the same Search commands, either F2 or Shift-F2. However, instead of typing a search string, you then press the appropriate function key or function key combination that you originally used to enter the formatting code.

For example, to find the first place in a document where you entered a font change, you press F2, press Ctrl-F8, and type **1** (the same key sequence you used to make the font change). You will then see the font change format code displayed as the search string:

-> Srch: [Font Change]

You then press F2 to initiate the search for the format code.

You can use WordPerfect's Search function to find any format code that you can enter (for example, you cannot search for a [SPg] code because only the program can enter it). However, when you access command menus as part of a search operation, the menu option selections do not always appear the same as they did when you entered the formatting code originally. All command menus that appear when performing a search or search and replace operation have their options arranged horizontally, but some of the original menus have their options arranged vertically.

For instance, in the [Font Change] search example in the preceding discussion, when you press Ctrl-F8 after pressing F2, the options are displayed as follows:

1 Font; 2 LPI; 3 JustOff; 4 JustOn; 5 UndrlnStyle; 6 Bin#; 7 Cmnd; 8 LnNum: 0

instead of in their usual vertical arrangement.

Also, sometimes you may have to enter an option number (or letter) different from the one you used to insert the format code originally. You must review the menu options carefully to select the format code you want to search for. Notice in the menu options just listed, for example, that you must type **7** to search for a Print command code ([Cmnd]) that you entered in the text, but you originally would have typed **A** from the Ctrl-F8 menu to enter this Print command.

Note that all format codes that are entered as search strings are identical to those used in the Reveal Codes window. For more information about searching for format codes, see "Searching for Formatting Codes" and "Macros to Search and Replace Formatting Codes" earlier in this chapter.

Search and Replace

> **KEY SEQUENCE**
>
> **Alt-F2**
> w/Confirm? (Y/N) **N** (or **Y**)
> - > Srch: <*search string*> **F2**
> Replace with: <*replacement string*> **F2**

When you perform a search and replace operation, WordPerfect matches the capitalization of the first letter of the words it finds. For example, if you ask it to search for *file list* and replace this phrase with *list files*, it will replace *File List* with *List files*, *file List* with *list files*, and so forth. This feature allows you to correctly replace words and phrases that are capitalized at the beginning of a sentence as well as lowercased within the text.

You can also search for words or phrases and replace them with substitute words or phrases that you specify. Again, the 59-character limit applies: You can search for up to 59 characters and replace them with as many as 59 characters, including spaces.

You can use the Search and Replace command to significantly simplify the typing of a document by creating a kind of glossary. To do this, you enter a specific abbreviation for an often-used term throughout the document and then use the Replace function to substitute each occurrence of this abbreviation with the word's unabbreviated form. For example, if you work for a firm named Nolan, Tuttle, Bronkowski and Associates, you might enter the abbreviation **NTBA** each time the firm's name is mentioned in a document. After you finish entering your text, you can then use the Replace function to search for all occurrences of *NTBA* and have the program replace them with Nolan, Tuttle, Bronkowski and Associates.

To make this procedure most efficient, you can use the Replace function without requiring confirmation for each replacement. However, you must be careful in such a case that the abbreviation you have selected never occurs within other words in the document (as in the example using NTBA). If it does, your replacement string will be introduced in places that are far from appropriate, and the procedure will end up wasting, instead of saving, time.

To perform a search and replace operation, you press Alt-F2. WordPerfect then asks you whether you want confirmation before it makes each replacement. The following prompt appears:

w/Confirm? (Y/N) N

If you enter **Y**, WordPerfect will ask you to confirm whether you want to make the replacement each time it finds the word or phrase you specified (the search string).

If you press Return to accept the No default selection, WordPerfect will replace each occurrence of the search string with whatever you specify as the replacement string. This can cause unexpected results in your document if you are not careful.

For example, if you instruct WordPerfect to search for

–> Srch: ins

and replace it with

Replace with: International Network Systems

as could be done in the press release shown in Figure 3.6, the unforeseen and unwanted results shown in the document in Figure 3.7 will be produced.

To carry out a search and replace operation, you first respond to the confirmation prompt, as already discussed. WordPerfect then prompts you for the search string—the word or phrase to search for. Be careful when you enter the search string not to press Return at the end unless you want WordPerfect to search for a hard return at the end of the string. Press F2 again (or press Esc) to enter the search string.

```
CONTACT:   JoAnn Miller
              -or-
           Frank Duncan
           (555) 201-7845


FOR IMMEDIATE RELEASE

     ins ANNOUNCES INNET NETWORK

     Modesto, Calif. -- ins today announced its INNET Network, a
PC network capable of supporting as many as 1500 PCs within a
radius of more than a mile and a half. Using telephone-style
cabling, the INNET can support 105 PCs within a 750-foot radius.
With data-grade cabling, the number rises to 250 in a 1200-foot
radius.
     ins has been instrumental in LAN research for the last five
years. Today's announcement insures ins a new place in the fast-
growing area of PC-based LANs. ins's president, Roy Newberry,
characterizes INNET as "an insuperable protocol just right for
today's needs."



C:\WP\BOOK\CHAP3\FIG3-6                    Doc 2  Pg 1  Ln 19    Pos 10
```

FIGURE 3.6: Using abbreviations while you create a document and then replacing them with their full forms later. In this document, *ins* has been used instead of *International Network Systems*, a company name. You should set WordPerfect to ask you for confirmation before each replacement. Otherwise you may get results similar to those in Figure 3.7.

WordPerfect then prompts you to enter the replacement string. Enter it, again being careful not to enter any formatting codes unless you want those codes to be inserted in your document. Press F2 again to begin the search and replace operation.

To return to the place in your document where you were before you began a search or a search and replace operation, press Ctrl-Home, Ctrl-Home (Go To).

REPLACING FORMATTING CODES

WordPerfect's Replace function is more limited when it comes to replacing format codes than its Search function is in locating them. For this reason, you will often need to create a macro that searches for the appropriate command and then simulates manual deletion and entry of the replacement formatting code. To see which format codes can be used as replacement strings, refer to Table 3.1 earlier in this chapter. You can also obtain additional information about creating macros that will replace those codes that cannot be used with WordPerfect's regular Replace function in the section entitled "Macros to Search and Replace Formatting Codes."

```
CONTACT:   JoAnn Miller
           -or-
           Frank Duncan
           (555) 201-7845


FOR IMMEDIATE RELEASE

    International Network Systems ANNOUNCES INNET NETWORK

    Modesto, Calif. -- International Network Systems today
announced its INNET Network, a PC network capable of supporting
as many as 1500 PCs within a radius of more than a mile and a
half. Using telephone-style cabling, the INNET can support 105
PCs within a 750-foot radius. With data-grade cabling, the number
rises to 250 in a 1200-foot radius.
    International Network Systems has been International Network
Systemstrumental in LAN research for the last five years. Today's
announcement International Network Systemsures International
Network Systems a new place in the fast-growing area of PC-based
LANs. International Network Systems's president, Roy Newberry,
characterizes INNET as "an International Network Systemsuperable
protocol just right for today's needs."

C:\WP\BOOK\CHAP3\FIG3-6                    Doc 2  Pg 1  Ln 20      Pos 50
```

FIGURE 3.7: The result of replacing *ins* with *International Network Systems* without confirming each replacement. Each occurrence of *ins*—including those in *instrumental, insures,* and *insuperable*—has been replaced with *International Network Systems.*

BLOCK OPERATIONS

WordPerfect's block feature allows you to perform operations on large sections of text instead of having to work word by word or line by line. Basically, a block is an area of text that you specify. It may be as small as one character or as large as your entire document. Using the block feature can save you much time and allow you to use the program more flexibly. For example, after you have marked text as a block, you can quickly

- Move it.
- Delete it.
- Underline it.
- Boldface it.
- Center it.
- Convert it to UPPERCASE (or lowercase).
- Print it.
- Sort the items within it.
- Search through it using search and replace.
- Mark it to be included in a list, table of contents, or index (see Chapter 7).
- Mark it for redlining or strikeout.
- Save it as a file by itself (to be inserted in another document).
- Append it to the end of another file.
- Check its spelling (see Chapter 12).

Marking a Block of Text

KEY SEQUENCE

Alt-F4 (highlight block with cursor)

To mark text as a block, press Alt-F4 (Mark Block). The message

Block on

will flash at the bottom of the screen. Position your cursor at the end of the text you wish to mark as a block by using any of the cursor movement techniques discussed in Chapter 1. You can then carry out any block operations.

To turn block marking off, press Alt-F4 again or press F1 (Cancel).

ALT-M: A MACRO TO MARK A BLOCK

Alt-M (for mark block) is a simple but useful macro that allows you to quickly mark a block of text so that you can delete or copy it.

Begin macro	*Macro name*	*Keystrokes*	*End macro*
Ctrl-F10	**Alt-M**	**Alt-F4 End**	**Ctrl-F10**

This macro marks the text from the cursor position to the end of the line as a block. To extend the block forward or backward, simply press ↓ or ↑ or use any of the cursor movement keys, including PgUp/PgDn, − / + , or Home Home ↑/↓, to mark large blocks of text.

CUTTING OR COPYING A MARKED BLOCK

KEY SEQUENCE

To move a marked block:
  Ctrl-F4 1 (reposition cursor) **Ctrl-F4 5**
To copy a marked block:
  Ctrl-F4 2 (reposition cursor) **Ctrl-F4 5**

After you have marked a section of text as a block by using Alt-F4, you can copy or move it to a new place in the document by pressing Ctrl-F4 (Move). When you press Ctrl-F4, you will see these block options:

1 Cut Block; 2 Copy Block; 3 Append; 4 Cut/Copy Column;
5 Cut/Copy Rectangle: 0

The first two allow you to cut or copy the highlighted block of text. Option 3 appends the highlighted block of text to the end of a file that you specify (see "Appending a Block to Another Document" earlier in this chapter). Option 4 is used when you are working with columns of text (see Chapter 4).

To move a marked block (see the previous reference entry for details), you select option 1, the Cut Block option, from this menu. This removes the highlighted text from the document and saves it in a buffer (a special memory location). To retrieve the block in a new place in the document, reposition the cursor at the place where you want the text to appear, press Ctrl-F4, and type **5** (the Retrieve option). To move the block to a second document in the other document window, press Shift-F3 (Switch) and then position the cursor at the place where the block is to in this document before pressing Ctrl-F4 and typing **5**.

To copy a marked block, you select option 2, the Copy Block option from this menu. When you select this option, WordPerfect copies the marked block into the same buffer used when moving a block. However, it does not remove the highlighted block from the screen during this copy process. To copy the block, reposition the cursor and then press Ctrl-F4 and type 5. To copy a block to a second document in the other document window, press Shift-F3 (Switch) and then position the cursor at the place where the block is to appear in this document before pressing Ctrl-F4 and typing 5.

Instead of using the preceding method to copy a marked block of text, you can just cut the block (using Ctrl-F4, 1) and retrieve it again in the same place without moving the cursor. Then you can reposition the cursor in the document where you want the block copied and retrieve it again (it remains in the buffer until you mark another block and cut or copy it using option 1 or 2 from the Ctrl-F4 Move menu). It is usually faster to copy text by cutting it, immediately reinserting it, and then inserting it again in its new location.

ALT-C: A CUT/COPY MACRO

A simple macro that can be combined with the Alt-M (mark block) macro presented earlier can speed up your copying and cutting operations.

Begin macro	*Macro name*	*Keystrokes*	*End macro*
Ctrl-F10	**Alt-C**	**Ctrl-F4 1**	**Ctrl-F10**

This macro simply cuts the block of text you have highlighted with the Alt-M macro. To use it, first press Alt-M to mark the block from the cursor's position to the end of the line, use the appropriate cursor movement keys to highlight all of the text you wish to include in the block, and then press Alt-C to cut the block.

ALT-I: AN INSERT MACRO

The following macro inserts cut or copied text at the location you specify in your document.

Begin macro	*Macro name*	*Keystrokes*	*End macro*
Ctrl-F10	**Alt-I**	**Ctrl-F4 5**	**Ctrl-F10**

Working together, the Alt-M (mark block), Alt-C (cut/copy), and Alt-I (insert) macros can save you a significant amount of time. Although they do not reduce the number of keystrokes substantially, they eliminate the time required to read the on-screen menus and decrease the chances that you might inadvertently select an incorrect option from the menus.

To use these macros to move a block of text, you press Alt-M, finish highlighting the block with the appropriate cursor movement keys, press Alt-C to cut the block, reposition the cursor to the place in the document where you want the block moved, and then press Alt-I to insert the block there. To copy the block, you execute Alt-I right after you use Alt-C to reinsert the block in its original position and then move the cursor to the place in the document where the block is to appear and execute Alt-I again to copy the block to its new position.

Cutting or Copying a Sentence, Paragraph, or Page

In addition to the cut and copy procedure, which can be used to move or copy any size block of text (described in the previous reference entry), WordPerfect offers you an alternate method for moving or copying a block composed of entire sentences, paragraphs, or pages. Depending on the situation, one or the other may be faster for you. If you need to copy or cut only the current sentence, paragraph, or page, you can use the following method.

KEY SEQUENCE

To move the sentence, paragraph, or page containing the cursor:
   Ctrl-F4 1 (for sentence) or **2** (for paragraph) or **3** (for page)
   1 (to cut) (reposition cursor) **Ctrl-F4 5**
To copy the sentence, paragraph, or page containing the cursor:
   Ctrl-F4 1 (for sentence) or **2** (for paragraph) or **3** (for page)
   2 (to copy) (reposition cursor) **Ctrl-F4 5**

To perform this type of cut and copy operation in WordPerfect, you use the Move menu. This menu appears when you press Ctrl-F4 (Move) before you mark a block using Alt-F4. The first three options on this menu allow you to indicate which portions of your text you wish to cut—a sentence, paragraph, or page:

   Move 1 Sentence; 2 Paragraph; 3 Page;

The last three options

   Retrieve 4 Column; 5 Text; 6 Rectangle

allow you to paste the cut material back into your document. Option 4 (Column) retrieves a column of text (see Chapter 4), option 5 retrieves regular text (ragged right or justified), and option 6 (Rectangle) retrieves a rectangular block of text (see Chapter 13).

To use this method for moving or copying one of these units of text, you follow these steps:

1. Press Ctrl-F4 (Move).

2. Type **1** to indicate that you wish to cut or copy the sentence that the cursor is on, **2** to cut or copy the paragraph the cursor is on (as illustrated in Figure 3.8), or **3** to cut or copy the entire current page.

3. When you press 1, 2, or 3, WordPerfect highlights the text that is going to be affected and prompts you for the operation you wish to perform:

   1 Cut; 2 Copy; 3 Delete: 0

   Type **1** if you wish to cut the text, **2** if you wish to copy it, and **3** if you wish to delete it. (If you type **0**, the cut/copy operation is canceled.) When you use either option 1 or 2, WordPerfect makes a copy of the selected text and stores it in the regular cut/copy buffer. If you select option 3, WordPerfect places the text in another buffer from which it can be retrieved using F1 (Cancel). If you cut or delete, the highlighted text disappears from the screen.

4. Move your cursor to the place in your document where you want the cut or copied text to appear.

5. Press Ctrl-F4 (Move) again. Type **5** to insert the text into your document at that point.

6. If you wish to reinsert a block of text that has been deleted, press F1 and type **1** to restore it at the cursor's position.

After you cut or copy text, you may need to use the space bar to insert additional spaces around your text. This is because WordPerfect considers a sentence to be the first letter of the sentence up to the next period, but not including the space after the period. It considers a paragraph to be all text between one [HRt] code and the next. (See Appendix B for a description of the special formatting codes WordPerfect uses.)

COMMANDS TO REDLINE AND STRIKE OUT TEXT

The Mark Text key, Alt-F5, allows you to mark text that others may have to review. The Redline function marks a vertical rule in the left margin; it is often used to indicate the position of new or revised text so that you or others may find it quickly. (Some printers will produce a plus sign instead of a vertical rule.) The Strikeout function does as its name implies: It inserts a dashed line through text that is tentatively to be deleted; others who review the document can find the marked text quickly.

```
Performance Appraisals

The key to managing your career at MagnaCorp is to understand the
performance and appraisals process thoroughly.  You need to know
-----------------------------------------------------------------
what others think of how well you are doing so that you can know
how to improve.

The performance appraisal cycle at MagnaCorp consists of both
informal and formal planning sessions.  In informal sessions,
both you and your manager sit down at least once every three
months and together work out a performance plan for the coming
period.  This plan details what is expected of you and indicates
goals for a specific time period.  It is important that this be a
two-way process:  you and your manager should feel free to
communicate and set mutual goals.  At least once a year, a formal
appraisal session will be held in which a formal evaluation will
be made and a rating assigned to your overall performance for the
year.

Opportunities for Advancement

The bulletin board outside the Personnel Department on the first
1 Cut; 2 Copy; 3 Delete: 0
```

FIGURE 3.8: Copying or cutting a sentence, paragraph, or page. In this figure, a paragraph has been selected to be copied (or cut). Because the highlighted material is stored in a memory buffer, a quick way to copy text is to cut it, immediately reinsert it, and then insert it in its new location.

Redlining Text

KEY SEQUENCE

To redline new text:
   Alt-F5 3
To redline existing text:
   Alt-F4 Alt-F5 3

To mark text for redlining and strikeout, you use Alt-F5 (Mark Text). When you press Alt-F5, the following prompt appears:

1 Outline; 2 Para #; 3 Redline; 4 Short Form; 5 Index; 6 Other Options:

Type *3* to begin redlining text. When you have finished typing the text you wish to highlight with a vertical bar in the left margin, press Alt-F5 3 again to turn off redlining.

To redline text you have already typed, mark the text as a block first (Alt-F4). Then press Alt-F5 3 as before. You will not be able to see the redlining on your screen, but it will be printed with your document. To check the position of the redlining, you can press Alt-F3 to see the formatting codes. The code for redlining is [RedLn]. To delete redlining, position the cursor to the right of the [RedLn] code and press Backspace. Then find the [r] code, which marks the end of the redlined text, and delete it also.

In Figure 3.9, text has been redlined, as you can see from the formatting codes. Figure 3.10 shows an example of the printed text with redlining.

Striking Out Text

KEY SEQUENCE

To strike out existing text:

Alt-F4 Alt-F5 4

To remove all redlined and struck-out text:

Alt-F5 6 6 (Version 4.2 only)

Alt-F5 4 (earlier versions)

```
informal and formal planning sessions.  In informal sessions,
both you and your manager sit down at least once every three
months and together work out a performance plan for the coming
period.  This plan details what is expected of you and indicates
goals for a specific time period.  It is important that this be a
two-way process: you and your manager should feel free to
communicate and set mutual goals.  At least once a year, a formal
C:\WP\BOOK\HANDBOOK                          Doc 2  Pg 3  Ln 8        Pos 16
informal and formal planning sessions.  In informal sessions,[SRt]
both you and your manager sit down at least once every [RedLn]three[SRt]
months and together work out a performance plan for the coming[SRt]
period[r]_.  This plan details what is expected of you and indicates[SRt]
goals for a specific time period.  It is important that this be a[SRt]
two[-]way process: you and your manager should feel free to[SRt]
communicate and set mutual goals.  At least once a year, a formal[SRt]
```

FIGURE 3.9: Using redlining within a document. This technique is useful to mark new or revised text that must be submitted to others for review. The [RedLn] code marks the text that has been redlined. This is a good way to bring changes—in this case, in the company's performance review period—to the attention of others.

Striking out text works in a way similar to redlining. To strike out text, however, you must first mark the text as a block with (Alt-F4). Figure 3.11 illustrates text that has been marked for strikeout; Figure 3.12 shows the printed version.

```
The performance appraisal cycle at MagnaCorp consists of both
informal and formal planning sessions.  In informal sessions,
both you and your manager sit down at least once every three
months and together work out a performance plan for the coming
period.  This plan details what is expected of you and indicates
goals for a specific time period.  It is important that this be a
two-way process:  you and your manager should feel free to
communicate and set mutual goals.  At least once a year, a formal
appraisal session will be held in which a formal evaluation will
be made and a rating assigned to your overall performance for the
year.
```

FIGURE 3.10: The redlined text as it appears when printed. (The redline inicator may appear as a plus sign, depending on your printer.) This technique is useful for highlighting material you wish others to review without having them read the entire document.

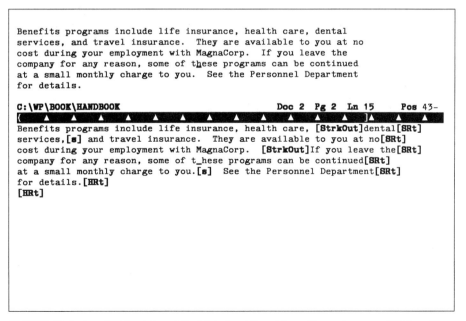

FIGURE 3.11: Text marked for strikeout. To delete the strikeout formatting codes, press Alt-F3, position the cursor to the right of the [StrkOut] and [s] codes, and press Backspace.

```
Benefits

Benefits programs include life insurance, health care, dental
services, and travel insurance.  They are available to you at no
cost during your employment with MagnaCorp.  If you leave the
company for any reason, some of these programs can be continued
at a small monthly charge to you.  See the Personnel Department
for details.
```

FIGURE 3.12: The printed paragraph with struck-out text. This technique is often used in legal applications in which others review what has been deleted.

When you have made your final decisions about the redlined or struck-out text, press Alt-F5 to delete the redline markings or the struck-out text. Enter **6** to select Other Options and then **6** to remove redlining and strikeout. The following prompt appears:

Delete Redline markings and strikeout text? (Y/N) N

Enter **Y** to delete all occurrences of redlined or struck-out text in your document. You can also search for the [RedLn] and [StrkOut] codes and delete the sections selectively.

KEEPING WORDS TOGETHER

KEY SEQUENCE

<first word> **Home Space bar** *<next word>*

Reveal Codes

[ ]

To keep words together so they will never be broken at the end of a line—if, for example, you change margin settings later—you can insert a nonbreak space (what WordPerfect calls a *hard space*). Dates, such as February 15, 1949; proper names and titles, such as Dr. Sandra S. Schuler; and certain parts of equations (see Chapter 11) usually should not be broken at the end of a line.

To insert a hard space, type the first word, press Home, press the space bar to insert a space, and then enter the second word. A hard, or nonbreaking, space is shown in the WordPerfect Reveal Codes window (accessed by pressing Alt-F3) as a space enclosed in square brackets, [ ]. To replace a hard space with one that will break across a line, you do not have to access the Reveal Codes window to locate this format code. Just move the cursor to the space that you wish to replace, press Del to remove it, and press the space bar, this time without pressing Home first.

USING HYPHENS, EM DASHES, AND EN DASHES

Four punctuation marks—the hyphen, the minus sign, the em dash, and the en dash—often cause confusion because, although they are typed in similar ways, when they are typeset they have different effects and are used for different purposes. If you are preparing material that is going to be typeset, you may want to pay particular attention to these four types of dashes.

- The em dash, also known as the long dash or simply as the dash, is typed as two hyphens with no space between them—when typeset, it appears as you see here. (The em dash is so called because in typesetting, it takes up approximately the same amount of space as the character *m* in the typeface that is being used.)

- The en dash, which is typed as a hyphen, is actually slightly longer than a hyphen when it is typeset. It is used to denote continuing numbers, as in dates (1987–88) or in page references (pages 546–50).

- The hyphen is used in word division and to punctuate compound words such as *self-evaluate* and *brother-in-law*. It is also used in manuscripts to indicate a minus or negative sign in mathematical expressions. However, when a minus sign is typeset, it is usually slightly longer than a hyphen, as in the expression A6 − A1.

Breaking em dashes, which consist of double hyphens, can cause errors in typesetting. To make sure that WordPerfect never breaks such a dash, type it as Home, − (hyphen, hyphen).

To indicate an en dash, simply type a hyphen. It is perfectly permissible to break elements joined by en dashes at the end of a line, so you do not have to specify them as never to be broken. You may need to specify to the typesetter that en dashes be used in specific places in your documents.

To indicate a negative or minus sign in mathematical expressions or enter a nonbreaking hyphen, type Home, - (hyphen) (see Chapter 11 for a discussion of additional mathematical symbols in WordPerfect).

HYPHENATION COMMANDS

KEY SEQUENCE

To turn on automatic hyphenation:
 Shift-F8 5 5 1 0 (or **Return**)
To turn on program-aided hyphenation:
 Shift-F8 5 4 1 0 (or **Return**)
To reset hyphenation zone:
 Shift-F8 5 3 <*value for left zone*> **Return** <*value for right zone*>
 Return 0 (or **Return**)
To turn hyphenation off:
 Shift-F8 5 2 0 (or **Return**)

REVEAL CODES

 [Hyph on]
 [Hyph off]
 [HZone Set: <*left zone setting*>**,** <*right zone setting*>**]**
 Soft hyphen (added by the program when you press Esc): —
 Cancel hyphen (added when you press F1 to avoid hyphenation): /

The default setting for WordPerfect is hyphenation off. If you want to use the program's Hyphenation command, you must turn it on and choose between aided and automatic hyphenation. To turn hyphenation on, you press Shift-F8 and type **5** to select the Hyphenation option. When you do, you will see the following menu options:

[HZone Set] 7,0 Off Aided 1 On; 2 Off; 3 Set H-Zone; 4 Aided; 5 Auto: 0

As you can see from the first part of this menu line, WordPerfect always informs you of the size of the hyphenation zone, whether hyphenation is on or off and what type of hyphenation is in use (aided or automatic) before it lists the five menu options attached to the Hyphenation menu.

To turn hyphenation on, you type **1**. Once you do this, you will see that Off changes to On in this line. If you press Return or type **0** to leave this menu and return to the document without making any further selections, WordPerfect will use aided hyphenation and its default hyphenation-zone settings of 7 and 0.

With aided hyphenation, WordPerfect will beep each time a word extends beyond the right margin and starts at or before the left hyphenation zone. You will then see this prompt:

Position hyphen; Press ESC

To the right of this prompt you will see the word the way WordPerfect will hyphenate it if you now press Esc. To change the place where the word is hyphenated, use the arrow keys ($\rightarrow$ and $\leftarrow$) to move the hyphen to the position you want the word to break (WordPerfect will not allow you to move the hyphen to the right if hyphenating any further to the right would cause characters to extend beyond the right margin). If you do not want the word to be hyphenated, press F1 (Cancel).

When you press F1, WordPerfect enters a [SRt] format code at the end of the line and a / format code (the cancel-hyphen code) at the beginning of the following line. If you change your mind and wish to hyphenate the word, delete the / code in the Reveal Codes window (accessed by pressing Alt-F3). You will again see the prompt with the word to be hyphenated.

To select automatic hyphenation, you type **5** to select the Auto option and then press Return or type **0** to leave the menu. When automatic hyphenation is on, WordPerfect will hyphenate any word that requires it without giving you a chance to change the place where it is hyphenated.

The third option on the Hyphenation menu, Set H-zone, is used to modify the settings of WordPerfect's hyphenation zones. WordPerfect maintains both left and right hyphenation zones. By selecting option 3, you can specify where these two zones (abbreviated H-zones) begin and end (see Figure 3.13). The default setting for the left H-Zone is 7, meaning that the zone begins seven spaces before the right margin setting (position 67 if the default margin setting is used). The default setting for the right H-Zone is 0, meaning that the zone ends at the right margin (position 74 if the default margin setting is used).

If a word begins before or right at the left H-Zone and continues past the right H-Zone, WordPerfect will prompt you for where to insert the hyphen if you are using aided hyphenation or will immediately hyphenate the word if you are using automatic hyphenation.

To enter new settings for the right and left hyphenation zones, you select option 3 from the Hyphenation menu. You will then be prompted

[HZone Set] 7,0 to Left =

Type a new value for the left H-Zone and press Return. You will then see the prompt

Right =

where you can enter a new value for the right H-Zone. If you just press Return instead of entering new values for either of these prompts, the default setting the prompt controls will remain in effect.

```
week.  An additional two floating holidays may be taken at your
discretion and with the approval of your manager.

Benefits

Benefits programs include life insurance, health care, dental
services, and travel insurance.  They are available to you at no
cost during your employment with MagnaCorp.  If you leave the
company for any reason, some of these programs can be continued
at a small monthly charge to you.  See the Personnel Department
for details.

Personal Leave

Personal time off with or without pay can be arranged for short
periods with the approval of your manager.  In addition, if you
have more than one year of service with MagnaCorp, you may be
granted longer periods of personal leave--to obtain an advanced
degree, for example, or to complete a specialized course of
study. Special types of leave with pay are covered in the
following sections.

Bereavement Leave.  Up to three days off with pay are granted in
the event of the death of a member of your immediate family.
[HZone Set] 7,0    to Left = 10 Right = _
```

FIGURE 3.13: Specifying the hyphenation zone. The smaller the zone, the more often the program will prompt you for hyphenation. If you are working with a document with narrow columns, you may want to use a smaller hyphenation zone. The right H-zone is usually left set to 0.

If you are typing a document in which hyphenation is extremely important, you can make the hyphenation zone small, which causes WordPerfect to prompt you more often for where you would like hyphens to occur. Also, if you are working with several justified text columns, as with newspaper or parallel columns, you will probably want to turn on the hyphenation feature so that you have more control over where words break and the program can space your lines more evenly.

> *Note:* Adjusting the right H-Zone setting is similar to releasing the right margin. If you change the default value from 0 to a larger value such as 3, Word-Perfect allows words to extend up to three spaces beyond the right margin. Making this type of adjustment to the right H-Zone would allow a long word that has been wrapped to the next line to shift up if it extends no more than three characters beyond the right margin.

Adjusting the right H-Zone setting is most helpful when you are using proportional spacing with justified margins on a letter-quality printer. Setting an H-Zone such as 0,3 can help reduce the amount of space between words in a line. Although your text will sometimes appear to extend beyond your right margin setting, when WordPerfect prints it, the program will try to fit all of the text within the margin by reducing the amount of space between words. Depending upon the font used and the right H-Zone value selected, this can help reduce uneven spacing overall. However, be aware that with some printers and fonts, changing the right H-Zone in this manner can cause some lines to actually extend beyond the right margin. This is especially true when you are justifying text columns. You will have to experiment with your printer and various right H-Zone settings to determine the balance that produces the best-looking documents.

If you are typing a document in which hyphenation does not particularly matter, you can simply leave the hyphenation feature off and type your document with a ragged-right margin, in which case WordPerfect will simply wrap a word that breaks at the end of one line to the next line, not hyphenating it at all.

You can also enter your entire document and then turn on hyphenation, performing all of your hyphenation at once. To turn on hyphenation for a document that you have already entered, move to the beginning of the document (press Home, Home, ↑). Press Shift-F8 (Line Format). From the menu, select 5, Hyphenation, and enter 1 to turn on hyphenation. To have the entire document hyphenated automatically, type 5 to select Auto hyphenation.

To maintain more control over where each word is hyphenated, leave the setting on Aided (if it has previously been changed to Auto, type 4 to return it to Aided). Each time WordPerfect comes across a word that is to be hyphenated, it will beep and prompt you to confirm its intended hyphenation. If you later change margin settings so that words you have indicated to be hyphenated are no longer in a position where they need a hyphen, they will not be hyphenated.

In the Reveal Codes window (Alt-F3), the soft hyphens entered whenever WordPerfect hyphenates a word appear as —. If you press F1 to avoid hyphenating a word, shifting the word to the following line, WordPerfect adds a cancel hyphen code (/) immediately before the word.

When you give the command to turn on hyphenation, WordPerfect enters the format code [Hyph on] into the text. When you give the command to turn hyphenation off, WordPerfect enters the code [Hyph off]. When you reset the H-Zone values, WordPerfect enters the code [HZone Set:]. Following the colon and separated by a comma, you will see the new left and right H-Zone values in effect.

If you ever delete a [Hyph on] code in the Reveal Codes window either deliberately or by mistake, hyphenation will immediately be turned off. However, this does not mean that the hyphens that were previously entered by the program when hyphenation was on will be eliminated; these will be affected only if you alter the [HZone Set] settings in a way that requires rehyphenation of some of the lines.

If you intend to change the [HZone Set] values from those you entered previously, be sure to position the cursor after the original [HZone Set] format code in the Reveal Codes window (you may even want to delete the original [HZone Set] code) before you press Shift-F8, type 5 and 3, and enter your new left- and right-zone values.

If you wish to rehyphenate a document that has been edited or in which you have changed the margin settings, you will probably want to first remove the soft-hyphen and cancel-hyphen codes that were entered during the first hyphenation operation. To do this, you must position the cursor at the very beginning of the document by pressing Home, Home, ↑ and turn off hyphenation by pressing Shift-F8, and typing **5**, **2**, and **0**.

Then begin a search and replace operation to remove the cancel-hyphen codes by pressing Alt-F2 and then Return to have WordPerfect replace without confirmation. For the search string, press Shift-F8, type **6** to choose the Align Char option, and then press F2 twice to begin the replace operation.

Finally, perform a second search and replace operation to remove the soft hyphens by positioning the cursor at the top of the document again and pressing Alt-F2 and then press Return to have WordPerfect replace without confirmation. For the search string, press Ctrl and the hyphen key. Then press F2 twice more to begin the replace operation.

After all of the hyphens have been removed, reposition the cursor at the beginning of the document (press Home, Home, ↑) and turn on hyphenation once more by pressing Shift-F8 and typing **5**, **1**, and **0** (also type **5** if you want to implement Auto hyphenation and the program is set to Aided, or **4** if you want to implement Aided hyphenation and the program is set to Auto).

Note: These techniques for rehyphenating a document will not have any substantial effect if you have not made extensive editing changes or changed the right margin in such a way that requires different hyphenation.

CREATING SPECIAL CHARACTERS BY USING OVERSTRIKE

KEY SEQUENCE

<*first character*> Shift-F1 3 <*overstrike character*>

REVEAL CODES

[Overstrk] <*overstrike character*>

WordPerfect can create and display many characters and graphic symbols on the screen. To use these special characters and assign them to keys on your keyboard, see Chapter 11. Chapter 11 also discusses using mathematical symbols and Greek characters.

However, your printer may not be able to print many of these special characters. In such cases, you can use WordPerfect's Overstrike feature to create special characters such as grave and acute accent marks, as in the word resumé.

To create such accent marks or special characters, you type the first character and then press Shift-F1 (Super/Subscript). Enter **3** for the Overstrike option and type the character that is to overstrike the first character.

The original character that is to be overstruck will no longer be visible on the screen. All that you will see is the second character that is to overstrike the first. When your document is printed, both will be printed in the same column position. If you press Alt-F3 to access the Reveal Codes window, you will see both characters. The second character to overstrike the first will be preceded by the [Overstrk] format code.

Note that you can always display the original character in the editing screen by moving the cursor to the left of the second, visible character. However, when you do this, the second character is no longer visible. You can only view both characters at one time on your screen in the Reveal Codes window.

For example, if your letter-quality printer does not print the zero with a slash through it ($\emptyset$) to differentiate it from the letter O, you could use the overstrike feature to accomplish this. To enter the number 10 in a document, for instance, you would type **10**, press Shift-F1, and then type **3**. As soon as you do this, the cursor will move back one position so that it is under the 0. Then you type the /. On your screen, you would now see this:

1/

However, when you press Alt-F3 and look at this number in the Reveal Codes window, you would see this:

10[Overstrk]/

The character that you wish to have overstrike the first should always follow the base character and be preceded by the [Overstrk] format code in the Reveal Codes window.

If you have already typed a word or number in the text and then decide to overstrike a character, you must be careful where you position the cursor before you press Shift-F1 (Super/Subscript). Be sure that the cursor is positioned to the right of the character that you wish overstruck before you press Shift-F1, type **3**, and enter the second character.

If the cursor was not in proper position when you issued the overstrike command, you will have to find and remove not only the [Overstrk] format code in the Reveal Codes window, but also the character that comes before it, for even after you remove the [Overstrk] code, this character will not be visible in the regular editing screen. The only way to redisplay this original character is to delete and reenter it.

Figure 3.14 shows several examples of the use of the overstrike feature to create special characters. Compare how the words using the overstrike characters

```
        The temperature was 30o C _1o.

        Please check my reservations at the Ch^teau de Balleroy.

        I sent my resum' in three weeks ago.

        We visited Finist're last year.
C:\WP\BOOK\CHAP3\FIG3-15                        Doc 2  Pg 1  Ln 6       Pos 10
(  ▲    ▲    ▲    ▲    ▲    ▲    ▲    ▲    ▲    ▲    ▲    ▲   ]▲   ▲    ▲
[TAB]The temperature was 30[SuprScrpt]o C +[Ovrstk]_1[SuprScrpt]o.[HRt]
[HRt]
[TAB]Please check my reservations at the Cha[Ovrstk]^teau de Balleroy.[HRt]
_[HRt]
[TAB]I sent my resume[Ovrstk]' in three weeks ago.[HRt]
[HRt]
[TAB]We visited Finiste[Ovrstk]'re last year.[HRt]
```

FIGURE 3.14: Four example sentences using WordPerfect's overstrike feature to create hybrid print characters. In the first, the + (plus) and _ (underscore) characters are used together to create a plus-or-minus symbol. In the second, the ^ (caret) is used to create the circumflex symbol that is used with many vowels in European languages (the *â* in *Château* here). The third and fourth examples use the apostrophe and the accent grave (often located on the key with the ˜ immediately to the right of the apostrophe on the keyboard) to create special accent marks for the letter *e*. Notice that only the overstrike character appears in the regular editing window, although the characters to be printed together both appear in the Reveal Codes window.

appear in the regular editing screen as opposed to in the Reveal Codes window. Figure 3.15 shows how the special characters created in this manner appear when printed.

ALT-V: A MACRO TO OVERSTRIKE CHARACTERS

If you find that you use the overstrike feature quite often to print special hybrid characters that are not supported by your printer, you may want to create and use the following macro. This macro, Alt-V, not only enters the overstrike command, but also positions the cursor correctly. However, for this macro to function correctly, you must always execute it with the cursor beneath the character to be overstruck.

Begin macro	*Macro name*	*Keystrokes*	*End macro*
Ctrl-F10	**Alt-V**	→ **Shift-F1 3**	**Ctrl-F10**

```
The temperature was 30° C ±1°.

Please check my reservations at the Château de Balleroy.

I sent my resumé in three weeks ago.

We visited Finistère last year.
```

FIGURE 3.15: A printout of the example sentences in Figure 3.14. By skillfully combining separate characters, you can make your printer produce a wide variety of special foreign-language and technical symbols that might not otherwise be possible.

To use this macro, you need to position the cursor directly beneath the character you wish to have overstruck before you press Alt-V. Then type your overstrike character. Also, make sure that WordPerfect is not in Overtype mode when you use this macro. The word processor is in Insert mode if "Overtype" is *not* displayed in the left corner of the status line.

SUMMARY

This chapter has discussed several editing techniques you will use as you revise and create documents in WordPerfect. The following references can direct you to more information about topics not covered in this chapter:

- For information about entering text, simple formatting, and basic text enhancements such as boldfacing, underlining, and centering, see Chapter 2, "Basic Formatting and Text Entry."
- For information about setting page formats, including headers and footers, see Chapter 4, "Page Formatting Techniques."
- For details about creating indexes, tables of contents, footnotes, and endnotes, see Chapter 7, "Creating Notes, Lists, Indexes, and Citations."
- For details about working with material in columns, see Chapter 8, "Page Composition: Working with Columns."
- For a discussion of how to sort more complex lists, see Chapter 10, "Sorting."
- For instructions about how to use the Speller and Thesaurus with your documents, see Chapter 12, "Using the Speller and Thesaurus."
- For an explanation of each for the formatting codes WordPerfect uses, see Appendix B, "Formatting Codes."

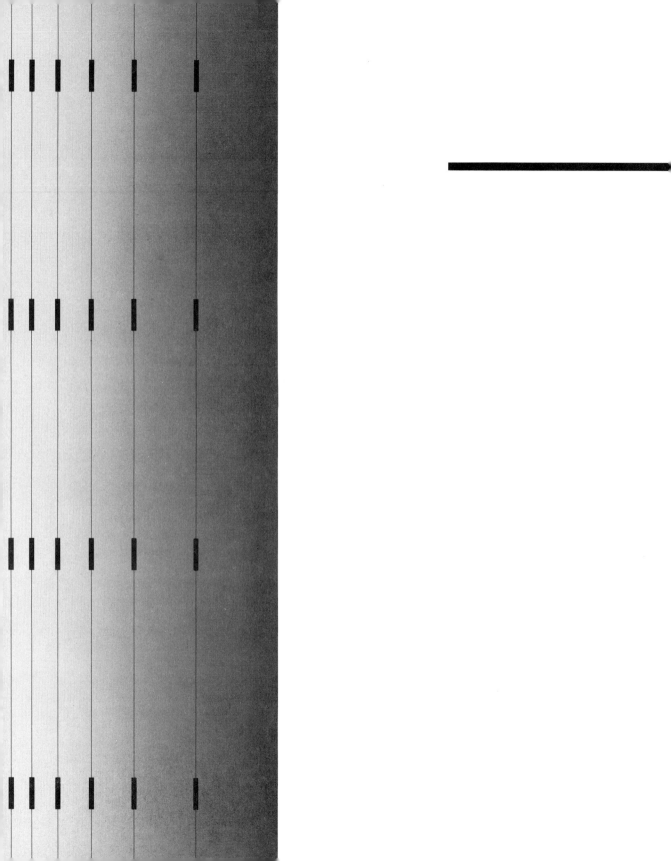

CHAPTER 4

PAGE FORMATTING TECHNIQUES

PAGE FORMATTING TECHNIQUES

This chapter presents WordPerfect's options for generating standard page layouts—using headers, footers, page numbers, various techniques for keeping lines of text on a page, and the Print Preview feature, which displays the page format on the screen as it will be printed. It also presents techniques for setting up tables by using the Tab key. For information about multiple-column layouts, see Chapter 8.

PAGE FORMATTING CONSIDERATIONS

When you have finished entering and editing the text of your document, you may find it beneficial to review your document's page layout before you print your work. When checking the paging, you will want to make sure that no widow or orphan lines have occurred and that no tables or sections of text that must be kept together on a page have been broken across two pages.

> *Note:* WordPerfect uses the terms *widow* and *orphan* as follows: A widow is the first line of a paragraph that appears alone at the bottom of a page, with the rest of the paragraph appearing at the top of the following page; an orphan is the last line of a paragraph that appears alone on the first line of a page, with all of its preceding text at the bottom of the previous page. When you turn on the program's Widow/Orphan protection (discussed later), WordPerfect does not allow either one of these situations to occur.

If your document contains headers and footers, you will want to make sure that their contents are correct and that they appear in the proper position on the page. This is especially true if you are using two headers (or footers) that alternate left and right on even- and odd-numbered pages of the document or in situations where you suppress them either temporarily or permanently.

Figure 4.1 shows you the typical page layout for an $8^{1}/_{2} \times 11$-inch printed page. In this illustration, the margins use the default left and right margin settings of 10 and 74 using pica type (10 characters per inch). Remember that the left margin setting of 10 really represents a print offset of 10 characters, which is equal to an inch when you use pica type. Unlike some other word processors you may have used, WordPerfect does not use a separate print offset command to left indent all of the text shown on the screen. Instead, it builds this offset into the left margin setting. Also, line length is determined by subtracting the right margin setting (plus 1) from the left margin setting. In Figure 4.1, the maximum line length is 65 characters, or $6^{1}/_{2}$ inches, leaving a right margin of 10 characters, equivalent to 1 inch.

MagnaCorp Employee Handbook

WELCOME

Welcome to MagnaCorp. We hope this employee handbook will help to guide you through your first few days here. In addition, it contains valuable information about employee services and benefits available to you. Ask your manager or call the personnel office if you have any questions for which you cannot find the answers in this handbook.

Work Day

The official work day at MagnaCorp is 8:30 a.m. to 5:00 p.m. Flexible hours can be arranged with your manager.

Parking

As parking is limited, please apply to the personnel office for a parking slot assignment.

Hours

Noon to 1 p.m. has been reserved as lunch hour for all employees. Some departments have chosen to take lunch from 11:30 to 12:30 or from 12:30 to 1:30; check with your manager.

Cafeteria

The company cafeteria, located on the third floor, is open from 7 a.m. until 2 p.m. daily. Breakfast is available for your convenience until 9:00. After 2 p.m., vending machines with cold sandwiches and salads are available.

Recreational Facilities

MagnaCorp participates in the city recreational plan and therefore its employees have access to the municipal gym located at First and Brannan Streets. The jogging track and par course in Grant Park are also nearby. Showers and lockers for company employees are located near the south entrance of the main lobby.

Vacation

Full-time permanent employees are eligible for two weeks of paid vacation after six months of continuous employment. During the first five years of service, you earn three weeks of vacation per year. After five years of service, you receive four weeks of vacation.

Credit Union

First Draft   Company Confidential

FIGURE 4.1: Typical page layout. The default left and right margin settings have been used in this figure so that you can see the spacing WordPerfect produces if you do not change any default settings. A header and footer have been added. When WordPerfect creates the header and footer, it subtracts whatever number of text lines it needs for the header and footer.

The top margin setting has been left at the default setting of 12 half-inch lines, or 1 inch. Notice that the header is not placed within this top margin. Unlike some word processors, WordPerfect deducts from the total number of text lines on a page to accommodate any header or footer rather than reducing the number of blank lines in the top and bottom margins.

You can add multiple-line headers or footers to a document. In fact, there is no explicit limit to the number of lines that can be devoted to either type of running title. Just remember that the longer the header or footer, the fewer the lines of text each page can accommodate and the longer the document will be.

Regardless of how many lines you define for a header, a header always includes one more blank line to separate it from the main body of text on the page. The same is true for a footer, except the blank line is added above the footer text rather than below it as with a header.

Numbering Pages

There are two ways of adding page numbers to a document: You can either use the special Page number command or add the page number to the header or footer you are using throughout the document. However, you should not use these techniques together for this would result in two sets of page numbers on every page.

To add automatic page numbers, you select option 1, Page Number Position, from the Page Format menu accessed by pressing Alt-F8. When you choose option 1, you must then choose from eight options that determine where the page numbers will appear on the page as well as the one option that allows you to have no page numbers (see "Page Numbering" later in this chapter for details about using these position options).

After you select the numbering position, WordPerfect inserts the [Pos Pg#:] format code into the document. Following the number symbol (#:), you will see the number of the position option that determines page-number placement in the document.

The one drawback to using the Page number command as opposed to including page numbering as part of a header or footer is that you cannot add the word *Page* to make the number appear, for example, as

Page 1

nor can you add chapter or section numbers before page numbers to print, for example,

Chapter 4-1

The Page number command adds only the numeral that WordPerfect supplies for the page number in its appropriate position on the page.

If you want your entire document to be numbered, position the cursor at the very beginning of the document before using the Page number command. If you do not want the page numbering to begin on the first page (if the first page of your document is a title page, table of contents, or list of figures, for instance), position the cursor at the beginning of the page where numbering is to begin (right before or after the [HPg] or [SPg] format code in the Reveal Codes window—Alt-F3) and then issue the command.

If you do not begin the page numbering on the first page, but you want to include the first page in the page number count, you must also adjust the beginning page number. For example, if your report contains a title page that should not have a page number printed on it but which should be included in the page count, making your first numbered page 2 instead of 1, you must use the New Page Number option on the Page Format menu.

When you press Alt-F8 and type **2** to select the New Page Number option, you will see the prompt

New Page #:

In this example, you would type **2** at the prompt and press Return. You will then see a prompt that allows you to choose between Arabic and Roman numerals:

Numbering Style: 1 Arabic; 2 Roman: 0

Most of the time you will select option 1, Arabic, to have your page numbers appear in the Arabic style: 1, 2, 3, and so on.

However, if you are numbering front matter such as a preface, introduction, table of contents, or list of figures, you may want to select option 2, Roman, to use small Roman numerals: i, ii, iii, and so on.

> *Note:* When using Roman style numbering, you still type the starting page number in Arabic numerals. For example, you type **1** or **5** when prompted for New Page Number and then select option 2 from the Numbering Style prompt to make i or v appear on the page.

If you are using Roman style numbering for just part of the document, remember to change the New Page Number and the Numbering Style when you come to the first page that is to be numbered using Arabic numerals. When you make the transition to Arabic numerals, remember to the set the page number to 1.

If you want your report to contain blank pages where illustrations, figures, or charts from another source will appear, you may want to add a blank page that will still contain a page number, or you may want to skip page numbers and then number the one containing the artwork with a typewriter or by hand.

If you wish to include a blank page that contains only the page number, position the cursor beneath the soft page break (shown by a line of hyphens) and press Ctrl-Return to insert a hard page break (shown by a line of equal signs). Make sure that no text is included between these two lines. The best way to accomplish this is to open the Reveal Codes window by pressing Alt-F3, position the cursor right after the [SPg] format code, and press Ctrl-Return to add the [HPg] format code. In the editing screen, the blank page will be represented by a blank line between a single line of hyphens and a double line of equal signs. When you position the cursor on this blank line, you will see the Pg indicator on the status line change to a new page number. To remove such a blank line, all you have to do is delete the [HPg] format code.

> *Note:* If you are not only adding a blank page for art but are also assigning the page a special page number out of sequence with the previous pages, make sure that the [Pg#] format code that is added when you use the New Page Number command is situated between the [SPg] and [HPg] format codes in the Reveal Codes window.

If you do not want to add a blank page that contains nothing but the page number, then just move the cursor to the beginning of the page that is to be numbered out of sequence and issue the New Page Number command. You can check the page numbers by checking the Pg indicator on the status line. To check the style and position of the page number, you need to use the print preview feature (see the section "Using Print Preview to Check the Page Layout" later in this chapter for details).

> *Note:* The Pg indicator in the status line functions even if you do not add page numbers to the document. However, be aware that if you do add page numbers and set a new beginning page somewhere after the first page, the Pg indicator is affected. This means that it is possible to have two different pages in the same document that have the same page numbers. For instance, if you turn on page numbering at the beginning of the document and later use the New Page Number command to start numbering again from page 1, as you scroll from the beginning of the document you will see the Pg indicator increase from 1 until it reaches the [Pg#:1] format code, where you will see it change back to Pg 1 again. If you use the Go To function (Ctrl-Home) to move to the beginning of a page by entering its page number in a document that has duplicate page numbers, you could find yourself at the wrong page.

If you change the left and right margin settings from their default values of 10 and 74, you will also have to adjust the page number's column positions if you want them correctly centered or left or right aligned at the top or bottom of the page. For example, if you change to a left margin of 5 and a right margin of 79, a left-aligned page number (top or bottom) will appear indented five spaces from the left margin. Likewise, a right-aligned page number will appear indented five spaces from the right margin, and a centered page number will remain centered, because you have moved the left and right margins equally.

To adjust the column positions of the page numbers, you select option 7, Page Number Column Positions, from the Page Format menu and type **2** to use the Set to Specified Settings option. You will then be prompted to enter new values for the left-aligned, centered, and right-aligned numbers.

When you see the prompt "L = ," you enter **5** and press Return to left align page numbers with the left margin in the preceding example. When you see the prompt "C = ," you enter **42,** and when you see the final prompt, "R = ," you enter **79.** This properly aligns your page numbers for the new margin settings, regardless of the position you select for your page numbers.

When you set new page number positions using the Page Number command, WordPerfect inserts the format code [Pg# Col:5,42,79] into the text. The values after the colon separated by commas represent the new left and right values that were entered. To have this code affect all of the numbered pages, you must make sure that it is located either right before or after the [Pos Pg#] format code in the text.

If you started page numbering from the first page of the document, you can find this code by moving the cursor to the very beginning of the document by pressing Home, Home, and the ↑ key. If you started page numbering somewhere else, you can use the Search feature to find the code. Press F2 (or Shift-F2 if you need to perform a reverse search), press Alt-F8, type **1** to select the Pos Pg# option, and press F2 again to initiate the search.

> *Note:* You can also use the Search function to quickly locate the [Pg#] format code if you ever need to check the page number you entered or the numbering style you used. To do this, press F2, press Alt-F8, and type **2** to select the Pg# option. Then press F2 again to initiate the search. When you see the code in the Reveal Codes window, you can see whether you used Arabic or Roman numbering because the page number appears in the specified style. For example, if the page number were 10, it would appear as 10 if you used Arabic and x if you used Roman numbering.

To suppress page numbering on any particular page of your document, you can use the Suppress for Current Page Only option (option 8) on the Page Format menu. If you want to turn off only the page numbering, you then select option 2 from the list of menu options that appears. If you also want to suppress the headers and footers that occur on the page, you select option 1. Before you use this command, make sure that the cursor is positioned at the top of the page (right after the [SPg] or [HPg] code in the Reveal Codes window). The page number count for the next page will be increased, even though no page number appears on the page where you used the Suppress for Current Page Only command. (For more details about the Suppress for Current Page Only option, see the reference entry "Suppressing Headers, Footers, and Page Numbers" later in this chapter.)

Working with Headers and Footers

Headers are headings that appear at the top of each page of a document, and footers are headings that appear at the bottom of each page. WordPerfect separates the header that you add to a document by a single blank line that appears between the header text and the main body of the document text. Likewise, it separates a footer from the main body of text by adding one blank line after the document text and before the text of the footer.

The Alt-F8 (Page Format) key sequence is used to set headers and footers and select their options. WordPerfect allows you to define multiple-line headers and footers. You enter the text of multiple-line headers and footers exactly as you want it to appear on the page. The left and right margin settings that are currently in effect for the text of the document also rule the alignment and word wrap of the header and footer text.

If you wish to increase the amount of blank space between a header and the main body of text, you need only add extra blank lines by pressing Return after you enter the header text and before you exit the definition screen. To increase the amount of blank space between the main body of text and a footer, add these blank lines at the beginning of the definition screen before you enter the footer text.

ALTERNATING HEADERS AND FOOTERS

WordPerfect allows you to add up to two headers and two footers for each document. It refers to these as Header A and B and Footer A and B, respectively. Normally, a report requires only one header (especially because the program allows you to create multiple-line headers that can contain various types of identifying information).

However, one common situation usually requires two headers (or footers)—when your report is going to be reproduced on both sides of a sheet of paper and later bound. In such a situation, you need to define one header for odd-numbered pages and another for even-numbered pages (as defined by the page numbering options where those override the default settings). Sometimes these two headers may contain slightly different information. The first header (that appears on odd-numbered pages) might identify the name of the report, and the second header (on the even-numbered pages) might identify the current chapter or section.

Even if your headers contain exactly the same identifying text, they require different formatting to make them appear at the appropriate margin, for instance, and so you still need to define both a Header A and Header B for the document. The header for the even-numbered pages will be justified with the left margin, and the header for the odd-numbered pages will be justified with the right margin.

If your headers contain page numbers, you will want to place the page number symbol (^B—entered by pressing Ctrl and typing **B**—see ''Adding Automatic Page Numbers and the Current Date'' later in this chapter) before the text of the header for even-numbered pages and after the text of the header for odd-numbered pages. For example, to add alternating headers that include page numbers to a business plan, you move the cursor to the beginning of the second page (assuming that the document has a title page) and enter the text for Header A on the definition screen as follows:

^B BUSINESS PLAN

Then you move the cursor to the beginning of the third page and enter the text for Header B as follows:

BUSINESS PLAN ^B

(Remember that you can automatically right align text on a line by issuing the command Alt-F6 before you enter the text. If you do not do this for text in the odd-page header, WordPerfect left aligns it in a field that begins to the right of the center of the page.)

When you define alternating headers A and B, not only do you format their text, but you also specify that one header (A or B) occurs only on even-numbered pages and that the other occurs only on odd-numbered pages. Remember that when you print a report containing alternating headers or footers, you can set the binding width to allow sufficient room on even- and odd-numbered pages for three-ring or spiral binding. To do this, you press Shift-F7 and type **3** to select the Options menu. From this menu, you type **3** again to select the Binding Width option (see Chapter 5 for details).

USING TWO NONALTERNATING HEADERS OR FOOTERS

You can also define and use two headers on pages of a report that is not going to be reproduced on both sides of the paper. Defining both a Header A and B (or Footer A and B) in a single document allows you to discontinue one of the headers while still printing the other. If you define a two-line header with the first line as Header A and the second line as Header B, you can discontinue Header B some place in the text while still retaining Header A, whereas if you define both lines as Header A, you cannot display one part without the other. If you discontinued Header A, no heading of any sort would be printed from that point on in the text.

When defining two headers (or footers), you must separate them in some fashion. If both headers are to occur on the same line, their text must remain separate and not overlap in any way. For example, you can enter the text for Header A flush left and that for Header B flush right (so long as they do not overlap when printed). To place the two headers on separate lines, you can enter Header A on the first line and a blank on the second line and then, when defining Header B, enter a blank line with a hard return followed on the second line by the text of Header B.

To discontinue one of the headers at any place in the document, you position the cursor at the top of the first page where the header is to be discontinued, press

Alt-F8, and type **6.** You then select the appropriate Type (**1** for Header A, **2** for Header B, and so on), type **0** to discontinue the header, and press Return to return to the document.

Using the Discontinue command has a different effect than using the appropriate option to turn off the header accessed by selecting the Suppress for <u>Current</u> Page Only option on the Page Format menu (Alt-F8). The Discontinue option suppresses the type of header selected from the specified page through the rest of the document, whereas Suppress for <u>Current</u> Page Only discontinues the header selected only on the specified page.

> *Note:* Because you can select only two headers or footers (regardless of whether you have them printed on every page or alternating pages), you cannot keep changing the text of the header (or footer) to reflect each new section in a document. You cannot, for example, have a report in which Header A identifies the chapter and Header B identifies each subsection. For such a case, although Header A would remain unchanged throughout the chapter, Header B might have to change every several pages. However, you cannot edit the text of Header B in just one place in a document. If you used the Edit option (4) to change the subsection name, this edit would change the text of Header B throughout the rest of the document, not just on the page where you entered it.

ADDING AUTOMATIC PAGE NUMBERING AND THE CURRENT DATE

Instead of using the Page Number command, you can have WordPerfect automatically number the pages of your report in the header or footer you define. This is done by entering the code ^B or ^N into the header or footer text. To do this, you position the cursor on the line where you want the page number to be printed and press either Ctrl-B or Ctrl-N. When you do this, the page number code will appear with a caret (or circumflex) preceding the capital letter *B* or *N,* depending upon which you use (Ctrl-N is a little easier to remember if you think of *N* as representing *number*).

When you have WordPerfect number the pages in a header or footer, you can also add text before the numerals. For instance, to print the page number preceded by the word *Page* in Footer A centered on every page, select **3** as the Type and **1** as the Occurrence. Then in the definition screen you press Shift-F6, type **Page,** press the space bar, and press Ctrl-N. The footer then appears as follows:

Page ^N

When the report is printed, the ^N will be replaced by the appropriate page number, such as Page 1, Page 2, and so on.

To enter a starting number different from the one that the program would use automatically, select New Page Number (option 2) on the Page Format menu just as you do when you assign a new starting number when you use WordPerfect's automatic page numbering commands (see "Numbering Pages" earlier in this chapter for details about the New Page Number option).

Suppose, for example, that you keep various chapters of a report in separate files but want to number all pages of the report consecutively. After printing the first chapter or using the Preview command to determine the last page number, you would edit the file containing the second chapter and then use the New Page Number command to enter the appropriate number for the first page of this chapter before you print it. Remember that you can always verify the page number assignment by checking the Pg indicator on the status line. If you use the New Page Number command to change the starting number of the second chapter from 1 to 43, the Pg indicator will then display 43 instead of 1.

In addition to adding automatic page numbering to the header or footer of a report, you can also insert the date or time. WordPerfect provides two options for inserting the current date and time: the Insert Text and Insert Function options. Selecting Insert Text (option 1) after pressing Shift-F5 (the Date key sequence) enters the date when the function is originally used. The Insert Function (option 3), on the other hand, inserts a date that is updated whenever you retrieve or print the document.

If you wish to date stamp your report so that the date is current whenever you print a copy of the report, you use the Insert Function instead of the Insert Text command. You can also time stamp your document using the Date Insert Function option. Whether or not the date or time is inserted and in what format depends upon the Date Format (option 2) in effect when you issue the Insert Function command. To find out how to format the date as you want it appear in the header, footer, or text of the document, see the reference entry "Inserting the Date into Headers and Footers" later in this chapter.

Techniques for Keeping Text Together on a Page

When you are checking the paging of a document prior to printing, you may find instances where soft page breaks (those entered by the program) split across two pages of text that you wish to remain on a single page. Common bad page breaks that you usually will want to correct involve widow and orphan lines, section headings at the bottom of pages separated from any of their text, and tables that are split apart.

WordPerfect offers several different methods for controlling these types of page-break problems. To avoid widows and orphans, you can use WordPerfect's Widow/Orphan protection. To avoid headings at the bottom of a page separated from their text, you can use the program's Conditional End of Page command. And to avoid splitting a table across two pages, you can use the program's Block Protect commands.

AVOIDING WIDOW AND ORPHAN LINES

To prevent the occurrence of widow and orphan lines throughout a document, you turn on the Widow/Orphan protection when you begin the document. To do this, position the cursor at the very beginning of the document (by pressing Home, Home, and the ↑ key), press Alt-F8 (the Page Format key sequence), and type **A** to turn on Widow/Orphan protection. From then on, WordPerfect automatically pages the document so that the first line of any paragraph does not appear alone on the last line of a page. It also pages so that the last line of any paragraph does not appear alone on the first line of a new page. To accomplish this, the program places page breaks above the first line of any paragraph that would otherwise have been widowed or orphaned. This causes the page on which the paragraph would otherwise have started to be short one or several lines.

If you later edit the document in such a way that widows or orphans no longer occur in paging, WordPerfect will ignore the Widow/Orphan format codes, and the pages previously affected will again have the standard number of lines.

If you do not want the document you are about to create to ever have widow or orphan lines, you can turn on Widow/Orphan protection as soon as you start the document at the time you set margins and line spacing. If you set the document format with a macro, you may want to include Widow/Orphan protection as one of the macro's commands.

USING THE CONDITIONAL END OF PAGE COMMAND

To get rid of other kinds of unwanted page breaks, such as those that occur when a section heading is placed on the last line of a page separated from any of its accompanying text, you can use the Conditional End of Page option (option 9) on the Page Format menu (Alt-F8). When you select this option, you are prompted to enter the number of lines to be kept together.

To use this command, position the cursor at the beginning of the line below the soft page break and count the number of lines (including blank lines) required to position the cursor on the line right above the heading that is not to appear alone on the page; then enter this number in response to the prompt for the number of lines to keep together that appears when you press Alt-F8 and type **9**.

If your only purpose is to avoid having a section head appear alone at the bottom of a page, just position the cursor at the beginning of the first line that occurs below the soft page break and press the ↑ key to move the page break to the first line above that heading. As you do this, count the number of times you need to press the ↑ key to position the cursor appropriately. This is the number you need to enter as the number of lines to keep together. Then press Alt-F8, type **9**, enter the number of times you pressed the ↑ key, and then press Return. When you press the ↓ key, the soft page break will be moved so that it occurs right above the heading.

If you are using line spacing other than single spacing, you need to multiply the number of times you press the ↑ key to move the cursor from the first line below the page break to the first line above the heading by the spacing number used. For instance, if you are using one-and-a-half spacing and you pressed ↑ six times, you enter the number of lines to keep together as **9** (1.5 × 6). If you are using double spacing, you enter **12** (2 × 6), and so on.

If you want to keep a specific block of text together, for instance, a section heading and the entire first paragraph that occurs below it, you use this same technique for determining the number of lines to be kept together. In this case, however, you must position the cursor at the beginning of the last line of the first paragraph before you press ↑ to reach the line where you enter the Conditional End of Page command.

Using the Conditional End of Page command is preferable to adding hard page breaks (by pressing Ctrl-Return), because its use will never cause an additional short page to be introduced into the text. If you insert a hard page break and then add sufficient lines of text to sections that precede it, you can end up with a very short page containing only a few lines that is inserted between the last soft page break the program added and the hard page break you added, because the program will break the page at the point where the hard page break occurs.

USING THE BLOCK PROTECTION COMMAND

Although you can use the Conditional End of Page command to keep together any number of lines (less than the maximum number of lines allowed on a page), WordPerfect offers an alternative means for keeping a block of text from ever being split across two pages: the Block Protect command. This command is easier to use than the Conditional End of Page command because it requires no line-number calculations.

To use Block Protect, you must first mark the block using Alt-F4 and the appropriate cursor movement keys. Then press Alt-F8, whereupon you will see the prompt

Protect Block? (Y/N) N

To protect the highlighted text, you type **Y.** The highlighting disappears, and WordPerfect places two Block Protect codes around the text: a [BlockPro:On] code before the beginning of the block and a [BlockPro:Off] at its end. (You can remove this block protection by deleting either of these two codes in the Reveal Codes window, accessed by pressing Alt-F3.)

The major difference between using the Conditional End of Page command and the Block Protect command is that when you use block protection, you can edit the block freely and still be assured that it will always be printed together on a page. For example, if you use the Conditional End of Page command to protect the present number of lines in a table and then add several new lines to the end of it, you could end up with the new lines orphaned on a new page. However, if you use the Block Protect command and then enter these lines (before, and not after, the [BlocPro:Off] code), this situation will never occur.

Most of the time, you will find it most efficient to use Conditional End of Page to eliminate widowed headings at the bottoms of pages and Block Protect to prevent tables and other like units of text from being split by page breaks.

When using the Block Protect command with a table or some other unit of text, be careful if you ever move the table to a new place in the document. It is very easy to forget to include one or the other of the [BlockPro] format codes when marking the text to be relocated. You should use the Reveal Codes window to locate these codes and position the cursor immediately in front of the [Block-Pro:On] code before you use Alt-F4 to highlight the block. Make sure that the cursor is positioned right after the [BlockPro:Off] code before you press the space bar to make the Reveal Codes window disappear. Press Ctrl-F4 and type **1** to cut the text and move it to the place you want it to appear; then press Ctrl-F4 and type **5** to retrieve the text.

If you ever move a protected block and find that it is missing either the [Block-Pro:On] or the [BlockPro:Off] code, delete the code that remains and then mark the block and reissue the Block Protect command.

Working with Tables

Although WordPerfect also has a special Columns feature that allows you to create both newspaper-style (wrapped) columns as well as parallel columns, many times you can create the kind of table you want simply by setting the appropriate margins and tab stops and using the Tab key to indent your columns. The only time you should not use this method but should use WordPerfect's parallel columns feature instead is when a table includes individual column entries that require more than a single line. So long as all column entries can be entered on single lines of the table, you can use the method described in this section. (For details about how to set up tables with parallel columns, see Chapter 8.)

When you begin to create a table, plan the longest entry each column will need to accommodate and set the tab stops accordingly. When setting your tab stops (see Chapter 2 for details about setting tabs), you must decide how you want the text aligned. WordPerfect supports left-aligned, right-aligned, centered, and decimal tabs (aligned around the current alignment character, which by default is the period).

Next, set the tab stops required in your table by first clearing the tabs to the end of the line and then typing the appropriate tab character (**L** for Left, **R** for Right, **C** for Centered, or **D** for Decimal) on the ruler line. If you want the left margin of your table to be before position 10, remember to press Home-← to move the cursor to the very beginning of the ruler line (position 0) before pressing Ctrl-End to clear the tabs to the end of the line and setting the types of tab stops the table requires (see "Setting Tabs" in Chapter 2 for more information).

You may also need to make the margins of the page slightly wider. You can set your tab stops before you change the margin settings. Just remember that if you do not set the proper left and right margins, the program will not use tabs that come before or after the margins. Sometimes you may have to change to a smaller type in order to fit all of the information in your table on a single page (see Chapter 5 for details about changing pitch). If you must use a smaller pitch, such as 12 (elite type) or 17 (compressed type) characters per inch, in the table, remember to increase the right and left margin settings accordingly.

As you set up your table, you can tell where to set tab stops by reading the position indicator on the status line. If you are working with complex tables, you may wish to keep the tab ruler visible at the bottom of the screen. To do so, press Ctrl-F3, type **1,** press ↑ once, and press Return.

You may also want to change the tab-alignment character used with any decimal tabs you set or in the Tab Align function (Ctrl-F6) with left-justified tabs (see Chapter 2 for details about the Tab Align command). In WordPerfect, this character is preset to the period so that all columns of figures you type are aligned on the decimal point (see Figures 4.2 and 4.3). You may want to use another character, such as the $ (dollar sign) or the : (colon). Or, if you are typing columns of equations, you may want to set the equal sign as the alignment character (see Chapter 11 for details about typing equations). To change the alignment character, press Shift-F8 and enter **6** for Align Char. Then enter the character on which you wish to align the columns in your table.

When working with tables, you can move quickly from column to column when your cursor is on the last (or first) character in a column by pressing the Ctrl-→ and Ctrl-← keys. WordPerfect considers a text column to be any text that is separated by tabs or tab-alignment characters.

CENTERING TEXT IN TABLES

If you have not set a special Center tab stop on the ruler, you can still have WordPerfect center the text that you enter in a particular column so long as the tab is a left-justified tab (marked L on the ruler line). To center column headings or items in table columns at such tab stops, press the Tab key to move the cursor to the appropriate left-justified tab and press Shift-F6 (the Center key sequence) before you type the column heading or table entry. Then type the entry, pressing Return to move down one line or Tab to move to the next column. When you do this, be careful that there is sufficient room to fit your centered entry between the left margin and other column entries on the same line.

```
Loan Rates                                      December 29, 1986


                    FIXED MORTGAGE              ADJUSTABLE MORTGAGE

                    Rate    Points              Rate     Points

SAVINGS AND LOANS

First Fed Savings   9.750%   2.00               8.875%   2.50

International Savings  9.625%  2.00             9.125%   2.00

Home Loan Savings   9.500%   3.00               8.875%   2.50

East Coast Federal  9.625%   2.50               9.375%   3.00




C:\WP\WPB\LOANTABL                      Doc 1  Pg 1  Ln 1      Pos 5
```

FIGURE 4.2: A mortgage rate table created using various kinds of tab stops. The FIXED MORTGAGE and ADJUSTABLE MORTGAGE column headings were centered by using the centering command (Shift-F6) at left-justified tabs. The Rate and Points headings were entered using standard left-justified tabs. The data for the percentage rate and points for each type of mortgage were entered using decimal tabs offset to the right of the tab stops for the Rate and Points headings (notice that these figures are aligned on the period).

Using this centering method in a table can sometimes eliminate the need to create two different ruler lines: one containing a set of tabs including Center tabs to align column headings and another below the first containing tabs to align the text of the table.

In the Reveal Codes window, column entries centered in this manner appear as follows:

[TAB][C]<*text*>[c]

To remove centering, position the cursor to the right of the [C] or [c] code and press Backspace. When you remove either of the centering codes, the text will reform so that it is left justified at the tab stop.

BLOCK PROTECTING THE TABLE

Once you have entered the text of your table, you will want to consider how it is paged in the document. If the table takes up a page or less (usually, one page contains 54 lines if you are using standard 8½ × 11-inch paper), you will want

```
                    FIXED MORTGAGE              ADJUSTABLE MORTGAGE

                Rate      Points             Rate       Points

‾
SAVINGS AND LOANS _____

First Fed Savings    9.750%    2.00              8.875%    2.50
C:\WP\WPB\LOANTABL                          Doc 1  Pg 1  Ln 7      Pos 5
(━━━━━━━━━━━━━━━━━━━━━━━━━━▲━━━━━━▲━▲━━━━━━━━━━━━▲━━━━━━━▲━▲━━━━━━━━━━━)
[TAB]   [TAB][C][U]FIXED MORTGAGE[c][u][TAB][TAB][TAB][C][U]ADJUSTABLE MORTGAGE[c
][u][HRt]
[HRt]
[TAB]Rate[TAB][TAB]Points[TAB]Rate[TAB][TAB] Points[HRt]
_[HRt]
[U]SAVINGS AND LOANS[Undrl Style:7][TAB][TAB][TAB][TAB][TAB][TAB][TAB][u][HRt]
[Tab Set:L5,L25,D29,L37,D4₿,L55,D59,L67,D7₿,L79][HRt]
First Fed Savings[TAB][A]9[a].750%[TAB][A]2[a].00[TAB][A]8[a].875%[TAB][A]2[a].5
0[HRt]
```

FIGURE 4.3: The first part of the mortgage rate table (shown in its entirety in Figure 4.2) with the format codes visible. Notice the [C] after the [TAB] codes. Although these items were centered on a regular left-justified tab, the format codes for a special Center tab on the ruler appear the same. In the Reveal Codes window, notice that the underlining style of the line containing the heading SAVINGS AND LOANS is specified as continuous single underlining (denoted by the 7 in the [Undrl Style] code). This continues the underlining across the next seven tab stops. In the line beneath this, new tabs were set, including decimal tabs (denoted by the D in the [Tab Set] code). The use of these decimal tabs is indicated by the [A][a] codes in the next line below.

to use WordPerfect's Block Protect feature to ensure that it is never split across two pages. To do this, mark the table as a block using Alt-F4 and the appropriate cursor movement keys. Then press Alt-F8 and type **Y** to indicate that you want the highlighted table block protected. Make sure to include column headings for the table as part of this block.

If your table is longer than a page, you are confronted with a different type of paging problem. Probably the best strategy is to allow the table to be paged as required by the line count until you have finished creating and editing the entire document. Then before printing your final document, review the table and decide where to add hard page breaks. These page breaks should be as close as possible to the bottom of the soft page break added by WordPerfect.

After you add your own page breaks (by pressing Ctrl-Return), you may want to copy the column headings from the beginning of the table to the top of the table data on the new page. After doing this, you should review how the page breaks affect the rest of the table to see if, and where, you need to make further page-break decisions.

Of course, your manual paging of a long table will likely become obsolete as soon as you edit the text of the document that precedes the table. In such a case, you must again review the paging of the table, removing hard page breaks and adding new ones where required. However, when a table runs longer than a single text page, none of WordPerfect's automated methods for keeping particular lines of text together on a single page will work satisfactorily.

EDITING TABLES

WordPerfect's Cut/Copy Column feature is very useful when you are editing tabular material. To move or copy a column in a table, you simply mark the column that you wish to move as a block (by pressing Alt-F4), press Ctrl-F4 (the Move key sequence), and then enter a **4** for Cut/Copy Column. When you enter **4,** the block highlighting adjusts to highlight only the column where the cursor is (Figure 4.5), and the following prompt appears:

1 Cut; 2 Copy: 0

Enter **1** to cut the column or **2** to copy it or press Return to select the 0 option if you see that the column is not highlighted properly. When you cut a column, the other columns in the table are repositioned.

Although this process appears fairly straightforward in theory, it can become fairly complicated in practice. You must exercise care when blocking a column that is to be moved or copied, or it will not be highlighted correctly. Most of the time, you should have the Reveal Codes window displayed before you attempt to mark a block and use the Cut/Copy Column command.

To illustrate how to use this command and what precautions are necessary, we will follow the steps for transposing the columns in the mortgage rate table illustrated in Figure 4.2. As this table was constructed, the fixed rates precede the adjustable rates. If you decide that you want the adjustable rates listed before the fixed rates, you can transpose these columns, eliminating the need to retype the data.

To do this you must first mark the two columns of data under the FIXED MORTGAGE heading and then cut them. You start by positioning the cursor at the beginning of the first column of data. In this case, you place the cursor beneath the *9* in 9.75% after First Fed Savings (you do not need to include the Rate and Points column headings as they are identical for both the fixed and adjustable columns).

As you work, you should have the Reveal Codes window displayed as in Figure 4.4. Notice there that the first mortgage rate for First Fed Savings is preceded by both [TAB] and [A] format codes (for decimal alignment), but the rate for International Savings in the next line is preceded only by an [A] code. Because the name *International Savings* is longer than the names of the other savings and loans, no extra tab was needed before the decimal tab.

Because of this, you must position the cursor after and not before the [A] format code before you begin to mark the block with Alt-F4. If the cursor is positioned after the [TAB] code preceding the [A] code, the block marked by WordPerfect will include part of the name *International Savings*. By positioning the cursor after the [A] code, you are telling WordPerfect that the column includes only the text after the decimal tab. After positioning the cursor properly, you can turn off the Reveal Codes display (by pressing the space bar).

> *Note:* If every savings and loan entry were followed by a [TAB] format code before the [A] code, make sure that the cursor is positioned right after the [TAB] code instead of after the [A] code. Doing this will save you quite a bit of work after cutting the columns. This is because the columnar data for the adjustable mortgages will move to align correctly under the Rate and Points column headings. Because you cannot include the [A] codes as part of the block, you have to manually delete the [TAB] code to make the remaining columnar data align properly before you retrieve the cut columns.

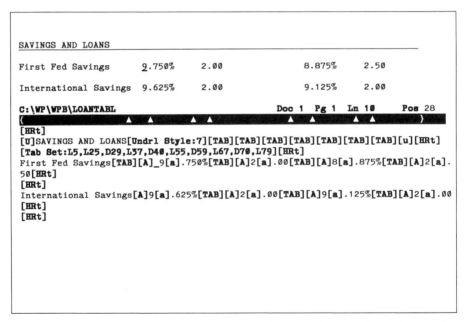

FIGURE 4.4: The Reveal Codes display used to determine where to mark a text column to be moved. To transpose the adjustable-mortgage rate column and the fixed-mortgage rate column, the fixed-rate data must first be marked as a column and cut. This causes the adjustable-rate data to move left to where the fixed-rate data was previously. The adjustable-rate information can now be reinserted to the right of the repositioned fixed-rate data. To begin the column-marking process, the cursor must be positioned correctly so that only the two columns of fixed-rate data will be cut. Because the percentage rate for International Savings did not require entry of a tab stop as was the case for all other companies, the cursor must be positioned after the first [A] code rather than before it for the columns to be marked properly (see the text for more details).

The next step is to indicate to the program where the column ends. To do this, you use the regular marking procedure by pressing Alt-F4 and the ↓ key until you come to the last line. However, at this point you must use the → key to extend the highlighting no further than the 0 in 2.50 (it could end right before the 2 or anywhere within the number). That is where the columns you want included in the block end. (In the Reveal Codes window, the cursor will be positioned between the 0 and the [TAB] format code.)

After indicating where the column ends, you press Ctrl-F4 and type **4** to use the Cut/Copy Column command. The marked block should then appear as is it does in Figure 4.5, which includes just the two columns of data for the fixed-rate percentages and points. Then you type **1** to cut the currently marked column.

Figure 4.6 shows the result of cutting the marked columns. Notice that removing the columns has caused the adjustable-rate percentages and points to move to the left, although they are not positioned correctly under the Rate and Points headings. To make them align correctly, you must turn on the Reveal Codes display again (by pressing Alt-F3) and delete the extra [TAB] code that precedes the

```
SAVINGS AND LOANS

First Fed Savings       9.750%     2.00            8.875%     2.50

International Savings   9.625%     2.00            9.125%     2.00

Home Loan Savings       9.500%     3.00            8.875%     2.50

East Coast Federal      9.625%     2.50            9.375%     3.00












1 Cut; 2 Copy; 3 Delete: 0
```

FIGURE 4.5: Columns blocked for cutting. Before pressing Ctrl-F4 and selecting the Cut/Copy Column option (4), the regular block-marking command, Alt-F4, was used. To block the columns, the cursor was first positioned at the very beginning of the first column in the block (see Figure 4.4) and then the highlighting was extended no further than the end of the last column to be included (in this case, the 0 in the 2.50 points for East Coast Federal). When Ctrl-F4 was pressed and option 4 was selected, the highlighting displayed only the columns included in the block, as shown here (rather than including the entire lines between the first and last column positions, as was the case before option 4, the Cut/Copy Column option, was selected). Figure 4.6 shows the table after the Cut option (1) was selected.

[A] format code. When you delete this tab code and press the ↓ key, you will see the data correctly repositioned. After deleting all of the extra [TAB] codes, you can turn off the Reveal Codes display and position the cursor at the end of the line containing the first savings and loan, First Fed Savings. If you press the End key once you are on this line, the cursor will move to immediately follow the 0 in 2.50. You then press the Tab key to insert the tab you just removed in its proper position. You must do this for each line of the table so that the columns that you are about to retrieve are positioned correctly.

After inserting your tabs at the end of each line, you then position the cursor at the end of the line containing First Fed Savings, and you reinsert the cut columns by pressing Ctrl-F4 and typing **4** (the Retrieve Column command). The last step simply requires editing the FIXED MORTGAGE and ADJUSTABLE MORTGAGE headings so that they appear in the appropriate columns. Figure 4.7 shows the revised table after all of these changes have been made.

As you can see from the foregoing discussion, moving columns in a table can be somewhat complicated. When working with columns, you must be aware of what formatting codes you are and are not including as part of the block. Many times, you will have to think ahead before you cut or retrieve a column. If you do

	Rate	Points	Rate	Points
SAVINGS AND LOANS				
First Fed Savings		8.875%	2.50	
International Savings		9.125%	2.00	
Home Loan Savings		8.875%	2.50	
East Coast Federal		9.375%	3.00	

C:\WP\WPB\LOANTABL   Doc 1   Pg 1   Ln 16   Pos 5

FIGURE 4.6: The table after the columns marked in Figure 4.5 have been cut. The effect of cutting the marked columns has been to move over the other two columns of data as shown. Notice, however, that they are not yet properly aligned under the Rate and Points column headings. To align them, you must remove an extra [TAB] format code from all of the lines. (Refer to the accompanying text for more information about this anomaly.)

not, when you remove the column or reinsert it in a new position, the data in the table may become quite jumbled.

WordPerfect can sort items within columns in a table. See Chapter 10 for information about this feature.

Centering Text Vertically on a Page

In WordPerfect, you can easily center title pages for reports as well as short, one-page letters vertically between the top and bottom of the page. To do this, you must first position the cursor at the very top of the page. You will almost always use vertical centering on the first page of the document, so this will usually correspond to the beginning of the document. To move the cursor to the top of the page, you press the Home key twice and then the ↑ key.

After you have positioned the cursor, you press Alt-F8 (the Page Format key sequence), type *3* to select the Center Top to Bottom option, and then press

```
Loan Rates                                        December 29, 1986


                    ADJUSTABLE MORTGAGE              FIXED MORTGAGE

                    Rate     Points              Rate     Points

SAVINGS AND LOANS  _____

First Fed Savings   8.875%   2.50               9.750%   2.00

International Savings 9.125% 2.00               9.625%   2.00

Home Loan Savings   8.875%   2.50               9.500%   3.00

East Coast Federal  9.375%   3.00               9.625%   2.50
    ─




C:\WP\WPB\LOANTABL                      Doc 1  Pg 1  Ln 17    Pos 5
```

FIGURE 4.7: The Loan Rates table in its final form after the adjustable and fixed mortgage figures have been transposed. This was done by properly aligning the fixed-rate figures under their column headings (see Figure 4.6), adding an extra tab at the end of each line, and then retrieving the cut columns containing the fixed rate figures (by positioning the cursor at the last tab stop in the first line of the table data and using Ctrl-F4 and option 4, the Retrieve Column command). The final step was editing the FIXED MORTGAGE and ADJUSTABLE MORTGAGE headings to reflect the transposed data. The Reveal Codes window was used to position the cursor after the [C][U] codes before deleting and inserting the correct headings.

Return to return to the document. When you do this, WordPerfect adds the format code [Center Pg] to your document. However, you will not see the effect of this code on the text. To see how the page will appear when printed, you can issue the Page Print Preview command by pressing Shift-F7, typing **6,** and then typing **2.** You will probably have to use the + (plus) and - (hyphen) keys to scroll the text up and down the page. Press F7 to exit the preview screen and return to the regular document.

When you are working with a title page that is followed by full pages of text, be sure and add a hard page break (by pressing Ctrl-Return) after the text that is to appear on the title page. If you do not, WordPerfect will include the text from subsequent pages in its vertical centering.

If you ever want to eliminate vertical centering for a letter or title page, all you have to do is display the Reveal Codes window, position the cursor right after the [Center Pg] code, and delete the code by pressing the Backspace key.

THE PAGE FORMAT KEY (ALT-F8)

Most of your formatting changes will be made through the Page Format menu shown in Figure 4.8 (key sequence Alt-F8).

```
Page Format

        1 - Page Number Position

        2 - New Page Number

        3 - Center Page Top to Bottom

        4 - Page Length

        5 - Top Margin

        6 - Headers or Footers

        7 - Page Number Column Positions

        8 - Suppress for Current page only

        9 - Conditional End of Page

        A - Widow/Orphan


Selection: 0
```

FIGURE 4.8: The Page Format menu (reached by pressing Alt-F8). This menu allows you to set page length, specify page numbers, add headers and footers, and specify other page formatting settings.

The Page Format menu gives you the following options:

1 Page Number Position specifies the location of page numbers.

2 New Page Number allows you to specify the number on which page numbering starts.

3 Center Page Top to Bottom allows you to center text vertically on a page.

4 Page Length allows you to change the length of the page as well as the number of text lines per page.

5 Top Margin allows you to specify a top margin other than the 1-inch default top margin.

6 Headers or Footers allows you to specify text to be printed at the top (header) or bottom (footer) of each page of your document.

7 Page Number Column Positions specifies the column position of the page number.

8 Suppress for Current page only allows you to turn off page numbering, headers, and footers for the current page.

9 Conditional End of Page allows you to specify a condition that must be met to keep lines of text together on one page.

A Widow/Orphan allows you to specify that an incomplete line not appear at the bottom of a page (widow) or at the top of a page (orphan).

Using Print Preview to Check the Page Layout

KEY SEQUENCE

To preview how the entire document will appear when printed:
   Shift-F7 6 1
To preview how the current page will appear when printed:
   Shift-F7 6 2
To toggle between the regular and previewed versions of the document:
   Shift-F3
To exit the previewed version and return to the regular document:
   F7

The current version of WordPerfect (Release 4.2) has a very valuable Print Preview feature that you can use to check page layout before you actually print a document. When you select the Preview command on the Print menu, WordPerfect redraws the document screen showing the document as it will appear when printed. To use this command, you press Shift-F7 (the Print command key sequence) and type **6** to select the Preview option. You are then presented with two menu options:

Preview: 1 Document; 2 Page: 0

You type **1** if you want to preview the contents of the entire document on screen or type **2** if you want to preview only the page that currently contains the cursor. After you select either option, you will see the message "Please Wait" as WordPerfect redraws the screen. Once WordPerfect has finished, you will see the document or the current page adjusted to show headers, footers, footnotes, page numbers, and all margins, including those for the left, right, top, and bottom margins. In Preview mode, you can also see right justification if you have justified part or all of the document.

> *Note:* In practice, it takes a long time for WordPerfect to prepare the preview of an entire document unless the document consists of only a very few pages. In a document of 50 pages or more, you may have to wait several minutes before you can see the document in Preview mode. Because of this long wait state, so uncharacteristic of WordPerfect, you should probably use the Preview command with the Page option rather than the Document option. By previewing several key pages individually, such as the title page, the first page where headers and footers occur, and any specially formatted pages where you have used Block Protect or the Conditional end of page commands, you should be able to spot any problem areas without having to preview the entire document.

When WordPerfect previews a document or document page, it places its text in a third document window that is available only when using the Print Preview feature. You can verify that you are previewing the way the document will print by checking the status line at the bottom of the screen. There you will see "Doc 3," regardless of whether the regular text of the document was retrieved in the first (Doc 1) or second (Doc 2) window.

You cannot edit the Print Preview version of the document in Doc 3. You can, however, use the Switch window command, Shift-F3, to toggle back and forth between the regular and preview versions.

When you are finished previewing the document or current page in the third document window, you can close it and return to the regular document by pressing F7 (the Exit key). Once you press F7, you cannot return to the preview version in Doc 3 without first accessing the Preview command again.

If you notice page layout changes when previewing the document that must be made before you print, you should make the necessary changes and then preview the page or document once more. Regular use of the Preview feature will save you a great deal of printing time, to say nothing of wasted paper. You can use the reference entries in this chapter to help you diagnose and correct particular page format problems.

ALT-L: A MACRO TO PREVIEW THE LAYOUT OF THE CURRENT PAGE

To save you time in previewing the current page, you might want to create and use the following macro. This can speed up the process of turning on the Print Preview feature to check the contents and placement of headers and footers as well as the general page layout.

Begin macro	*Macro name*	*Keystrokes*	*End macro*
Ctrl-F10	**Alt-L**	**Shift-F7 6 2**	**Ctrl-F10**

To use this macro to preview the way the current page will appear when printed, press Alt-L. When the "Please Wait" message disappears from the screen, you will see the current page in document window 3 (Doc 3). You can scroll up and down and move the cursor left and right to check its contents and layout. When you are finished, press F7 to return to the regular document window. If you want to edit your document, press Shift-F3 instead.

PAGE NUMBERING

WordPerfect allows you to specify both the position and the style of page numbers. You may, for example, want to keep page numbers out of the way by putting them in the lower-right or lower-left corner of the page. You may also want to emphasize them by centering them at the top of the page, or you may want to include them in your headers or footers. If you are working with a document that is going to be printed on both sides of the page and bound, you may want to alternate the position of the page number on right-hand and left-hand pages so that the page number is always in the same relative position.

Options 1, 2, 7, and 8 on the Page Format menu involve page numbers; they are discussed in the following sections. You can also insert page numbers into headers and footers (see "Inserting Headers and Footers" later in this chapter) and suppress page numbering on any given page (see "Suppressing Headers, Footers, and Page Numbers" later in this chapter).

Page Number Position

KEY SEQUENCE

To add page numbers in the top left of every page:
Alt-F8 1 1 0 (or **Return**)
To add page numbers centered at the top of every page:
Alt-F8 1 2 0 (or **Return**)

To add page numbers in the top right of every page:
    Alt-F8 1 3 0 (or **Return**)
To add page numbers alternating left and right at the top:
    Alt-F8 1 4 0 (or **Return**)
To add page numbers at the bottom left of every page:
    Alt-F8 1 5 0 (or **Return**)
To add page numbers centered at the bottom of every page:
    Alt-F8 1 6 0 (or **Return**)
To add page numbers at the bottom left of every page:
    Alt-F8 1 7 0 (or **Return**)
To add page numbers alternating left and right at the bottom of every page:
    Alt-F8 1 8 0 (or **Return**)

REVEAL CODES

Sets position of page numbers:
    [**Pos Pg#:** <*page numbering position code* (1–8)>]

When you press Alt-F8, the Page Format key sequence, Option 1 allows you to specify the page number position. You can place page numbers in the following positions:

- At the left, right, or center of the top of each page

- At the left, right, or center of the bottom of each page

- Alternating left and right at the top of each page

- Alternating left and right at the bottom of each page

You can also choose option 0 on the Page Numbering menu to have no page numbers, the default selection.

If you select either option 4, Top alternating left & right, or option 8, Bottom alternating left & right, page numbers will appear on the left side of left-hand (usually even-numbered) pages and on the right side of right-hand (usually odd-numbered) pages, as shown in Figure 4.9.

Employee Handbook

Recreational Facilities

MagnaCorp participates in the city recreational plan and therefore its employees have access to the municipal gym located at First and Brannan Streets. The jogging track and par course in Grant park are also nearby. Showers and lockers for company employees are located near the south entrance of the main lobby.

Vacation

Full-time permanent employees are eligible for two weeks of paid vacation after six months of continuous employment. During the first five years of service, you earn three weeks of vacation per year. After five years of service, you receive four weeks of vacation.

Credit Union

MagnaCorp's credit union is located on the third floor. Hours are 9 to 6 p.m. daily. The credit union observes all national and bank holidays, whereas the company may or may not follow the same schedule.

Holidays

MagnaCorp designates five official holidays each year. These are New Year's Day, Memorial Day, Independence Day, Labor Day, and Thanksgiving Day. In addition, the company closes for Christmas week. An additional two floating holidays may be taken at your discretion and with the approval of your manager.

Benefits

Benefits programs include life insurance, health care, dental services, and travel insurance. They are available to you at no cost during your employment with MagnaCorp. If you leave the company for any reason, some of these programs can be continued at a small monthly charge to you. See the Personnel Department for details.

Personal Leave

Personal time off with or without pay can be arranged for short periods with the approval of your manager. In addition, if you have more than one year of service with MagnaCorp, you may be granted longer periods of personal leave--to obtain an advanced degree, for example, or to complete a specialized course of study. Special types of leave with pay are covered in the following sections.

2

FIGURE 4.9: Page numbers alternating positions on left and right pages when the document is bound (option 8).

Bereavement Leave. Up to three days off with pay are granted in the event of the death of a member of your immediate family.

Military Leave. Members of armed forces reserve units or the National Guard may be eligible for two weeks of annual training leave.

Jury Duty. Paid leave to serve on a jury will be granted for the term required. MagnaCorp will reimburse you the difference between juror pay and your regular salary.

Leave for Illness

Sick leave is normally accrued at the rate of one day per month. In special circumstances, extended leave can be arranged through your manager. If you are hospitalized, your salary is covered by disability insurance from the first day of hospitalization.

Performance Appraisals

The key to managing your career at MagnaCorp is to understand the performance and appraisals process thoroughly. You need to know what others think of how well you are doing so that you can know how to improve.

The performance appraisal cycle at MagnaCorp consists of both informal and formal planning sessions. In informal sessions, both you and your manager sit down at least once every three months and together work out a performance plan for the coming period. This plan details what is expected of you and indicates goals for a specific time period. It is important that this be a two-way process: you and your manager should feel free to communicate and set mutual goals. At least once a year, a formal appraisal session will be held in which a formal evaluation will be made and a rating assigned to your overall performance for the year.

Opportunities for Advancement

The bulletin board outside the Personnel Department on the first floor contains up-to-date listings of job openings within the company and at field locations throughout the country. Whenever possible, openings are filled from within the company. If you see a position for which you feel you are qualified, check with the Personnel Department.

Educational Aid

MagnaCorp offers educational opportunities to employees at all

3

FIGURE 4.9: Page numbers alternating positions on left and right pages when the document is bound (option 8) (continued).

Changing the Column Position for Numbers

KEY SEQUENCE

To specify new left, center, or right page number positions (in tenths of an inch):

Alt-F8 7 2 L = <*left value*> **Return C** = <*center value*> **Return**
R = <*right value*> **0** (or **Return**)

To reset left, center, and right page number positions to initial values:

Alt-F8 7 1 0 (or **Return**)

REVEAL CODES

Sets new column positions for left-, center-, and right-aligned page numbers (both top and bottom):

[**Pg Col#:** <*left value, center value, right value*>]

Whenever you change the margins in your documents, you must also specify the new left, right, and center column positions (option 7) so that the page number will be correctly aligned on the page. For example, if you are designing a page layout in which paragraphs are indented, you might want the page number to be aligned flush left on one of the columns.

When you select option 7 for Page Number Column Position, you are presented with the menu shown in Figure 4.10. Select 2 to change the character position. The left position currently is set to 10, the center position to 42, and the right position to 74. Type the character positions for your new left, right, and center settings (or simply change the setting of the page number position you are going to use). From that point on in your document, page numbers will appear at the character position (column position) you specified. For example, if you change the center setting to 30 and specify option 2 (Top center) for the page number position, page numbers will appear at character position 30 at the top of each page.

To make sure that page numbers appear in the same position throughout your document, move to the beginning of your document (Home, Home, ↑) before specifying page number positions or altering the default settings.

```
Reset Column Position for Page Numbers

  (L = Left Corner, C = Center, R = Right Corner)

     1 - Set to Initial Settings (In tenths of an inch)
              L=10 C=42 R=74

     2 - Set to Specified Settings

Current Settings

     L=10 C=42 R=74




Selection: 0
```

FIGURE 4.10: Changing the page number column position. This menu allows you to specify where the page number appears on the page. If you want page numbers to appear in the same relative position on each page of your document, make sure that you return to the beginning of your document before you use this menu to change the page number position.

Specifying New Page Numbers and Changing from Arabic to Roman

KEY SEQUENCE

To specify a number at which to begin page numbering using Arabic numbers:
Alt-F8 2 <*new page number*> **Return 1 0** (or **Return**)

To specify a number at which to begin page numbering using Roman numerals:
Alt-F8 2 <*new page number*> **Return 2 0** (or **Return**)

REVEAL CODES

Sets numbering style to Roman numerals:
[Pg#:ii]

Sets new page number:
[Pg#: <*page number value*> **]**

You frequently may want to specify that page numbering begin with a certain number. For example, you may want to number chapters or sections of a report or book consecutively but want to store each chapter or section as a separate file. Option 2 on the Page Format menu lets you specify which page number is to begin each section.

When you select option 2, the following prompt appears at the bottom of the screen:

> **Selection: 2**
> **New Page #:**

When you enter the page number on which you want page numbering to begin, another prompt appears:

> **Selection: 2**
> **Numbering Style 1 Arabic; 2 Roman: 0**

To change from Arabic numbers (1, 2, 3, and so forth) to lowercase Roman numerals (i, ii, iii), enter **2.** Roman numerals are often used for the front-matter pages—title page, copyright page, table of contents, foreword, and preface—of a book or long report. You can number these pages with Roman numerals and then switch back to Arabic, beginning with 1, for the body of the book or report. If all you want to do is change to Roman numerals, simply enter **1** as the new page number.

INSERTING HEADERS AND FOOTERS

Headers and footers are lines of text printed at the top (header) or bottom (footer) of your document page. They are often used to identify the title of a document, to indicate the date on which the document was created, or to specify a message (for instance, "Company Confidential").

Defining Headers and Footers in a Document

KEY SEQUENCE

To create headers or footers:
> **Alt-F8 6** <*type* (**1** for Header A, **2** for Header B,
> **3** for Footer A, **4** for Footer B)>
> <*occurrence* (**1** for Every page, **2** for Odd pages, **3** for Even pages>
> <*header or footer text*> **F7 0** (or **Return**)

REVEAL CODES

[Hdr/Ftr: <*type number*> , <*occurrence number*> ;
   <*header or footer text*>]

With WordPerfect, you can have both headers and footers on each page, and each header or footer can be longer than one line (for an example, see Figure 4.11). Word-Perfect automatically leaves one line of space between the header (or footer) and the text. To add more space between the text and the header or footer, insert hard returns at the end of your header or at the beginning of your footer.

To create a header or footer, use option 6 from the Page Format menu. You will see the screen shown in Figure 4.12.

When you create a header or footer, you must first select the type of header or footer you wish to create. You type **1** for Header A if you are creating your first header and **2** for Header B if you are creating your second header. Likewise, type **3** to create Footer A and type **4** to create Footer B, your first and second footers, respectively.

You create two headers A and B (or footers) if you want their text to alternate on even- and odd-numbered pages of the document. You usually do this when a document will be reproduced on both sides of each sheet of paper so that the header on odd-numbered pages will appear in the same place on the page as it does on even-numbered pages. If your document will be reproduced on only one side of each sheet of paper, you just need to create one header or footer (A) for the document.

The second list on the screen allows you to indicate the occurrence, or placement, of the header or footer you are defining on the page. You select option 1 if you want the header or footer to be printed on each page of the document. You select option 2 if you want it to be printed only on odd-numbered pages and option 3 if you want it to be printed only on even-numbered pages.

If you are using only one header in the document, you select A as the Type by entering **1** and Every Page as the Occurrence by entering **1** again. You will then be presented with a full editing screen on which to enter the text of the header (or footer). When entering the header (or footer) text, you can use the same print enhancements and alignment features as you can when entering any text in the document. For instance, if you want the text of the header (or footer) to be centered and underlined, you press Shift-F6 followed by F8 and then type the text, press F8, and press Return. After you have finished, you press F7 to exit the Header/Footer editing screen and then type **0** or press Return to return to the document.

If you are using two headers that are to alternate between odd- and even-numbered pages, you select A as the Type for the first one and Odd Pages as the Occurrence by typing **1** and **2** on the Header/Footer options screen. When you enter the text for the header, you will usually want to right align it by pressing

Employee Handbook--page 1

WELCOME

Welcome to MagnaCorp. We hope this employee handbook will help to guide you through your first few days here. In addition, it contains valuable information about employee services and benefits available to you. Ask your manager or call the personnel office if you have any questions for which you cannot find the answers in this handbook.

Work Day

The official work day at MagnaCorp is 8:30 a.m. to 5:00 p.m. Flexible hours can be arranged with your manager.

Parking

As parking is limited, please apply to the personnel office for a parking slot assignment.

Hours

Noon to 1 p.m. has been reserved as lunch hour for all employees. Some departments have chosen to take lunch from 11:30 to 12:30 or from 12:30 to 1:30; check with your manager.

Cafeteria

The company cafeteria, located on the third floor, is open from 7 a.m. until 2 p.m. daily. Breakfast is available for your convenience until 9:00. After 2 p.m., vending machines with cold sandwiches and salads are available.

Recreational Facilities

MagnaCorp participates in the city recreational plan and therefore its employees have access to the municipal gym located at First and Brannan Streets. The jogging track and par course in Grant park are also nearby. Showers and lockers for company employees are located near the south entrance of the main lobby.

Vacation

Full-time permanent employees are eligible for two weeks of paid vacation after six months of continuous employment. During the first five years of service, you earn three weeks of vacation per year. After five years of service, you receive four weeks of vacation.

Credit Union

CONFIDENTIAL: For Management Review Only

FIGURE 4.11: Document with both headers and footers. Remember that headers and footers take up the space normally allowed for text, so you may want to adjust the number of lines per page if you are using complex headers and footers in a document.

```
Header/Footer Specification

    Type                           Occurrence
    1 – Header A                   0 – Discontinue
    2 – Header B                   1 – Every Page
    3 – Footer A                   2 – Odd Pages
    4 – Footer B                   3 – Even Pages
                                   4 – Edit


    Selection: 0                   Selection: 0
```

FIGURE 4.12: The Header/Footer Specification screen. You can specify two separate headers and footers for each page in your document. This allows you to create different headers and footers for right (odd) and left (even) pages in your documents.

Alt-F6 before typing it. If you are adding page numbers as part of the header, you then press Ctrl-B to add the page numbers after entering the identifying text.

After pressing F7, you type **6** again to create your second header and select B as the Type and Even Pages as the Occurrence by typing **2** and *3* on the Header/ Footer options screen. When you enter the text of the header for the even numbered pages, you leave it left aligned. If you are adding pages numbers as part of this header, you then press Ctrl-B before you type the identifying text. Figure 4.13 shows the effect of having one header on even-numbered pages and another on odd-numbered pages.

After you select where you want a header or a footer and the header or footer types, a blank screen appears. Here you can type the text of your header or footer, using boldfacing, underlining, or other text enhancements. To make your header or footer flush right on the page, press Alt-F6 when your cursor is on the first character in the header. Remember also that your header can be longer than one line, but that the longer the header, the fewer text lines you are allowed on the page. When you have finished typing the text of your header or footer, press F7 to exit from the header screen.

Because you will almost always want the headers and footers you specify to appear on all pages of your document, be sure to move your cursor to the beginning of the document (Home, Home, ↑) before pressing Alt-F8. If you do not

Employee Handbook--page 2

MagnaCorp participates in the city recreational plan and
therefore its employees have access to the municipal gym located
at First and Brannan Streets. The jogging track and par course
in Grant park are also nearby. Showers and lockers for company
employees are located near the south entrance of the main lobby.

Vacation

Full-time permanent employees are eligible for two weeks of paid
vacation after six months of continuous employment. During the
first five years of service, you earn three weeks of vacation per
year. After five years of service, you receive four weeks of
vacation.

Credit Union

MagnaCorp's credit union is located on the third floor. Hours
are 9 to 6 p.m. daily. The credit union observes all national
and bank holidays, whereas the company may or may not follow the
same schedule.

Holidays

MagnaCorp designates five official holidays each year. These are
New Year's Day, Memorial Day, Independence Day, Labor Day, and
Thanksgiving Day. In addition, the company closes for Christmas
week. An additional two floating holidays may be taken at your
discretion and with the approval of your manager.

Benefits

Benefits programs include life insurance, health care, dental
services, and travel insurance. They are available to you at no
cost during your employment with MagnaCorp. If you leave the
company for any reason, some of these programs can be continued
at a small monthly charge to you. See the Personnel Department.

Personal Leave

Personal time off with or without pay can be arranged for short
periods with the approval of your manager. In addition, if you
have more than one year of service with MagnaCorp, you may be
granted longer periods of personal leave--to obtain an advanced
degree, for example, or to complete a specialized course of
study. Special types of leave with pay are covered in the
following sections.

Bereavement Leave. Up to three days off with pay are granted in
the event of the death of a member of your immediate family.

Military Leave. Members of armed forces reserve units or the

FIGURE 4.13: Using different headers on odd- and even-numbered pages. If you are printing a long
report that is going to be bound, you may want to specify two different headers or footers so that
headers or footers appear in the outside margins rather than at the bound edge (gutter) of each page.

Employee Handbook--page 3

National Guard may be eligible for two weeks of annual training
leave.

Jury Duty. Paid leave to serve on a jury will be granted for the
term required. MagnaCorp will reimburse you the difference
between juror pay and your regular salary.

Leave for Illness

Sick leave is normally accrued at the rate of one day per month.
In special circumstances, extended leave can be arranged through
your manager. If you are hospitalized, your salary is covered by
disability insurance from the first day of hospitalization.

Performance Appraisals

The key to managing your career at MagnaCorp is to understand the
performance and appraisals process thoroughly. You need to know
what others think of how well you are doing so that you can know
how to improve.

The performance appraisal cycle at MagnaCorp consists of both
informal and formal planning sessions. In informal sessions,
both you and your manager sit down at least once every three
months and together work out a performance plan for the coming
period. This plan details what is expected of you and indicates
goals for a specific time period. It is important that this be a
two-way process: you and your manager should feel free to
communicate and set mutual goals. At least once a year, a formal
appraisal session will be held in which a formal evaluation will
be made and a rating assigned to your overall performance for the
year.

Opportunities for Advancement

The bulletin board outside the Personnel Department on the first
floor contains up-to-date listings of job openings within the
company and at field locations throughout the country. Whenever
possible, openings are filled from within the company. If you
see a position for which you feel you are qualified, check with
the Personnel Department.

Educational Aid

MagnaCorp offers educational opportunities to employees at all
levels. Tuition refunds are available to full-time employees for
courses at accredited institutions. To make sure that a course
for which you plan to enroll will be covered, consult your
manager or the Personnel Department.

FIGURE 4.13: Using different headers on odd- and even-numbered pages. If you are printing a long report that is going to be bound, you may want to specify two different headers or footers so that headers or footers appear in the outside margins rather than at the bound edge (gutter) of each page. (continued)

position the header or footer at the beginning of the document, it will appear only on pages that follow the page where it was inserted.

HD: A Macro to Enter a Header (Or Footer)

You can write a macro to automate the process of inserting headers or footers into standard documents you create. The following macro takes advantage of WordPerfect's ability to pause during a macro so that you can insert text—in this case, the chapter number. This macro inserts a header that will appear in the upper-right corner of each page of your document, as shown in Figure 4.14.

Begin macro	*Macro name*	*Keystrokes*	*End macro*
Ctrl-F10	**HD**	**Alt-F8 6 1 1 Alt-F6**	**Ctrl-F10**
		Chapter <space>Ctrl-PgUp	
		Return Return	
		Ctrl-B Return Alt-F6	
		Version: <space>	
		Shift-F5 1	
		F7 Return	

To use this header, position the cursor at the very beginning of the document (by pressing Home, Home, ↑), press Alt-F10, type **HD**, and press Return. When you hear a beep, type the number of the chapter and press Return. The macro will then insert the automatic page numbering symbol (^B) and enter the word *Version:* along with the date.

You can easily customize this macro to your own needs by substituting *Section* for *Chapter* (or some more appropriate heading) and deleting *Version:* or omitting the current date. These keystrokes for entering the header can also be combined with those that set the margins and tab stops when you start a new document. For more information about creating and using macros, especially macros that pause for user input, see Chapter 14.

Editing Headers

REVEAL CODES

To edit a header or footer:

Alt-F8 6 *<type number>* **Return 4** (edit text of header or footer) **F7 0**
(or **Return**)

Chapter 20-1
Version: January 6, 1987

A business, once it gets beyond the entrepreneurial stage,[1] next faces the challenge of organizing and managing itself as a stable company.[2] Managers who heretofore were rewarded for initiative and ingenuity are now penalized for outstepping the boundaries of corporate rules; employees who in the past were rewarded for their willingness to challenge established theory must now follow corporate canons. In this stage of business growth a radical change in the employee-manager mix may be noted.[3]

At the same time the business is facing this challenge, it meets yet another challenge: managing for future growth. A dynamic business cannot be allowed to stagnate; it must always be planning for the future. The future, in such a case, may mean diversification rather than the former concentration on a narrow set of goals. Yet another type of managerial thinking is required: that of long-range planners.[4]

These different types of idealists must manage a new set of assumptions to manage for current stability while planning for future expansion. Such planners must be able to juggle one set of conservative assumptions while at the same time exercising a plan of highly imaginative proportions that concerns five- and ten-year growth plans and beyond. Such thinkers are scarce; when found, they command excellent salaries.

---

[1]See Paul L. Salomon, _The Entrepreneurial Mind_ (Chicago: Row-Martin, 1987).

[2] Saul C. Guttman, _Stages in Business Growth_ (Hoffman: Baltimore, 1987), p.198

[3]This is also the time of most rapid employee expansion, so the mix in personality types may pass unnoticed.

[4]Eldon R. WainWright, _Long-Range Planning for Corporate Policy_ (Harrison & Ball: New York, 1987).

FIGURE 4.14: Sample header added with the HD macro. This macro inserts the page number, the word _Version_, and the date the document is printed in the upper-right corner of each page.

WordPerfect makes it easy for you to edit headers and footers once they have been created without having to reselect them and retype them. Simply press Alt-F8, type 6 (for Headers and Footers), enter the number of the Type that corresponds to the header or footer you wish to edit, and select option 4, the Edit option. WordPerfect presents you with a screen showing the current placement and content of your header or footer and automatically returns the cursor to the beginning of the document (or to the position where you inserted the header or footer). Simply edit or retype the information you want to change; then press F7 to exit.

Inserting Page Numbers into Headers and Footers

KEY SEQUENCE

Ctrl-B (or **Ctrl-N**)

To insert automatic page numbering into your headers and footers, press Ctrl-B (or Ctrl-N) at the position in the header or footer where you want the page number to appear. For example, to use the footer

Preliminary Report
Page 1

you type

Preliminary Report
Page Ctrl-B

The Ctrl-B keystrokes will appear on your screen as ^B. Each page of your document will then automatically be numbered by the program, starting from 1 (to change the number on which page numbering starts, refer to the discussion "Numbering Pages" earlier in this chapter.)

Inserting the Date into Headers and Footers

KEY SEQUENCE

To insert the System date in the format Month, DD, YYYY with the date fixed:

Shift-F5 1

To insert the System date in the format Month, DD, YYYY with the date updated whenever you retrieve or print the document:

Shift-F5 3

To insert the System time in the format HH:MM AM/PM with the time fixed:

Shift-F5 2 7:8 0 Return 1

To insert the System time in the format HH:MM AM/PM with the time updated whenever you retrieve or print the document:

Shift-F5 2 7:8 0 Return 3

REVEAL CODES

When you select option 3, Insert Function, from the Date menu:

[**Date:** *< current date/time format codes >*]

You may want to insert the date into the headers or footers of your documents you create so that you can keep a record of each draft. You will probably also want to date the memos, business letters, and reports you create. Pressing Shift-F5 allows you to insert the current date or time from your computer's internal clock (or the date and time that you enter when you start the computer). Using this command, WordPerfect will automatically insert the current date for you in a format that you specify.

To insert the current date at the cursor location, press Shift-F5. The following prompt appears:

Date 1 Insert Text; 2 Format; 3 Insert Function: 0

Type **1** to insert the date (as determined by your computer's internal clock) at the cursor location.

To change the format of the date, type **2.** The screen shown in Figure 4.15 appears.

The default format is month, day, year, as in August 15, 1987. However, you can change this format by entering the number of the format shown on the screen. You can specify whether

- The month appears as a number or as a word
- Four digits or two digits of the year are used
- The day of the week is spelled out
- A 12-hour clock or a 24-hour clock is used
- Minutes and A.M. or P.M. are used

The order in which you type the format numbers and the punctuation you use to enter them determines how dates and times appear in your documents. Table 4.1 shows you all of the possibilities using the Format option.

PATTERN	FORMAT CODES	EXAMPLE
For dates without leading zeros:		
Month DD, YYYY	3 1, 4	March 1, 1988
Weekday Month DD, YYYY	6 3 1, 4	Tuesday March 1, 1988
MM/DD/YYYY	2/1/4	3/1/1988
MM/DD/YY	2/1/5	3/1/88
DD/MM/YY	1/2/5	1/3/88
Report Date: MM/DD/YY	Report Date: 2/1/5	Report Date: 3/1/88
For dates with leading zeros:		
Month, DD, YYYY	3 %1, 4	March 01, 1988
MM/DD/YY	%2/%1/5	03/01/88
For time without leading zeros:		
HH:MM AM/PM	8:9 0	1:7 PM
HH:MM (24 hr. clock)	7:9	13:7
For time with leading zeros:		
HH:MM AM/PM	%8:%9 0	01:07 PM
For date and time:		
MM/DD/YY - HH:MM AM/PM	%2/%1/5 - 8:%90	03/01/88 - 1:07 PM

TABLE 4.1: Date Format Options

For example, to specify that dates appear in the format 2/16/45, you enter

2/1/5

Refer to the numbers in Figure 4.16. You will see that 2 indicates Month (number), 1 indicates Day of the month, and 5 indicates Year (last two digits).

You can specify the time format in the same way. Your date and time formats cannot be longer than 29 characters. Unless you specify a time format, WordPerfect will insert only the date when you press Shift-F5, **1**. Whatever pattern you use here will continue to be used each time you press Shift-F5, **1** until you exit WordPerfect. You can permanently change the date format by using the Setup menu, selecting option 2, Change Initial Settings, and then pressing the Date key sequence, Shift-F5. You then enter the code numbers and punctuation you want used as the default values and press Return (see Chapter 16 for more information about the Setup menu options).

```
Date Format

    Character    Meaning
        1        Day of the month
        2        Month (number)
        3        Month (word)
        4        Year (all four digits)
        5        Year (last two digits)
        6        Day of the week (word)
        7        Hour (24-hour clock)
        8        Hour (12-hour clock)
        9        Minute
        0        am / pm
        %        Include leading zero for numbers less than 10
                   (must directly precede number)

    Examples:  3 1, 4      = December 25, 1984
               %2/%1/5 (6) = 01/01/85 (Tuesday)
Date Format: 3 1, 4
```

FIGURE 4.15: WordPerfect's Date Format screen. You can select other date formats by entering the number of the format shown on the screen. Dates you enter will be formatted as you have specified until you exit the program or change the date format again.

AM: A MACRO TO INSERT THE CURRENT TIME USING A 12-HOUR CLOCK

Begin macro	Macro name	Keystrokes	End macro
Ctrl-F10	**AM**	**Shift-F5 2**	**Ctrl-F10**
		8: %9 0 Return 1	

FD: A MACRO TO RETURN TO FULL DATE FORMAT

Begin macro	Macro name	Keystrokes	End macro
Ctrl-F10	**FD**	**Shift-F5 2**	**Ctrl-F10**
		3 1, 4 Return	

To use this macro, press Alt-F10 and type **FD.** You will then be presented with the menu options

Date 1 Insert Text; 2 Format; 3 Insert Function: 0

Press Return to simply change the format back to full date format or type **1** to enter the date at the cursor's position.

Deleting Headers and Footers

KEY SEQUENCE

F2 Alt-F8 6 F2 Backspace

REVEAL CODES

[Hdr/Ftr]

When you insert headers and footers into a document, WordPerfect also inserts the formatting code [Hdr/Ftr:] for them (see Figure 4.16). Because the headers and footers do not appear on your screen (they appear only on your printed documents or when you use the Print Preview feature), you may sometimes need to search for these codes to remove or edit headers and footers.

To search for a header or footer in a document, press F2 (or Shift-F2 if you are searching backward), press Alt-F8, and type **6.** This enters [Hdr/Ftr] as the search string. Then press F2 to initiate the search. To delete the header or footer located by the program, press Backspace. If you turn on the Reveal Codes window by pressing Alt-F3 when you perform the search, you can view the text of the header or footer. This will help you determine if you want to delete the header or footer.

> *Note:* Searching for the occurrence of a header or footer in a document is not the same as searching the text of the header or footer. When you want to search (or search and replace) the text of a header or footer, you need to perform an extended search by pressing Home before you press F2 and enter the search string. In Chapter 3, see the section "Using the Search Commands to Find Formatting Codes" for more information about locating occurrences of formatting codes and the section "Performing an Extended Search" for more information about searching the text of headers and footers.

You also need to change headers and footers whenever you change margins in your document, because headers and footers are not automatically updated to reflect the new margin settings. All you have to do is search for the occurrence of the header/footer formatting codes as just described and follow the steps required to edit headers and footers without actually making any changes (although you can make changes if you want to).

To do this, Press Alt-F8, type **6,** enter the number of the type of header or footer (shown in the [Hdr/Ftr] format code in the Reveal Codes window), type **4** to select the edit option, press F7, and press Return to return to the document. When you perform this procedure, WordPerfect will then calculate the new positions of your headers and footers.

```
WELCOME

Welcome to MagnaCorp. We hope this employee handbook will help to
guide you through your first few days here.  In addition, it
contains valuable information about employee services and
benefits available to you.  Ask your manager or call the
personnel office if you have any questions for which you cannot
C:\WP\BOOK\F4-1                              Doc 2  Pg 1  Ln 1      Pos 10
( ▲    ▲    ▲    ▲    ▲    ▲    ▲    ▲    ▲    ▲    ▲    ]▲    ▲    ▲
_[Hdr/Ftr:1,1;[A][B]MagnaCorp Employee Handbook[b]][Hdr/Ftr:3,1;First Draft[A]Co
mpany Confidential]WELCOME[U][HRt]
[W/O On][u][HRt]
Welcome to MagnaCorp. We hope this employee handbook will help to[SRt]
guide you through your first few days here.  In addition, it[SRt]
```

FIGURE 4.16: Formatting codes for a header. To reveal the formatting codes, press Alt-F3. To search for a header or footer code, press F2 and specify Hdr/Ftr as the search string.

Suppressing Headers, Footers, and Page Numbers

KEY SEQUENCE

To suppress page numbering, the header, or the footer on current page:

Alt-F8 8 1 Return 0 (or Return)

To suppress only page numbering on current page:

Alt-F8 8 2 Return 0 (or Return)

To print page number at bottom center on current page only:

Alt-F8 8 3 Return 0 (or Return)

To suppress only the header or footer on current page:

Alt-F8 8 4 Return 0 (or Return)

To suppress only Header A on current page:

Alt-F8 8 5 Return 0 (or Return)

To suppress only Header B on current page:

Alt-F8 8 6 Return 0 (or Return)

To suppress only Footer A on current page:

Alt-F8 8 7 Return 0 (or Return)

To suppress only Footer B on current page:
   Alt-F8 8 8 Return 0 (or **Return**)

Note: You can also select multiple items to be suppressed after pressing Alt-F8,
8 by typing the appropriate numbers with a plus sign (+) between them—for
instance, you can type **3 + 5 + 6** to print the page number at the bottom center
of the current page and suppress Headers A and B.

REVEAL CODES

[Suppress: *<suppress option number(s)>*]

You may sometimes not want headers, footers, and page numbers to appear
on certain pages of your document, such as the title page, the first pages of chapters, pages that contain full-page illustrations, or the first page of a business letter.
WordPerfect allows you to suppress these special formats.

   To suppress headers, footers, and page numbers on a page, position your cursor at the top of the page (just under the dashed line that marks the page break on
your screen). Then press Alt-F8 and select option 8 (Suppress for Current page
only). The screen shown in Figure 4.17 appears.

```
Suppress Page Format for Current Page Only

   To temporarily turn off multiple items, include a "+" between menu entries.
   For example 5+6+2 will turn off Header A, Header B, and Page Numbering
   for the current page.

      1 - Turn off all page numbering, headers and footers

      2 - Turn page numbering off

      3 - Print page number at bottom center (this page only)

      4 - Turn off all headers and footers

      5 - Turn off Header A

      6 - Turn off Header B

      7 - Turn off Footer A

      8 - Turn off Footer B

Selection(s): 0
```

FIGURE 4.17: The Suppress Page Format screen. Selections made from this screen will be suppressed
on the page of the document where your cursor is positioned.

Note: You can choose option 3 to have the page number appear at the bottom center of the current page. This is useful, for example, for the first page of each chapter or the opening page of a report.

If you want to suppress headers, footers, and page numbers on more than one page—for example, in an entire appendix at the back of your document—you turn off the individual formatting through the separate formatting options. For example, to suppress page numbering, select option 0 on the Page Number Position option screen (Alt-F8 1 0). To suppress headers or footers, use option 0 (Discontinue) on the Header/Footer Specification screen (Alt-F8 6 0).

CENTERING PAGES TOP TO BOTTOM

KEY SEQUENCE

Alt-F8 **3 0** (or **Return**)

REVEAL CODES

[Center Pg]

WordPerfect allows you to have text automatically centered on a page top to bottom. This feature comes in handy for such documents as cover pages, title pages, and short letters (see Figure 4.18).

To center a page vertically (top to bottom), position the cursor at the beginning of the page, before any codes that you may have inserted. (Press Alt-F3 to see the formatting codes; then use the arrow keys to move the cursor to the beginning of these codes). Press Alt-F8 and choose option 3, Center Page Top to Bottom.

This command is often used to vertically center the title page of a report or paper. To use it, type the title information, insert a hard page break (by pressing Ctrl-Return), move the cursor to the beginning of the document by pressing Home, Home, and the ↑ key (if the title page is not the first page of the document, make sure that the cursor is at the very top of the page, right next to the [HPg] or [SPg] format code), press Alt-F8, and type **3**.

To delete page centering, press Alt-F3 to see the formatting codes. Position the cursor to the right of the Center Page code [Center Pg] and press Backspace.

INSERTING PAGE BREAKS

Although WordPerfect automatically breaks pages according to the number of lines per page (54 text lines is the default value, but you can change it by pressing Alt-F8, 4 to change the Page Length option), there may be times when you want to

```
Memo to:  All departments
From:  Business office

Effective immediately, the following procedures are necessary to
obtain work requisitions for hiring contract employees:


1.  Notify the business office 30 days before any new-hire
contract employee begins employment.

2.  Prepare a Cost Estimate worksheet showing projected
length of employment, renumeration, and estimated
termination date.

3.  Obtain signoffs from the relevant department managers in
whose departments the contract employee will be working (see
Form 23-799).

4.  Submit a completed Form 34-110 indicating that the
proposed employee is a bona fide contractor; attach local
business license if required.
```

FIGURE 4.18: Centering pages top to bottom (Alt-F8, 3). This feature is useful for positioning the text and headings of a letter vertically on the printed page.

begin a new page at a certain point, to insert a completely blank page, or to break a page so that certain lines of text—for example, items in a list—are kept on the same page.

WordPerfect allows you to specify a new page (insert a hard page break). It also has three features—Conditional End of Page, Block protection, and Widow/Orphan protection—that allow you to specify text that must be kept on the same page. Be aware when you use any of these methods that you may not always have exactly the same number of text lines per page throughout your document. Word-Perfect will break pages as required to keep the text you specified together.

Specifying a New Page

KEY SEQUENCE

To insert a hard page break:
   Ctrl-Return

REVEAL CODES

   [HPg]

To begin a new page at a particular point, position the cursor there and press Ctrl-Return. A double dashed line indicating the beginning of the new page will appear across your screen.

To delete a page break, position the cursor in the first column of the line just underneath the break and press Backspace. You can also press Alt-F3 to see the formatting codes and then backspace over the page break code, which is [HPg] (for hard page).

The page breaks that WordPerfect automatically inserts appear on your screen as a line of single dashes. The formatting code for those page breaks is [SPg] (for soft page). To change these page breaks, you must change the number of lines per page (see Chapter 2 for specific information about changing the page length).

Keeping Lines Together at the End of a Page

KEY SEQUENCE

   Alt-F8 9 *<number of lines to keep together>* **Return**

REVEAL CODES

[CndlEOP: <*number of lines*>]

WordPerfect also has a feature, Conditional End of Page, that allows you to specify that a certain number of lines be kept together on one page. You may want to use this feature when you have a list that should not be broken, or when you have a heading that you want to keep with at least a few lines following it. In addition, when you insert an illustration you may want to indicate a minimum number of text lines to appear below it.

When you use the Conditional End of Page feature, WordPerfect will keep the text lines that you specify together, even if it means breaking a page early and placing the lines on the next page.

To indicate text that should not be broken onto two pages, first move the cursor to the line just above the lines that you want to keep together. Press Alt-F8 and type **9** (for Conditional End of Page). Then enter the number of lines to keep together.

Block Protection

KEY SEQUENCE

Alt-F4 (highlight block) **Alt-F8** Block Protect? (Y/N) **Y**

REVEAL CODES

[BlockPro:On]
[BlockPro:Off]

As an alternate method of indicating lines that should be kept on the same page, you can also mark text as a block and then indicate that the block be kept together. This method is often faster, particularly if you use a mark-block macro such as the one presented in Chapter 3.

Figure 4.19 shows a situation in which block protection is useful. To keep the tabular rows and columns together, you mark the table as a block using Alt-F4 and the cursor keys and then press Alt-F8. The prompt

Protect Block? (Y/N) N

appears at the bottom of your screen. Enter **Y** to turn block protection on for the highlighted text. That text will then not be broken at the end of the page. Word-Perfect will break the page early if necessary in order to keep the specified block on the same page.

```
International Savings  9.625%     2.00          9.125%    2.00

Home Loan Savings      9.500%     3.00          8.875%    2.50
_
East Coast Federal     9.625%     2.50          9.375%    3.00


C:\WP\BOOK\CHAP4\FIG4-2                   Doc 1  Pg 1  Ln 15    Pos 5
[        ▲      ▲      ▲  ▲            ▲     ▲      ▲  ▲        ]
[BlockPro:On]International Savings[A]9[a].625%[TAB][A]2[a].00[TAB][A]9[a].125%[T
AB][A]2[a].00[HRt]
[HRt]
Home Loan Savings[TAB][A]9[a].500%[TAB][A]3[a].00[TAB][A]8[a].875%[TAB][A]2[a].5
0[HRt]
_[HRt]
East Coast Federal[TAB][A]9[a].625%[TAB][A]2[a].50[TAB][A]9[a].375%[TAB][A]3[a].
00[BlockPro:Off][HRt]
[HRt]
[HRt]
```

FIGURE 4.19: Using block protection to keep elements of a table together on the same page. The program will not break text within this block if it needs to begin a new page; instead, it will break the page before the block begins and create a short page.

To delete block protection, press Alt-F3 to see the formatting codes and delete either the [BlockPro:On] at the very beginning of the block of text you marked or the [BlockPro:Off] code at its very end.

Widows and Orphans

KEY SEQUENCE

To turn Widow/Orphan protection on:
  Alt-F8 A Y 0 (or **Return**)
To turn Widow/Orphan protection off:
  Alt-F8 A N 0 (or **Return**)

REVEAL CODES

  [W/O On]
  [W/O Off]

WordPerfect has a feature called Widow/Orphan protection that enables you to instruct the program not to leave a single line of text by itself as the last line of a page (widow) or as the first line of a page (orphan).

To turn on Widow/Orphan protection, move the cursor to the beginning of the document (you will probably want this protection on for the entire document). Then press Alt-F8 A (for Widow/Orphan) and enter **Y.**

To turn off Widow/Orphan protection, move to the beginning of your document and use the same key sequence as you used to turn Widow/Orphan protection on and type **N.** The default setting is off.

When you use Widow/Orphan protection (or any of the other page break methods presented in the preceding sections) you may not always get exactly the same number of text lines per page. WordPerfect will insert page breaks as required to keep the text you specified together on the same page.

SUMMARY

This chapter has presented a variety of techniques that are commonly used for formatting pages. For information about how to set margins and tabs, adjust the page length, and change from justified to ragged right margins, see Chapter 2, "Basic Formatting and Text Entry." For information about how you can use other page formats for tables of contents and lists, see Chapter 7, "Creating Notes, Lists, Indexes, and Citations." For information about creating and using parallel and newspaper-style columns as well as preparing page layouts for printed documents, see Chapter 8, "Page Composition: Working with Text Columns."

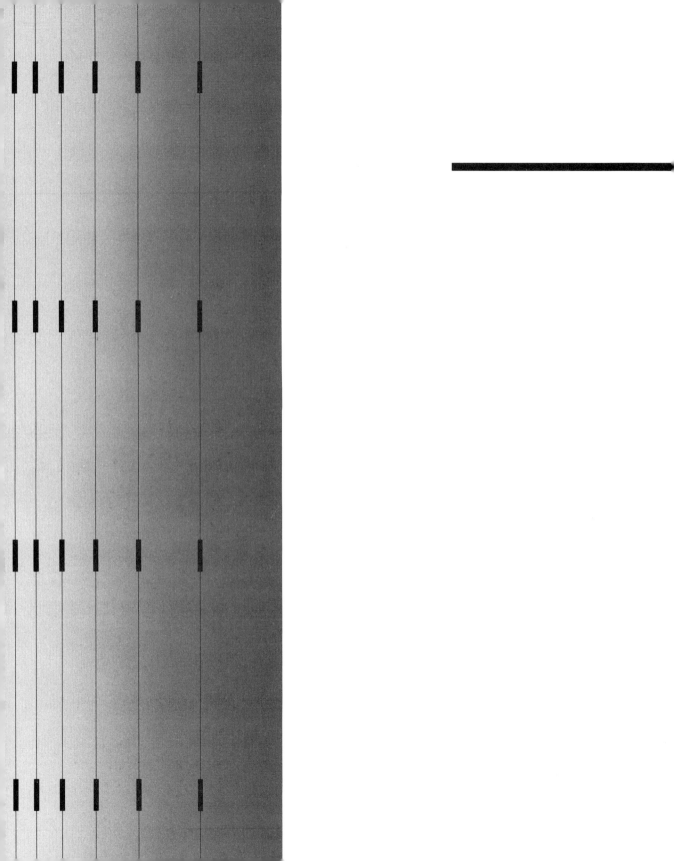

PRINTING

PRINTING

WordPerfect gives you a variety of methods with which to print your documents—so many, in fact, that they may be confusing at first. However, each of these printing methods is designed to handle a particular task and thus give you more flexibility with the program. You can, for example, print

- An entire document, either one that you have retrieved or one that you have not retrieved
- The current page on your screen
- Selected pages or a range of pages
- A marked block of text
- The contents of the current screen

This chapter details all of these methods by which you can print in Word-Perfect and explains the print options that are available to you. These options include changing printers (that are already installed), setting the number of copies, setting the binding width, and changing print fonts (including using proportional spacing).

For information about how to print to disk to create an ASCII file, see Chapter 15. For information about how to install new printers and to permanently set up new default printing options, see Chapter 16.

PRINTING METHODS—AN OVERVIEW

WordPerfect offers a variety of ways to print. We will examine each of these methods before we discuss the printer control and print options available to you. Table 5.1 summarizes WordPerfect's printing methods.

Regardless of the printing method you choose, WordPerfect performs all of its printing in the background, allowing you to return to editing as soon as you have issued the appropriate printing command. Because all printing methods support background printing, you never need to wait until a print job is finished before you return to WordPerfect to create a new document or edit an existing one.

TO PRINT	KEY SEQUENCE
From the Printer Control screen	**Shift-F7 4 P** <*file name*> **Return**
A range of pages	**Shift-F7 4 P** <*file name*> <*page numbers to print separated by commas, range of page numbers to print separated by hyphens*> **Return**
A document on the List Files screen	**F5 Return** (highlight document) **4**
A group of documents on the List Files screen	**F5 Return** (highlight each List document) * (to mark it) **4 Y**
The entire document on the screen	**Shift-F7 1**
The page on the screen	**Shift-F7 2**
The text on the screen	**Shift-PrtSc**
A block of text	**Alt-F4** (highlight block) **Shift-F7 Y Alt-F4**

TABLE 5.1: WordPerfect's Printing Methods

Quick Draft Printing (Printing an Unsaved Document)

WordPerfect allows you to print the document that is currently in RAM—the document you have just been working on—even if you have not saved it. You can print the entire document or only the current page. You might want, for example, to try out a special printing effect or simply print a quick note that you do not want to save on a disk. You can print only one copy at a time using this method.

To print the document currently in memory, Press Shift-F7. The following menu appears at the bottom of the screen:

1 Full Text; 2 Page; 3 Options; 4 Printer Control; 5 Type-thru; 6 Preview: 0

Type **1** to print the entire document or **2** to print the current page only. You can suspend printing while your document is printing by pressing Shift-F7 and typing **4** to reach the Printer Control screen; then type **S** to execute the Stop Printing option. The technique for aborting printing is discussed in more detail later in this chapter.

By using option 3 on the Print menu before you make your printout, you can change the printer, the number of copies, or the binding width for the document printed. You can also obtain an on-screen preview of the printed document by selecting option 6 from this menu (see Chapter 4 for more information about using the Print Preview feature).

When you print either the full text or the current page of the document in memory, WordPerfect creates a temporary copy of the file in RAM or, if there is insufficient free memory, on the current disk. If you are printing the full text of a particularly long document, you may receive the disk-full error message when you press Shift-F7 and type **2**. This occurs whenever the current disk does not have enough free space to accommodate the temporary copy of the file in RAM. In such a case, you will have to use one of the two methods for printing a document that has been saved on disk (see "Printing All or Part of a Saved Document" later in this chapter).

Using WordPerfect Like a Typewriter

You can also use WordPerfect like a typewriter by selecting the Type-thru option (number 5) from the Print menu. This feature is most useful when you need to print an envelope or mailing label that you do not want to save. When you use Type-thru printing, you have the option of having either each character or each line echoed to the printer as you type it.

You select these two options from the menu that appears when you press Shift-F7 and type **5**:

Type-thru printing: 1 by line; 2 by character: 0

Once you have selected either line-by-line or character-by-character Type-thru printing, you will see the screen shown in Figure 5.1.

Most of the time you will find it more convenient to print line by line rather than character by character. This is because when you print character by character, you cannot correct any typing mistakes. Also, your printer may not support WordPerfect's character-by-character Type-thru printing.

When you print line by line, the line of text that you enter is not printed until you press Return. This gives you time to catch any typing errors on the line and correct them before you press Return to send the text to the printer.

When you use WordPerfect's Type-thru printing, you will find that text editing is not handled the same way it is during normal document creation and editing. With the Type-thru feature, the program is always in Typeover mode, and it cannot be put into Insert mode. Also, many cursor movements and deletion commands, such as Ctrl-← and Ctrl-→ to move a word at a time and Ctrl-Backspace to delete a word, will not work. When you are editing a line of text in Type-thru mode, the only ways to move the cursor are by using the → and ← keys, and the only ways to delete text are by using the Del and Backspace keys.

To position the print head horizontally on the paper before you print, you can use either the space bar or the → key. If your printer will not advance the print head when you press the → key in character-by-character mode, use the space bar. Likewise, use the space bar when you are in line-by-line mode.

```
This line will be printed as soon as I press Return._




Line Type-thru Printing

Function Key        Action

Move                Retrieve the previous line for editing
Print Format        Do a printer command
Enter               Print the line
Exit/Cancel         Exit without printing







                                                          Pos 53
```

FIGURE 5.1: The Line Type-thru screen. By using this screen, you can make WordPerfect operate much like a typewriter. Note, however, that each line that you type is printed only when you press Return, which allows you to correct typing errors before you send the line to the printer. On some printers, you can also have each character printed as you type.

To position the print head vertically on the paper, press the ↓ key to advance the paper up to the line where you want the printing to start. If you are using line-by-line Type-thru printing, then type the line as you want it and press Return to have it printed. To end Type-thru printing and return to the regular document editing window, you press either F7 (Exit) or F1 (Cancel).

Printing All or Part of a Saved Document

In addition to being able to print a document in memory, WordPerfect gives you two methods for printing a document that has already been saved: You can use the Print option on the List Files menu (F5 Return 4), or you can use the Print a document option on the Printer Control screen (Shift-F7 4 P). When you use either of these methods, remember that WordPerfect will print the document as it was last saved on the disk. If you have the document you want to print in RAM and have made changes to it that have not been saved, these will not be reflected in the printout unless you save the document again (by pressing F10 and Return) before using either of these printing commands.

PRINTING FROM THE LIST FILES SCREEN

To print the entire document, you can print either from the List Files screen or from the Printer Control screen. However, you will generally find using the List Files screen much easier because you do not need to type the file name, and the List Files screen lets you more quickly add files to the queue when you want to print a group of files in the same directory.

To print a document located in the current directory or on the active data disk, you press F5 (the List Files key). Then move the cursor highlight to the name of the file that you want to print and type **4** to select the Print option. As soon as you select this option, you may (by pressing F1) return to creating or editing another document.

To print more than one file, you can mark each file name listed by moving the cursor highlight to it and typing * (an asterisk). To mark the file, WordPerfect places an * right after the byte count in the file listing. To mark all files for printing, press Home-PrtSc. After you have marked all of the files you want printed in this manner, type **4** to select the Print option. You will receive the message

Print Marked Files? (Y/N) N

You type **Y** to have WordPerfect place the marked files in its print queue (in the order in which they were marked) and begin printing the first one.

If you need to stop the printing, delete one of the files in the queue, or advance one of the files to the head of the queue, you must enter a command from the Printer Control screen. To access this screen, you press Shift-F7 and type **4** to select the Printer Control option. See the following section for a discussion of how to accomplish these tasks using the options listed on this menu.

PRINTING FROM THE PRINTER CONTROL SCREEN

If you want to print only a part of a document, you must print it from the Printer Control screen. In addition to allowing you to print just part of a document, this method gives you greater control over printing than does the others. Specifically, this screen contains options to

- Stop (S) and resume (G) printing.
- Cancel a specific print job or all jobs in the queue (C).
- Rush a specific print job to the top of the queue (R).
- Display all of the files that you have placed in the print queue (D).
- Change the printer to be used, number of copies, or binding width for all jobs in the queue from the Select Print Options menu (1).
- Display all of the printers that have been installed and the eight fonts WordPerfect supports (2).

- Install new printers for use with WordPerfect (3).

To reach the Printer Control screen, you select option 4 from the Print menu (accessed by pressing Shift-F7). Figure 5.2 shows this screen.

To print a document from this screen, you select the Print a Document option by typing **P.** You will then receive the prompt

Document name:

Here you type the name of the document you wish to print. If the document is not in the current directory, enter its full path name. If it is the current directory, you need not include the drive and directory specifications as part of the name.

If you misspell the name of the file, or if the file name you enter is not in the directory that you specified, you will receive the message "ERROR: File not found" when you press Return. If you cannot determine the source of the error and need to refer to a directory listing, you must press F1 or Esc to exit the Printer Control screen and then press F5. (Once you locate the file name, you can print the file directly from the List Files screen unless you want to print only a part of it.)

After you enter a valid file name and press Return, you receive the prompt

Page(s): All

```
Printer Control
                                C - Cancel Print Job(s)
1 - Select Print Options        D - Display All Print Jobs
2 - Display Printers and Fonts  G - "Go" (Resume Printing)
3 - Select Printers             P - Print a Document
                                R - Rush Print Job
Selection: 0                    S - Stop Printing


Current Job

Job Number: n/a                 Page Number:  n/a
Job Status: n/a                 Current Copy: n/a
Message:     The print queue is empty

Job List

Job  Document          Destination        Forms and Print Options




Additional jobs not shown: 0
```

FIGURE 5.2: The Printer Control screen. This screen allows you to select printers as well as to control the printing process.

To print the entire document, all you have to do is press Return. However, if you want to print only a range of pages, you must indicate this by entering the numbers of the first and last pages to be printed separated by a hyphen. For example, if you want to print only pages 48 through 50, you indicate this by typing **48-50** in place of the word *All* in the Page(s): prompt.

In Version 4.2 of WordPerfect, you can specify individual, discontinous pages as well as ranges of pages to be printed. For example, you can print just pages 6, 9, and 21 to 24 from a document by entering **6,9,21-24** in response to the Page(s): prompt. See "Printing through the Printer Control Screen" later in this chapter for more information about specifying individual and ranges of pages to be printed.

Selecting an Alternate Printer

Before you print a document from the Printer Control screen, you can use option 1 on the Printer Control menu to display the Print Options menu. From this menu, you select the first option (Printer Number) to change the printer to be used. WordPerfect allows you to choose from among six different printer numbers. Each printer number represents a printer definition that determines either the kind of printer or the type of font to be used.

Fonts and Printer Types

For each printer definition, WordPerfect gives you a choice of eight different fonts. Depending upon the printer type, a font can represent a typeface such as Courier Bold, Courier Light, or Courier Italics; a different type size, such as 8, 12, 24, or 36 points, in the same type style; or the kind of spacing used, such as proportional spacing or fixed-pitch (for instance, 10, 12, or 15 pitch) spacing. What fonts are available for a particular printer and what they do depend greatly upon the type of printer.

With dot-matrix printers the font selected can determine the type size (compressed, regular, or expanded), the typeface (draft, near letter quality, or a downloaded font), or the type style (roman, italic, and so on) as well as the type of spacing (fixed versus proportional spacing).

With impact letter-quality printers that use daisy wheels or thimbles, the font chosen can determine the typeface (Gothic, Courier, and so on), the type style (roman, italics, and so on), and the type of spacing (fixed versus proportional). However, with this type of printer, a change in font necessitates a change in the printing element.

With laser printers, the font used can determine the typeface (Times Roman, Helvetica, Gothic, and so on), the type style (roman, italics, and so on), the print weight (regular or medium, light or bold), the type size (10, 12, 18, or 30 points, for instance), and the type of spacing (fixed-pitch or proportional spacing). Most laser printers, such as the HP LaserJet Plus, require you to use either a special cartridge or downloaded font to effect a font change. (Downloaded fonts are often referred to as *soft fonts* because they come on a disk and their printer codes must be copied to the memory of the laser printer before they can be used.)

SWITCHING FROM A DRAFT TO A LETTER-QUALITY PRINTER

By using the Printer Number option, you can switch from your draft printer to your letter-quality printer when you are ready to obtain a final printout. Usually, when you have both a draft and a letter-quality printer, the draft printer is installed as printer 1, the default printer, and the letter quality printer is installed as printer 2 because it is used less frequently. To change to the letter-quality printer (either an impact or laser printer), you need only change the printer number from 1 to 2 before printing.

When you select this first option on the Printer Control screen, you will see the menu options shown in Figure 5.3. To change the printer, you type **1** to select the Printer Number option and then enter the number of the printer. If you have more than one letter-quality printer attached to your system (commonly the case when WordPerfect is run in a network), the printer you wish to use may not be number 2.

VERIFYING A PRINTER'S NUMBER

If you are ever uncertain about the number assigned to a particular printer or whether the printer has been installed to work with WordPerfect, you can check this by selecting option 2, Display Printer and Fonts, on the Printer Control screen (Shift-F7). When you select this option, WordPerfect displays the name and type of each of the six printers it supports in numerical order (three to a screen display).

Under the line that contains the printer number, name, and type (continuous, hand fed, or sheet fed), you will see descriptions of each of the eight type fonts that WordPerfect supports for that particular printer definition—see Figure 5.4, which shows the first screen that appears when you select the Display Printers and Fonts option. If you have not installed six printers (the maximum) for use with WordPerfect, you will notice that any printer with a number that you have not yet assigned is shown either as a standard printer or a DOS text printer. The DOS text printer is usually printer 6 unless you change it. This printer prints a file to the disk.

```
Select Print Options

    1 - Printer Number              3

    2 - Number of Copies            1

    3 - Binding Width (1/10 in.)    0




















Selection: 0
```

FIGURE 5.3: The Select Print Options screen. This screen allows you to indicate which printer you want to use and to specify the number of copies to be printed and the binding width (the inside margin).

Installing a New Printer

If the printer you wish to use is not listed on either of the two screens of printers, or if you are installing WordPerfect for the first time, you can install the printer by pressing Shift-F7, typing **4** to get to the Printer Control screen, and selecting option 3, Select Printers. When you select this option, you will see a screen similar to the one shown in Figure 5.5. This screen lists all of the printers with definitions currently in the file WPRINTER.FIL and fonts currently in the WPFONT.FIL file. For a new number to be assigned to a printer, the printer must be listed on this screen.

To add a new printer definition to this file, you must have a copy of the Word-Perfect Printer disk available (Version 4.2 has two Printer disks, Printer 1 and Printer 2). First press the ↓ key until the printer number you wish to assign to the new printer definition appears after the word *Printer* at the bottom of this screen. Then press the PgDn key to assign a new printer definition.

WordPerfect will inform you if it cannot find the printer definition files and will tell you to place a copy of the WordPerfect Printer disk in your disk drive. After you have done so, type the letter of the drive (**A** or **B**) to have the program read the printer definitions from the disk. These printer definition files are listed in alphabetical order. Scroll the list up with the PgDn key until you locate the name of your

```
 1:  Standard Printer          Continuous

            1 ASCII/Line Ptr        2 ASCII/Line Ptr
            3 ASCII/Line Ptr        4 ASCII/Line Ptr
            5 ASCII/Line Ptr        6 ASCII/Line Ptr
            7 ASCII/Line Ptr        8 IBM Graphics

 2:  IBM Graphics Printer      Continuous

            1 IBM Graphics          2 IBM Graphics
            3 IBM Graphics          4 IBM Graphics
            5 IBM Graphics          6 IBM Graphics
            7 IBM Graphics          8 Dot Matrix 1/60

 3:  Epson FX                  Continuous

            1 Epson FX&Type3        2 Dot Matrix 1/60
            3 Epson FX NorPS        4 Epson FX ItaPS
            5 Epson FX&Type3        6 Epson FX&Type3
            7 Epson FX&Type3        8 Epson FX&Type3




 Press any key to continue_
```

FIGURE 5.4: The first screen that appears when you select the Display Printers and Fonts option (2) on the Printer Control screen. You can install up to six printers to use with WordPerfect.

```
 Printer Definitions in C:\WP\WPRINTER.FIL

      1  Standard Printer         2  DOS Text Printer
      3  Epson FX












                                 PgDn for Additional Printer Definitions
                                 Exit when Done
      Printer 1                  Cancel to Ignore Changes
      Using Definition: 3        Arrow Keys to Change Printer Number
```

FIGURE 5.5: The Printer Definitions screen accessed by selecting option 3, Select Printers, on the Printer Control screen.

printer and the model with characteristics closest to those of the printer you are using. Then enter its number and press Return.

You will then be prompted to enter the type and number of the printer port. The default value is 0, for LPT1, the first parallel printer port. If the printer whose definition you just chose is connected to another parallel port, select either LPT2 or LPT3. If the printer has a serial interface, choose the appropriate number from the four COM ports listed.

When defining a printer that uses a serial interface, you must also indicate the baud rate, parity, stop bits, and character length. All of these settings should be in your printer manual. If you cannot find them, try running the printer with the baud rate set to 9600, the parity set to none, the number of stop bits set to 1, and the character length set to 8. If these settings do not work, experiment with various changes in the baud-rate and parity values before trying alternate stop-bit and character-length values.

After you finish entering these values or immediately after you specify a port if you selected a line printer (LPT1, LPT2, or LPT3), you will be prompted to select the type of paper feed for the printer. The three selections are 1 for a continuous-feed printer, 2 for a hand-fed (single-sheet printing) printer, and 3 for a sheet-fed printer. If your printer has a sheet feeder and you select 3, you will be presented with the options shown in Figure 5.6. These include the number of extra lines required between pages to eject pages properly, the column position of the left edge of the paper, the number of bins, and the sheet feeder type.

If your sheet feeder documentation does not include information regarding the number of lines between pages and where the page platen is positioned on the page, accept the default settings of 24 lines and column position 26. If, after test printing a document, these settings do not work for your feeder, return to this option and experiment with new values.

> *Note:* If you are using one of the printer definitions for the HP LaserJet Plus or LaserJet Series II, select option 1 for continuous feed, even though this printer has a sheet feeder (notice in Figure 5.6 that the HP LaserJet Plus is not listed). If you use either type 17 (HP LaserJet) or 19 (HP LaserJet 500 +), printing will be shifted too far to the right on the page. For additional information about using LaserJet printers, see Appendix C.

After you have indicated the type of paper feed, WordPerfect copies the completed definition to the WPRINTER.FIL file and the fonts associated it with it to the WPFONT.FIL file, and it assigns to the printer definition the printer number that was displayed when you chose the printer definition. You can then select option 2, Display Printers and Fonts, to view the type fonts that you can use with the printer or option 1, the Select Print Options, to use the newly installed printer to print your document.

> *Note:* When installing new printers in Version 4.2, try to find the printer definition on the Printer 1 disk before you look on the Printer 2 disk. The Printer 1

disk has 144 printer definitions, including one for the Laserwriter printer. If you do not find the printer you want on this first disk, wait until the red light goes out on the disk drive and then replace the Printer 1 disk with the Printer 2 disk and press the PgDn key again. Note that many of the 96 printer definitions on the Printer 2 disk are listed as limited-support printers. This means that their definitions were written from printer manuals, and that Word-Perfect Corporation does not have the printers in house and therefore offers only limited phone support for them.

ASSIGNING PRINTER NUMBERS TO DEFINITIONS

You can use the Select Printers option (3) on the Printer Control screen to copy as many printer definition files from your Printer 1 and 2 disks to your WPRINTER.FIL file as you have room for on your WordPerfect System disk, even though you can have only six different definitions installed at a time. (If you are using WordPerfect on a hard disk, you are restricted only by the amount of free space in the WordPerfect directory.) For instance, if you are

```
Sheet Feeder Information
      Number of Extra Lines Between Pages (12 LPI):  1
      Column Position of Left Edge of Paper (10 Pitch):  26
      Number of Sheet Feeder Bins (1-7):  1

Sheet Feeder Type

    1 NEC 3550 Single/Dual            2 NEC 3515/5515/7715 Single/Dual
    3 Rutishauser Single Bin          4 Rutishauser Dual Bin
    5 Diablo (Ziyad) Single/Dual      6 Qume Single Bin
    7 Brother HR-15/HR-25/HR-35       8 NEC 3500R/10/20/30 Single/Dual
    9 Xerox 2700 Laser               10 IBM 5218 Dual Bin/Envelope Feed
   11 Seitz Tek ST-125               12 Pagemate II/III
   13 Pagemate I                     14 BDT LetterMate I,II,III
   15 Epson LQ-1500 Single/Dual      16 Canon A1
   17 HP LaserJet                    18 Ziyad PaperJet 400
   19 HP LaserJet 500+               20 IBM Pageprinter 3812
   21 BDT MF-850 3 bin Laser Feeder  22 BDT MF-830 6 bin Laser Feeder
   23 BDT MF-830 6 bin La (continued) 24 Diablo D80IF




Selection: 1          (Use the PRINTER program to define a new sheet feeder)
```

FIGURE 5.6: Selecting a sheet feeder as part of a printer definition file. When setting up a printer definition, you need to indicate the number of lines to add between pages (to eject the paper properly), the column position at which the left edge of the paper is positioned, the number of bins the printer has, and the type of feeder the printer uses. If your sheet feeder is not listed among those on this screen, you can use the PRINTER program to define and add its type to this list (see the section "Creating and Modifying Printer Definitions" later in this chapter).

using an HP LaserJet Plus with WordPerfect, you can choose from more than a dozen printer definitions for just this one printer. Depending upon the amount and type of cartridges and soft fonts you own, you can easily need to use more than six printer numbers.

In such a situation, you can use the Select Printers option to reassign one of the printer numbers to the definitions that have already been copied from the Printer 1 or 2 disk. To do this, you press Shift-F7 and type **4** to get to the Printer Control screen. From there, you type **3** to get to the Printer Definitions screen.

From this screen, select the printer number that you wish to use by pressing the → or ← key (the → key increases the number and the ← decreases it). Then type the number of the printer definition you wish to use as it is listed at the top of this screen. When you press Return, you will then have to indicate the port and the type of forms to be used. If you select one of the serial ports (COM1 through COM2), you will also have to define the baud rate, parity, number of stop bits, and character length as well as the form type. As soon as you finish defining these parameters and the type of paper feed, you will be returned to the Printer Definitions screen. From there you press F7 (Exit) to save the new printer-number definition and to return to the Printer Control screen.

CONTROLLING THE PRINT QUEUE

The letter options C through S in the column at the right of the Printer Control screen are used to control documents once they have been sent to the print queue. Any time you send a file to the printer, regardless of the printing method used, WordPerfect gives it a print-job number and lists it in the job list on the Printer Control screen. Any additional files you specify for printing are added to the list in the order in which you specified them.

If you specify that a document is to be printed from memory (from either document window 1 or 2), WordPerfect indicates this by displaying (Screen) in the Document column in place of the document's file name. If you specify that a document is to be printed from the disk, the program displays the document's full file name (including the path) in the Document column.

Because the Printer Control screen has room to display only the top three print jobs in the queue, this screen includes the indicator

Additional jobs not shown: 0

at the bottom. If the number after the colon is other than zero, then there are other print jobs not currently visible on the screen. To display these, you type **D** to select the Display All Print Jobs option.

The first document listed in the job list is always the one that is currently being printed. The Printer Control screen lists such information as the job number, document name, and type of form used by this document under the Job List heading, and it gives you information about the current job's progress and status beneath the Current Job heading. From the current job information, you can find out the number of the page and the copy currently being printed. This information can help you gauge when the current document will finish printing and when the next copy of it or the next document in the queue will begin printing.

To halt a printing operation to adjust the paper or ribbon, for example, you type **S** to select the Stop Printing option. Whenever you use this command, the Job Status listing will show

Waiting for a "GO"

and the Message listing will read

Fix printer—Reset top of form—Press "G" to continue

As soon as you fix the problem and type **G** to restart the printing, the Job Status listing will again display "Printing," and the Message area will display "None."

If you ever want to speed up the printing of a document by sending it to the top of the queue, you use the Rush Print Job command. When you select this option by typing **R**, you are prompted as follows:

Rush which job?

WordPerfect displays the last job number as the suggested one to send to the top of the queue. If you wish to rush a different print job, you type its number over the number that is currently displayed. As soon as you press Return, you receive a second prompt:

Interrupt Current Job? (Y/N) N

If you wish to print your rush job right away, you type **Y**. WordPerfect will respond by suspending the printing of the current document and will begin printing your rush job. As soon as the rush job is finished, WordPerfect will return to the document whose printing was suspended and finish it before printing any other jobs in the queue. If you just press Return, the program will not begin printing your rush job until after it has finished printing the job that was current when you selected the R command.

To take a job out the queue, you use the Cancel Print Job(s) option. When you type **C**, the prompt

Cancel which job? (* = All Jobs)

appears under the Selection heading. If you want to cancel only a single print job, you just enter its number and press Return. If you want to cancel all of the jobs in the queue (including the current one), you type ***.** You must then also type **Y** to confirm this cancellation in response to the prompt

Cancel all print jobs? (Y/N) N

Be careful not to press Return out of habit after you type * for this would answer no to the "Cancel all print jobs?" prompt. After you type **Y**, you may see this message appear very briefly beneath the Selection heading:

Press ENTER if printer does not respond

If the current job continues to print even after you have cancelled all of the print jobs in the queue, pressing the Return key as indicated by this message usually causes it to stop immediately.

ALT-I: A MACRO TO IMMEDIATELY INTERRUPT PRINTING

Unlike other programs that you may have used that require only two keystrokes, such as Ctrl-Break, to interrupt or suspend printing, WordPerfect requires four keystrokes (Shift, F7, 4, and S) to halt printing. To speed up this process and, perhaps, make the keystrokes easier to remember (especially when you are panicking over a paper jam), you can create a macro called Alt-I (for Interrupt printing).

Begin macro	Macro name	Keystrokes	End macro
Ctrl-F10	**Alt-I**	**Shift-F7 4 S**	**Ctrl-F10**

To use this macro, you must first be in one of the document windows. If you are at the List Files screen, you must press F1 before you use this macro. To stop the printing, press Alt-I. This takes you immediately to the Printer Control screen and enters an S to stop the printing. Remember that you must type **G** from this screen when you want to restart printing.

TESTING YOUR PRINTERS

Before you print many documents with WordPerfect, you may want to test your printer's capabilities with the PRINTER.TST and PRINTER2.TST files on the Learning disk. These allow you to see whether your printer is capable of printing such effects as boldface, italics, underlining, overstrike, superscripts and subscripts, double underlining, tab aligning, column centering, redlining, various pitches, and various line drawing features.

To test your printer, place a copy of your WordPerfect Learning disk in one of your floppy disk drives (drive A or B) and access the printer control screen by pressing Shift-F7 and typing **4**. Then type **P** and enter **PRINTER.TST** prefaced by the appropriate drive letter. For example, if you placed the Learning disk in drive A, you enter

A:PRINTER.TST

as the file to print. Then press Return to accept the default selection (All).

If you have installed more than one printer, you will want to reprint this file using each printer attached to your system. To do this, change the printer number temporarily by typing **1** twice followed by the number of the printer you wish to test. Then press Return and reprint the PRINTER.TST file.

After you have printed the contents of PRINTER.TST, you may want to print the file named PRINTER2.TST. This file contains two sections: one that prints each of the available fonts in various pitches such as 10, 12, 15, and 13, and one that prints sample boxes using various fonts that mix single and double lines. By printing the PRINTER2.TST file, you can obtain a sample of all of the fonts available for the printer and ascertain whether the printer supports WordPerfect's line and box drawing capabilities.

PRODUCING SPECIAL PRINTING EFFECTS

Most of the time you can change pitches and font numbers in your text to produce print enhancements in addition to the more common boldfaced, underlined, and super- and subscripted text. For instance, if you are using the definition for an Epson FX printer, Font 3 will produce proportionally spaced print. By entering font changes in the text, you can exert a great deal of control over the final printed output.

However, if the definition for your printer does not include a font that produces an effect that you know your printer is capable of, you can still produce the effect in the document. You can do this by using the Insert Printer Command on the Print Format screen to enter the appropriate printer code in the document.

Changing Pitches and Fonts in a Document

To change the font in effect, you press Ctrl-F8 (Print Format) and select option 1. This allows you to set both a new pitch and a new font. Remember that pitch refers to the number of characters in 1 inch of a line of text. To set pitch, you enter the number of characters per inch.

Fonts are determined by the printer definition assigned to the printer number you are using. Remember that only eight fonts are available for each printer definition. You can always check to see which fonts are available for a particular printer number by pressing Shift-F7 and typing **4** and then **2**. When setting the font (Ctrl-F8 1), you enter the number between 1 and 8 that represents the typeface or type style that you wish to use.

PROPORTIONAL SPACING IN A DOCUMENT

In proportional spacing, each character is spaced according to its width. For example, an *m* takes up more space than an *i*. Your printer may be capable of proportional spacing. To find out, you can run the PS.TST file located on the Learning disk. Press Shift-F7 and type **4** (Printer Control) and **P**. Then enter the file name **PS.TST** and press Return to print all of the file. (If the Learning disk is in a drive other than the default drive, be sure to include it as part of the file name—for instance, A:PS.TST.)

To indicate proportional spacing, you enter the pitch number followed by an asterisk and the font number. For example, 13*,3 indicates a proportionally spaced pitch and font, and 13,2 indicates nonproportional spacing. (The font number of the proportionally spaced font is usually 3.) To see which fonts are defined for proportional spacing, press Shift-F7, select option 4 (Printer Control), and then select option 2. A screen similar to the one shown in Figure 5.4 appears (it will be defined for the printer or printers you are using). The letters *PS* indicate proportional spacing for dot-matrix and daisy-wheel printers. If you are using a laser printer such as the HP LaserJet, LaserJet Plus, or LaserJet Series II, the PS code will not appear as part of the font description. To determine whether a particular font is proportionally spaced, you must consult the documentation that accompanied your cartridge or soft-font set.

If you are using a daisy-wheel printer, you will need to change the element (either a print wheel or thimble) to get proportional spacing. If your entire document is to be printed in a proportionally spaced font, you should make this change before you send the document to the printer, first entering the proper font-change code at the beginning of the text.

If you mix fixed and proportionally spaced fonts in a single document, WordPerfect automatically stops printing when it reaches the font-change code that requires you to change the element. It beeps to alert you that printing has been halted. After you replace the element with the one associated with the proportionally spaced font called for, you must select the Go option from the Printer Control screen (Shift-F7 4 G) to restart printing. You will have to repeat this procedure of halting the printer and switching elements if the document returns to fixed spacing or use a new font that calls for either a different type style (such as italics) or typeface (such as Gothic).

If you are using a dot-matrix or laser printer, you will need to insert the appropriate cartridge or to download the appropriate font to get proportional spacing.

ENTERING PRINTER CODES IN A DOCUMENT

If the printer definition supplied by WordPerfect does not support a printing enhancement you wish to use, you can enter the appropriate Escape or Control codes directly in the text. To enter a printer code in your document, you press Ctrl-F8 (Print Format) and type **A** to select the Insert Printer Command option.

At the Cmnd: prompt, you enter the appropriate printer code in ASCII code. To find the appropriate code, you must consult your printer manual. Most printer codes are initiated by the ASCII code for the Escape key. Thus, they are referred to as *Escape sequences.*

Printer manuals often list Escape sequences in three different ways: in ASCII, decimal, and hexidecimal code. For example, the following alternative codes for turning near-letter-quality mode on and off might be listed in a dot-matrix printer manual:

> **ASCII—ESC** x *n*
> **DEC.—27 120** *n*
> **HEX.—1B 78** *n*

In this example, you substitute either 1 or 0 for *n* in the code. Entering **1** turns on near-letter-quality mode, and entering **0** turns it off. If you were to use Word-Perfect's Printer Command to turn on near-letter-quality mode, you would have to mix the ASCII and decimal code forms.

The rule for when to use the ASCII code form and when to use the decimal code form is simple: Any character whose ASCII code number is less than 32 or greater than 126 must be entered in decimal form. Any character whose ASCII code number is between 32 and 126, inclusive, can be entered in either ASCII or decimal form. You can use the ASCII code chart in Appendix A of this book to look up the ASCII code numbers of the characters you want to use.

When you enter an ASCII code in decimal form in the text of your document, you must enclose the decimal number in a pair of angle brackets. For instance, in the previous example, the Escape sequence to turn on near-letter-quality mode is ESCx1. Appendix A shows that the ASCII decimal code for ESC is 27, that for x is 120, and that for 1 is 49. Because 27 is less than 32, you must enter it in angle brackets as <27>. Because both x and 1 are between 32 and 126, you can enter them as ASCII characters (that is, exactly as you would enter them into the text of any document). Thus, you would enter the following Escape sequence after the Cmnd: prompt:

> **Cmnd: <27>x1**

It is important to note that the case of letter characters (such as x in this example) entered in a printer Escape sequence is crucial. The printer command here would not work if you entered X (uppercase) in place of x (lowercase). This is because X has the ASCII code number 088, and x has the ASCII code number 120.

A printer code entered as an ASCII code will not be visible in the text of your document. To verify that it has been entered correctly, you must access the Reveal Codes window by pressing Alt-F3. The format code for sending a printer command is [Cmnd:]. The code you entered will appear after the colon and before the last square bracket. For example, the Escape sequence to turn on near-letter-quality mode would appear in the Reveal Codes window, as

[Cmnd: <27>x1]

You can also use the printer command feature to have WordPerfect read in the file of a program that downloads fonts into the printer's memory (a technique used by some dot-matrix printers as well as by laser printers). If you have created a BASIC program that sends the Escape sequences required to load a soft font, you can have WordPerfect send the font to the printer when WordPerfect encounters the appropriate [Cmnd:] code.

To do this, you must press Ctrl-F8 and type **A** as you do when defining any other printer command. However, instead of entering ASCII codes after the Cmnd: prompt, you press Shift-F10 (Retrieve) and type the complete name of the program file for downloading the fonts. Make sure that you include the drive letter and path as part of the file name if the file is not located on the same disk or directory as the document where you enter this special printer code. After you enter the name of the program file, press Return twice. In the Reveal Codes window (Alt-F3), you will see <126> preceding the file name that you entered.

This special code tells WordPerfect to retrieve the program file when you print the document. Once the fonts contained in this program file are downloaded, your printer will be able to produce them in the rest of the document whenever it encounters [Font Change:] codes that use them.

Note: You must enter the Retrieve File code <126> by pressing Shift-F10 after the Cmnd: prompt. You cannot enter it by typing the number 126 surrounded by angle brackets.

To locate special printer codes that you have entered into the text of your document, you can use the Search feature (using either forward or backward search, as required). Press F2 and then press Ctrl-F8 and type **7** to enter [Cmnd:] as the search string. Printer command format codes can be deleted by positioning the cursor in the Reveal Codes window either immediately before the [Cmnd:] code or immediately after it and then pressing either the Del or Backspace key.

CREATING AND MODIFYING PRINTER DEFINITIONS

A wide variety of printers and special fonts can be used with WordPerfect simply by copying their definitions from the Printer 1 or Printer 2 disk and assigning them printer numbers (see "Installing a New Printer" earlier in this chapter). However, if you are technically inclined, you can create your own definitions for printers or fonts that are not listed on either Printer disk. To do this, you use a special utility program called PRINTER.EXE. If you are using Version 4.1 of WordPerfect, this program is located on your Learning disk. If you are using Version 4.2, you will find it on your Printer 2 disk.

In Version 4.1, the documentation for this program is on the Learning disk in a file called PRINTER.MAN. To obtain a hard copy of this 36-page printer manual, print it as you would any other WordPerfect document. In Version 4.2, the documentation for this utility progam can be found in the typeset manual entitled "Defining a Printer Driver."

This manual tells you how to use the WordPerfect PRINTER program, which allows you to change and add to WordPerfect's printer definitions and character tables. Printer definitions are a table of codes WordPerfect uses to implement right justification, underlining, super- and subscripts, and so forth for specific printers. Character tables contain information about character widths and positioning information for proportional spacing. They translate characters from the screen into strings to be sent to the printer.

Whenever you use the PRINTER program to configure a new printer or font for use with WordPerfect, be sure that you work with copies, not originals, of your WPRINTER.FIL and WPFONT.FIL files. Creating a new printer definition is difficult work at best, and it is very easy to make changes that can render one of your printer definitions useless. If you do your work on a copy, you will still be able to print documents with existing definitions until you get all of the bugs out of your new definition.

If you are using WordPerfect on a floppy disk system, copy both the WPRINTER.FIL and FONT.FIL files from your System disk; if you are using the program on a hard disk, copy both files from your WordPerfect program directory (\WP) onto a formatted disk. Then copy the PRINTER.EXE program. If you are using Version 4.2, also copy the PRHELP.EXE file (found on your Printer 2 disk) to this disk. Now make the drive containing this floppy disk (A or B) current and while in DOS enter the startup command

PRINTER

As soon as the program is loaded into memory, you will see the main menu of the Printer Definition program shown in Figure 5.7. The first two options on this menu give you help—either general help or help specific to the codes used in the printer definitions. The next three options (3, 4, and 5) allow you to examine or redefine your new printer definitions.

Usually, you will need to use only option 3, Printer Definitions, to define a new type or printer or to assign a new set of fonts to a printer definition. As soon as you select 3, you are presented with a list of all of the printer definitions currently in your WPRINTER.FIL file. The following options also appear at the bottom of the screen:

A. Create B. Edit C. Delete D. Rename E. Exit E

To create a new printer definition, you choose option A. You will be prompted to enter a new name for this printer definition. When you do, type a name that describes the printer type, typefaces, and type styles associated with the definition

```
╔══════════════════════════════════════════════════════════════╗

   ███████ PRINTER:  WordPerfect Printer Definition Program ███████



        Please Choose One:

              1. General Information and Help

              2. Explanation of Special Codes Used in This Program

              3. Printer Definitions (Examine, Change)

              4. Character Tables (Examine, Change)

              5. Sheet Feeder Definitions (Examine, Change)

              0. Exit

        Selection: 0




╚══════════════════════════════════════════════════════════════╝
```

FIGURE 5.7: The main menu of the PRINTER program used when setting up new printer or bin definition files for use with WordPerfect.

(use the existing names as guides). After you press Return, you are prompted to enter the current printer to use as a pattern. Type the number of the printer definition listed on the screen that most closely resembles the one you are about to define. If you are just defining new fonts to be used, choose the number of the printer definition that contains the fonts currently defined for that type of printer.

When you press Return, the program displays a new menu with 10 options (1—9 and A). If you are defining a new type of printer, you will need to consult both your printer documentation and the documentation for the PRINTER program as you examine the settings for each of these options. If you are just defining new fonts to be used, you can confine your choices to options 8— Selecting Fonts (Fonts 1—4) and 9—Selecting Fonts (Fonts 5—8) (and possibly A—Character Tables for Fonts).

Be very sure that you understand how to enter code changes for each option before you proceed. The special codes (listed in the documentation and when you choose option 2) must be entered by pressing the Alt key and the appropriate letter, and ASCII Escape sequences must be entered from the keyboard just as you enter printer commands (see "Entering Printer Codes in a Document" earlier in this chapter).

After you have finished creating the new printer definition, select the 0 option (Return) to return to the main menu and then select Exit to save your changes and return to the operating system prompt. Then copy the revised WPRIN-TER.FIL and WPFONT.FIL files onto a working copy of your WordPerfect System disk (preferably not the one you usually use to run WordPerfect). Start WordPerfect using this disk and press Shift-F7 and type **4** to get to the Printer Control screen. From there select option 3 and redefine one of the printer numbers to use the new printer definition that you just created. Finally, select that printer using option 1 on the Printer Control screen and print a sample document using the P option.

> *Note:* If your new printer definition uses downloaded fonts, be sure to exit WordPerfect (you can use the Shell function—Ctrl-F1 1) and download all of the fonts that you will be using before you try to print a sample document with the new printer definition. Also, add all necessary font-change codes (Ctrl-F8 1) to the document before you test print it.

For more detailed information about creating a new printer definition using the PRINTER program, refer to the section "Creating a New Soft Fonts Printer Definition" in Appendix C. This section steps you through the creation of new printer definitions for the HP LaserJet Plus and Series II printers using soft fonts not currently defined on the Printer 1 disk.

PRINTING THE DOCUMENT IN MEMORY

When you print the document that is currently in RAM, you have several options. These include printing all of the document or only the current page, changing the printer to be used, specifying the number of copies to be printed, and changing the binding width (inside margin).

Print Options

KEY SEQUENCE

To print the entire document in memory:
    Shift-F7 1
To print only the current page on the screen:
    Shift-F7 2
To change the printer to be used before printing:
    Shift-F7 3 1 *<printer number>* **0** (or **Return**)**1** (to print entire document)
        or **2** (to print current page)
To increase the number of copies before printing:
    Shift-F7 3 2 *<number of copies>* **0** (or **Return**) **1** (to print entire
        document) or **2** (to print current page)

To change the binding width before printing:

Shift-F7 3 3 <*binding width in tenths of an inch*> **0** (or **Return**) **1** (to print entire document) or **2** (to print current page)

In WordPerfect, the Print key sequence is Shift-F7. When you press this sequence, the following menu appears at the bottom of the screen:

1 Full Text; 2 Page; 3 Options; 4 Printer Control; 5 Type-thru; 6 Preview: 0

To print the text of the entire document on the screen (that is, in RAM), you type **1** to select the Full Text option. To print just the current page, you type **2** to select the Page option.

Before you print either the page or the entire document in memory, you can temporarily modify the print options that control the printer used, the number of copies printed, and the binding width. To do this, you type **3** to select the Options menu. You are then presented with three options:

1 - Printer Number	**1**
2 - Number of Copies	**1**
3 - Binding Width (1/10th in)	**0**

To change the printer number, you type **1** and the number of the printer that you wish to use (see "Verifying a Printer's Number" for information about how to review printer numbers). To change the number of copies, you type **2** followed by the number of copies. You can enter a number between 2 and 99.

You use the third option, Binding Width, when a document is to be reproduced on both sides of the paper and is going to be bound. WordPerfect uses the new binding-width value you set with this option to shift the text on left pages (even) to the left by the specified amount and to shift the text on right pages (odd) to the right by the specified amount. When entering the binding width, you enter fractional values in tenths of an inch. For example, to set a temporary binding width of $1\frac{1}{2}$ inches, you enter **15** (that is, 15 tenths of an inch).

After you change any of the values on the Options menu screen, you are returned to the Print menu options, where you can choose option 1 or 2 to print either the entire document or the current page. After you send the document to the printer using one of these options, you can continue editing your document. However, changes that you then make in the document will not be included in the printout.

PRINTING THROUGH THE PRINTER CONTROL SCREEN

> **KEY SEQUENCE**
>
> To print an entire document from a disk:
> **Shift-F7 4 P** <*document name*> Page(s): (All) **Return**
> To print specific pages and/or a range of pages in a document on a disk:
> **Shift-F7 4 P** <*document name*> Page(s):   <*pg–pg,pg,pg,...*>
> **Return**

To print a document that has been saved on a disk, you select option 4, Printer Control, from the Print menu (accessed by pressing Shift-F7). Doing this brings you to the Printer Control screen where you first set the print options, such as the printer to be used, the number of copies, and so forth (see "Using Printer Control" later in this chapter). Then

1. Type **P** (for Printing).
2. Enter the document name.
3. Specify the beginning and ending pages to print (press Return to print the entire document).

You can halt printing at any time or specify a rush job. See "Stopping a Print Job" and "Rush Printing" later in this chapter.

You can specify that only certain pages from a document are to be printed. To do so, you enter the starting and ending page numbers at the prompt. If you press Return for the ending page number, WordPerfect will print the document to the last page it contains.

The Printer Control Screen

The Printer Control screen (Shift-F7 4) allows you to control printing, see the current status of your print jobs, and verify or change the print queue. It is illustrated in Figure 5.2. No matter what method of printing you use (except Shift-PrtSc to print the screen contents), you use this screen to halt printing, set print options, and view the status of your print jobs.

The top section of the Printer Control screen presents a variety of options to control printing:

1 Select Print Options allows you to specify the printer number, number of copies, and binding margins.

2 Display Printers and Fonts allows you to verify the printers you have installed and review the fonts that currently work with your equipment.

3   Select Printers allows you to change the number and type of printers, direct printer output to different ports or to a disk file, and specify baud rate.

Other options allow you to stop and start specific print jobs:

C   Cancel Print Job(s) allows you to cancel (terminate) print jobs. Typing an asterisk terminates all print jobs.

D   Display All Print Jobs displays information about all current print jobs, not just the three jobs that normally are shown.

G   Go (Resume Printing) restarts a print job that you have stopped or that the program has halted to allow you to change paper, for example.

P   Print a Document prints the document that you specify. You can also specify a range of pages to print instead of an entire document.

R   Rush Print Job allows you to interrupt the current print job and specify that another document begin printing.

S   Stop Printing stops (temporarily halts) the current print job but does not cancel it. To restart the job, enter **G** for Go.

The middle portion of the Printer Control screen displays information about the current print job. It shows the job number, the page the printer is on, the number of copies, and the job status. Messages about your print jobs also appear here.

The job list at the bottom of the screen contains information for only three print jobs—the current job and the next two in the queue. If you have additional jobs, you can type **D,** Display All Print Jobs, to see a list of all print jobs.

Selecting Printer Options

Option 1 on the Printer Control screen allows you to select a printer to use, specify the number of copies to be printed, and specify any extra binding width you may need if your document is to be bound. These print options you select are in effect only temporarily, until you quit WordPerfect.

CHANGING PRINTERS (TEMPORARILY)

> **KEY SEQUENCE**
>
> **Shift-F7 4 1 1** *<printer number>*

You can specify that WordPerfect use different printers for different jobs. For example, you may print drafts on a dot-matrix printer but want to change to a letter-quality printer or a laser printer for the final version.

To change printers temporarily, press Shift-F7, type **4,** and type **1** twice. Then enter the number of the printer you wish to use.

SPECIFYING THE NUMBER OF COPIES TO PRINT

> **KEY SEQUENCE**
>
> **Shift F7 4 1 2** *<number of copies>* **Return (0** or **Return** to leave the screen)

You often may want to print more than one copy of your document. Word-Perfect will print as many copies as you indicate (up to 99 maximum), while freeing you to return to other documents or begin work on a new document.

CHANGING BINDING MARGIN WIDTH

> **KEY SEQUENCE**
>
> **Shift-F7 4 1 3** *<binding width>* **Return (0** or **Return** to leave the screen)

When two-sided documents are bound, especially if they are very bulky, they are sometimes difficult to open sufficiently to read the text that is near the inside margins (the gutter). WordPerfect allows you to shift text that is on lefthand (even-numbered) pages to the left and shift righthand (odd-numbered) pages to the right to provide a wider inside margin. You can specify new margins in 0.1-inch increments.

To do so, select option 1, Select Print Options, from the Printer Control screen. You can either select Options (option 3) from the Print menu (Shift-F7) or select option 4 to go to the Printer Control screen. Enter **3** for Binding Width and then enter the size of the inside margin you wish to use. For example, to increase the default 1-inch margin by half an inch (to 1½ inches), you enter **15**.

DISPLAYING PRINTERS AND FONTS

> **KEY SEQUENCE**
>
> **Shift-F7 4 2**

From time to time, you may wish to review the printers you have installed to work with WordPerfect and see which typefaces are available to you. To verify printers and fonts, press Shift-F7, enter **4**, and choose option 2, Display Printers and Fonts. The screen shown in Figure 5.4 appears. This screen shows the printers available to you as well as the typefaces (fonts). The letters *PS* next to a font name indicate proportional spacing. Two numbers are shown: one for sheet-fed paper and one for continuous-feed paper. This screen shows only the printers that are currently installed. To delete a printer or install additional printers, you use option 3, Select Printers.

CHANGING INSTALLED PRINTERS

> **KEY SEQUENCE**
>
> **Shift F7 4 3**

You can use option 3, Select Printers, on the Printer Control screen to install new printers or delete a printer you have already installed. To install an additional printer, your Printer disk must be inserted into one of your floppy disk drives. WordPerfect will prompt you to indicate the drive letter so that it can read the printer driver information when you press the PgDn key.

For detailed information about how to install a new printer, refer to "Installing a New Printer" earlier in this chapter.

Using Printer Control

WordPerfect lets you control the printers you are using in a variety of ways. For example, you can print only certain pages, suspend printing temporarily, cancel one or all of your print jobs, or insert a rush job to the head of the print queue. You can press Esc to leave the Printer Control screen and return to the normal editing screen while WordPerfect continues to print the jobs you have specified.

PRINTING SELECTED PAGES OF A DOCUMENT

> **KEY SEQUENCE**
>
> **Shift-F7 4 P** <*document name*> **Return** <**N,N,**> or <**N->** or
> <**-N**> or <**N-N**> **Return**

You often may want to print only a few pages of a long document instead of the entire document. For example, you may have modified only a few pages, or you may wish to see only one section. To enter the page range, you type the starting and ending page numbers, separated by a dash, over the (All) that appears after the Page(s): prompt. To print specific pages, you enter the starting page numbers separated by commas. To print from a specific page to the end of the document, you enter the starting page number followed by a dash. To print from the beginning of the document up to and including a specific page, you enter a dash followed by the ending page number. When entering any of these combinations, be sure not to enter any spaces between the numbers and the dash or commas used.

If your document has page numbers that use Roman instead of Arabic numerals, you can still have just specific pages or ranges of these pages printed. In this case, you indicate the page numbers by entering the appropriate lower-case letters instead of numbers. Table 5.2 shows you various combinations that can be entered at the Page(s): prompt and the results of each.

CANCELING A PRINT JOB

KEY SEQUENCE

Shift-F7 4 C <*job number* or * > **Return**

Entering C (for Cancel) while the Printer Control screen is displayed allows you to cancel a print job. When WordPerfect prompts you for which job to cancel, enter the job number of the document that is printing or the job you want to cancel and press Return. You may need to press Return again if your printer does not respond. If you are using a large printer buffer, several seconds may elapse before your printer stops printing what has already been sent to it. To cancel all print jobs, enter an asterisk (*) and press Return.

ENTRY	RESULT
Page(s): 4	Prints only page 4 of the document.
Page(s): 6,12	Prints pages 6 and 12 of the document.
Page(s): 2-6,17	Prints pages 2 through 6 and page 17 of the document.
Page(s): 10-	Prints from page 10 to the end of the document.
Page(s): -5	Prints from the beginning of the document through page 5.
Page(s): x-xii	Prints Roman numeral pages 10 through 12.
Page(s): iv,2-5,iv-x	Prints the first Roman numeral page iv, Arabic numeral pages 2 through 5, and finally the second Roman numeral pages iv through x.

TABLE 5.2: Entering Selected Pages to Be Printed

STOPPING A PRINT JOB

> **KEY SEQUENCE**
>
> To suspend printing:
> **Shift-F7 4 S**
> To resume printing:
> **G**

You can halt a print job temporarily—for example, to adjust the paper if you see that it is not feeding properly—by pressing S when the Printer Control screen is displayed. This interrupts printing but does not cancel the job. When you are ready to start printing again, type **G** (for Go). WordPerfect may ask you to reset the top of the printing form or give you some other message in the message area of the Printer Control screen. If printing does not resume as soon as you press G, check this area for any messages.

RUSH PRINTING

> **KEY SEQUENCE**
>
> **Shift-F7 4 R** <*job number*> **Y**

You can move a job to the front of the print queue by pressing R at the Printer Control screen. WordPerfect will prompt you for the number of the job to rush (you can type **D** to display all print jobs). Enter the job number and press Return. If you respond **Y** to the Interrupt prompt, WordPerfect will immediately print your rush job and then resume printing the job it was working on. If you answer **N**, WordPerfect will print the rush job as soon as it completes the job it was printing.

PRINTING A DOCUMENT FROM THE LIST FILES SCREEN

> **KEY SEQUENCE**
>
> To print a document in the current working directory:
> **F5 Return** (highlight document) **4**
> To batch print a number of documents in the current directory:
> **F5 Return** (highlight each document) ***** (to mark each document)
> **4** Print Marked Files? (Y/N) **Y**

> To print a document not in the current working directory:
> **F5 Return** (highlight directory) **Return Return**
>   (highlight document) **4**

You can view the names of all the documents you have created and specify documents to be printed from the List Files screen (Figure 5.8). Press F5 and Return to view this screen. To print a document listed on this screen, move the cursor highlight to the document's name and enter **4** to select the Print option on the List Files menu.

To have WordPerfect consecutively print (batch print) a group of documents listed on this screen, you must mark each document to be printed by highlighting it and then typing an * (asterisk) to mark it. To mark all files in the directory, press Home-PrtSc. After you have marked all of the document files you wish to print, you type **4** to select the Print option. WordPerfect then responds with this prompt:

Print Marked Files? (Y/N) N

When you type **Y**, WordPerfect begins printing the documents in the order in which they were marked. The program places all marked files in its print queue in the order they were marked.

```
02/19/87  09:40            Directory C:\WP\BOOK\*.*
Document Size:    84501                    Free Disk Space:  3829760

. <CURRENT>    <DIR>                 .. <PARENT>    <DIR>
CH12     .     <DIR>  01/01/87 12:03  CHAP1     .   <DIR>  11/28/86 10:02
CHAP11   .     <DIR>  01/04/87 13:22  CHAP13    .   <DIR>  01/18/87 13:01
CHAP2    .     <DIR>  12/12/86 11:52  CHAP3     .   <DIR>  12/24/86 11:53
CHAP4    .     <DIR>  01/03/87 11:27  CHAP6     .   <DIR>  12/03/86 08:08
CHAP7    .     <DIR>  12/08/86 13:42  CHAP8     .   <DIR>  01/15/87 08:09
ALT-A    .MAC      27 01/26/87 07:46  ALT-L   .MAC      20 01/26/87 07:54
ALT-Z    .MAC       2 01/04/87 08:53  ALTA    .MAC       9 11/27/86 09:47
ALTB     .MAC       9 11/27/86 09:43  ALTC    .MAC       9 11/27/86 09:43
ALTF     .MAC      35 11/26/86 18:50  ALTL    .MAC      25 01/26/87 07:52
ALTQ     .MAC      31 12/29/86 07:54  ALTR    .MAC       9 11/27/86 09:44
ALTT     .MAC      11 12/16/86 08:09  ALTZ    .MAC       2 01/04/87 08:54
AUPRO    .        403 10/27/86 16:53  C       .BAT      60 12/05/86 08:45
CH1      .      55561 11/28/86 09:20  CH11    .      16893* 01/04/87 12:46
CH13     .      2116* 01/18/87 13:10  CH15    .      24771* 02/13/87 08:41
CH15     .BK!   24355 02/11/87 10:34  CH15A   .BK!   24304 02/11/87 10:20
CH15FIGS.        464 02/11/87 14:02   CH15FIGS.BK!    1652 02/11/87 13:56
CH15HDS  .        560* 02/11/87 13:55 CH16    .      27334 02/13/87 08:20
CH16     .BK!   27001 02/11/87 18:05  CH16FIGS.        373 02/11/87 14:03

1 Retrieve; 2 Delete; 3 Rename; 4 Print; 5 Text In;
6 Look; 7 Change Directory; 8 Copy; 9 Word Search; 0 Exit: 6
```

FIGURE 5.8: Printing documents from the List Files screen. You can print all the documents you mark with an asterisk (*). To print only one document, highlight its name and select option 4 (Print).

If you need to use a printer control at any time, you can press Shift-F7 and enter **4** to go to the Printer Control screen. There you can interrupt printing by typing **S**, specify a rush job in the print queue by typing **R**, or cancel the printing of all documents in the queue by typing **C**.

You print documents in other subdirectories by highlighting the directory name and pressing Return twice. You then highlight the document file you want to print and type **4**. Again, if you want to print a group of files listed in this subdirectory, mark all of the files with an asterisk before typing **4**. If you want to return to the current directory, highlight .. <PARENT> <DIR> and press Return (see Chapter 6 for more information about changing directories in WordPerfect).

> *Note:* If you are using Version 4.1 or an earlier version, you cannot change directories in this manner. Instead, you must highlight the subdirectory name and enter **6** to use the Look option. Then you can mark the document or documents to be printed as described in the preceding discussion.

When you have finished selecting documents to be printed, press F1 (Cancel) or Esc to return to your document or to begin work on a new document.

PRINTING A BLOCK OF TEXT

KEY SEQUENCE

Alt-F4 (highlight block) **Shift-F7**
Print Block? (Y/N) **Y Alt-F4**

You can also quickly print a specified block of text without using the Printer Control screen. To do so, mark the block (Alt-F4) and then press Shift-F7. Enter **Y** at the prompt "Print marked block? (Y/N) N." Press Alt-F4 to return to your document; you do not have to wait until the block is printed.

PRINTING THE SCREEN CONTENTS

KEY SEQUENCE

To start:
    Shift-PrtSc
To abort:
    Ctrl-Break

You can also print the contents of the current screen. To do so, press Shift-PrtSc. Some graphics characters that appear on your screen may be translated by your printer into symbols it can print.

This procedure does not require using WordPerfect's Printer Control screen; to abort printing before the current screen is printed, you press Ctrl-Break.

DIRECT PRINTING (USING TYPE-THRU)

KEY SEQUENCE

To print directly line by line:
Shift-F7 5 1 <*text*> **Return F7** (to exit Type-thru)
To print directly character by character:
Shift-F7 5 2 <*text*> **F7** (to exit Type-thru)

WordPerfect's Type-thru feature allows you to use your keyboard as you would a typewriter. The text you type is not saved, however, but is sent directly to the printer. If you are filling out a form, you can use this feature to advance to the line on which you wish to type, filling out the entire form that way. Likewise, you can use Type-thru mode to address an envelope or a label. (For details about addressing large numbers of envelopes and labels using WordPerfect's Merge feature, see Chapter 9.)

You have a choice of using either character-by-character or line-by-line Type-thru printing. The line-by-line option is usually the best choice because it gives you an opportunity to correct each line before you send it to the printer (by pressing Return).

Some printers, however, especially some of the laser printers such as the Canon and the HP LaserJet, cannot use the Type-thru feature. Others, especially dot-matrix printers, can only accept line-by-line Type-thru printing.

To use the Type-thru feature, press Shift-F7 and enter **5**. The following prompt appears:

Type-thru printing: 1 by line; 2 by character: 0

Enter **1** if you want the characters you type to be sent to the printer only when you press Return. Enter **2** if you want each character to go to the printer as it is typed, much as characters do when you use a typewriter. Remember, however, that you cannot correct characters if you use option 2.

PRINTING TO DISK

KEY SEQUENCE

To print a document to a file called DOS.TXT using the DOS Text printer definition:
Shift-F7 4 1 1 6 Return

To print a document to a disk file using one of the other printer definitions:
Shift-F7 4 3 *<printer number>* **Return 8** *<file name of DOS text file>*
Return 1 (for Single Sheet or **2** for Continuous or **3** for Sheet
Feeder) **F7**

WordPerfect can output a document file to a new disk file (to print to a disk)
rather than to your printer. The new disk file created with this operation is essentially a DOS text (ASCII) file that also contains all of the printing control codes
required to print it as it was formatted by WordPerfect.

The resulting file can be printed from the DOS operating system without having a copy of WordPerfect running. This allows you to print WordPerfect documents on a printer attached to another computer that does not even have
WordPerfect on it.

To output a document file to a disk, you access the Printer Control screen by
pressing Shift-F7 and typing **4.** From there select option 3 (Select Printers). On
the Printer Definitions screen, select the printer number that represents the
printer definition for the type of printer that will be used to print the file.
Remember that the correct printer defintion may differ from the one you use to
print documents on the printer (or printers) attached to your computer.

You may need to press either the ← or → key to change the printer number
(pressing → increases the printer number, and pressing ← decreases it) until you
have selected the proper printer definition (listed beneath the printer number).
When the printer number is correct, press Return.

The Printer Port screen now appears. From this screen, select option 8
(Device or File Pathname) and then type a file name under which the DOS text
file version of your document will be stored. If you do not specify a new path
name, WordPerfect will save the document in the default directory. When naming the file, you can use the same file name and add the extension .TXT to
differentiate it from the original document file. After you enter the file name and
press Return, you will be prompted to indicate the type of paper feed for the
printer. Select 1 if the printer uses continuous feed, 2 if it uses single-sheet feed,
or 3 if it uses its own automatic sheet feeder.

After you select the type of feeder, you will be returned to the Printer Definitions screen. Press F7 (Exit) to return to the Printer Control screen. From this
screen, you select the file to be printed to the disk just as you select any file for
printing. Type **P,** type the name of the file, and press Return to accept the (All)
default value, or enter the range of pages to be printed and then press Return. As
soon as you do, WordPerfect will save the file you designated to be printed in a
disk file under the name you gave it when you selected option 8 on the Printer
Port screen.

To obtain a hard copy of the DOS text file, you can use either the DOS COPY
or PRINT command. When you use the DOS COPY command, you must

specify the name of the file and the device where the file is to be sent. For instance, if the file is named LETTER.TXT and the printer you want to print it on is attached to the first parallel interface (LPT1), you enter the COPY command at the DOS prompt as follows:

COPY LETTER.TXT PRN

As soon as you press Return (assuming that the printer is on line), the DOS text file under that name is output to the printer connected to the first parallel port. If the printer you want to use is connected to a serial port, you modify the PRN designation to either COM1 or COM2 (depending upon the number of the serial port to which the printer is attached).

To use the DOS PRINT command, you merely type the command followed by the file name. For instance, to use the PRINT command to output the file in the previous example, you enter

PRINT LETTER.TXT

If this is the first time you have issued the PRINT command during a work session, you will receive the prompt

Name of list device [PRN]

Press Return if the printer is attached to the first parallel port. Indicate a different device by entering the port type and number—for instance, LPT2, LPT3, COM1, or COM2.

> *Note:* Do not use the DOS PRINT command to print your DOS text file if you exit WordPerfect to get to the operating system by using the DOS Shell command (Ctrl-F1 1). If you do use PRINT, the computer will fail, and you will be unable to return to WordPerfect without restarting the computer and reloading WordPerfect. You can, however, safely use the COPY command to print your DOS text file and afterward return directly to WordPerfect.

WordPerfect also offers another way to create a DOS text file that can be printed directly from the operating system instead of from within WordPerfect using one of its print commands. When you use this method, you select the DOS text printer as the printing device and do not give the file a name. WordPerfect automatically saves the resulting file under the name DOS.TXT.

To create a DOS.TXT file, you press Shift-F7 and type **4** to access the Printer Control screen. From this screen, type **1,** which takes you to the Select Print Options screen. From this screen, select option 1 (Printer Number) and enter the number of the DOS text printer. This will be 6 unless you have reassigned this number to another printer definition.

Press Return to return to the Printer Control screen. From there, type **P** and enter the name of the file you want to print. After you indicate whether you want the entire file or just part of it printed, WordPerfect will save your document in a new DOS text file named DOS.TXT.

After creating a DOS.TXT file in this manner, you can use either the DOS COPY or PRINT command to print its contents directly from the operating system prompt. When you print DOS.TXT, you will find that it is formatted as it appeared on the screen. However, the printout will lack any special print enhancements, such as boldfacing or underlining, that you used. If the document you wish to print on a remote printer contains such printing enhancements, you must use the method in which you define the appropriate printer definition and assign the DOS text file a new name.

CHANGING PRINTING OPTIONS

Printing options affect the style and appearance of your documents rather than the way you control the printers that you have defined for use with Word-Perfect. WordPerfect's Print Format menu (Figure 5.9) contains *printing* options, as opposed to *printer* options, that you can change. It allows you to specify different pitches and fonts, change the number of lines per inch from 6 to 8, select right justification, change the underlining style, specify sheet feeder bins, and insert special printer commands. To use the Print Format menu, press Ctrl-F8.

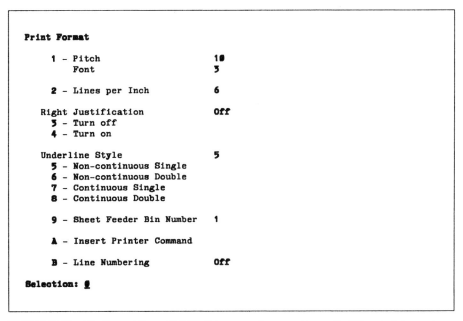

FIGURE 5.9: The Print Format Menu (Ctrl-F8). This menu allows you to specify different pitches and fonts, change the number of lines per inch from 6 to 8, select right justification, change the underlining style, specify sheet feeder bins, and insert special printer commands.

All of these options remain in effect only until you quit WordPerfect. The next time you start WordPerfect, the default settings will be used. If there are certain settings you would like to use in many documents that you create, you can write macros that set them for you (see Chapter 14).

Changing Pitch and Font

KEY SEQUENCE

To change the pitch and font:
    Ctrl-F8 1 *<pitch* (in characters per inch)*>* **Return** *<font number>*
        Return 0 (or **Return**)
To view a description of the font number:
    Shift-F7 4 2

REVEAL CODES

[**Font Change:** *<pitch number>* , *<font number>*]

To change the pitch (number of characters per inch) and font (type style) in which your document will be printed, you use the Font option on the Print Format menu (accessed by pressing Ctrl-F8 and typing **1**).

To change the pitch, you simply type over the default pitch number of 10 and press Return. To change the font, type the number of the font you wish to use. (To see a list of the fonts that you can currently use, select option 2, Display Printers and Fonts, on the Printer Control screen by pressing Shift-F7 and typing **4** and **2**.) If the font that you wish to use is proportionally spaced, be sure to enter an asterisk after the pitch number (for instance, enter **11*** for 11 characters per inch in proportionally spaced type).

You may sometimes have to change pitch (the number of characters per inch), even though all you want to do is change the font, because the font may have a different pitch (number of characters per inch). WordPerfect normally uses 10-pitch type. Your printer manual contains information about the pitch of the fonts it supplies. You can also print the PRINTER.TST document to see the various fonts and pitches available to you (for information about how to run the printer test, see "Testing Your Printers" earlier in this chapter). Be sure to print this document with each printer that you are using.

When you change the pitch, you must also change the margin settings if you want to maintain 1-inch margins. For example, to use 12-pitch type and keep

1-inch left and right margins, you need to reset the margins to L = 12 and R = 89, as there are 12 characters per inch in 12-pitch type.

To calculate the new margin setting with a different pitch, you multiply the width of the paper times the pitch. For example, to calculate new margins for 15-pitch type on 8 ½ × 11-inch paper, you multiply 8.5 by 15 to get 127.5 characters per line. The new left margin will then be 15, and the new right margin will be 112. To reset the margins, you press Shift-F8 and type **3** (for more information about resetting margins, see Chapter 2).

Changing the Number of Lines per Inch

KEY SEQUENCE

Ctrl-F8 2 8 (or **6**)

WordPerfect also allows you to change the number of lines per inch (vertical line spacing) from 6 lines per inch to 8 lines per inch. Changing this setting allows you to use less leading, or space between lines, in your printed documents.

However, when you change the number of lines per inch, you must also change the number of text lines per page if you want to keep the same relative top and bottom margins. You do this by pressing Alt-F8 and entering **4** to change page length.

If you are using standard 8½ × 11-inch paper and you change to 8 lines per inch, you should change the number of text lines to 72. (The paper is 11 inches long, so there are then 88 lines per page. You will need 16 lines for 1-inch top and bottom margins, which leaves 72 text lines.) Likewise, if you print at 8 lines per inch on 11 × 14-inch paper, you must change the number of text lines to 96. (See Chapter 2 for details about how to change the top and bottom margins.)

At present, 6 and 8 lines per inch are the only possible settings. To change from the default of 6 lines per inch to 8 lines per inch, enter Ctrl-F8, type **2,** and enter **8** (or enter **6** to change back to the default setting).

Using Right Justification

KEY SEQUENCE

To turn off right justification:
  Ctrl-F8 3
To turn on right justification:
  Ctrl-F8 4

When the program performs proportional spacing and justification and expands and compresses type, WordPerfect uses a method called *HMI* (horizontal motion index) to determine the distance the print head moves when the next character is printed. Most dot-matrix printers do not support HMI but instead use microspacing, in which the print head moves only in increments of 1, 2, 4, 8, or 16 units. If your printer supports neither HMI nor microspacing, it probably uses a method called *space fill*, in which full spaces are added between words to justify each line. Except when you use hyphenation, WordPerfect fills the spaces between words using one of these methods (see "Using Hyphenation" in Chapter 3).

Print the PRINTER.TST file on the Printer disk to see the effects of right justification with your printer. You cannot see right justification on your screen unless you use the Preview option (6) on the Print menu (for details about how to use this command, see Chapter 4). The default setting is right justification.

Though you may not always want all text right justified, you may often want certain portions of your document (for example, quoted material) to be right justified.

Specifying Sheet Feeder Bins

KEY SEQUENCE

Ctrl-F8 9 <*bin number*> **Return 0** (or **Return**)

REVEAL CODES

[**Bin#:** <*bin number*>]

Specifying the sheet feeder bin number allows you to switch between feeding letter-size paper kept in one bin and legal-size paper kept in another bin. If you press Ctrl-F8, type **9,** and change the bin number, WordPerfect inserts the formatting code [Bin#:] into your document at that point.

This bin-switching feature is also useful if you keep letterhead in one bin and plain paper in another. For instance, if you keep letterhead in bin 1 and plain paper in bin 2, you can print the second and all subsequent pages of a letter from bin 2 by positioning the cursor at the top of the second page and then pressing Ctrl-F8, typing **9** (to select the Sheet Feeder Bin Number option), and typing **2** (to switch to the second bin). When you press Return to set the new bin number, WordPerfect places the format code [Bin#:2] in the document at the cursor's position. When the letter is printed, the first page will be printed on the letterhead paper in the first sheet feeder bin, and all following pages will be printed on the plain paper in the second bin.

Using Special Printer Commands

KEY SEQUENCE

Ctrl-F8 A Cmnd: *<printer control code>*

You can insert special printer codes that turn on special effects your printer is capable of. To use special printing effects beyond the usual font changes and printing enhancements such as underlining, boldfacing, and the like, you must insert a code that WordPerfect sends to your printer to tell it what to do. These codes are specific to each printer, and you must consult your printer manual for a list of the codes used.

You enter the ASCII code for the printing effect you want. You cannot enter ASCII codes less than 32 or greater than 126 directly from the keyboard but must enter their decimal equivalents enclosed in angle brackets. Remember that ASCII codes are case sensitive: Uppercase **A** (ASCII code 065) is not the same as lowercase **a** (ASCII code 097), for example. (Appendix A lists ASCII codes and the characters or names they represent.)

For example, to enter the sequence Esc # for your printer, you do not enter the letters **esc** or press the Esc key. Instead, you enter the decimal ASCII equivalent of Esc, **27**, enclosed in angle brackets and followed by the # symbol. To do this, you press Ctrl-F8, type **A,** and then enter <27># after the Cmnd: prompt. The format code entered for this printer command (visible only in the Reveal Codes window—Alt-F3) would appear as [Cmnd:<27>#].

See "Entering Printer Codes in a Document" earlier in this chapter for more detailed information about using printer codes to obtain desired printing effects.

Advancing the Printer a Number of Lines

KEY SEQUENCE

Shift-F1 6 *<number of lines>* **Return**

REVEAL CODES

[AdvLn: *<number of lines>*]

Although WordPerfect's line advance feature is most often used to advance the printer up or down by half lines when creating equations (see Chapter 11), you can also use it to tell the printer to advance a certain number of lines. This feature is useful if, for example, you have stored your company letterhead in a macro and want to position the letterhead a certain number of lines down from the top of the page.

To instruct the printer to advance a certain number of lines when your document is printed, press Shift-F1. The following prompt appears:

1 Superscript; 2 Subscript; 3 Overstrike; 4 Adv Up; 5 Adv Dn; 6 Adv Ln: 0

Enter **6** and then enter the number of lines you want the printer to advance before printing the text that follows. You will not see the spaces on your screen. To verify them or delete the Line Advance command, press Alt-F3 to reveal the formatting codes, position the cursor to the right of the [AdvLn:] code, and press the Backspace key.

SUMMARY

This chapter has presented the various options WordPerfect provides to facilitate printing. Other chapters discuss more specialized printing topics.

For information about producing and printing special mathematical and foreign-language symbols by entering their ASCII codes in a document and using the Line Advance feature, see Chapter 11, "Mathematics, Equations, and Special Symbols." For information about producing and printing special characters by using WordPerfect's Overstrike feature, see Chapter 3, "Editing Techniques."

For information about using WordPerfect with the HP LaserJet, LaserJet Plus, or LaserJet Series II printer, see Appendix C. Note that this appendix also contains specific information about creating a new printer definition for soft fonts using the PRINTER program. This information might be helpful to you in creating your own printer definitions, even if you do not own a LaserJet printer.

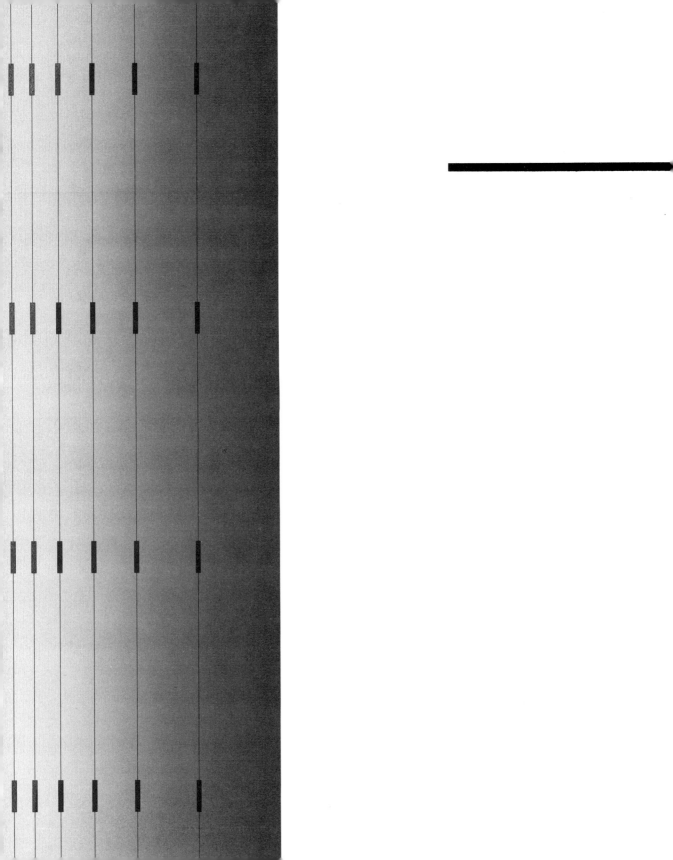

CHAPTER 6

FILE MANAGEMENT TECHNIQUES

FILE MANAGEMENT TECHNIQUES

This chapter presents techniques and reference information for managing the document files that you create with WordPerfect. The file-management topics covered in this chapter include

- Rules and conventions for naming document files
- Password protecting documents
- Creating and organizing document files in directories
- Locating specific documents for editing
- Performing housekeeping chores such as deleting files, renaming documents, and making backup copies of your data disks

In Chapter 1, you will find information about saving the document files that you create in WordPerfect. In Chapter 2, you will find information about retrieving files for editing. In Chapter 15, you will find information about creating ASCII files. Otherwise, you will find all of the other pertinent information about managing WordPerfect documents in this chapter.

NAMING FILES

To name a file in WordPerfect, you follow the DOS file-naming conventions. WordPerfect follows the same rules that DOS does for naming files; they are summarized here for your reference.

- A file name can consist of from one to eight characters.
- These characters may be the letters A-Z or the numerals 0-9.
- In addition, you can use the symbols $ & # @ ! ' ` ~ ( ) { } - _ ^
- You cannot use the symbols ? . " / \ [ ] : ¦ < > + = , *
- You cannot use spaces within a file name.
- You may add an optional extension consisting of a period (.) followed by from one to three additional legal characters, as defined above.

In general, a file name cannot exceed eight characters and may be any combination of letters, numbers, and symbols, with the exceptions listed above. You can enter a file name in lowercase letters; WordPerfect will automatically convert them to uppercase letters.

In addition to following the rules outlined here, you should not begin the name of a file with {WP} because the WordPerfect program uses special auxiliary files that begin with these characters.

WordPerfect does not automatically assign extensions to the files it creates (other than macro files, to which it automatically gives the extension .MAC). If you are creating a file for a special purpose—for example, generating a DOS text file to be used in another program, you may want to assign it a three-letter file extension such as .ASC (for ASCII) so that you can quickly identify such files later.

Meaningful File Names

Eight characters are not a lot in which to communicate what a file contains. The name 10-27LTR may help you remember that you wrote a letter on the 27th of October, but it does not tell you to whom you wrote the letter or why. As a general rule, use abbreviations that are meaningful to you. If you write few letters, and if October 27 was a special day, 10-27LTR may be a perfectly meaningful name for you.

Using Wildcard Characters

You often may not remember the exact name of a file, or you may want to specify that WordPerfect search for all files or a group of files without listing each one individually. WordPerfect allows you to use characters called *wildcards* to represent a character or a group of characters when you search for a file, instead of having to know the exact file name or having to type each file name separately. The question mark (?) represents any single character, and the asterisk (*) represents any combination of characters.

For example, if you know that the file you are looking for begins with the letters *RPT* (for report), you can enter

RPT*

in response to a search prompt, and WordPerfect will search for all files beginning with RPT and ending in any other combination of letters, such as RPT1_87 or RPTMAY, for example.

The wildcard combination *.* represents any combination of characters plus any extension. It is automatically supplied with some of WordPerfect's search prompts, such as the DIR prompt that appears when you press F5 (List Files), as discussed later in this chapter. This combination of wildcard characters means that all files will be shown.

The following examples show several ways in which you can use wildcard characters.

Wildcard combination:	**WordPerfect searches for:**
LTTR?	All files beginning with LTTR and ending in one more character, such as LTTR1.
LTTR??	All files beginning with LTTR and ending in one or two more characters, such as LTTR1, LTTRBA, and LTTR87.
LTTR*	All files beginning with LTTR and ending in any combination of characters (up to a total of eight), such as LTTR1_8, LTTRBOB, LTTR2, and LTTR1A.
LTTR*.*	All files beginning with LTTR and ending in any combination of characters (up to a total of eight) plus any three-character file extension, such as LTTR87.ASC, LTTR87, LTTRBOB, and so forth.
.	All files with or without any extensions.

Be careful when you use wildcards. If you use them with commands such as Copy or Delete, you may change your file system in ways that you do not anticipate.

Password Protecting Your Files

WordPerfect allows you to password protect the document files you create. In the parlance of the program, password protecting a file is referred to as "locking a file." The options for locking a file are located on the Document Conversion, Summary and Contents screen accessed by pressing Ctrl-F5. From this screen, you select option 4, the Locked Document Format Save option, to save the document in the current window under a password. (In Version 4.1, this option is number 3, Lock and save current document.)

When you select this option, WordPerfect will prompt you for a password:

Enter Password:

You can enter a password up to 75 characters long. (WordPerfect masks the display of the characters you enter for the password on the editing screen so that you will be typing blind.) After you press Return, you are prompted to reenter the password you just typed:

Re-Enter Password:

You must type the password exactly as you just entered it (note that WordPerfect matches only the sequence or spelling of the letters and disregards any difference in case). Again, WordPerfect does not display the characters that you enter on your screen.

If you fail to verify the password in this manner, you will receive the error message "ERROR: Incorrect Password." You will receive the original password prompt, where you can enter another password that you will then have to verify.

If you verify the password, WordPerfect will prompt you to enter a document name if the document has not been saved before. If the document has already been saved, WordPerfect will suggest the original file name. If you wish to save the document under the same name, you type **Y** in response to the Replace? prompt. However, you may save the password-protected file under a new file name if you wish. To do this, you simply edit the file name as it is displayed on the screen.

To retrieve a password-protected file, you can either press Shift-F10 (Retrieve) in the editing screen or Ctrl-F5 and select option 5 (Retrieve Locked Document Format). (In Version 4.1, this option is number 4—Unlock and retrieve a locked document.)

In either case, you will be prompted to enter the password assigned to the file after you enter the file name. You can also retrieve a password-protected file by highlighting its name on the List Files screen (F5), selecting option 1 (Retrieve), and then entering the password.

Regardless of the retrieval method you use, if you do not enter the password correctly, you will receive the error message "ERROR: File is locked" and be prompted to enter the file name again. If you cannot reproduce the password that you assigned to the document, you will not be able to retrieve it for editing or printing.

WordPerfect does not allow you to print a password-protected document from disk (using either the Print option on the Printer Control or List Files screen). The only way to print a locked file is to successfully retrieve it (by entering the correct password) and then use the Print key sequence (Shift-F7) and select either Full Text (1) or Page (2) option. This means two things: If you forget the password, you cannot obtain another printout of the document, and you should never password protect a document that is too large to print from RAM memory (see Chapter 5 for details).

> *Note:* You can still rename, copy, and delete password-protected files without having to give the password. However, remember that files that you rename or copy to new disks or directories are still password protected and will require you to enter the correct password before you can retrieve them for editing or printing.

To remove password protection, or "unlock" a file, you must retrieve the file using one of the methods described here and then save it. When you are prompted to enter the password, just press Return. From then on, you will be able to retrieve the file without having to enter a password, and you can print the file from the disk as well as from memory.

Locating Files for Editing and Printing

To get an alphabetical list of all files on the disk in the default drive (if you save your documents on a floppy disk) or the default directory (if you save your documents on a hard disk), press the function key F5 (List Files) and press Return.

The List Files screen that you then see displayed is divided into three parts:

- A header section that gives you the date, time, name of the default directory, size in bytes of the current file in memory, and amount of unused space in bytes that remains on the default drive.

- A directory listing section that gives you a complete list of all of the files on the default directory in two columns. This listing is preceded by the names of any directories attached to the default directory (this includes the parent as well as any subdirectories). Directories are indicated by the <DIR> code. The list of files that follows includes the file name, file name extension, size in bytes, and date and time of the last update. This list is arranged alphabetically by file name.

- A third section that contains the command options available on the List Files screen. There are 10 options on this menu:

1 Retrieve; 2 Delete; 3 Rename; 4 Print; 5 Text In; 6 Look; 7 Change Directory; 8 Copy; 9 Word Search; 0 Exit: 6

To move through the list of file names on the screen, you can use the ↑ and ↓ keys to move the highlight up and down one file at a time or the PgUp and PgDn keys to move it up and down a screenful at a time. To move directly to the last file name in the list, press Home, Home, and the ↓ key. To move up to the first file, press Home, Home, and the ↑ key. To move the highlight back and forth between the two columns, use the ← and → keys.

You can also quickly locate a particular file in the list just by typing the first few characters of its name. WordPerfect has a Word Search feature that is activated as soon as you start typing. It tries to match the letters entered with files in the listing. For example, to locate a file named TABLE2-1 that is not visible in the first screen display of the files, you need only type **T**. This takes the cursor highlight to those files that begin with the letter *T*. If TABLE2-1 is not the first file in the directory that begins with *T*, you can continue typing more letters (such as **ABL**), or you can use the ↓ key to exit Word Search and move the highlight directly down to the name of the file you want.

VIEWING THE CONTENTS OF FILES FROM THE LIST FILES SCREEN

By selecting 6, the Look option (the default option in Version 4.2) on the List Files menu, you can display the contents of the file whose name is currently highlighted. This feature is most helpful when you need to view some of the contents of a file to ascertain if it is the document you want to edit or print. When you highlight the name of a file and press Return (in Version 4.2) or type **6** (in Version 4.1 or 4.2), WordPerfect displays the first part of the document on the editing screen. At the bottom of the screen, you will see the messages

NOTE: This text is not displayed in WordPerfect format. Press any key to continue.

The first message (in inverse video) is there to let you know that you cannot edit the text that you see on the screen in any way. If you need to see more of the file to identify it, you can scroll through it by pressing either the ↓ or PgDn key. Pressing any other key will return you immediately to the List Files screen.

You can also use the Look option to temporarily change to a new directory to locate documents listed there. To do this, you move the cursor highlight to the name of the directory whose listing you wish to see and type **6** (you can also just press Return in Version 4.2). Remember that selecting the Look option to see the contents of a new directory does not change the default directory as does using option 7, Change Directory (see the section ''Creating and Using Document Directories'' that follows for more information about changing directories). To return to the directory listing of the default directory, you have only to press F1 to return to your document and then press F5 and Return again.

SEARCHING FILES FOR SPECIFIC CONTENTS

Besides having WordPerfect display the contents of a particular file in the current directory, you can have WordPerfect search the files for a particular word or phrase. This helps you quickly locate files whose names you no longer remember but for which you know some identifying phrase or keywords. To have the program list only those files that contain the keywords or phrase you remember, you use the List Files Word Search option (9). When you select this command, you can enter a search string that contains up to a maximum of 20 characters. When entering this search string, be aware that upper- and lowercase letters are considered to be the same by the program.

For example, you can use the Word Search command to locate all documents that have anything to do with Hewlett Packard Corporation by selecting option 9 from the List Files screen and entering **''Hewlett Packard''** in response to the prompt

Word Pattern:

(You must enclose the word pattern in quotation marks if it contains a space, comma, semicolon, or single or double quotation marks.) After you press Return, WordPerfect searches all of the files in the current directory for the presence of the phrase *Hewlett Packard*. After it has finished, it will list on the screen only those files that contain these words.

When using the Word Search option to locate specific files, you can use the *** and **?** wildcard characters (see the previous section, "Using Wildcard Characters," for details). For example, if you have forgotten exactly how you spelled *Hewlett* in your documents, you can enter the word pattern as

"H?wl* Packard"

In this example, WordPerfect will match the search string if you began the name with *He* or *Hu* as well as if you ended it with *let, lat,* or *lett.*

Also, this feature allows you to use the logical operators AND and OR represented by the semicolon (or single blank space) and comma, respectively. For instance, if you want to narrow the search to only those documents in which you mention both Hewlett Packard AND their product the HP LaserJet, you enter the Word Pattern as

"Hewlett Packard";"HP LaserJet"

On the other hand, to locate documents where you mention either Hewlett Packard OR the HP Laserjet, you can modify the Word Pattern to

"Hewlett Packard","HP LaserJet"

Once WordPerfect has searched all of the files and returns a screen listing of only those files that contain your search string, you can obtain a hard copy by pressing Shift-PrtSc. To locate a specific document within this restricted list, you can use the Look option (6) to review the contents of each.

> *Note:* You can use more than a single AND or OR logical operator in the search string you enter so long as it does not exceed 20 characters total. However, you must understand the logic you employ. Consider these examples:
>
> - If you enter **Ash,Berry,Singer**, your document must contain the name Ash, Berry, *or* Singer.
> - If you enter **Ash;Berry;Singer**, your document must contain all three names: Ash, Berry, *and* Singer.
> - If you enter **Ash;Berry,Singer**, your document must contain *either* both the names Ash and Berry *or* just that of Singer alone.
> - If you enter **Ash,Berry;Singer**, your document must contain *either* the name Ash *or* those of both Berry and Singer.

Creating and Using Document Directories

If you are using WordPerfect on a hard disk system, you can keep your documents in subdirectories below the one that contains the WordPerfect program files. In fact, you can set up many such subdirectories in which you keep related documents. For example, if you do word processing for many people in the office, you can have a directory for each person. When you type a letter or memo for one person, you make his or her directory current before creating the document. You can also set up subdirectories based on the type of document, regardless of who created it. For instance, you can have a directory for proposals, another for letters, and so on.

When you need to create such data directories, you can do so from within WordPerfect using F5 (List Files), instead of using the DOS MD (Make Directory) command. You can also make a document subdirectory current for saving or retrieving documents from within WordPerfect rather than having to use the DOS CD (Change Directory) command.

There are two methods for making a particular data directory current. You can press the function key F5 and press Return. WordPerfect will display all of the directories attached to the current directory (they carry the designation <DIR> in the second column). To make a different directory current, move the highlight block to its name and press Return twice. Select option 7 (Change Directory) from the menu and press Return when prompted with the new current directory. Then press F1 (Cancel) or Esc to begin creating a new document.

You can also press the function key F5 and type = (the equal sign). When you first press F5, WordPerfect displays the name of the current directory at the bottom of the editing screen and the message "(Use = to change default directory)." For example, if you press F5 after starting WordPerfect in the directory named WP, you will see

Dir C:\WP*.*

on the left side of the screen. (The *.* is a DOS operating system convention that means show all of the files regardless of file name or file-name extension.) If you press Return at this point, WordPerfect will display an alphabetical list of all program files in this directory.

To change the current directory, type = (the equal sign from the top row of the keyboard). This changes the screen display to

New directory = C:\WP

and places the cursor beneath the C. To change directories, you can completely retype the directory name or simply edit it. For example, if you wish to create a new letter for Bob and you have set up a directory to contain all of his documents, you can type

C:\WP\BOB

and press Return, or you can use the ← or End key to move the cursor to the end of C:\WP and just type **\BOB** before pressing Return.

As soon as you press Return, WordPerfect displays the new directory, including the DOS wildcard characters; for example,

C:\WP\BOB*.*

Press Return again to display all of the files in this directory that can be accommodated in one screen view. All of the files created in the directory are listed in alphabetical order, from left to right and down each line. You can press F1 (Cancel) or Esc to return to the document editing screen, where you can begin your new document.

Regardless of the method you use, once you have made a particular directory current, all of the documents you create and save will automatically be located in it. You can also use these methods to change the current directory when you wish to retrieve a document for editing that is located in a directory different from the one that is current.

In Version 4.2, once you name a document at the time you save it, the name of the document including the full path name (that is, showing exactly where the document is located on the hard disk by displaying all of the directories before the file name) is displayed on the last line of the screen. If you wish to save the edited document in a directory different from the one in which it was created, you must edit its file name by modifying the directory path when saving the file.

For instance, if you retrieve a document named C:\WP\BOB\IBMPROP and you wish to save the edited version in Mary's directory, you must modify its name to C:\WP\MARY\IBMPROP when you save it. From then on during editing, the file name at the bottom of the screen will read C:\WP\MARY\IBMPROP. However, the current directory will continue to be C:\WP\BOB. If you were to start a new document in the second window that you saved, it would be located in Bob's directory.

You can also create new WordPerfect subdirectories in which to save your documents. To do this, you press the F5 (List Files) key and type = followed by the full name of the directory. When you press Return, WordPerfect asks whether it should create a new directory if the directory you specify does not currently exist. For example, if you press F5 and type = and then type

C:\WP\DOUG

and you have not yet created a directory for Doug, WordPerfect will respond

create C:\WP\DOUG (Y/N) N?

To have WordPerfect create this new directory, you need only type **Y**. WordPerfect will then create the new directory. However, it will not simultaneously make this directory current. If you wish to change to this directory, you still must use one of the methods for changing directories described previously. (For more information about how to set up new directories and change directories within WordPerfect, refer to Chapter 6.)

CD: A Macro to Make a New Document Directory Current

You can use WordPerfect's macro facility to set up a macro that will prompt you for the name of the subdirectory you wish to make current. You create this macro while the directory C:\WP is still current.

Begin macro	*Macro name*	*Keystrokes*	*End macro*
Ctrl-F10	**CD**	**F5 = C:\WP End**	**Ctrl-F10**
		Ctrl-PgUp	
		Return Return	
		Return Return	

When you invoke this macro, you press Alt-F10 and type **CD.** When you hear the beep, type the name of the directory attached to the WordPerfect directory that you wish to make current. Precede its name with a backslash; for example, enter **\BOB**. When you press Return, WordPerfect will display a list of all files in the new current directory. You can then retrieve a file for editing by moving the highlight bar to the file name and pressing Return, or you can press F1 (Cancel) or Esc to create a new document to be stored in this directory.

Using the List Files Menu to Perform Common Housekeeping Chores

In addition to using the List Files screen to obtain a directory listing of files, to retrieve or print a particular document, or to make a new data directory or drive current, you can use the List Files menu to perform common housekeeping chores, including

- Deleting files
- Renaming files
- Copying files to a new data disk or directory

Although all of these file-management tasks can be accomplished by using appropriate DOS commands in the operating system, you may find it easier to do them from within WordPerfect using the List Files options. This is especially true if you are unfamiliar with the syntax required when using the DOS RENAME and COPY commands. In the following sections, you will find entries for the List File options for renaming, deleting, and copying files as well as for the DOS RENAME, DEL, and COPY commands.

Renaming a File

> **KEY SEQUENCE**
>
> **F5** (List Files) (select directory) **Return** (highlight file) *3*
> New Name: < *new file name* > **Return**

You can rename a file that you have already named either by using the DOS RENAME command (see "Renaming a File from DOS" later in this chapter) or by selecting option 3, Rename, from the List Files screen. You may, for example, want to rename files when you move them to a different directory or subdirectory (see "Working with Directories" later in this chapter), or you may want to assign more meaningful names for long-term storage.

To rename a file,

1. Press F5 (List Files). A prompt appears at the bottom of the screen asking if you want to search the default directory, which is the directory you specified to hold the program files when you initially set up the program (see Figure 6.1). To see a list of the files in this directory, press Return. Alternatively, you can type the path name of the directory you wish to search.

```
Opportunities for Advancement

The bulletin board outside the Personnel Department on the first
floor contains up-to-date listings of job openings within the
company and at field locations throughout the country.  Whenever
possible, openings are filled from within the company.  If you
see a position for which you feel you are qualified, check with
the Personnel Department.


Educational Aid

MagnaCorp offers educational opportunities to employees at all
levels.  Tuition refunds are available to full-time employees for
courses at accredited institutions.  To make sure that a course
for which you plan to enroll will be covered, consult your
manager or the Personnel Department.




Dir C:\WP\FILES\*.*                    (Use = to change default directory)
```

FIGURE 6.1: Using the F5 (List Files) key. The prompt that appears when you press F5 (List Files) asks whether you want to search the default directory.

2. When a screen similar to the one shown in Figure 6.2 appears, move the highlight to the file you wish to rename. Type *3* to select option 3, Rename, from the menu at the bottom of the screen.

3. Enter the new file name, as shown in Figure 6.3; then press Return. The file listing changes to reflect the new name. Press Esc, F1 (Cancel), 0, or F7 (Exit) to return to your document.

WORKING WITH DIRECTORIES

If you are using WordPerfect on a hard disk, all program files will be kept in their own directory. Because the hard disk offers a very large storage area, you usually can locate files more easily if you organize them in divisions called *directories*. You can think of these directories as analogous to file drawers in a single filing cabinet. Within each drawer, you store many file folders. Likewise, each directory can contain many files, each with a unique file name.

When you start WordPerfect, all of the documents you create will automatically be saved in the current directory (C:\WP). Most often, you will want to save your documents in separate directories. These are usually attached to the directory that contains the WordPerfect program files.

```
12/02/86  18:04              Directory C:\WP\FILES\*.*
Document Size:     5779                    Free Disk Space:   7266304

. <CURRENT>   <DIR>                   .. <PARENT>   <DIR>
MSCHS    .      <DIR>   10/14/86 10:12   0        .CAP    4256  10/02/86 13:05
123SS    .       1010   08/14/86 12:54   123SS    .BK!     943  08/06/86 13:08
A        .CAP    4256   10/02/86 13:05   ADDRESS  .PF       12  10/10/86 15:18
ADDRESS  .SF      821   10/10/86 15:29   ALTA     .MAC       9  09/25/86 08:50
ALTB     .MAC       9   09/25/86 08:52   ALTC     .MAC       9  09/25/86 08:53
ALTD     .MAC      17   11/27/86 08:20   ALTE     .MAC      13  09/25/86 08:47
ALTF     .MAC      33   09/30/86 08:15   ALTH     .MAC      28  09/30/86 07:55
ALTL     .MAC      23   09/25/86 10:09   ALTN     .MAC       3  10/09/86 08:39
ALTO     .MAC       5   08/12/86 08:52   ALTQ     .MAC      46  11/27/86 07:52
ALTR     .MAC      18   10/08/86 09:40   ALTT     .MAC       4  08/12/86 08:56
ALTV     .MAC      13   08/12/86 11:23   ALTW     .MAC       5  08/12/86 08:50
ALTY     .MAC       5   08/12/86 08:51   ALTZ     .MAC      10  10/16/86 10:24
APP      .MAC      12   11/13/86 17:32   APPB     .        2063  11/13/86 17:14
CH1HDS   .       1717   11/22/86 10:05   CHAPTER8 .ASC   18688  10/29/86 10:40
COPYRITE .       2246   11/13/86 11:30   COPYRITE .ASC    2304  11/13/86 11:30
ESCROW   .        639   10/21/86 20:09   FIG1-10  .CAP    4256  11/20/86 09:05
FIG1-9   .CAP    4256   11/20/86 09:02   IO       .MAR     853  10/27/86 22:01
IO_ASCII .MAR     896   10/27/86 22:03   KARIN    .        1715  10/09/86 19:58

1 Retrieve; 2 Delete; 3 Rename; 4 Print; 5 Text In;
6 Look; 7 Change Directory; 8 Copy; 9 Word Search; 0 Exit: 6
```

FIGURE 6.2: The F5 (List Files) screen. This screen lists the names of all files stored in the default directory. To view the contents of another directory, move the cursor to highlight the directory name, type **6** (Look), and press Return.

In fact, you can set up many of these directories in which you keep related documents. For example, if you do word processing for many people in the office, you can have a directory for each person. When you type a letter or memo for one person, you make his or her directory current before creating the document. You could also set up directories based on the type of documents they contain, regardless of who created them. For instance, you could have a directory for proposals, another for letters, and so on.

You can also view the contents of other directories, delete files, copy files, print files, retrieve DOS text files (ASCII files), look at the contents of files, look in other directories, change the default directory, and search through files for a specific word of phrase. Each of these techniques will be discussed in subsequent sections.

Creating a Directory

> **KEY SEQUENCE**
>
> **F5** (List Files) **Return 7** <*new directory name*> **Y Return**
>
> or
>
> **F5** (List Files) = <*new directory name*> **Return Y**

```
12/02/86  18:04              Directory C:\WP\FILES\*.*
Document Size:     5779                      Free Disk Space:   7266304

. <CURRENT>   <DIR>                  .. <PARENT>   <DIR>
MSCHS    .    <DIR>    10/14/86 10:12  0        .CAP    4256  10/02/86 13:05
123SS    .    1010     08/14/86 12:54  123SS    .BK!     943  08/06/86 13:08
A        .CAP  4256    10/02/86 13:05  ADDRESS  .PF       12  10/10/86 15:18
ADDRESS  .SF    821    10/10/86 15:29  ALTA     .MAC       9  09/25/86 08:50
ALTB     .MAC     9    09/25/86 08:52  ALTC     .MAC       9  09/25/86 08:53
ALTD     .MAC    17    11/27/86 08:20  ALTE     .MAC      13  09/25/86 08:47
ALTF     .MAC    33    09/30/86 08:15  ALTH     .MAC      28  09/30/86 07:55
ALTL     .MAC    23    09/25/86 10:09  ALTN     .MAC       3  10/09/86 08:39
ALTO     .MAC     5    08/12/86 08:52  ALTQ     .MAC      46  11/27/86 07:52
ALTR     .MAC    18    10/08/86 09:40  ALTT     .MAC       4  08/12/86 08:56
ALTV     .MAC    13    08/12/86 11:23  ALTW     .MAC       5  08/12/86 08:50
ALTY     .MAC     5    08/12/86 08:51  ALTZ     .MAC      10  10/16/86 10:24
APP      .MAC    12    11/13/86 17:32  APPB     .        2063  11/13/86 17:14
CH1HDS   .     1717    11/22/86 10:05  CHAPTER8 .ASC   18688  10/29/86 10:40
COPYRITE .     2246    11/13/86 11:30  COPYRITE .ASC    2304  11/13/86 11:30
ESCROW   .      639    10/21/86 20:09  FIG1-10  .CAP    4256  11/20/86 09:05
FIG1-9   .CAP  4256    11/20/86 09:02  IO       .MAR     853  10/27/86 22:01
IO_ASCII .MAR   896    10/27/86 22:03  KARIN    .        1715  10/09/86 19:58


New Name: realty.asc_
```

FIGURE 6.3: Renaming a file. The name you type for the file at the prompt in the lower-left corner will be the one it will have until you change it again. Be sure to include any extension you wish the file to have. For example, if the file is a DOS text file, you may wish to give it the extension .ASC (for ASCII). WordPerfect will automatically give any macro files you create the extension .MAC.

You often may want to create a new directory to store groups of related files. WordPerfect allows you to create new directories from within the program. (You can also create a new directory from DOS using its MD command; see "Exiting to DOS through the WordPerfect Shell" later in this chapter.)

To create a new directory, press F5 (List Files); then press Return to see the List Files screen. Type **7** to select the Change Directory option. When the prompt

New Directory =

appears, enter the name of the new directory you wish to create. You will be asked to confirm whether you want to create a new directory. Type **Y** to confirm your selection and tell WordPerfect to create the new directory.

The new directory name will appear on the List Files screen. Remember, it will be a subdirectory of the directory you are currently in. For example, if you are in a subdirectory named \WP\FILES and you create a new directory named BOOK, this new directory will be a subdirectory of the FILES subdirectory, and its path name will be \WP\FILES\BOOK.

You can also press F5 (List Files) and type = , followed by the full name of the directory. When you press Return, WordPerfect prompts you to create a new directory if it finds that the directory does not currently exist. For example, if you press F5, type = , and then type

C:\WP\DOUG

and you have not yet created a directory for Doug, WordPerfect will respond with

create C:\WP\DOUG (Y/N) N?

To have this new directory created, you need only type **Y**. WordPerfect will then create a new subdirectory named DOUG. However, it will not simultaneously make this directory current. If you wish to change to this directory, you must use one of the methods for changing directories described in the following sections.

Making a Directory Current (Changing Directories)

KEY SEQUENCE

F5 Return (highlight directory name) **Return Return**

or

F5 = <*directory name*> **Return Return**

or

F5 Return 7 <*directory name*> **Return Return**

To make a new directory current for retrieving a document, you can use one of three methods:

- Press F5 (List Files) and then press Return. WordPerfect will display all of the directories attached to the current directory (they carry the designation <DIR> in the second column). To make a different directory current, highlight its name and press Return twice.
- Press F5 (List Files), type = , and enter the directory name.
- Press F5 and Return and then select option 7, Change Directory, from the List Files screen; then enter the directory name in response to the prompt.

Using Path Names

In Version 4.2, once you name a document, its full path name (that is, a list of the directories and subdirectories showing where the file is located on the hard disk) is displayed on the last line of the screen. If you wish to save the edited document in a directory different from the one in which it was created, you must modify its path name.

For instance, if you retrieve a document named C:\WP\BOB\IBMPROP and you wish to save the edited version in Mary's directory, you must modify the path name to **C:\WP\MARY\IBMPROP** when you save the file. From then on during editing, the file name at the bottom of the screen will read C:\WP-\MARY\IBMPROP. However, the current directory will continue to be C:\WP\BOB. If you were to start a new document in the second window and save it, it would be located in Bob's directory.

Changing the Default Directory

KEY SEQUENCE

F5 (List Files) = *<new default directory>*
F5 (List Files) **Return 7** *<new default directory>*

The default directory is the directory name that appears whenever you press F5 (List Files). If you are working on a long project, such as a report containing several sections or a book with many chapters, you may want to change the default directory in which your files are stored.

If you press the function key F5 and type = (equal sign), you can change the default directory. When you first press F5, WordPerfect displays the name of the current directory at the bottom of the editing screen and the message

"(Use = to change default directory)". For example, if you press F5 after starting WordPerfect in the directory named WP, you will see

Dir C:\WP*.*

on the lower-left side of the screen. (The *.* means list all of the files in that directory; see "Using Wildcards Characters" earlier in this chapter.) If you press Return at this point, WordPerfect displays an alphabetical list of all of the program files in this directory.

To change the current directory, type = . The screen display changes to

New directory = C:\WP

and the cursor moves to beneath the C. To change the default directory, you can completely retype the directory name, or you can simply edit it. For example, if you wish to create a new letter for Mary and you have set up a directory to contain her documents, you can type

C:\WP\MARY

and press Return (Figure 6.4). You can also use the ← or End key to move the cursor to the end of C:\WP and just type \MARY before pressing Return.

```
Opportunities for Advancement

The bulletin board outside the Personnel Department on the first
floor contains up-to-date listings of job openings within the
company and at field locations throughout the country.  Whenever
possible, openings are filled from within the company.  If you
see a position for which you feel you are qualified, check with
the Personnel Department.


Educational Aid

MagnaCorp offers educational opportunities to employees at all
levels.  Tuition refunds are available to full-time employees for
courses at accredited institutions.  To make sure that a course
for which you plan to enroll will be covered, consult your
manager or the Personnel Department.




New Directory = C:\WP\MARY_
```

FIGURE 6.4: Changing the default directory. To change the directory so that a different directory name will appear when you press F5 (List Files), type = and enter the name of the new directory when prompted to do so.

As soon as you press Return, WordPerfect displays the new directory, including the DOS wildcard characters; for example,

C:\WP\MARY*.*

Press Return again to display all of the files in this directory that can be accommodated in one screen view. All of the files created in the directory are listed alphabetically, from left to right and down each line. You can press F1 (Cancel) or Esc to return to the document editing screen.

You can also change the default directory from the List Files screen. To do so, type **7** (Change Directory) and enter the full path name of the new directory that you want to designate as the default working directory.

Regardless of the method you use, once you have made a particular directory current, all of the documents you create and save will automatically be located in it. You can also use these methods to change the current directory when you wish to retrieve for editing a document that is located in a directory different from the one that is current.

Deleting a Directory

KEY SEQUENCE

F5 Return < select directory or enter *directory name* > 2 Y

You can delete an empty directory from within WordPerfect or from DOS (see "Exiting to DOS through the WordPerfect Shell" later in this chapter). You must delete all files within a directory (except the **.** and **..** directories, which simply represent the current and parent directories) before you can delete the directory. (See "Deleting Files" later in this chapter for instructions regarding how to delete files.)

To delete a directory, highlight its name on the List Files screen. Press F5 and then Return; then move the cursor to the appropriate directory. You can type **6** (Look) and press Return to view the contents of other directories. Then type **2** (Delete) and type **Y** to confirm. If the directory contains files that have not been deleted, you will receive the prompt

ERROR: directory not empty

Go to the directory by using option 6 (Look) and pressing Return; then delete any files the directory contains. You can then return to the previous screen by highlighting the parent directory (marked ..< PARENT > < DIR >), use option 6 (Look), and delete the directory you have just emptied.

Viewing the Contents of a Directory

KEY SEQUENCE

F5 Return (highlight directory) **6 Return**
F5 = *<directory name>* **Return**

WordPerfect allows you to see the names of files each directory contains. This feature is very helpful when you are searching for a file that may be in a subdirectory several levels down. When the List Files screen is visible, you can view the contents of a directory simply by moving the cursor to highlight it, typing **6** (Look), and pressing Return. You can then view the contents of any subdirectories that directory contains by using the same procedure. Figures 6.5 and 6.6 illustrate the process of viewing the directory contents in WordPerfect.

You can also view the contents of a specific directory by pressing = and typing the name of the new directory at the prompt at the bottom of the screen. When you press Return, the screen will display the files contained in that directory, just as in Figures 6.5 and 6.6.

```
01/30/87  16:16            Directory C:\WP\*.*
Document Size:         0                    Free Disk Space:   5246976

. <CURRENT>    <DIR>                .. <PARENT>    <DIR>
4WORD    .     <DIR>   09/25/86 09:45   BILLING .     <DIR>   12/02/86 18:09
BOOK     .     <DIR>   10/27/86 14:08   FILES   .     <DIR>   08/08/86 08:22
QA2      .     <DIR>   08/06/86 10:27   10      .LRN    148   09/25/85 15:58
1X       .MAC    13    09/25/85 15:58   20      .LRN    154   09/25/85 15:58
2COL     .MAC    12    08/06/86 13:12   2X      .MAC     13   09/25/85 15:58
30       .LRN   148    09/25/85 15:58   3X      .MAC     13   09/25/85 15:58
40       .LRN   136    09/25/85 15:58   4X      .MAC     13   09/25/85 15:58
5X       .MAC     3    09/25/85 15:58   ALTB    .MAC      1   07/27/86 12:01
ALTC     .MAC     2    07/27/86 13:09   ALTE    .MAC     11   09/29/86 15:18
ALTF     .MAC     7    07/27/86 12:28   ALTG    .MAC      7   08/06/86 11:39
ALTH     .MAC    13    09/29/86 15:11   ALTI    .MAC      2   07/27/86 12:07
ALTJ     .MAC     5    07/27/86 13:17   ALTK    .MAC      5   07/27/86 12:24
ALTL     .MAC    24    07/27/86 11:50   ALTM    .MAC      2   07/27/86 12:20
ALTO     .MAC     4    07/28/86 11:37   ALTP    .MAC      4   07/27/86 12:03
ALTQ     .MAC     5    07/27/86 12:27   ALTR    .MAC      3   07/27/86 12:22
ALTS     .MAC     8    07/27/86 12:33   ALTT    .MAC      4   07/27/86 12:58
ALTU     .MAC     1    07/27/86 12:02   ALTV    .MAC      8   07/27/86 12:57
ALTW     .MAC     3    07/27/86 12:18   ALTX    .MAC      2   07/27/86 12:05

1 Retrieve; 2 Delete; 3 Rename; 4 Print; 5 Text In;
6 Look; 7 Change Directory; 8 Copy; 9 Word Search; 0 Exit: 6
```

FIGURE 6.5: Viewing the contents of a directory. In this figure, the directory BILLING has been highlighted. When **6** is typed (to indicate Look), the contents of this directory will appear on the screen, as shown in Figure 6.6.

Checking the Contents of Files before You Retrieve Them

KEY SEQUENCE

F5 Return (move cursor to file name) **6** (or **Return**)

WordPerfect has a very useful feature that allows you to display the contents of a document before you retrieve it. This allows you to make sure that the document you are retrieving is indeed the one you are looking for before you actually bring it to the editing screen.

When you have highlighted a document name (rather than a directory name; see "Viewing the Contents of a Directory" earlier in this chapter) on the List Files screen and you type **6** (for Look), the program displays one screenful of the text of the document, as shown in Figure 6.7.

When you use this feature, you can scroll downward through the document only by using either the ↓ or PgDn key. If you press any other key, the program will immediately return you to the List Files screen. If you have added a Document Summary screen to your document, you will see it displayed prior to the first text in the document, even if you have turned off its display (see Chapter 2 for details about creating a Document Summary screen).

```
12/02/86  18:23              Directory C:\WP\BILLING\*.*
Document Size:         24                   Free Disk Space:    7188480

. <CURRENT>     <DIR>                  .. <PARENT>     <DIR>
RECEIVE .       <DIR>    12/02/86 18:23     ACCOUNTS.        2845  11/27/86 09:08
CASHIN  .       20127   10/27/86 14:29     LTTR12-2.         359  12/02/86 18:15
LTTR12-3.          10   12/02/86 18:18     LTTR12-7.          11  12/02/86 18:18
MAGNACOR.        5778   12/02/86 18:01     MEMO12-4.         323  12/02/86 18:18
PAYABLES.        3923   09/29/86 09:11




1 Retrieve; 2 Delete; 3 Rename; 4 Print; 5 Text In;
6 Look; 7 Change Directory; 8 Copy; 9 Word Search; 0 Exit: 6
```

FIGURE 6.6: The contents of the BILLING directory. Other subdirectories within this subdirectory (such as RECEIVE) can be viewed by typing **6** and pressing Return. To return to the previously viewed directory, highlight the directory named .. <PARENT>.

Searching for a File Containing Specific Text

> **KEY SEQUENCE**
>
> **F5 Return** (highlight directory or file within directory) **9**
> Word Pattern: <*search string*> **Return**

Another useful feature of the WordPerfect program is that it allows you to search through all the files in one directory to find a specific word or phrase (up to 20 characters). If you know that a file contains a particular word but cannot remember the name of the file it is in, this feature can be very handy.

When you search a directory for a file containing a specific word or phrase that contains punctuation (a comma, semicolon, or quotation marks) or spaces, you must enter the word or phrase to be searched for in quotation marks.

You can also use wildcards (see "Using Wildcard Characters" earlier in this chapter) to enlarge the search pattern. For example, if you are searching for a file containing an address for a company and you are sure that its name began with *South-* but do not remember whether its full name is *Southwestern, Southeastern,* or *Southern,* you can enter the word pattern as **South***.

```
Filename C:\WP\BOOK\HANDBOOK                         File Size:      5778
WELCOME

Welcome to MagnaCorp. We hope this employee handbook will help to
guide you through your first few days here.  In addition, it
contains valuable information about employee services and
benefits available to you.  Ask your manager or call the
personnel office if you have any questions for which you cannot
find the answers in this handbook.

Work Day

The official work day at MagnaCorp is 8:30 a.m. to 5:00 p.m.
Flexible hours can be arranged with your manager.

Parking

As parking is limited, please apply to the personnel office for a
parking slot assignment.

Hours

Noon to 1 p.m. has been reserved as lunch hour for all employees.
NOTE: This text is not displayed in WordPerfect format.
Press any key to continue_
```

FIGURE 6.7: Viewing the contents of a document before you retrieve it. You c n use the Look option (option 6) of the List Files screen to view one screenful of a document's contents before you retrieve it to make sure it is the document you want. To return to the List Files screen, press any key on the keyboard. You can move through a document thus displayed only by pressing either the ↓ or PgDn key.

You can further expand or restrict a word search by using semicolons and blank spaces (which stand for AND) or commas (which stand for OR). For example, to search for files that contain both *invoice* and *past due,* you enter

invoice;"past due"

To search for files that contain either the word *invoice* or the phrase *past due,* you enter

invoice,"past due"

For files containing *October* and either *invoice* or *past due*, you enter

invoice,"past due"; October

Figures 6.8 through 6.10 illustrate the process of searching for a word pattern. In Figure 6.8, the program is being instructed to search the directory BILLING for the phrase *past due;* Figure 6.9 shows the file names that appear. The location of the phrase in the file is displayed in Figure 6.10.

To search for a word pattern,

1. Press F5 (List Files) Return.

2. Highlight the directory you wish to search or highlight any file name in the directory.

```
12/02/86  18:39            Directory C:\WP\BILLING\*.*
Document Size:        364                    Free Disk Space:    7143424

. <CURRENT>    <DIR>                 .. <PARENT>    <DIR>
RECEIVE  .    <DIR>    12/02/86 18:23   ACCOUNTS.       2845   11/27/86 09:08
CASHIN   .    20127    10/27/86 14:29   LTTR12-2.        359   12/02/86 18:15
LTTR12-7.       364    12/02/86 18:30   LTTR12-7.BK!     361   12/02/86 18:29
MAGNACOR.      5778    12/02/86 18:01   MEMO12-4.        323   12/02/86 18:18
PAYABLES.      3923    09/29/86 09:11   SCREEN15.CAP    4256   12/02/86 18:30
SCREEN17.CAP   4256    12/02/86 18:37   SCREEN18.CAP    4256   12/02/86 18:38
SCREEN19.CAP   4256    12/02/86 18:39






Word Pattern: past due_
```

FIGURE 6.8: Searching a directory for a word pattern. The directory BILLING is being searched for the phrase *past due*. All files containing that phrase will be listed on the screen that appears in Figure 6.9.

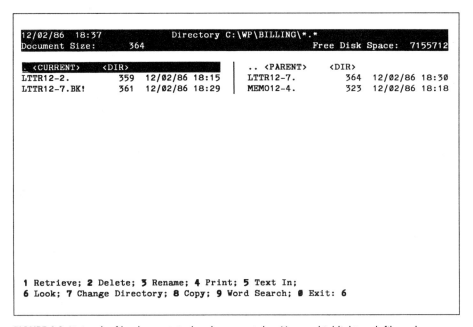

```
12/02/86  18:37              Directory C:\WP\BILLING\*.*
Document Size:       364                      Free Disk Space:  7155712

. <CURRENT>    <DIR>                .. <PARENT>    <DIR>
LTTR12-2.        359  12/02/86 18:15    LTTR12-7.        364  12/02/86 18:30
LTTR12-7.BK!     361  12/02/86 18:29    MEMO12-4.        323  12/02/86 18:18
```

```
1 Retrieve; 2 Delete; 3 Rename; 4 Print; 5 Text In;
6 Look; 7 Change Directory; 8 Copy; 9 Word Search; 0 Exit: 6
```

FIGURE 6.9: Listing the files that contain the phrase *past due.* You can highlight each file and press Return to see the occurrence of the phrase *past due* within the file.

3. Type **9** (for Word Search). The following prompt appears at the bottom of the screen.

   Word Pattern:

4. Enter the word pattern.
5. Press Return.

The program searches the current directory and lists the name of each file that contains the word or phrase. You can then move the cursor to each document and press Return or 6 (Look) to verify which document is the one you are looking for; the page containing the word or phrase is presented when you press Return.

COPYING FILES

KEY SEQUENCE

F5 Return (highlight file name) **8** <*drive name* and/or *path name*>

```
Filename C:\WP\BILLING\LTTR12-7                    File Size:        364
Marshall Mobile Homes
3422 West Bayshore
Mountain View, CA 94303

Dear Client:

The attached copies of current invoices show that your account
number 455-1180 is over sixty days past due.  Please call us at
555-3400, extension 772, to discuss arrangements for late
payments and to avoid incurring additional fees.

Sincerely,

T. R. Mason
Finance Department




NOTE: This text is not displayed in WordPerfect format.
Press any key to continue_
```

FIGURE 6.10: Viewing the contents of the file. The portion of the file containing the phrase being searched for—in this case, *past due*—is shown on the screen.

WordPerfect's List Files screen (displayed when you press F5 and press Return) also allows you to copy files. This feature is very useful when you need to move a document into a different directory or copy a file onto a floppy disk so that you can use it as a backup or transfer it to a hard disk at another location. You can also use this feature to rename a document by making a copy of it under a different name.

If you only want to copy a file under its same name in a different drive or directory, you do not have to retype the name. Simply indicate the drive or directory onto which you want the file copied.

You can copy several files at once by marking each with an asterisk before you type **8** for option 8 (Copy).

To copy a file (or several files),

1. Press F5 (List Files), press Return, and highlight the file you wish to copy or mark them with asterisks if there are several files. (You can display different directories by moving the highlight to their names, typing **6** (Look), and pressing Return to view their contents.)

2. Type **8** for option 8 (Copy). The following prompt will appear:

    Copy This File To:

You can simply type a drive name followed by a colon to copy each file under its same name to a disk on another drive. For example, if you want to copy a file named LTTR27 to a floppy disk in drive A, you type

A:

at the prompt, and the file will be copied under the name LTTR27 onto the disk in drive A.

If you want to copy a file to another directory, you must use the path name that indicates where you want the file to be copied. For example, to copy LTTR27 to a subdirectory named BOB on drive C (your current location), you type

BOB

You can rename the file by giving it a new name at the prompt. For example, to rename LTTR27 as BOB27 and copy the file to the BOB subdirectory, you enter

BOB\BOB27

When you have finished copying files to their appropriate directories, you can use option 2, Delete, to delete the files from the directory you have just copied them from.

DELETING FILES

KEY SEQUENCE

F5 *< directory name >* **Return** (highlight file) **2 Y**

To delete files within WordPerfect, you use the F5 (List Files) key and specify the directory containing the file(s) you wish to delete. Note that you can also go directly to the List Files screen and use option 6 (Look) to examine the contents of directories and files to determine which you want to delete. When the List Files screen appears, highlight the file you wish to delete and type **2** (for Delete). To delete several files, move the highlight to each and type * (asterisk), as shown in Figure 6.11. Then type **2** for option 2 (Delete). You will be prompted to confirm whether you want to delete the files you have indicated.

MAKING BACKUP COPIES

WordPerfect gives you several ways to safeguard your work by backing up files to another disk and by creating duplicate copies of files on the same disk. The following sections examine these methods.

```
12/02/86  19:06               Directory C:\WP\BILLING\*.*
Document Size:        364                        Free Disk Space:   7106560

  . <CURRENT>    <DIR>                .. <PARENT>    <DIR>
  RECEIVE .      <DIR>   12/02/86 18:23    ACCOUNTS.       2845  11/27/86 09:08
  CASHIN  .      20127   10/27/86 14:29    LTTR12-2.        359  12/02/86 18:15
  LTTR12-7.        364   12/02/86 18:30    LTTR12-7.BK!     361  12/02/86 18:29
  MAGNACOR.       5778   12/02/86 18:01    MEMO12-4.        323  12/02/86 18:18
  PAYABLES.       3923   09/29/86 09:11    SCREEN15.CAP    4256* 12/02/86 18:30
  SCREEN17.CAP   4256*   12/02/86 18:37    SCREEN18.CAP    4256* 12/02/86 18:38
  SCREEN19.CAP   4256*   12/02/86 18:39






  Delete Marked Files? (Y/N) N
```

FIGURE 6.11: Marking several files to be deleted. You can delete several files at a time by marking each with an asterisk before you type 2 to delete them. You can also use this method to copy and print several files at the same time.

Disk Backup Copies

You should always back up your work by making a copy of it and keeping the copy in a place separate from the one where you normally store your files. If you are using a two-disk-drive system, this means copying important files onto other floppy disks and storing them in a covered place away from heat, light, and magnetic sources. If you are using a hard disk system, this means establishing a backup system whereby you store important files on floppy disks and store those disks in a location separate from your hard disk. (See "Backing Up a Hard Disk" later in this chapter.) Backing up your disks is a precaution you should take in addition to backing up your files. If a disk gets damaged, the files it contains may be unusable. Keeping a separate disk backup copy can save you from having to recreate a great deal of work.

Automatic Backup

The WordPerfect program can create automatic backup files for you on the disk you have specified to contain your program files. The program provides an Automatic Timed Backup feature that allows you to set the number of minutes between each automatic save operation.

If you save the document when you exit the program at the end of your work session, the special file named {WP}BACK.1, in which your edits are saved, is automatically erased. However, if you experience some kind of problem that prevents you from exiting WordPerfect normally, this special file is retained. You can then rename it and use it as your working copy of the document. Using this feature means that the only edits you can possibly lose are those between the time the last automatic save operation occurred and the time you experienced the power interruption or computer failure.

Original Backup

WordPerfect also provides an Original Backup feature to automatically save two copies of a document that has been edited: one copy of the document in its original form and the other containing all of your editing changes. If you use this feature, you must have sufficient storage space on your data disk to accommodate both an edited and unedited version of the document.

> *Note:* Both the Automatic Timed Backup and the Original Backup features are inactive when you first use WordPerfect. To activate them, you must start WordPerfect by using the Setup menu (WP/S). For a complete description of how to set these features, refer to Chapter 16.

CHECKING DISK SPACE

KEY SEQUENCE

To check the amount of free space in the current directory or the size of the current document:

F5 Return

The top of the List Files screen, which you view by pressing F5, indicates the amount of available disk space at the Free Disk Space: prompt (Figure 6.12) at the top right of the screen. At the left side of the same line, it also lists the size (in bytes) of the current document.

In Figure 6.12, you can see that the document currently being edited uses 376 bytes, and 7,118,848 bytes of space are still available in the directory WP\BILL-ING. In addition, the size of each document in the directory is listed below as part of the file listing.

If you save your WordPerfect documents on a disk in a floppy disk drive (either drive A or drive B), you can use this information about document size and free disk space to make sure that there is still sufficient space on the disk to save the document you are currently editing. For a document to be successfully saved on a disk, the document size must be less than or equal to the amount of free disk space.

```
12/02/86  19:10                 Directory C:\WP\BILLING\*.*
Document Size:        376                       Free Disk Space:   7118848

. <CURRENT>    <DIR>                .. <PARENT>    <DIR>
RECEIVE .     <DIR>   12/02/86 18:23   ACCOUNTS.       2845  11/27/86 09:08
CASHIN  .     20127   10/27/86 14:29   LTTR12-2.        359  12/02/86 18:15
LTTR12-7.       364   12/02/86 18:30   LTTR12-7.BK!     361  12/02/86 18:29
MAGNACOR.      5778   12/02/86 18:01   MEMO12-4.        323  12/02/86 18:18
PAYABLES.      3923   09/29/86 09:11




    1 Retrieve; 2 Delete; 3 Rename; 4 Print; 5 Text In;
    6 Look; 7 Change Directory; 8 Copy; 9 Word Search; 0 Exit: 6
```

FIGURE 6.12: Checking the size of the current document and the amount of unused disk space in the default directory. As you can see from the figure, the current document uses 376 bytes, and 7,118,848 bytes are still available in the directory WP\BILLING.

PASSWORD PROTECTING A DOCUMENT

If you work with sensitive material or material to which many others have access, you may want to place password protection on some of your files so that only you or those you authorize (by giving them the password) can open those files. A password can contain up to 75 characters.

It goes without saying that you should keep a record of the passwords you assign to files so that you can open these files again. The program does not provide a way for you to open files you have locked unless you use the correct password, so to protect yourself, keep a written (and up-to-date) record of your passwords in a safe place.

Locking a File

KEY SEQUENCE

Ctrl-F5 4 *<password> <password>* (Version 4.2)
Ctrl-F5 3 *<password> <password>* (earlier versions)

To lock a file, you press Ctrl-F5 to view the Text In/Out menu. Select option 4 (in Version 4.2; select option 3 in earlier versions) and enter the password twice. Word-Perfect does not display the password on the screen, so it asks you to enter it twice to protect against typing errors. After you have locked a file in this way, WordPerfect will prompt you to enter the password twice each time you save the file.

Retrieving a Locked File

KEY SEQUENCE

Shift-F10 <*file name*> **Return** <*password*>

or

F5 1 <*file name*> **Return** <*password*>

or

Ctrl-F5 5 <*file name*> **Return** <*password*> (Version 4.2)
Ctrl-F5 4 <*file name*> **Return** <*password*> (earlier versions)

To retrieve a file that you have locked, you can use any of the standard retrieval methods in WordPerfect:

- You can press Shift-F10, enter the name of the file, and enter the password when prompted to do so.
- You can retrieve the file by displaying the List Files screen, highlighting the file name, and entering **1** (for Retrieve).
- You can (in Version 4.2) use the Text In/Out screen to retrieve the file (option 5).
- You can (in earlier versions) use the Text In/Out screen (Ctrl-F5) to retrieve the file and unlock it (see "Removing Password Protection" later in this chapter).

Once you have retrieved a locked file, you can edit it just as any other Word-Perfect document. The major difference between it and other documents you create in WordPerfect is that you must always print it from the screen. This feature prevents others from printing a locked file.

Printing a Locked File

KEY SEQUENCE

To print the entire document:
Shift-F7 1

To print the displayed page:
Shift-F7 2

To print a locked file, you must have it displayed on your screen. Press Shift-F7 (Print) and select either option 1 to print the entire document or option 2 to print the page that is displayed.

Because the program loads the entire locked document into memory in order to print it, you may not have sufficient RAM to print long locked documents. If you work with these types of documents often, save them in smaller sections of, for example, 10 pages each. That way you will probably never have a problem with memory allocation when you print locked documents.

Removing Password Protection

Whenever you wish to remove password protection from a particular file in Version 4.2, you must save the document without using its password. To save the file, press F10 and Return (assuming that you wish to save the file under the same file name). You will then be prompted to enter the password. Instead of typing the original password, you press Return and then type **Y** to replace the file. When WordPerfect saves the file this time, it will do so without the password. Thereafter, you can retrieve this document just as you do any document file that is not password protected.

EXITING TO DOS THROUGH THE WORDPERFECT SHELL

KEY SEQUENCE

To go to DOS:
Ctrl-F1 1
To return to WordPerfect:
EXIT Return

If you have sufficient RAM, you can temporarily exit to DOS while in WordPerfect. You may, for example, need to format some disks or use another program such as Lotus 1-2-3 or dBASE III Plus. (See Chapter 15 for details about transferring data between WordPerfect and other software programs that you use.)

To exit to DOS through the Shell command, press Ctrl-F1 (Shell) and select option 1 (Go to DOS). While you are in DOS you can use any of its commands to carry out tasks. For example, you can copy, rename, or delete files or format new data disks. When you have finished working in DOS, type **EXIT** to return to WordPerfect.

If you type **WP** to return to WordPerfect from DOS instead of typing **EXIT**, you will receive a "Directory is in use" error message. Type **1** to exit and then type **EXIT** to return to WordPerfect.

Renaming a File from DOS

To rename a file from DOS, you use the RENAME (REN) command. (you can always exit temporarily to DOS by pressing Ctrl-F1 and selecting option 1, Go to DOS; see the previous section.) Be sure to enter the complete path name if the drive containing the file you want to rename is not the current drive, or if the directory containing the file is not the current directory. Use any extensions that the file has or that you want it to have. For example, to change a file name from TEST to MACROS, you enter

REN TEST MACROS

to rename the file on the current drive and the current directory. Enter

REN A:TEST.MAC MACROS.MAC

to rename the file TEST.MAC on drive A. As you can see, it is much simpler and faster to use WordPerfect's List Files feature to first locate a file and then rename it.

BACKING UP A HARD DISK AND RESTORING FILES

If you are using WordPerfect on a hard disk, you will sometimes need to back up files from the hard disk. In addition, you will often need to transfer files to floppy disks so that you can move them to a different workstation without a hard disk—to a computer in a colleague's office or at home, for example.

In an office environment, you should make it a practice to back up files to floppy disks daily, just in case of a hard disk failure. For your own personal use, you should follow this rule of thumb: Back up what you do not want to lose. If you have spent a long time creating a file and do not want to lose that work and effort, be sure to back it up.

These backup copies are in addition to the backup files WordPerfect creates and saves for you (see "Making Backup Copies" earlier in this chapter as well as Chapter 16 for details about using the Setup menu to specify automatic backup). The WordPerfect backup files are also stored on the hard disk, which will not do you any good if you have a hard disk failure.

You can back up the contents of an entire hard disk (which you might want to do, for example, before physically moving the computer). You can also back up the contents of a directory or document file. The following sections briefly explain the procedures used to back up and restore files in each of these situations. For additional information, refer to *Power User's Guide to Hard Disk Management* by Jonathan Kamin (SYBEX, 1987).

Backing Up a Hard Disk

To back up the entire contents of a hard disk (named drive C), including all subdirectories, use the following command in DOS:

BACKUP C:\ A: /S

If your hard disk is drive D or some other drive, you would use that drive letter instead of the C in the preceding command. The /S argument ensures that all subdirectories are backed up. You will be prompted to insert additional floppy disks as necessary.

To back up only those files that have been modified since the last backup, use the command

BACKUP C:\ A: /S/M

To use this command effectively, you must always answer the system date and time prompts accurately. Otherwise the system has no way of keeping track of when each file was last modified.

Restoring files to the hard disk follows a similar procedure. Use the command

RESTORE A: C:\ /S

to restore files (including the contents of subdirectories) contained on a floppy disk in drive A to a hard disk named drive C.

Backing Up a Directory

To back up only the contents of a certain directory to a floppy disk in drive A, you use the command

BACKUP C: <*directory name*> A:

This backs up all the files in the directory whose name you specify. You will be prompted to insert additional floppy disks as necessary.

To restore a backed-up directory to the hard disk (if, for example, you are transferring files from one hard disk to another), you use the command

RESTORE A: C: <*directory name*> /P

The /P argument tells DOS to prompt you for each file to restore. You may, for example, want to restore some files but not others.

Backing Up a File

You can also choose to back up only one file from the hard disk to a floppy disk. The command to do this is

BACKUP C: *<file name>* **A:**

This backs up a file on the hard disk (drive C) to a floppy disk in drive A. If the floppy disk in drive A already has files on it, use the command

BACKUP C: *<file name>* **A: /A**

The /A tells DOS to append files to the contents of the floppy disk, not overwrite them.

Likewise, to restore a file to the hard disk, you must use the RESTORE command. You can simply enter

RESTORE A: C: *<file name>*

SUMMARY

This chapter has explored many of the techniques you can use for managing your files in WordPerfect as well as in its operating system, DOS. You have seen how to

- Name and rename files
- Work with directories
- Save, retrieve, copy, delete, and print files
- Work with more than one file at once
- Make several different kinds of backup copies

The topic of file management encompasses many techniques. Other chapters that contain related material are

- Chapter 1, "WordPerfect's Startup Commands, Editing Screen, and Keyboard Layout"
- Chapter 5, "Printing Documents"
- Chapter 15, "Importing and Exporting Documents"
- Chapter 16, "Installation, Setup, and Startup Options"

The next part of this book explains many specialized word processing features that you may or may not use in your work. Included are chapters on creating listings and citations, working with multicolumn material, merge printing, sorting, and using mathematics and equations in WordPerfect. You may wish to explore these chapters selectively as you need the material in them.

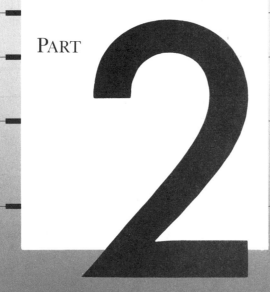

PART

2

SPECIALIZED WORD
PROCESSING FEATURES

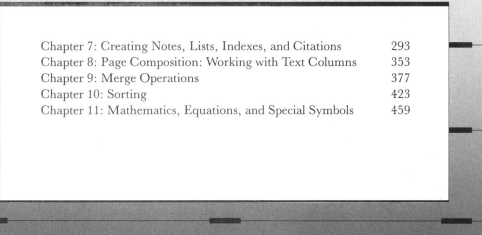

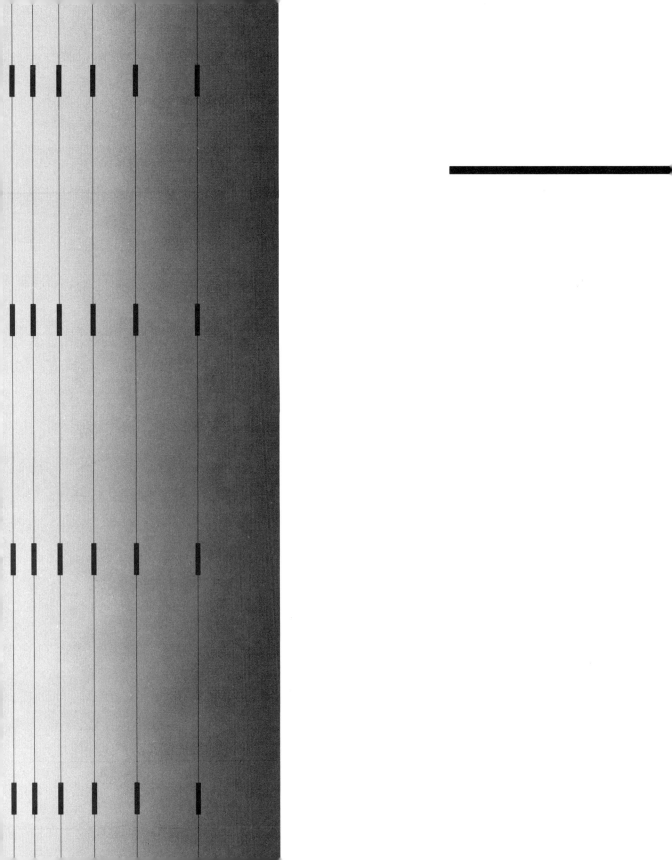

CHAPTER 7

CREATING NOTES, LISTS, INDEXES, AND CITATIONS

CREATING NOTES, LISTS, INDEXES, AND CITATIONS

ordPerfect contains several built-in functions that streamline specialized word processing tasks required in certain occupations. For example, it can

- Create footnotes and endnotes
- Create tables of contents
- Create and reorganize lists
- Generate outlines
- Generate indexes
- Create concordances (Version 4.2)
- Number lines (Version 4.2)
- Create citations (Version 4.2)
- Generate a table of authorities (Version 4.2)

If your work calls for any of these specialized functions, you will appreciate the tools WordPerfect gives you. For example, if you create documents such as long business reports or professional papers that require a table of contents as well as tables of tables and figures, footnotes, and indexes, you will find WordPerfect's specialized features indispensable. If you are in the legal profession, you will often use WordPerfect's automatic line numbering feature as well as its ability to mark citations and generate tables of authorities.

This chapter discusses the techniques used to generate these special formats in your documents. If you do not use any of these formats in your work, you may wish to turn to another chapter in this part of the book that discusses a specialized technique applicable to the tasks you do. Chapter 8 discusses using multicolumn layouts, which you will find useful if you prepare newsletters, manuals, or brochures. Chapters 9 and 10 explain techniques used for merge printing and sorting, which have a variety of applications in all fields, and Chapter 11 contains information about using mathematics, equations, and special symbols within WordPerfect.

FOOTNOTES AND ENDNOTES

If your work requires you to create footnotes—notes that appear at the bottoms of pages—and endnotes—notes that appear at the end of a document or at the end of each chapter or section in a document—you will appreciate the many features that WordPerfect provides.

When you create footnotes, WordPerfect automatically inserts them at the bottom of the page. Figure 7.1 illustrates an example of a page with several footnotes. If the note and the line referencing the note will not fit on the same page, WordPerfect automatically breaks the page and carries the footnote and its reference line to the next page.

When you add or delete a note, WordPerfect automatically renumbers all of your notes for you. That way you never have to worry about searching through your documents and changing the note numbering system each time you change your notes.

Endnotes are simply footnotes that are printed at the end of a document rather than as footnotes on the page where their reference occurs. When endnotes are printed, their reference numbers appear on the same line as the note (Figure 7.2), whereas footnote numbers will be superscripted if your printer can print superscripts. The sciences generally use this type of reference list rather than footnotes, and this system is becoming increasingly popular in other fields as well. Some people believe that documents using this system are more readable than those that use footnotes because readers are not interrupted by references they may not need.

Another system of annotating a document uses both footnotes and endnotes: footnotes that explain or further clarify material on the page and endnotes that provide a list of references or suggestions for further reading. If you choose this system, you will want to change the system of footnote numbering to use different symbols from those you use for endnotes; you may also want to specify that footnote marking start over again on each new page; see "Numbering Notes by Page" later in this chapter.

When you create a note (using Ctrl-F7 1 for footnotes and Ctrl-F7 5 for endnotes), you simply type it into the text where you want it to appear. WordPerfect gives you a full screen in which to create the footnote. There is, practically speaking, no limit to the size of the footnote you can create—WordPerfect allows you to create a 16,000-character footnote if you choose. When you return to the editing screen, you see only the footnote number, not the text of the footnote itself. You can press Alt-F3 (Reveal Codes) to see the first 50 characters of the note, as shown in Figure 7.3. To see the note in its entirety, you must select the option to edit it (Ctrl-F7 2 or 6).

The default settings for footnotes create notes like the ones shown in Figure 7.1: Numbering begins with an Arabic 1, footnotes appear at the bottoms of pages, there is a 2-inch rule between footnotes and the text of the document, the

A business, once it gets beyond the entrepreneurial stage,[1] next faces the challenge of organizing and managing itself as a stable company.[2] Managers who heretofore were rewarded for initiative and ingenuity are now penalized for outstepping the boundaries of corporate rules; employees who in the past were rewarded for their willingness to challenge established theory must now follow corporate canons. In this stage of business growth a radical change in the employee-manager mix may be noted.[3]

At the same time the business is facing this challenge, it meets yet another challenge: managing for future growth. A dynamic business cannot be allowed to stagnate; it must always be planning for the future. The future, in such a case, may mean diversification rather than the former concentration on a narrow set of goals. Yet another type of managerial thinking is required: that of long-range planners.[4]

These different types of idealists must manage a new set of assumptions to manage for current stability while planning for future expansion. Such planners must be able to juggle one set of conservative assumptions while at the same time exercising a plan of highly imaginative proportions that concerns five- and ten-year growth plans and beyond. Such thinkers are scarce; when found, they command excellent salaries.

[1]See Paul L. Salomon, <u>The Entrepreneurial Mind</u> (Chicago: Row-Martin, 1987).

[2] Saul C. Guttman, <u>Stages in Business Growth</u> (Hoffman: Baltimore, 1987), p.198

[3]This is also the time of most rapid employee expansion, so the mix in personality types may pass unnoticed.

[4]Eldon R. WainWright, <u>Long-Range Planning for Corporate Policy</u> (Harrison & Ball: New York, 1987).

FIGURE 7.1: Footnotes on a printed page. WordPerfect will break pages to keep footnotes on the page to which they refer unless you instruct it otherwise. You can also change the default 2-inch rule that separates footnotes from text.

```
1.Carruthers, R. M., et al., Establishing a Value-Added
Performance Appraisal System (New York: Abbott Press, 1987).

2.Stein, J. M., "A Dual System of Performance Appraisal," in The
Immediate Manager 18:22-35 (April 1987).

3.McKnight, S. L., and Harrington, T.L., Corporate Strategies
for the Twentieth Century (Indianapolis: Hubris Publishers, 1987).

4.Stephens, R. W., Motivation: The Inner-Directed Search (New
York: Abbott Press, 1986).
```

FIGURE 7.2: Endnotes printed at the end of a document. WordPerfect automatically numbers endnotes for you. If you delete a note or add a new one, WordPerfect adjusts the numbering system.

```
A performance appraisal system has, among others, the following
goals1:
        To assess actual performance
 _      To motivate employees
        To provide a system of rewards (and punishments)2
        To open a channel of feedback between employee and manager

C:\WP\BOOK\CHAP7\NOTES                        Doc 1  Pg 1  Ln 7      Pos 10
[ ▲   ▲    ▲    ▲    ▲    ▲    ▲    ▲    ▲    ▲    ▲    ]▲   ▲    ▲
A performance appraisal system has, among others, the following[SRt]
goals[Note:Foot,1;[Note #]See Carruthers et al., Establishing a Value[-]Added ..
. ]:[Index:Performance Appraisal System;Goals of][HRt]
[TAB]To assess actual performance [HRt]
_[TAB]To motivate employees[HRt]
[TAB]To provide a system of rewards (and punishments)[Note:Foot,2;[Note #]Klein
and Stephens report an interesting sideligh ... ][HRt]
[->Indent]To open a channel of feedback between employee and manager[HRt]
[HRt]
```

FIGURE 7.3: Viewing the contents of a note by pressing Alt-F3. When you press Alt-F3 near the position of a note, WordPerfect displays the first 50 characters of the note. To see the rest of the note, press any noncursor key; then press Ctrl-F7 and select option 2 (for a footnote) or option 6 (for an endnote).

footnote number is superscripted, and footnotes are single spaced with one line between each note. You have several options for changing these default settings:

- You can change the line spacing within footnotes to space and a half, double spacing, and so forth.

- You can change line spacing between footnotes, also in half-line increments.
- You can change the system of numbering from Arabic numerals to letters, symbols, or words, such as *Note:*.
- You can change the numbering system so that WordPerfect begins numbering each time a new page begins.
- You can specify the number of lines that are to be kept together when WordPerfect must break the last part of a footnote onto the following page. In Version 4.2, you can also specify that a "(Continued...)" message be inserted when WordPerfect splits footnotes between pages.
- You can specify that a rule be inserted across the bottom of the page to separate footnotes from text, or you can specify that no rule be used.

The default settings for endnotes create endnotes at the end of your document, using Arabic numerals with periods and single spacing the notes. If you want endnotes to appear on a page by themselves, move the cursor to the end of your document (Home Home ↓) and press Ctrl-Return to insert a new page before you print the document.

If you change the margins of a document that contains notes, the program does not automatically reset the margins of footnotes and endnotes for you. To make sure your footnote and endnote margins are correct, move to the beginning of your document (Home Home ↑) and perform a word count (Ctrl-F2 6). This automatically updates the margin settings in the notes as well as in the headers and footers. If you prefer, you can search for each footnote or endnote and simply exit from it without making any changes; this process also updates the margin settings but takes a little longer. When you use this method, you may wish to give your notes a final review at the same time, making any necessary changes.

The following sections explain the techniques used in working with footnotes and endnotes. As the procedures are the same in both cases—with the exception of certain option numbers—both footnotes and endnotes will be referred to as *notes* unless one or the other is specifically meant.

Creating a Note

KEY SEQUENCE

Footnotes:
   Ctrl-F7 1 <*note*> **F7**
Endnotes:
   Ctrl-F7 5 <*note*> **F7**

REVEAL CODES

[Note]

You can create a note at any position in your text. WordPerfect automatically starts numbering with 1. If you want to begin with a different number, or if you want to use letters or symbols instead of Arabic numbers in your notes, see "Changing the Note Numbering System" later in this chapter. If you want to use words to indicate notes (such as *Note:*), see "Using Strings to Indicate Notes" later in this chapter.

To create a note, you use the Ctrl-F7 key sequence. The following menu appears:

**1 Create; 2 Edit; 3 New #: 4 Options; 5 Create Endnote;
6 Edit Endnote: 0**

When you create a footnote (by selecting option 1), the screen shown in Figure 7.4 appears. (The screen is identical for endnotes, except that the 1 in the upper-left corner has a period following it because endnotes are not numbered with superscripts.)

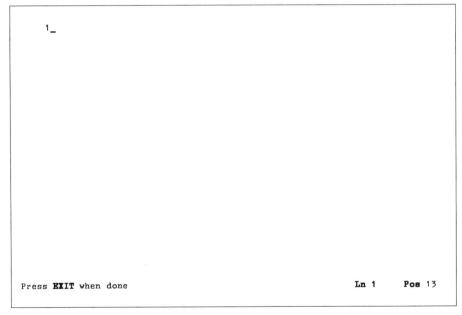

FIGURE 7.4: The footnote editing screen. There is almost no limit to the size of the notes you can create in WordPerfect. The screen for creating and editing endnotes is the same except that the 1 in the upper-left corner is followed by a period (1.).

You can enter a footnote of any length that you wish. When WordPerfect formats the page, it subtracts the number of lines the footnote requires from the number of text lines, including the headers and footers that must appear on the page. If WordPerfect cannot fit all of the footnote on the page that contains the line to which it refers, it will keep a minimum of two lines of the footnote on the page, plus a blank line to separate the footnote from the rule, before beginning a new page. For example, if you have an eight-line footnote on a page that can hold only five lines of the footnote, three lines of it will be carried to the bottom of the next page. You can change the minimum number of lines to be kept on the first page; you can also specify that WordPerfect insert the message "(Continued...)" when it breaks footnotes. See "Specifying How Footnotes Break" later in this chapter.

When you press F7 (Exit) to return to the editing screen after creating a note, the note number appears as shown in Figure 7.5. When your document is printed, footnote numbers (or letters or symbols) will be printed as superscripts (assuming your printer has that capability); endnotes will be referenced in text as superscripts, but their numbers will be on the same line as the text in the reference list (see Figure 7.2).

```
A performance appraisal system has, among others, the following
goals1:
        To assess actual performance
   _    To motivate employees
        To provide a system of rewards (and punishments)2
        To open a channel of feedback between employee and manager

A well-designed performance appraisal system has as its foremost
characteristic that there be no surprises--that is, that ongoing
communication between employee and manager be so thorough as to
let both know where they stand at all times.

Scheduling Performance Appraisals

Such results can only be achieved by a system of frequent
meetings, both formal and informal, between employees and their
managers. Securing commitment to the goals of this process
facilitates communication and establishes a climate that is
conducive to change and growth within a corporation3.

In technical white-collar industries, many companies have found
that a bi-weekly system of informal meetings combined with a
formal review every six months produces satisfactory results.
Usually, however, a system in which formal meetings occur more
C:\WP\BOOK\CHAP7\NOTES                    Doc 1  Pg 1  Ln 7      Pos 10
```

FIGURE 7.5: Note numbers as they appear in your document on the editing screen. These numbers (or symbols, if you are not using the default numbering system) normally appear as superscripts in the printed document.

Editing a Note

> **KEY SEQUENCE**
>
> Footnote:
> **Ctrl-F7 2** <*footnote number*> **Return** (edit footnote) **F7**
> Endnote:
> **Ctrl-F7 6** <*endnote number*> **Return** (edit endnote) **F7**

To edit a note, you do not have to position the cursor on the note number. When you press Ctrl-F7 and select option 2 (to edit a footnote), you will see the prompt

Ftn#?

Type the number of the note you wish to edit.

Likewise, when you edit an endnote, you receive the prompt

Endn#?

when you select option 6. You can thus step through all the notes in your document if you choose and review or edit the contents of all of the notes.

When you edit a note, all of WordPerfect's features, including any macros you have created, are available to you. When you spell check your document using options 2 or 3 of the Spell feature, WordPerfect spell checks each note in the order it occurs in your text.

Deleting a Note

> **KEY SEQUENCE**
>
> (position cursor on note number) **Del**

To delete a note from a document, position the cursor on the note number and then press Del. You can also press Alt-F3 (Reveal Codes) to see the format code WordPerfect has inserted for the note and simply backspace over it. Each time you insert a note into your document, WordPerfect inserts the code [Note], as shown in Figure 7.6. You can use the program's Search feature (F2) to search for each occurrence of the [Note] code and delete notes. WordPerfect automatically renumbers notes each time you delete one.

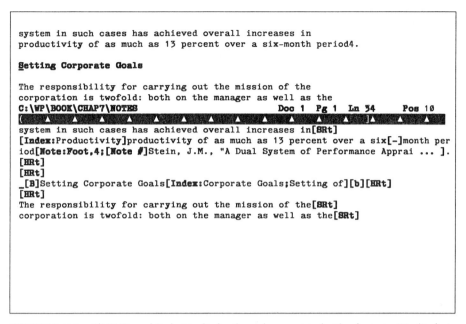

FIGURE 7.6: Using Alt-F3 (Reveal Codes) to display the codes associated with a footnote. WordPerfect automatically supplies the number of the footnote in the code. To delete a footnote from your document, you can display the footnote codes, position the cursor to the right of the codes, and press Backspace. You can also search your document for [Note] codes and delete them without displaying them.

To search for [Note] codes, you must generate the formatting symbol at the prompt

> −>Srch:

1. Position the cursor at the beginning of the document (press Home Home ↑) and press F2 (Search).

2. When the Search prompt appears, press Ctrl-F7 and select option 1, Footnote/Endnote. The Search prompt will then display

> −>Srch:[Note]

3. When WordPerfect finds a note, you can delete it by pressing Backspace. The program displays the prompt

> **Delete Note? (Y/N) N**

> Enter **Y** to delete the note. Press F2 again to have WordPerfect search through your document for the next occurrence of the [Note] code.

Simply typing [**Note**] at this prompt will cause the program to search your document for any occurrences of the word *Note* in brackets in your text.

Changing Note Options

When you select option 4 from the Footnote menu (Ctrl-F7), the screen shown
in Figure 7.7 appears. As you can see, there are many options you can use with
footnotes and endnotes. The following sections explain each of these and illustrate how you can use them in documents you create.

Be sure to return to the beginning of your document (by pressing Home
Home ↑) before you change note options so that the options you select will apply
to all the notes in your document.

CHANGING LINE SPACING IN NOTES

KEY SEQUENCE

Ctrl-F7 4 1 *<number>* **Return F7** (Exit)

The default spacing for notes is single spacing; you can select other line spacing for your notes, using half-line increments. For example, to use space-and-a-
half spacing in notes, enter **1.5**, for double spacing, enter **2**, and so forth.

```
Footnote Options

     1 - Spacing within notes              1
     2 - Spacing between notes             1
     3 - Lines to keep together            3
     4 - Start footnote numbers each page  N
     5 - Footnote numbering mode           0
     6 - Endnote numbering mode            0
     7 - Line separating text and footnotes 1
     8 - Footnotes at bottom of page       Y
     9 - Characters for notes              *
     A - String for footnotes in text      [SuprScrpt][Note]
     B - String for endnotes in text       [SuprScrpt][Note]
     C - String for footnotes in note           [SuprScrpt][Note]
     D - String for endnotes in note        [Note].

     For options 5 & 6:          For option 7:
        0 - Numbers                 0 - No line
        1 - Characters              1 - 2 inch line
        2 - Letters                 2 - Line across entire page
                                    3 - 2 in. line w/continued strings

Selection: 0
```

FIGURE 7.7: The Footnote Options screen. WordPerfect allows you to style many different aspects of
notes, including how they are printed and what numbering system they use. Despite the name of this
screen, its options apply to endnotes as well.

CHANGING LINE SPACING BETWEEN NOTES

> **KEY SEQUENCE**
>
> **Ctrl-F7 4 2** *<number>* **Return F7** (Exit)

The default setting for spacing between notes is 1, which means that there will be one line of space between notes. If you would like additional space between notes, enter **1.5** (for one and a half lines of space between notes) or **2** (for two lines of space between notes), for example.

SPECIFYING HOW FOOTNOTES BREAK

> **KEY SEQUENCE**
>
> **Ctrl-F7 4 3** *<number>* **Return F7** (Exit)

WordPerfect will keep at least three lines of a footnote on the same page as its reference before beginning a new page (the default setting) unless you specify otherwise. You can enter a new number for the minimum number of lines you want to appear together on the same page. If you never want footnotes to be split, enter a number greater than the number of lines in the longest footnote.

In Version 4.2, option 7 also lets you specify that a "(Continued...)" message appear when a footnote is split. When the footnote continues on the next page, it begins with "(...Continued)" (see "Changing the Line That Separates Footnotes from Text" later in this chapter).

NUMBERING NOTES BY PAGE

> **KEY SEQUENCE**
>
> **Ctrl-F7 4 4 Y F7** (Exit)

WordPerfect allows you to specify whether it is to number notes consecutively throughout a document (the default setting) or whether you want it to begin numbering with 1 or a beginning symbol each time it begins a new page. Enter **Y** to begin numbering each time the program begins a new page.

For example, if you are using explanatory notes as footnotes (indicated by symbols) and using endnotes as reference notes (numbered as Arabic numerals), you will probably want to use this option. If you use symbols, WordPerfect repeats them; for example, the symbol * becomes ** the second time it is used,

✱✱✱ the third time, and so forth. Starting the system over each time a new page begins prevents a long string of symbols (such as ✱✱✱✱✱) from occurring in text. See the next section for details about how to change the system of symbols, letters, and numbers WordPerfect uses in notes.

CHANGING THE NOTE NUMBERING SYSTEM

KEY SEQUENCE

Footnotes:
> **Ctrl-F7 4 5 0** (numbers) or **1** (characters) or **2** (letters)

Endnotes:
> **Ctrl-F7 4 6 0** (numbers) or **1** (characters) or **2** (letters)

You can change the system of note numbering WordPerfect uses to either symbols (option 1) or lowercase letters (option 2). If you choose to use symbols, WordPerfect uses an asterisk for notes.

You can also specify a series of up to five symbols for WordPerfect to use. For example, to use the system ✱, @, and # to indicate footnotes, follow these steps, which combine several options:

1. Press Ctrl-F7 and select option 4.
2. Select option 5 (footnote numbering); then enter **1** for Characters and **9** for Characters with notes (see Figure 7.8).
3. Enter ✱ @ #; then press Return twice. Note that you can also press Return and F7 (Exit) or simply press F7 (Exit) twice.

CHANGING THE LINE THAT SEPARATES FOOTNOTES FROM TEXT

KEY SEQUENCE

> **Ctrl-F7 4 7 0** (no line) or **1** (2-inch line) or **2** (line across page)
> **3** (continued option)

WordPerfect allows you to change the default 2-inch rule that separates footnotes from text either to no rule or to a rule that extends across the page. In Version 4.2 you can also specify whether to have the program insert "(Continued...)" when a footnote must be split to another page. If you select this option, the text of a footnote that is split ends with "(Continued...)" and begins with "(…Continued)" on the next page. Figure 7.8 also illustrates the suboptions available with option 7 on the Footnote Options menu.

PLACING FOOTNOTES IN TEXT

KEY SEQUENCE

Ctrl-F7 4 8 N F7 (Exit)

If you do not always want your footnotes to appear at the bottoms of pages, you can change the footnote placement setting (option 8). If you enter **Y** instead of **N**, WordPerfect places footnotes two lines below the last text on the page, even if it is not a full page. Figure 7.9 illustrates a sample document in which this option has been selected. If you leave the option set to N, WordPerfect will always insert footnotes at the bottoms of pages, even if the page contains only a few lines of text.

```
Footnote Options

    1 - Spacing within notes              1
    2 - Spacing between notes             1
    3 - Lines to keep together           3
    4 - Start footnote numbers each page N
    5 - Footnote numbering mode          1
    6 - Endnote numbering mode           0
    7 - Line separating text and footnotes 1
    8 - Footnotes at bottom of page      Y
    9 - Characters for notes             *@#
    A - String for footnotes in text     [SuprScrpt][Note]
    B - String for endnotes in text      [SuprScrpt][Note]
    C - String for footnotes in note            [SuprScrpt][Note]
    D - String for endnotes in note      [Note].

    For options 5 & 6:           For option 7:
        0 - Numbers                  0 - No line
        1 - Characters               1 - 2 inch line
        2 - Letters                  2 - Line across entire page
                                     3 - 2 in. line w/continued strings


Selection: 0
```

FIGURE 7.8: Changing the symbol system WordPerfect uses for footnotes. Instead of using an asterisk as the symbol to indicate footnotes, you can specify up to five different symbols to be used. Each will be repeated the next time it is used. For example, the system *, @, # in the figure will be **, @@, and ## the second time the symbols are used in the same document. The suboptions available for option 7, Line separating text and footnotes, also allow you to specify whether footnotes that are split between pages end and begin with a (Continued…) notation (Version 4.2).

```
can grow--in other words, a direction in which the employees can
make greater contributions to the company.  Employees, however,
often perceive this direction to be one in which they can better
themselves (in other words, command higher salaries), not
realizing that corporate goals are ideally merely a superset of
their own.@@



             ─────────────────

     @@See Stephens, R.W., Motivation: The Inner-Directed Search (New
York: Abbott Press, 1986)
```

FIGURE 7.9: Changing the placement of footnotes. You can have WordPerfect insert footnotes two lines below the last line on pages that contain less than a full page of text.

USING STRINGS TO INDICATE NOTES

KEY SEQUENCE

Ctrl-F7 4 A-D <*string*> **F7** (Exit)

If you prefer that your notes be marked with a string (a sequence of characters)—for example, *Note:*—instead of a sequence of numbers, symbols, or individual letters, you can use options A through D on the Footnote Options menu to specify the string.

For example, to change the footnote numbering system so that a pound sign (#) appears as the note reference within the text, but the string "*Note:* See" appears to introduce the footnote itself, follow this procedure:

1. Press Ctrl-F7 and select option 4.
2. Enter **9** (for Characters for notes); then enter # and press Return.
3. Enter **C** (for String for footnotes in note) and press Del (to delete the [SuprScrpt] code). Move the cursor to the right of the [Note] code, press F8 (to begin underlining), and type **Note:**. Then press F8 again to turn off underlining. Enter a space and type **See** (*See* followed by a space); then press Return.

Your screen should look like the one in Figure 7.10. Figure 7.11 shows how a printed document using this system would appear.

```
Footnote Options

    1 - Spacing within notes              1
    2 - Spacing between notes             1
    3 - Lines to keep together            3
    4 - Start footnote numbers each page  N
    5 - Footnote numbering mode           1
    6 - Endnote numbering mode            0
    7 - Line separating text and footnotes 1
    8 - Footnotes at bottom of page       Y
    9 - Characters for notes              #
    A - String for footnotes in text      [SuprScrpt][Note]
    B - String for endnotes in text       [SuprScrpt][Note]
    C - String for footnotes in note      [Note][Undrline]Note:[u]   See
    D - String for endnotes in note       [Note].

    For options 5 & 6:              For option 7:
        0 - Numbers                     0 - No line
        1 - Characters                  1 - 2 inch line
        2 - Letters                     2 - Line across entire page
                                        3 - 2 in. line w/continued strings


Selection: 0
```

FIGURE 7.10: Changing the symbol used for footnotes and using the string *"Note:* See " to begin each footnote. If you use only a few notes in your documents, you may wish to use this method. You can use any string you like, such as *WARNING:* or *For further reference, see ...,* depending on your application.

If you want to change the format codes that insert notes ([Note]) and position them (such as [SuprScrpt]), choose option C and then press the key that corresponds to the code you want to change. For example, to change the code for the string to be used for footnotes in the note, which is [SuprScrpt] [Note] (in boldface on your screen), press Ctrl-F7 and select option C; then press Ctrl-F7 and type **1.** (1 followed by a period). This changes the way that notes appear so that they will not be superscripted.

Notes on Using the Mark Text Menus in Earlier Versions of WordPerfect

The Version 4.2 Mark Text menus, which are used for outlining, paragraph numbering, creating indexes and concordances, and generating tables of contents and authorities—several of which are new features added to Version 4.2 of WordPerfect—are slightly different from those in earlier versions of the

The Performance Appraisal System

A performance appraisal system has, among others, the following
goals:
    To assess actual performance
    To motivate employees
    To provide a system of rewards (and punishments)
    To open a channel of feedback between employee and manager

A well-designed performance appraisal system has as its foremost
characteristic that there be <u>no surprises</u>--that is, that ongoing
communication between employee and manager be so thorough as to
let both know where they stand at all times.

Scheduling Performance Appraisals

Such results can only be achieved by a system of frequent
meetings, both formal and informal, between employees and their
managers. Securing commitment to the goals of this process
facilitates communication and establishes a climate that is
conducive to change and growth within a corporation.

In technical white-collar industries, many companies have found
that a bi-weekly system of informal meetings combined with a
formal review every six months produces satisfactory results.
Usually, however, a system in which formal meetings occur more
often has been found to be more workable in areas of those
companies in which production and/or assembly of components is
the prime goal. Stein reports that a dual performance appraisal
system in such cases has achieved overall increases in
productivity of as much as 13 percent over a six-month period.

Setting Corporate Goals

The responsibility for carrying out the mission of the
corporation is twofold: both on the manager as well as the
employee. At the same time, the perspective differs. The
manager is responsible for providing a direction in which the
employee can grow--in other words, a direction in which the
employees can make greater contributions to the company.
Employees, however, often perceive this direction to be one in
which they can better themselves (in other words, command higher
salaries), not realizing that corporate goals are ideally merely
a superset of their own.#

———————————

#<u>Note:</u> See Stephens, R.W., <u>Motivation: The Inner-Directed Search</u>
(New York: Abbott Press, 1986)

FIGURE 7.11: A printed document using the system described in the text. The string *"Note:"* now replaces symbols, characters, and letters in footnotes, and footnotes are indicated in text by the # symbol.

program. If you are using an earlier version, your Mark Text (Alt-F5) menu will appear as follows:

1 Outline; 2 Para #; 3 Redline; 4 Remove; 5 Index; 6 Define; 7 Generate: 0

The Version 4.2 Mark Text menu appears as

1 Outline; 2 Para #; 3 Redline; 4 Short Form; 5 Index; 6 Other Options: 0

In Version 4.2, additional options and a new screen (Other Mark Text Options)—which replaces the earlier Text Marking Definition Screen—have been added, but in most cases keystrokes stay the same. Where a keystroke sequence is different in Version 4.2 than in earlier versions, this chapter presents both sequences.

CREATING A TABLE OF CONTENTS

WordPerfect can create tables of contents for you and print them when your documents are printed. For the program to create a table of contents, you must mark each heading that you want to appear in the table of contents by using the Mark Text key sequence (Alt-F5).

> *Note:* Alt-F5 presents options for making tables of contents only if you have first marked a block of text. If you have not marked a block of text, the program assumes that when you press Alt-F5 you want to create an outline or use one of WordPerfect's other options.

You can mark up to five levels of headings to be included in the table of contents. Because you probably will not want to take the time to do this as you are writing, you should make a habit of marking the headings you wish to appear in the table of contents with a special attribute—such as boldface or underlining—that you do not use anywhere else in your document. That way you can quickly search for those headings and mark them for the table of contents when you are ready to create it by searching for the [B] or [U] code. You can also write a macro to search for the headings, assuming you have used a unique text attribute for them, and generate the table of contents for you. Such a macro will be presented later in this chapter; for more information about creating and using macros, see Chapter 14.

After you have marked the headings you wish to be included in the table of contents, you define how you want the table of contents page to be formatted. Each level of heading can use one of five different numbering and formatting styles. Figure 7.12 illustrates some of the various formats you can use in a table of contents.

```
 _                      CONTENTS


WELCOME  . . . . . . . . . . . . . . . . . . . . . . . . .      1
        Work Day  1
        Parking  1
        Hours  1
        Cafeteria  1
        Recreational Facilities  1


PAID LEAVE . . . . . . . . . . . . . . . . . . . . . . .        1
        Vacation  1
        Holidays  1
        Personal Leave  2
              Bereavement Leave (2); Military Leave (2); Jury
              Duty (2)
        Leave for Illness  2


CREDIT UNION . . . . . . . . . . . . . . . . . . . . . . .      2


BENEFITS . . . . . . . . . . . . . . . . . . . . . . . . .      2


PERFORMANCE APPRAISALS . . . . . . . . . . . . . . . . . .      2
        Opportunities for Advancement  3
C:\WP\BOOK\CHAP7\CONTENTS                   Doc 2  Pg 1  Ln 1        Pos 10
```

FIGURE 7.12: Various tables of contents formats. You can use no page numbers or place page numbers in parentheses. Page numbers can follow the entries or appear flush right preceded by dot leaders (or not preceded by dot leaders—not shown). You can have the lowest defined level of heading displayed in wrapped format, as is shown here. Each level of heading can use a different style.

Marking Text for a Table of Contents

> **KEY SEQUENCE**
>
> **Alt-F4** (Mark Block) **Alt-F5** (Mark Text) **1** *<heading level>*

> **REVEAL CODES**
>
> **[Mark:ToC,*n*] [EndMark:ToC,*n*]**

You can mark up to five levels of headings to be included in a table of contents. You can use WordPerfect's Search feature (F2) to find headings if you have previously marked them with a special character, such as @ or #, or have used a unique text attribute, such as boldfacing or underlining, that does not appear anywhere else in your document. If you use the procedure described here to mark headings for tables of contents, you can search for those headings later by pressing F2 (Search) and then pressing Alt-F5 (Mark Text) and selecting option 1. For each heading you want included in the table of contents, follow these steps:

1. Press Alt-F4 to mark the heading as a block.
2. Press Alt-F5 (Mark Text). The following prompt appears:

Mark for: 1 ToC; 2 List; 3 Redline; 4 Strikeout; 5 Index; 6 ToA: 0

3. Select option 1. The following prompt appears:

ToC Level:

Enter the level of the heading (from 1 to 5). WordPerfect inserts formatting codes as shown in Figure 7.13.

TOC: A MACRO FOR MARKING A TABLE OF CONTENTS

The following macro assumes that you have used boldface for each heading in your text that you wish to include in the table of contents and that you have not used boldface anywhere else in the document. (If it finds an occurrence of boldface that is not a heading, you will need to exit from the macro and restart it.) It searches for each occurrence of the [B] code and pauses to allow you to enter the appropriate level for each heading.

Begin macro	*Macro name*	*Keystrokes*	*End macro*
Ctrl-F10	**TOC**	**F2 F6 F2 Alt-F4 End Alt-F5 1 Ctrl-PgUp Return 1 Return Alt-F10 TOC Return**	**Ctrl-F10**

This is a chaining macro that repeats itself each time you press Return until no more occurrences of the [B] code are found. See Chapter 14 for more information about creating and using macros.

Defining the Style for a Table of Contents

KEY SEQUENCE

Alt-F5 6 2 <*options*> (Version 4.2)
Alt-F5 6 6 <*options*> (earlier versions)

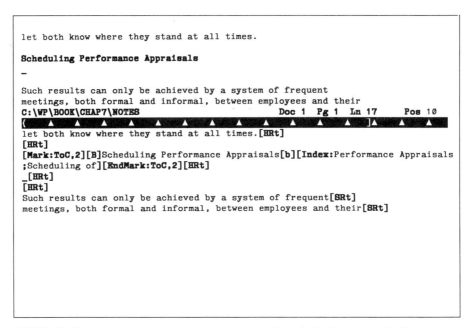

```
let both know where they stand at all times.

Scheduling Performance Appraisals
-

Such results can only be achieved by a system of frequent
meetings, both formal and informal, between employees and their
C:\WP\BOOK\CHAP7\NOTES                    Doc 1  Pg 1  Ln 17     Pos 10
```

```
let both know where they stand at all times.[HRt]
[HRt]
[Mark:ToC,2][B]Scheduling Performance Appraisals[b][Index:Performance Appraisals
;Scheduling of][EndMark:ToC,2][HRt]
_[HRt]
[HRt]
Such results can only be achieved by a system of frequent[SRt]
meetings, both formal and informal, between employees and their[SRt]
```

FIGURE 7.13: Formatting codes inserted when you mark text for a table of contents. WordPerfect keeps track of each level of heading by the level number you assign to it.

REVEAL CODES

[DefMark:ToC,*n*] [EndDef]

You need to create a page for your table of contents, which normally appears near the beginning of a document. If you want a title page as the first page of your document, create the title page first; then insert a hard page break (Ctrl-Return) and position the cursor just below the break so that the table of contents will follow the title page. (When you generate a table of contents, it appears at the position where you define its style.) If you are not using a title page, move the cursor to the beginning of the document (Home Home ↑) and then insert the hard page break for the table of contents. You will also probably want to center a heading—such as CONTENTS—for the table of contents.

To define the format of the contents page,

1. Press Alt-F5 (Mark Text) and select option 6 (Other Options; select Define in earlier versions). The Other Mark Text Options screen appears (Figure 7.14).

2. Select option 2 (Define Table of Contents). The Table of Contents Definition screen appears (Figure 7.15).

```
Other Mark Text Options

    1 - Define Paragraph/Outline Numbering

    2 - Define Table of Contents

    3 - Define List

    4 - Define Table of Authorities

    5 - Define Index

    6 - Remove all Redline Markings and all Strikeout text from document

    7 - Edit Table of Authorities Full Form

    8 - Generate Tables and Index




Selection: 0
```

FIGURE 7.14: The Other Mark Text Options screen (Version 4.2). You also use this screen to define formats for indexes, lists, and tables of authorities.

3. Enter the number of heading levels you are using in the table of contents (**1–5**).

4. At the prompt

    Display last level in wrapped format? (Y/N) N

    enter **N** (or press Return) if you want each heading on a separate line. If you enter **Y**, WordPerfect displays the headings with the highest heading level number as one wrapped line, with the headings and page numbers separated by semicolons, as was shown in Figure 7.12.

5. Select the page number position style you wish to use for each level by entering the appropriate code.

Option 1 prints headings only, with no page numbers. If you choose option 2 or 3, page numbers will occur next to headings, and with option 3, they will be in parentheses. Options 4 and 5 place page numbers flush right, with or without dot leaders.

Generating a Table of Contents

KEY SEQUENCE

Alt-F5 (Mark Text) **6 8 Y** (Version 4.2)

```
Table of Contents Definition

    Number of levels in table of contents (1-5): 0



                        Page Number Position
       Level 1
       Level 2
       Level 3
       Level 4
       Level 5


       Page Number Position
       1 - No Page Numbers
       2 - Page Number Follow Entries
       3 - (Page Numbers) follow Entries
       4 - Flush Right Page Numbers
       5 - Flush Right Page Numbers with Leaders
```

FIGURE 7.15: The Table of Contents Definition screen. You can specify a different numbering style for each of five levels of headings. Option 1 prints headings only, with no page numbers. If you choose option 2 or 3, page numbers will occur next to headings, and with option 3, they will be in parentheses. Options 4 and 5 place page numbers flush right, with or without dot leaders.

For the first table of contents (earlier versions):
    Alt-F5 (Mark Text) **7 Y**
For subsequent tables of contents (earlier versions):
    Alt-F5 (Mark Text) **7 N Y**

When you have defined a style for your table of contents, press Alt-F5 (Mark Text), select option 6 (Other Options), and then select option 8 (Generate Tables and Index). (In earlier versions of WordPerfect, option 7 is Generate.) If you have marked text for other lists or tables, such as a table of authorities, or if you have marked index entries, WordPerfect will generate those at the same time. It is not necessary, however, to wait until you have marked these other tables and index entries so that everything is generated at once; you can generate a table of contents before you have marked any of the other items. WordPerfect generates a table of contents, list, or index for each [DefMark] it finds. You will see the prompt

Existing tables, lists, and indexes will be replaced. Continue? (Y/N): Y

Enter **Y** (or press Return) to tell WordPerfect to delete any existing tables and generate the new ones.

In earlier versions of WordPerfect, this prompt is

Have you deleted your old Table of Contents, Lists and Index? (Y/N) N

If you enter **N**, WordPerfect will delete your old lists for you, but it will prompt you for confirmation before it deletes the block containing the old table of contents.

The first time you generate a table of contents, WordPerfect creates it at the position of your cursor, where you defined the style of the table of contents. The prompt

Generation in progress: Counter: (number)

appears while the program is generating the table of contents.

Deleting Existing Tables of Contents, Lists, and Indexes

Each time WordPerfect generates a table of contents—or any other kind of list, such as a table of authorities or an index—it searches for a [DefMark] code and uses that code to generate the list.

In earlier versions of the program, if you have previously generated a table of contents, list, or index, you must be sure to respond **N** to the prompt

Have you deleted your old Table of Contents, Lists, and Index?

If you have already generated a table of contents, list, or index but have not deleted it and you respond **Y** to this prompt, WordPerfect will generate two tables of contents, lists, or indexes: one for each [DefMark] code that it finds. In addition, if you have redefined some aspect of the style—such as the page number position—you need to locate and delete the [DefMark] code that the program inserts at the beginning of the old table of contents, list, or index; otherwise, the program will also generate two page numbers: one in the old style and the other in the style you have most recently defined.

In Version 4.2 of WordPerfect, the program's prompt before generating a table or index is

Existing tables, lists, and indexes will be replaced. Continue? (Y/N): Y

so you do not have to worry about a correct response to the prompt. However, if you have changed styles or generated tables of contents, lists, or indexes elsewhere in your text where you no longer want them, you will need to use the following procedure to locate those [DefMark] codes and delete them.

To remove the old [DefMark] code from previously generated lists, tables of contents, or indexes,

1. Press F2 (Search); then press Alt-F5 (Mark Text).
2. Select option 7 [DefMark] from the menu that appears.
3. Press F2 to begin the search.

4. When the program locates the [DefMark] code, delete it (by backspacing over it). You will see the prompt

Delete [DefMark]? (Y/N) N

Enter **Y** to delete the code.

5. Press Alt-F5 (Mark Text) and use option 6 to define the new style where you want the table of contents to appear.

6. Select option 8 (option 7 in earlier versions) to generate the new tables and index.

If you have any difficulty generating subsequent tables of contents, lists, or indexes, there may be extra [DefMark] codes in your text. Use the procedure just described to find and delete them. Remember, after you generate the first table of contents, list, or index at the position of the cursor, subsequent tables, lists, and indexes will be generated at that same location, because it will contain a [DefMark] code.

Revising a Table of Contents, List, or Index

If you have changed the text in your document since you last generated a table of contents, list, or index, you may need to remark the entries. WordPerfect allows you to search for the particular [Mark] code for each entry you have marked.

1. Press F2 (Search); then press Alt-F5 (Mark Text).

2. From the following menu that appears, select the appropriate option to find the [Mark] code that begins the item you want to search for.

1List/Toc 2Par# 3Index 4Redln 5StrkOut 6Par#Def
7DefMark 8EndDef 9ToA: 0

3. Press F2 to begin the search.

4. When the program finds the [Mark] code, delete it (by backspacing over it). You will see the prompt

Delete [Mark]? (Y/N) N

Enter **Y** to delete the code.

5. Press Alt-F4 (Mark Block); then press Alt-F5 (Mark Text) and option 1 to mark the table of contents.

For example, if you are searching for table of contents codes, the cursor will stop at each occurrence of the [Mark:ToC:*n*] code (*n* is the level of the heading you indicated when you marked the text). If all your headings are marked correctly—that is, surrounded by [Mark:ToC,*n*] and [EndMark:ToC,*n*] codes—you are ready to generate the new table of contents. Position the cursor where you want the table of contents to appear and generate it as described in the preceding section.

If you also want to change the style of a table of contents, list, or index, you need to search for its [DefMark] code, delete it, and define the new style as described in the appropriate sections for tables of contents, lists, and indexes in this handbook. The new table, list, or index will be generated at the point in your document where the style is defined.

CREATING AND REORGANIZING LISTS

WordPerfect can create lists for you: It will keep track of five different lists—each as long as you like—for each document.

The items in a list do not have to be next to each other but can be scattered throughout your document; for instance, you can create a list of figures or tables from captions within your document. However, an item can be included in only one list.

The procedure for marking a list and having WordPerfect generate it is similar to that used for creating a table of contents (see the preceding discussion): You mark the items to be included in the list, define the style of the list, and then instruct WordPerfect to generate the list for you. The sections that follow explain the procedure for creating and reorganizing lists.

Creating a List

KEY SEQUENCE

Alt-F4 (Mark Block) **Alt-F5** (Mark Text) **2** *<list number>*

REVEAL CODES

[Mark:List,*n*] [EndMark:List,*n*]

You can mark up to five separate lists in a document. You can use WordPerfect's Search feature (F2) to locate list items. You can also search if you have previously marked them with a special character, such as @, or have used a unique text attribute that does not appear anywhere else in your document, such as boldfacing or underlining. For each list item that you want to include, follow these steps:

1. Press Alt-F4 and use the cursor movement keys to mark the list item as a block.

2. Press Alt-F5 (Mark Text). The following prompt appears:

   Mark for 1 ToC; 2 List; 3 Redline; 4 Strikeout; 5 Index; 6 ToA: 0

3. Select option 2. When the following prompt appears, enter the number of the list (from **1** to **5**):

   List#:

Defining the Style for a List

KEY SEQUENCE

Alt-F5 6 3 *<list number>* *<option number>* (Version 4.2)
Alt-F5 6 *<list number>* *<option number>* (earlier versions)

REVEAL CODES

[DefMark:List,*n*] [EndDef]

You need to create a page for your list, probably at the end of the document. You may want to insert a hard page break (Ctrl-Return) so that the list will begin on a new page. Move the cursor to the end of the document (Home Home ↓) and then insert the hard page break.

To define the format of the list,

1. Press Alt-F5 (Mark Text) and select option 6 (Other Options). The Other Mark Text Options screen appears.

2. Select option 3 (Define List). In Version 4.2, the following prompt appears:

   Enter List Number: (1-5)

   (In earlier versions of the program, the Text Marking Definition screen appears instead of the Other Mark Text Options screen, and you must select an option for the appropriate list number.)

3. Enter the number of the list you want the marked item to be included in. The List Definition screen appears (in all versions of WordPerfect; see Figure 7.16).

4. Select the style you wish to use by entering the appropriate option number, as shown in Figure 7.16.

Option 1 prints list items only, with no page numbers. You will probably use this option unless you are creating a table of tables or a table of figures for a

```
List 1 Definition

     1 - No Page Numbers
     2 - Page Numbers Follow Entries
     3 - (Page Numbers) Follow Entries
     4 - Flush Right Page Numbers
     5 - Flush Right Page Numbers with Leaders

















  Selection: 0
```

FIGURE 7.16: The List Definition screen. You will most often use option 1, which generates list items without page numbers. The other options create lists similar to tables of contents, with page numbers that indicate which page of your document each item is on.

document. If you choose option 2 or 3, page numbers will occur next to list items, and with option 3, they will be in parentheses. Options 4 and 5 place page numbers flush right, with or without dot leaders.

Generating a List

KEY SEQUENCE

Alt-F5 (Mark Text) **6 8 Y** (Version 4.2)
For the first list (earlier versions):
Alt-F5 (Mark Text) **7 Y**
For subsequent lists (earlier versions):
Alt-F5 (Mark Text) **7 N Y**

When you have defined a style for each of your lists, press Alt-F5 (Mark Text), select option 6 (Other Options), and then select option 8 (Generate Tables and Index). If you are using an earlier version of WordPerfect, select option 7 (Generate). If you have marked text for other lists or tables, such as a table of authorities, or if you have marked index entries, WordPerfect will generate those at the same time. It is not necessary, however, to wait until you have marked those items so that everything is generated at once; you can generate a list before you have marked any of the other items. WordPerfect will generate a list, table of contents, or index for each [DefMark] it finds.

In Version 4.2 of WordPerfect, the program prompts you before generating a list:

Existing tables, lists, and indexes will be replaced. Continue? (Y/N): Y

In earlier versions of WordPerfect, this prompt is

Have you deleted your old Table of Contents, Lists and Index? (Y/N) N

If you enter **N**, WordPerfect deletes your old list for you, but it will prompt you again before it deletes the block containing the old lists. If you respond incorrectly to the prompt, you may need to remove the [DefMark] codes for any existing lists you have previously created. See "Deleting Existing Tables of Contents, Lists, and Indexes" earlier in this chapter.

When you have responded to the Text Marking Definition prompts, the first time you generate a list, WordPerfect creates it at the position of your cursor. Later, when you generate the list again, it will be created at the position of the [DefMark] code.

The prompt

Generation in progress: Counter: (*number*)

appears while the program is generating the list. The counter number indicates the number of list items in your document.

Revising a List

If you have revised items in your lists since you last generated the lists, you may have inadvertently deleted one of the [Mark:List,*n*] or [EndMark:List,*n*] codes (*n* is the number of the list). Refer to the section "Revising a Table of Contents, List, or Index" earlier in this chapter for the procedure to follow to make sure that your lists are correct before you generate them.

WORKING WITH OUTLINES

Many people who write find that outlining is a useful aid in organizing their work. However, they often avoid the task because of the difficulty in manually keeping an outline accurate. WordPerfect can automatically maintain outlines you create with the program and change the level and numbering of items as necessary. Of course, you can also create short outlines by simply typing the material as you want it to appear, but when you work with long outlines, you will probably want to use WordPerfect's built-in outlining feature.

In fact, you can use WordPerfect's outlining feature as an idea processor, similar to programs such as ThinkTank. After you have created a basic outline, you can add major points to it, indenting sublevels as ideas occur to you. You can then write the document following the outline, and you can be assured that all the points you listed are covered. If you are maintaining "boilerplate" or standard text in separate files, you can even insert merge codes to have the program insert the appropriate paragraphs or sections at print time. (See Chapter 9 for additional ideas regarding how you can use WordPerfect's merge print feature.)

As you soon discover when you use Outline mode, the Tab and Return keys work differently than they usually do. Pressing Return adds an outline level number to a paragraph, and pressing Tab lowers a paragraph to the next outline level (for example, from 1 to a). This allows you to quickly reorganize your work, with WordPerfect keeping track of the outline level numbers for you.

WordPerfect's default outlining style is the one you probably learned in school:

    I.
        A.
            1.
                a.
                    (1)
                        (a)
                            i)

You can use more than seven levels; the seventh-level definition is used for the levels after the seventh, and each level is indented one additional tab stop. There are also two other numbering styles built into the program: paragraph style, which uses the system 1., a., i., (1), (a), (i), 1); and legal style (sometimes called *mil spec*), which numbers each paragraph and level sequentially as 1, 1.1, 1.1.1, and so forth. You can change the system of numbering and punctuation; see "Customizing a Numbering Style" later in this chapter.

Creating an Outline

KEY SEQUENCE

For the first entry:
    Alt-F5 (Mark Text) **1 Return**
For subsequent entries:
    Return or **Tab**

REVEAL CODES

[Par#]

After you have turned on Outline mode (by pressing Alt-F5 and selecting option 1, Outline), each time you enter characters or a space and then press Return, a new outline number is generated in your text. To generate a number at a lower level, you press the Tab key. For example, to create an entry numbered (a) (assuming you are using the default style for outlining), you press Tab five times after pressing Return for the first-level number.

So long as you are in Outline mode, the prompt

Outline

appears in the lower-left corner of your screen. To turn off Outline mode, press Alt-F5 (mark Text) and select option 1, Outline, again.

To indent text without entering an outline number or letter when you are in Outline mode, press the space bar before you press the Tab key. You can also use the Indent key sequence (Shift-F4) to indent text without inserting outline numbers.

To create the short outline shown in Figure 7.17, you follow these steps:

1. Press Alt-F5 (Mark Text) and select option 1, Outline. Press Return to insert the first level number, I.

2. Enter the first heading, **Year-End Results**. Press Return and then press Tab to change the II that appears to an A.

3. Enter the heading **Comparison with Fiscal 1987**. Press Return and then Tab to enter the B.

4. Enter the heading **Estimate for Fiscal 1988**. Then press Return. This time, press Tab twice to indent the next head.

5. Enter **Best Case:** and then press the space bar and then the Tab key to insert a tab.

6. Enter **Early/Late Analysis** and press Return. Then press Tab twice and enter **Worst Case**.

7. Press Return to insert the II; then enter the heading **General Market Trends**.

8. Press Return to insert the III; then enter the heading **Outlook for the Future**.

You can continue to outline up to 13 levels (the last 7 are numbered with lowercase Roman numerals) in this way until you turn Outline mode off by pressing Alt-F5 and selecting option 1 again. To change the outlining style, see "Changing the Style of Outline and Paragraph Numbering" later in this chapter.

When you delete or insert items in an outline, WordPerfect automatically renumbers your outline for you.

```
    I. Year-End Results
        A. Comparison with Fiscal 1987
        B. Estimate for Fiscal 1988
            1. Best Case:  Early/Late Analysis
            2. Worst Case
   II. General Market Trends
   III.Outlook for the Future              _




    C:\WP\BOOK\CHAP7\OUTLINE                    Doc 1  Pg 1  Ln 9      Pos 40
```

FIGURE 7.17: A short outline created in Outline mode. In Outline mode, pressing the Return and Tab keys enters outline numbers for you. Pressing Return enters a number at the first level; the program then indents and inserts a lower-level number each time you press Tab.

To delete an outline number, position the cursor on it and press Del. You can also backspace over an outline number to delete it. WordPerfect inserts the formatting code [Par#] each time it generates an outline number.

NUMBERING PARAGRAPHS

WordPerfect can automatically number paragraphs for you. You can use it to number paragraphs or items in a list, and it will keep track of the numbers for you. When you add or delete items or paragraphs, WordPerfect renumbers the rest of them. The paragraphs or items you number do not have to be next to each other; they can be scattered throughout your document.

If you are writing numbered instructions or test questions, this feature is especially useful because you can insert or delete steps or questions and the program will automatically correct the numbering system.

If you use automatic paragraph numbering, each time you press the Tab key, WordPerfect inserts a paragraph number at a progressively lower level. The numbering style the program uses depends on the tab stop the cursor is at. For example, if the cursor is at the left margin, WordPerfect inserts I. (for level 1). If you have pressed Tab once, it labels the paragraph A. (level 2); if you have pressed Tab twice, it labels the paragraph 1. If you use fixed paragraph numbering, WordPerfect also automatically inserts a new number, but the paragraph level does not change. See "Using Fixed Numbering" later in this chapter.

Automatic Paragraph Numbering

KEY SEQUENCE

Alt-F5 2 <*level number*> or **Return**

To number paragraphs automatically, press Alt-F5 and select option 2 (Para #). The prompt

Paragraph Level (ENTER for Automatic):

appears. If you type a level number, such as **1**, all the paragraph numbers the program enters for you will be level-1 numbers. When you press Return, Word-Perfect will insert a paragraph number. To enter progressively lower levels of paragraph numbers, press the Tab key until you reach the level you want. Then press Alt-F5, select option 2, and enter the level number or press Return.

Using Fixed Numbering

KEY SEQUENCE

Alt-F5 (Mark Text) **2** <*level number*>

REVEAL CODES

[Par#:n]

The Reveal Codes screen for the outline shown in Figure 7.17 is presented in Figure 7.18. The code

[Par#:Auto]

indicates that WordPerfect is automatically numbering for you. You can turn off automatic numbering so that each time you enter a paragraph number, it will be generated at the same level. Fixed numbering is the method you normally will use when you are writing numbered test questions or preparing a questionnaire, for example, and you want to be able to renumber quickly when adding to or deleting from the list.

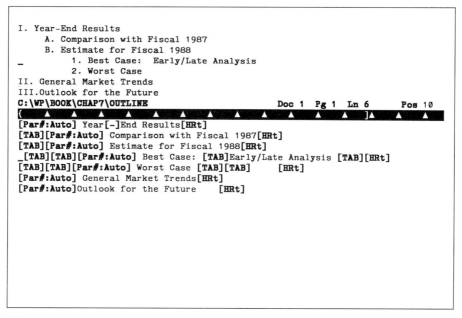

```
I. Year-End Results
     A. Comparison with Fiscal 1987
     B. Estimate for Fiscal 1988
 _        1. Best Case:   Early/Late Analysis
          2. Worst Case
II. General Market Trends
III.Outlook for the Future
C:\WP\BOOK\CHAP7\OUTLINE                         Doc 1  Pg 1  Ln 6      Pos 10
```

[Par#:Auto] Year[-]End Results[HRt]
[TAB][Par#:Auto] Comparison with Fiscal 1987[HRt]
[TAB][Par#:Auto] Estimate for Fiscal 1988[HRt]
_[TAB][TAB][Par#:Auto] Best Case: [TAB]Early/Late Analysis [TAB][HRt]
[TAB][TAB][Par#:Auto] Worst Case [TAB][TAB]   [HRt]
[Par#:Auto] General Market Trends[HRt]
[Par#:Auto]Outlook for the Future   [HRt]

FIGURE 7.18: The Reveal Codes screen for the outline shown in Figure 7.17. The word *Auto* in the code indicates that WordPerfect is using automatic outline numbering. To use fixed numbering, press Alt-F5 (Mark Text) and select option 2, Para #. Then enter the number of the level or style you want to use.

When you use fixed numbering, WordPerfect does not change the level of paragraph numbers automatically when you press Tab in front of them. However, it adjusts all paragraph numbers if you delete or add a new numbered paragraph. (It does not change the paragraph numbers until you press Return for the new addition or deletion.)

The level you indicate at the prompt determines the style of numbering the program uses. It uses whatever style you have chosen for that level. For example, to enter Arabic numbers you enter *3*, because level 3 of the default numbering style is Arabic numbers. See "Changing the Style of Outline and Paragraph Numbering" later in this chapter for details about how to change the numbering style or specify a custom style to suit your needs.

Figure 7.19 illustrates the results you can get by using fixed numbering. In this figure, the fifth level of outline style—in which numerals are enclosed in parentheses—was indicated by entering a *5* at the prompt

Paragraph Level (ENTER for automatic):

Figure 7.20 illustrates the results of inserting a new paragraph in the list. WordPerfect automatically renumbers the rest of the numbered items for you.

```
(1)  Define the term recession and explain its probable
     consequences. (20 minutes)

(2)  What historical evidence is presented by the monetarists to
     support the argument that the money supply is the key to the
     monetary system? (15 minutes)

(3)  In what year was the Federal Reserve Board created?
```

```
Paragraph Level (ENTER for automatic): 1_
```

FIGURE 7.19: The prompt for using fixed numbering. If you turn off automatic numbering by entering a level number (from 1 to 7), the number the program enters stays the same when you press the Tab key. (With automatic numbering, the numbering level changes when you move the cursor to the left of the number and press Tab.)

ALT-P: AN AUTOMATIC PARAGRAPH NUMBERING MACRO

If you use fixed paragraph numbering often, you may want to write a macro to speed up entry of the key sequences each time you create a new numbered paragraph. The following macro, Alt-P, automates the process for you. It assumes that you are using the default style for paragraph/outline numbering and that you want to number paragraphs with Arabic numbers and periods (1., 2., 3., and so forth). (See the next section, "Changing the Style of Outline and Paragraph Numbering," for more information.)

Begin macro	*Macro name*	*Keystrokes*	*End macro*
Ctrl-F10	**Alt-P**	**Alt-F5 2 3**	**Ctrl-F10**
		Return	

CHANGING THE STYLE OF OUTLINE AND PARAGRAPH NUMBERING

The program contains many options for paragraph numbering, as shown in Figure 7.21. You can define styles for seven different levels, using four

```
(1)  Define the term recession and explain its probable
     consequences. (20 minutes)

(2)  What historical evidence is presented by the monetarists to
     support the argument that the money supply is the key to the
     monetary system? (15 minutes)

(3)  Define the term inflation and discuss its effects (35
     minutes)_

(4)  In what year was the Federal Reserve Board created?




C:\WP\BOOK\CHAP7\QUEST                          Doc 1  Pg 1  Ln
```

FIGURE 7.20: Inserting a new numbered paragraph. If you insert a new paragraph by pressing Alt-F5 (Mark Text), selecting option 2, Para #, and pressing Return (or entering a fixed level), WordPerfect will automatically renumber paragraphs you have entered in this way when you delete one or add a new one to the list.

punctuation options and six numbering styles. The default style is style 2, Outline; in this style, the seven different levels are represented as

> I.
>   A.
>   1.
>   a.
>   (1)
>   (a)
>   i)

If you select style 1, Paragraph Numbering, your outlines and paragraphs will be numbered in the style 1., a., i., (1), (a), i) 1). Legal Numbering, style 3, provides the sequence 1., 1.1., 1.1.1., and so forth.

To use paragraph numbering, follow these steps:

1. Press Alt-F5 (Mark Text) and select option 6 (Other Options).

2. When the Other Mark Text options screen appears, select option 1 (Define Paragraph/Outline Numbering). The Paragraph Numbering Definition screen appears, as shown in Figure 7.21.

```
Paragraph Numbering Definition

    1 - Paragraph Numbering, e.g. 1. a. i. (1) (a) (i) 1)
    2 - Outline Numbering, e.g. I. A. 1. a. (1) (a) i)
    3 - Legal Numbering, e.g. 1. 1.1. 2.2.1 etc.
    4 - Other

Selection: 0

Levels:              1   2   3   4   5   6   7
  Number Style:      0   2   4   3   4   3   1
  Punctuation:       1   1   1   1   3   3   2

Number Style                       Punctuation
0 - Upper Case Roman               0 - #
1 - Lower Case Roman               1 - #.
2 - Upper Case Letters             2 - #)
3 - Lower Case Letters             3 - (#)
4 - Numbers
5 - Numbers with previous levels separated by a period

Starting Paragraph Number (in Legal Style): 1
```

FIGURE 7.21: The Paragraph Numbering Definition screen (Version 4.2). There are basically three different types of paragraph numbering: outline style (I., A., and so on), paragraph style (1., a., and so on), and legal style (1, 1.1, and so on, also sometimes called *mil spec*). You can also customize the numbering system if you prefer.

3. Select a numbering style from the options on the screen or create a style of your own (see "Customizing a Numbering Style" later in this chapter).

For example, to select legal style, enter *3*; then, for legal style, enter the paragraph number at which you want numbering to start. If you are numbering chapters of a book that are kept in separate files, you can enter *5* to begin numbers in Chapter 5 with a 5 (5.1, 5.1.1, and so on) (Figure 7.22).

Customizing a Numbering Style

You can instruct WordPerfect to use a numbering system of your own for paragraph and outline numbering. To do so, Press Alt-F5 (Mark Text) and select option 6 (Other Options); then select option 1 (Define Paragraph/Outline Numbering). Select option 4 (Other) from the Paragraph Numbering definition screen; then enter any combination of styles and symbols from the choices available to you for the seven levels. For example, to begin paragraph/outline numbering with (A), type *2* and then *3* at the Level-1 listing.

```
Paragraph Numbering Definition

    1 - Paragraph Numbering, e.g. 1. a. i. (1) (a) (i) 1)
    2 - Outline Numbering, e.g. I. A. 1. a. (1) (a) i)
    3 - Legal Numbering, e.g. 1. 1.1. 2.2.1 etc.
    4 - Other

Selection: 3

Levels:                1   2   3   4   5   6   7
    Number Style:      0   2   4   3   4   3   1
    Punctuation:       1   1   1   1   3   3   2

Number Style                              Punctuation
0 - Upper Case Roman                      0 - #
1 - Lower Case Roman                      1 - #.
2 - Upper Case Letters                    2 - #)
3 - Lower Case Letters                    3 - (#)
4 - Numbers
5 - Numbers with previous levels separated by a period

Starting Paragraph Number (in Legal Style): 5
```

FIGURE 7.22: Instructing the program to begin paragraph numbering using a number other than 1. In the figure, **Legal** style was selected; then **5** was entered as the number with which to begin numbers. Paragraphs and outlines will be numbered in the style 5., 5.1, 5.1.1., and so forth.

CREATING INDEXES

You create an index of a document you have written in WordPerfect by marking each occurrence of the items you want to include in the index. The program prompts you for the heading you wish the item to appear under in the index and also allows you to specify a subheading for the entry. It inserts an [Index:] code for each entry you make and keeps track of the page numbers on which the entries appear. When you ask WordPerfect to generate the index, it searches for the [Index:] codes and creates the index in the style you have selected. Figure 7.23 shows a sample index.

You can select several different index styles, just as you can select different styles for tables of contents and lists. You can also use WordPerfect's index feature to create a list of key words for a glossary; they will automatically be alphabetized when the index is generated.

To delete a term from an index, you must delete the [Index:] code associated with it. To search for these codes, press F2 (Search); then press Alt-F5 (Mark Text) and enter 3 (for Index). You can also search directly for the word or phrase you wish to delete or change. See Chapter 3 for additional information about searching through WordPerfect documents.

```
Communication
     Employee-manager  2
     Facilitating  3
Corporate goals
     As superset of employee goals  4
     Setting of  4
Performance Appraisal System  2
     Formal review  3
     Goals of  2
     Informal meetings  3
Performance Appraisals
     Bi-weekly system  3
     Scheduling of  2
Perspective, manager-employee  4
Productivity  3
```

FIGURE 7.23: A sample index created with WordPerfect. You can select the style of numbering that is to be used for headings and subheadings (note that headings and subheadings must use the same styles). Selecting no page numbering is useful if you want to create a list of key words rather than an index.

The word or phrase as it is listed in the index does not have to be the same as it appears in the text. For example, you might want to index the phrase *textile technology* as *technology, textile* in the index. WordPerfect allows you to change the phrasing of the index item when it prompts you for the index heading and subheading (see Figure 7.24). It also allows you to indicate more than one heading under which to index the item.

The concordance feature of Version 4.2 of WordPerfect allows you to list all the words or phrases that you want to include in the index. (In earlier versions of the program, you can use the Search function (F2) to speed up the process of searching for words you wish to index; in fact, you can write macros to speed up the process even further—see Chapter 14.) If you create a concordance file, WordPerfect will search through your document for each occurrence of the words in the concordance file and mark it for inclusion in the index. If you have specified that the item be indexed under another word or phrase, WordPerfect will use the word or phrase you have specified instead of the exact wording of the item that it finds in text.

No matter which version of the program you are using, it is generally wise to plan an index before you begin to mark entries for it. Keeping a list of headings under which you want to organize your entries helps ensure you do not have entries that are worded differently but actually cover the same material. For example, you might decide to create an entry for *Twentieth-century economists* but halfway through the process change the wording to *Economists, twentieth century.*

```
communication between employee and manager be so thorough as to
let both know where they stand at all times.

Scheduling Performance Appraisals_

Such results can only be achieved by a system of frequent
meetings, both formal and informal, between employees and their
                                     Doc 1  Pg 2  Ln 17     Pos 43
```
▓ ▲ ▲ ▲ ▲ ▲ ▲ ▲ ▲ ▲ ▲ ▲ ▲]▲ ▲ ▲ ▓
```
communication[Index:Communication;Employee-manager] between employee and manager
 be so thorough as to[SRt]
let both know where they stand at all times.[HRt]
[HRt]
[B]Scheduling Performance Appraisals[b][Index:Performance Appraisals;Scheduling
of][Index:Performance Appraisals]_[HRt]
[HRt]
Such results can only be achieved by a system of frequent[SRt]
meetings, both formal and informal, between employees and their[SRt]
```

FIGURE 7.24: Changing the wording of an index entry from the way it appears in text. In this figure, *Scheduling Performance Appraisals* has been marked to appear in the index as *Performance Appraisals, Scheduling of.*

Keeping such a list—perhaps in a second window for easy reference—can help you remember how you have organized your entries. Figure 7.25 illustrates the use of a second window containing a list of headings. (See Chapter 3 for details about creating and using two windows at the same time.)

Marking Items for an Index

KEY SEQUENCE

Alt-F5 (Mark Text) **5 Return** or *<heading>* Return

REVEAL CODES

[Index:;]

You can mark items for an index in one of two ways: by following the procedure outlined here or by creating a concordance file (if you are using Version 4.2 or a later implementation of WordPerfect). The procedure used for creating and using a concordance file is described here.

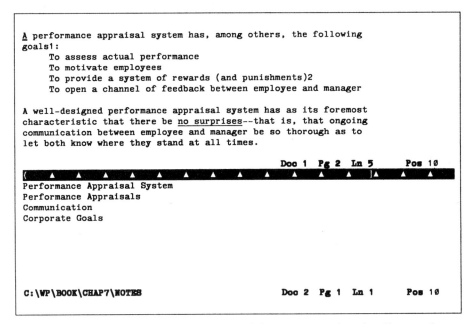

```
A performance appraisal system has, among others, the following
goals1:
     To assess actual performance
     To motivate employees
     To provide a system of rewards (and punishments)2
     To open a channel of feedback between employee and manager

A well-designed performance appraisal system has as its foremost
characteristic that there be no surprises--that is, that ongoing
communication between employee and manager be so thorough as to
let both know where they stand at all times.

                                  Doc 1  Pg 2  Ln 5        Pos 10
 ▲   ▲   ▲   ▲   ▲   ▲   ▲   ▲   ▲   ▲   ▲  ]▲   ▲   ▲
Performance Appraisal System
Performance Appraisals
Communication
Corporate Goals




C:\WP\BOOK\CHAP7\NOTES                     Doc 2  Pg 1  Ln 1     Pos 10
```

FIGURE 7.25: Keeping index entries worded consistently by using a second window. The second window contains the wording of the main headings that you have decided in advance that you want to include in your index.

An indexing macro has not been included here for three reasons: (1) A simple indexing macro is included in the WordPerfect program documentation (Lesson 2 of Macro Chaining); (2) the concordance feature in Version 4.2 accomplishes basically the same thing as a macro, but is more flexible and sophisticated; and (3) creating an index usually involves a sequence of judgments that a macro cannot make. A macro can locate every occurrence of a phrase and mark it for inclusion in an index, but it cannot supply cross references such as *See also* and *See* (although the concordance feature can cross reference to a limited extent). Neither can it reword index entries to fit the best phrasing for the entry. It cannot, for example, reword *Types of Performance Appraisals* to *Performance Appraisals, Types of,* and it cannot transpose *John R. Sommers* to *Sommers, John R.* for inclusion in an index. Unless you are creating a very simple index in which you are marking only single words or set phrases, it is wiser to search, using F2, for words or phrases you wish to index so that you can judge which entry is to appear under which topic heading in the index.

To mark items for an index,

1. Locate the word or phrase you wish to include in the index. Position the cursor on it or on the space following it. If you are indexing a phrase, you must first mark it by pressing Alt-F4 (Mark Block) and highlighting the phrase.

2. Press Alt-F5. The following menu appears:

Mark for: 1 ToC; 2 List; 3 Redline; 4 Strikeout; 5 Index; 6 ToA: 0

3. Select option 5, Index. The following prompt appears:

Index Heading:

This prompt is followed by the phrase you marked or the word the cursor is on. If you want the entry to appear in the index just as it does where it is highlighted, press Return. WordPerfect automatically capitalizes the first letter of an index heading and lowercases subheading entries unless the word was capitalized in the text. If you want the word or phrase to appear differently in the index, type it or edit it as you wish it to appear. For example, if WordPerfect presents

Index Heading: John Kenneth Galbraith

and you wish the entry to be

Galbraith, John Kenneth

enter **Galbraith, John Kenneth** as the index heading. (You can also enter any *See* and *See also* references at this point by typing them at the appropriate heading or subheading level.)

4. The program then prompts you for a subheading. If you accepted the default word or phrase as the heading, you can type a subheading or simply press Return for no subheading. If you entered a different word or phrase for the heading, WordPerfect will present the default word or phrase as the subheading. You can press Return to accept it, type over the word WordPerfect presents and substitute the one you wish to use, or delete the subheading if you do not want one.

5. Repeat this process for each word or phrase you want to include in your index.

Figure 7.24 illustrates how WordPerfect inserts format codes with your index entries.

You can search for words or phrases to index in your document by using WordPerfect's Search feature (see Chapter 3) to locate each occurrence in your document. If you are using Version 4.2 or a later implementation of Word-Perfect, you can use the Concordance feature (see the following section) to search for and mark index entries.

If you are revising index entries, search while you are in the Reveal Codes screen (Alt-F3) so that you can see the index entries you have created.

Creating Concordances (Version 4.2)

> **KEY SEQUENCE**
>
> (open new document) **Alt-F5** (Mark Text) *5* <*entries*>

A concordance file is simply a file containing all the words and phrases you wish WordPerfect to search for and mark as index entries. To use such a file, you specify the name of the concordance file associated with a document when you define the style of your index. When WordPerfect generates the index, it uses the named concordance file as the basis on which to search your document, mark index entries, and generate the index. Both the concordance file and the document you are indexing should be in your default directory. Although you can automate the indexing process by creating a concordance file, creating one can be very time consuming if you have a large number of cross references or references that should appear in a form different from the way they appear in the text (as *Smith, John* instead of *John Smith,* for example). Such complex concordance files can also be tedious to revise. The most efficient use of a concordance file is to index specific words and phrases exactly as they appear in text.

It is easy to create very large concordance files, especially if you are indexing many entries under several different headings. The size of the concordance file WordPerfect can handle is limited by the amount of memory available when you generate the index. If the program does not have sufficient memory, it will prompt you about whether you want to continue. If you enter **Y**, the amount of material that has been indexed to that point will be created as an index. Typing **N** cancels the index-generation process. If memory limitation is a problem, you may need to break your document into smaller files in order to index it. To keep page numbering correct, you can specify the page number on which each file after the first is to begin by pressing Alt-F8 (Page Format) and selecting option 2 (New Page Number).

If you use large concordance files, you can speed up the process of generating indexes by sorting the concordance file alphabetically before you generate the index. See Chapter 10 for additional information.

To use a concordance file, enter the words or phrases you wish to index exactly as they appear in your document. If you want an entry to appear in the index with a different wording or under a different heading, you must also use Alt-F5 to define these forms as index entries. For example, in Figure 7.26 *John Kenneth Galbraith* is the phrase as it appears in the document. By looking at the format codes, you can see that the phrase has been marked in the index as a heading as well as a subheading under *Economists, twentieth-century. Galbraith* has also been specified as a search string in the concordance. When the index is generated, all occurrences of *John Kenneth Galbraith* or *Galbraith* will be indexed under *Galbraith,*

John Kenneth or *Economists, twentieth-century.* The form of the entry in the final index follows the capitalization of the coded index entry, although WordPerfect will search for instances of both upper- and lowercase words in the document.

To create a concordance file,

1. Open a new document.

2. Enter the words or phrases you want to use in the index as headings, as subheadings, or as entries by themselves. Press Return after you enter each one.

3. Then go back and mark each entry with the appropriate index marks by pressing Alt-F5 (Mark Text) and selecting option 5, Index (you will need to block phrases first; see "Marking Items for an Index" earlier in this chapter). If you want an entry to appear as a subheading under another heading, mark it as a subheading for that heading. If you want the item also to appear as an entry by itself, you must mark it as a heading as well.

In Figure 7.26, *Galbraith, John Kenneth* has been marked as a subheading as well as a heading. Figure 7.27 illustrates the final index.

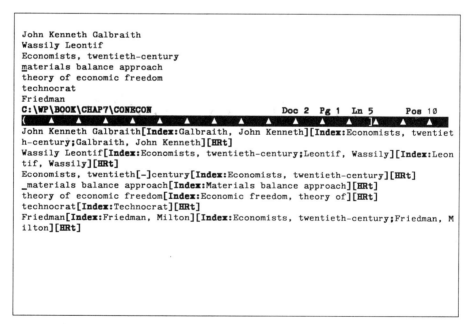

FIGURE 7.26: Marking items in a concordance file. You mark items in a concordance file in the same way that you mark items in a document you are indexing. The program uses this file as the basis on which to search the actual document and mark the occurrences of the words and phrases that are listed in the concordance file. In this figure, the item *Galbraith, John Kenneth* has been marked both as a heading and as a subheading under *Economists, twentieth-century.*

Defining the Style of an Index

KEY SEQUENCE

Alt-F5 (Mark Text) **6 5** *<concordance file name>* **Return** *<option>*
(Version 4.2)
Alt-F5 (Mark Text) **6 8** *<option>* (earlier versions)

REVEAL CODES

[**DefMark:Index,***n*]

Defining the style for an index is a simple process:

1. Press Alt-F5 (Mark Text) and select option 6 (other Options).

```
During the twentieth century, several economists became known for
their work on the materials balance approach.  In particular,
Wassily Leontif expounded this theory...
================================================================================
Milton Friedman and John Kenneth Galbraith became known for their
innovative theories in...
================================================================================
Galbraith and Leontif, in particular, personified...
The concept of the technocrat encompasses several aspects of...

Friedman's solution to the problem was to...
================================================================================
Economists, twentieth-century
     Friedman, Milton  2, 3
     Galbraith, John Kenneth  2, 3
     Leontif, Wassily  1, 3
Friedman, Milton  2, 3
Galbraith, John Kenneth  2, 3
Leontif, Wassily  1, 3
Materials balance approach  1
Technocrat  3



C:\WP\BOOK\CHAP7\TEST                    Doc 2  Pg 4  Ln 1      Pos 10
```

FIGURE 7.27: The index generated from the concordance file shown in Figure 7.26. This partial document illustrates that the program recognizes possessives (*Friedman's,* on page 3) as well as complete words and phrases listed in the concordance file. Note also that because of the way the index entries were listed in the concordance file, the format *last name, first name* has been generated in the index, although the format in the document is *first name, last name.*

2. Select option 5 (Define Index). The following prompt appears:

Concordance filename (Enter = none):

Enter the name of the concordance file, if you are using one; otherwise, press Return. The screen shown in Figure 7.28 appears.

3. Select the option number corresponding to the style you wish to use.

The index style options are similar to the list style options. Select option 1 if you do not want WordPerfect to print the page number on which the index entry appears. (This is the style you would use if you were preparing a list of key words, for example.) If you select option 2, page numbers follow the index entries. Option 3 produces page numbers after entries also, but the page numbers will be in parentheses. Options 4 and 5 produce page numbers flush right on the index page, with or without dot leaders.

If you want a columnar index, you must insert the column codes and turn the Columns feature on in the text (with Alt-F7) just before the [DefMark:Index] code. See Chapter 8 for details.

```
Index Definition

   1 - No Page Numbers
   2 - Page Numbers Follow Entries
   3 - (Page Numbers) Follow Entries
   4 - Flush Right Page Numbers
   5 - Flush Right Page Numbers with Leaders

















Selection: 0
```

FIGURE 7.28: The Index Definition screen. The options available here are similar to the page number definition options you can select for tables of contents, except that you cannot use different numbering styles in heading and subheading entries. You cannot wrap subheadings as you can the lowest levels of headings in tables of contents.

Generating an Index

KEY SEQUENCE

Alt-F5 (Mark Text) **6 8 Y** (Version 4.2)
Alt-F5 (Mark Text) **7 Y** or **N Y** (earlier versions)

REVEAL CODES

[DefMark:Index] [EndDef]

To generate an index, first move the cursor to the end of the document you are indexing (Home Home ↓). Press Ctrl-Return to insert a hard page break. The index will be generated at this point.

1. Press Alt-F5 (Mark Text) and select option 6, Other Options. For Version 4.2 or later implementations, select option 8, Generate Tables and Index. (If you are using an earlier version of the program, select option 7, Generate).

2. In Version 4.2, The following prompt appears:

   Existing tables, lists, and indexes will be replaced.
   Continue? (Y/N): Y

   Type **Y** (or press Return) to have WordPerfect generate the new index for you, replacing any existing index.
   In earlier versions of WordPerfect, this prompt is

   Have you deleted your old Table of Contents, Lists and Index?
   (Y/N) N

   If you enter **N**, WordPerfect deletes your old index for you, but it will prompt you again before it deletes the block containing the old index. If you respond incorrectly to the prompt, you may need to remove the [DefMark] codes for any existing indexes you have previously created. See "Deleting Existing Tables of Contents, Lists, and Indexes" earlier in this chapter.

Revising Index Entries

If you have revised items for your index since you last generated it, you may have inadvertently deleted one of the [Index:] codes. Refer to the section "Revising a Table of Contents, List, or Index" earlier in this chapter for the procedure to follow to make sure that your index entries are correct before you generate them.

Automatic Line Numbering (Version 4.2)

KEY SEQUENCE

Ctrl-F8 B *<options>* **Return Return**

REVEAL CODES

[LnNumOn][LnNumOff]

Line numbering is used in many types of documents, especially in the legal profession. Version 4.2 of WordPerfect allows you to specify that lines be automatically numbered in the documents you create. Although the line numbers do not appear on the editing screen, they will be present when your document is printed (see Figure 7.29).

You can select whether to include blank lines in the line count and whether numbering begins with 1 when a new page begins (the default) or continues consecutively throughout the document. You can also specify how far from the left edge of the paper you want the line numbers to appear. Another option lets you specify how often you want lines to be numbered—for example, every fifth line, and so forth.

To number the lines in a document, move the cursor to the position in your document where you want line numbering to begin. Press Ctrl-F8 (Print Format). The screen shown in Figure 7.30 appears.

To turn on line numbering at the cursor position, type **2** (the default is 1 for no line numbering). If you want blank lines to be skipped, type **3** and enter **N** at the Count blank lines? option. WordPerfect automatically includes blank lines as it numbers lines unless you tell it not to.

You can also choose to have lines numbered in increments you specify. For example, suppose you want to number only every other line or every fifth line. To do so, type **4** and enter the number of lines you want WordPerfect to skip before it numbers the next line. To have the program number every five lines, enter **5**; WordPerfect will number lines 5, 10, 15, 20, and so forth.

The fifth option on the Line Numbering menu allows you to indicate where you want WordPerfect to print the line numbers. WordPerfect measures the distance from the left margin in terms of tenths of an inch and automatically inserts line numbers 6/10 of an inch from the left margin unless you specify otherwise. To begin line numbers 1.5 inches from the left margin, select option 5 and enter **15**.

If you want line numbering to continue sequentially throughout your document, enter **6** and type **N**. WordPerfect begins line numbering with 1 on each new page unless you change this option.

```
1  Carney & Kellahan

2  125 West Main St.

3  Redwood City, CA 94035

4

5  (415) 555-1244

6

7  Attorneys for Petitioner

8

9

10           SUPERIOR COURT OF THE STATE OF CALIFORNIA

11

12                     COUNTY OF SAN MATEO

13
14  Estate of        )
15  Wilma M. Cohen,)              No. 774921
16       deceased.)
17  _____)
18

19           PETITION FOR PROBATE OF WILL

20

21           To the Honorable Superior Court of the State Of

22  California in the County of San Mateo:

23           The petition of RALPH W. PATTON respectfully shows:

24           That WILMA M. COHEN died on the 30th day of October,

25  1986, in the City of Half Moon Bay, County of San Mateo, State of

26  California; that said decedent was at the time of her death a

27  resident of the County of San Mateo, State of California, and

28  left an estate therein consisting of real and personal property;
```

FIGURE 7.29: Line numbering in a legal document. You can also number lines in selected portions of a document if you do not want each line in the entire document to be numbered.

```
Line Numbering

    1 - Turn off                         Off
    2 - Turn on

    3 - Count blank lines?                Y

    4 - Number every n lines, where n=    1

    5 - Position of number from left edge: 6
            (in tenths of an inch)

    6 - Restart numbering on each page?   Y









Selection: _
```

FIGURE 7.30: The Line Numbering screen. The default condition is that each line is numbered regardless of whether you have selected double spacing, single spacing, or some other spacing interval.

To stop line numbering, position the cursor at the point where you want line numbering to stop, press Ctrl-F8 (Print Format) B, and type **1**. You can also use F2 to search for the [LnNumOn] codes within your document and delete them or use Alt-F3 (Reveal Codes) to locate the line number formatting codes and backspace over them.

USING CITATIONS AND TABLES OF AUTHORITIES (VERSION 4.2)

If you work in the legal profession, you will appreciate WordPerfect's built-in Table of Authorities feature. It allows you to search a legal document for citations that you specify and mark them wherever they occur in the document, including in footnotes and endnotes. WordPerfect can then generate a table of authorities for you that lists each citation in the document and the page numbers on which it appears.

When you first mark a citation to be included in a table of authorities, WordPerfect asks you to define the full form of the citation. The *full form* is the way the citation will be listed in the final table of authorities. You can also specify a short form for the citation—a capsule version of the full form. WordPerfect then allows you to use the short form to indicate all subsequent occurrences of the citation in your document. Using the short form speeds up the process of marking citations;

some citations can be quite long, running several lines. Only one short form can be associated with each full form, so if you are working in a long document with many citations, it is wise to keep a list of the short forms you are using, perhaps in a second window.

In a table of authorities, citations are usually grouped into sections by type: statutes, cases, articles, text, and so on. You can specify up to 16 different sections for the table, and you can define a different format for each section. It is also wise to assign section numbers to the various types of citations you will be using before you begin, because WordPerfect will prompt you for the appropriate section number when you mark each citation. You can keep a list of the section types by number in a second window for easy reference.

After you have marked all the citations in your text file that you want included in the table of authorities, you create a page for the table.

You then define the style for the table, just as you do for tables of contents, lists, and indexes, and instruct WordPerfect to generate the table for you. A sample table of authorities is shown in Figure 7.31; the exact format for legal citations varies from state to state, but you can define WordPerfect's format to meet your needs.

```
                    TABLE OF AUTHORITIES


STATUTES                                            Page:

Business and Professional Code, Section 6009 . . . . . . . . . 2

Business and Professional Code, Sections 2-101 and 2-102 . . . 1

CASES

Adams v. State Bar of California, 811 Cal. 933 (1986)  . . . . 1

Belli v. State Bar of California, 609 Cal. 788 (1985)  . . . . 1

ARTICLES

Martin, Legal Advertising, 13 A.B.A.J. 110 (1986)  . . . . . . 2


===========================================================================
                SUPREME COURT FOR THE STATE OF CALIFORNIA
MARTIN ERICKSON,               )
            Petitioner,        )        NO. 956201
C:\WP\BOOK\CHAP7\BRIEF                          Doc 1  Pg 1  Ln 16     Pos 10
```

FIGURE 7.31: A sample table of authorities. A table of authorities lists all the citations referred to in a legal document. Citations are grouped into sections by type—for example, federal and state statutes, cases, and secondary sources such as legal encyclopedias and periodicals.

Marking Citations for a Table of Authorities

KEY SEQUENCE

Alt-F4 (Mark Block) **Alt-F5** (Mark Text) **6** <*section number*> **Return**
or **Return** (to accept default short form)
Alt-F5 (Mark Text) **4** (to enter short form)

REVEAL CODES

[ToA:;[*short form*];] [ToA:;[*short form*]; <*full form*>]

To generate an accurate table of authorities, WordPerfect has to know where each citation occurs. You can mark citations in the body of the document as well as in any footnotes or endnotes you have created.

If the document you are working with contains footnotes and endnotes, you should use WordPerfect's extended Search feature (available in Version 4.2) to search for citations; it searches through notes as well as headers and footers. To specify an extended search, press Home and then press F2 (Search).

When you have located a citation you wish to mark for inclusion in the table of authorities, be sure to mark it as a block (Alt-F4) before you press Alt-F5 (Mark Text). If you have not marked a block in your document, the correct Mark Text menu will not appear.

The first occurrence of a citation should be marked in its entirety—that is, using its full form. This is the way the citation will be listed in the table of authorities. After you have specified the full form, you can specify a short form, which is an abbreviated version of the full form. Thereafter you can use the short form in place of the full form by pressing Alt-F5 (Mark Text) and selecting option 4 (Short Form). WordPerfect presents the last short form you defined, and you can simply press Return to accept it.

WordPerfect also expects you to indicate in which section of the table of authorities you want each citation to be included—whether it is a federal or state statute, a case, or whatever other type of citation it may be. You are prompted for the appropriate section number when you mark the citation.

When you mark a citation, WordPerfect gives you a chance to edit it, for example, to specify italics or underlining and to indent the line as you wish it to appear in the table. A full-form citation can be up to 30 lines long.

To mark citations for inclusion in a table of authorities,

1. Move to the beginning of the document (Home Home ↑). Press F2 (Search) and specify the citation you wish to find in the document. (See Chapter 3 for techniques you can use when searching.) If your document

contains footnotes or endnotes, press Home F2 to use WordPerfect's Extended Search feature, which searches through notes as well as through the body of the document.

2. Mark the first occurrence of the citation in its full form by pressing Alt-F4 (Mark Block) and highlighting the entire citation.

3. Press Alt-F5 (Mark Text). The following menu appears:

   Mark for: 1 ToC; 2 List; 3 Redline; 4 Strikeout; 5 Index; 6 ToA: 0

   Select option 6, ToA.

4. The following prompt appears:

   ToA section # (press Enter for short form only):

   For the first occurrence of the citation, enter the number of the section in which you want the citation to be listed in the table of authorities. If this is not the first occurrence and you have already defined a short form, then you simply press Return to have WordPerfect mark the citation and its section number for you.

5. For the first occurrence of the citation, WordPerfect presents you with an editing screen in which you can edit the full form of the citation. At this point you can insert text attributes such as boldfacing or underlining and style the citation as you want it to appear in the table of authorities. A sample full-form citation on the editing screen is shown in Figure 7.32.

6. When you have edited the full form of the citation, press F7 (Exit). Word-Perfect then presents you with a suggested short form on the prompt line (see Figure 7.33). You can shorten the short form even further or accept the program's suggestion by simply pressing Return.

7. Press F2 (or Home F2) to resume the search or change the search string; press F2 again to actually begin the search.

8. When the program stops at the next occurrence of the citation, press Alt-F5 (Mark text) and select option 4 (Short Form). The program displays the short form you have defined. Press Return to accept it and mark the citation in the document.

Continue in this way until all occurrences of the citation in your document have been marked. Then move to the beginning of your document and search for the next citation that you wish to include in the table of authorities.

TOA: A MACRO FOR MARKING CITATIONS IN A TABLE OF AUTHORITIES

After you have defined and edited the full form of a citation to be included in the table of authorities, you can use the following macro to speed up the search

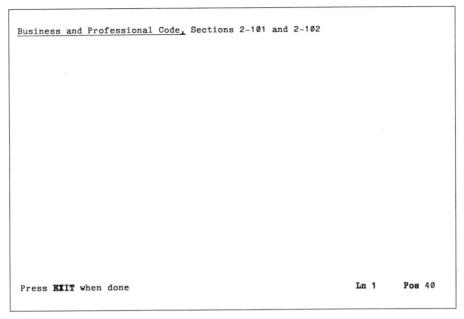

FIGURE 7.32: The citation editing screen. WordPerfect presents this editing screen so that you can edit the first occurrence of a citation. The full form of any citation may be up to 30 lines long.

for each occurrence of it. To use this macro, define the short form of the citation as a word or phrase that will always appear in your text—for example, *Calif. vs. Knight* or simply *Knight.* The macro searches for each occurrence of the string and marks it to be included in the section you have specified for the full form. Be sure to use a unique short form for each citation—that is, one that you do not use for other citations in other sections. Also make sure that the short form you use is sufficient to identify the citation as opposed to an occurrence of a proper noun in your document. For example, suppose you specify a citation's short form as Ackerman, but there are other occurrences of the word *Ackerman* in your text. If you have used text attributes such as boldfacing or underscoring to indicate citations in the document, be sure to include them in the short form; this will help WordPerfect locate only citations and not other occurrences of the search string.

Begin macro	*Macro name*	*Keystrokes*	*End macro*
Ctrl-F10	**TOA**	**Home F2 Ctrl PgUp Return Return** *<short form>* **F2 Alt-F5 4 Return Alt-F10 TOA Return**	**Ctrl-F10**

```
                    STATEMENT OF THE CASE
          The California State Legal Advisory Board has
recommended that Martin Erickson be suspended from the practice
of law for an alleged violation of the Business and Professional
Code, Sections 2-101 and 2-102. Erickson petitions the California
Supreme Court to review the Board's recommendation.
          The California State Legal Advisory Board heard the
case pursuant to American Bar Association regulations.  The
California Supreme Court is authorized to hear this petition for
review under Business and Professions Code Section 6009.
                   STATEMENT OF FACTS
          Petitioner, MARTIN ERICKSON, placed advertisements in
the Palo Alto Times Tribune and the Peninsula Register offering
his services to the public in the event of a DWI (Driving While
Intoxicated) arrest. These advertisements appeared on Wednesday,
March 18, 1986, in the Business sections of both publications.
          On July 5, 1986, after an evidentiary hearing, the Legal
Advisory Board issued a recommendation suspending petitioner from
the active practice of law for a period of three months on the
basis that he had violated the Business and Professional Code.
Motion was then made to the Superior Court of the County of Santa
Clara to issue such a ruling.  The Court so ruled on August 1,
1986.
Enter Short Form:  Business and Professional Code, Sections
```

FIGURE 7.33: The prompt to enter the short form of a citation. Using the short form speeds up the process of marking text for a table of authorities. Each citation may have only one unique short form associated with it. You may want to use a second window to keep track of the short forms you have assigned.

This macro, named TOA, is to be used after you have indicated in which section a citation is to appear and have specified the full form of the citation, including any editing for abbreviations or text attributes such as underscoring or boldfacing. The macro performs an extended search through your document for the short form you enter at the beep. It then finds the next occurrence of that short form and marks it to be included in the section you specified when you indicated and edited the full form. The macro repeats itself until the program finds no more occurrences of the short form in the text.

Defining the Style of a Table of Authorities

KEY SEQUENCE

Alt-F5 6 4 *<section number>* *<options>*

Formatting a table of authorities is slightly different from formatting other special pages in your document, such as tables of contents, lists, and indexes. You need to define the sections the table is to contain (up to 16) as well as specify the table style—whether it is to use dot leaders between citations and page numbers and how much space to allow between citations, for example.

In addition, a table of authorities is normally placed after a cover sheet and table of contents (which may be called an *index* or *subject index*), so you may wish to define these pages first. You may then want to change the page numbering of your document so that numbering begins with 1 on the first page of the actual document (see Chapter 4 for instructions about how to change page numbering.)

To define the style of a table of authorities,

1. Move to the beginning of your document (Home Home ↑) or to the location where you want the table of authorities to be generated.

2. Press Ctrl-Return to insert a hard page break. Position the cursor on the new page and type the heading you want for the table, such as **Table of Authorities**; press Return twice to move to a new line.

3. Define each section you want included in the table: Enter the section name (such as **CASES** or **STATUTES**). Press Alt-F6 (Flush Right) to align the heading Page: at the right margin and enter **Page:**. Press Return to move to a new line. Then press Alt-F5 (Mark Text) and select option 6, Other Options. Select option 4, Define Table of Authorities, enter the section number at the prompt, and press Return.

4. Select the style you wish to use in that section from the options that appear (see Figure 7.34). You can choose whether to use dot leaders, allow underlining, and allow space between citations. WordPerfect then prepares a table of authorities similar to the one in Figure 7.31. Press Return to return to the document.

Repeat this process for each section you want to include in the table of authorities. Figure 7.35 illustrates how WordPerfect inserts formatting codes as you set up a table of authorities.

Generating a Table of Authorities

KEY SEQUENCE

Alt-F5 6 8 (**Y** or **N**)

REVEAL CODES

[DefMark:ToA] [EndDef]

```
Definition for Table of Authorities 1


    1 - Dot leaders                        Y

    2 - Allow underlining                  N

    3 - Blank line between authorities     Y







Selection: _
```

FIGURE 7.34: Defining the style of a table of authorities. The options for a table of authorities are more limited than those for other types of tables and lists. You can choose whether to use dot dealers, allow underlining, and allow space between citations.

When you have marked each citation and specified the style for the table of authorities, Press Alt-F5 (Mark Text) and select option 6, Other Options. Then select option 8, Generate Tables and Index, to generate the table of authorities as well as any other tables, lists, or indexes you have defined. See "Deleting Existing Tables of Contents, Lists, and Indexes" earlier in this chapter for a discussion of other factors you should take into account when generating tables in a document that already contains tables and lists.

SUMMARY

This chapter has presented a variety of specialized techniques that you may need to use when you work with certain types of documents. You have seen how to

- Create notes
- Work with lists
- Use automatic line numbering
- Number paragraphs and outlines automatically
- Create tables of authorities

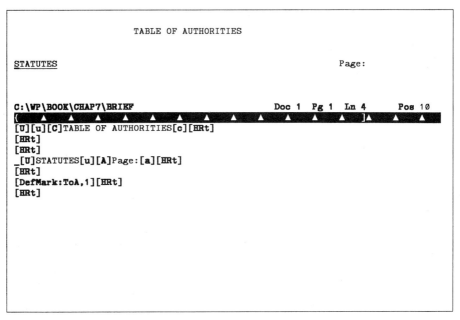

```
                        TABLE OF AUTHORITIES


STATUTES                                                Page:



C:\WP\BOOK\CHAP7\BRIEF                      Doc 1  Pg 1  Ln 4     Pos 10
[U][u][C]TABLE OF AUTHORITIES[c][HRt]
[HRt]
[HRt]
_[U]STATUTES[u][A]Page:[a][HRt]
[HRt]
[DefMark:ToA,1][HRt]
[HRt]
```

FIGURE 7.35: Reveal codes for a table of authorities. You can also use text attributes such as boldfacing, underlining, and centering for the headings of each section of a table of authorities.

Other chapters that may contain related material of interest to you are

- Chapter 3, "Editing Techniques," which presents techniques used to search through documents.
- Chapter 4, "Page Formatting Techniques," which presents instructions for specifying page numbering.
- Chapter 10, "Sorting," which presents techniques used to sort items in lists.
- Chapter 14, "Creating and Using Macros," which presents techniques used to write macros.

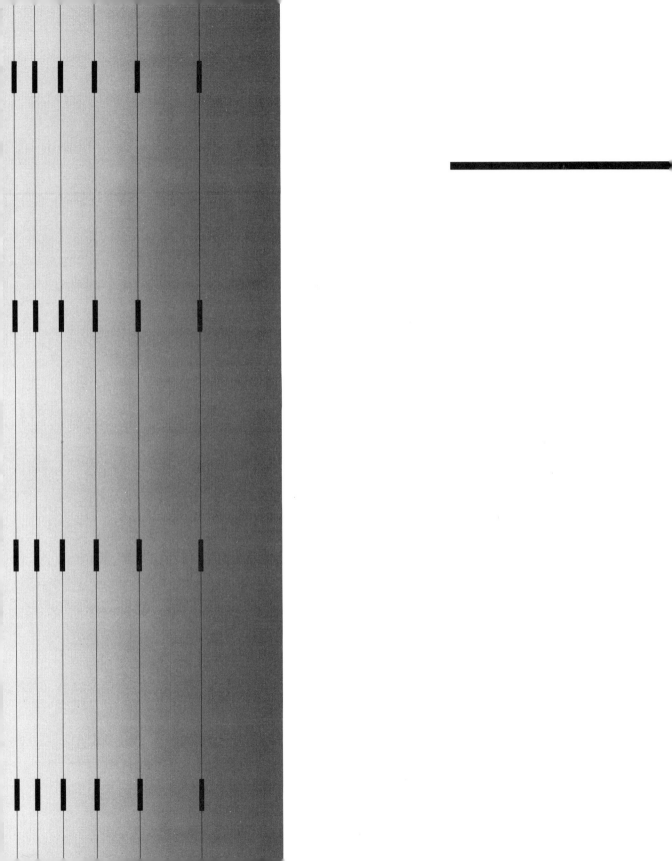

CHAPTER 8

PAGE COMPOSITION: WORKING WITH TEXT COLUMNS

PAGE COMPOSITION: WORKING WITH TEXT COLUMNS

WordPerfect can automatically format two different types of text columns for you: newspaper-style columns (sometimes called *winding* or *snaking* columns) and parallel columns. Newspaper columns are used whenever it does not matter where the material in the column ends, because the program wraps the text to the top of the next column. Parallel columns are used whenever the material in the columns should remain next to each other on the same page.

For example, you will probably want to use WordPerfect's newspaper columns feature to create columns of text for a newsletter or handbook or to generate a multicolumn index. Parallel columns can be very useful for such items as brochures, in which product descriptions and prices must stay next to each other, or agendas, in which dates and times must stay parallel to notes on what is taking place. Parallel columns are also often used in script writing, in which stage directions occupy one column and dialogue is presented in a second, parallel column. Indeed, you will want to use parallel columns to construct tables whenever the data in one or more columns requires more than a single line.

This chapter discusses how you use both types of text columns and shows you how changes you make to text in one column can affect text in other columns as well. Refer to "Working with Tables" in Chapter 4 for information about constructing tables with tab stops.

It is important to note that in WordPerfect, text columns are not the same as columns you set with tabs or columns you define as math columns, and the techniques you use with each of these types of columns are slightly different. For information about working with tabs, see Chapter 2; for techniques using math columns, refer to Chapter 11.

PAGE COMPOSITION

Because you can mix text columns with regular one-column formats, Word-Perfect gives you a great deal of flexibility in page composition. For example, you could begin a page with a one-column format, switch to two or three newspaper-style columns, switch back to a one-column format, and then change to two parallel columns, all on the same page. Figure 8.1 illustrates a sample page that uses a mix of column layouts.

Unlike many other programs, WordPerfect (Version 4.1 and later implementations) displays columns on the screen exactly as they will be formatted on the printed page, so you can see the effects of changes you make in page layouts. In Version 4.2, you can even use a special feature called Column Display to view one column at a time on your screen, which speeds up moving from one column to the next as you make changes.

WordPerfect also automatically calculates and displays column margin settings for you, so for copy fitting you have only to look at the screen and make any adjustments you think are necessary. It will automatically calculate evenly spaced columns for you and adjust spacing between columns to whatever setting you specify.

```
                              WELCOME

    Welcome to MagnaCorp. We hope this employee handbook will help to
    guide you through your first few days here.  In addition, it
    contains valuable information about employee services and
    benefits available to you.  Ask your manager or call the
    personnel office if you have any questions for which you cannot
    find the answers in this handbook.


                        ITEMS OF INTEREST

    Work Day                        Recreational Facilities

    The official work day at        MagnaCorp participates in the
    MagnaCorp is 8:30 a.m. to 5:00  city recreational plan and
    p.m.  Flexible hours can be     therefore its employees have
    arranged with your manager.     access to the municipal gym
                                    located at First and Brannan
    Parking                         Streets.  The jogging track
                                    and par course in Grant Park
    As parking is limited, please   are also nearby.  Showers and
    apply to the personnel office   lockers for company employees
    for a parking slot assignment.  are located near the south
    C:\WP\BOOK\HANDBOOK                     Doc 2  Pg 1  Ln 1      Pos 45
```

FIGURE 8.1: Intermixing columns and regular text. The columns were specified as newspaper-style columns, which means that WordPerfect will continue to wrap text from one column to the next until you turn Column mode off. When Column mode is on and you wish to return to regular text format, press Alt-F7 and select option 3 to turn Column mode off.

Along with text columns, WordPerfect contains several other features you can use for page composition to create various effects. These include

- Setting different headers and footers for right (even) and left (odd) pages (see Chapter 4)
- Changing fonts for larger headings (see Chapter 5)
- Creating borders and using graphics characters (see Chapter 13)
- Changing the binding width for documents that are going to be printed and bound (see Chapter 5)

After you review the material in this chapter, you may want to explore some of these additional techniques to use with text columns.

WORKING WITH COLUMNS

The basic process of creating text columns in WordPerfect is straightforward: You first define the type of columns you want to use—including the number of columns per page, the spacing between them, and so forth—turn Column mode on, type the text for the columns, and turn Column mode off again. Once you have created a column definition, you can use it anywhere in your text by simply turning Column mode on.

Because the program treats each type of text column—newspaper and parallel—in a slightly different way, you may have unexpected results when you edit them unless you understand just how the program handles each. The following sections discuss how WordPerfect treats newspaper and parallel text columns.

Newspaper Columns

With newspaper-style columns, when you reach the bottom of the first column, the cursor moves to the top of the next column on the same page. When you fill one page with columns, the cursor moves to the beginning of the first column on the next page. When you add text to the columns, text below the new text is pushed down through the columns and to the next page if necessary. If you look at the Reveal Codes for newspaper-style columns, you will see that what is happening is that WordPerfect is inserting a soft page code [SPg] at the end of each column (Figure 8.2).

When you fill one page with newspaper-style columns, WordPerfect moves the cursor to the leftmost column at the beginning of the next page. In this way, you can continue to write columnar material or add to existing material, and it will automatically flow through the columns. Newspaper-style columns are therefore very easy to edit and manipulate.

Because the program treats each newspaper-style column as a separate page, you will notice that some commands operate a little differently from the way they do in normal editing mode. For example, if you press the delete-to-end-of-page key sequence (Ctrl-PgDn) while in newspaper-style columns, the program will delete the lines from the cursor position to the end of the column. It will not remove text in the other columns on the same page.

With newspaper columns, you can instruct the program to keep a block of text together and not divide it between columns by turning on block protection (Alt-F4 Alt-F8 Y). If you do so, WordPerfect will keep the text you marked as a block within the same column, but it may have to break a column early to do so, resulting in a short column.

To end a newspaper-style column at a specific point, simply position the cursor where you want the column to end and press Ctrl-Return. If you are not in the rightmost column, this does not force a page break, as you might expect, but inserts a hard page code [HPg] in the text at the bottom of that column. The cursor then moves to the top of the next column, where you can begin entering more text or revise the text that is already there. If you press Ctrl-Return while you are in the rightmost column of newspaper-style columns, the program breaks the page and moves the cursor to the beginning of the next page.

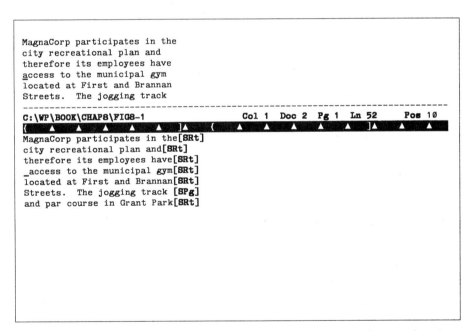

FIGURE 8.2: Reveal Codes for newspaper-style columns. WordPerfect inserts a soft page code at the end of each column. When you display Reveal Codes (Alt-F3) while in Column mode, only the codes for the column the cursor is on are displayed. You can check the status line to make sure you are viewing the codes for the column you want to examine.

Parallel Columns

When using parallel columns, WordPerfect behaves in a slightly different way: Instead of inserting a soft page break at the end of each column, it defines each parallel column with block protection (Figure 8.3). Parallel columns are designed for text that is next to each other to remain in the same relative position. As a result, you should be careful to use parallel columns only on a page-by-page basis—in other words, use parallel columns only for groups of text that occupy less than one page.

When you enter text in parallel columns, you indicate the end of one column and the beginning of the next by pressing Ctrl-Return. Unlike with newspaper columns, which will continue to flow to the correct column, with parallel columns you should always insert a hard page break code by pressing Ctrl-Return at the end of each column. If you reach the end of a page, the cursor will wrap to the beginning of the first column on the next page, which disrupts the parallel arrangement of the text, as illustrated in Figure 8.4.

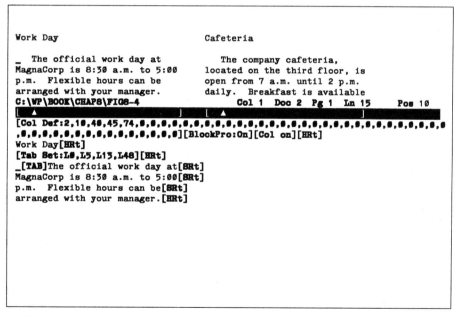

FIGURE 8.3: Reveal Codes for parallel columns. The format codes differ from those for newspaper columns: WordPerfect turns on block protection at the beginning of each set of parallel columns, uses a soft page break between columns within the parallel column area, and turns off block protection at the end of the parallel column area when you press Ctrl-Return. Here you can also see the [Col Def] code WordPerfect inserts when you define columns. The first number indicates the number of columns; the rest are the left and right margin settings of each pair of columns. Zeros appear where no columns have been defined.

```
of leave with pay are covered          informal sessions, both you
in the following sections.              and your manager sit down at
                                        least once every three months
Bereavement Leave.  Up to three         and together work out a
days off with pay are granted           performance plan for the
in the event of the death of a          coming period.  This plan
member of your immediate                details what is expected of
family.


------------------------------------------------------------------------------

you and indicates goals for a
specific time period.  It is
important that this be a two-
way process:  you and your
manager should feel free to
communicate and set mutual
goals.  At least once a year, a
formal appraisal session will
be held in which a formal
evaluation will be made and a
rating assigned to your overall
performance for the year.

C:\WP\BOOK\CHAP8\FIG8-1                  Col 1  Doc 2  Pg 2  Ln 44      Pos 10
```

FIGURE 8.4: Parallel columns incorrectly wrapping to the top of the next page. To avoid this situation, always press Ctrl-Return to end a group of parallel columns before you reach the bottom of the page. If you need to continue parallel columns across pages, press Ctrl-Return to break them at an appropriate point, insert a blank line in each unwanted column on the next page (by pressing Return and then Ctrl-Return), and continue to type the text.

Because the program operates in this way, editing parallel columns can cause unexpected results in your page layouts. If you try to add text to a column that is already full, the text at the bottom of the column will wrap into the beginning of the next column instead of simply flowing downward within the same column.

Working in Column Mode

When you are in Column mode (indicated by Col on the status line) Word-Perfect provides a different status line that indicates the current column as well as the current line and position to help you keep track of where the cursor is. If you have several columns on the screen, you may need to check the status line from time to time to determine the location of the cursor. This is especially true if you are using Reveal Codes, because WordPerfect displays only the Reveal Codes for the column the cursor is on (Figure 8.5). Although the codes are presented under the leftmost column, they may apply to material in other columns.

When you are in Column mode in WordPerfect, a few of the program's other features do not operate. The Footnote feature, for example, is not available; neither is the program's Sorting feature. If you need to sort columnar material—as,

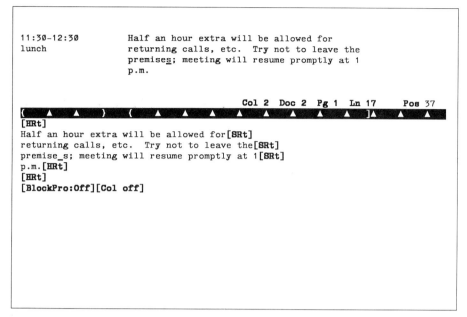

```
11:30-12:30          Half an hour extra will be allowed for
lunch                returning calls, etc.  Try not to leave the
                     premises; meeting will resume promptly at 1
                     p.m.


                                     Col 2  Doc 2  Pg 1  Ln 17      Pos 37
( ▲    ▲    )  ( ▲    ▲    ▲    ▲    ▲    ▲    ▲    ▲    ]▲    ▲    ▲
[HRt]
Half an hour extra will be allowed for[SRt]
returning calls, etc.  Try not to leave the[SRt]
premise_s; meeting will resume promptly at 1[SRt]
p.m.[HRt]
[HRt]
[BlockPro:Off][Col off]
```

FIGURE 8.5: Using Reveal Codes with two columns. The program displays the codes for the column the cursor is in, but they appear under the leftmost column. Check the status line to make sure which column you are viewing. You can also press Alt-F7 (Math/Columns) and select option 5 (Column Display) to display only one column at a time on the screen.

for example, in a glossary or index—be sure to sort it before you convert it to columns, or change the columns back to regular text format by deleting the [Col on] code. (See Chapter 10 for more information about sorting.) In addition, only single spacing within columns is possible (although there is a way to get around this limitation; see "Double Spacing Text in Columns" later in this chapter), and decimal tabs are not operative. If you need to create columns of numbers aligned on the decimal point, either use the Tab key or use Word-Perfect's Math columns feature, which also allows you to make calculations on the columns of numbers (see Chapter 11 for details about working with math columns in WordPerfect).

If you are working with newspaper-style columns, you may often run across a situation in which columns are not of equal length on the same page. If you want equal columns, you can simply press Alt-F8 (Page Format), select option 4 (Page Length), and reset the number of text lines. The number of text lines should be exactly divisible by the number of columns you have. For example, if you are working with a three-column page, the number of text lines should be divisible by 3; if you have four columns, the number of text lines should be divisible by 4, and so forth. The default page setting is 54 single-spaced lines, which is divisible by 3; for four columns, you might want to change the page length to 52 lines. If one of your columns will be short, common practice is to make it the last column.

You can have up to 24 columns on a page (Version 4.2; five if you are working with an earlier version), but if you are printing on standard 8½ × 11-inch paper, you will find that four columns is about the maximum you will want to use, unless you are working with very short entries, such as in an index. With three or four columns five spaces apart, lines are long enough to be easily read without too much hyphenation. (To improve hyphenation, you may want to turn right justification off in narrow columns by pressing Ctrl-F8, the Print Format key sequence, and selecting option 3.) With over three columns per page, you will probably also want to set a new hyphenation zone so that word spacing will be more equal when columns are right justified. The hyphenation zone is normally set to 7, but in very narrow columns you may want to change it to 4 (see "Hyphenation Commands" in Chapter 3). If you set the H-zone to 4, WordPerfect will beep when a word four positions from the right margin extends beyond the right margin. You can then set the hyphen or press F1 (Cancel) if you do not want the word to be hyphenated.

When you work with columns, you may also want to set a tab for paragraph indents. Figure 8.6 illustrates a situation in which paragraph indents were used

```
Work Day                         Recreational Facilities

   The official work day at         MagnaCorp participates in
MagnaCorp is 8:30 a.m. to 5:00   the city recreational plan and
p.m.  Flexible hours can be      therefore its employees have
arranged with your manager.      access to the municipal gym
                                 located at First and Brannan
Parking                          Streets.  The jogging track
                                 and par course in Grant Park
   As parking is limited,        are also nearby.  Showers and
please apply to the personnel    lockers for company employees
office for a parking slot        are located near the south
assignment.                      entrance of the main lobby.

Hours

   Noon to 1 p.m. has been       Vacation
reserved as lunch hour for all
employees.  Some departments     _
have chosen to take lunch from      Full-time permanent
11:30 to 12:30 or from 12:30     employees are eligible for two
to 1:30; check with your         weeks of paid vacation after
manager.                         six months of continuous
C:\WP\BOOK\CHAP8\FIG8-1          employment. During the first
                                             Col 2  Doc 2  Pg 1  Ln 30      Pos 45
```

FIGURE 8.6: Using tabs for paragraph indents within columns. Because WordPerfect treats each column as a separate page, you must set tabs at the beginning of each column if you want to use settings other than the default of a tab every five spaces. Here indents are set at three spaces.

within columns. If you are working with very narrow columns, however, you may want to simply press Return one extra time at the end of each paragraph to insert an additional line of space between paragraphs. Otherwise the first line in each paragraph will be even shorter than the rest of the lines in the column, which may cause difficulties in formatting right-justified material.

WordPerfect will calculate and display margin settings for columns. If you wish, you can override them. For example, you may want newspaper columns to use different margin settings, as shown in Figure 8.7.

Moving between Columns

When Column mode is on, the cursor moves a little differently from the way it moves in normal Editing mode. Instead of using the Tab key to move between columns, you move between columns by using the Goto key sequence (Ctrl-Home) plus the → or ← arrow key. In addition, Goto-Home (Ctrl-Home Home) plus the ← key moves the cursor to the first column on the page, while Goto-Home plus the → key moves the cursor to the last column on the page. You will find that using these key sequences is much faster than moving the cursor

```
                      ITEMS OF INTEREST

Work Day               Cafeteria

   The official work       The company cafeteria, located on
day at MagnaCorp is    the third floor, is open from 7 a.m.
8:30 a.m. to 5:00      until 2 p.m. daily.  Breakfast is
p.m.  Flexible hours   available for your convenience until
can be arranged with   9:00.  After 2 p.m., vending machines
your manager.          with cold sandwiches and salads are
                       available.
_
Parking                Recreational Facilities

   As parking is           MagnaCorp participates in
limited, please apply  the city recreational plan and therefore
to the personnel       its employees have access to the
office for a parking   municipal gym located at First and
slot assignment.       Brannan Streets.  The jogging track
                       and par course in Grant Park are also
Hours                  nearby.  Showers and lockers for company
                       employees are located near the south
   Noon to 1 p.m. has
C:\WP\BOOK\CHAP8\FIG8-3                Col 1  Doc 2  Pg 1  Ln 21      Pos 10
```

FIGURE 8.7: Mixing different column-margin settings. Although this technique is more often used with parallel columns, you can create newspaper columns of varying width as well to add interest and variety to your page layouts.

through the text to reach the beginning or end of the columns. Table 8.1 summarizes all of these cursor movement key sequences.

In addition, because scrolling through several columns can take some time, WordPerfect allows you to display only one column on the screen so that you can work with it more easily. To do so, you press Alt-F7 (Math/Columns), select option 5 (Column Display), and then type **N** at the prompt "Display columns side by side?" This key sequence is a toggle: To see all the columns once again, repeat the sequence, selecting **Y** instead of **N** at the prompt.

Defining Text Columns

When you create a column definition, you do not have to use it right away. Instead, you can set up your page layout at the beginning of a document and then, at any point in the document, switch to the column format you have defined by turning Column mode on. This allows you to alternate between text formats on the same page of your document without having to redefine columns each time you use them.

Entering Text in Columns

To enter a starting number different from the one that the program would use automatically, select New Page Number (option 2) on the Page Format menu just

KEY SEQUENCE	RESULT
Ctrl-Home → or ←	Moves cursor between columns
Ctrl-Home Home ←	Moves to the first column
Ctrl-Home Home →	Moves to the last column
→	Moves to the first character of the next column when the cursor is on the last character in one column
←	Moves to the last character of the previous column when the cursor is on the first character in one column
Ctrl-Return	Ends a column and moves to the next column; in a rightmost newspaper-style column, also creates a page break
Note: Other cursor control key sequences work as they do in Editing mode and scroll all columns simultaneously.	

TABLE 8.1: Cursor Movement in Column Mode

Return. In Column mode, this does not cause a page break, as you might expect, unless you are in a rightmost column. It simply moves the cursor to the top of the next column and begins a new column. If you press Ctrl-Return when the cursor is in the rightmost column on a page, it moves the cursor to the beginning of the first column on the next page, and the program inserts a hard page break.

If you are working with parallel columns, you should always end them by pressing Ctrl-Return at the end of each one to insert a hard page break code (see "Parallel Columns" earlier in this chapter for an illustration explaining why).

You may also notice that WordPerfect does not allow you to move the cursor through an empty column by using the arrow keys. Use the space bar to move through an empty column.

In Column mode, most of the cursor movement key sequences operate normally (exceptions are listed in Table 8.1). Pressing End moves the cursor to the end of the line, pressing Home Home ↑ moves the cursor to the beginning of the document, and so forth.

Mixing Columns and Standard Text

In WordPerfect, it is easy to intermix standard text that flows from the left to the right margin with text that is presented in columns. After you have set column definitions (which can be done at any point earlier in the document), you can simply turn Column mode on (Alt-F7, option 3) and begin typing text in columns. When you finish entering the text you want in columns, turn Column mode off by pressing Alt-F7 and selecting option 3 again. If you want columns of even lengths, you may wish to change the number of lines per page or simply press Ctrl-Return at the end of each column where you want the column to break.

Converting One-Column Text to Two Columns

You often may want to convert text that has already been entered in one column into two-column format, or for ease in entering text, you may want to enter text in one column and then convert it to two or three columns. To do so, use the following procedure:

1. Count the length of the longest line you will need in the two-column format. For example, if you are converting a list of names and addresses, count the number of characters in the longest address line, which usually contains the most characters. For a quick count, you can look at the status line at the bottom of the screen and subtract the left margin setting.

2. Move the cursor to the beginning of the text you want to convert into columns.

3. Define the columns with at least the width of the longest line that you determined in step 1.

4. Turn Column mode on (Alt-F7 3). Move the cursor to the end of the text you want to reformat and then turn Column mode off (by pressing Alt-F7 3 again).

Be aware of the limitations of a standard $8\frac{1}{2} \times 11$-inch page. More than four columns can be difficult to read, as word breaks occur frequently in such narrow columns.

After you have inserted a new column definition for text that has already been entered in one-column format, remember that you must turn Column mode on (option 3 on the Math/Columns menu) and then press ↓ to move the cursor into the text area in order for the reformatting to take place. You may also want to press Ctrl-Return at appropriate places in the reformatted material to produce better column breaks and more even column alignment.

Double Spacing Text in Columns

Although WordPerfect does not normally allow mixing double and single spacing within text columns, you can get around this limitation by first highlighting the block of text you want double spaced and then searching for each soft return ([SRt]) at the end of each line (pressing Ctrl-M inserts a [SRt] code) and replacing each soft return with a double hard return ([HRt][HRt]) to create double spacing.

To do this, you first press Alt-F4 and then highlight all of the text in the column to be double spaced. You then press Alt-F2 to begin the search and replace operation. Press Ctrl-M to enter the search string, [SRt]. Press F2 and press Return twice to enter the replacement string, [HRt][HRt]. Finally, press F2 again to perform the search and replace operation. Text you alter in this way will not be right justified, however, as illustrated in Figure 8.8.

Retrieving Material into Text Columns

When the cursor is positioned in the column where you want retrieved text to appear, you can retrieve a file into that position. You can also open a new document window (Shift-F3), retrieve a file, and cut or copy selected portions of it into your column. When Column mode is on, WordPerfect will reformat the new text according to the [Col Def] that appears before the columns in the text.

Editing Columns

To cut or copy text columns in WordPerfect, you mark the text as a block (Alt-F4) and use Move (Ctrl-F4) to cut or copy it. You do not use the Cut, Copy, or

```
Recreational Facilities
                                 Vacation
    MagnaCorp participates in
                                    Full-time permanent
the city recreational plan and   employees are eligible for two
                                 weeks of paid vacation after
therefore its employees have     six months of continuous
                                 employment. During the first
access to the municipal gym      five years of service, you
                                 earn three weeks of vacation
located at First and Brannan     per year. After five years of
                                 service, you receive four
Streets.  The jogging track      weeks of vacation.

and par course in Grant Park

are also nearby.  Showers and

lockers for company employees

are located near the south

entrance of the main lobby.

C:\WP\BOOK\CHAP8\FIG8-4          Col 1  Doc 2  Pg 2  Ln 2      Pos 10
```

FIGURE 8.8: Mixing double and single spacing in text columns. To achieve this effect, you perform a search and replace operation for each [SRt] code in the text you want double spaced, replacing the [SRt] codes with [HRt][HRt].

Retrieve Columns options, which can be misleading. These options work only on columns you have set with the Tab key and columns you have defined as math columns.

When you define a block in Column mode, press → to move to the next column. If you are at the top of a column, pressing ↓ takes you to the bottom of the previous column.

If you are editing newspaper columns, simply make whatever additions or deletions you think are necessary. WordPerfect reformats newspaper columns automatically, wrapping each one down (snaking) throughout the columns and across pages of columns. You may not see all the reformatting until you move the cursor through the columns.

If you are editing parallel columns, be aware that major changes are not possible. It is best to use parallel columns only on a page-by-page basis and simply create a new page at the appropriate breaks (by turning off Column mode and pressing Ctrl-Return). If you attempt to insert text into a column that is already full, the text will wrap onto the leftmost column on the next page instead of wrapping down the same column on the new page.

Because WordPerfect considers text columns to be pages, all the page commands (such as Delete to End of Page) work within columns. For example, pressing

Ctrl-PgDn deletes all the lines from the cursor position to the end of the column instead of all the lines from the cursor position to the end of the page.

You can turn Widow/Orphan Protection on within a column (Alt-F8, option A) so that single lines will not be left at beginnings or ends of columns. See Chapter 4 for more information about using WordPerfect's Widow/Orphan Protection feature.

You can shorten the length of columns by changing the number of text lines per page (Alt-F8, option 4). To keep columns of equal length, specify a page length that is divisible by the number of columns.

To return columnar material to the normal one-column format, delete the [Col on] code. Press Alt-F3 to reveal the codes and then position the cursor to the right of the [Col on] code and backspace over it.

Changing Column Definitions

To change a column definition, you must first delete the old column definition code. You can use WordPerfect's Search feature to locate any [Col Def] codes you may have inserted into your text. To do so,

1. Press F2 (Search); then press Alt-F7. The following menu appears:

   Math: 1 Def 2 On 3 Off 4 + 5 = 6 * 7 t 8 T 9 !
   A N Column: B def C On D Off 0

   Select option B. WordPerfect will locate the next occurrence of a [Col Def] code in your text.

2. Press Alt-F3 to see the Reveal Codes. Position the cursor to the right of the [Col Def] code you no longer wish to use and press Backspace to delete it.

3. Change the column definition (see "Defining Text Columns" earlier in this chapter).

When you delete a column definition, the page is reformatted to whatever one-column text format you are using. After you set a new column definition and move the cursor through the text, the page will be reformatted back into columns.

WORKING WITH NEWSPAPER AND PARALLEL COLUMNS

Entering newspaper and parallel text columns in documents you create in WordPerfect requires the following steps:

1. Position the cursor at the beginning of the area you want to define as columns or at any point in your document before the area you want to define as columns.

2. Define the columns (see the next section, ''Defining Columns of Text'').

3. Turn on Column mode.

4. Enter the column text (see ''Entering Text in Columns'' earlier in this chapter).

5. Turn off Column mode.

The sections that follow present techniques for each of these steps.

Defining Columns of Text

KEY SEQUENCE

To define newspaper columns:

Alt-F7 4 Y (or **N**) <*number of spaces between columns*> **Return 1**
    <*number of columns*> **Return** <*margin settings* or **Return**> **F7**

To define parallel columns:

Alt-F7 4 Y (or **N**) <*number of spaces between columns*> **Return 2**
    <*number of columns*> **Return** <*margin settings* or **Return**> **F7**

REVEAL CODES

[**Col Def:** <*number of columns defined*>, <*margin settings*>,...]

You use a similar procedure to define newspaper-style columns and parallel columns. The main difference is that for parallel columns, you specify that groups of text be kept together on a page (by responding **Y** to the prompt ''Do you want groups kept together on a page?''). Parallel columns are often not of equal width, so you may also want to specify different column margins for this type of column.

To define either type of text column,

1. Position the cursor at the beginning of the area you want to define. To create a column definition, you can actually position the cursor at any earlier point in the document, including the beginning of the document. When you turn Column mode on (by pressing Alt-F7 and selecting option 3), the last column definition you specified will be used.

2. Press Alt-F7 and select option 4 (Column Def). The screen shown in Figure 8.9 appears. This screen is the one that appears in Version 4.2 of WordPerfect; in earlier versions of the program, only five columns per page were possible. Version 4.2 allows for 24 columns per page.

```
Text Column Definition

     Do you wish to have evenly spaced columns? (Y/N) N
     If yes, number of spaces between columns:
     Type of columns: 1
          1 - Newspaper
          2 - Parallel with Block Protect

     Number of text columns (2-24): 0

     Column    Left     Right     Column    Left     Right
       1:                           13:
       2:                           14:
       3:                           15:
       4:                           16:
       5:                           17:
       6:                           18:
       7:                           19:
       8:                           20:
       9:                           21:
      10:                           22:
      11:                           23:
      12:                           24:
```

FIGURE 8.9: The Column Definition screen. Version 4.2 of WordPerfect allows you to define up to 24 columns per page. If you are working with a laser printer in which a variety of type styles and sizes are available, you will appreciate the flexibility of the additional columns (earlier versions of the program allowed only five columns per page).

3. Respond to the prompt

   Do you wish to have evenly spaced columns? (Y/N)

   with either **Y** or **N**, depending on the effect you want to create. If you respond **Y**, WordPerfect will ask you how many spaces to leave between columns and calculate margin settings for your columns. Enter the number of spaces you wish to leave between columns and press Return. If you respond **N** (or when you enter the number of spaces between columns), the program moves to the following prompt:

   Type of Columns: 1
   1—Newspaper
   2—Parallel with Block Protect

   If you want newspaper columns, choose 1, the default value, by pressing Return. For parallel columns, type **2** and press Return.

4. At the next prompt, enter the number of text columns you want to use. In Version 4.2 of WordPerfect, you can specify from 2 to 24 columns; in earlier versions, you can specify from 2 to 5.

5. Enter the left and right margin settings for your column. If you responded **Y** to the first prompt, WordPerfect will calculate these margin settings for you. Simply press Return to accept them. If you want to use other margin settings for your columnar material, enter those settings here.

6. Press F7 to exit.

Note: Version 4.1 of WordPerfect displays a slightly different prompt for choosing the type of columns you wish to use. Instead of choosing a number (**1** for Newspaper and **2** for Parallel), you answer either **N** or **Y** to the prompt

Do you want groups kept together on a page? (Y/N)

To set up Newspaper columns, press Return to choose the N default. To set up Parallel columns, you type **Y** and press Return.

You may receive the following error message when defining text columns:

Error: Text columns can't overlap

This message appears when you have set column margins incorrectly. You will need to enter new margin values.

The first number in the [Col Def] code that appears when you define columns is the number of columns you have specified. Thereafter, each pair of numbers indicates the margin settings for each column. You can have up to 24 columns; if you do not use a column setting, zeros appear as the margin settings for that column.

If you try to turn Column mode on before you have defined the type and number of columns to be used (that is, before WordPerfect meets a [Col Def:] code), you will receive the error message

ERROR: No text columns defined

To delete the column format in effect (either Newspaper or Parallel) and return the text to regular line formatting, open the Reveal Codes window (Alt-F3) and delete the [Col on] code positioned before the text that is formatted in columns.

Turning Columns On and Off

KEY SEQUENCE

Alt-F7 *3*

REVEAL CODES

[Col on]
[Col off]

After defining your columns, you can select option 3 (Column On/Off) from the Math/Columns menu (accessed by Alt-F7) to begin entering text in columns, or you can simply resume typing if you are not ready to enter columnar material yet. When you want to switch to columns, press Alt-F7 (Math/Columns) and select option 3 (Column On/Off) to turn Column mode on.

Moving between Text Columns

KEY SEQUENCE

To move between columns:
    Ctrl-Home → or ←
To move to the first column:
    Ctrl-Home Home ←
To move to the last column:
    Ctrl-Home Home →
To move to the first character of the next column when the cursor is on the last character in one column:
    →
To move to the last character of the previous column when the cursor is on the first character in one column:
    ←
To end a column and move to the next column:
    Ctrl-Return

Before you enter text, you may want to reset the hyphenation zone (if you are working with very narrow columns) or set a tab for a paragraph indent.

Ending Newspaper and Parallel Columns

KEY SEQUENCE

    Ctrl-Return

REVEAL CODES

For newspaper columns:
    [Hpg]

For parallel columns:
[BlockPro:Off][Col off]
[HRt]
[BlockPro:On][Col on]

You can end a newspaper column at any point and go on to the next column or to the next page. To end a column, press Ctrl-Return. Unless you are in the last (rightmost) column on the page, WordPerfect will insert a hard page code and move the cursor to the next column. If you are in the rightmost column when you press Ctrl-Return, WordPerfect will insert a hard page break and move the cursor to the leftmost (first) column on the next page.

In Parallel Column mode, pressing Ctrl-Return simply moves the cursor from one column to the next. It does not insert a hard page break if you press it while in the rightmost column, as it does with newspaper columns. If you reach the end of a page while in Parallel Column mode, WordPerfect moves the cursor to the top of the next (leftmost) column on the next page rather than to the top of the same column on the next page.

With parallel columns, WordPerfect uses block protection so that groups of related columns will be kept together on the same page. If a group of parallel columns needs to be split across pages, WordPerfect inserts a soft page break and moves the beginning of the columns to the top of the next page. Make sure that the material you enter can all fit on one page or specify where it is to break, as shown in Figure 8.10.

Displaying One Column at a Time

KEY SEQUENCE

To display one column at a time:
Alt-F7 5 N
To display columns side by side:
Alt-F7 5 Y

Because scrolling through large numbers of columns can be time consuming, you may want to display each column by itself on the screen. In Version 4.2 of WordPerfect, you can view one column at a time by selecting option 5 (Display Columns) from the Alt-F7 (Math/Columns) menu. To return to a side-by-side display, press Alt-F7 again, select option 5, and answer **Y** to the prompt

Display columns side by side? (Y/N)

```
Thursday, September 17

9 a.m.                 New employee orientation.  Be prepared to
Employee               give a brief summary of your work experience
Relations              to the rest of the group.
Council
                       Coffee break will be scheduled after the film
                       presentation.

                       Call-forward phones to extension 3550.




11:30-12:30            Half an hour extra will be allowed for
lunch                  returning calls, etc.  Try not to leave the
                       premises; meeting will resume promptly at 1
                       p.m.



=============================================================================
Friday, September 18

7:30 a.m.              Breakfast meeting with vice presidents at
                       Rotunda Restaurant
C:\WP\BOOK\CHAP8\FIG-P                      Doc 2  Pg 1  Ln 3      Pos 10
```

FIGURE 8.10: Parallel columns on one page. When you reach the end of a page using Parallel Column mode, WordPerfect wraps the cursor to the beginning of the leftmost column on the next page instead of continuing it down the rightmost column. For this reason, be sure that text you enter can be broken across pages as has been done here. Column mode was turned off. A hard page break was inserted, and Column mode was turned on again. One other way around this limitation is to insert a "(Continued...)" line at the top of the leftmost column on the next page or press Return to insert a blank line in that column.

NEW: A MACRO FOR TWO-COLUMN NEWSPAPER COLUMNS

The following macro automatically formats your document into two evenly spaced newspaper-style columns and puts you in Column mode so that you can immediately begin typing text in columns.

Begin macro	Macro name	Keystrokes	End macro
Ctrl-F10	**NEW**	**Alt-F7 4 Y 5** **Return 1 2** **Return F7 3**	**Ctrl-F10**

PAR: A Macro for Two-Column Parallel Columns

The following macro automatically formats your document into two evenly spaced parallel columns and puts you in Column mode so that you can immediately begin typing text in columns.

Begin macro	*Macro name*	*Keystrokes*	*End macro*
Ctrl-F10	**PAR**	**Alt-F7 4 Y 5**	**Ctrl-F10**
		Return 2 2	
		Return F7 3	

Summary

This chapter has presented the techniques you use when working with text columns—either newspaper or parallel columns—in WordPerfect. For additional information see

- Chapter 2, "Basic Formatting and Text Entry," for information about setting and using tabs in WordPerfect
- Chapter 4, "Page Formatting Techniques," for details about setting the hyphenation zone, using the Widow/Orphan Protection feature, and using different headers and footers on facing pages
- Chapter 5, "Printing," for information about changing the binding within printed documents
- Chapter 10, "Sorting," to see how to sort material before you format it into columns
- Chapter 11, "Mathematics, Equations, and Special Features," for information about using math columns and performing calculations on columns of numbers
- Chapter 13, "Line and Box Drawing," for techniques you can use to enhance newsletters, brochures, or whatever you create with WordPerfect's Column feature

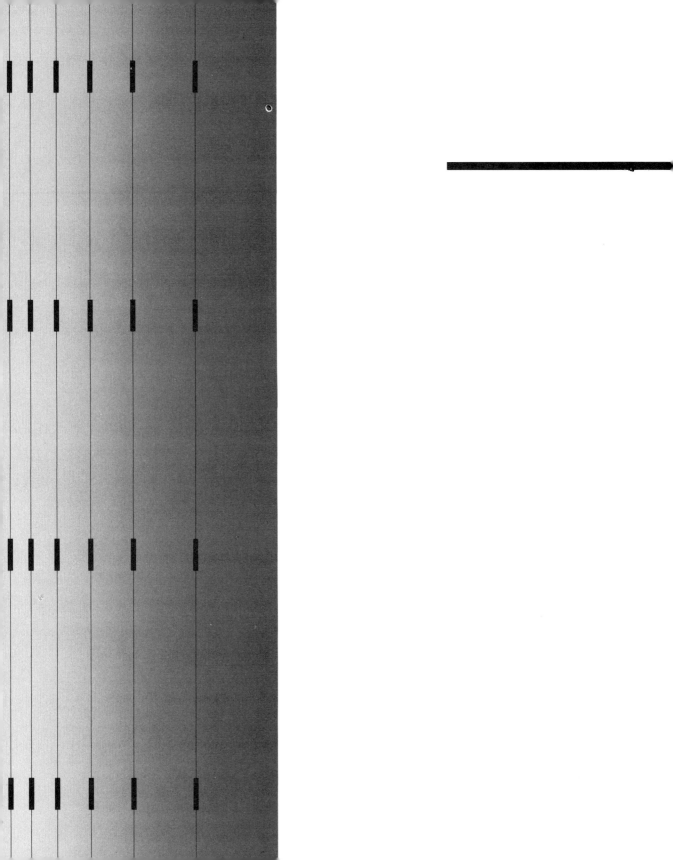

MERGE OPERATIONS

MERGE OPERATIONS

This chapter discusses WordPerfect's merge capabilities, starting with traditional mail merge applications such as the production of form letters and mailing labels, forms printing, and the creation of reports. The chapter also discusses how you can use the Merge feature to perform document assembly using standard text from several different files.

WordPerfect's Merge feature includes many options. This chapter presents information about how to use these options to perform merge operations directly from the keyboard, send merged information directly to the printer, execute macros from a merge operation, and create menu-driven merge operations.

You often will want to sort the data in a secondary merge file before you execute a merge operation. To do this, you use WordPerfect's Sort feature. For specific information about sorting, refer to Chapter 10.

If you wish to use data from other software programs, such as Lotus 1-2-3 and dBASE III PLUS, in WordPerfect merge operations, you must first convert this data into the format used by the secondary merge file. To find out how to do this, refer to Chapter 15.

THE BASIC MERGE OPERATION

WordPerfect merge operations essentially involve two files: (1) a secondary merge file that contains a list of data items arranged in an unvarying order and (2) a primary merge file that contains both standard text and data variables that will be replaced with specific data items from the secondary merge file when the merge operation is performed. If you have used merge printing with other word processors, you may know the secondary merge file as the *data file* and the primary merge file as the *master document*.

During the merge operation, WordPerfect creates a new file that contains information from both the secondary and primary merge files. For instance, when you create form letters, the new file created during the merge operation will contain one letter for each set of data in the secondary merge file. In each letter generated, all data variables that you designated in the primary merge file will be replaced with the appropriate data items from the secondary file. Once the merge file has been created, you can print it or edit it just as you do any other WordPerfect document.

Preparing the Secondary Merge File

To prepare the secondary merge file, you must select the data items you wish to include and decide upon the order in which they are to be maintained. Both aspects of the secondary merge file are important. Because this file represents a special kind of data file, the elements it contains and the way they are structured must not vary throughout the file.

For instance, suppose that you are creating a client address file that you will ultimately use to generate form letters as well as mailing labels and to address envelopes. Undoubtedly, you will want to include the company name, street address, city, state, and zip code for each of your clients. In addition, you may want to include the name of your primary contact at the company and the appropriate personal title, such as Mr., Ms., or Mrs.

Each of these items of information has to be represented in the same way in the new secondary merge file. However, not all of these items require their own data variable, or *field*. A single field can contain several items of information, so long as these items are always used as a single unit in any merge operation.

For example, you will likely always use the city, state, and zip code for each client as a unit either in the inside address in form letters or on the envelopes or mailing labels generated through merging. However, you will not likely always use the contact person's first and last name and personal title as a unit. For example, in the salutation of the letter, you may use either just the person's title and last name or just the person's first name. You might address the letter to Mr. Smith ("Dear Mr. Smith") or directly to John ("Dear John"), but not to Mr. John Smith ("Dear Mr. John Smith"). When you set up a secondary merge file, you must very carefully consider which items must be kept separate, and which can be combined into single fields in the secondary merge file.

> *Note:* If you will be importing data into the secondary merge file from other sources, for instance, databases maintained in Lotus 1-2-3 or stand-alone database management systems such as dBASE III PLUS or RBASE:5000, the secondary merge file fields must be structured like those of the source database. For example, if dBASE III Plus maintains your client database and this file has three separate fields for the city, state, and zip code data, you will have to use the same three individual fields in the secondary merge field.

The group of fields that you maintain for each of your clients in the secondary merge file is referred to collectively as a *record*. Every record in the secondary file must have the same number of fields, though some of the fields can be empty. Thus, however you finally decide to set up the fields, you will need to reserve a place for each of them in the secondary merge file, even if you do not yet have information for them.

WordPerfect has its own way of identifying the fields and records in the secondary merge file. All data entered in each field must be placed on its own line, and the data must be terminated by a Merge R (Return) code. To designate the end of one record and the beginning of another, you must terminate the record information with a Merge E (End) code. This code must appear by itself on its own line.

You can enter the Merge Return code in one of two ways: either by pressing F9 (marked Merge R on the keyboard template) or by pressing Ctrl-R and Return. Pressing F9 is more convenient because doing so not only enters the Ctrl-R code but also enters a hard return. If you use the Ctrl-R method, you must manually press Return to move to the next line so you can enter a new field or another Merge E code.

The Merge Return code is displayed on the screen as ^R. However, you cannot produce this code by entering the caret (Shift-6) and the letter *R*. Although the result of using this key combination would appear identical to you on the screen, WordPerfect does not recognize ^R as a Merge Return code unless it was produced by pressing F9 or Ctrl-R Return.

To enter the Merge E code to mark the end of a record, you press either Shift-F9 (marked Merge E on the keyboard template) or Ctrl-E and Return. Again, using Shift-F9 is more convenient than using Ctrl-E because WordPerfect automatically enters the Merge E code and a hard return at the same time. If you use the Ctrl-E method, you must manually press Return.

Figure 9.1 shows the structure and the merge codes in a client secondary merge file. The first record in the file does not contain actual data. Rather, its purpose is to identify all of the fields in each record of this file by number and name. (The ^N code above the field name, COMPANY NAME, prevents WordPerfect from ever using the data in this first *dummy record* during any merge operation.) Notice that each field is entered on its own line and is marked with a Merge R (^R) code, and that after the last field the end of the record is marked by a Merge E (^E) code.

Notice also that when there is no information for a field, as is the case in field 3 (STREET ADDRESS 2) for ABC Contracting, a Merge R code still marks the field's place. If this Merge Return were omitted from the secondary merge file, its absence would prevent proper use of the subsequent fields in this record. WordPerfect keeps track of individual fields by numbering their placement in the record (see "Preparing the Primary Merge File" that follows). Without a Merge R code for the empty field 3, the city, state, and zip code field (4) would become the third field, the contact person's first name would become the fourth field, the contact person's last name would become the fifth field, the contact person's title would become the sixth field, and this record would not have a seventh field. As a result, the wrong information in this record would be merged into the primary file wherever fields 3 through 7 were used.

The number of records that a secondary merge file can hold is limited only by available disk space. Nevertheless, if you maintain truly large data files with thousands of records, you will probably find such files unwieldy to edit and maintain. In that event, you will find it advantageous to divide the secondary merge

```
^N
1 - COMPANY NAME^R
2 - STREET ADDRESS 1^R
3 - STREET ADDRESS 2^R
4 - CITY, STATE  ZIP^R
5 - CONTACT'S FIRST NAME^R
6 - CONTACT'S LAST NAME^R
7 - PERSONAL TITLE^R
^E
ABC Contracting^R
1345 Seventh Street^R
^R
Berkeley, CA  94707^R
Jim^R
Wagoner^R
Mr.^R
^E
Speedo Printing^R
221 Avenue of the Americas^R
Suite 456^R
San Francisco, CA  94111^R
Allan^R
Grill^R
Mr.^R
A:\CLIENT.SF                        Doc 1  Pg 1  Ln 1      Pos 10
```

FIGURE 9.1: The secondary merge file for a client address file. This file tracks seven fields (or items) of information for each record (or client) it contains. The first record is used only to identify the number and name of each field. The ^N code (indicating advance to the next record) above the COMPANY NAME field identifier prevents WordPerfect from ever using the data in this record in a merge operation. Notice that information for each of the seven fields is entered on its own line and that each field is terminated with a Merge R (Return) code, shown as ^R. Even when there is no information for a particular field, as is the case in this figure in the second street address field for ABC Contracting, a Merge R code must still be entered to mark the place for that field. Also, notice that the end of each record is marked with a Merge E (End) code, shown as ^E.

file into several smaller files. For instance, if you maintain the records in a client file in alphabetical order by company name (see Chapter 10 for information about sorting secondary merge files), you can split the file in two so that one contains those companies whose names begin with the letters A–M, and the other contains those that begin with the letters N–Z.

When you save the data you have entered in a secondary merge file (just as you save any WordPerfect document: by pressing either F10 or F7), you may want to include the extension .SF to mark the file as a secondary merge file. Although this is not essential, adding this extension to all secondary merge files helps you easily distinguish them from regular documents in a directory listing.

Preparing the Primary Merge File

You can create several different primary merge files to use with a single secondary merge file. For instance, in the client data file example, you might set up two primary merge files: one to generate a letter for each client in the secondary merge file, and one to address the mailing label for each letter.

The primary merge file that contains the form letter includes both standard text that does not vary from letter to letter as well as data variables (fields), which are taken from each record in the secondary merge file and, therefore, change as each letter is generated. It is the appropriate use of these data variables throughout the letter that personalizes its content.

To indicate where the contents of a particular field are to be merged into the text of the letter, you use WordPerfect's Merge Codes key sequence, Alt-F9. When you press Alt-F9, you are presented with the following merge options:

$$^C;\ ^D;\ ^F;\ ^G;\ ^N;\ ^O;\ ^P;\ ^Q;\ ^S;\ ^T;\ ^U;\ ^V:$$

As with the Merge R (^R) and Merge E (^E) codes, each begins with the Ctrl character symbol (^) to mark it as a merge code. From this menu, you select **^F** by typing **F** (Insert Field). As soon as you do, the following prompt appears:

Field Number?

In response, you enter the number of the field whose data variable you want inserted into the text. Fields in the secondary merge file are numbered sequentially beginning with 1. The numbering of the fields ends when WordPerfect reaches the Merge E (^E) code that marks the end of one record in the file and the beginning of the next.

> *Note:* If you are using Version 4.1 of WordPerfect, the Merge Codes options displayed when you press Alt-F9 are the same and are listed in the same order. However, each code is preceded by an option number or letter (1–9, A, B, and C). In this release, to select a particular merge code option, you enter the option number or letter instead of the letter of the merge code you wish to use, as you do in Version 4.2. For example, in Version 4.1 you type 3 instead of F to insert a field in the text.

Figure 9.2 shows a sample primary merge file that will generate a form letter for each record in the client secondary merge file. Below the date are the merge codes to insert fields 1 through 4. Together, these fields make up the inside address.

To add the merge code for inserting field 1 on the third line of the letter, you place the cursor at the beginning of the line, press Alt-F9, type **F**, type **1**, and press Return. WordPerfect automatically adds the carets before the F and after the 1 so that the code is entered in the letter as ^F1 ^. The first field in the client secondary merge file contains the name of the company. When WordPerfect generates the letters for each customer during the merge operation, it will replace the ^F1 ^ code with the actual company name.

In a similar manner, the merge codes for fields 2, 3, and 4 are added to the letter. Notice, however, that the merge code for field 3 contains a question mark

```
July 14, 1987

^F1^
^F2^
^F3?^
^F4^

Dear ^F7^ ^F6^:

Please take a moment out of your busy schedule to look over the
enclosed price list, which contains many exciting specials that I
can offer your firm for a limited time only.  As you will see,
most of our paper products are offered at prices well below
retail (in fact, some are just pennies above wholesale cost!).

In addition, if you order now, I will make ^F1^ one of my valued
corporate accounts.  This unique status will entitle your company
to a revolving charge account with American Paper Products
(please complete the credit application and return it with your
first order) as well as liberal volume discounts on top of the
already incredible prices offered to you.

Thank you for your time.  I look forward to serving you at ^F1^
and hope to take care of all your paper product needs.
A:\FORMLTR.PF                              Doc 1   Pg 1   Ln 1      Pos 10
```

FIGURE 9.2: Sample form letter to be used with the client secondary merge file to generate personalized letters to each customer in the file. Each of the ^F*n* merge codes (where *n* is the number of the field) will be replaced during the merge operation with the data entered into that field in the secondary merge file. Notice that the ^F1^ merge code is used several times (in the heading and in the first line of the second and third paragraphs). The name of the company to which the letter is addressed will appear in each of these positions.

immediately before the final caret (^F3? ^). This question mark prevents Word-Perfect from adding a blank line in a letter when the third field in the record is blank (this is a Version 4.2 feature that will not work with earlier releases of WordPerfect). It is added to field 3 because not all of the records use a second line in the street address. Similarly, in your merge applications, you should add a question mark to the ^F merge codes of all field numbers in a primary merge file whenever any secondary merge file entries are empty (marked only by a Merge R code). (For more information, see the next section, "Performing the Merge Operation.")

In the salutation of this letter, two new fields are inserted: ^F7^, which will be replaced with a personal title such as Mr., Ms., or Mrs. from field 7 (PERSONAL TITLE); and ^F6^, which will be replaced with the contact person's last name from field 6 (CONTACT'S LAST NAME). The result will be the more polite salutation that addresses a person by title and last name, for example, "Dear Mr. Smith."

The only other use of data variables is in the body of the letter, where the two insertions of field 1 (^F1 ^) enter the company name in the first lines of the second and third paragraphs. As you can see in this example, you can reuse a single data variable from the secondary merge file as often as you need to.

You must be very careful when you insert merge codes that you enter the correct field number in each case. As you create the primary merge file, you may find it helpful to refer to a printout of your secondary merge file that has all of the fields of a sample record numbered. You should also double check your work by printing a copy of the primary merge file (Shift-F7 1), substituting real data from each of the fields used in the copy.

You save a primary merge file just as you do any other WordPerfect document. When naming the file, you may want to give the file name the extension .PF to mark it as a primary merge file. Just as adding the .SF extension to a secondary merge file makes its function clear, so too adding the .PF extension will alert you to the fact that the file contains data variables and should be used only with WordPerfect's Merge feature.

Performing the Merge Operation

After you have prepared both the primary and secondary merge files, you can perform the merge operation at any time. However, before you actually give the Merge command, your editing window should be blank. If the text of your primary or secondary merge file (or any other document) is displayed on your screen, you should either switch to the other document window (Shift-F3) or use the Exit command (F7 Return Return Y N) to clear the screen.

The reason that you need a blank screen is that WordPerfect, unlike most other word processors, does not output the results of a merge operation directly to the printer. Instead, it creates a new file in the current document window that contains a copy of the primary merge file for each record in the secondary file. After this file has been created, you can save it and print it just as you do any other WordPerfect document.

To perform a merge operation, you press Ctrl-F9 (Merge/Sort). When you do, you are presented with three options:

1 Merge; 2 Sort; 3 Sorting Sequences: 0

Type **1** to initiate the merge, and you are prompted to enter the name of the primary merge file to use:

Primary File:

Enter the file name of your primary merge file (be sure to add the .PF extension if you used it) and press Return. You are then prompted to enter the name of the secondary merge file:

Secondary File:

As soon as you enter the name of the file containing the secondary merge data you wish to use, WordPerfect begins the merge operation.

While data from the two files are being processed and the new file is being generated, you will see the message * Merging * displayed in the lower-left corner of the screen. As soon as the merge operation is completed, the cursor will move to the very end of the file. You can press PgUp to review the contents of the new file page by page from the end to the beginning of the file, or you can press Home twice and ↑ to go directly to the beginning of the file and then press PgDn to review the file from beginning to end. During the merge operation, WordPerfect automatically places hard page breaks between each copy of the primary merge file (each letter, form, report, envelope, mailing label, and so on).

Figure 9.3 shows the top of the first letter generated by merging the form letter in Figure 9.2 with the records in the client data file shown in Figure 9.1. Because the first record, containing the field numbers and names, was preceded by a ^N (Next Record) merge code, it was ignored, and the first letter generated was for the second record, that of ABC Contracting.

```
July 14, 1987

ABC Contracting
1345 Seventh Street
Berkeley, CA  94707

Dear Mr. Wagoner:

Please take a moment out of your busy schedule to look over the
enclosed price list, which contains many exciting specials that I
can offer your firm for a limited time only.  As you will see,
most of our paper products are offered at prices well below
retail (in fact, some are just pennies above wholesale cost!).

In addition, if you order now, I will make ABC Contracting one of
my valued corporate accounts.  This unique status will entitle
your company to a revolving charge account with American Paper
Products (please complete the credit application and return it
with your first order) as well as liberal volume discounts on top
of the already incredible prices offered to you.

Thank you for your time.  I look forward to serving you at ABC
Contracting and hope to take care of all your paper product
needs.
                                     Doc 1   Pg 1   Ln 1        Pos 10
```

FIGURE 9.3: The top of the first form letter created with WordPerfect's Merge feature. This letter to ABC Contracting required only three lines for the inside address (there was no entry for field 2, STREET ADDRESS 2). Because the merge field code contained a question mark (^F3? ^; see Figure 9.2), WordPerfect suppressed the blank line that otherwise appears when a field inserted into a primary merge file is empty for a particular record. Notice how the occurrences of the company name (^F1 ^) in the body of letter blend in—WordPerfect automatically realigns the paragraphs to accommodate the substitution.

Notice in Figure 9.3 where data were inserted in the primary merge file to create the final letter. Also notice that the use of the question mark in field 3 (^F3? ^ in Figure 9.2) prevented a blank line from being inserted between the line containing the street address and the line containing the city, state, and zip code below it. Contrast this with Figure 9.4, which shows the top of the second letter, to Speedo Printing; this letter used all four lines for the inside address.

You can abort a merge operation at any time before it is finished by pressing F1 (Cancel). This causes WordPerfect to stop merging and to write any letters or forms that have been completed to the screen. To reexecute the merge operation, you press F7 (Exit) and answer no to the prompt about saving the new document. Then you can make whatever changes you want to either the primary or secondary merge file and reissue the Merge command (Ctrl-F9 1).

After you have checked the results of the merge operation, you can print the file right away (Shift-F7 1) or save it under a new file name and print it later.

```
July 14, 1987

Speedo Printing
221 Avenue of the Americas
Suite 456
San Francisco, CA  94111

Dear Mr. Grill:

Please take a moment out of your busy schedule to look over the
enclosed price list, which contains many exciting specials that I
can offer your firm for a limited time only.  As you will see,
most of our paper products are offered at prices well below
retail (in fact, some are just pennies above wholesale cost!).

In addition, if you order now, I will make Speedo Printing one of
my valued corporate accounts.  This unique status will entitle
your company to a revolving charge account with American Paper
Products (please complete the credit application and return it
with your first order) as well as liberal volume discounts on top
of the already incredible prices offered to you.

Thank you for your time.  I look forward to serving you at Speedo
Printing and hope to take care of all your paper product needs.
                                        Doc 1  Pg 2  Ln 1        Pos 10
```

FIGURE 9.4: The top of the second form letter created with WordPerfect's Merge feature. Notice that in contrast to the letter to ABC Contracting (shown in Figure 9.3), the letter to Speedo Printing required four lines for its inside address because of the suite number in the third field. Whenever you perform a merge operation in which some of documents require data from a particular field and others do not, you need to enter ? after the field number in the primary merge file.

Merging Directly to the Printer

When you perform a merge operation, the entire contents of the file in the current document window generated by this operation is held in the computer's memory (if you lose power before you save the new document, it will be lost). If the number of records in your secondary merge file is quite large, your computer can possibly run out of memory before WordPerfect generates all of the merged copies. If this happens, WordPerfect terminates the merge operation as soon as the computer's available memory is used up, much like when you press F1 to abort a merge operation.

To avoid having only a part of your secondary merge file processed, you can add special merge option codes at the end of the primary merge file. You can add these codes on the last line containing text by inserting a space between them and the last text on the line, or you can add them on their own line at the end of the file.

You first add the merge code, ^T (Type), which instructs WordPerfect to send all merged text up to this code to the printer and then to clear this text from the computer's memory. You then must add the merge codes ^N and ^P^P to instruct WordPerfect to move to the next record and generate and print the document for this and subsequent records until all of the records in the secondary merge file are processed. The ^N (Next Record) merge code tells WordPerfect to process the next record in the file. The pair of ^P (Primary File) merge codes tells WordPerfect which primary merge file to use next. When you do not enter any file name between the pair of ^P codes, WordPerfect uses the same primary merge file again.

The ^N^P^P merge code combination is required with the ^T code to prevent WordPerfect from entering an extra page break. When the ^T merge code is used alone, the printer automatically advances to the beginning of the next page when it finishes printing each merged document. This page break sends a form feed to the printer, which results in a blank page between each merged document. When you enter the entire sequence

^T^N^P^P

at the end of your primary merge file, extra blank pages are suppressed as WordPerfect prints each of your merged documents. Printing automatically stops when the program processes the last record or when it reaches a ^Q (Quit) code in the secondary merge file.

When you use this method to print your merged documents directly to the printer, you can stop the printing at any time by accessing the Print Control screen (Shift-F7 4) and typing **S** (Stop). When you are ready to begin merge printing again, reset the printhead at the top of the form and type **G** (Go) from this screen. The program will begin printing the current document from the top of the page. If you wish to cancel the merge printing, type **C** (Cancel) and press

Return if the print job document is listed on the screen as (Merge). You may have to press Return a second time to make the printer stop.

If you did not abort the merge operation before you stopped the merge printing, WordPerfect restarts the merge operation as soon as you return to the editing screen. In this event, press F1 to cancel the merge operation and return to the Print Control screen again. Once there, select the Cancel option a second time. When you return to the editing screen, the merge operation will not recommence.

Merging from the Keyboard

When you want to generate only a few letters, forms, or reports and you do not need to save the variable data, you can enter data directly from the keyboard during a merge operation. You do this by entering a special merge code, ^C (Console), wherever you want WordPerfect to pause the merge operation to allow you to manually enter text. After you have entered the text, press F9 (Merge R), and WordPerfect will continue the merge operation.

The ^C merge code can be used in either the primary or secondary merge file. You use it in the *primary* merge file when you need to fill in the text for a particular field for all of the documents generated by the merge operation. This amounts to having to manually enter the data for that field in the merge document generated for every record in the secondary merge file.

To use the Console feature, you simply enter the ^C merge code in the text of the primary merge file where you would normally enter an insert-field merge code. For example, assume that you replace the ^F7^ and ^F6^ insert-field merge codes with a ^C merge code in the primary merge file, as shown in Figure 9.5. When you execute the merge operation (using the client secondary merge file), WordPerfect will generate the complete text of the first letter to ABC Contracting on your screen. With the cursor positioned immediately after the word *Dear* in the salutation (the ^C merge code will disappear), the merge operation will pause until you press F9. At that point, you can enter the title and name of the person to whom you wish to address the letter. As soon as you press F9 (Merge R) to continue the merge operation, the rest of the substitutions for ^F1^ in the body of the letter will be made, and the next letter will be generated on your screen. Again the merge operation will pause when it encounters the ^C merge code, positioning the cursor after the word *Dear* in the salutation and waiting until you press F9. The merge operation will continue in this manner until all of the records in the secondary merge file are processed.

You use the ^C merge code in the *secondary* merge file when you want WordPerfect to pause the merge operation to allow you to enter text for a field or fields of only specific records. Rather than pausing as it generates the merge document for each record, as it does when you use ^C in a primary file, WordPerfect stops only when it processes a record in which some of the fields contain a ^C merge code.

```
July 14, 1987

^F1^
^F2^
^F3?^
^F4^

Dear ^C:

Please take a moment out of your busy schedule to look over the
enclosed price list, which contains many exciting specials that I
can offer your firm for a limited time only.  As you will see,
most of our paper products are offered at prices well below
retail (in fact, some are just pennies above wholesale cost!).

In addition, if you order now, I will make ^F1^ one of my valued
corporate accounts.  This unique status will entitle your company
to a revolving charge account with American Paper Products
(please complete the credit application and return it with your
first order) as well as liberal volume discounts on top of the
already incredible prices offered to you.

Thank you for your time.  I look forward to serving you at ^F1^
and hope to take care of all your paper product needs.
A:\FORMLTR.PF                                Doc 1   Pg 1   Ln 1        Pos 10
```

FIGURE 9.5: Using the ^C merge code in a primary merge file. Here, a ^C merge code has been substituted for the ^F7^ and ^F6^ insert-field merge codes in the primary merge file. Instead of taking the data for the salutation for each merge letter from the records of the secondary merge file, WordPerfect will halt merge processing while the operator enters this information manually. During this pause, the cursor will be located in the column where the ^ (control character) of the ^C merge code appears in the figure. When the salutation is typed and the operator presses F9, the merge operation will continue, pausing again at the same position in each new letter.

For instance, assume that you edit the secondary merge file containing the client records and replace the entries for fields 5 (CONTACT'S FIRST NAME), 6 (CONTACT'S LAST NAME), and 7 (PERSONAL TITLE) with ^C merge codes just as in the Speedo Printing record (see Figure 9.6). When you perform the merge operation with the form letter primary file that uses fields 7 (^F7^) and 6 (^F6^) in the salutation, WordPerfect will still generate the first letter, using ABC Contracting's record, automatically.

However, when WordPerfect processes the record for Speedo Printing, it will display the text on your screen, position the cursor after the word *Dear,* and pause the merge operation. It will wait for you to enter the person's title from the keyboard (the ^F7^ insert-field code will no longer appear on the screen, although the ^F6^ code will still be visible). As soon as you enter the title and press F9 (Merge R), the ^F6^ code will disappear, the cursor will move right one space, and the merge operation will pause again. Here, you enter the last name of the person you are addressing in the salutation. When you press F9 to continue the merge operation, WordPerfect will make the field 1 (^F1^) substitutions for

```
^N
1 - COMPANY NAME^R
2 - STREET ADDRESS 1^R
3 - STREET ADDRESS 2^R
4 - CITY, STATE  ZIP^R
5 - CONTACT'S FIRST NAME^R
6 - CONTACT'S LAST NAME^R
7 - PERSONAL TITLE^R
^E
ABC Contracting^R
1345 Seventh Street^R
^R
Berkeley, CA  94707^R
Jim^R
Wagoner^R
Mr.^R
^E
Speedo Printing^R
221 Avenue of the Americas^R
Suite 456^R
San Francisco, CA  94111^R
^C^R
^C^R
^C^R
A:\CLIENT.SF                                 Doc 1  Pg 1  Ln 1       Pos 10
```

FIGURE 9.6: Using the ^C merge code in a secondary merge file. Here, the code replaces the entries for the first name, last name, and personal title of the contact person only in the record for Speedo Printing (at the bottom of the figure). During the merge operation, WordPerfect will pause to allow the operator to enter these items only when it generates the Speedo Printing merge letter. The first letter, to ABC Printing, does not contain any ^C merge codes and so will be generated without any operator input from the keyboard.

this letter and then automatically generate the rest of the letters for the remaining records.

Displaying Messages on the Screen

You can also use another merge code, ^O (for On-screen), with the ^C merge code to have WordPerfect display a particular message or prompt whenever it pauses the merge operation. For example, when you use the ^C merge code to enter the salutation of your form letters from the keyboard (as shown in Figure 9.5), you can have WordPerfect display a message indicating that the merge operation has paused and prompting you (or a fellow worker) to enter the name of the addressee. You enter your message prompt enclosed in a pair of ^O merge codes followed by the ^C merge code in the primary merge file. You enter these codes immediately after the *Dear* in the salutation, as follows:

Dear ^OMerge Paused! Enter name and press F9 ^O ^C:

When you perform the merge operation, the message "Merge Paused! Enter name and press F9" will be displayed on the last line of the screen in double intensity. The cursor will also be positioned immediately after the word *Dear* in the salutation to allow you to enter the person's title and name.

When you create your on-screen messages and prompts using ^O codes followed by the ^C merge code, you can use up to 48 characters. Any characters beyond 48 will not appear because they run into the document, page, and line position prompt that always appears on the screen on this same line.

The ^O^O merge codes can be combined with other WordPerfect merge options. You can use them to display a message that prompts you to enter the name of the primary and secondary files to be used in an upcoming merge operation, or you can use them to display a message that prompts you to enter the name of a macro to be executed at the end of the merge operation. For more information about possible applications, see the sections "Filling Out Forms," "Macros in Merge Operations," and "Creating Menus" that follow.

Creating Envelopes and Mailing Labels

Once you have created the secondary merge file that contains all of the records you need to use in a merge operation, you can use this file not only to generate the form letters but also to create the mailing labels or to address the envelopes needed to send these letters. To do so requires only that you create an additional primary merge file containing all of the insert-field merge codes you need in the correct order.

For example, to generate mailing labels or envelopes for the advertising letters generated from the client secondary file, you begin by entering the following insert-field merge codes in a new document:

> ^F1^
> ^F2^
> ^F3?^
> ^F4^
> Attn: ^F7^ ^F5^ ^F6^

Each of these insert-field merge codes, with the exception of ^F7^ ^F5^ ^F6^ on the last line, must be entered on a separate line terminated with a hard return (Return). To enter the field number, you press Alt-F9, type **F** and the number of the field you wish to use, and press Return.

Once you have created this new primary file containing only the fields to be inserted, you save it and then execute the merge operation (Ctrl-F9 1) using this new file as the primary file and the file containing the client records as the secondary file. Figure 9.7 shows the result of this merge operation.

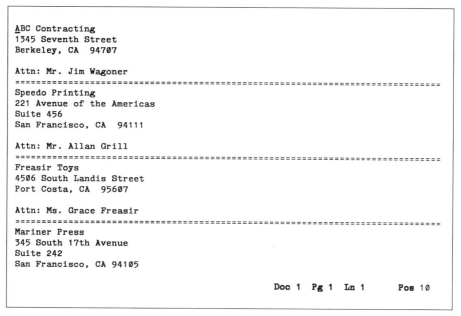

```
ABC Contracting
1345 Seventh Street
Berkeley, CA  94707

Attn: Mr. Jim Wagoner
================================================================================
Speedo Printing
221 Avenue of the Americas
Suite 456
San Francisco, CA  94111

Attn: Mr. Allan Grill
================================================================================
Freasir Toys
4506 South Landis Street
Port Costa, CA  95607

Attn: Ms. Grace Freasir
================================================================================
Mariner Press
345 South 17th Avenue
Suite 242
San Francisco, CA 94105


                                        Doc 1  Pg 1  Ln 1      Pos 10
```

FIGURE 9.7: Executing a merge operation to print mailing labels or envelopes for the form letters. This figure shows the first four mailing labels (the same file can be used to address envelopes) that were generated by using a new primary merge file. This file simply contains the proper insert-field merge codes (plus the text *Attn:* in the last line) arranged to fit the mailing address format. Notice here again that some of the addresses contain three lines, and others contain four. Nevertheless, because the ? was entered in the insert-field merge code (^F3? ^) for the sometimes-blank field, WordPerfect accommodates either format.

Once the merge operation is completed, you must establish the correct format settings for the size of mailing labels or envelopes you are using before you send this new document to the printer. If you want to print continuous-feed mailing labels, you will have to adjust the page length and top, left, and right margin settings.

DETERMINING FORMAT SETTINGS FOR MAILING LABELS

To determine the correct settings for printing mailing labels,

1. Measure the length from the top of one mailing label to the next and the width of your mailing label (note that you must take into account the space between labels or errors in advancing lines will accrue). To determine the overall character width, multiply the width of the label in inches by the pitch you are using. For example, if you are using the default of 10 pitch, you multiply the width by 10. If you are using 12 pitch, you multiply the width by 12.

2. Decide how far you want the address indented from the left edge of the label. To determine the left margin setting, multiply this figure in inches by the pitch you are using. For example, if you want the address indented half an inch and you are using 10-pitch type, you multiply the pitch by .5.

3. Subtract the left margin setting from the overall width in characters to determine the setting for the right margin.

4. Multiply the length by 6 (for 6 lines per inch) to determine the form length.

5. Determine the number of lines you need for a top margin and subtract this number from the form length to determine the number of text lines.

Before setting the page format for labels, make sure the cursor is at the top of the file (Home Home ↑) so the codes will take effect.

For example, if your mailing labels are 1½ inches (from top to top) × 4 inches, you want to print using 10-pitch type, and you want the addresses indented half an inch from the left edge of the label, you use the following settings:

Margins **(Shift-F8 3)**

   Left margin: **5**

   Right margin: **35**

Page length **(Alt-F8 4 3)**

   Form length: **9**

   Number of text lines: **7**

Top margin **(Alt-F8 5)**

   Number of half-lines: **4** (equivalent to 2 lines)

Because the label is 4 inches wide, the overall width in characters is 40 (4 × 10). To establish a left margin indent of half an inch, you set the left margin at 5 (.5 × 10). To determine the right margin setting, you subtract the overall width in characters from the left margin setting (40 − 5). To enter these new margin settings, you press Shift-F8, type **3** (Margins), and enter **5** for the left margin and **35** for the right margin.

Because the length from label to label is 1½ inches, the form length is 9 lines (1.5 × 6). To center the text vertically on the label, you can have no more than 2 lines for the top margin. To determine the number of text lines per page, you subtract the form length from the top margin (9 − 2). To set the new page length, you press Alt-F8, type **4** (Page Length), and type **3** (Other). Then enter **9** as the new form length and **7** as the number of text lines per page. When you return to the Page Format menu, type **5** (Top Margin) and enter **4** as the number of half lines. Because the top margin is set in half lines, you must enter a number that is twice the number of lines you want as the top margin.

After you have set the margins and page length to suit the dimensions of the labels you are using, you are ready to send your merged document to the printer. To do this, align the printhead so that it is at the very top of the first label, press Shift-F7 (Print), and type **1** (Full Text). If you think that you may want to rerun these labels before you update the secondary merge file and perform a new merge operation, you should save the document before exiting WordPerfect.

> *Note:* If your secondary file contains so many records that WordPerfect cannot complete the merge operation due to insufficient computer memory, you will have to send the labels to the printer with the ^T^N^P^P merge codes added to the end of the file. See the section "Merging Directly to the Printer" earlier in this chapter for details about how to use these codes.

If you use multiple-column labels (two, three, or more columns of labels on a page), you will have to set up text columns using WordPerfect's Parallel Column feature. In this case, the number of labels across the page determines the number of columns to specify, and the left margin setting determines the amount of space between your columns. You will also have to determine the correct column width, which must be long enough to accommodate your longest address entry. See Chapter 8 for more information about setting and using parallel columns.

DETERMINING FORMAT SETTINGS FOR ENVELOPES

If you want to address legal-size envelopes, you will have to hand feed each one into your printer. First set the left margin to 40 and the right margin to 80 by pressing Alt-F8 4, selecting option 3, and entering these two settings. Then set the top margin to 0 by pressing Alt-F8, selecting option 5, and entering this setting. Finally, position the cursor on the first page of the document (press Home twice and the ↑ key if the cursor is not on the first page).

To print your envelopes, place the first one in the printer and move it up so that the printhead is at the exact place where you want the first line of the address to print. Then press Shift-F7 and select option 2 (Page). After the first address has been printed, press PgDn to move the cursor to the second address, position your next envelope as before, and press Shift-F7 and select option 2. Repeat this procedure until all of your envelopes are addressed.

> *Note:* Some printers will give a paper-out signal when you try to print envelopes (because they are so short). If this is the case, you will have to consult your printer documentation to find out how to disable the paper-out sensor before attempting this procedure.

Filling Out Forms

In addition to creating form letters, printing mailing labels, and addressing envelopes, you can use WordPerfect's merge capabilities to fill out forms. The information that is entered into particular blanks on the form can come from either a secondary merge file or the keyboard or from a combination of these sources.

When using the Merge feature to complete a form that you have designed in WordPerfect, you should set up the form, including all headings and tabs stops, before you insert the required merge codes. If you will be using a secondary merge file to complete part or all of the blanks in the form, you should use the insert-field merge code (Alt-F9 F) and enter the appropriate field number where you want the text to begin. The same is true if you will be entering ^C merge codes to allow you to fill in some or all of the blanks from the keyboard.

Figure 9.8 shows a simple form designed and executed in WordPerfect. This form uses data from various fields of a secondary merge file to fill out all but the last blank. When WordPerfect comes to this blank during the merge operation, it displays the on-screen prompt "Enter 'Yes' or 'No' and then Press F9" and pauses to allow you to enter a yes or no response.

```
 _      Business Data

       Legal Name:  ^F1^

       Address:      ^F2^

       City: ^F3^              State: ^F4^    Zip: ^F5^

       Federal Tax I.D. #:      ^F6^

       Social Security Number:  ^F7^

       Is business a corporation?  ^OEnter "Yes" or "No" and then
Press F9^O^C




A:\FORM1099.PF                              Doc 1  Pg 1  Ln 1      Pos 10
```

FIGURE 9.8: A simple form that is filled out using both data from a secondary file and information typed from the keyboard. Notice that the last entry (where the operator designates whether or not the business is a corporation) contains a prompt enclosed in a pair of ^O merge codes as well as a ^C merge code to temporarily pause the merge operation. This instruction about how to fill in this blank and continue the merge operation appears on the last line of the screen when the merge operation is paused.

Using Preprinted Forms

If you are using WordPerfect's Merge feature to fill out preprinted forms, your primary file will contain only the appropriate merge codes, much like a primary file for printing mailing labels or addressing envelopes. When you enter the merge codes, either to insert a specific field from a secondary file or to pause the merge operation so you can enter information from the keyboard, their line and column placement in the primary file is critical. If you enter the codes on the wrong line or begin at the wrong column position, the merged data may print over the headings and will not properly fill in the blanks when you print the merged document.

To help identify the correct line and column position for each merge code, you can insert one of the preprinted forms in a typewriter, positioning the printhead at the left edge of the paper on the first line of the form. Then count the number of carriage returns you must enter to reach each line that contains blanks to be filled in. You can then use these line numbers to determine where to place each merge code. You should also count the number of spaces required to move the printhead from the left edge of the paper to the position on each line where the printing for each blank is to begin.

Alternatively, you can use a ruler to measure the form's margins, the location of the lines containing blanks, and the position on each line where merge codes are to be placed.

Regardless of the method you use, be sure that you take into account Word-Perfect's default left and right margins settings of 10 and 74 as well as the pitch and lines-per-inch settings that will be used in printing. Although it may take some experimentation to get all of these settings just right, once you have worked out the proper placement for each code, you will never have to change the settings unless the preprinted form is revised.

When you merge data from a secondary merge file, be sure that the fields do not contain more characters than will fit on the blanks where the fields will be merged. You must also keep in mind the maximum number of characters per blank when you fill in the blanks from the keyboard (remember, you will not see the blanks on your computer screen).

If you wish, you can enter a short message between a pair of ^O merge codes for each blank to indicate the type of entry that is required from the keyboard. Place the pair of ^O merge codes and your messages immediately before the ^C merge code that pauses the merge operation.

If you are going to add message prompts, do not add them until after you have made sure that all of the ^C merge codes for each blank in your preprinted form are correctly positioned. Then make sure that WordPerfect is still in Insert mode, position the cursor beneath the caret of each ^C, and enter the first ^O (Alt-F9 O or Ctrl-O) followed by the text of your message and the final ^O code. Do the same thing for each blank for which you wish to add a message. Adding message prompts will displace the ^C merge codes on your screen. However, when you execute the merge operation, the messages between the ⌃O codes will appear at the bottom of the screen, and the ⌃C code will appear in its correct position.

Creating Reports

You may occasionally want to obtain a report listing all of the records in a secondary merge file. To do this, you first need to create a primary merge file that lists the fields in the order in which you want them to appear in printed form. Often, you will want to have all of the information in each record arranged on a single line of the report. In addition, you will probably want to include column headings that identify each item. After you have created this primary file, you simply execute the merge operation using this primary file along with the appropriate secondary file.

For example, to obtain a report listing for all of the clients in your secondary file, you can set up the following primary file:

Company	Address	Contact
⌃F1⌃	⌃F2 ⌃F3 ⌃ ⌃F4 ⌃	⌃F7 ⌃ ⌃F5 ⌃ ⌃F6 ⌃
⌃N⌃P⌃P		

Be sure that your right margin setting is sufficient to accommodate the entire record on a single line. You must insert ⌃N ⌃P ⌃P codes at the end of the file to suppress page breaks between the records. If you do not do this, the merge document prints each record on a separate page.

PERFORMING MORE COMPLEX MERGE OPERATIONS

WordPerfect includes other merge codes that make it possible to accomplish much more complex operations than we have looked at thus far. In the following sections, you will find information about how to perform merges that assemble the merge document from several different primary files, how to create a secondary file through a merge operation, how to place macros in merge files for execution when the merge operation terminates, and how to create menu-driven merge operations.

Assembling Documents

You can use WordPerfect's Merge feature to automatically assemble documents whose parts are stored in separate files of their own. This application is often useful when you construct form letters or legal documents composed of standard paragraphs that require only slight modification during the merge operation.

To have WordPerfect assemble a final document from several different primary files during a merge operation, enclose the name of the primary file to be used in a pair of ^P merge codes. The ^P merge code, like the ^O merge code, is always paired.

Figure 9.9 shows a primary merge file named ASSEMBLE.PF that constructs a merged document from three different primary files. The first file, HEADING.PF, contains a merge code (^D) that inserts the system date into the letter as well as several insert-field merge codes that create the inside address and salutation from data in the client secondary merge file (used in the previous merge examples). Its contents are shown in Figure 9.10.

The second file, LTRBODY.PF, contains most of the standard text for the letter as well as a ^C merge code that allows you to specify how long the special prices are in effect and an insert-field merge code (^F1^) that supplies the name of the company to whom the letter is addressed. The contents of this file are shown in Figure 9.11. The third file, CONCLUS.PF, contains an on-screen message that prompts you to enter the name of the salesperson sending the letter. Its contents are shown in Figure 9.12.

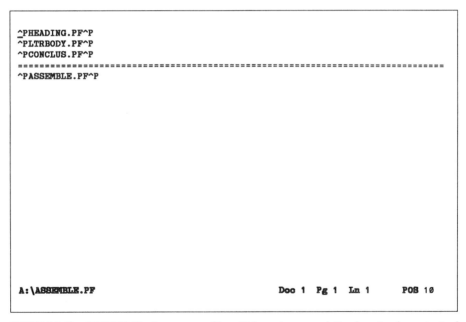

```
^PHEADING.PF^P
^PLTRBODY.PF^P
^PCONCLUS.PF^P
================================================================================
^PASSEMBLE.PF^P




A:\ASSEMBLE.PF                              Doc 1  Pg 1  Ln 1      POS 10
```

FIGURE 9.9: The ASSEMBLE.PF primary merge file, which creates merge letters by using the contents of three external primary merge files: HEADING.PF, LTRBODY.PF, and CONCLUS.PF. The ^P merge codes that surround each of these file names instruct WordPerfect to use their contents in the merge operation. In addition, as WordPerfect processes the contents of these files, it will follow whatever merge codes they contain. The hard page break (shown by the line of equal signs) and the ^PASSEMBLE.PF ^P merge codes chain the merge operation, causing it to begin document assembly again until the operator terminates the merge operation (F1).

```
_^D

^F1^
^F2^
^F3?^
^F4^

Dear ^F7^ ^F6^:
```
```
A:\HEADING.PF                          Doc 1  Pg 1  Ln 1      POS 10
```

FIGURE 9.10: The contents of the HEADING.PF primary merge file used in the document assembly. This file creates a standard inside address and salutation using data from each record in the secondary file.

Notice in Figure 9.9 that ASSEMBLE.PF is itself listed between a pair of ^P merge codes at the bottom of the file after a hard page break (designated by the line of equal signs). The addition of this page break and these ^P codes causes the merge operation to loop continuously, allowing you to construct merged letters from the component files, until WordPerfect reaches the end of the secondary merge file, or until you press Shift-F9 (Merge E) to terminate the operation.

SELECTING THE PRIMARY FILES TO BE USED

The document assembly procedure performed in the preceding example does not vary. During the merge operation, WordPerfect always uses the same primary files. The only differences among the letters produced by the merge operation result from the various data variables taken from the client secondary file records and the individual responses entered from the keyboard.

However, you can easily make this type of merge operation more flexible by combining the ^O, ^P, and ^C merge codes in a slightly different way to have WordPerfect prompt you during the merge operation for the names of different primary files to use. This feature will make document assembly a dynamic process, allowing you to select from among a variety of prepared primary files to suit the document you are constructing.

```
Please take a moment out of your busy schedule to look over the
enclosed price list, which contains many exciting specials that I
can offer your firm only until ^C.  As you will see, most of our
paper products are offered at prices well below retail (in fact,
some are just pennies above wholesale cost!).

In addition, if you order now, I will make ^F1^ one of my valued
corporate accounts.  This unique status will entitle your company
to a revolving charge account with American Paper Products
(please complete the credit application and return it with your
first order) as well as liberal volume discounts on top of the
already incredible prices offered to you.




A:\LTRBODY.PF                              Doc 1  Pg 1  Ln 1      Pos 10
```

FIGURE 9.11: The contents of the LTRBODY.PF primary merge file used in the document assembly. It contains a ^C merge code to allow the operator to slightly alter the text of each letter to tailor it to the company to which it is sent. The ^F1^ code takes the company name from the same record in the secondary file that is used to generate the inside address. The contents of the heading will appear on the screen when the operator enters the date on which the special offer expires.

You could use this technique in the preceding example to select the text for each letter as it is being assembled during the merge operation. Instead of always using the text in the file LTRBODY.PF, as you must now, you could then designate the primary file to be used for the body of the letter.

Figure 9.13 shows how this is done. Notice that in place of the merge codes ^PLTRBODY.PF^P in the third line, the ASSEMBLE.PF primary file now contains

^U^O Enter the complete name of the letter file to use: ^P^C^P^O

The ^U (for Update screen) writes the contents of the merge letter on the screen. This allows you to see to whom the letter is addressed and, thus, decide which primary file to use—that is, which type of letter to send.

After the ^U merge code, an on-screen message prompt is introduced with a ^O code. When the merge operation is executed, the prompt

Enter the complete name of the letter file to use:

without the ^O codes, will appear at the bottom of the screen.

However, notice that the pair of ^O merge codes enclose not only this prompt but also a pair of ^P merge codes, which themselves enclose a ^C merge code.

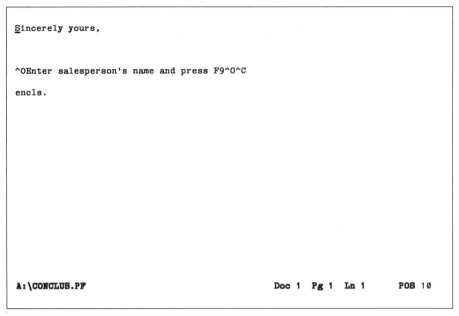

```
Sincerely yours,


^OEnter salesperson's name and press F9^O^C

encls.
```

```
A:\CONCLUS.PF                              Doc 1  Pg 1  Ln 1      POS 10
```

FIGURE 9.12: The contents of the CONCLUS.PF primary merge file used in the document assembly. This primary file contains the merge codes that pause the merge operation and prompt the operator to enter the salesperson's name and then press F9 to continue the merge operation. This prompt will appear on the last line of the screen, and the cursor will be positioned at the beginning of the signature line during the merge operation.

The ^C merge code pauses the merge operation to allow you to respond to the prompt that is still displayed on the screen (this is why the ^P ^C ^P codes precede the final ^O code). The response that you enter is interpreted by WordPerfect as the name of a primary merge file because it is enclosed in a pair of ^P codes.

When you initiate a merge operation using this version of the ASSEMBLE.PF file, WordPerfect generates the heading of the letter from the HEADING.PF file and then displays the inside address and salutation on the screen. It then pauses and prompts you for the name of the primary file to use in generating the body of the letter (shown in Figure 9.14). After you select the appropriate primary merge file (assuming that you have prepared several alternative primary files), enter its name and press F9, WordPerfect uses the CONCLUS.PF file to generate the conclusion of the letter. After you enter the correct signature name from the keyboard and press F9 again, WordPerfect repeats the entire process for a new letter. This process continues until either all of the records in the secondary merge file are used or you press Shift-F9.

Note: You can easily adapt this technique to other applications, from assembling contracts to preparing examinations, making them as complex as you

```
^N
^PHEADING.PF^P
^U^OEnter the complete name of the letter file to use:   ^P^C^P^O
^PCONCLUS.PF^P
==============================================================================
^PASSEMBLE.PF^P
```

A:\ASSEMBLE.PF   Doc 1 Pg 1 Ln 1   POS 10

FIGURE 9.13: Creating a more flexible document assembly procedure. This figure shows essentially the same merge codes as in Figure 9.9 with one significant difference. During this document assembly, the operator will be prompted to enter the name of the primary file to be used for the body of the letter. This allows the user to choose from various "boilerplate" texts that print slightly different versions of the letter. The ^U merge code writes the heading on the screen, and the ^C merge code pauses the merge operation to allow the user to enter the name of the primary file to be used. Word-Perfect accepts the entry as the name of a primary file because the ^C is between a pair of ^P codes.

need. Although this example was purposely kept simple and so employs only one prompt for the primary file to use, you can add as many such prompts as you need to assemble the final document.

SELECTING THE SECONDARY FILES TO BE USED

The preceding examples have all assumed that you need to use only a single secondary merge file during the entire merge operation. This may not always be the case. To change the secondary file, you use a pair of ^S merge codes. These work just like the ^P merge codes, only you enter the name of a secondary merge file between them.

When you use the ^S merge codes to switch to a new secondary file (different from the one you name when you initiate the merge operation with Ctrl-F9 1), you should place them before any insert-field merge codes (^Fn ^ , where n is the field number) in the primary file that will use data from this new secondary file.

In addition to entering the name of the secondary file to be used, you can have

WordPerfect prompt you for the name of the secondary file by adapting the technique introduced in the preceding section. You simply use ^S merge codes instead of ^P codes. For example, you could enter

^U ^O Enter the name of the secondary file to use: ^S ^C ^S ^O

to halt the merge operation and display the message

Enter the name of the secondary file to use:

During this pause you can designate a new secondary merge file, which will be used as soon as you press F9 to continue the merge operation.

Creating a Secondary File through a Merge Operation

You can use WordPerfect's Merge feature to help you build your secondary files. By combining the ^O and ^C merge codes with a new merge code, ^V,

```
February 27, 1987

ABC Contracting
1345 Seventh Street
Berkeley, CA  94707

Dear Mr. Wagoner:


^OEnter the complete name of the letter file to use:  ^P^C^P^O
^PCONCLUS.PF^P
===============================================================================
^PASSEMBLE.PF^P






Enter the complete name of the letter file to use:  ADLTR2.PF_
```

FIGURE 9.14: The flexible document assembly merge operation in progress. Here, the contents of the heading primary file have been written to the screen, and the prompt for the name of the primary file to be used to generate the body of the letter can be seen. In this case, the primary file ADLTR2.PF has been entered by the operator. When the operator presses F9, WordPerfect will insert the text of this primary file into the body of the letter, and the rest of the merge operation will continue. Just as before, the merge operation will be repeated for each record in the secondary file. However, before each new letter created, the operator will be asked to choose the primary file to use to generate the body of the letter.

you can essentially automate the procedure of adding records to any of your secondary merge files. The ^V merge code (for Insert—Ctrl-V toggles Insert mode on and off in many programs) inserts merge codes into the file you are creating.

Figure 9.15 illustrates this technique, here used to add records to the client secondary merge file introduced earlier in this chapter in the section ''Preparing the Secondary Merge File'' (see Figure 9.1). The first pair of ^O merge codes followed by the ^C code simply displays the message

Press F9 after each entry - Press F9 now to continue

Notice the general pattern used after this first message to prompt you to enter data for each field in the record:

$$^\wedge O < message > {}^\wedge O {}^\wedge C {}^\wedge V {}^\wedge R {}^\wedge V$$

You are already familiar with the ^O and ^C merge codes. These merely display the message between the ^O codes at the bottom of the screen and pause the merge operation to allow you to enter the required text.

```
^OPress F9 after each entry - F9 now to continue^O^C^OEnter the
Company Name^O^C^V^R^V
^OEnter the Street Address^O^C^V^R^V
^OEnter the Suite, Mail stop number or press F9^O^C^V^R^V
^OEnter the City, State (as CA) & Zip Code^O^C^V^R^V
^OEnter the First name of the Contact person^O^C^V^R^V
^OEnter the Last name of the Contact person^O^C^V^R^V
^OIndicate the person's Title as Mr., Ms., or Mrs.^O^C^V^R^V
^V^E^V^OShift-F9 if done - F9 to add another record^O^C
^PCLIENT.INP^P




A:\CLIENT.INP                        Doc 1  Pg 1  Ln 1      POS 10
```

FIGURE 9.15: Executing a merge operation using on-screen prompts to build a secondary merge file. This file is named CLIENT.INP. The .INP extension marks it as a special primary file that facilitates client secondary file data entry. The ^V merge codes insert the merge code ^R or ^E into the document as soon as you press F9 to continue the merge operation. Notice that the operator is prompted to enter data for each field in the record. The ^PCLIENT.INP^P in the last line causes the entire merge operation to be repeated until the operator presses Shift-F9, thus allowing multiple records to be entered without using a macro or reexecuting the merge operation.

To these have been added a pair of ^V merge codes surrounding a ^R (Merge R) code. As soon as you enter the text and press F9 to continue the merge, the ^V codes insert the ^R code at the end of your entry. This automates the process of terminating each field entry with a ^R merge code (entered by pressing F9 when you add records to a secondary merge file manually).

To use this primary merge file to create the client secondary file, you simply press Ctrl-F9 and type **1** to start the merge operation. When prompted for the name of the primary file to use, you enter **CLIENT.INP** (the file name given to this example file; the .INP extension marks this as an input file). When you are prompted for the name of the secondary file to use, you press Return to bypass this prompt.

As soon as the CLIENT.INP file is loaded, you will see the general message prompt indicating that you are to press F9 after making each field entry (see Figure 9.16). When you press F9, WordPerfect clears the ^OEnter the Company Name ^O ^C codes from the first line of the file and displays the message

Enter the Company Name

without the ^O codes on the last line of the screen. Only the ^V ^R ^V codes remain in the first line of the file. As soon as you enter the name of the company

```
^OEnter the Company Name^O^C^V^R^V
^OEnter the Street Address^O^C^V^R^V
^OEnter the Suite, Mail stop number or press F9^O^C^V^R^V
^OEnter the City, State (as CA) & Zip Code^O^C^V^R^V
^OEnter the First name of the Contact person^O^C^V^R^V
^OEnter the Last name of the Contact person^O^C^V^R^V
^OIndicate the person's Title as Mr., Ms., or Mrs.^O^C^V^R^V
^V^E^V^OShift-F9 if done - F9 to add another record^O^C
^PCLIENT.INP^P
```

Press F9 after each entry – F9 now to continue   Doc 1   Pg 1   Ln 1   POS 10

FIGURE 9.16: Commencing the merge operation to add records to a secondary file. When you start this merge operation, the initial prompt giving the operator general instructions about how to proceed is immediately displayed on the last line of the screen. As soon as the operator presses F9, this prompt is replaced by the prompt to enter the company name.

and press F9, WordPerfect inserts the ^R (Merge R) code immediately after your entry and displays the prompt for the street address, pausing to allow you to make this entry on the second line of the file.

This process of prompting, pausing, and inserting the ^R merge code continues until WordPerfect reaches the line containing

^V ^E ^V ^OShift-F9 if done - F9 to add another record ^O ^C

The ^V codes insert the ^E (Merge End) code that marks the end of the record in the secondary file. The on-screen prompt

Shift-F9 if done - F9 to add another record

(shown in Figure 9.17) appears. If you press F9, the ^PCLIENT.INP ^P merge codes on the line below start the merge process all over again. If you press Shift-F9, the merge operation terminates.

After you terminate the merge operation, all that is required is for you to erase the ^PCLIENT.INP ^P in the last line and append the records you have created to an existing secondary file (CLIENT.SF in this case). To do this, you first

```
Signet Products, Inc.^R
4562 14th Avenue^R
^R
San Francisco, CA  94103^R
Marjorie^R
McPherson^R
Ms.^R
^E_`
^PCLIENT.INP^P




















Shift-F9 if done - F9 to add another record     Doc 1  Pg 1  Ln 8      Pos 12
```

FIGURE 9.17: Finishing the first record in the merge operation that adds records to a secondary file. In this figure, the operator has responded to all of the prompts for specific field data. In addition, the ^V ^E ^V merge codes have entered the ^E (Merge E) code into the file. Currently, the message indicating how to exit or to add another record is displayed at the bottom of the screen. If the operator presses F9, the ^PCLIENT.INP ^P codes cause the merge operation to be repeated. If the user presses Shift-F9, the merge operation terminates, and the ^PCLIENT.INP ^P codes are ignored. The operator must be sure to erase these codes before appending the record to the secondary file.

mark the new records as a block by positioning the cursor at the beginning of the file (Home Home ↑) and then pressing Alt-F4 and Home Home ↓. Then press Ctrl-F4 (Move), select option 3 (Append), and enter **CLIENT.SF**, the name of secondary merge file. These steps can be accomplished by using a macro, as discussed in the following section. Note that you should always exit the CLIENT.INP file without saving it, or the input prompts will be destroyed.

Macros in Merge Operations

You can have a macro executed upon the termination of any merge operation. To do this, you enclose the name of the macro within a pair of ^G merge codes (for Go To *macro*). You enter the macro's file name between the pair of ^G merge codes exactly as it appears in the WordPerfect directory listing, less the file extension .MAC. For example, if your macro is named ALTL.MAC (executed manually by pressing Alt-L), you enter it in the merge file as ^GALTL^G. If your macro is named SORT.MAC (executed manually by pressing Alt-F10, typing **SORT**, and pressing Return), you enter it as ^GSORT^G.

It is important to understand that regardless of where in the primary merge file these ^G codes are placed, the macro they enclose will not be executed until the merge operation terminates. In other words, you cannot have WordPerfect execute the macro at the onset of the merge operation or during the merge operation. Also, you can call for the execution of only a single macro at the completion of a merge operation (although the macro can itself call other macros—see Chapter 14 for more information about how to chain macros).

In some primary merge files, the placement of a macro enclosed in ^G merge codes within the file is crucial. For example, if your primary file assembles documents or repeats by using a pair of ^P merge codes, you place the Go To macro statement before the pair of ^P merge codes. That way, WordPerfect will read the Go To macro statement before it uses the new primary file (or files). Although the macro will not be executed until the merge operation called for in the new primary file is completed, the macro will be not be overlooked because WordPerfect reads (and remembers) the Go To macro statement before it reads and executes the ^P merge codes.

Figure 9.18 shows the primary merge file, introduced in the previous discussion, that facilitates the addition of records to the client secondary merge file, this time with a Go To macro statement. The ^GAPPEND^G added immediately after the ^V^E^V merge codes (in the second-to-last line of the file) executes a macro named APPEND whenever the user terminates the macro by pressing Shift-F9 (Merge E). Notice that the macro name enclosed in a pair of ^G merge codes is placed before the ^PCLIENT.INP^P codes on the last line. This ensures that the macro will be read before the merge operation is repeated. If the ^G merge codes were placed after the pair of ^P codes, the APPEND macro would never be executed.

```
^OPress F9 after each entry - F9 now to continue^O^C^OEnter the
Company Name^O^C^V^R^V
^OEnter the Street Address^O^C^V^R^V
^OEnter the Suite, Mail stop number or press F9^O^C^V^R^V
^OEnter the City, State (as CA) & Zip Code^O^C^V^R^V
^OEnter the First name of the Contact person^O^C^V^R^V
^OEnter the Last name of the Contact person^O^C^V^R^V
^OIndicate the person's Title as Mr., Ms., or Mrs.^O^C^V^R^V
^V^E^V^GAPPEND^G^OShift-F9 if done - F9 to add another record^O^C
^PCLIENT.INP^P
```

A:\CLIENT.INP   Doc 1 Pg 1 Ln 1   POS 10

FIGURE 9.18: Adding a macro to be executed upon termination of a merge operation that adds records to the client secondary merge file. This macro, APPEND, is executed only when the operator presses Shift-F9 to terminate the merge operation. When this happens, the macro deletes the ^PCLIENT.INP ^P merge codes, blocks the records that have been created, and appends these records to the client secondary file. Notice the placement of the ^GAPPEND ^G merge codes. They are placed before the on-screen message codes and the codes that repeat the merge operation to ensure that the macro is not ignored (see the accompanying text for more information).

The keystrokes contained in the APPEND macro are as follows:

Begin macro	Macro name	Keystrokes	End macro
Ctrl-F10	**APPEND**	**↓ Home ←**	**Ctrl-F10**
		Ctrl-End	
		Home Home ↑	
		Alt-F4 Home Home ↓	
		Ctrl-F4 3	
		CLIENT.SF Return	

When you do terminate the merge operation, signaling that you do not want to add any more records to the secondary file, the APPEND macro first deletes the ^ PCLIENT.INP ^P merge codes on the last line. Then it moves the cursor to the beginning of the file (Home Home ↑), turns on blocking (Alt-F4), and highlights all of the text to the end of the document (Home Home ↓). Finally, it accesses the Move menu (Ctrl-F4), selects option 3 (Append), and specifies CLIENT.SF as the file to append your records to. In effect, this macro performs all of the cleanup tasks that you would normally do once you have executed this merge operation either by executing such a macro or manually performing these keystrokes.

> *Note:* Do not forget that the macro files executed from merge files must be available to WordPerfect during the merge operation. If your merge files are on a separate data disk, make sure all of the macros they use are on the same disk. If your merge files are in a particular WordPerfect subdirectory on your hard disk, make sure that the macros are also in this directory.

Creating Menus

You can also run merge operations from menus that you create by skillfully combining the ^O, ^C, and ^G merge codes. When you create a menu for a merge application, you can display it, including all of its options, by placing it between a pair of ^O merge codes. Within the pair of ^O merge codes, you place the ^G merge codes. Within the pair of ^G merge codes, you enter the first part of the macro name followed by a ^C code.

The simplest menu to create uses numbered options from which to select. The number chosen determines which macro is executed. To create such a menu, you name all of the macros associated with the menu the same except for the last character, to which you assign a number corresponding to the menu option it executes.

Figure 9.19 shows an example of this type of menu. Here you see a simple menu with five options that execute the most common tasks associated with various merge operations using the client secondary file. Notice that the entire menu—the title, numbered options, and the prompt—is enclosed within the ^O merge codes. To indent your menu options on the screen, as was done in this example, you must use spaces instead of tab stops. You can use the Esc key repeat function—pressing Esc, typing **25** (or whatever number of spaces you want your indentation to be), and pressing the space bar—to help you make these indentations.

Immediately before the second ^O merge are ^G merge codes surrounding the macro name MERGE, followed by a ^C code. This pauses the merge operation to allow you to enter the number of the option you wish to use. This entire set of codes, ^GMERGE^C^G, is placed immediately before the final ^O merge code.

Figure 9.20 shows how the menu appears when a merge operation is executed using the merge menu. When you select a number and press F9, the number is appended to MERGE. For example, if you type **1** to choose the option Add records to a secondary file, the macro named MERGE1 is executed. If you type **2** to select the Perform merge option, the macro named MERGE2 is executed, and so on.

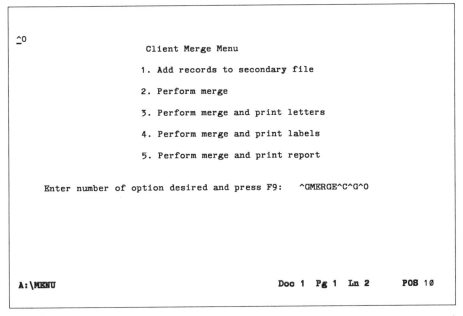

FIGURE 9.19: Creating the client merge menu. Notice that the entire menu—the title, the options, and the prompt—are enclosed in ^O merge codes. The ^GMERGE^C^G merge codes are also placed before the final ^O code. This displays the first part of the macro name (MERGE), with the cursor immediately after it, on the last line of the screen with the rest of the prompt message when the menu merge operation is executed (see Figure 9.20).

Each macro created for this menu begins a different merge operation. For example, MERGE1, executed by selecting option 1 (Add records to secondary file), contains the keystrokes

Ctrl-F9 1 CLIENT.INP Return Return

which initiate the merge operation, enter CLIENT.INP as the primary file to be used, and bypass the prompt for the name of the secondary file. At that point the MERGE1 macro terminates, and the merge operation controlled by the merge codes in CLIENT.INP takes over. This is the merge operation that prompts you as you add new records to the client secondary file. (To review the CLIENT.INP primary file, refer to the discussion and figures in "Creating a Secondary File through a Merge Operation" earlier in this chapter.)

If you choose the second option, Perform merge, the MERGE2 macro is executed. This macro contains the keystrokes

Ctrl-F9 1 ASSEMBLE.PF Return CLIENT.SF Return

which start the merge operation and then enter ASSEMBLE.PF as the primary file and CLIENT.SF as the secondary file to be used. At that point the MERGE2

```
                    Client Merge Menu

               1. Add records to secondary file

               2. Perform merge

               3. Perform merge and print letters

               4. Perform merge and print labels

               5. Perform merge and print report


        Enter number of option desired and press F9:   MERGE_
```

FIGURE 9.20: The client merge menu as it appears on the screen during execution. Notice that the cursor appears immediately after the macro name MERGE. When the operator enters the number of the option to use, it is appended to the macro name. When the operator then presses F9 to continue the merge operation, WordPerfect executes that macro which, in turn, initiates the appropriate merge operation (see the accompanying text for details about how these macros work).

macro terminates, and the merge operation controlled by the merge codes in ASSEMBLE.PF takes over. The merge operation in the ASSEMBLE.PF file allows you to choose from among various primary merge files to tailor your letter to the particular addressee retrieved from the client secondary file. (To review the ASSEMBLE.PF merge operation, refer to the discussion and figures in "Assembling Documents" earlier in this chapter.)

In a similar manner, the macros for options 3, 4, and 5 (named MERGE3, MERGE4, and MERGE5 respectively) initiate their own merge operations. The macro MERGE3, executed when you choose option 3, initiates a merge operation using a primary file that sends each of the merged letters to the printer (using the ^T^N^P^P merge codes—refer to "Merging Directly to the Printer" earlier in this chapter to review their use).

The macro MERGE4, executed when you choose option 4, begins a merge operation using another merge file. This merge file contains the codes to perform the standard mailing label merge operation using MAILABEL.PF and CLIENT.SF with one difference: it also contains its own macro that specifies the correct margin and page-length settings for mailing labels and sends the document to the printer. The macro MERGE5, executed when you choose option 5, is very similar except that it uses a primary file set up to produce a standard report listing; it also contains its own macro that sets the printing parameters and then sends the document to the printer.

If you want your menu redisplayed after you use one of its options, you create a macro that starts the merge operation and then insert the ^G merge codes to have that macro executed when the particular merge operation terminates. For example, the menu shown in Figure 9.20 can be activated by executing an Alt-M macro. This macro, similar to those that execute the various menu options, simply initiates the merge operation (Ctrl-F9 1), supplies the name of the primary file containing the menu (MENU in this case), bypasses the prompt for a secondary file, and then terminates.

To activate the merge menu, you simply add the following statement to the merge file that runs a particular menu option:

^GALTM^G

You must make sure that this pair of ^G merge codes is placed in the primary merge file so that WordPerfect reads this statement before it executes any codes that initiate the use of new primary or secondary files (refer to "Macros in Merge Operations" earlier in this chapter for details).

Not all of the menus that you create will have options that are executed by macros enclosed in ^G merge codes. In fact, you may create some menus in which each menu option executes a merge operation, using either a specific primary or secondary file. In such cases, you nest a pair of ^P (for primary file) or ^S (for secondary file) merge codes that contain the ^C code (Pause) within the pair of ^O codes that display the menu structure and list its options. For example, if you place the statement

^PMERGE^C^P

before the final ^O merge code, the menu option number you select completes the name of the primary file to be used. This merge file could itself contain the appropriate Go To macro codes that reactivate the menu or activate a new menu containing various suboptions.

By transferring control in this way, from macro to merge file and back to macro, you can create sophisticated menu systems that include as many levels and suboptions as you need. For more ideas about how to create menu-driven merge applications, see *WordPerfect Tips and Tricks* by Alan R. Neibauer (SYBEX, 1986).

BASIC MERGE CODES

KEY SEQUENCE

To separate fields in the secondary merge file with a Merge R code:
F9 or **Ctrl-R Return**

To separate records in the secondary merge file with a Merge E code:

Shift-F9 or **Ctrl-E Return**

To insert a field in the primary merge file:

Alt-F9 F *<field number>* **Return**

To eliminate blank lines when a field is empty (Version 4.2 only):

Alt-F9 F *<field number>*? **Return**

REVEAL CODES

Merge R code:

^R[HRt]

Merge E code:

^E[HRt]

Insert-field code:

^F*<number>* **^**

To perform a basic merge operation in WordPerfect, you must create and use two different files: a secondary merge file that contains all of the data to be substituted into each merged document and a primary merge file that indicates where each item from the secondary file is to be placed.

To create the secondary merge file,

1. Place each information item (or field) on its own line or lines terminated with a Merge R (Return) code. You enter this code by pressing F9 or Ctrl-R and Return. The Merge R code appears on the screen as ^R.

2. Even if you do not have information for a particular field, you must still enter a Merge R code to mark its position in the record. Do this by pressing F9 (or Ctrl-F9 and Return) without making any text entry.

3. Indicate where each record to be used in the merge operation ends by entering a Merge E (End) code on a separate line. This is done by pressing Shift-F9 or Ctrl-E and Return. Each ^E merge code demarcates the boundary of a single record, which contains all of the fields that you maintain for one entity (client, employee, account, and so on) on their own lines above the ^E code. The Merge E code appears on your screen as ^E.

Each record in the secondary file must contain the same number of fields (that is, Merge R codes), regardless of whether any particular field contains data. In other words, there must always be the same number of Merge R codes preceding the Merge E marker throughout the entire secondary file. WordPerfect identifies a particular field by number. Fields are numbered sequentially beginning with 1 for the first data item terminated with a Merge R code.

When you save the secondary file, you can indicate its type by adding the file name extension .SF (secondary file) at the end of the file name.

To create the primary merge file to be used with the secondary file that you have created,

1. Begin a new document. Enter all of the text that is not to vary from merge document to merge document, just as you normally would.

2. Indicate any places where you want information to be supplied from the secondary merge file by entering an insert-field merge code. You do this by pressing Alt-F9, typing **F**, entering the appropriate field number, and pressing Return. Be sure that you indicate the correct field number or the wrong information will be substituted from the secondary file during the merge operation. The insert-field merge code is shown on your screen by ^F*n*^, where *n* is the field number that you entered.

When indicating where data from a particular field in the secondary file is to be placed in the primary file, you can reuse the same field number as many times as necessary. Be sure to insert any required spaces or constant punctuation such as commas or colons (not included in the data entry for the field) between the insert-field merge codes just as though they were actual text rather than special codes.

If you are using Version 4.2 of WordPerfect, you can append a ? (question mark) to the end of the field number when you enter the insert-field merge code to keep the program from inserting blank spaces or lines for empty fields. In other words, if some of the records in the secondary file do not have entries for a particular field, adding a question mark to its field number will prevent unwanted blanks from appearing in the merge document that uses its information.

When you save the primary file, you can indicate its type by adding the extension .PF (primary file) at the end of the file name.

To perform the merge operation,

1. Clear the current editing screen or switch to a new, unused document window (Shift-F3).

2. Press Ctrl-F9 and select 1 (Merge) to begin the merge operation.

3. In response to the prompt Primary file:, enter the complete file name of the primary merge file you wish to use and press Return.

4. In response to the prompt Secondary file:, enter the complete file name of the secondary merge file you wish to use and press Return.

WordPerfect will display the message * Merging * at the bottom of your screen. When the merge operation is completed, the resulting document will contain an individual merged document for each record in the secondary file. Each merged document (form letter, mailing label, report listing, and so on) will be separated by hard returns. You can then save this new composite document and print it later or send it directly to the printer.

If your secondary file is quite large, you may find that WordPerfect is unable to complete the merge operation for all of the records in the secondary file. In such a case, you will have to edit your primary document, adding merge codes to send each merged document directly to the printer. See "The ^T (Type) Merge Option" that follows for details about how to do this.

OTHER MERGE OPTION CODES

KEY SEQUENCE

To pause a merge operation to enter text from the keyboard:
    Alt-F9 C or **Ctrl-C**

To enter the system date:
    Alt-F9 D or **Ctrl-D**

To execute a macro upon completion of a merge operation:
    Alt-F9 G *<macro name>* **Alt-F9 G** or **Ctrl-G** *<macro name>* **Ctrl-G**

To use the next record in a secondary file in a merge operation:
    Alt-F9 N or **Ctrl-N**

To display a message or prompt on the screen:
    Alt-F9 O *<message>* **Alt-F9 O** or **Ctrl-O** *<message>* **Ctrl-O**

To specify a new primary document to be used in a merge operation:
    Alt-F9 P *<file name>* **Alt-F9 P** or **Ctrl-P** *<file name>* **Ctrl-P**

To quit a merge operation:
    Alt-F9 Q or **Ctrl-Q**

To specify a new secondary document to be used in a merge operation:
    Alt-F9 S *<file name>* **Alt-F9 S** or **Ctrl-S** *<file name>* **Ctrl-S**

To send all previously merged text directly to the printer:
    Alt-F9 T or **Ctrl-T**

To update the screen with merge data:
    Alt-F9 U or **Ctrl-U**

To insert merge codes into the document being created:
    Alt-F9 V *<merge code>* **Alt-F9 V**

WordPerfect offers many optional merge codes that you can use to adapt the merge operation to special requirements. The following sections explain the basic function of each one. In addition, you can refer to the figures and discussions in the earlier sections of this chapter for examples illustrating their use.

The ^C (Console) Merge Option

The ^C merge code temporarily halts the merge operation in process. This allows you to enter data directly from the keyboard into the merge documents being created. To continue the merge operation once you have finished adding text, you press F9. You insert the merge code into your primary or secondary document by pressing Alt-F9 and typing **C** or by pressing Ctrl-C.

The ^C pause is often combined with paired ^O merge codes, primarily to keep the message prompt or menu options on the screen and to allow you to enter your response. You insert the ^C code immediately after the final ^O merge code.

The ^C merge code can also be combined with the ^G, ^P, and ^S merge codes, primarily to allow you to specify the name of the macro, primary, or secondary file to use. In this case, it is entered within any of these paired codes.

The ^D (Date) Merge Option

The ^D merge code inserts the system date (the date entered in DOS when you start the computer) into your merge file. Usually you will use this code to insert the date in a primary merge file instead of entering the date manually or with WordPerfect's Date insert function (Shift-F5 1). When you execute the merge operation, WordPerfect will substitute the full date (such as January 11, 1955) wherever a ^D appears. This date is automatically updated to the current date each time you execute a merge operation using a primary document that contains it. To enter this merge code into your merge file, press Alt-F9 and type **D** (or press Ctrl-D).

The ^G (Go To Macro) Merge Option

The ^G merge option is always paired. Between the pair of ^G merge codes, you place the name of the macro that is to be executed when the merge operation terminates. For example, if you want the macro Alt-M to be executed as soon as the merge operation called for in a primary file is complete, you enter

^GALTM^G

in the primary file. If your macro does not use the Alt key with a single alphabetical letter, you enter its initials or full name between the pair of ^G merge codes. To enter these codes, press Alt-F9 and type **G** (or press Ctrl-G), enter the name of the macro (do not enter the .MAC file extension), and press Alt-F9 and type **G** (or press Ctrl-G) again.

When you enter such a code into a merge file, WordPerfect must read it before it uses another primary file or performs a loop using the same primary file (designated by a pair of ^P merge codes). Also, you can only have one macro executed in this manner. Therefore, you can enter only one pair of ^G merge codes in your merge file. Refer to the section "Macros in Merge Operations" earlier in this chapter for information about the placement and use of macros.

The ^N (Next Record) Merge Option

The ^N merge code tells WordPerfect to use the next record in the designated secondary file. If the program does not find a next record in the file, WordPerfect terminates the current merge operation. To enter the ^N merge code, press Alt-F9 and type **N** (or press Ctrl-N).

You can place the ^N code above a particular record in the secondary file to cause WordPerfect to skip that particular record in the merge operation.

You can also combine the ^N code with a pair of ^P merge codes in the primary file to suppress unnecessary page breaks between merged documents—for example,

^N^P^P

This group of codes is often used with the ^T merge code to prevent unnecessary form feeds (blank pages) between printed merge documents—see "The ^T (Type) Merge Option" that follows.

The ^O (On-screen Message) Merge Option

The ^O merge option is always paired. Between the pair of ^O merge codes, you place the text of the message or prompt you want displayed on the screen. To enter these merge codes, press Alt-F9 and type **O** (or press Ctrl-O), enter the text of your message as well as any other merge codes to be included, and press Alt-F9 and type **O** (or press Ctrl-O) again.

The ^O code is combined with a ^C pause code to keep a message on the screen until you press F9 (otherwise you never get a chance to read the message and respond to it). For example, if you enter

^OEnter the date of sale: ^O^C

in a primary file when you perform the merge operation, WordPerfect will pause the operation and display

Enter the date of sale:

on the last line of the screen in double intensity. This message will remain on your screen until you press F9. The ^O merge codes are also used to display a menu of options on the screen. For more information about using ^O merge codes to display prompts, refer to "Displaying Messages on the Screen" and "Assembling Documents" earlier in this chapter. For more information about how to use ^O codes to create menu-driven merge operations, refer to "Creating Menus," also presented in a previous section.

The ^P (Primary File) Merge Option

The ^P code is always paired. Between the pair of ^P merge codes, you place the complete name of the primary merge file that you want inserted. If you do not specify a file name between the pair of ^P merge codes, WordPerfect uses the current primary file. To insert these merge codes, press Alt-F9 and type **P** (or press Ctrl-P), enter the file name (if you are using other than the current file), and press Alt-F9 and type **P** (or press Ctrl-P) again.

You can combine ^P merge codes with the ^N code to cause the current merge operation to loop continuously (somewhat like the way you can chain macros) until all of the records in the designated secondary file are processed. If you combine this grouping of merge codes with the ^T code, WordPerfect will send all of the merge documents directly to the printer—see "The ^T (Type) Merge Option" that follows.

The ^P merge codes can also be used to designate a new primary file to be used during the current merge operation. To do this, you enter the complete file name between the pair of ^P codes. When WordPerfect encounters these merge codes, it uses the newly designated primary document in the merge operation and follows the codes it contains until its merge operations are complete. Then the program returns to the original primary file (this is somewhat like the way a program returns to a calling program after a subroutine is executed in a programming language). Refer to "Selecting the Primary Files to Be Used" earlier in this chapter for more information about this application.

The ^Q (Quit) Merge Option

The ^Q merge code terminates a merge operation. You may enter this code into either a primary or secondary merge file. However, most often you will use it to restrict the records to be processed in a merge operation. In such a case, you place the code in the secondary merge file on its own line immediately before the beginning (first field) of the first record that you do not want included. When WordPerfect encounters this merge code, it terminates the merge operation, thus ignoring all records that come after the ^Q merge code. To enter the ^Q merge code, press Alt-F9 and type **Q** (or press Ctrl-Q).

The ^S (Secondary File) Merge Option

The ^S merge code is always paired. Between the pair of ^S merge codes, you place the complete name of the secondary merge file that you want inserted.

If you do not specify a file name between the pair of ^S merge codes, Word-Perfect uses the current secondary file. To insert these merge codes, press Alt-F9 and type **S** (or press Ctrl-S), enter the file name, and press Alt-F9 and type **S** (or press Ctrl-S) again.

You use the ^S merge codes to designate a new secondary file to be used during the current merge operation. You enter the complete file name between a pair of ^S codes in the primary file at the place where new data is to be substituted.

When WordPerfect encounters the ^S merge codes, it uses the newly designated secondary document in the merge operation and follows the codes it contains until its merge operations are complete. Refer to "Selecting the Secondary Files to Be Used" earlier in this chapter for more information about this application.

The ^T (Type) Merge Option

The ^T merge code sends all of the text merged to the point where the code is placed directly to the printer. After the text is sent to the printer, it is cleared from the computer's memory.

This code is most often used to print each merged document as it is generated in cases in which it is not possible or desirable to create a large merged document containing every record in the secondary file. To enter the ^T merge code, press Alt-F9 and type **T** (or press Ctrl-T).

Usually you will combine the ^T merge code with the ^N code and a pair of ^P codes. This combination, ^T^N^P^P, ensures that each record in the second document is processed and prevents the insertion of extra form feeds between the documents as they are printed. For more information about using ^T, refer to "Merging Directly to the Printer" earlier in this chapter.

The ^U (Update) Merge Option

The ^U merge option rewrites the screen, causing the merge document currently being generated to be displayed on your screen. To enter this option, press Alt-F9 and type **U** (or press Ctrl-U).

This option is often used in applications in which the merge document is assembled from several merge files. In such applications, being able to see the merged document from the first file often helps you decide which file to use next. You will often combine the ^U code with the ^O, ^C, and ^P merge codes. For examples, refer to "Selecting the Primary Files to Be Used" and "Selecting the Secondary Files to Be Used" earlier in this chapter.

The ^V (Insert Code) Merge Option

The ^V merge code is always paired. It inserts any merge codes enclosed within a pair of ^V codes into the document currently being created. You enter these codes by pressing Alt-F9 and typing **V** (you *cannot* press Ctrl-V), pressing Alt-F9, typing the letter of the merge code to be inserted, and pressing Alt-F9 and typing **V** again.

The ^V merge code is quite useful when you are performing a merge operation that adds records that you can transfer to an existing secondary merge file. For this application, you enclose a ^R (Merge R) and a ^E (Merge E) code in ^V merge codes. For an illustration, refer to "Creating a Secondary File through a Merge Operation" earlier in this chapter.

SUMMARY

This chapter discussed WordPerfect's Merge feature. You will undoubtedly want to use this feature with the Sort and Select features presented in the next chapter. The Sort and Select features offered by WordPerfect allow you to arrange the records you maintain in your secondary files as well as to create more limited files that contain only the records that meet the conditions you specify.

Although WordPerfect gives you the ability to perform three kinds of sorts—line, paragraph, and merge sorts—it is the merge sort that you will probably use most often, especially as your applications for WordPerfect's Merge feature expand. For this reason, you will want to become thoroughly familiar with all aspects of merge sorting covered in Chapter 10.

Other chapters of possible interest include the following:

- Chapter 8, "Page Composition: Working with Text Columns," discusses how to set up column formats that you can use when printing multiple-column mailing labels.

- Chapter 11, "Math and Equations," discusses how to perform mathematical calculations in documents that can be used in merge operations to automate invoicing and other applications requiring calculations.

- Chapter 15, "Using WordPerfect with Other Software," discusses how to import data maintained in other programs, such as Lotus 1-2-3, and stand-alone database management systems, such as dBASE III Plus, into WordPerfect secondary merge files.

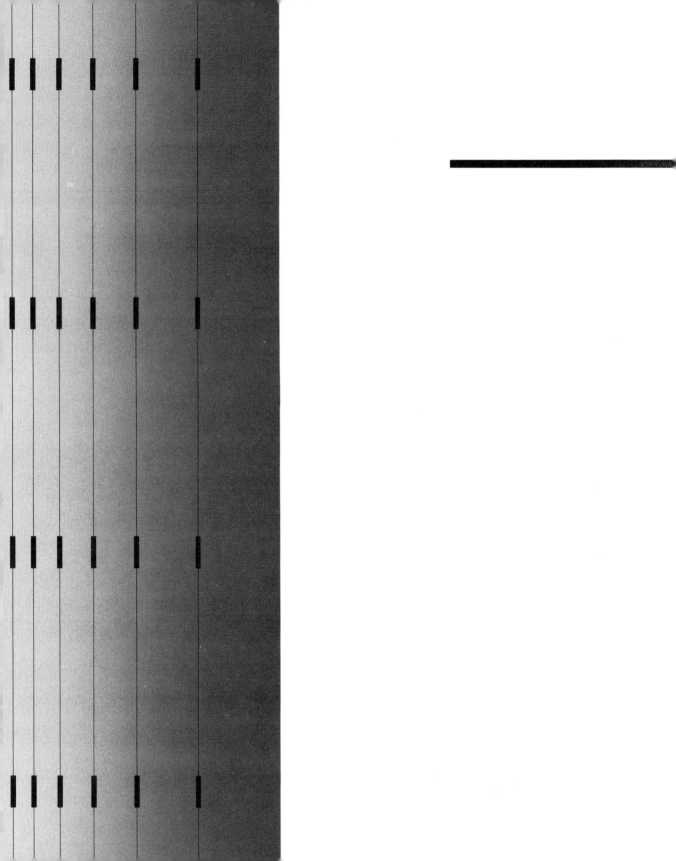

SORTING

SORTING

his chapter presents the sorting operations that you can perform with WordPerfect. WordPerfect enables you to perform three kinds of sorts:

- Merge sorts, which are performed on records in a secondary merge file
- Line sorts, which are performed on data organized into tables
- Paragraph sorts, which are performed on text separated by at least two hard returns or a hard page break

With WordPerfect's Sort feature, you can rearrange almost any kind of text that the program produces, thus making a separate program to alphabetize any of the data listings you use unnecessary. You can use the Sort feature to organize text or numbers in the tables you create and to reorganize paragraphs throughout your document.

If you regularly use mail merge, you will find the merge sort function invaluable. In addition to enabling you to order the records in the secondary file in the way you want the letters and mailing labels produced (usually in order by zip code), it also allows you to select just specific records (such as only those records containing Ohio in the state field. For more information about performing mail-merge operations with WordPerfect, see Chapter 9.

PRINCIPLES OF SORTING

Before you begin using WordPerfect's Sort feature, you should be familiar with the terms that it uses. Without a background in data processing, you may find its Sort menu a little daunting at first. However, once you grasp the underlying principles and have gained a little experience performing various kinds of sorts, you will find sorting a quite straightforward process.

Sorting Keys

The fundamental element of sorting is the *sort key*. The key is the data item that determines the new order of all data that is sorted. Suppose that you have just entered the following list of names:

Elizabeth Mundel
Allan Grill
Jay Snyder
Susan Kelly
Shane Gearing
Judy Ziajka
Susan Nurse
David Kolodney

and you now want to arrange this list alphabetically by last name. Your list contains two data items for each person: a first and last name. To have WordPerfect sort this list as you want it to, you designate the second data item, the last name, as the sort key. Using the last name as the key sorts the list as follows:

Shane Gearing
Allan Grill
Susan Kelly
David Kolodney
Elizabeth Mundel
Susan Nurse
Jay Snyder
Judy Ziajka

If you make the first name the key, the sort produces this list:

Allan Grill
David Kolodney
Elizabeth Mundel
Jay Snyder
Judy Ziajka
Shane Gearing
Susan Nurse
Susan Kelly

You may often need to use more than one key when you sort. In the preceding example, all of the last names in the list are unique. However, not all of the first names in the list are unique, as there are two *Susan*s in the list. Notice that the final order in which the two *Susan*s appear is not completely alphabetical (*Nurse* is listed before *Kelly*) because WordPerfect sorted the list using just the first name as the key.

If you want to make sure that the list is arranged in a completely alphabetical order regarding both the first and last names, you have to sort the list again. You will still use the first name as your first (or *primary*) key, but in addition, you will also designate the last name as the second (or *secondary*) key. When the list is sorted using two keys, the duplicates in the primary field (the *Susan*s) will be sequenced by the secondary key (their last names) so that *Susan Kelly* will precede *Susan Nurse*.

WordPerfect allows you to use up to nine different keys in sorting. Very seldom, if ever, will you need to use all nine keys to arrange all of the duplicate items in a list in the way you want. However, there are many situations that require the use of multiple keys.

For instance, suppose that you have a table listing the employees and their supervisors in all departments of a company and this table currently is arranged in no particular order. If you want to arrange the table alphabetically first by department, then by supervisor, and finally by employee's last name, you will have to use at least three, and possibly four, sorting keys.

First, you can designate the column containing the departments as the primary key. However, this key is bound to yield many duplicate items (there many be 50 or more employees in a single department). To order the employees within each department, you can designate the column containing the supervisors' names as the secondary key. Again, there are bound to be many employees who have the same supervisor. To order the employees who have the same supervisor, you can define the column holding the last names as the third key. Finally, if some of the employees have the same last name, you can define the column containing first names as the fourth key.

When you sort data in WordPerfect, you will have to make these types of determinations in all but a few cases. Only when you know that the data you want the list sorted by contains no duplicates (as when you sort by social security numbers or account numbers) can you be sure that using just one key will result in the desired arrangement.

Sort Order

Another important principle in sorting is the *sort order*. There are two basic kinds of sort order: ascending (from lowest to highest) and descending (from highest to lowest). WordPerfect can sort alphanumeric data (consisting of any types of characters: letters, numbers, and special symbols) as well as strictly numeric data (consisting solely of numbers).

When you sort alphanumeric data in ascending order, WordPerfect follows a sequence in which punctuation and special symbols (such as @, #, and $) precede numbers, and numbers (arranged from lowest to highest) precede letters (arranged in alphabetical, or A–Z, order). When you sort alphanumeric data in descending order, this sequence is reversed. Letters (arranged in Z–A order) precede numbers (arranged from highest to lowest), which precede punctuation and symbols.

You use WordPerfect's Numeric Sort option when the data you are arranging consists only of numbers. When you sort numeric data in ascending order, WordPerfect arranges it in a strict sequence of lowest to highest value. This means that any negative values (those prefaced by a minus sign) precede any positive values, however small. When you sort numeric data in descending order, just the opposite is true, as WordPerfect arranges the data in a strict sequence of highest to lowest value.

Ascending sort order is the default setting for any type of sort operation in WordPerfect. When you change the sort order to descending, WordPerfect uses this order in all subsequent sorting operations performed during your work session until you change the setting back to ascending order.

THE LINE SORT

When your data is arranged in a tabular format consisting of columns and rows, you use the line sort. You must group the individual data items and place them in columns of the table, separating each column by at least one tab setting (using either Tab or Indent) for the line sort to work properly. Any column of information (or *field*) in the table can be used as a sort key. However, for the sort to work, each column must contain only one type of information.

Also, for the sort to work, you must make sure that the table ruler contains only the tab stops required to reach each column and that these tabs are spaced far enough apart to accommodate all of the entries in any one column.

Figure 10.1 shows a vacation accrual table containing seven different fields, including the employee's identification number in the first column and the number of vacation days in the seventh column. Each field is separated by a single tab. All of the tabs except that of the vacation days field left align the columns, separating them by the [TAB] format code. The last field uses a decimal tab, which separates it from the previous field with [A][a] alignment codes.

To sort the information in this table, you use WordPerfect's Line Sort feature. If you want to arrange the information alphabetically by employee name, you designate the second field, the last-name column, as the primary key. Notice, however, that three people have the last name *Smith*. To order these duplicate items, you must also define a secondary key, the third field, which contains the first names.

To do this, you press Ctrl-F9 (Merge/Sort) and select option 2 from the following menu:

1 Merge; 2 Sort; 3 Sorting Sequences: 0

```
1004    Nelson      Steven    F.    11    06-02-84    14.3
1324    Carrington  Neil      T.    10    03-02-86     7.1
1073    Smith       Thomas    A.    12    10-03-83    14.3
1289    Tudor       Carol     M.    10    12-03-84    17.8
1233    McGill      David     P.    10    01-04-84    16.8
1323    Wadsworth   Sharon    G.    12    01-04-86     7.1
1415    Watson      Sean      A.    10    07-05-85    14.3
1325    Smith       Mary      A.    11    03-05-86     7.1
 233    Smith       Sandra    B.    12    02-16-80    31.4
 788    Kaye        Peter     A.    11    05-16-82    29.4
1066    Olsen       Phillis   G.    12    04-17-83    26.4
1059    Allen       Holly     M.    11    03-18-83    23.4
1407    Farner      Kenneth   E.    12    04-20-85    14.3
 534    Drew        Mary      J.    10    03-24-81    26.4
```

```
C:\WP\WPB\VACATION                        Doc 2  Pg 1  Ln 1      Pos 10
```

FIGURE 10.1: The vacation accrual table before line sorting. When performing a line sort, you must arrange the items of information (the fields) in columns separated by the same number of tabs. In this table, each column is separated by a single left-align tab. Notice that each column contains the same type of information. During sorting the rows (records) will be reordered according to the key that is defined.

When you do, this prompt appears:

Input file to sort: (Screen)

If you press Return without entering a file name, WordPerfect will apply the sort you are about to define to all of the data in the document in the current document window (or editing screen). If you want to sort a file that is on the disk and not currently in the document window, you type its complete file name over the default specification, (Screen). Usually, you will want to retrieve the document that contains the data you want to sort before you begin the sort operation and, therefore, will accept the (Screen) default selection by simply pressing Return.

> *Note:* Always make sure that you have saved your document in memory before you sort its information using the (Screen) default for the input file. That way, if you make a mistake when defining the sorting parameters, you will still have a copy of the information in its original order.

When you press Return, you are prompted for the name of a new file to which the sorted data should be output:

Output file for sort: (Screen)

Again, the default selection is the screen. If you do not wish to save the sorted data in a new disk file, you simply press Return. If you do want to save the sorted file, type the name of a new file name over the (Screen) default specification.

Often, you will want to accept the (Screen) default here, too. This allows you to view the results of the sort operation and make sure that the information is arranged exactly as you want it before you save the file. If you find that you used an inappropriate key or did not define enough keys to obtain the desired sort, you can then abandon the file in memory (F7 N N), retrieve the original file, and redefine the sort operation.

When you press Return, WordPerfect automatically splits the editing window display. In the lower window, it displays the Sort by Line screen (shown in Figure 10.2). At the bottom of this screen are the Sort menu options:

1 Perform Action; 2 View; 3 Keys; 4 Select; 5 Action; 6 Order; 7 Type: 0

WordPerfect supports three types of sort: line, paragraph, and merge. It always indicates the type of sort it will perform in two places in the lower window. The type of sort is centered between a line of hyphens immediately below the ruler line that divides the windows, and it also is listed under the heading *Type of Sort* at the bottom right of the screen above the Sort menu options. Although the line sort is the default sort type, WordPerfect retains any change made to this setting. Therefore, you should always check these areas to make sure that the program is set to perform the kind of sort you want. If it is not, select option 7 (Type) and select the correct option from among these choices:

Sorting Type: 1 Merge; 2 Line; 3 Paragraph: 0

Notice in Figure 10.2 that WordPerfect has already entered default values for the first key, leaving the other eight keys blank. The information for the first key is as follows:

Key Typ Field Word
  1   a   1   1

Under the heading *Typ,* for *Type,* the letter *a* appears, indicating an alphanumeric sort. When you redefine the value for this key, or add new keys, you can specify a numeric sort by entering an *n* instead of an *a* in this column.

The next two columns for the first key both contain the number 1. When you define a line sort, you can indicate not only the number of the field (column) to be used as the key, but also the number of the word in that field.

Fields and words are numbered sequentially from left to right across the line. For example, in Figure 10.1, the column containing employees' identification numbers is field 1, the one containing employees' last names is field 2, and so on.

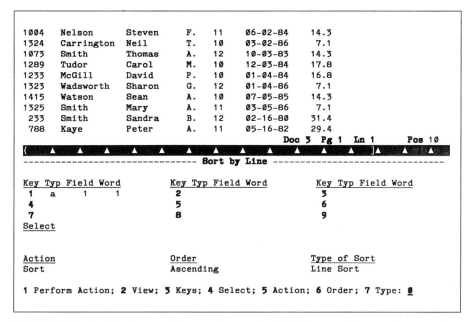

FIGURE 10.2: Starting the line sort of the vacation accrual table. When you define a sorting operation, WordPerfect splits the editing screen into two windows, as shown here. The default selection is Sort by Line. The program also suggests default settings for the first key. To change these, or to define other keys to be used, you select option 3 (Keys) from the Sort menu. Notice that below the keys, the Sort by Line screen displays the action, order, and type of sort. You can change any of these default settings by choosing the appropriate Sort menu options.

None of the fields in the vacation accrual table have more than one word as WordPerfect counts words. For WordPerfect to consider an item in a field as a word, it must be separated from other items in the same field by spaces. WordPerfect considers a field entry that contains several elements separated by punctuation, such as commas and hyphens, but no spaces, as a single word.

For instance, although the date-hired field (6) is made up of three elements (month, day, and year), because these elements are separated by hyphens and not spaces, they cannot be counted as individual words. You cannot use the Word setting to put the table in order by the year hired unless you replace the hyphens with spaces. For example, if the dates hired were entered as

06 02 84
03 02 86

and so on, you could sort the table by year hired by using the third word (the digits of the year) of the sixth field as the sort key. You would designate this key in the Line Sort screen as

Key Typ Field Word
  1   a   6   3

In fact, if you entered the date with spaces instead of hyphens (or slashes, as in 06/02/84), you could easily arrange this table by the entire date hired (month, day, and year). To do this would require the use of three keys, each using field 6 with a different word. The keys for this sort would appear in the Line Sort screen as follows:

Key	*Typ*	*Field*	*Word*	*Key*	*Typ*	*Field*	*Word*	*Key*	*Typ*	*Field*	*Word*
1	a	6	3	2	a	6	1	3	a	6	2

Key 1 sorts the table by the digits of the year hired (word 3). Next, key 2 sorts those records that share the same year by the month (word 1). Finally, key 3 sorts those records that share both the same year and month by the day.

> *Note:* Even though the dates in field 6 are entered entirely with numbers, you do not need to change the type of sort from *a* (alphanumeric) to *n* (numeric) in order to have WordPerfect sort integers (whole numbers) correctly. Do not forget that *a* stands for *alphanumeric* and not for ascending order.

When the fields in your table contain only one word as they do in the vacation accrual table, you need not change the default Word setting of 1. However, to have WordPerfect sort the vacation accrual table in alphabetical order by employee name, you do have to change the number of the field for key 1 and add the information for key 2.

To do this, you select option 3 (Keys) from the Sort menu. WordPerfect then places the cursor under the Typ column for key 1. You can press either Return or → to move to the next key column. If you need to move to a previous key column, you press the ← key. If you have defined keys in the rows below, you can use the ↑ and ↓ keys to move the cursor back and forth between keys on different lines.

Figure 10.3 shows how the keys for this sort are specified. For this sort, you use two alphanumeric fields, the last name and the first name fields, so you do not change the default *a* (alphanumeric). To move to the column for the field number, you press →. To change the field number for key 1 from 1 to 2, you press → and type **2**. Even though the cursor is positioned immediately after the 1, when you type **2**, the 2 replaces the 1 as the field number.

Next, you press → twice, once to to move to the Word column and a second time to bypass it and move to the key 2 definition. As soon as you press → a second time, WordPerfect fills in its default settings for this key: *a* for the Typ, 1 for the Field, and 1 for the Word. Here, you need to change the Field number from 1 to 3. After moving the cursor to the Field column for this key and entering the new value, you press F7 (Exit) to return to the Line Sort menu options.

Before you perform any sorting operation by selecting option 1 (Perform Action) from the menu, you should always check the key definitions and the Action, Order, and Type of Sort settings that are listed at the bottom of the Sort screen immediately above it.

```
1004    Nelson      Steven    F.    11    06-02-84    14.3
1324    Carrington  Neil      T.    10    03-02-86     7.1
1073    Smith       Thomas    A.    12    10-03-83    14.3
1289    Tudor       Carol     M.    10    12-03-84    17.8
1233    McGill      David     P.    10    01-04-84    16.8
1323    Wadsworth   Sharon    G.    12    01-04-86     7.1
1415    Watson      Sean      A.    10    07-05-85    14.3
1325    Smith       Mary      A.    11    03-05-86     7.1
 233    Smith       Sandra    B.    12    02-16-80    31.4
 788    Kaye        Peter     A.    11    05-16-82    29.4
                                      Doc 3  Pg 1   Ln 1        Pos 10
```

```
----------------------------- Sort by Line -----------------------------

Key Typ Field Word        Key Typ Field Word        Key Typ Field Word
 1   a    2     1           2   a    3_    1          3
 4                          5                         6
 7                          8                         9
Select


Action                    Order                     Type of Sort
Sort                      Ascending                 Line Sort

Type: a = Alphanumeric; n = Numeric;  Use Arrows;  Press EXIT when done
```

FIGURE 10.3: Defining the keys for a line sort operation. Because this table is to be sorted alphabetically by last name and first name, two keys are defined. The first key uses field 2, which contains the last names. The second key uses field 3, which contains the first names. Both of these fields in the table contain only one word, so the Word setting is left at 1 for both keys. Because both of these keys contain only alphabetical information, the Typ setting is left at the default setting *a* (for alphanumeric).

The Action column tells you whether you are about to perform a sort, a sort and select, or a select operation (see "Selecting Records" later in this chapter for information about using the Select operation). The Order column tells you whether the sort will be arranged in ascending or descending order. To change the Order column to Descending from the default setting of Ascending, you select option 6 (Order) and enter **2** (Descending). The Type of Sort column tells you the type of sort, which must be line sort in order to correctly sort this table. To change this from the Line Sort default setting, you select option 7 (Type). To specify a paragraph sort, you then select option 3 (see "The Paragraph Sort" that follows for information about when and how to use this sort type). To specify a merge sort, you select option 1 (see "The Merge Sort" later in this chapter for information about when and how to use this sort type).

Figure 10.4 shows the table after the sort has been performed by selecting option 1 (Perform Action) from the menu. As soon as you choose 1, WordPerfect displays a counter indicating the number of records sorted (this may appear too briefly for you to read it if there are only a few records to sort). When the sorting operation is finished, WordPerfect automatically clears the Sort window and returns to the normal full-screen document window.

WordPerfect uses a split-screen window arrangement whenever you sort data (it places your document in a special window marked Doc 2). If you have text in both document windows, this window is marked Doc 3, just as it is when you use the Print Preview feature. The Sort menu contains a View option (2), which you can use to move the cursor to the data in the window above. This allows you to scroll through the data using all of the normal scrolling keys. However, you cannot edit the data in this window. If you see something that requires editing, you must exit the sorting operation completely (using F1). To return to the Sort menu after scrolling through the document to be sorted, you press F7 (Exit).

Sorting a Block

In the sort operation outlined in the previous discussion, the entire contents of the document (which contained only the tabular data to be sorted) was used. Most of the time when you perform a line sort, and many times when you perform a paragraph or merge sort, you will not want to sort all of the information in the document.

In such cases, you alter the sorting procedure slightly by first marking the data to be included in the sort with WordPerfect's Block feature before you select the

```
1059   Allen       Holly     M.   11   03-18-83   23.4
1324   Carrington  Neil      T.   10   03-02-86    7.1
 534   Drew        Mary      J.   10   03-24-81   26.4
1407   Farner      Kenneth   E.   12   04-20-85   14.3
 788   Kaye        Peter     A.   11   05-16-82   29.4
1233   McGill      David     P.   10   01-04-84   16.8
1004   Nelson      Steven    F.   11   06-02-84   14.3
1066   Olsen       Phillis   G.   12   04-17-83   26.4
1325   Smith       Mary      A.   11   03-05-86    7.1
 233   Smith       Sandra    B.   12   02-16-80   31.4
1073   Smith       Thomas    A.   12   10-03-83   14.3
1289   Tudor       Carol     M.   10   12-03-84   17.8
1323   Wadsworth   Sharon    G.   12   01-04-86    7.1
1415   Watson      Sean      A.   10   07-05-85   14.3




C:\WP\WPB\VACATION                    Doc 2  Pg 1  Ln 1        Pos 10
```

FIGURE 10.4: The vacation accrual table after sorting. Notice that all of the records have been re-arranged. The primary key, which used the last-name field, controlled the new order of the records except in the case of the three duplicate last names of *Smith*. Their order was controlled by the secondary key, which sorted on the first names.

Sort feature. For example, Figure 10.5 shows the vacation accrual table sorted by employee name, this time including the column headings, line separators, and table numbering required for it in the final report. To use the Line Sort feature to sort the employee data again, this time by department number and the number of vacation days accrued, you have to sort a block that contains just the data rather than sorting the entire document.

To do this, you position the cursor at the beginning of the first ID number in line 8 and press Alt-F4 (Block). Then you use the ↓ key to highlight all of the records down to that of Sean Watson in line 18. When the block is correctly marked, you press Ctrl-F9 (Merge/Sort). This time, WordPerfect opens the Line Sort window without requiring you to select the Sort option (2) from the Merge/Sort menu.

To sort records in the table by department number and vacation days, you enter **5** (which contains the department numbers) as the field for key 1, and you enter **7** (which contains the vacation days) as the field for key 2. However, because the vacation days field contains fractional numbers, you must change the type of sort from *a* (alphanumeric) to *n* (numeric).

You can apply the alphanumeric sort type only to fields containing numbers when the values are all expressed in whole numbers of equal length, such as zip

```
 -

                        Vacation Accrual
                       Departments 10 - 12

 ID      Last       First      M  Dept   Date        Vacation
 No.     Name       Name       I  Code   Hired       Days

 1324    Carrington Neil       T.  10    03-02-86     7.1
  534    Drew       Mary       J.  10    03-24-81    26.4
 1407    Farner     Kenneth    E.  12    04-20-85    14.3
  788    Kaye       Peter      A.  11    05-16-82    29.4
 1004    Nelson     Steven     F.  11    06-02-84    14.3
 1066    Olsen      Phillis    G.  12    04-17-83    26.4
 1325    Smith      Mary       A.  11    03-05-86     7.1
  233    Smith      Sandra     B.  12    02-16-80    31.4
 1073    Smith      Thomas     A.  12    10-03-83    14.3
 1323    Wadsworth  Sharon     G.  10    01-04-86     7.1
 1415    Watson     Sean       A.  10    07-05-85    14.3

                         Table 6.2


 C:\WP\WPB\VACATION                    Doc 2  Pg 1  Ln 1      Pos 10
```

FIGURE 10.5: Final vacation accrual table as it appears in the text of the report. Titles, column headings, table number, and even line separators (created with the Line Draw feature) have been added to the table data. If any records in the table require reordering, you must limit the sort to just those records by defining them as a block before you use the Sort command (Ctrl-F9).

codes. Whenever the numbers contain decimals, as in this case, or when a field contains dollars and cents figures (without the $) or numbers of unequal length (for example, 2, 17, 130), you need to use the numeric type of sort. If you do not, WordPerfect will not sort the records on this key. Figure 10.6 shows the key definitions used to perform this new record sort.

Figure 10.7 shows the records in this table after the sort has been performed. Notice that only the records included in the block (the records in lines 8 to 18) were reordered. If a line sort had been performed on the entire document, Word-Perfect would have rearranged not only these records but also the titles, columns, and even the line separators with disastrous consequences for the table.

THE PARAGRAPH SORT

You use the paragraphs sort when data is separated by at least two hard returns: one to end the paragraph and the other to enter a blank line. The data can also be separated by hard page breaks (Ctrl-Return). This kind of sort can be be applied to

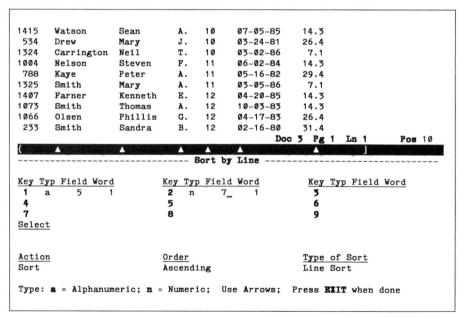

FIGURE 10.6: The key definitions required to sort the records in the vacation accrual table first by department number and then by the number of vacation days accrued. Before the sorting operation was begun and these two keys were defined, just the records in the table were marked as a block. Notice that the type of the secondary key using the vacation days field (the last field in the table) has been changed from alphanumeric to numeric (*n*). This was necessary because this field contains fractional numbers expressed as decimals.

either the entire document (in other words, all of the paragraphs) or just specific paragraphs in the document that have been previously marked as a block.

The paragraph sort differs only slightly from the line sort discussed in the previous section. Figure 10.8 shows a document containing descriptions of several movies for a movie guide. As you can see, these were not entered in alphabetical order by movie. However, because each description is entered as a paragraph below a heading, you can use WordPerfect's Paragraph Sort feature to order them.

In sorting the paragraphs, you will want to use the movie title, entered as a short line, as the key. Even though the titles are followed by a hard return, the paragraph description below them will be moved when the document is sorted. This is because WordPerfect's paragraph sort marks the information to be re-arranged by at least *two* hard returns, one to end the paragraph and another to enter a blank line. Because the movie titles are terminated by a single hard return, WordPerfect considers them and their paragraph descriptions as a single unit for purposes of sorting.

To begin the paragraph sort operation, you mark the paragraphs (assume that just this group of movies beginning with the letter C is to be sorted) and press Ctrl-F9. When WordPerfect opens the Sort window, it will still be set to Line Sort, the program default selection. In addition, if you have done any previous sorting during

```
                          Vacation Accrual
                        Departments 10 - 12

    ID      Last        First     M    Dept    Date        Vacation
    No.     Name        Name      I    Code    Hired       Days

    1324    Carrington  Neil      T.   10      03-02-86      7.1
    1415    Watson      Sean      A.   10      07-05-85     14.3
     534    Drew        Mary      J.   10      03-24-81     26.4
    1325    Smith       Mary      A.   11      03-05-86      7.1
    1004    Nelson      Steven    F.   11      06-02-84     14.3
     788    Kaye        Peter     A.   11      05-16-82     29.4
    1323    Wadsworth   Sharon    G.   12      01-04-86      7.1
    1407    Farner      Kenneth   E.   12      04-20-85     14.3
    1073    Smith       Thomas    A.   12      10-03-83     14.3
    1066    Olsen       Phillis   G.   12      04-17-83     26.4
     233    Smith       Sandra    B.   12      02-16-80     31.4

                           Table 6.2



    C:\WP\WPB\VACATION                    Doc 2  Pg 1  Ln 8      Pos 10
```

FIGURE 10.7: The vacation accrual table after the records were sorted by department number and vacation days accrued. Now the records in this table are in ascending order by department number and vacation days. Because this sort was applied only to the records in the table and not to the entire file, none of the headings were disturbed by this operation.

```
The Clairvoyant
TV reporter sets out to find the truth when a psychic art student
draws sketches of three murder victims before their gruesome
murders. R-Language, violence. (1983). June 20.

Cocoon
Ron Howard's heartwarming look at age and extraterrestrials. Don
Ameche won the Academy Award for Best Supporting Actor for his
portrayal of the leader of a "geriatric set" in search of the
"fountain of youth." PG13-Language. (1985) June 1, 9.

The Candidate
Robert Redford stars as an ambitious young lawyer who runs for
senator and, in the process, alienates his wife and finds himself
alienated from his own views on the world. PG. (1972). June 15.

Camelot
Lerner and Loewe's acclaimed musical with Richard Harris as the
ill-fated King Arthur of the Round Table. G. (1967) June 18.

Cimmarron
Heroic family adventure set during the last days of the American
frontier. Based on Edna Ferber's great novel of the same name.
With Irene Dune. PG. (1931). June 3, 6.
A:\GUIDE                                    Doc 1  Pg 1  Ln 1      Pos 10
```

FIGURE 10.8: Movie descriptions before sorting with the Paragraph Sort feature. The descriptions, including their titles and accompanying paragraphs, are each separated by two hard returns. The first return marks the end of the paragraph, and the second enters a blank line separating one paragraph from the next.

the work session, the key settings for the last sort that you defined will still be displayed (WordPerfect remembers all sort settings until you exit the program).

To change the type of sort from Line to Paragraph Sort, you select option 7 (Type) and select option 3 (Paragraph Sort). When you do this, you will see Paragraph Sort listed under the heading *Type of Sort,* and Sort by Paragraph displayed between the line of hyphens under the ruler line demarcating the windows.

The key definition columns are slightly different for a paragraph sort than for a line sort. In addition to the three columns of information, Typ, Field, and Word, the paragraph sort also has a fourth column, Line. The definition for the first key is

Key	Typ	Line	Field	Word
1	a	1	1	1

When you define a key for paragraph sorting, you not only designate the number of the field (marked by tab settings just as when you perform a line sort) and the word, but also the number of the line that is to be used. Paragraph lines are counted sequentially from the first line of the paragraph (below the blank line containing the second hard return) to the last line of the paragraph (containing the first hard return and immediately above the blank line containing the second hard return).

Reverse Field Sorting

To sort the movie descriptions by title, you need to define only a single key. For this key, you will use line 1 and field 1 (the default settings). To order these titles correctly, you will want WordPerfect to ignore the definite article *The* whenever it occurs first in a movie title (so that *The Candidate* precedes *Cimmarron*, and *The Clairvoyant* precedes *Cocoon*). WordPerfect will not do this if you use 1 as the Word setting. It will observe a strict alphabetical order for the first word in each title, thus placing *The Candidate* and *The Clairvoyant* at the end of the document.

To get around this problem, you can use WordPerfect's reverse field sorting. In this type of sorting, you designate the word to be used in a particular field by entering the Word setting as a negative value. This tells WordPerfect to reverse the word count order; instead of counting from left to right from the beginning of the field, WordPerfect counts from right to left from the end of the field. The number you enter before the minus sign tells WordPerfect how many words to advance to the right. When you apply reverse field sorting to a specific field in a line or paragraph sort, WordPerfect counts backward from the end of the field, advancing right one word (a word must be marked by spaces) for each number after the minus sign.

For example, entering − **1** as the Word setting when defining the key for this paragraph sort tells WordPerfect to use the first Word to the right of the end of field 1. When the movie title consists of just a single word, this amounts to the same thing as designating 1 as the Word setting. However, when the title contains two words, *The* followed by the movie's name, the program uses the second word (the movie's name) instead of the first word (*The*) in the first field of the first line of each paragraph.

> *Note:* You can use reverse word order in this way only when the word you want used as the key appears in all fields in the same relative position when counted from right to left. In other words, it works in the preceding example because the name of the movie (starting with *C*) is always picked up by the − 1 setting, whether or not its title is preceded by an article. However, if the movie *Citizen Kane* was included in the descriptions, this technique would not work for it. The − 1 setting would tell WordPerfect to sort its paragraph by the word *Kane* instead of *Citizen,* thus placing the movie's description at the very end of the sorted titles beginning with the letter *C.*

Figure 10.9 shows the final definition for key 1 required to sort the movie descriptions in the correct alphabetical order. Figure 10.10 shows the descriptions after they have been sorted using this key. Notice that because reverse field sorting was used to define the word to be used in line and field 1, the movie titles and their summaries are in the proper order, even when the titles begin with *The.*

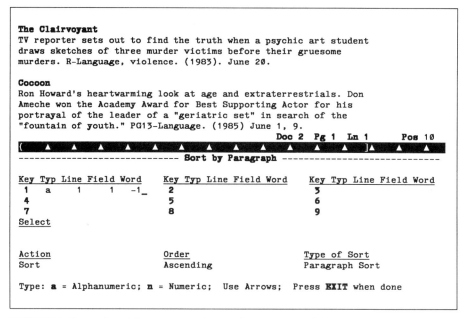

```
The Clairvoyant
TV reporter sets out to find the truth when a psychic art student
draws sketches of three murder victims before their gruesome
murders. R-Language, violence. (1983). June 20.

Cocoon
Ron Howard's heartwarming look at age and extraterrestrials. Don
Ameche won the Academy Award for Best Supporting Actor for his
portrayal of the leader of a "geriatric set" in search of the
"fountain of youth." PG13-Language. (1985) June 1, 9.
                                        Doc 2  Pg 1  Ln 1        Pos 10
( ▲   ▲   ▲   ▲   ▲   ▲   ▲   ▲   ▲   ▲   ▲   ▲  ]▲   ▲   ▲
-------------------------------- Sort by Paragraph ---------------------------

Key Typ Line Field Word    Key Typ Line Field Word    Key Typ Line Field Word
 1   a    1     1    -1_     2                          3
 4                           5                          6
 7                           8                          9
Select


Action                     Order                       Type of Sort
Sort                       Ascending                   Paragraph Sort

Type: a = Alphanumeric; n = Numeric;  Use Arrows;  Press EXIT when done
```

FIGURE 10.9: The sort key definition required to sort the paragraphs alphabetically by movie title. In order to sort the movie descriptions by the part of their names that begins with the letter *C,* ignoring the article *The* at the beginning of a title, the Word number is specified as −1. This tells the program to count each word from right to left from the end of the field (see the accompanying text for an explanation of how this works).

THE MERGE SORT

As useful as you will find WordPerfect's line and paragraph sorting, if your work involves mail merge operations, you will undoubtedly come to rely upon WordPerfect's third kind of sort, the merge sort. This type of sorting is designed to be used only with secondary merge files. It recognizes individual fields within the records by Merge R codes and individual records within the file by Merge E codes (see Chapter 9).

When you define the sort keys for merge sort, just like when you define them for a paragraph sort, WordPerfect allows you to designate the type as either *a* or *n,* as well as the number of the field, the number of the line in the field, and the number of the word to use within the field. The only difference between defining a key for a merge sort and for a paragraph sort is that in a merge sort, the field number column precedes the line number column.

In a merge sort, the field number is equivalent to the number you would use to designate the field in a primary document. You change the line number from the default setting of 1 only when the field consists of multiple lines terminated by hard returns but not Merge R codes.

```
Camelot
Lerner and Loewe's acclaimed musical with Richard Harris as the
ill-fated King Arthur of the Round Table. G. (1967) June 18.

The Candidate
Robert Redford stars as an ambitious young lawyer who runs for
senator and, in the process, alienates his wife and finds himself
alienated from his own views on the world. PG. (1972). June 15.

Cimmarron
Heroic family adventure set during the last days of the American
frontier. Based on Edna Ferber's great novel of the same name.
With Irene Dune. PG. (1931). June 3, 6.

The Clairvoyant
TV reporter sets out to find the truth when a psychic art student
draws sketches of three murder victims before their gruesome
murders. R-Language, violence. (1983). June 20.

Cocoon
Ron Howard's heartwarming look at age and extraterrestrials. Don
Ameche won the Academy Award for Best Supporting Actor for his
portrayal of the leader of a "geriatric set" in search of the
"fountain of youth." PG13-Language. (1985) June 1, 9.
A:\GUIDE                                    Doc 1  Pg 1  Ln 1        Pos 10
```

FIGURE 10.10: Movie descriptions sorted with the paragraph sort. Notice that because reverse field sorting (− 1) was used in the Word setting, the movie descriptions are now arranged in proper order; any occurrence of *The* as the first word in the title was ignored in the sort operation.

To select merge sorting, you select option 7 (Type) from the Sort menu and enter **1** (Merge Sort). The default settings for key 1 will appear as follows (unless you have changed the key settings previously in the same work session):

Key	Typ	Field	Line	Word
1	a	1	1	1

You can perform a merge sort on just a particular set of records by marking them as a block or on the entire secondary merge file. Usually you will perform a merge sort on the contents of the entire secondary file. This is an occasion when you might want to output the results of the sort not to the screen but, rather, to a new file. Also, if your secondary file is quite large, you may have to designate the name of the secondary file as the input file to be sorted and then enter a new file name in which to save the sorted results, thus completely bypassing on-screen sorting.

Figure 10.11 shows the first few records of the client secondary file (used in the merge examples in Chapter 9) before any of its records have been sorted.

Note: The first dummy record identifying the field numbers and names has been removed to prevent its being sorted along with the actual records.

```
ABC Contracting^R
1345 Seventh Street^R
^R
Berkeley, CA  94707^R
Jim^R
Wagoner^R
Mr.^R
^E
Speedo Printing^R
221 Avenue of the Americas^R
Suite 456^R
San Francisco, CA  94111^R
Allan^R
Grill^R
Mr.^R
^E
Freasir Toys^R
4506 South Landis Street^R
^R
Port Costa, CA  95607^R
Grace^R
Freasir^R
Ms.^R
^E
C:\WP\WPB\CLIENT.SF                    Doc 2  Pg 1  Ln 1      Pos 10
```

FIGURE 10.11: The first few records of the client secondary merge file before sorting. In sorting these records, fields are counted by Merge R codes (^R) just as they are when fields are inserted into a primary merge file.

To sort these records in alphabetical order by company name, you use the merge sort with the first key set to the default values. By default, an alphanumeric sort is performed using the first word in the first line of the first field. The first field in the secondary file contains the name of the company. Because the first field of this file contains only one line, the Line setting is left at 1, and because the first word of the company name is the most significant, the Word setting is left at 1.

Figure 10.12 shows the results of this sort. If you scroll through this file, you will find only one record that is not in its proper order: that of The Consulting Group. Because the first word (*The*) of the company field was used, this company is placed after Speedo Printing instead of after ABC Contracting where it belongs. To rectify this, you must use WordPerfect's Move command to move the record (including its Merge E code) to the appropriate position. You cannot use WordPerfect's Sort feature to have this done automatically (reverse field sorting will not work in this situation).

If you wanted to use this secondary file in a mail merge operation, you would probably want to resort it, this time ordering its records by zip code. To do this, you would use another merge sort, this time defining the zip code as the key. In

```
ABC Contracting^R
1345 Seventh Street^R
^R
Berkeley, CA  94707^R
Jim^R
Wagoner^R
Mr.^R
^E
Fine Stationary^R
345 Alder Lane^R
^R
Northridge, CA 95670^R
Gene^R
Johnson^R
Mr.^R
^E
Freasir Toys^R
4506 South Landis Street^R
^R
Port Costa, CA  95607^R
Grace^R
Freasir^R
Ms.^R
^E
C:\WP\WPB\CLIENT.SF                    Doc 2  Pg 1  Ln 1       Pos 10
```

FIGURE 10.12: The first part of the client secondary file after its records have been sorted alphabetically by company name. To accomplish this sort, only a primary key (key 1)—the first word in field 1—needed to be defined. This sorted the records by the first name of each company.

these records, the zip code is always the last word in the fourth field. You would then define the first sort key, using reverse field sorting, as follows:

Key	Typ	Field	Line	Word
1	a	4	1	−1

When the sort has been performed and the secondary file is used in a mail merge operation, each form letter and mailing label will be generated in ascending order by zip code, making it easier to bundle and send a mass mailing.

SELECTING RECORDS

WordPerfect's Select feature can be used to restrict a sort to just those records that meet specific conditions. Usually you will need to use the Select feature when performing a merge sort, although it is possible to use it when performing a line or paragraph sort.

Using Simple Conditions to Sort and Select Records

When you set up the conditions by which records are selected, you specify the number key followed by the condition that must be met. You construct this condition using one of the logical operators recognized by WordPerfect. Table 10.1 shows you the special symbols and logical operators used by WordPerfect when setting up conditions for the Select feature.

For the select operation to work, you must have already defined the key (using option 3 on the Sort menu) before you enter a selection condition. If you have not previously defined the key, you will receive the error message "ERROR: Key not defined" after you construct the condition.

To set up a selection condition after you have defined all of the sort keys, you choose option 4 (Select) from the Sort menu. The cursor then moves to the first position below the heading *Select,* where you enter the condition. When you enter your condition, you do not need to enter spaces between the operators that you use, although you can enter them if they make the condition easier for you to read. (However, when you use a two-character logical operator such as $>$ = , $<$ = , or $<>$, do *not* follow it with a space, or an error message will appear.)

The first part of the condition always consists of the word *key* followed by the number of the sort key that the selection is to be applied to. Then you enter a logical operator symbol followed by the value that sets the condition. This value can

SYMBOL	FUNCTION	EXAMPLE
=	Equal to	key1 = IL
< >	Not equal to	key1 < >CA
>	Greater than	key1 >M
<	Less than	key2 <50.00
> =	Greater than or equal to	key1 > =74500
< =	Less than or equal to	key2 < =H
*	Logical AND	key1 = IL * key2 <60600
+	Logical OR	key1 = IL + key3 >1000.00
g	Global selection	keyg = Mary

TABLE 10.1: Symbols and Logical Operators Used in Selecting Records

be a number or letter if you are using an alphanumeric sort, or any numeric value if you are using a numeric sort.

For example, if you want to sort and include only those records in the client secondary file with a zip code greater than or equal to 94500, you first set the type of sort to Merge Sort (option 7 and 1). Then you set the first key to sort by zip code by selecting option 3 (Keys) and entering the following values:

Key	Typ	Field	Line	Word
1	a	4	1	−1

Finally, you select option 4 (Select) and enter the following condition for key 1:

key1 > = 94500

You press F7 to return to the Sort menu.

As soon as you press F7, the action on the Merge Sort screen changes from Sort to Select and Sort. When you select option 1 (Perform Action), WordPerfect not only sorts all of the records with zip codes 94500 or higher, but it also eliminates from the file any records with zip codes lower than 94500.

Figure 10.13 shows the first part of the client secondary file after this sort and select operation. Notice that only records with zip codes 94500 or higher appear here, and that all of the records visible are properly sorted according zip code.

Using Compound Conditions to Sort and Select Records

When you prepare selection conditions, you can create compound conditions by using the logical AND and OR operators between simple conditions. WordPerfect uses the * (asterisk) as the AND logical operator and the + (plus sign) as the OR logical operator. Be careful that you use *, *not* +, to mean AND when you set up compound conditions.

When you set up a compound AND condition, both parts of the condition must be met. For example, if you want to restrict the sorted records to those with zip codes between 94500 and 94800, you can enter this compound condition using the AND logical operator (*) as follows:

key1 > = 94500 * key1 < = 94800

This statement means "select only those records with zip codes (defined in key 1) greater than or equal to 94500 *and* less than or equal to 94800." When the sort and select operation is performed, WordPerfect will sort only those records with zip codes between, and including, these values. All other records will be discarded.

You can also create compound conditions using the OR logical operator to join simple conditions. For example, suppose you want to use only those records with state fields OR, CA, and WA in a mailmerge operation. To select these

```
Meyer & Associates^R
1456 Franklin Street^R
#1201^R
Oakland, CA 94600^R
Judy^R
McDonald^R
Ms.^R
^E
Lauder and Sons^R
45 South Pickett Avenue^R
#45^R
Berkeley, CA 94702^R
Jennifer^R
Hawkins^R
Mrs.^R
^E
ABC Contracting^R
1345 Seventh Street^R
^R
Berkeley, CA 94707^R
Jim^R
Wagoner^R
Mr.^R
^E
C:\WP\WPB\CLIENT1.SF                    Doc 2  Pg 1  Ln 1      Pos 10
```

FIGURE 10.13: The first part of the client secondary file after the records have been selected and sorted by zip code greater than or equal to 94500. Notice that no records with zip codes below 94500 now appear in this file. Also notice that the records visible in this figure (those with zip codes above 94500) are now sorted in strict zip code order.

records and sort them by zip code, you would still use the zip code field as the primary key, but in addition, you would define a second key for the state field. This key will not affect the outcome of the sort; it simply allows you to set up a select condition).

After defining these two keys, you would enter the following compound select condition, using simple conditions referring to key 2, which defines the state field, separated by the OR logical operator (+):

key2 = OR + key2 = CA + key2 = WA

This statement means "select only those records with the state (defined in key 2) defined as OR *or* CA *or* WA." When these records are selected, they are still sorted by the primary key, defined as the zip code.

The foregoing examples have all used the same key number in the compound conditions. This does not have to be the case. You can set conditions in which, for example, a value must be met or exceeded in one key field as well as be equal to another value in a second field. For example, if you have a secondary file that tracks the credit limit of your customers as well as address information, you can set up a condition selecting only records with a credit limit of $2,500.00 or more and the state field defined as New York. Assuming that you have defined the state field as key 1 and the credit limit field as key 2, you enter the select statement as

key1 = NY * key2 > = 2500.00

This statement means "select only those records with the state (defined in key 1) defined as NY *and* the credit limit (defined in key 2) greater than or equal to $2,500.00." Remember that because the credit limit field contains dollars and cents (fractional numbers), you set the sort type for key 2 to *n* (for numeric).

Sometimes when constructing compound conditions, you will have to use parentheses to adjust the phrasing of the simple conditions. WordPerfect evaluates selection conditions from left to right. To have WordPerfect evaluate a pair of simple conditions as a unit before it evaluates other conditions in the statement, you enclose the pair in parentheses. For instance, if you want to expand the selection conditions cited in the last example to choose the records in which the state is either New York or Massachusetts and the credit limit is between $2,500.00 and $5,000.00, you enter the following compound statement:

(key1 = NY + key1 = MA) * key2 > = 2500.00 * key2 < = 5000.00

This statement means "select only those records in which the state (defined in key 1) is either NY *or* MA, *and in either case,* in which the credit limit (defined in key 2) is greater than or equal to $2,500.00 *and* less than or equal to $5,000.00." Without the parentheses around the first OR condition of the statement, WordPerfect would interpret the statement to mean "select only those records in which the state is NY (and the credit limit is anything) *or* in which the state is MA *and* the credit limit (for the MA records only) is between $2,500.00 and $5,000.00." The AND condition defining the range for the credit limit would be applied to only those customers who live in Massachusetts. When creating complex compound conditions, you should consider the phrasing of your statement if the records are not selected as you intended.

Performing a Global Selection Operation

In addition to the operators illustrated in the previous examples, there is one more special character that you should be familiar with. This is the global selection character, g. You enter the g in place of a key number as **keyg.** Unlike all other situations in which you use the Select command, when you use keyg, you do not need to have previously defined any sort keys.

The global selection character instructs WordPerfect to select all records where the condition following keyg is met, regardless of the field. For example, the statement

keyg = Smith

selects all records in which *Smith* occurs in any field of the secondary file. It selects the record if *Smith* is the second word in the company name (as in The Smith Company), if *Smith* is the surname in the contact name field, and so on.

When you have performed a sort and select operation, you will probably want to save the results in a new file. If you did not change the default sort output setting from (Screen) to a new file name when you began the sort operation, you can still save the results in a new file by pressing F7, typing **Y,** and then editing the suggested file name before pressing Return. Then you can use the records in this new file whenever you need to in your merge operations.

Selecting Records without Sorting Them

Usually you will want to sort the records at the same time that you select them. However, if this is not the case, you can have WordPerfect select just the records that meet your conditions without sorting them. To do this, you define your keys and selection conditions just as you do when you both sort and select records. However, after you have finished both these steps and have returned to the Sort menu, you select option 5 (Action). When you choose this option, you are presented with two menu options:

Action: 1 Select and Sort; 2 Select Only: 0

To select just the records meeting the conditions you have set, you select option 2. As soon as you choose this option, you are returned to the Merge Sort screen. Beneath the Action heading, you will see that the word *Select* has replaced the words *Sort and Select.* When you select option 1 (Perform Action) from the Sort menu, WordPerfect eliminates from the file all records that do not meet the selection conditions. However, those records that remain will still be in the same order as they were before you executed the select-only operation.

USING THE SORT COMMANDS

KEY SEQUENCE

File Sort
To sort a file:
Ctrl-F9 2
To select the input file to sort:
(Screen) **Return** or *<name of file to sort>* **Return**

To select the output file for sort:

(Screen) **Return** or *<name of sorted file to create>* **Return**

To select the sort type:

7 (Type) **1** (Merge Sort) or **2** (Line Sort) or **3** (Paragraph Sort)

To scroll through the records before sorting:

2 (View) **F7**

To select the sort keys:

3 (Keys) Typ **a** (alphanumeric) or **n** (numeric)

<field number> <line number (for paragraph and merge sort)*>*

<word number (for all keys)*> F7*

To change the sort order:

6 (Order) **1** (Ascending) or **2** (Descending)

To select the records to be sorted:

4 (Select) **keyn** *<condition>* **F7** *(Note:* n represents the number of a key previously defined with option 3, Keys.)

To perform the sort operation as defined:

1 (Perform Action)

Block Sort

To sort a block:

Alt-F4 (highlight block with cursor keys) **Ctrl-F9**

To select the sort type:

7 (Type) **1** (Merge Sort) or **2** (Line Sort) or **3** (Paragraph Sort)

To scroll through the records before sorting:

2 (View) **F7**

To select the sort keys:

3 (Keys) Typ **a** (alphanumeric) or **n** (numeric)

<field number> <line number (for paragraph and merge sort)*>*

<word number (for all keys)*> **F7***

To change the sort order to descending:

6 (Order) **1** (Ascending) or **2** (Descending)

To select the records to be sorted:

4 (Select) **keyn** *<condition>* **F7** *(Note:* n represents the number of a key previously defined with option 3, Keys.)

To perform the sort operation as defined:

1 (Perform Action)

Sort Sequence

To modify the sorting sequence:
    Ctrl-F9 3 1 (for US/European) or **2** (for Scandinavian) **0** (or **Return**)

Conditional Sort

To select specific records from a file (without sorting):
    Ctrl-F9 2
To select input file to sort:
    (Screen) **Return** or <*name of file to use*> **Return**
Output file for sort:
    (Screen) **Return** or <*name of file to create*> **Return**
To select the sort keys:
    3 (Keys) Typ **a** (alphanumeric) or **n** (numeric)
    <*field number*> <*line number* (for paragraph and merge sort)>
        <*word number* (for all keys)> **F7**
To enter the selection condition:
    4 (Select) **keyn** <*condition*> **F7** (*Note:* n represents the number of a key
        previously defined with option 3, Keys.)
To restrict to selection only:
    5 (Action) **2** (Select Only)
To perform the select operation as defined:
    1 (Perform Action)

    WordPerfect's Sort feature allows you to perform three kinds of sorting. Each
kind calls for its own special formatting:

- For a line sort, data is organized into columns and rows, as in a spreadsheet.
  Each row forms a record, and each column is separated by a tab setting.

- For a paragraph sort, the data to be sorted is separated by two (or more)
  hard returns or a hard page break (Ctrl-Return).

- For a merge sort, the data is arranged in the same field and record format
  as used in a secondary merge file. In this format, each field is terminated
  by a Merge R (^R) code, and each record in the file is terminated by a
  Merge E (^E) code.

Accessing the Sort Command

To sort a file by any of these three methods, you press Ctrl-F9 (Merge/Sort) and select option 2 (Sort). You will then be prompted for the name of the input file to sort. WordPerfect will suggest the default selection (Screen). If you press Return to accept this selection, WordPerfect will sort the file in memory. If you wish, instead, to sort a file on disk, you enter the complete file name and press Return.

After indicating the source of the data to be sorted, you are prompted to indicate where you want the sorted data output. Again, WordPerfect will suggest (Screen) as the output destination. If you wish to save the data in a disk file, you enter the file name before you press Return.

Selecting the Type of Sort

After you indicate the source and destination of the sort, you are presented with the Sort by Line screen. Sort by Line is the default sort type. At the bottom of this screen, you will see the following sort options:

1 Perform Action; 2 View; 3 Keys; 4 Select; 5 Action; 6 Order; 7 Type: 0

If you wish to perform a different kind of sort, select option 7 (Type). When you do, you are presented with these options:

Sorting Type: 1 Merge; 2 Line; 3 Paragraph: 0

To select Merge Sort, enter **1.** To select Paragraph Sort, enter **3.** Whenever you change the type of sort using these options, the new type is displayed on the sorting screen beneath the heading *Type of Sort,* and between the line of hyphens immediately below the ruler line.

Defining the Sort Order

The default sorting order used by WordPerfect is ascending. WordPerfect uses a sort order in which special characters and numbers precede letters, all arranged in ascending order (regardless of case). If you wish to change the sort order to descending, select option 6 (Order) from the Sort menu. When you do, you are presented with these options:

Sorting Order: 1 Ascending; 2 Descending: 0

To change the sort order from ascending to descending, select option 2. To change the order from descending to ascending, select option 1. WordPerfect always lets you know the order that is in effect on the sorting screen. Either Ascending or Descending is listed below the heading *Order* above the sorting menu options.

Defining the Sort Keys

To sort data in a file, you must designate the key, or keys, on which to sort it. WordPerfect lets you define up to nine keys for any one sorting operation. If all of the data in the field you will be using as the key is unique, you do not need to define more than one key. However, if the data include duplicate items, you may want to define another key that determines their order in the file.

To define the sort key, or keys, to be used, you select option 3 (Keys) from the Sort menu. WordPerfect places the cursor in the Typ column of the first key. It also fills in default values for this first key, which you can modify. To move the cursor to a new column of a key or to a new key, you press Return or the → key. If you have filled in several keys, you can use any the four cursor movement key to move back to a previously defined key.

When you define a sort key, you begin by defining the type of data that will be sorted as either alphanumeric (consisting of both text and numbers) or numeric (numbers only). WordPerfect always supplies the default setting *a* (for alphanumeric). To change this setting to numeric, you merely type **n** over the *a* (the editor is not in Insert mode).

Use the numeric setting only when all the data in the field you are using as the key consists of numbers. Note that if the data consists of integers (whole numbers) only, and all data items are of equal length, you can use either the numeric or alphanumeric setting. However, if the data in the key field contains fractional numbers (in decimal form) or numbers of unequal length, you must use numeric setting.

Besides the type of data, you must indicate which data field is to be used as the key. How you define this field depends upon the type of sort you want to perform. When you perform a line sort, you must designate the number of the field and, further, the number of the word within the field to be used. In a line sort, each field must be separated by either a tab or a specific indent.

Fields are numbered beginning with 1 from left to right across the line. Likewise, words are numbered beginning with 1 from left to right across the field (column). However, you can also indicate the position of a word by a negative number. When you preface an integer with a minus sign, WordPerfect counts the words from right to left from the end of the field. This is referred to as reverse field sorting (for applications for this type of sorting, see ''Reverse Field Sorting'' earlier in the chapter).

WordPerfect considers an item of text as an individual word only if it is separated by spaces. WordPerfect considers any text items joined by hyphens, slashes, or some other kind of punctuation to be a single word for purposes of sorting. If the field that you are using as the key contains only one word, you leave the number of the word set at 1. However, if the field contains more than one word, such as the first and last name of each employee, you designate which word is to be used by entering its position number.

When you perform a paragraph sort, in addition to designating the number of the field and the number of the word in the field, you must also designate the number of the line to be used. WordPerfect counts line numbers starting with 1 for the first line of the paragraph (denoted by two hard returns or a hard page break before it) and ending with the last line in the paragraph (denoted by two hard returns or a hard page break following it).

In a paragraph sort, the number of the field is always 1 unless you have entered separate columns of information within the paragraph separated by a tab or indent. When specifying the number of the word, you count beginning with 1 from left to right across the line. You can also use reverse field sorting for a paragraph sort by entering a negative value when defining the sort key.

When defining the keys for a merge sort, you enter the field, line, and word numbers just as you do for a paragraph sort. Because a merge sort is used with a secondary merge file, each field is marked by a Merge R code (^ R). The end of each record is marked by a Merge E code (^ E). The fields are numbered from 1, just as they are when they are used in a primary merge document (sequentially down the page until the Merge E code is reached). If some fields in your secondary merge file use more than one line (lines terminated by hard returns instead of Merge R codes), you may have to adjust the line number when defining the key. The number of the word in each field is counted just as it is for a line or paragraph sort.

When defining a sort operation, you can use the View option (2) on the Sort menu to scroll through the data in the document any time before you perform the sort operation. When scrolling through the data, you can use any cursor movement key or key combination that you normally use to move through a document. However, you cannot edit data when using the View option (this option works exactly like the Look option on the List Files menu). To return to the Sort screen, you press F7 (Exit).

When you have defined the type of sort, the sort order, and the sort keys to be used, you select option 1 (Perform Action) to sort your data. Before you do any sorting, you should always save a copy of your document. That way, you will have an unsorted version of the file to use should you make any errors in defining the sort operation. As soon as WordPerfect has sorted your data, the Sort window will disappear, and you will be returned to the full-screen document window.

Block Sorting

To sort only part of the data in a file, you need to first mark the data to be included in the sort as a block. To do this, move the cursor to the first character to be included, press Alt-F4 (Block), and use the appropriate cursor movement keys to highlight the rest of the data you want sorted.

When marking the data to be included in a line sort, be careful not to include any column headings that you may have entered to identify the data in the table. After the block is properly marked, press Ctrl-F9 (Merge/Sort). The Sort by Line screen will appear. You can then define the type of sort, order, and keys just as when you sort the contents of an entire file (see the previous section for details).

Selecting the Records to Be Sorted

WordPerfect also allows you to set up conditions that select the records to be sorted. To use the Select feature, you must first define the sort keys that you wish to use. Then select option 4 (Select) from the Sort menu. The cursor will be placed beneath the Select column heading. There, you enter the condition that must be met followed by the number of the key to which the condition is applied. When entering the condition, you separate the key number by the appropriate logical operator (see Table 10.1), followed by a value.

For example, to select and sort only records in which the last name begins with any letter *M* through *Z,* you define the last-name field as the key. If the key number is 1, you enter this selection condition as follows:

key1> = M

Notice that the word *key* precedes the key number, and that spaces are not entered between the elements of the condition. You can enter spaces between parts of a condition if you prefer.

You can also enter numerical conditions, provided that the field contains numbers (in some cases, you must also set the type of field to *n*). For instance, if key 2 is the amount-due field, you can select and sort just the records in which the amount due is greater than $500.00 by entering

key2>500.00

WordPerfect allows you to construct compound conditions by separating simple conditions with either * (asterisk) for AND or + (plus) for OR. To select and sort the records in which the amount due is between $650.00 and $2,500.00, you enter

key2> = 650.00 * key2< = 2500.00

WordPerfect also allows you to perform a global selection. To do this, you do not enter a key number, but instead, you enter **keyg** followed by the condition. When you use keyg, WordPerfect selects all records in the file, in any field (not just those used in defining keys) in which the condition is met. For example, to select and sort all records in which the word *Illinois* occurs, you enter

keyg = Illinois

When you perform the sort operation, WordPerfect selects all records in which *Illinois* occurs anywhere in any of its fields. For instance, it will select the record if *Illinois* occurs in the address field, the state field, or even the company-name field. (For more examples of selection conditions and more information about using logical operators, refer to "Selecting Records" earlier in this chapter.)

After you enter your selection condition, press F7 (Exit) to return to the Sort menu. Select option 1 (Perform Action) to have WordPerfect select and sort your records. When you enter a sort condition, WordPerfect retains it (as well as any key definitions) for the duration of your work session. If, later in the same session, you wish to perform a sort operation that does not require the selection condition, be sure to choose the Select option and delete the existing condition (use the Del key) before you choose the Perform Action option.

WordPerfect also lets you just select records without sorting them. To do this, you still must define the necessary keys and enter the selection condition as previously described. However, before you select option 1 (Perform Action), you select option 5 (Action). When you do this, WordPerfect presents these options:

Action: 1 Select and Sort; 2 Select Only: 0

Select option 2 (Select Only). Then when you choose the Perform Action option, WordPerfect will eliminate all records that do not meet the selection condition, although their arrangement will be unchanged from the order in which they were originally entered.

Changing the Sorting Sequence

WordPerfect includes a sorting option that allows you to change the normal US/European sorting sequence used to Scandinavian. You use the Scandinavian sorting sequence when the data you want to sort contains foreign language characters, such as æ, Æ, ö, and ê.

To change the sorting sequence, you press Ctrl-F9 and select option 3 (Sorting Sequence). You are then presented with these options:

Sorting Sequence: 1 US/European; 2 Scandinavian: 0

To select the Scandinavian sorting sequence, choose option 2 from this menu. To return to the US/European sorting sequence (the normal dictionary sort order for languages using the Roman alphabet without any foreign-language characters), select option 1.

Note: The term *Scandinavian sorting sequence* is somewhat of a misnomer because in the English-language version of WordPerfect, the IBM extended character set cannot produce special characters like the thorn (equivalent to *th* at the beginning of a word) used by some Scandinavian languages. To produce the foreign-language characters available in the IBM extended character set, you can either enter their ASCII codes (see Appendix A) by pressing the Alt key and typing the code number from the 10-key numeric pad or assign the characters to various Ctrl-*letter* or Alt-*letter* key sequences (Ctrl-F3 3) and then enter them by pressing Ctrl or Alt and the appropriate letter key (see Chapter 11 for details).

SUMMARY

The data to which you apply WordPerfect's Sort and Select features always must be organized in your documents in some special way. To find information about how to format and enter the data you need to sort, you can refer to the following chapters.

- Chapter 3, "Editing Techniques," presents information about marking blocks of text.
- Chapter 4, "Page Formatting Techniques," presents information about setting up tables using tabs.
- Chapter 8, "Page Composition: Working with Text Columns," presents information about setting up tables with parallel columns.
- Chapter 9, "Merge Operations," presents information about setting up secondary merge files.
- Chapter 11, "Mathematics and Equations," presents information about setting up tables that contain calculations.
- Chapter 15, "Using WordPerfect with Other Software," presents information about importing data created in spreadsheet or database management programs either as tables or as records in a secondary merge file.

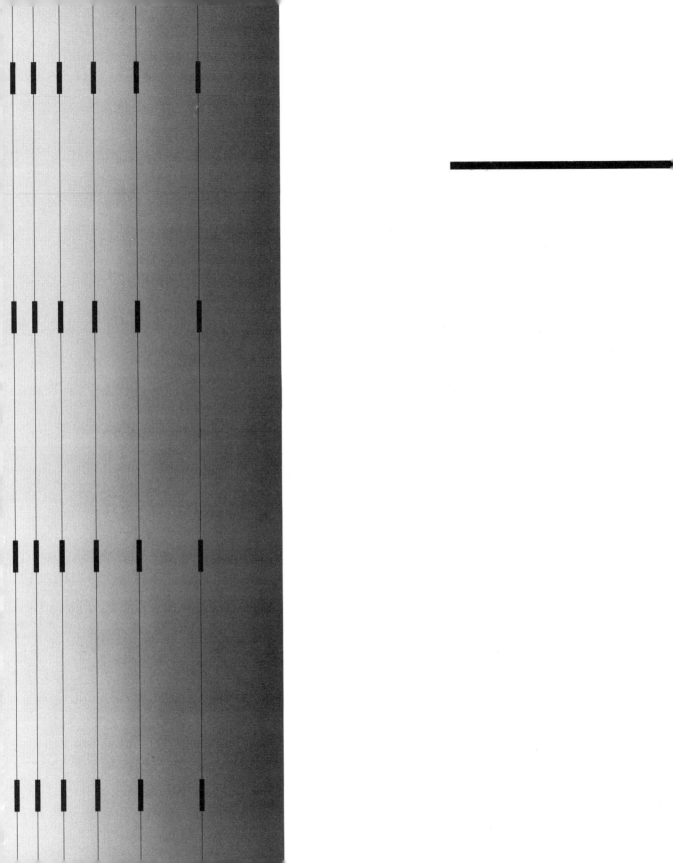

MATHEMATICS, EQUATIONS, AND SPECIAL SYMBOLS

MATHEMATICS, EQUATIONS, AND SPECIAL SYMBOLS

You can use WordPerfect as a calculator for simple mathematical functions such as addition, subtraction, multiplication, and division. The program can also calculate totals, subtotals, grand totals, and averages on numbers in columns. In addition, you can write formulas that perform mathematical operations on columns of numbers. Although these relatively simple mathematical functions cannot substitute for the capabilities a full-featured spreadsheet or database management program can give you, they can allow you to bring spreadsheet or database data into WordPerfect and manipulate it further—for example, to calculate percentages of change, extended totals, or discounts. If you do very many of these kinds of calculations in WordPerfect, you may want to obtain MathPlan, which is WordPerfect Corporation's spreadsheet program. MathPlan is completely compatible with WordPerfect; in fact, many of the key sequences are the same.

WordPerfect also offers features that simplify mathematical typing as well as special symbols such as foreign-language punctuation marks and currency symbols. This chapter explains how you can use all of these special features in the documents you create in WordPerfect.

USING WORDPERFECT'S MATHEMATICAL FEATURES

WordPerfect's mathematical features can be used in two basic ways:

- Without defining columns as special Math columns, you can calculate totals, subtotals, and grand totals for a column of numbers, as illustrated in Figure 11.1.
- If you define columns as Math columns, you can write formulas that perform specific computations across rows of columns.

In either case, you turn WordPerfect's Math mode on (Alt-F7, option 1) to perform calculations and then turn it off when you are finished calculating. When you are in Math mode (indicated by the Math prompt in the lower-left corner of the screen), the program works a little differently from when it is in other modes. First, when you enter text in Math mode, WordPerfect uses the decimal point as the alignment character. Characters that you type appear to the left of the cursor until you type a decimal point. Cutting columns of text while you are in Math mode also requires you to use a slightly different technique from the one used in normal text mode. In addition, there are certain restrictions you must be aware of when you define columns as Math columns so that the program will perform calculations accurately.

The following sections discuss general techniques for using WordPerfect's mathematical features and give you a few hints about using these techniques. For step-by-step procedures for each specific task, see the reference entries at the end of this chapter.

Working with Mathematics in WordPerfect

Without predefining columns as Math columns, you can calculate different types of totals for numbers. This feature is often useful when you have imported data that you want to total from a spreadsheet or database (see Chapter 15) or simply want to perform calculations on numbers you have entered into a document—in an order letter or invoice, for example.

```
Order Number        Amount

021389              $54.54
912670              $198.75
667120              $25.51

Subtotal            278.80+

From PO#4485        $t217.89

Total               496.69=_




Math                                    Doc 2  Pg 1  Ln 11    Pos 38
```

FIGURE 11.1: Performing calculations on simple columns of numbers. You can calculate totals, subtotals, and grand totals for columns of numbers without first defining the columns as special math columns. The *t*, +, and = symbols will not appear when the document is printed.

Setting Tabs for Math Columns

When Math mode is on, WordPerfect uses the decimal point as the alignment character. After you press Tab, characters that you type appear to the left of the cursor. Because of this, you may find it more convenient to first type in normal text mode any column headings you wish to use as labels and then define the columns that will be used in the Math portion of your document. With the headings in place on your screen, you can see more easily where to set tabs for your Math columns, as shown in Figure 11.2.

Math Column Definitions

You can define up to 24 columns (A through X) as Math columns and designate any four of them to contain formulas. Columns that contain formulas are called *calculation columns* (type 0); they will display the results of the calculations you specify when you tell WordPerfect to calculate. Calculated columns contain an exclamation point (!) until the program calculates results; they then display

```
Employee  Starting  $Increase  Current    %Increase
Number    Salary               Salary

4231      $26000    $9600      35,600.00!   26.97!
4423      $23500    $2000      25,500.00!    7.84!
4389      $22000    $3750      25,750.00!   14.56!
```

```
.................L........L.........L.........L.................................
0123456789012345678901234567890123456789012345678901234567890123456789012345678
       20        30        40        50        60        70        80
Delete EOL (clear tabs); Enter number (set tab); Del (clear tab);
Left; Center; Right; Decimal; .= Dot leader; Press EXIT when done.
```

FIGURE 11.2: Setting tabs for Math columns. When Math mode is on, whatever you enter is aligned at the tab setting. When you set up Math columns, be sure to clear all tabs on the line (by pressing Shift-F8 1 and then pressing Ctrl-End) and then set new ones at the positions where you want each column to end; otherwise, your columns will not align as you want them to. (The exclamation points in the figure indicate calculations that WordPerfect has made.)

results with an exclamation point next to them. These exclamation points do not appear when the document is printed.

You can define three other types of columns: *Numeric columns* (type 2) hold the data you wish to perform calculations on. WordPerfect defines all columns to be numeric columns when you turn Math mode on unless you specify otherwise. *Text columns* (type 1) contain labels or descriptions and are ignored in calculations. *Total columns* (type 3), which are a special type of calculated column, display subtotals, totals, and grand totals; you can use this type of column to display totals separately from the columns that hold the data, as illustrated in Figure 11.3.

WordPerfect performs subtraction by adding positive and negative numbers. When you define Math columns, you select how you want negative numbers to be displayed—either in parentheses—for example, (48.00)—or with a minus sign—for example, − 48.00. (Financial reports often use the parentheses convention.) Numbers that you enter in parentheses will be considered negative if you do not change the setting to a minus sign.

In Version 4.2 of WordPerfect, you can designate any number in a column to be considered negative when calculations are made by inserting an *N* before the number. This feature is often useful if you need to total a group of numbers and then subtract them from another group of numbers. You can total the first group

```
Order Number       Amount     Total

021389             54.54_
912670            198.75
667120             25.51

Subtotal          278.80+

From PO#4485      t217.89

Total                        496.69=




Math                                   Doc 2  Pg 1  Ln 3     Pos 37
```

FIGURE 11.3: Using a total column to display totals. You can use total columns to display selected subtotals, totals, and grand totals in separate columns instead of at the bottom of the column on which the calculations are made.

and then designate that total as negative (by inserting an *N* before it). From then on, that total will be considered a negative number in calculations.

Calculating Totals

WordPerfect allows you to calculate various types of totals, both within columns that have not been defined as Math columns and within Math columns as well. In addition, you can further define Math columns as total columns so that totals can be displayed in a column separate from the columns that hold the numbers they total.

The program uses the following operators:

- The plus sign (+) calculates the subtotal of all numbers that occur after the previous subtotal.
- The equal sign (=) totals all subtotals.
- The asterisk (*) totals all totals (calculates a grand total).

In addition, you can specify any number in the column to be considered as a subtotal by beginning it with a *t* or specify any number to be considered a total by beginning it with a *T*. This feature is useful when you are working with columns in which numbers have previously been totaled or subtotaled without using the + or = operators, as in Figure 11.4. You can specify those numbers to be included in any further grand totals, totals, or subtotals you calculate.

Version 4.2 of WordPerfect allows you to designate any number in a column to be considered a negative number (and therefore subtracted) when it is used in calculations. To do so, enter an *N* before the number. In earlier versions, you indicate a negative number only by either placing a minus sign (−) before it or enclosing it in parentheses.

Calculating Totals and Averages in Rows

WordPerfect's Math feature includes several built-in formulas that allow you to calculate totals and averages of rows of numbers in numeric (data) or total columns.

- The addition symbol (+) calculates the total of all the numbers in the row that are in numeric columns.
- The + / symbol calculates the average of all the numbers in the row that are in numeric columns.
- The = symbol calculates the total of all the numbers in the row that are in total columns.

```
Order Number        Amount     Total

021389              54.54
912670             198.75
667120              25.51

Credit             N50.00

Subtotal           228.80+

‾
From PO#4485       t217.89


Total                         446.69=




Math                                    Doc 2  Pg 1  Ln 10     Pos 10
```

FIGURE 11.4: Specifying a negative number in Version 4.2. The *N* before the credit amount indicates that the program should consider the following number to be negative. Because WordPerfect subtracts by adding positive and negative numbers, the credit amount is subtracted when the subtotal is calculated.

- The = / symbol calculates the average of all the numbers in the row that are in total columns.

These special operators work on numbers to their right and left across the entire row—not just on numbers to the left. If you are not aware of this, you can obtain confusing results.

Tips on Using WordPerfect's Math Feature

When you use WordPerfect's Math feature, be sure to delete all tab settings and set new ones before you begin. Even if you are using the Math feature only in its simplest form, the tab stops that are preset at every five spaces are too close together for most columns of numbers. WordPerfect considers whatever is between two tab stops to be a column, starting with the first tab stop. In other words, column A begins at the first tab stop, and what is typed at the left margin before a tab stop is set is not considered to be a column (see Figure 11.5). If you do not understand this distinction and write formulas involving columns, you may wind up with inaccurate results, because your column designations will not be correct.

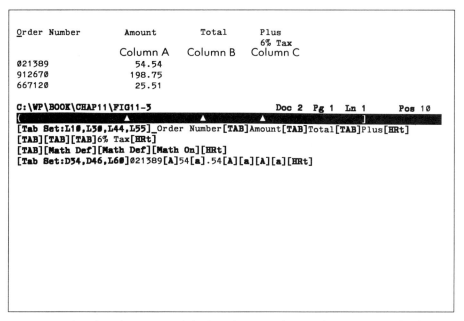

```
Order Number        Amount       Total      Plus
                                            6% Tax
                    Column A   Column B   Column C
021389                54.54
912670               198.75
667120                25.51


C:\WP\BOOK\CHAP11\FIG11-5                    Doc 2  Pg 1  Ln 1      Pos 10
(            ▲              ▲          ▲              ]
[Tab Set:L18,L38,L44,L55]_Order Number[TAB]Amount[TAB]Total[TAB]Plus[HRt]
[TAB][TAB][TAB]6% Tax[HRt]
[TAB][Math Def][Math Def][Math On][HRt]
[Tab Set:D34,D46,L68]021389[A]54[a].54[A][a][A][a][HRt]
```

FIGURE 11.5: The column beginning with the first tab stop is column A when you use WordPerfect's Math feature. When you use the Math feature, be sure first to clear all tab stops by pressing Shift-F8 (Line Format), selecting option 1 or 2 (Tabs), and pressing Ctrl-End; then set the new tab stops you want to use. Note that two different tab settings are used: one for the text headings and one for the math columns themselves. Tabs you set for math columns align on the decimal point (or whatever alignment character you specify), even though you may set them with the Tab key, which produces the **L** symbol (for left aligned) on the screen. WordPerfect's Align Char = prompt appears in the lower-left corner of the screen when you are in an area that the program considers to be a column.

When you use the Math feature, you need to remember a few general rules:

- Be sure to reset the tabs before you begin so that you will know which column is column A, which is column B, and so forth, and so that the columns will be wide enough for the numbers you are going to use.

- Sketch your columns on a sheet of paper so that you can keep track of which is column A, which is column B, and so forth, or label each column outside the [Math On] area as you work and delete the letter designator later. The columns themselves will not be visible when you use the Math Definition screen. Because column A does not always begin at the left margin (the first column on the screen) but instead begins at the first tab stop, it can be confusing to remember which column is which when you begin entering data.

- If you prefer, you can set Math tabs after you turn Math mode on. Press Alt-F3 to see the existing tab settings; then set new math tabs for your numerical columns. That way you can align math tabs with any column-heading tabs you may have set outside the Math area.

- If you reset any tabs while you are working—for example, if you realize you need to add a new column—be sure to press Alt-F3 (Reveal Codes) to check the placement of the new [Tab Set] code. WordPerfect uses the code that is closest to the data in your document.

- Do not enter any numbers that are to be calculated unless you see the Align Char = message in the lower-left corner of the screen. It indicates that you are in a column that the Math feature can operate on instead of in a column next to the left margin.

- When you write a formula that contains column letters as variables, do not use any spaces in the formula.

- WordPerfect performs calculations from left to right. To tell WordPerfect to calculate a sequence of operations first, enclose them in parentheses.

- In columns where calculated values are to appear (those columns that you define as calculated columns), WordPerfect will insert an exclamation point (!) when you press Tab to enter the column. Anything you enter into these columns will be disregarded, as they are to hold calculated values only. If you do not want a row in that column to be used in the calculation, delete the ! before you select option 2 (Calculate) from the Math/Columns menu (Alt-F7) when you turn Math mode on.

- If you have difficulty getting calculations to appear, it may be because you did not press Tab to enter each calculation column you defined before you pressed Alt-F7 (Math/Columns) and selected option 2 to calculate. Before you calculate, make sure that an exclamation point is visible in each column that is to hold calculations, including columns you have defined as totals columns. Also remember that you must be within the area defined as a math area—between the [Math On] and [Math Off] codes—in order to make calculations.

- Any time you change numbers in numeric columns or formulas in calculated columns or move, cut, or copy Math columns, be sure to recalculate your results by pressing Alt-F7 (Math/Columns) and selecting option 2 (Calculate). Option 2 will not appear as Calculate unless you are within the [Math On] area and can see the Math prompt in the lower-left corner of the screen.

- Once you have defined math columns (inserted a [MathDef] code into your document), that definition will be used each time you turn Math mode on, even if you are in a different part of your document, unless you specify another Math definition.

TYPING EQUATIONS

If your work requires you to do mathematical or statistical typing, you will find WordPerfect's several alternative methods for creating subscripts and superscripts and using special symbols very useful. The factor that determines which of WordPerfect's methods you use will probably be your printer. Although you can see on the screen all of the characters the IBM keyboard can generate, the printer you are using may not be able to print them all. In addition, some printers are not capable of reverse line feeds, which are required to use the Line Advance feature.

Before you begin to type equations, you should test your printer to find out what it is capable of, as is discussed in Chapter 5. If it will not produce the effects you want, you may wish to check your printer manual to see if you can adjust it in any way. For example, if your printer operates only with tractor feed, it may not produce enough friction to advance the paper the small amount required for sub- and superscripts. In such a case, you can try lowering the platen to increase the friction, or the printer may have a switch inside that you need to set.

If you run PRINTER.TST (described in Chapter 5) on your printer, you will be able to see which symbols your printer will not print. You may need to create these by using Overstrike (Shift-F1, option 3) instead of trying to generate them from their ASCII codes.

There are basically two aspects of mathematical typing that cause problems: line spacing and special symbols. WordPerfect offers several solutions to each, so you should pick the method that works best with the equipment you have.

Line Spacing in Mathematical Typing

When you write equations, you often need to use subscripts or superscripts that appear slightly above or below the baseline of the equation, as in the following formula:

$$\frac{X^2 \ = \ (n \ - \ 1)^n}{a_2}$$

In WordPerfect, there are three basic methods for creating these effects:

- Subscript and Superscript features (Shift-F1, options 1 and 2)
- Advance Up and Advance Down features (Shift-F1, options 4 and 5)
- Half-line spacing (Shift-F8 4)

In addition, if you write complex equations, you may wish to define an area of text for half-line spacing and then create the equation in Typeover mode within that area.

Each of these methods has advantages and disadvantages; in addition, some of these methods may not be suitable for use with your printer. Test each one with your printer before deciding which works best for you.

Using the Subscript and Superscript Features

You can use WordPerfect's Subscript and Superscript features (Shift-F1, options 1 and 2) to create sub- and superscripts directly. Different printers produce different effects when they print sub- and superscripts, so test your printer first to make sure it is capable of producing the effects you need. In WordPerfect, subscripts and superscripts are not displayed in their correct placement on the screen; you can only detect their presence by the letters S for superscript and s for subscript that appear on the screen when you create them or by viewing the Reveal Codes screen (Alt-F3), where subscripts appear as [SubScrpt] and superscripts appear as [SuprScrpt] (Figure 11.6).

If your printer does not print sub- and superscripts, or if you would like to be able to see an indication of them on the screen, you can use half-line spacing instead. With this method, you will need to place sub- and superscripts on separate lines. With half-line spacing, subscripts and superscripts appear on the screen a full line below or above the basic equation, although they actually will be

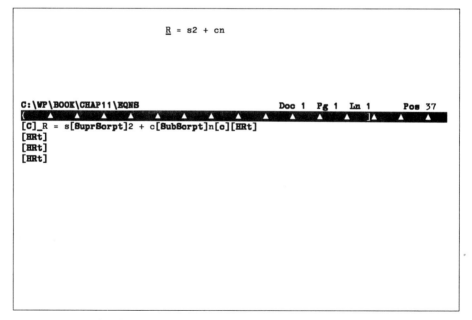

FIGURE 11.6: Reveal codes for sub- and superscripts. Subscripts and superscripts are not displayed on the screen; to check for their formatting codes, press Alt-F3.

printed a half line below or above. If you are working with complex equations with more than one level of subscript or superscript, you will want to use this method.

The Advance Features

If your printer does not produce satisfactory sub- and superscripts, you can use WordPerfect's Advance features to move text up or down a half line at a time. Options 4 (Adv Up) and 5 (Adv Dn) on the Super/Subscript menu (Shift-F1) are toggles. To use these options, you must turn the feature on before you type the text you want to appear on a different line and then turn the feature off when you have finished typing the text for that line. Although you do not see directly on the screen the subscripts and superscripts you create this way, an arrowhead in the lower-left corner of the screen indicates when you are in either of these modes, and you can view the Reveal Codes to check your work. As shown in Figure 11.7, the Advance Up and Advance Down codes appear around each entry you make. This method has the advantage that you can type directly any number of characters to be sub- or superscripted without marking them as a

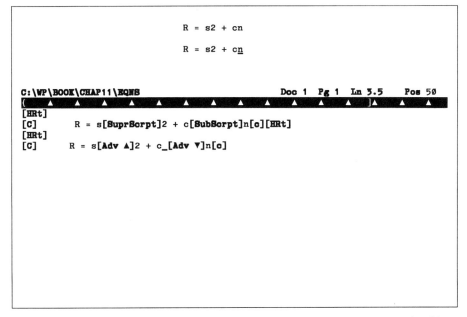

FIGURE 11.7: Viewing Reveal Codes for Advance Up and Advance Down. Your printer must be able to perform reverse line feeds to use this method; test your printer before you decide to use these features. The Ln indicator in the lower-right corner of the screen indicates your position as you use the Advance Up and Advance Down features. As you can see, the on-screen effects of using sub- and superscripts are similar, but the formatting codes are different.

block. However, you must remember to use an equal number of Advance Up and Advance Down commands to return to the base line of your equation. The Ln indicator in the lower-right corner of the screen shows your position. Make a note of the line number on which you start creating an equation so that you can be sure to return to the proper line.

Writing Complex Equations

When you write equations with several levels of sub- and superscripting, you will probably find it most convenient to first set up half-line spacing and then define a space in which to create the equation. You can then move the cursor through this space and enter the equation in Typeover mode. If you use this method, be sure to delete characters by using the space bar to type over them instead of pressing Del or Backspace; using Del or Backspace may insert incorrect spacing into your equation. This method has the advantage that you can see a representation of your equation on the screen with indications of the line spacing, as shown in Figure 11.8. Although sub- and superscripts are spaced one line apart, half-line spacing will be used when your document is printed. Test your printer to see whether it is capable of half-line spacing before you decide to use this method.

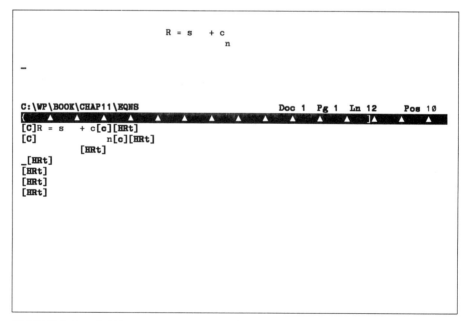

FIGURE 11.8: Using half-line spacing to create complex equations. The sub- and superscripts in this equation will be printed a half line below and above the base line when the document is printed.

Using Italics in Equations

In mathematical equations, variables are usually indicated by italics. Your printer is probably capable of producing italics, but you need to insert a printer command into your text to tell the printer to turn italics on. To do so, press Ctrl-F8 (Print Format) and select option A (Insert Printer Command). Then enter the code your printer uses to turn on Italic mode.

Likewise, when you have finished using italics, you must turn Italic mode off by inserting the command your printer uses to turn italics off. Your printer manual will contain these codes. (Also see Chapter 5 for a discussion of how to use ASCII codes to turn on print enhancements in your text.) The latter portion of this chapter contains two macros you may wish to adapt for your printer to turn italics on and off.

Using Special Mathematical Symbols

WordPerfect allows you to use many special mathematical symbols that are not on your IBM keyboard. If you use any of these symbols often, you can assign them to Ctrl- or Alt-*key* combinations so that they will be typed whenever you press that key sequence. The only limiting factor may be your printer, so before you do much mathematical typing, run the PRINTER.TST (described in Chapter 5) to see which characters your printer cannot print. You may need to create certain characters by using Overstrike mode rather than by generating them from the keyboard.

Because you will probably use Alt-*key* sequences for macros, you should assign mathematical and special symbols to Ctrl-*key* combinations instead. However, if you do not use very many macros but do want a full range of mathematical symbols available to you directly from the keyboard, you can use Alt-*key* sequences as well. WordPerfect allows you to use any combination of letter keys (A through Z) with both the Alt and Ctrl keys to generate mathematical and special symbols.

> *Note:* Be sure not to use Ctrl in combination with B, E, F, R, X, and V; these combinations are used by WordPerfect to generate page numbers and for other specific purposes. In addition, Ctrl-C, D, G, N, O, P, Q, S, T, U, and V are used in merge printing. If you use merge printing, do not use these codes.

If you have assigned any macros to Alt-*key* combinations and later assign a symbol to that key combination, the macro will not work until you undo the key assignment by reassigning the number 0 to that combination.

You can also assign graphics symbols for line and box drawing (see Chapter 13) to keys on your keyboard by using the same procedure as for mathematical symbols (see the section "Assigning Special Symbols to Keys" later in this chapter). Likewise, if you do foreign-language typing, you can use the same procedure to assign special punctuation symbols and diacritical marks to keys on your keyboard.

IBM Graphics Characters

Your IBM (or IBM-compatible) keyboard can generate 169 special characters, although your printer may not be able to print them all. To see these characters, press Ctrl-F3 (Screen) and select option 3 (Ctrl/Alt keys). The screen shown in Figure 11.9 appears. The lower portion of the screen contains the special characters. Each character is assigned a number, which you read from the numbers down the column on the left side and across the row on top, beginning with zero. Numerals in boldface indicate tens. For example, the inverted question mark is 168, which you read by reading down the column to 150 and then counting across the row to position 168.

When the Ctrl/Alt keys screen is displayed, you can assign any of the special symbols to Ctrl- or Alt-*key* combinations on your keyboard. Make sure your printer is capable of producing these symbols before you assign them to keys on your keyboard. Table 11.1 presents some of the most frequently used key assignments for mathematical symbols. Note that some of them, such as the integral sign, are in two parts; you must assign the codes for each part and then use the Alt- or Ctrl-*key* combinations you have assigned to enter them separately.

Key	Value	Key	Value	Key	Value	Key	Value
Alt-A	0	Alt-N	0	Ctrl-A	0	Ctrl-N	0
Alt-B	0	Alt-O	0	Ctrl-B	0	Ctrl-O	0
Alt-C	0	Alt-P	0	Ctrl-C	0	Ctrl-P	0
Alt-D	0	Alt-Q	0	Ctrl-D	0	Ctrl-Q	0
Alt-E	0	Alt-R	0	Ctrl-E	0	Ctrl-R	0
Alt-F	0	Alt-S	0	Ctrl-F	0	Ctrl-S	0
Alt-G	0	Alt-T	0	Ctrl-G	0	Ctrl-T	0
Alt-H	0	Alt-U	0	Ctrl-H	0	Ctrl-U	0
Alt-I	0	Alt-V	0	Ctrl-I	0	Ctrl-V	0
Alt-J	0	Alt-W	0	Ctrl-J	0	Ctrl-W	0
Alt-K	0	Alt-X	0	Ctrl-K	0	Ctrl-X	0
Alt-L	0	Alt-Y	0	Ctrl-L	0	Ctrl-Y	0
Alt-M	0	Alt-Z	0	Ctrl-M	0	Ctrl-Z	0

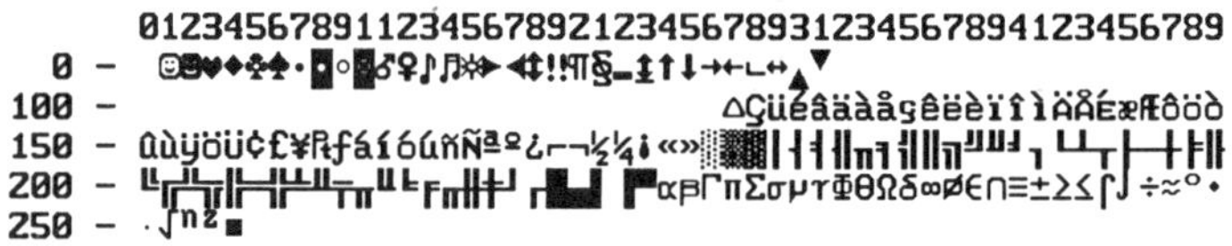

Press key to be defined (Press **Exit** to return): _

FIGURE 11.9: The Ctrl/Alt keys screen. You can assign any of these graphics, mathematical, or foreign-language symbols to Ctrl- or Alt-*key* combinations on your keyboard. If you assign any of them to an Alt-*key* sequence that is being used by a macro, the macro will not operate until you undo that key assignment by using this menu to assign it the number 0.

DESCRIPTION	NUMBER	SYMBOL
up arrow	24	↑
down arrow	25	↓
right arrow	26	→
left arrow	27	←
bi-arrow	29	↔
case 1/2	171	$\frac{1}{2}$
case 1/4	172	$\frac{1}{4}$
alpha	224	α
beta	225	β
Gamma	226	Γ
pi	227	π
Sigma	228	Σ
sigma	229	σ
mu	230	μ
tau	231	τ
Pi	232	Π
Theta	233	Θ
Omega	234	Ω
delta	235	δ
infinity	236	∞
phi	237	ϕ
epsilon	238	ε
intersect	239	$\cap$
identical to	240	$\equiv$
plus or minus	241	$\pm$
greater than or equal to	242	$\geq$
less than or equal to	243	$\leq$
upper integral	244	$\lceil$
lower integral	245	$\rfloor$
division	246	$\div$
approximately equal to	247	$\approx$
degree	248	$\circ$
multiplication	249	$\bullet$
dot	250	$\cdot$
root	251	$\sqrt{}$
n superscript	252	^{n}
2 superscript	253	^{2}

Note: Most printers cannot print characters with codes from 1 to 31; these codes are reserved for special commands.

TABLE 11.1: Special Mathematical Symbols You Can Assign to Your Keyboard

FOREIGN-LANGUAGE TYPING

WordPerfect also offers special options for foreign-language typing. If you do only a small amount of foreign-language typing, you can simply use Overstrike to create characters such as ñ or é. However, you can save keystrokes and perhaps create better printed effects if you assign these graphics symbols directly to Alt- or Ctrl-*key* combinations on your keyboard. See "Using Special Mathematical Symbols" earlier in this chapter for a discussion of this technique; see "Assigning Special Symbols to the Keys" later in this chapter for step-by-step instructions on how to assign key combinations.

Table 11.2 presents some common foreign-language symbols you may wish to assign to key combinations on your keyboard. If you need to use a symbol not listed there, you may be able to create it by using Overstrike. See "Creating Special Symbols by Using Overstrike" later in this chapter.

WORDPERFECT'S MATH FEATURES

Working with math columns in WordPerfect is a six-step process:

1. Clear the tabs and set new ones corresponding to the columns you wish to use. You may define up to 24 columns (A through X), and four of them can contain formulas that specify operations on other numeric columns.

2. Define each column as a text, numeric, calculation, or total column. Numeric columns contain data you wish to make calculations on; calculation columns contain the formulas and display the results of the calculations; and total columns calculate subtotals, totals, and grand totals of data in other columns. Text columns contain labels and are not used in calculations.

3. Turn on the Math feature (Alt-F7 1). This option is a toggle; when you have finished your calculations, you must turn it off.

4. Enter the text and data into the columns you have defined.

5. Instruct WordPerfect to make the calculations by selecting option 2 (Calculate) when the Math feature is on. If Math mode is not on, or if your cursor is not in the Math area, the menu containing the Calculate option will not appear.

6. Turn the Math feature off by pressing Alt-F7 and selecting option 1 again.

If all you want to do is calculate totals of numbers in columns, you do not need to define Math columns (step 2). See the section "Calculating Totals and Averages" later in this chapter.

NAME	NUMBER	SYMBOL
Cedilla C	128	Ç
umlaut u	129	ü
acute e	130	é
circumflex a	131	â
umlaut a	132	ä
grave a	133	à
ring a	134	å
cedilla	135	ç
circumflex e	136	ê
umlaut e	137	ë
grave e	138	è
umlaut i	139	ï
circumflex i	140	î
grave i	141	ì
Umlaut A	142	Ä
Ring A	143	Å
Acute E	144	É
Danish ae	145	æ
Danish AE	146	Æ
circumflex o	147	ô
umlaut o	148	ö
grave o	149	ò
circumflex u	150	û
grave u	151	ù
umlaut y	152	ÿ
Umlaut O	153	Ö
Umlaut U	154	Ü
cent	155	¢
pound	156	£
yen	157	¥
peseta	158	Pt
franc	159	*f*
acute a	160	á

TABLE 11.2: Foreign-Language Symbols and Diacritical Marks

NAME	NUMBER	SYMBOL
acute i	161	í
acute o	162	ó
acute u	163	ú
tilde n	164	ñ
Tilde N	165	Ñ
inverted question mark	168	¿
inverted exclamation point	173	¡
guillemets	174, 175	» «

TABLE 11.2: Foreign-Language Symbols and Diacritical Marks

The reference sections that follow discuss each of these six steps. A step-by-step example is presented in the section "Example: Working with Math Columns" later in this chapter.

Defining Math Columns

KEY SEQUENCE

Alt-F7 2 *<definitions>* F7

REVEAL CODES

[Math Def]

After you have cleared tabs and set new ones, you should define the Math columns. When you press Alt-F7 and select option 2 (Math Def), the screen shown in Figure 11.10 appears. From it you select the definitions for each of the columns you will be using.

The rows under the row labeled A through X (for each column you can define) indicate the type of column (calculation, text, numeric, or total), the symbol to be used with negative numbers (either parentheses or the minus sign), and the number of digits that are to be displayed after the decimal point (up to four).

All columns are predefined as numeric columns (type 2). To change a column's definition, move the cursor to its letter by using the arrow keys. Enter **0** if the column is to contain a formula, enter **1** if the column is to contain only text, and enter **3** if the column is to contain a calculated total. If you have defined the column as type 0, when you press Return the cursor moves down to the Calculation Formulas section of the screen to allow you to enter the formula for the calculation. For example, to calculate what percentage the number in column B is of the number in column C, you would enter B/C*100, as shown in Figure 11.10.

Note that you enter the special operators used for totals and averages in the columns themselves, not in the Math Definition screen.

When you have finished defining all the columns you are going to use, press F7 to exit to the menu. Only four columns can be defined for calculations.

If you need to change the math definitions you have assigned, you should delete the old [Math Def] code. See ''Revising Math Definitions'' later in this chapter.

Entering Data

KEY SEQUENCE

Alt-F7 1 <*data*>

```
Math Definition          Use arrow keys to position cursor

Columns                  A B C D E F G H I J K L M N O P Q R S T U V W X

Type                     2 2 0 2 2 2 2 2 2 2 2 2 2 2 2 2 2 2 2 2 2 2 2 2

Negative Numbers           ( ( ( ( ( ( ( ( ( ( ( ( ( ( ( ( ( ( ( ( ( ( (

# of digits to           2 2 0 2 2 2 2 2 2 2 2 2 2 2 2 2 2 2 2 2 2 2 2 2
the right (0-4)

Calculation    1    C    B/C*100
Formulas       2
               3
               4

Type of Column:
    0 = Calculation    1 = Text    2 = Numeric    3 = Total

Negative Numbers
    ( = Parenthesis (50.00)        - = Minus Sign  -50.00

Press EXIT when done
```

FIGURE 11.10: The Math Definition screen. Here column C has been defined as a calculation column (type 0). You can use from one to four calculation columns to perform calculations on numeric columns (type 2). You enter the formulas you want to use in the Calculation Formulas area, using the column letters as the variables in the formula. In the figure, column B will be divided by column C and multiplied by 100.

Be sure to turn Math mode on before you begin to enter data on which you want to perform calculations. Only the data you enter in Math columns, which begin with the first tab setting, can be used in calculations. Although you do not need to define Math columns first if you are only totaling columns of numbers, you should be sure to reset all tabs before you begin so that numbers do not overlap in columns. WordPerfect's tabs are set every five spaces, and the numbers you work with often will be longer than five characters, including spaces.

When Math mode is on, WordPerfect uses the decimal point as the alignment character. After you press Tab, characters that you type appear to the left of the cursor.

When you move the cursor by tab spacing to a column you have defined as a calculation column, an exclamation point (!) appears. This indicates that WordPerfect is going to perform a calculation in that column, so do not enter anything there.

You will need to enter any currency symbols (such as **$**) and commas to separate thousands manually; unlike many spreadsheet programs, WordPerfect's Math feature does not have an option that defines entries as currency and formats them for you.

Moving between Columns

KEY SEQUENCE

To move between columns:
   Ctrl-← or **Ctrl-→**
To move to the beginning of the first text column:
   Ctrl-Home Home ←

When Math mode is on, you move between columns by using a combination of the Ctrl key and the right and left arrow keys. Pressing Home and ← after the Ctrl-Home (Goto) sequence takes you to the beginning of the first text column.

Calculating Totals and Averages

KEY SEQUENCE

   Alt-F7 1 *<data>* **Alt-F7 2 Alt-F7 1**

REVEAL CODES

   [Math On] [Math Off]

WordPerfect contains built-in formulas that allow you to calculate subtotals, totals, grand totals, and averages. If you are totaling numbers down a column, you do not need to define math columns first. You simply enter the symbol for the operation at the point in the column where you wish the operation to be performed. A plus sign (+) calculates subtotals, an equal sign (=) calculates totals, and an asterisk (*) calculates grand totals. You can also enter **T** before a number to indicate that it is to be considered a total when the results are calculated, or you can enter **t** to indicate that a number is to be considered a subtotal. In Version 4.2, you can enter **N** before a number to indicate that it is to be considered a negative number.

To get totals, subtotals, and grand totals from simple columns of numbers (not predefined as Math columns),

1. Clear and then reset the tabs. When Math mode is on, WordPerfect aligns tabs on the alignment character, which is the period (.) unless you change it.

2. Turn the Math feature on: Press Alt-F7 (Math/Columns) and select option 1 (Math On). The following prompt appears in the lower-left corner of the screen:

   Math

3. Press the Tab key to move to the first column. Then enter the numbers you wish to work with. When you press the period (.) to indicate a decimal point, the numbers will align on that decimal point.

4. Wherever you want a subtotal to be calculated in that column, insert a plus sign (+), either from the numeric keypad or from the top row of your keyboard. WordPerfect will subtotal each number in the column after the last plus sign. Where you want a total of the subtotals, enter an equal sign (=). If you want any numbers to be considered as totals or subtotals even if no calculation has been performed on them—which may be useful if you are working with imported data on which totals and subtotals have already been calculated—enter **t** before any additional subtotals and **T** before any additional totals. If you want to calculate a grand total— the total of all the totals—enter an asterisk (*).

5. To tell WordPerfect to make the calculations you have specified, press Alt-F7 (Math/Columns) and select option 2 (Calculate). (You can select this option at any time to have the program perform calculations, for example, as you enter the numbers.) WordPerfect displays double question marks (??) if it cannot make a calculation. If this occurs, recheck your Math Definition screen to make sure that the column references in any formulas you have written are correct.

6. Turn Math mode off by selecting option 1 (Math Off) from the Math/Columns menu.

Turning Math mode on and off inserts the codes [Math On] and [Math Off] into your document. If you later need to edit your figures, you can search for these codes by pressing Alt-F7 (Math/Columns) and selecting option 1 after you press F2 (Search).

Displaying Totals in Separate Columns

If you have defined Math columns (see "Defining Math Columns" earlier in this chapter), you can display subtotals, totals, and grand totals in separate columns. To do so, you simply define the column or columns that you wish to hold the total calculations as total columns (type 3) and type the +, =, or * symbol in your document in the column where you want the calculation to appear (see Figure 11.11).

Using Special Operators for Row Calculations

You can use certain special operators to compute the totals and averages of rows. To do so, define the column that is to hold these special operators as a

```
Order Number        Amount      Total

021389               54.54
912670              198.75
667120               25.51

Subtotal            278.80+

Total                           496.69=




Math                                    Doc 2  Pg 1  Ln 9      Pos 10
```

FIGURE 11.11: Displaying a total in a separate column. If you define a column as a total column by using the Math Definition screen, you can display various types of totals there. Unlike when you enter a calculation formula in the Math Definition screen, you enter the symbol used for the type of total you want in the appropriate column in your document after you have defined Math columns.

calculation column (type 0). Then, when the cursor moves to the Calculation Formulas area of the Math Definition screen, enter any one of the special operators listed here.

- The addition symbol (+) calculates the total of all the numbers in the row that are in numeric columns (type 2).
- The + / symbol calculates the average of all the numbers in the row that are in numeric columns (type 2).
- The = symbol calculates the total of all the numbers in the row that are in total columns (type 3).
- The = / symbol calculates the average of all the numbers in the row that are in total columns (type 3).

These special operators work on numbers to their right and left, across the entire row—not just on numbers to the left. If you are not aware of this, you can obtain confusing results. Figure 11.12 illustrates a situation in which an average has been calculated across a selected row.

```
Sales Summary--Third Quarter

                 August          September          October          Quarterly
                                                                      Average

Income
_
 Sales           37500           48500              39750

 Leases          19500           18500              21250            19,750!

 Total           19,500+         56,000+            58,750+




Math                                               Doc 2  Pg 1  Ln 7       Pos 5
```

FIGURE 11.12: Making calculations across rows. WordPerfect contains four special operators that make calculations across rows. These calculations are made either on every number in each numeric column or on every number in each total column, depending on the operator you select. Here averages have been computed for the lease figures in the Leases row. Because the other average figures were not wanted, the exclamation points that appeared in the calculation column for the other rows were deleted. Otherwise, averages would have been computed for sales and totals as well.

If you do not want a calculation to be performed on a certain row, you can delete the ! that appears in the calculation column for that row, as was done in the figure.

These special formulas should be used by themselves; no other formulas should appear in the column that contains them.

Making Other Calculations

KEY SEQUENCE

Alt-F7 2 <*definitions*> Alt-F7 1 Alt-F7 2

You can specify calculations on numeric columns (type 2). To do so, you define the column in which you want these calculations to occur as type 0 (calculation) and enter the formula you want to use in the Calculation Formulas part of the Math Definition screen. When you write formulas, do not use any spaces in them—for example, write *C/B+D*.

WordPerfect calculates from left to right. To tell WordPerfect to calculate a sequence of operations first, enclose them in parentheses.

Example: Working with Math Columns

To illustrate how WordPerfect's math features work, here is a simple example that incorporates most of the program's basic math techniques. You can apply these same techniques to more complex math columns that involve additional computations.

This example demonstrates

- Clearing and setting tabs for math columns
- Defining a math column
- Turning Math mode on and off
- Entering data in math columns
- Getting a subtotal and total
- Displaying a total in a separate column
- Indicating an additional subtotal
- Using a formula for computation

To create the example shown in Figure 11.13, take the following steps:

1. Set text tabs at positions 10, 30, 44, and 55.

2. Enter the headings **Order Number, Amount Total,** and **Plus 6% Tax,** as shown in Figure 11.13.

3. Press Alt-F7 2 to define the math columns. When the Math Definition screen appears, fill it out as shown in Figure 11.14. Column B is a total column, so it is type 3; column C holds a formula, so it is type 0. When the cursor moves to the Formula Calculation area, enter the formula for column C as **1.06∗B.** Press F7 to exit the Math Definition screen and enter the [Math Def] code into your document.

4. Turn Math mode on by pressing Alt-F1 and selecting option 1 (Math On).

5. Press Shift-F8 (Line Format) and select option 1 or 2 to set tabs. Press Home Home ↑ to make sure you are at the beginning of the tab ruler line; then press Ctrl-End to delete all tabs to the end of the line. Set new tabs at positions 34, 46, and 60. You can simply press Tab to set the tabs or enter the position numbers and press Return; then press F7 (Exit). Any tabs you set while Math mode is on will be considered decimal tabs unless you change the alignment character (See Chapter 2 for a more detailed discussion of setting tabs).

6. Enter the data as shown in Figure 11.13.

```
Order Number        Amount

021389               54.54
912670              198.75
667120               25.51

Subtotal               +

From PO#4485        t217.89

Total




Math                                    Doc 1  Pg 1  Ln 11    Pos 10
```

FIGURE 11.13: Sample math columns example. Although relatively simple, this example illustrates the basic techniques required to create more complex math columns and formulas. Follow the step-by-step instructions in the text to practice these techniques.

```
Math Definition              Use arrow keys to position cursor

Columns                      A B C D E F G H I J K L M N O P Q R S T U V W X

Type                         2 3 0 2 2 2 2 2 2 2 2 2 2 2 2 2 2 2 2 2 2 2 2 2

Negative Numbers             ( ( ( ( ( ( ( ( ( ( ( ( ( ( ( ( ( ( ( ( ( ( ( (

# of digits to               2 2 2 2 2 2 2 2 2 2 2 2 2 2 2 2 2 2 2 2 2 2 2 2
the right (0-4)

Calculation    1    C        1.06*B
Formulas       2
               3
               4

Type of Column:
     0 = Calculation    1 = Text     2 = Numeric    3 = Total

Negative Numbers
     ( = Parenthesis (50.00)         - = Minus Sign  -50.00

Press EXIT when done
```

FIGURE 11.14: The Math Definitions screen for the example. Column A has been left as a numeric column (type 2). Column B has been defined as a total column (type 3), and column C, which contains the formula 1.06*B, is a calculation column (type 0). In any math definition, only four columns can hold formulas.

Because the leftmost column does not occur after a tab, WordPerfect ignores it in any calculations it makes. If you have columns that contain headings or labels that occur after a tab setting, you can define them as text columns (type 1), and WordPerfect will ignore them in calculations too. When you press Tab to enter the **Plus 6% Tax** column, WordPerfect will insert exclamation points. Because you do not need a line total for each of these items, press Backspace to delete the exclamation points, leaving only the one at the bottom of the column.

The *t* before the "From PO4485" figure indicates that WordPerfect is to consider this number a subtotal, even though it has not calculated it. Enter an equal sign (=) in the Total column to indicate that WordPerfect should calculate the total of all the subtotals here.

7. When your table resembles the one in Figure 11.13, press Alt-F7 (Math/ Columns) and select option 2 to make the calculations. You screen should then look like the one in Figure 11.15. After the calculations have been made, press Alt-F7 (Math/Columns) and select option 1 to turn Math mode off.

```
Order Number        Amount      Total       Plus
                                            6% Tax

Ø21389               54.54
912670              198.75
667120               25.51

Subtotal            278.80+

From PO#4485       t217.89

Total                           496.69=      526.49!




Math                                    Doc 1  Pg 1  Ln 4      Pos 10
```

FIGURE 11.15: The completed example with the subtotal, total, and calculation. Additional calculations that would have been displayed in column C were removed by deleting all but one exclamation point (!) in that column.

Revising Math Definitions

KEY SEQUENCE

Alt-F7 2 <*column definition*> **F7**

REVEAL CODES

[Math Def]

WordPerfect enters special codes when you define Math columns. If you need to revise the math definition later, you can use the program's Search feature to search for the [MathDef], [Math On], [Math Off], + (subtotal), = (total), * (grand total), *t* (subtotal designator), *T* (total designator), ! (calculation), or *N* (negative number designator) codes. To use this feature, press F2 (Search); then press Alt-F7. The following menu appears:

Math: 1 Def 2 On 3 Off 4 + 5 = 6 * 7 t 8 T 9 !
A N Column: B Def C On D Off 0

You can press the number or letter of the option to search for the next occurrence of it in your document. (Only options 1 through A pertain to Math features.) For example, to search for the next Math definition, you enter **1**; to search for the next calculation column, you enter **!**.

You will often want to change the definitions of math columns so that you can add new columns of data, delete columns, or move columns to new locations. With your cursor positioned before the [Math On] code (press Alt-F3 to see the codes), you can delete the old [Math Def] code. Then press Alt-F7 (Math/Columns) and select option 2 (Math Def) to change any column definitions that you wish. Remember to recalculate by using the new definition before you move to another part of your document.

If you want to revise a Math Definitions screen you have already defined, position the cursor to the right of the [MathDef] code before you press Alt-F7 and select option 2 (Math Def). You can then use the cursor movement keys to position the cursor on the settings you wish to change. To edit a formula, place the cursor on the 0 that defines the column holding the formula and reenter 0. The cursor will move to the Calculation Formulas section of the screen, where you can edit the formula or delete it by pressing F1 (Cancel).

Remember that if you add, delete, or move columns, you will also need to revise the formulas that involve them.

Editing Math Columns

KEY SEQUENCE

To cut a column:
   Alt-F4 (position cursor) **Ctrl-F4 4 1**
To copy a column:
   Alt-F4 (position cursor) **Ctrl-F4 4 2** (position cursor) **Ctrl-F4 4**
To move a column:
   Alt-F4 (position cursor) **Ctrl-F4 4 1** (position cursor) **Ctrl-F4 4**

REVEAL CODES

[Math On] [Math Off]

You cut, copy, and move Math columns in much the same way that you cut, copy, and move blocks of text, but the highlighting the program first shows you may be a little confusing if you are not used to it.

1. Move the cursor to any point in the first row of the column and press Alt-F4 (Block). Remember that Math columns begin at the first tab stop, not at the left margin.

2. Move the cursor to the last row in the column. All the columns will be highlighted, but in the next step the program will restrict the highlighting to the current column.

3. Press Ctrl-F4 (Move) and select option 4 (Cut/Copy Column). Word-Perfect will highlight only the column the cursor is on. Select option 1 to cut the column or option 2 to copy it.

4. If you are copying or moving a column, position the cursor in the column to the right of where you want the new column to go. Then press Ctrl-F4 (Move) and select option 4 to retrieve the column.

5. If the editing you have just done requires any new calculations, recalculate the columns by pressing Alt-F7 and selecting option 2 (Calculate). Remember that when you move Math columns, the letters that designate them also change, which means that you may need to edit formulas that involve those columns.

When you manipulate Math columns that are separated by horizontal lines that you have inserted for clarity, such as those that divide headings (labels) from the numeric section of a table, you are likely to lose those lines during the cut, copy, and move operation. When your columns are in the positions where you want them, you can insert those lines again.

See Chapter 4 for further information about working with columns in tables.

MATHEMATICAL AND STATISTICAL TYPING

Because WordPerfect is designed to be used with many different printers of varying capabilities, it offers alternative methods for accomplishing special types of typing such as mathematical and foreign-language typing. Test your printer with the PRINTER.TST program (discussed in Chapter 5) to see what it is capable of before deciding on a specific technique for mathematical typing.

Using the Sub/Superscript Feature

KEY SEQUENCE

For a superscript:
   Shift-F1 1
For a subscript:
   Shift-F1 2

REVEAL CODES

[SuprScrpt] [SubScrpt]

When you press WordPerfect's Sub/Superscript key sequence, the following menu appears:

1 Superscript; 2 Subscript; 3 Overstrike; 4 Adv Up; 5 Adv Dn; 6 Adv Ln: 0

If you select 1 (for Superscript) or 2 (for Subscript), the next character that you type will be printed a half line above or below the base line of what you are typing. An uppercase S appears in the lower-left corner of the screen for superscripts; a lower-case s appears for subscripts. These indicators disappear when you start typing. You will not see the superscript or subscript elevated or lowered on the screen, but if your printer is capable of half-line advances, you will see the sub- or superscripts when your document is printed. They will appear on the screen as shown in Figure 11.16.

```
                         R = s2 + cn

                         R = s2 + cn

  ─
                              2
                         R = s   + c

C:\WP\BOOK\CHAP11\EQNS                    Doc 2  Pg 1  Ln 4.5    Pos 10
[C]R = s[SuprScrpt]2 + c[SubScrpt]n[c][HRt]
[HRt]
[C]R = s[Adv ▲]2[Adv ▼] + c[Adv ▼]n[c][HRt]
[Spacing Set:0.5]_[HRt]
[C]2[c][HRt]
[C]R = s   + c[c][HRt]
[HRt]
```

FIGURE 11.16: Subscripts and superscripts on the screen. Although these characters are not in their correct positions now, they will be raised or lowered one half line in the printed version of the document. To see whether such numerals are subscripts, superscripts, or footnotes, press Alt-F3 (Reveal Codes). The codes for sub- and superscripts are illustrated in the figure, as are those for Advance Up and Advance Down, another method for creating subscripts and superscripts. The third equation was created by using half-line spacing, which indicates sub- and superscripts one line above and below the base line on the screen. When the equation is printed, the sub- and superscripts will be raised or lowered only half a line.

If you want to use subscripts or superscripts of more than one character, type the sequence of characters. Mark them with the Mark Block key sequence (Alt-F4) and then press Alt-F1 and select option 1 or 2.

If you do much mathematical typing, you may want to write macros that put you in Subscript or Superscript mode or create standard-sized spaces in which you can use half-line spacing. Macros Alt-S and Alt-Z, presented in the next sections, are relatively simple, but they can save you many keystrokes and allow you to concentrate on typing the equation at hand rather than formatting the space.

ALT-S: A SUPERSCRIPTING MACRO

Begin macro	*Macro name*	*Keystrokes*	*End macro*
Ctrl-F10	**Alt-S**	**Shift-F1 1**	**Ctrl-F10**

Macro Alt-S puts you in Superscript mode; the next character you type after you press Alt-S will be superscripted. To use this macro with more than one character, type the characters that are to be superscripted and mark them as a block (Alt-F4) (or use a Mark Block macro, as was discussed in Chapter 3). Then, when you use the Alt-S macro, the entire block will be superscripted.

ALT-Z: A SUBSCRIPTING MACRO

Begin macro	*Macro name*	*Keystrokes*	*End macro*
Ctrl-F10	**Alt-Z**	**Shift-F1 2**	**Ctrl-F10**

Macro Alt-Z puts you in Subscript mode; the next character you type after you press Alt-Z will be subscripted. To use this macro with more than one character, type the characters that are to be superscripted and mark them as a block (Alt-F4) (or use a Mark Block macro, as was discussed in Chapter 3). Then, when you use the Alt-Z macro, the entire block will be subscripted.

Using Advance Up and Advance Down to Create Superscripts and Subscripts

KEY SEQUENCE

To advance up:
Shift-F1 4
To advance down:
Shift-F1 5

REVEAL CODES

[Adv Up] [Adv Dn]

Options 4 (Adv Up) and 5 (Adv Dn) on the Super/Subscript menu (Shift-F1) are toggles that move text up or down a half line at a time. To use these options, you must turn the feature on before you type the text you want to appear above or below the line and then turn the feature off when you have finished typing that text. Although you cannot see the spacing on the screen, it will appear in your document if your printer is capable of reverse line feeds.

When you use either of these modes, an arrowhead in the lower-left corner of the screen indicates whether you are using Advance Up or Advance Down. This arrowhead disappears as soon as you start typing. The Ln indicator at the lower-right of the screen shows your position in terms of line numbers. Remember to use an equal number of Advance Up and Advance Down commands to return to the base line of your equation. If an equation has many levels, note the line number on which the equation starts so that you can be sure to return to the proper line.

In Figure 11.16, the second equation was created by using Advance Up and Advance Down. Note the line number, 4.5, at the lower-right and the pairs of codes around each sub- and superscript. After you type a subscript or superscript, to return to the base line of the equation you must press Shift-F1 and select option 4 (Adv Up) or option 5 (Adv Dn) again.

Using Half-Line Spacing in Equations and Formulas

KEY SEQUENCE

Shift-F8 4 .5

REVEAL CODES

[Spacing Set: 0.5]

You can also create spacing in equations by changing to half-line spacing. Type the characters that appear on the superscripted lines first; then type the base-line characters. Finally, type the subscripted characters. The third equation in Figure 11.16 was created by using half-line spacing. This method has the advantage of allowing you to see the relative spacing of the equations and formulas you type, but equations typed in this way can be awkward to correct if you notice an error later.

If you type many equations or very complex equations, you will probably want to use the method described in the next section.

Using Half-Line Spacing in Complex Equations

If you first set WordPerfect to half-line spacing and then define a blank area in which to work, you can move the cursor around in this area by using the arrow keys and the space bar without changing the spacing of other characters. This makes it easy to edit equations as you type them in Typeover mode.

To create a blank space 65 characters wide and 16 half lines (8 lines) deep in which half-line spacing has been set, use the following steps:

1. Press Shift-F8 (Line Format), select option 4 (Spacing Set), and enter **.5** (for half-line spacing).

2. Press Ctrl-F8 (Print Format) and select option 3 to turn off right justification. Press F7 to exit.

3. Press Esc, enter **65,** and press the space bar to insert a line 65 characters wide.

4. Press Ctrl-F3 (Screen), select option 2 (Line Draw), and then select option 6 (Move).

5. Press Esc, enter **15,** and press ↓ to insert 16 blank half lines of space into your document. You can see the Ln indicator change at the lower-right of the screen.

6. Press F7 to return to your document; then press Ins to enter Typeover mode.

To use this procedure, you cannot be at the end of your document; there must be space available for you to work in. (You can create additional space by pressing Return.) Note in the preceding key sequence that you enter Line Draw mode, using the Ctrl-F3 2 6 key sequence (see Chapter 13 for additional details about using line and box drawing in WordPerfect). You also turn off right justification (using Ctrl-F8 3) so that your equations will not be right justified. You may wish to center your equations (using Shift-F6) or indent them a certain number of spaces from the left margin.

The preceding key sequence inserts a line 65 characters wide into your document. If you are not working with a 65-character line, change the number after the first Esc (see step 3) to whatever line width you are using. If you want more or fewer half lines, change the number after the second Esc (see step 5) to the number of half lines you need for the equation you are writing.

After you press F7, you are returned to your document. You can use the arrow keys and the space bar to position the cursor within the space you have just defined and begin typing your equation in Typeover mode. If you use this method, be sure to delete spaces by using the space bar instead of Del or Backspace; using Del or Backspace may insert incorrect spacing into your equation.

While you are in this area, you can use the Overstrike option on the Sub/Superscript menu (Shift-F1) to create special characters (see the section "Creating Special Symbols by Using Overstrike" later in this chapter), or you can use any special symbols you have assigned to keys on your keyboard (see "Assigning Special Symbols to Keys" later in this chapter).

If you frequently write equations, you should probably write a macro that automatically defines a standard-sized space in which half-line spacing is set. Macro Alt-E in the next section creates such a space, as described in the preceding steps, for you.

ALT-E: A MACRO FOR INSERTING EQUATIONS

Begin macro	*Macro name*	*Keystrokes*	*End macro*
Ctrl-F10	**Alt-E**	**Shift-F8 4 .5 Return**	**Ctrl-F10**
		Ctrl-F8 3 F7	
		Esc 65 space bar	
		Ctrl-F3 2 6	
		Esc 15 ↓ F7 Ins	

If you wish to modify macro Alt-E for a different line width or a different number of half lines, see the comments in the preceding section.

After you enter this macro, press Alt-E; you can write equations within the resulting space by using the arrow keys and space bar to position the cursor exactly where you want it. You will find that you can create quite complex equations in this way, as illustrated in Figure 11.17. While you are in the space you have created with this macro, you can use other special features, such as Overstrike (option 3 on the Shift-F1 menu) to create special characters not found on the keyboard. You can also use other mathematical symbols the program can generate (see "Creating Special Symbols by Using Overstrike" later in this chapter).

Using Italics in Mathematical Formulas

> **KEY SEQUENCE**
>
> **Ctrl-F8 A** *<printer command>*

> **REVEAL CODES**
>
> **[Comnd: $<n>n$]**

In mathematical formulas, variables are usually printed in italics, as in the following equation:

$$\frac{X^2 = (n - 1)^n}{a_2}$$

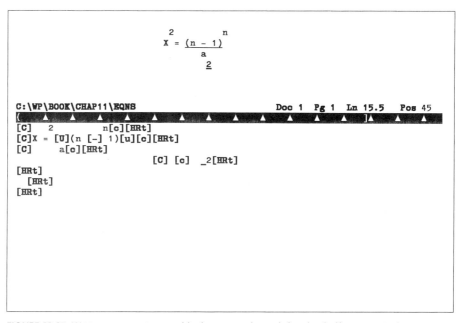

FIGURE 11.17: Writing an equation in a blank area you have defined as half spacing. In the equation illustrated, the rule was inserted by turning on underlining (F8). Each line of the equation was centered by pressing Shift-F6. You can first write an equation and then mark it as a block to center it, but you may sometimes find that the spacing changes when the program centers a complex equation.

In WordPerfect, you can press Ctrl-F8 and select option 1 (Command) to change the appropriate font to turn on italics.

Because turning italics on and off requires a certain number of keystrokes, you may wish to write a macro to handle this task. For example, most printers use Font 4 for italics and Font 1 for regular type. Macros ITO and ITX, described in the next sections, can be used to turn italics on and off.

ITO: A MACRO TO TURN ITALICS ON

Begin macro	Macro name	Keystrokes	End macro
Ctrl-F10	**ITO**	**Ctrl-F8 1 Return 4 Return F7**	**Ctrl-F10**

This macro is named ITO (for *italics on*) to help you remember that you are turning Italic mode on. Use option 2 on the Printer Control screen to determine the font number for italics on your printer. Whatever you type until you turn Italic mode off will appear in italics when printed.

ITX: A MACRO TO TURN ITALICS OFF

Begin macro	*Macro name*	*Keystrokes*	*End macro*
Ctrl-F10	**ITX**	**Ctrl-F8 1 Return 1 Return F7**	**Ctrl-F10**

This macro is named ITX (for *italics off*) to help you remember that you are turning Italic mode off. Use option 2 on the Printer Control screen to determine the font number for regular type on your printer. After you use this macro, whatever you type will appear in regular typeface.

SPECIAL SYMBOLS

Your IBM keyboard can generate 169 special characters and symbols—mathematical operators and characters as well as diacritical marks, punctuation symbols, and international currency symbols—that can be viewed on the screen. To use these characters in documents you create in WordPerfect, you must assign them to an Alt- or Ctrl-*key* combination.

Most printers can print most of these characters. (Characters with codes in the range 1 to 31 are normally used for control commands and therefore are usually not printable). Before you assign special characters and symbols to key sequences on your keyboard, check to see whether your printer can print them.

If you assign an Alt-*key* combination that is currently being used as a macro name, that macro will not operate until you uninstall the special character's Alt-*key* combination (see "Uninstalling Special Symbols" later in this chapter).

Assigning Special Symbols to Keys

KEY SEQUENCE

Ctrl-F3 3 <*key combination*> <*code number*> **F7**

When you press Ctrl-F3 (Screen) and select option 3 (Ctrl/Alt keys), the screen shown in Figure 11.18 appears. Each symbol or character is assigned a number, which you read from the numbers down the column on the left side and across the row on top, beginning with zero. Numerals in boldface indicate tens. For example, the inverted question mark is 168, which you read by reading down the column to 150 and then counting across the row to position 168.

```
Key    Value    Key    Value    Key    Value    Key    Value
Alt-A  246_     Alt-N  0        Ctrl-A 0        Ctrl-N 0
Alt-B  0        Alt-O  0        Ctrl-B 0        Ctrl-O 0
Alt-C  0        Alt-P  0        Ctrl-C 0        Ctrl-P 0
Alt-D  0        Alt-Q  0        Ctrl-D 0        Ctrl-Q 0
Alt-E  0        Alt-R  0        Ctrl-E 0        Ctrl-R 0
Alt-F  0        Alt-S  0        Ctrl-F 0        Ctrl-S 0
Alt-G  0        Alt-T  0        Ctrl-G 0        Ctrl-T 0
Alt-H  0        Alt-U  0        Ctrl-H 0        Ctrl-U 0
Alt-I  0        Alt-V  0        Ctrl-I 0        Ctrl-V 0
Alt-J  0        Alt-W  0        Ctrl-J 0        Ctrl-W 0
Alt-K  0        Alt-X  0        Ctrl-K 0        Ctrl-X 0
Alt-L  0        Alt-Y  0        Ctrl-L 0        Ctrl-Y 0
Alt-M  0        Alt-Z  0        Ctrl-M 0        Ctrl-Z 0

       0123456789112345678921234567893123456789 4123456789
  0 -
100 -
150 -
200 -
250 -

Press key to be defined (Press Exit to return):
```

FIGURE 11.18: Assigning a key sequence to a special character. Here the division sign, code 246 from the table, is being assigned to the Alt-A key combination. After it has been assigned to this key combination, a division sign will appear in your document whenever you press Alt-A. When you read the table, be sure to count from zero, not from 1. Every tenth number appears in boldface on your screen.

To assign one of these characters either to a Ctrl-*key* or Alt-*key* combination, press the key combination you want the symbol to have. For example, to assign the division sign (code 246) to the Alt-A combination, press Alt-A and enter **246** in the table at the top of the screen.

Note: Be sure not to use Ctrl in combination with B, E, F, R, X, and V because these combinations are used by WordPerfect to generate page numbers and for other specific purposes. In addition, Ctrl-C, D, G, N, O, P, Q, S, T, U, and V are used in merge printing. If you use merge printing, do not use these codes.

Uninstalling Special Symbols

KEY SEQUENCE

Ctrl-F3 3 < *key combination* > **0 F7**

To uninstall an Alt- or Ctrl-*key* combination you have assigned, you reassign the number 0 to that combination on the Ctrl/Alt key menu. When the screen shown in Figure 11.9 is displayed, enter the key combination you wish to uninstall. Then enter **0** as its numeric assignment.

After you have uninstalled a key combination that generates a special symbol, that key combination can then be used for another special symbol or, in the case of Alt-*key* combinations, for a macro. Any macros you have previously named with that Alt-*key* combination will now work again.

Creating Special Symbols by Using Overstrike

KEY SEQUENCE

<*base character*> **Shift-F1** 3 <*superimposed character*>

REVEAL CODES

[Ovrstk]

When you run the PRINTER.TST described in Chapter 5, you may discover special symbols that your printer cannot print. In such a case, you may wish to create these symbols by using Overstrike, which is option 3 on the Sub/Superscript menu (Shift-F1). You may also want to use this option if you work with special symbols relatively infrequently and do not want to devote an Alt- or Ctrl-*key* combination to a symbol (see "Assigning Special Symbols to Keys" earlier in this chapter).

When you select option 3, Overstrike, from the Sub/Superscript menu (Shift-F1), the next character you type will overstrike the character you have just typed. You will only see the last character on the screen, but if you press Alt-F3 (Reveal Codes), you will be able to see that both characters are present and will appear in your document when it is printed.

Figure 11.19 illustrates several symbols that can be created with the Overstrike method, and Table 11.3 lists other combinations that you may find useful.

You can use Overstrike mode in combination with sub- and superscripts if you need subscripts and superscripts placed above and below each other on the same line. Many printers provide sub- and superscripts in a smaller size than the main text; test your printer to see the effects it produces before you use this method extensively.

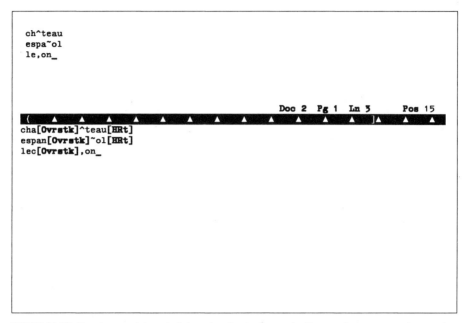

FIGURE 11.19: Creating special symbols by using Overstrike mode. If your printer cannot print certain symbols, you may be able to use Overstrike mode to create them. Although only the last character typed appears on your screen, both characters will appear when the document is printed.

FIRST ENTRY	SECOND ENTRY	RESULTING CHARACTER
o, a, e, u, or i	^	ô, â, ê, û, or î
o, a, e, u, or i	''	ö, ä, ë, ü, or ï
o, a, e, u, or i	´	ó, á, é, ú, or í
o, a, e, u, or i	`	ò, à, è, ù, or ì
n	~	ñ
c	,	ç
Y	=	¥
c	l	¢

TABLE 11.3: Symbols You Can Create by Using Overstrike

SUMMARY

This chapter has presented techniques you can use when typing mathematical and statistical documents as well as when doing foreign-language typing. It also shows you how to perform mathematical operations on data in columns and rows within WordPerfect.

The next part of this book explores some additional techniques you can use to enhance documents you create with WordPerfect. Chapter 12, "Using the Speller and Thesaurus," introduces you to built-in features of the WordPerfect program that you can use to check your documents for errors and also use as aids while you write. Chapter 13, "Line and Box Drawing," discusses techniques you can use to create charts and forms as well as to enhance documents with graphics characters. Chapter 14, "Creating and Using Macros," shows you in detail how you can write macros of your own to streamline and customize the work you do with WordPerfect.

SUPPLEMENTAL WORD
PROCESSING FEATURES

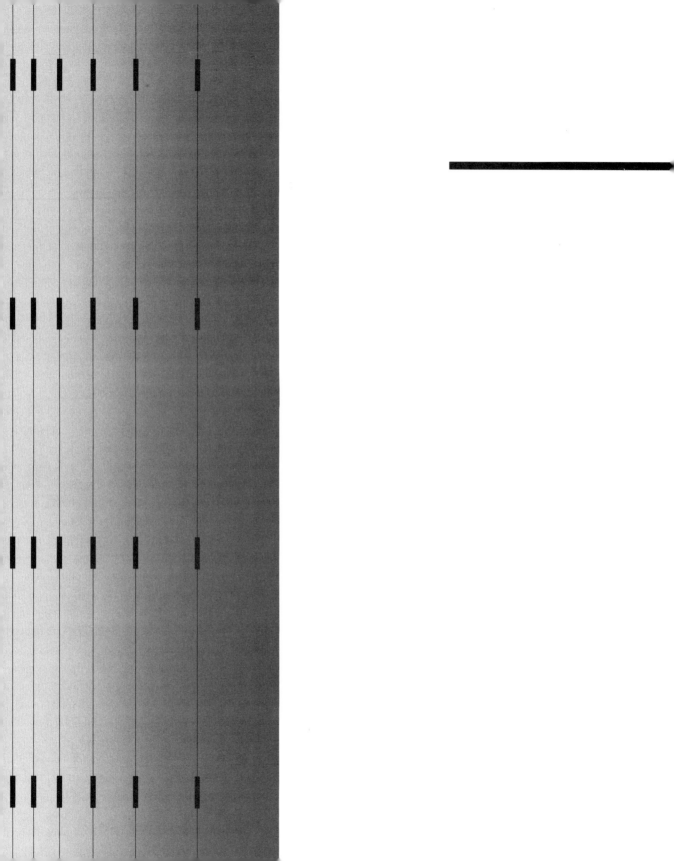

CHAPTER 12

USING THE SPELLER AND THESAURUS

USING THE SPELLER
AND THESAURUS

T his chapter presents WordPerfect's Speller and Thesaurus utilities. Word-Perfect contains both a built-in dictionary and a thesaurus to help you as you write and to check your work when it is done. You can use the Speller to check your documents for typographical errors after you have finished writing or, because you can specify a word to look up, you can use it to check the spellings of words you are unsure about as you are writing. You can use the Thesaurus to see alternative adjectives, nouns, and verbs (synonyms) for a word as well as antonyms, or words that have an opposite meaning. This feature can be especially helpful to you if you are struggling for just the right word in a particular context.

OVERVIEW OF WORDPERFECT'S SPELLER AND THESAURUS

WordPerfect's Speller actually consists of three dictionaries: a common word list of 1550 of the most often used words, a main word list of approximately 100,000 more words, and a supplemental dictionary consisting of all the words you add as you write. You can create additional custom dictionaries to suit your needs, which you may want to do if you write in a specialized field. In addition, you can tailor WordPerfect's dictionary to suit your own needs by adding the words you habitually mistype to its common word list, thereby speeding up the spell-checking process.

The Thesaurus consists of approximately 10,000 *headwords,* which are the basic words you can look up. WordPerfect will display many more words as suggested alternatives, but the headwords, which appear with a dot next to them, are linked to other references, which means that you can continue to explore alternative words until you find the one that best suits your needs. Figure 12.1 illustrates a Thesaurus screen presenting suggested alternatives for the word *stage.*

Use the Speller if

- You are unsure about the spelling of a word.
- You want to correct typographical errors and misspelled words in your document.

Use the Thesaurus if

- You are unsure about which word to use in a particular context.
- You are unsure about the meaning of a word. Seeing other related words, including any antonyms (opposites), will help you define it.
- You would like to see a group of related words (nouns, verbs, and adjectives) that could be used in place of a word or with a word in your document.

HOW WORDPERFECT'S SPELL CHECKER WORKS

When checking the spelling of a word, WordPerfect's Speller first checks a common word list of approximately 1550 words. If it does not find the word there, it next checks its main word list of over 100,000 more words.

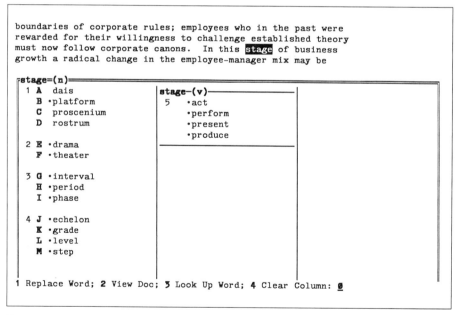

```
boundaries of corporate rules; employees who in the past were
rewarded for their willingness to challenge established theory
must now follow corporate canons.  In this stage of business
growth a radical change in the employee-manager mix may be

┌stage=(n)════════════════════════════════════════════════════┐
│ 1 A   dais            │ stage-(v)───────────┐                 │
│   B ·platform         │ 5   ·act            │                 │
│   C   proscenium      │     ·perform        │                 │
│   D   rostrum         │     ·present        │                 │
│                       │     ·produce        │                 │
│ 2 E ·drama            │                     │                 │
│   F ·theater          │                     │                 │
│                       │                     │                 │
│ 3 G ·interval         │                     │                 │
│   H ·period           │                     │                 │
│   I ·phase            │                     │                 │
│                       │                     │                 │
│ 4 J ·echelon          │                     │                 │
│   K ·grade            │                     │                 │
│   L ·level            │                     │                 │
│   M ·step             │                     │                 │
│                                                               │
│ 1 Replace Word; 2 View Doc; 3 Look Up Word; 4 Clear Column: 0 │
```

Figure 12.1: Using the Thesaurus. Here the word *stage* has been looked up. As you can see, WordPerfect presents alternative nouns and verbs that could be used in place of the word in your document. To see other lists of suggested words, enter the letter corresponding to a word in the list; words with dots next to them, such as *period* and *level* in the figure, are cross referenced to other word lists.

When you use the Speller, WordPerfect checks your document for words it does not recognize. When it encounters one of these, it presents the message "Not Found!" and displays a list of possible spellings (if it finds any near matches), as shown in Figure 12.2. You can simply press the letter corresponding to the correct word; WordPerfect inserts it into the document for you so that you do not have to manually correct the spelling. If the word you intended is not on the list—or if WordPerfect has been unable to find a word spelled similarly to the one you have typed—you can have WordPerfect search for words that sound like the word it has highlighted. In Figure 12.3, for example, WordPerfect has presented phonetic alternatives for the highlighted word.

The Speller menu also offers a word count option, which is useful in two very different situations. First, and most obviously, it allows you to get a count of the words in your document, which can be useful if you are writing a document of a specific number of words for a journal or term paper. However, getting a word count of your document is also a quick way to make sure that any changes you have made in margin settings are reflected in the document's headers and footers (see Chapter 4).

Because you will probably often use words WordPerfect's Speller does not know—especially proper names and specialized terms you use in your work—the program makes it easy for you to add words to the dictionary. Each time you select

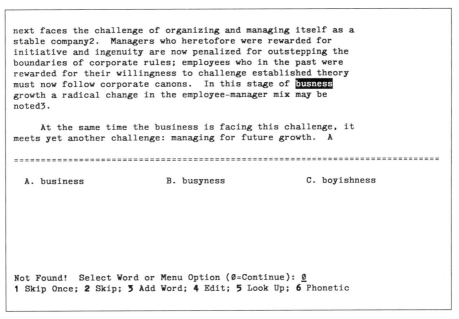

Figure 12.2: Presenting a list of suggested alternatives for a mistyped word. If WordPerfect presents a full screen of alternatives (A through X), press Return to display any additional alternatives.

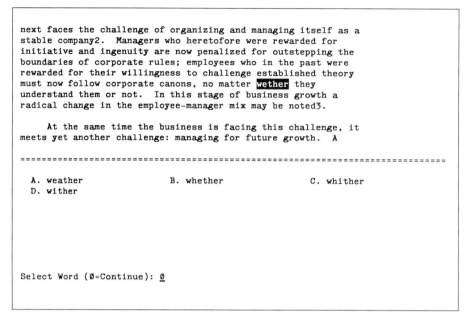

```
next faces the challenge of organizing and managing itself as a
stable company2.  Managers who heretofore were rewarded for
initiative and ingenuity are now penalized for outstepping the
boundaries of corporate rules; employees who in the past were
rewarded for their willingness to challenge established theory
must now follow corporate canons, no matter wether they
understand them or not.  In this stage of business growth a
radical change in the employee-manager mix may be noted3.

    At the same time the business is facing this challenge, it
meets yet another challenge: managing for future growth.  A

========================================================================

    A. weather              B. whether              C. whither
    D. wither




    Select Word (0=Continue): 0
```

Figure 12.3: Phonetic alternatives for a word. WordPerfect can search for words that sound like the word you have typed. If you are a habitually poor speller rather than an inaccurate typist, this feature can be especially useful.

option 3 (Add Word) from the Speller menu, WordPerfect adds that word to its supplemental dictionary, {WP}LEX.SUP. You can view this supplemental dictionary and edit it as you would any other document you create in WordPerfect. The dictionary {WP}LEX.SUP is automatically created in the directory containing WordPerfect utilities the first time you use the Add word option. You can also create other custom supplemental dictionaries of your own and specify that they be used instead of the regular supplemental dictionary. If you are working with two floppy drives instead of a hard disk and use a large supplemental dictionary, you may want to create several smaller supplemental dictionaries and copy the Speller (SPELL.EXE) plus your specialized dictionary onto one floppy disk.

Note that WordPerfect's Speller cannot check words that you have spelled correctly but may have used incorrectly, such as *weather* and *whether*. If you are in doubt about the use of these words, you may want to use the Speller's Look Up option (option 5) to look up such words; WordPerfect will then present you with a list of possible alternatives, even if the words are spelled correctly.

When you look up a word, you can use the question mark (?), asterisk (*), and hyphen (-) wildcard characters in place of letters you are unsure of. The question mark stands for any one letter, and the asterisk or hyphen represents a sequence of letters. For example, by entering ***tion-** you could look up all words beginning with any combination of letters, containing the string *tion*, and ending in any combination of letters.

The Speller can also check for double words—words that occur twice in a row in your documents, such as *the the* and *and and.* In addition, you can have the program ignore words containing numbers if your work requires you to write many phrases such as *the F2 key*; otherwise, WordPerfect will query you each time it sees a word containing a numeral.

USING THE SPELLER

When you use WordPerfect's Speller, it is wise to save your document first. The program checks the version that is currently in RAM (random-access memory). Also remember to save your document after you have spell checked it so that the changes you indicated as you used the Speller will become part of the saved version of your document.

To use WordPerfect's Speller, press Ctrl-F2 (Spell). You can select whether to check the word the cursor is on, a block that you have marked with Alt-F4 (Mark Block), the page the cursor is on, or the entire document as it appears on the screen. (When you instruct WordPerfect's Speller to check an entire document, it checks all portions of your document, including headers and footers, but it does not check index entries.) You can also instruct WordPerfect to look up a word that you type in response to a prompt or to count the words in your document. In addition, you can have the program use another main or supplemental dictionary that you have created (see ''Working with Other Dictionaries'' later in this chapter). If you have WordPerfect check the spelling of a word and it finds that the word is correct, you receive no on-screen notification; the cursor simply moves to the beginning of the next word.

When you use WordPerfect's Speller, you are presented with a screen whose lower half contains the suggested alternatives for any incorrect word Word-Perfect finds, as was shown in Figure 12.2. The top half shows where in your document WordPerfect found the suspect word. You cannot easily toggle between the two screens to edit your document, however. If you want to enter the document portion of the screen, you must either press F7 (Exit) or select option 4 (Edit). If you choose option 4, you may then edit the word that is presented or simply use the → or ← key to move from that word to the part of the sentence or paragraph that you wish to edit. While you are working with the spell checker, only the → and ← keys, along with Backspace and Del, are available as cursor movement keys. You cannot use most of the other cursor movement techniques, such as Go To (Ctrl-Home), End, and Ctrl-Backspace. You can change from Insert to Typeover mode, however.

To exit from the Speller, press F1 (Cancel). The program will present a word count of the text it has spell checked up to that point. Save your document if you want the changes introduced with the Speller to be incorporated into the saved version.

Because the Speller basically matches patterns, it quickly finds words in which only one or two letters are incorrect or out of place—such as *atble* for *table* or *procided* for *provided,* for example. It also catches more complex typographical errors and misspellings—it will suggest *document* as a replacement for *dicumenty,* for example.

The Speller ignores numbers, but it will stop at alphanumeric words—such as *F3*—and display the following menu:

Not Found! Select Word or Menu Option (0 = Continue)
1 2 Skip; 3 Ignore words containing numbers; 4 Edit

You can select option 3 (Ignore words containing numbers). If you select this option, WordPerfect will not query any typos in words such as *d9ocment,* however. If you habitually make such mistakes, be on the lookout for them.

Wordperfect's Speller will not suggest appropriate replacements for mistyped words containing symbols, such as *l;etter.* It considers only the portion of the word occurring after the symbol. It will query these words, but you must correct them manually. Likewise, it does not suggest appropriate replacements for words that have been run together, such as *specifythat.* It will query them, but you must correct them manually by pressing →, moving the cursor to the letter where the next word is to begin, pressing the space bar, and pressing Return to accept the new words.

WordPerfect's Speller will locate words that occur twice in a row. When it does, it presents the following menu:

Double word! 1 2 Skip; 3 Delete 2nd; 4 Edit; 5 Disable double word
checking

You can select option 3 to delete the second occurrence, or you can leave the words in place (options 1 and 2). Option 5 allows you to turn this feature off so that the program will not query you at double words.

You may notice as you use the Speller that sometimes the choices are presented in alphabetical order and sometimes they are not. This is because WordPerfect first looks in the common word list and then in the main word list. Both lists are stored in alphabetical order. The supplemental dictionary, which contains all the words you tell the program to add to its dictionary, is also maintained in alphabetical order, so unless your choices are all being pulled from one word list, you will not always see them in alphabetical order. You may also sometimes see duplicate words presented as choices if you have added a word to a supplemental dictionary that is in one of the other word lists as well, or if a word is in both the main and common word lists. After you have used the Speller for a while, you will be able to tell which list your commonly mistyped words are in by the amount of time it takes the program to display the choices on the screen.

If one of the words the Speller presents is the word you want, press the letter next to the word. WordPerfect then inserts the word into your text; you do not have to manually retype it or correct the incorrect letters. The program automatically capitalizes the word as it has been typed in your document. If you have mistyped *The* as *Hte* , WordPerfect will correct it as *The,* although its suggested replacement will be *the*.

If none of the words match the one you intended, press Return to see any additional word lists WordPerfect may find. For example, if WordPerfect presented you with a full screen of words, pressing Return may bring up additional alternatives that could not be displayed. WordPerfect sometimes will also present words beginning with other letters if you press Return. If words beginning with *c* are displayed, for example, pressing Return may bring up a list of words beginning with *k*.

If the Speller cannot locate a near match for a word, the blinking cursor moves from just under the double dashed line to the 0 at the end of the first menu line. If the cursor moves to this position, you know that WordPerfect has checked all its lists and cannot match the word. Press the → key to move the document screen and begin correcting the word manually.

WORKING WITH OTHER DICTIONARIES

If you are working with a floppy disk system and have space limitations, you may want to create and maintain several different supplemental dictionary–main dictionary combinations. For example, if you write articles for medical journals as well as popular science reviews, you might want to maintain a medical dictionary on a separate floppy disk. This disk should contain a copy of the Speller program (SPELL.EXE) and a copy of the main dictionary (LEX.WP) as well as the supplemental dictionary of medical terms. Each time you receive a "Dictionary Full" message indicating that you are out of RAM (see "'Dictionary Full' Messages" later in this chapter), you can add the supplemental dictionary to the main dictionary on that disk by using the Speller Utility (see "Editing Dictionaries" later in this chapter.) To help you remember which dictionary is which, you can simply label the floppy disk *Medical Dictionary*.

You can create a new main dictionary, but when you do so, it will not contain the 100,000 or so words in WordPerfect's main dictionary. If space is not a consideration, it is best to simply add words to your main dictionary. If you have space limitations, you can create separate supplemental dictionaries (see "Creating a New Supplemental Dictionary" later in this chapter). WordPerfect allows you to specify which main dictionary and supplemental dictionary to use (option 4 on the Speller menu) when you spell check a document.

"Dictionary Full" Messages

As you use the Speller, WordPerfect adds the words you specify to a supplemental dictionary called {WP}LEX.SUP. It also adds the words you skip to a list that it keeps in memory. When the RAM space you are working with becomes full—as it may when you are working with a large document, for example—you will receive the message "Dictionary Full." In such a case, you should add the words in the supplemental dictionary to the main dictionary (see "Using the Speller Utility" later in this chapter).

THE SPELLER UTILITY

A separate program, the Speller Utility, is provided on the Speller disk. This program allows you to create new dictionaries or edit both the common word list and the main word list in WordPerfect's built-in dictionary. It also allows you to display the common word list on the screen and perform word and phonetic lookup operations.

Because you may sometimes inadvertently add misspelled words to the dictionary by selecting option 3 (Add Word) from the Speller menu and then adding the supplemental dictionary to the main dictionary, the ability to delete words from the dictionary can be very useful to you. Likewise, it can be very useful for deleting words that you never use but which WordPerfect maintains as correct in the main dictionary. For example, *id* is a common typing error for *is,* but because the main dictionary lists *id* as a correct word (which it is, if you are writing in the field of psychology or related sciences), WordPerfect will not query you for the typographical error *id.* If you never use *id* or other main-dictionary words likely to appear in your documents as typing errors, you can delete them from the dictionary, and WordPerfect will recognize them as mistakes.

It is also handy to be able to add words directly to either the main dictionary or the common word list. WordPerfect's Speller Utility allows you to add or delete words directly from the keyboard or from a file containing a word list. When you create such a file, each word must be separated by a hard return, but the words do not have to be alphabetized.

You can also increase the speed of the spell-checking process by adding words you habitually mistype or misspell to the common word list instead of the main dictionary. The Speller Utility allows you to determine which list a word is in as well as to look up a word directly.

You can use the Speller Utility to

- Change dictionaries that you use
- Create new dictionaries
- Add words to the main dictionary's word lists

- Delete words from the main dictionary's word lists
- Optimize new dictionaries (by locating and formatting their words)
- Display the common word list
- Check the location of a word—whether it is in the common word list or the main word list

The Speller Utility's main menu (Figure 12.4) allows you to perform many housekeeping functions for the dictionaries you use.

Speller Utility Options

Option 1 on the Speller Utility allows you to change to another dictionary before using any of the other options or to create new dictionaries. Remember that any new dictionary you create will not contain WordPerfect's 100,000 or so entries unless you make a copy of the main dictionary and add words to it. If for some reason you do need to create an entirely new dictionary, you can use the procedure described in "Creating a New Main Dictionary" later in this chapter.

Option 2 (Add words to dictionary) allows you to add words to the current dictionary. Normally you would type **{WP}LEX.SUP** to add words from the

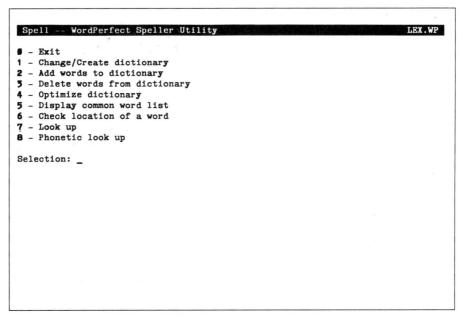

```
Spell -- WordPerfect Speller Utility                           LEX.WP

0 - Exit
1 - Change/Create dictionary
2 - Add words to dictionary
3 - Delete words from dictionary
4 - Optimize dictionary
5 - Display common word list
6 - Check location of a word
7 - Look up
8 - Phonetic look up

Selection: _
```

Figure 12.4: WordPerfect's Speller Utility. This menu allows you to perform housekeeping duties for the dictionaries you create and maintain in WordPerfect.

current supplemental dictionary to the main dictionary (or common word list). You can also add words directly from the keyboard or from another file containing a word list you have created.

Option 3 (Delete words from dictionary) allows you to delete words you enter from the keyboard or to delete words in a file containing a word list you have created.

Option 4 (Optimize dictionary) is used when you create a new dictionary. It instructs WordPerfect to alphabetize the words the new dictionary contains and format them properly. You should use this option only when you are creating a new dictionary.

Option 5 displays the common word list, which is a list of 1550 of the most commonly used words. WordPerfect displays the list in alphabetical order, one screen at a time; you can exit from this display by pressing F1 (Cancel). Option 6 allows you to determine whether a word is in WordPerfect's dictionary, and if it is, whether it is in the common word list or the main word list.

Options 7 and 8 allow you to look up a word you specify, either by its actual spelling or its phonetic spelling. With option 7 (Look up) you can use the wild-card characters * and ? to check spellings you are unsure of. For example, if you know the word *receive* is spelled either *receive* or *recieve,* you can enter *rec??ve.*

Using the Speller Utility

When you use the Speller Utility to add words to (option 2) or delete them from (option 3) a dictionary, no matter how few or how many words, the process will take up to 20 minutes (a shorter time for the smaller common word list) because WordPerfect must resort the entire dictionary. The program does not execute the add or delete operation until you exit from the Add or delete menu (option 5 on both menus).

If you have a floppy disk system, the Speller disk (the one containing SPELL-.EXE) must be in drive A. Drive A must not contain any customized dictionary you may have made, the main dictionary (LEX.WP), or any supplemental dictionaries. Your data disk should be in drive B. If you have a hard disk, the Speller Utility should be in the same directory as the WordPerfect program files, WP.EXE.

USING THE THESAURUS

Using WordPerfect's Thesaurus is a quick way to see a list of nouns, adjectives, and verbs that have meanings similar to that of a word in your document. To use the Thesaurus, you can first position the cursor on or after the word you wish to look up. When you press Alt-F1 (Thesaurus), you will see three columns containing various words as well as several lines of your text that surround the word you are looking up (Figure 12.5). (If you are using a floppy disk system, the Thesaurus disk must be in drive B before you press Alt-F1.)

The word you are looking up is presented in boldface at the beginning of each group of nouns, adjectives, or verbs. WordPerfect then presents several alternatives for that word that have the same or similar meanings. A word with a dot to its left (like *history* in Figure 12.5) is called a headword, and you can look up further references to it through the Thesaurus. If you press the letter next to any of the headwords, further lists of suggested alternatives will appear. For example, to display the screen for the headword *over*, shown in Figure 12.6, the letter *G* was pressed from the screen in Figure 12.5.

You can move between the columns by using the ← and → keys. The ↑ and ↓ keys as well as the PgUp and PgDn keys scroll the columns vertically. The Home (Home Home ↑) and End key combinations (Home Home ↓) take you to the beginning and end of the Thesaurus entry.

You can replace the word in your document with any of the words in the list by selecting option 1 (Replace Word) from the Thesaurus menu and typing the letter corresponding to the word you wish to use instead. You can also return to view your document—for example, to get a better idea of the context in which the word was used—by selecting option 2 (View Doc). Although you cannot edit

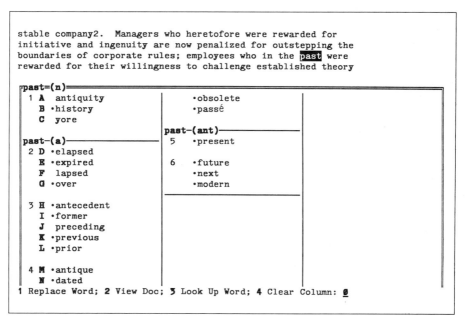

Figure 12.5: Using the Thesaurus. Here WordPerfect is presenting a list of alternative nouns and adjectives for the word *past* as well as antonyms—words such as *future* and *present* that mean the opposite of *past*.

your document while using option 2, you can return to the Thesaurus by pressing Exit (F7), or you can continue to use the Thesaurus by pressing Alt-F1 again to look up another word. You can press Return, Exit (F7), or Cancel (F1) to return to the Thesaurus.

If the word you are looking for is not on the list, try selecting other headwords (those with a dot next to them) and looking up their synonyms. You can also enter a word for the Thesaurus to look up that is not a headword (option 3, Look Up Word). If you use this method, you will find that the Thesaurus is a very useful tool and will take you through many different levels of meanings. If your screen becomes cluttered with too many alternative words, you can use option 4 (Clear Column) to clear the column the cursor is in and make room for more synonyms of another headword.

To use the Thesaurus with a two-floppy-disk system, replace the data disk in drive B with the Thesaurus disk. When you have finished looking up words and making any replacements within your document, replace your data disk in drive B and save your document. If you use the Thesaurus extensively, you may want to copy it onto your data disk so that you do not have to swap disks. Use the DOS COPY command to copy TH.WP, which is the Thesaurus program.

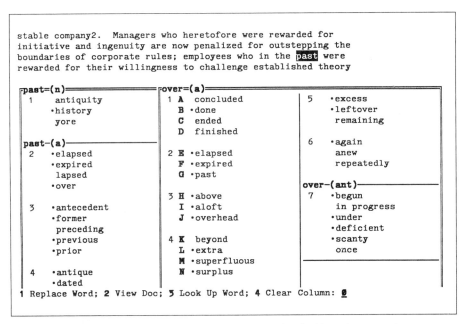

Figure 12.6: Looking up a headword. Headwords, which are identified by a dot next to them, are connected to lists of related words. To see synonyms for a headword, press the letter corresponding to the word. WordPerfect's Thesaurus contains approximately 10,000 headwords. In this figure, the letter G was typed to see related words for the headword *over* (listed in Figure 12.5). Notice that the related words for *over* listed in the second and third columns include a group of antonyms, listed under 7.

If you are using the Thesaurus on a hard disk, WordPerfect will first look for TH.WP, the Thesaurus program, in the same directory as the WordPerfect program, WP.EXE. If it does not find it there, it will prompt you for the full path name of the location where the Thesaurus is stored.

INSTALLING THE SPELLER AND THESAURUS ON A FLOPPY DISK SYSTEM

When you use WordPerfect with a floppy disk system, the WordPerfect Program disk is in drive A and the data disk is in drive B. You must use the Setup program to tell WordPerfect that the Speller will also be in drive B. To do so,

1. With the DOS A> prompt displayed on your screen, put the WordPerfect Program disk in drive A and the Speller disk in drive B.
2. Enter **WP/S** to bring up the Setup menu.
3. Select option 1 (Set Directories or Drives for Dictionary and Thesaurus Files). The following prompt appears:

    Where do you plan to keep the dictionary (LEX.WP)?
    Enter full path name:

4. Enter **B:**.
5. You will then be prompted to enter the path name for the supplemental dictionary and the Thesaurus. Enter **B:** at each of these prompts.
6. When you have specified drive B for the dictionaries and the Thesaurus, enter **0** to exit from the Setup menu and begin WordPerfect. To return to DOS, press F7 and respond to the WordPerfect exit prompts.

From now on, when you want to use the Speller or Thesaurus, you must remove your data disk from drive B and insert the Speller disk. You can then press Ctrl-F2 to use the Speller or Alt-F1 to use the Thesaurus. When you have corrected your document, remove the Speller disk and reinsert the data disk in drive B before you save your document. If you forget to remove the Speller disk and save the corrected document on the Speller disk instead of on the data disk, simply insert the data disk, save the document again, insert the Speller disk, and delete the saved document from it (see Chapter 6 for details about saving and deleting files).

As you use the Speller, WordPerfect adds the words you add to a supplemental dictionary called {WP}LEX.SUP. It also adds the words you skip to a temporary area in memory. When this space becomes full, you will receive the message "Dictionary Full." In such a case, you should add the words in the supplemental dictionary to the main dictionary. See "Using the Speller Utility" earlier in this chapter for instructions about how to do this if you work with large supplemental dictionaries.

INSTALLING THE SPELLER AND THESAURUS ON A HARD DISK SYSTEM

If you have a hard disk and you intend to keep the Speller and Thesaurus in a directory other than the default directory, you need to instruct WordPerfect about which directory contains the Speller and Thesaurus. You do this during the setup procedure.

To run the setup procedure,

1. At the C> prompt, enter **WP/S**.

2. Select option 1 (Set Directories or Drives for Dictionary and Thesaurus Files). The following prompt appears:

   Where do you plan to keep the dictionary (LEX.WP)?
   Enter full path name:

3. Enter the full path name of the directory where you intend to keep the Dictionary and Thesaurus, if you intend to keep them in a directory other than the default directory (the one containing WP.EXE). For example, if you plan to use a subdirectory named SPELL under the directory \WP, enter **C:\WP\SPELL.**

4. You will then be prompted to enter the path name for the supplemental dictionary and the Thesaurus. Enter the same full path name for each of these prompts; your work will be simplified by keeping all three together.

5. When you have specified the correct path name for the dictionaries and the Thesaurus, enter **0** to exit from the Setup menu and begin WordPerfect. To return to DOS, press F7 and respond to the exit prompts.

From then on, all you have to do to use the Speller is press Ctrl-F2. To use the Thesaurus, press Alt-F1.

THE SPELLER

If you have a floppy disk system, the Speller disk should be in drive B, and you should have retrieved the document you want to check. Do not remove the Speller disk from drive B while you are checking your document.

If you have a hard disk, the Speller (SPELL.EXE) should be in the same directory as the WordPerfect program files (WP.EXE).

Looking Up a Word

KEY SEQUENCE

To check a word's spelling:
   Ctrl-F2 1
To look up alternative spellings:
   Ctrl-F2 5

If you wish to check the spelling of the word the cursor is on, press Ctrl-F2 (Spell) and select option 1. If the cursor moves on to the next word, the current word is spelled correctly. If the spelling is incorrect, WordPerfect will present a list of possible alternatives. Press the letter corresponding to the word you wish to use or, if the correct alternative is not displayed, press → to begin editing the word manually.

If you wish to look up alternative spellings of a word, select option 5 (Look Up) and type a word or word pattern at the prompt. WordPerfect then presents all the close combinations of that pattern it can find in its dictionaries. You can press the letter corresponding to the word you wish to use if it is displayed.

Checking a Page

KEY SEQUENCE

   Ctrl-F2 2

If you want to check for misspellings and typographical errors only on the page on which the cursor appears, you can use option 2 of WordPerfect's Speller menu. You may want to do this if you have checked the entire document and then returned to a certain page to make corrections or additions, for example.

Checking a Document

KEY SEQUENCE

   Ctrl-F2 3

Selecting option 3 from the Speller menu allows you to check your entire document, including headers, footers, footnotes, and endnotes. It does not, however, check index entries. You can exit from the spell-checking process at any time by pressing F1 (Cancel); the changes you have made up to that point will be retained in your document. Be sure to save your document if you wish to save those changes.

For a discussion of the types of errors WordPerfect locates, see "Using the Speller" earlier in this chapter.

When you use the Speller, WordPerfect checks your document for words it does not recognize. When it encounters one of these, it displays the message "Not Found!" and a list of possible spellings (if it finds any near matches), as shown in Figure 12.7. You can simply press the letter corresponding to the correct word; WordPerfect inserts it into the document for you so that you do not have to manually correct the spelling. If the word you intended is not on the list—or if WordPerfect has been unable to find a word spelled similarly to the one you have typed—you can have WordPerfect search for words that sound like the word it has highlighted by selecting option 6 (Phonetic).

To manually correct a word, select option 4 (Edit) or simply press → to move the cursor onto the highlighted word; then correct the word. While you are working with the spell checker, only the → and ← keys, along with Backspace and Del, are available as cursor movement keys. You cannot use most of the other cursor

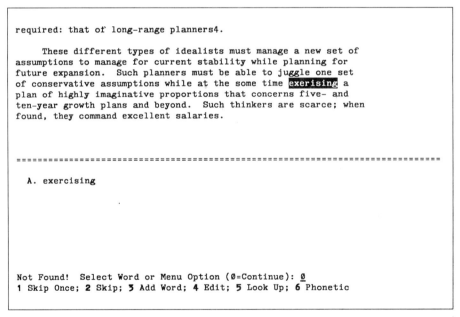

```
required: that of long-range planners4.

    These different types of idealists must manage a new set of
assumptions to manage for current stability while planning for
future expansion.  Such planners must be able to juggle one set
of conservative assumptions while at the some time exerising a
plan of highly imaginative proportions that concerns five- and
ten-year growth plans and beyond.  Such thinkers are scarce; when
found, they command excellent salaries.



===========================================================================

  A. exercising




Not Found!  Select Word or Menu Option (0=Continue): 0
1 Skip Once; 2 Skip; 3 Add Word; 4 Edit; 5 Look Up; 6 Phonetic
```

Figure 12.7: Using the Speller. Note that although WordPerfect has caught the misspelling of *exercising*, it has not caught the correctly spelled but incorrectly used word *some* (instead of *same*) just to the left. If a word is correctly spelled and is in WordPerfect's dictionary, the program will not query you about its spelling.

movement techniques, such as Goto (Ctrl-Home), End, or Ctrl-Backspace. You can change from Insert to Typeover mode, however.

The Speller ignores numbers, but it does stop at alphanumeric words—such as *F3*—and display the following menu:

> **Not Found! Select Word or Menu Option (0 = Continue)**
> **1 2 Skip; 3 Ignore words containing numbers; 4 Edit**

WordPerfect's Speller also locates words that occur twice in a row. When it does, it presents the following menu:

> **Double word! 1 2 Skip; 3 Delete 2nd; 4 Edit; 5 Disable double word**
> **checking**

You can select option 3 to delete the second occurrence, or you can leave the words in place (options 1 and 2). Option 5 allows you to turn this feature off so that the program does not query you at double words.

Getting a Word Count

KEY SEQUENCE

Ctrl-F2 6

To obtain a quick count of the words in your document, use option 6 of the Speller menu. This is also a good way to make sure that your entire document is properly formatted with any margin changes you may have made. Because WordPerfect checks headers and footers when it performs a word count, it implements in the headers and footers any changes in margin settings (see "Setting Headers and Footers" in Chapter 4).

USING THE SPELLER UTILITY

To use the Speller Utility, you must first exit to DOS either by exiting Word-Perfect (F7) or using the DOS Shell command (Ctrl-F1 1). If you are using a floppy disk system, insert the Speller disk in drive A and a data disk in drive B. When WordPerfect executes the Speller Utility to create a new dictionary, it creates it in drive B. It then deletes the old version of the main dictionary from the Speller disk in drive A and recopies the dictionary in drive B back into drive A.

Note: If the disk in drive A does not have sufficient space, WordPerfect will cancel the transfer of the new dictionary from drive B to drive A. In such a case, you need to delete extra files that may be on the Speller disk and then use the DOS COPY command to transfer the updated dictionary from the disk in drive B to the disk in drive A. You can also simply use the dictionary disk that is in drive B as your dictionary disk. Remember to label the disk properly if you choose to use this method.

If you are using WordPerfect on a hard disk system, make sure that the directory containing the LEX.WP file is current before issuing the following Speller Utility Startup command.

To use the Speller Utility at the DOS prompt,

1. Enter **SPELL** and press Return.
2. When the Speller Utility's main menu (shown in Figure 12.4) appears, select the option(s) you wish to use, one at a time, and supply any other necessary information the program prompts you for. (The options are presented in the following sections.)
3. When you have selected all the options you wish to use, enter **0** (Exit).

Adding or deleting words (options 2 and 3) may take as long as 20 minutes because the program alphabetizes and formats any new dictionary entries.

Changing Dictionaries

KEY SEQUENCE

B>**SPELL Return 1**

If you wish to switch the current dictionary to another one—to update it, for example—select option 1 on the Speller Utility menu. The prompt

Name of Dictionary to use:

appears. If you want to update a dictionary you have already created, enter its name—for example, **LEGAL.LEX**—at this prompt. If you want to create a new dictionary, enter its name at this prompt (see the next sections). WordPerfect will carry out all the options you subsequently select from the Speller Utility menu on the dictionary you specify here. If you are simply updating the main default dictionary (LEX.WP), you do not need to use this option.

Creating a New Main Dictionary

KEY SEQUENCE

B>**SPELL Return 1**

If you wish to create a new dictionary, select option 1 on the Speller Utility menu. The prompt

Name of Dictionary to use:

appears. Enter the name of the dictionary you wish to create, using the extension **.LEX.** WordPerfect displays the prompt

Create a new dictionary named <*file name*.LEX> (Y/N) N?

Press **Y** to create the new dictionary, which will be empty at this point.

The name of the current main dictionary is displayed in the upper-right corner of the screen. When you change to or create another dictionary, its name is displayed there.

> *Note:* When you create a new dictionary, it will not contain the 100,000 or so words in WordPerfect's main dictionary. You can delete the main dictionary by naming another, smaller dictionary LEX.WP. To be safe, always work with a copy of the main dictionary on a separate floppy disk or in a separate directory on the hard disk. If space is not a consideration, it is best to simply add words to your main dictionary. If you work with a floppy disk system, you may wish to create different versions of the main dictionary and keep them on separate floppy disks.
>
> You must then add words to your new dictionary (see the sections that discuss editing dictionaries later in this chapter). After you have added words, select option 4 to optimize the new dictionary. During this process WordPerfect alphabetizes the dictionary entries and formats them so that they may be used.

Creating a New Supplemental Dictionary

To create a new supplemental dictionary, you simply create a new document containing the words you want to include, each separated by a hard return. *Make sure that the words are spelled correctly.* When you save the document, give it a name, such as LEGAL.SUP, that helps you remember that it is a supplemental dictionary.

To use a different supplemental dictionary, select option 4 (Change Dictionary) when you run the Speller. When you are prompted to do so, enter the full path name of the supplemental dictionary you wish to use.

If you are working with a floppy disk system, you may wish to create several specialized dictionary disks by copying the Speller (SPELL.EXE) plus each specialized supplemental dictionary onto one floppy disk.

Editing a Main Dictionary

> **KEY SEQUENCE**
>
> B>SPELL Return 2

You can add words to a dictionary—either the main dictionary, LEX.WP, or other main dictionaries you have created—and delete words from it directly from the keyboard or by using a file containing the words you wish to add or delete. You may, for example, inadvertently add a word that is misspelled to the supplemental dictionary while spell checking your document and then later add the supplemental dictionary to the main dictionary, thus inserting a misspelled word into the main dictionary. You can use the Speller Utility to delete those words.

You may also want to add words you often mistype to the common word list to speed up the spell-checking process.

When you select option 2 from the Speller Utility main menu, the Add Words menu appears on the screen, as shown in Figure 12.8. Option 3 presents the Delete Words menu; it works the same way and has the same options as the Add Words menu.

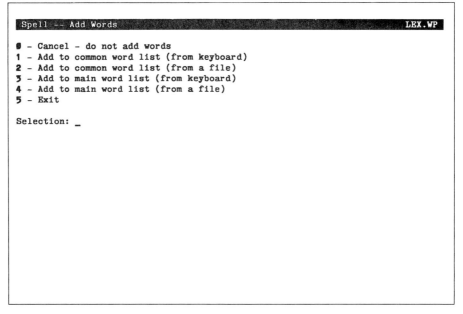

```
 Spell -- Add Words                                        LEX.WP
 ⬤ - Cancel - do not add words
 1 - Add to common word list (from keyboard)
 2 - Add to common word list (from a file)
 3 - Add to main word list (from keyboard)
 4 - Add to main word list (from a file)
 5 - Exit

 Selection: _
```

Figure 12.8: The Add Words menu. This menu allows you to add words to the main dictionary. If you receive the message "Dictionary Full" as you work, you need to add the words contained in the supplemental dictionary ({WP}LEX.SUP) to the main dictionary. This menu allows you to do so.

From the Add Words menu, you can select option 1 or 2 to add words to the common word list from the keyboard. The common word list is the one that WordPerfect checks first, so if you are adding words that you will use often, select one of these options. (If you are adding words to the common word list from the default supplemental dictionary, select option 2 and enter **{WP}LEX.SUP** as the name of the file when prompted to do so.)

Options 3 and 4 allow you to add words directly from the keyboard or from a file to the main word list. If you are updating the main dictionary from the default supplemental dictionary, use option 4 and enter **{WP}LEX.SUP** when prompted for a file name. Otherwise, enter the name of the file containing the words you wish to add. The words in the file should be separated by hard returns, but they do not need to be in alphabetical order. If you want to add words to a dictionary other than the main dictionary, you must first use option 1 on the main Speller Utility menu to change to that dictionary.

Select option 0 to return to the Speller Utility menu without making any changes; select option 5 to run the Add Words program and to exit from the Add Words menu.

Editing a Supplemental Dictionary

You can edit the default supplemental dictionary, {WP}LEX.SUP, or any other supplemental dictionary you create just as you would any other Word-Perfect document. Simply retrieve it by using List Files (F5) or by pressing Shift-F10 (Retrieve).

If you receive the message "Dictionary Full" while you are using the Speller, you need to add the supplemental dictionary to the main dictionary. See "Editing a Main Dictionary" earlier in this chapter.

Displaying the Common Word List

KEY SEQUENCE

B>**SPELL Return 5**

Because WordPerfect's Speller checks the common word list first, you may want to view the contents of this list and add words that you habitually mistype to it to speed up the checking process. For example, *document* is a word often mistyped, but because of the time WordPerfect takes to match its pattern and suggest alternatives for it, this word is in the main word list instead of the common word list.

When you select option 5 from the Speller Utility menu, WordPerfect displays the common word list in alphabetical order, one screen at a time (Figure 12.9).

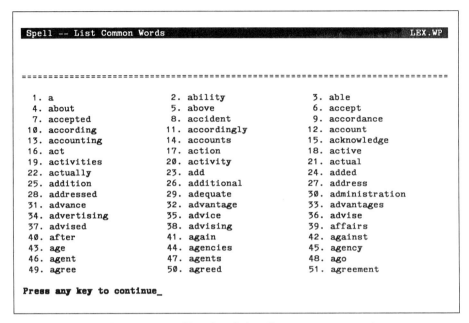

```
Spell -- List Common Words                                              LEX.WP
================================================================================

   1. a                       2. ability              3. able
   4. about                   5. above                6. accept
   7. accepted                8. accident             9. accordance
  10. according              11. accordingly         12. account
  13. accounting             14. accounts            15. acknowledge
  16. act                    17. action              18. active
  19. activities             20. activity            21. actual
  22. actually               23. add                 24. added
  25. addition               26. additional          27. address
  28. addressed              29. adequate            30. administration
  31. advance                32. advantage           33. advantages
  34. advertising            35. advice              36. advise
  37. advised                38. advising            39. affairs
  40. after                  41. again               42. against
  43. age                    44. agencies            45. agency
  46. agent                  47. agents              48. ago
  49. agree                  50. agreed              51. agreement

Press any key to continue_
```

Figure 12.9: Viewing the common word list. If you habitually mistype certain words, you may want to check this list to be sure that these words are included in it. WordPerfect checks this list first, so adding the words you typically misspell to it may speed up the spell-checking process.

You can press any key to move through the list (in a forward direction only). To exit from viewing the list, press F1 (Cancel). You cannot edit this list directly; to add words to it or delete words from it, use options 2 and 3 on the Speller Utility menu (see the sections that discuss editing dictionaries earlier in this chapter).

Checking the Location of a Word

KEY SEQUENCE

B>**SPELL Return 6**

To check whether a word is in the common word list or the main word list, use option 6 on the Speller Utility menu. You will receive the prompt

Word to check:

Enter the word you want to check. WordPerfect responds with either

Found in main dictionary

or

Found in common word list

You can check any number of words. Press F1 (Cancel) to return to the Speller Utility menu.

Looking Up Words with the Speller Utility

KEY SEQUENCE

To look up the spelling of a word:
   B>**SPELL Return 7**
To look up a word phonetically:
   B>**SPELL Return 8**

You can also use the Speller Utility to look up a word directly. You can use the question mark (**?**) and asterisk (*****) wildcard characters in place of letters you are unsure of. The question mark stands for any one letter, and the asterisk represents a sequence of letters. For example, if you want to check the spelling of *reprieve* but are unsure of whether the word is spelled *repreieve, repreive,* or *reprieve,* you can enter **repr*ve** to see a list of correctly spelled words beginning with *repr-* and ending in *-ve* (Figure 12.10).

Use option 8 to look up a word phonetically, just as you would in the Speller program.

USING THE THESAURUS

If you have a floppy disk system, the Thesaurus disk should be in drive B, and you should have retrieved the document you want to check. See "Installing the Speller and Thesaurus on a Floppy Disk System" earlier in this chapter.

If you are using a hard disk, you should have instructed WordPerfect about where you are storing the Thesaurus if you are not keeping it in the same directory as the WordPerfect program files (WP.EXE). See "Installing the Speller and Thesaurus on a Hard Disk System" earlier in this chapter.

Viewing Alternative Words

KEY SEQUENCE

Alt-F1

```
┌──────────────────────────────────────────────────────────────────────────┐
│▐Spell -- Match Pattern                                             LEX.WP▌ │
│                                                                            │
│ Word Pattern: _                                                            │
│                                                                            │
│ =========================================================================  │
│                                                                            │
│    1. reprehensive      2. representative      3. repressive               │
│    4. reprieve          5. reprobative         6. reproductive             │
│    7. reprove                                                              │
│                                                                            │
│                                                                            │
│                                                                            │
│                                                                            │
│                                                                            │
│                                                                            │
│                                                                            │
│                                                                            │
└──────────────────────────────────────────────────────────────────────────┘
```

Figure 12.10: Looking up a word through the Speller Utility. This process works the same way as looking up a word in the Speller program.

You can view alternative nouns, adjectives, and verbs for words in your document or for words you type in response to a prompt. There are several ways to look up a word:

- Move the cursor to the word and press Alt-F1 (Thesaurus).
- Press Alt-F1 (Thesaurus), press Return, and select option 3 (Look Up Word).
- If you are in the Thesaurus, select option 2 (View Doc), move the cursor to the word you want to look up, and press Alt-F1 (Thesaurus).

While you are in the Thesaurus,

- To view the context of the words in your document, select option 2 (View Doc). To return to the Thesaurus after viewing the document, press Return, F1 (Cancel), or F7 (Exit).
- To view groups of related words, type the letter corresponding to any of the headwords (those with dots to their left).
- To clear a column and make room for additional alternate words, move to the column and select option 4 (Clear Column).
- To exit from the Thesaurus without replacing any words, press Return, F1 (Cancel), or F7 (Exit).

If you wish to replace a word in your document with any of the suggested words, select option 1 (Replace Word) from the Thesaurus menu. You will be prompted to type the letter corresponding to the word in the display on the screen. When you do so, WordPerfect inserts the word in your document at the location of the cursor.

SUMMARY

This chapter has shown you how to use WordPerfect's Speller and Thesaurus to get the most from these built-in aids as you work. In addition, you have seen how you can use the Speller Utility to create custom dictionaries and tailor Word-Perfect's main dictionary to suit your needs.

Chapter 13, "Line and Box Drawing," discusses techniques you can use to create forms and charts directly within WordPerfect, and Chapter 14, "Creating and Using Macros," discusses how you can write your own macros, which can be great time savers.

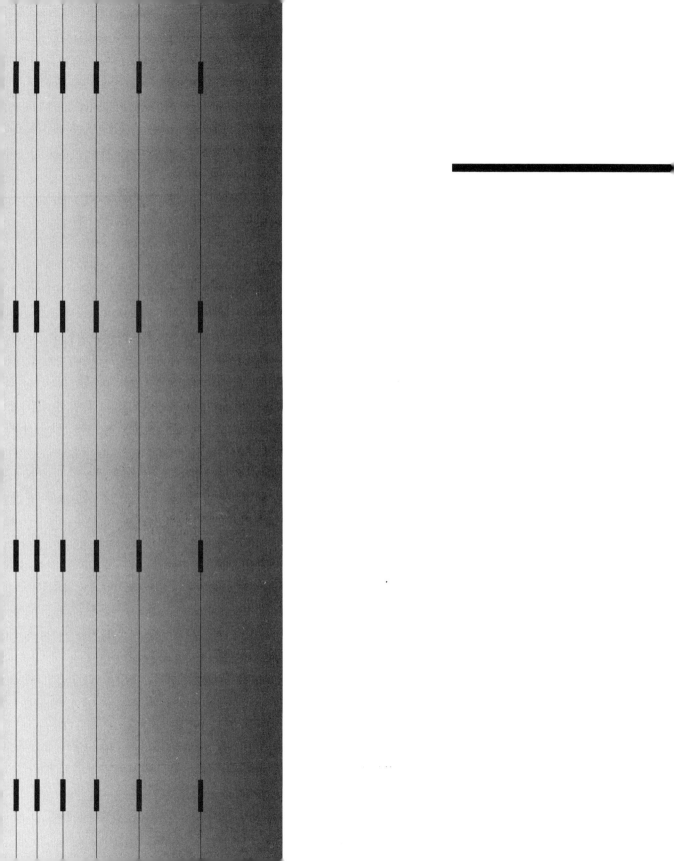

LINE AND BOX DRAWING

LINE AND BOX DRAWING

Not only does WordPerfect process words for you, but it also allows you to create simple graphics—such as charts, forms, and graphs—in your documents. If you are creating newsletters or brochures, you can use the program's graphics features to add interest to your page layouts, create borders around areas where artwork will be inserted, and highlight portions of the page to attract the reader's attention. You can even use WordPerfect to create fairly complex forms, complete with boxes and rules. In addition, you can create special mathematical symbols, such as brackets for large matrices, by using WordPerfect's Line Draw feature.

Because you can save the graphics you create, you can use simple shapes over and over again without having to create them each time from scratch. If you use standard graphics shapes often—such as in organization charts that change monthly, for example—you may want to use WordPerfect's macro capabilities to generate these shapes wherever you need them in your documents.

This chapter explains the techniques you use to create graphics with Word-Perfect's line and box drawing feature. If you create newsletters or other documents in which you use text columns, you may want to explore the techniques discussed in Chapter 8. If your primary interest is in using line drawing with forms, especially those for making simple calculations—such as invoices and order forms—you may want to review the techniques discussed in Chapter 11 to see how to set up your forms so that calculations can be performed within them. You may also want to investigate the possibility of using merge codes in forms you create with WordPerfect so that standard information will automatically be inserted; Chapter 9 discusses how to use merge codes in forms you design with line and box drawing.

USING GRAPHICS IN WORDPERFECT

WordPerfect's line and box drawing feature allows you to use the graphics characters that your printer is capable of printing to create a variety of relatively simple graphs, charts, and forms, such as the one illustrated in Figure 13.1. You can draw using single lines, double lines, or asterisks, or you can select up to eight different types of alternate drawing characters. In addition, you can use any of the IBM graphics characters that your printer can print in the drawings you create.

Printer Considerations

Because your screen can probably display many more characters than your printer can handle, you should run the PRINTER.TST described in Chapter 5 to see which graphics characters are available to you. Most dot-matrix printers can print many of the IBM graphics characters, but letter-quality printers, such as daisy-wheel printers, are limited to the characters that are on their print wheels. If you have a laser printer, Font 8 usually contains the graphics characters. Because WordPerfect Corporation is constantly updating the WordPerfect Printer program for use with additional printers, check with WordPerfect Corporation to make sure that you have the most recent Printer program.

You will also want to test your printer to determine the correct vertical-to-horizontal ratio to use for drawing squares. Boxes that appear square on the screen may not be square when they are printed because the representation on the screen does not show the same ratio used when a document is printed. Moving the cursor a certain number of spaces vertically is not the same as moving it the same number of spaces horizontally; the cursor moves a greater distance vertically. You can try out your printer by drawing what appears to be a square on the screen and then pressing Shift-F7 (Print) and choosing option 2 (Page) to see immediately whether the box

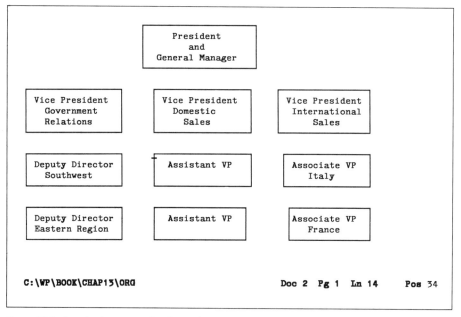

Figure 13.1: Sample chart created with WordPerfect's line and box drawing feature. You can draw "freehand" on the screen, or you can create a variety of shapes and store them in a file from which you can cut and paste the shapes you need. If you use graphics often, you can write macros that generate basic graphics shapes for you.

you have drawn is printed as a square or not. Many dot-matrix printers use a 5:3 vertical to horizontal ratio; that is, a box that is 5 spaces deep and 3 spaces wide (or 10 spaces by 6 spaces, or 15 spaces by 9 spaces, and so forth) will print as a square. Figure 13.2 illustrates the differences in screen representation and printed results using an Epson FX-85 dot-matrix printer. Use a similar test with your printer to determine the correct ratio for squares.

Getting Ready to Draw

Any complex drawing or form you want to create requires a little forethought. You may find it convenient to sketch a diagram on graph paper before you begin so that you can determine the exact line number on which to place graphic elements. The default document page size (for $8\frac{1}{2}$ × 11-inch paper) is 65 characters wide by 51 lines high. If you need more space than this, you can change to condensed font (see Chapter 5), which usually gives you up to a 132-character width to work with on $8\frac{1}{2}$ × 11-inch paper.

Even if you decide not to sketch out your form or chart completely, you should estimate the longest line of text that each box or area needs to contain. You can

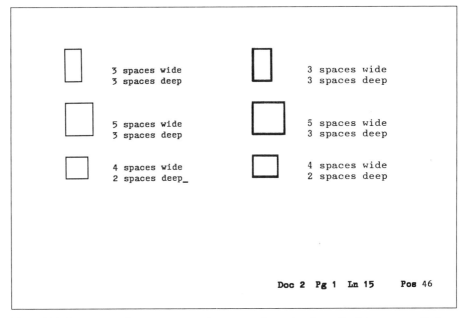

Figure 13.2: Determining the correct way to draw rectangles so that they will print as squares. Rectangles as represented on the monitor screen do not have the same proportions when they are printed. Part (a) of this figure illustrates a variety of shapes as they appear on the screen; part (b) shows how they appear when printed. Exact proportions may vary, depending on the type of printer you are using.

simply type a sample entry on the screen and draw a box around it; in most cases, this is the fastest way to estimate length.

Drawing Graphics

When you draw within WordPerfect, you are actually in Typeover mode. Characters that you draw replace any other characters that may be on the screen. Because of this, you may want to enter text for your charts and forms first and then draw the rules around them.

In addition, if you return later to add text to drawings, you must be sure to press the Ins key to go into Typeover mode. (When Typeover mode is on, the word *Typeover* appears in the lower-left corner of the screen.) If you remain in Insert mode, you will get unexpected results, as illustrated in Figure 13.3.

Any format codes you have inserted on the screen can produce unexpected results in Box and Line Drawing mode. For example, if you use Shift-F6 to center text and then later attempt to enclose this text in a box, the rule you draw will not extend over the [C] code on the line where it is present. You will need to exit Line Draw mode (press F7), press Alt-F3 to view the format codes, position the

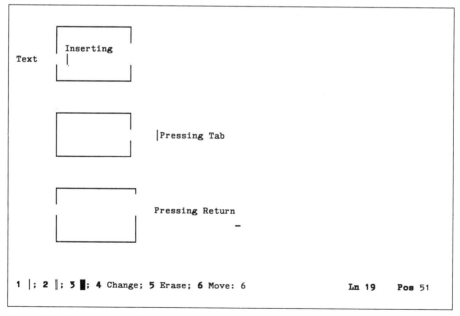

Figure 13.3: Entering text into box drawings while in Insert mode. As you can see, inserting text or pressing Tab or Return destroys the graphic arrangement. For this reason, be sure to enter text into graphics you create in WordPerfect by first pressing Ins to go into Typeover mode. In Typeover mode, you can add many graphics enhancements, such as legends, to graphs.

cursor to the right of any codes that are causing trouble, and press Backspace to delete these codes. At that point you may also need to reposition text on the screen. For this reason, it is better to first create the shape that you want to center and then mark it as a block (with Alt-F4) before you press Shift-F6 to center it.

When you are using Line and Box Drawing (Ctrl-F3 2), the end of the menu line indicates which option you have chosen. For example, option 1 (the default) is the current choice on the following menu:

1 ¦ ; 2 ¦¦ ; 3*; 4 Change; 5 Erase; 6 Move: 1

Options 1, 2, and 3 present the graphics characters that are available for you to draw with. Option 5 allows you to erase characters, and option 6 lets you move the cursor through graphics characters without erasing them. Option 4 allows you to change the graphics character used by option 3. If you select option 4, you are presented with eight alternative graphics characters. You can select one of these to replace option 3 on the previous menu, or you can select option 9 (Other) to enter the ASCII code for any other graphics character your printer will print. To see the list of possible codes and the characters they represent, exit from Line Draw mode by pressing F7 (Exit) and then press Ctrl-F3 (Screen) and select option 3 (Ctrl/Alt Keys) from the menu. The chart that appears at the bottom of the screen contains the codes for the IBM graphics characters, as illustrated in Figure 13.4. Remember, however, that your printer may not be able to print all of these characters; before you use them, run PRINTER.TST as described in Chapter 5 to determine which characters your printer can print.

Mixing Graphics and Text

Because any format codes that may be present on the screen can get in the way of line drawings, it is usually wise to create your graphics in a separate document, perhaps in a second window, and cut and paste them into the location where you want them in a document. To cut and paste a graphics drawing, you simply mark its beginning and end (opposite corners) with Alt-F4 (Mark Block), press Ctrl-F4 (Move), and select option 5 (Cut/Copy Rectangle). Position your cursor at the location in your document where you want the graphic image, press Ctrl-F4 (Move), and select option 6 (Move Rectangle).

Working with Forms

WordPerfect's Line Draw feature can be very useful for creating forms. You can use graphics characters to draw attention to important areas of the form that must be filled in or to block out sections that are to be kept blank, as shown in Figure 13.5. You can even create forms that will perform calculations on the

Key	Value	Key	Value	Key	Value	Key	Value
Alt-A	0	Alt-N	0	Ctrl-A	0	Ctrl-N	0
Alt-B	0	Alt-O	0	Ctrl-B	0	Ctrl-O	0
Alt-C	0	Alt-P	0	Ctrl-C	0	Ctrl-P	0
Alt-D	0	Alt-Q	0	Ctrl-D	0	Ctrl-Q	0
Alt-E	0	Alt-R	0	Ctrl-E	0	Ctrl-R	0
Alt-F	0	Alt-S	0	Ctrl-F	0	Ctrl-S	0
Alt-G	0	Alt-T	0	Ctrl-G	0	Ctrl-T	0
Alt-H	0	Alt-U	0	Ctrl-H	0	Ctrl-U	0
Alt-I	0	Alt-V	0	Ctrl-I	0	Ctrl-V	0
Alt-J	0	Alt-W	0	Ctrl-J	0	Ctrl-W	0
Alt-K	0	Alt-X	0	Ctrl-K	0	Ctrl-X	0
Alt-L	0	Alt-Y	0	Ctrl-L	0	Ctrl-Y	0
Alt-M	0	Alt-Z	0	Ctrl-M	0	Ctrl-Z	0

```
    012345678911234567892123456789312345678941234567 89
  0 -
100 -
150 -
200 -
250 -
```

Press key to be defined (Press **Exit** to return): _

Figure 13.4: ASCII codes for IBM graphics characters. You can view this chart by selecting option 3 from the Screen menu (Ctrl-F3). To read the ASCII value, locate the symbol you want to use. Then read down the column on the left and across the row at the top. Every tenth numeral is presented in bold-face on the screen. For example, the ASCII value for a double border is 185.

screen. For example, it would be quite simple to insert codes into the form in Figure 13.5 that will subtotal down the columns and across the rows and produce a total at the bottom. Other applications include calculating the prices of orders (price × quantity), adding sales tax to subtotals, adding standard shipping and handling charges to totals, and so forth. Chapter 11 discusses how you can set up columns of numbers so that WordPerfect can make simple calculations on them.

Another interesting application for forms you create in WordPerfect involves using merge codes with them. In this way you can produce customer names and addresses in invoice forms, merge product information into bills of lading, and so forth. See Chapter 9 for techniques you can use to automate your forms.

WordPerfect's Line Advance command, option 6 on the Subscript/ Superscript (Shift-F1) menu, allows you to command the printer to advance to a certain line on the page without having to repeatedly press Return in your document. If your printer supports this feature, you can print forms you create on letterhead, simply instructing the printer to advance to the first line below the letterhead. Figure 13.6 displays the Reveal Codes for this command.

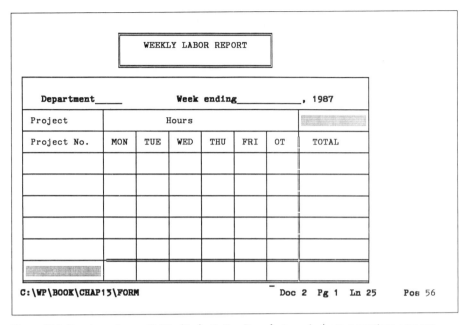

Figure 13.5: Creating a form with WordPerfect's Line Draw feature. As the text mentions, you can further enhance forms by using merge codes to insert additional information or by using WordPerfect's Math feature to perform calculations on columns of numbers.

Creating Graphics Macros

If you often use a standard set of graphics symbols—such as rectangles for charts—you may want to either create macros that will produce them or store the shapes in separate files and cut and paste them from these files as needed. Several graphics macros that you can use or modify for your own needs are presented later in this chapter.

Revising Graphics

To erase lines when the Line Draw feature is on, select option 5 on the menu line. Then you simply move the cursor over the lines and text you wish to erase. If Line Draw is off, you can erase by using the space bar to type over graphics or use the Del or Backspace key.

If you look at the Reveal Codes for a graphic image, as shown in Figure 13.7, you will see that WordPerfect inserts [HRt] at the end of each line you draw. You can therefore cut or copy portions of your drawings by using the program's Cut/Copy Rectangle feature.

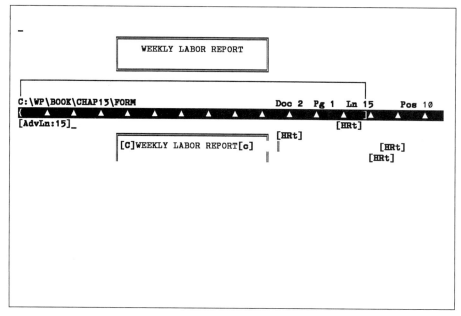

Figure 13.6: Using Line Advance in a form created with WordPerfect. Line Advance (Shift F1, option 6) allows you to specify a line number for the printer to move directly to. This command is often used for filling out standard (preprinted) forms, but you can also use it in the forms you create with Word-Perfect's Line Draw feature to move the printer directly to the next area to be printed.

You cut graphics or portions of graphics by marking the graphic image as a block using Alt-F4 and the ↓ and → keys, pressing Ctrl-F4 (Move), and selecting option 5 (Cut/Copy Rectangle). If you are moving the graphic image, select option 6 (Move Rectangle) when you have positioned the cursor where you want the graphic image to be placed.

CREATING GRAPHICS IN WORDPERFECT

WordPerfect allows you to create simple graphics that can be used in graphs, charts, and forms. With a little imagination, you can create templates for standard graphics shapes and cut and paste them into your documents. You can also combine WordPerfect's Line Draw feature with merge codes and mathematical calculations to "automate" many types of business forms and documents.

Drawing Simple Graphics

KEY SEQUENCE

Ctrl-F3 2 *<options>* **F7**

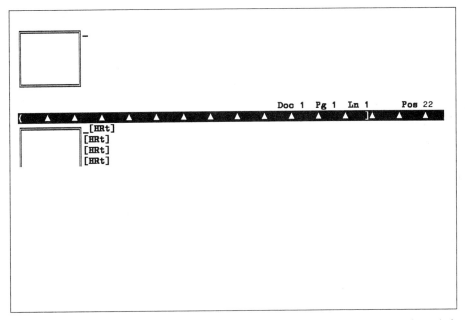

Figure 13.7: Reveal Codes for a graphic image. WordPerfect inserts a hard return ([HRt]) at the end of each line you draw, thus creating a rectangle. These shapes can then be cut and copied by using the program's Cut/Copy Rectangle key sequence.

To draw simple graphics in WordPerfect, press Ctrl-F3 (Screen) and select option 2 (Line Draw). When you are in WordPerfect's Line Draw mode, the following menu line appears:

1 | ; 2 | | ; 3 *; 4 Change; 5 Erase; 6 Move: 1

Selecting option 1, 2, or 3 allows you to choose among drawing single lines, double lines, or asterisks, as shown in Figure 13.8. Selecting option 4 allows you to select up to eight different types of alternate drawing characters, as shown in Figure 13.9. In addition, you can use any of the IBM graphics characters that your printer can print (see "Changing Graphics Characters" later in this chapter).

If you select option 5, the cursor will erase each character it passes through. Selecting option 6 allows you to move the cursor through your drawing without changing anything. When you are in Line Draw mode, the option you have selected appears at the end of the menu line, as shown in Figure 13.8. To exit Line Draw mode and enter text, press F7 (Exit) or F1 (Cancel). Pressing F1 does not erase any drawings you have created.

To enter text in drawings you have created, you should be in Typeover mode. (Press Ins to go into Typeover mode; you will see the word *Typeover* in the lower-left corner of the screen.) If you remain in Insert mode, which is WordPerfect's

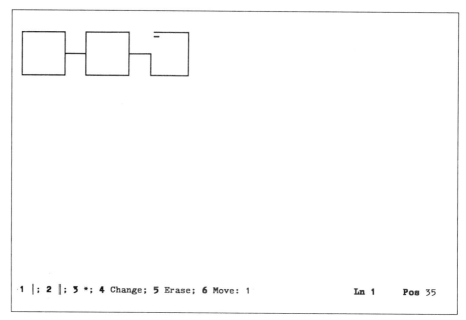

Figure 13.8: Using WordPerfect's Line Draw feature. Options 1, 2, and 3 indicate different types of line you can draw. You can change option 3 to another character or symbol. While you are in Line Draw mode, the number at the end of this menu indicates which option you have chosen. Press F7 (Exit) to leave Line Draw mode.

default setting, lines will be pushed to the right as you type, and pressing Return, Tab, or the space bar will insert spaces into your graphics.

You can also type text for your graphics first, enter Line Draw mode, and then draw lines around the text you have already entered.

Creating a Graph

WordPerfect's Line Draw feature allows you to create bar and stacked-bar graphs. The program cannot connect lines at any angle other than 90 degrees, however, so you cannot create pie charts and line graphs.

Figure 13.10 illustrates a sample graph you can create with WordPerfect. Options 1, 2, and 4 from the menu presented when Change (option 4) is selected from the Line Draw menu were used to create the bars in the graph and the legend indicators in the upper-right corner. After the lines and bars were drawn, F7 was pressed to exit Line Draw mode; Ins was then pressed to enter Typeover mode, as indicated in the lower-left corner of the screen. The text for the figure title and labels was then entered.

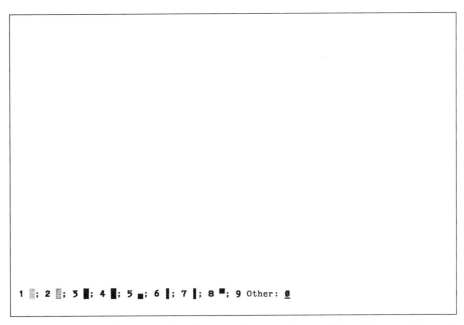

1 ▦; 2 ▦; 3 █; 4 █; 5 ▪; 6 ▐; 7 ▐; 8 ▀; 9 Other: <u>0</u>

Figure 13.9: Selecting alternate graphics characters. You can select any of these characters to be used as option 3 on the Line Draw menu, or you can specify another character or symbol by entering its code as described in the text or by pressing a key on the keyboard.

BIGBOX: A MACRO FOR A LARGE RECTANGLE

The following macro creates a large rectangle—10 characters deep by 25 characters wide. It is suitable for use in charts and diagrams in which you need several lines of text within a box. The Esc sequence tells WordPerfect to repeat an operation the number of times you define for the Esc key (see "Using Escape with Line Draw" later in this chapter for details).

Figure 13.11 illustrates the results of this macro.

Begin macro	*Macro name*	*Keystrokes*	*End macro*
Ctrl-F10	**BIGBOX**	**BIGBOX Return**	**Ctrl-F10**
		Ctrl-F3 2 1	
		Esc 10	
		↓ Esc 25	
		→ Esc 10	
		↑ Esc 25	
		← F7	

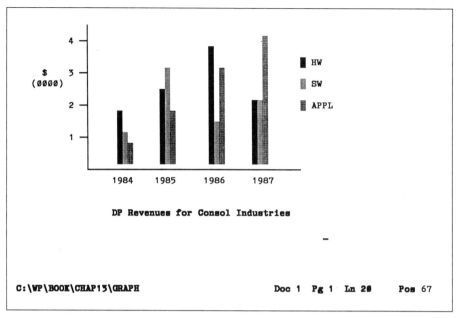

Figure 13.10: Sample graph you can create with WordPerfect's Line Draw feature. Although the program does not support pie charts and line graphs, which require slanted or curved lines, you can create stacked-bar and bar graphs such as this one to enhance your WordPerfect documents.

SMBOX: A MACRO FOR A SMALL RECTANGLE

Similar to the BIGBOX macro presented above, this macro creates a small rectangle at the point in your document where the cursor is when you invoke it. This smaller rectangle is suitable for use in charts that contain two lines of text, for instance, organization charts that contain a person's name and title. This macro will draw a box that is four lines deep and 15 characters wide. To increase the width of the box for longer names and titles, use a number larger than 15 in the macro. (Remember, these rectangles will have slightly different proportions when printed; test them on your printer and adjust the proportions accordingly.)

Figure 13.11 illustrates the results of this macro.

Begin macro	*Macro name*	*Keystrokes*	*End macro*
Ctrl-F10	**SMBOX**	**SMBOX Return**	**Ctrl-F10**
		Ctrl-F3 2 1	
		Esc 4	
		↓ Esc 15	
		→ Esc 4	
		↑ Esc 15	
		← F7	

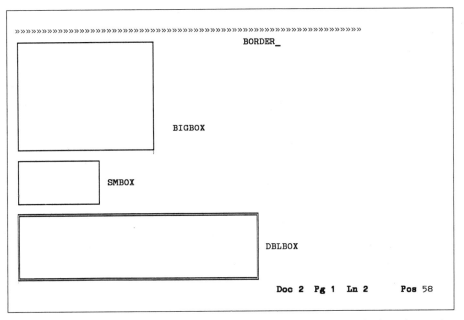

Figure 13.11: Using the macros described in the text. BIGBOX was used to create the large box, and SMBOX was used to create the smaller box. The double-rule box was created with DBLBOX, and the border was generated with BORDER. You can save these graphics shapes in a file, perhaps naming it GRAPHICS, and copy them into your documents wherever you choose, or you can simply invoke the macro to create each shape in your documents.

DBLBOX: MACRO FOR A RECTANGLE WITH A DOUBLE BORDER

You often may want to highlight graphics boxes—to draw attention to the portion of a chart containing sales totals, for example, or the major topics on an overhead transparency. This macro uses the double-rule character to create a banner-type box with a double border. To change the proportions of the box, simply use other numbers in place of the 6 (depth) and 45 (width) in the macro.

To center this box in a chart or document, mark it as a block (Alt-F4); then press Shift-F6 (Center) and respond **Y** to the Center (Y/N)? prompt.

Begin macro	*Macro name*	*Keystrokes*	*End macro*
Ctrl-F10	**DBLBOX**	**DBLBOX Return**	**Ctrl-F10**
		Ctrl-F3 2 2	
		Esc 6	
		↓ Esc 45	
		→ Esc 6	
		↑ Esc 45	
		← F7	

BORDER: MACRO FOR A 65-CHARACTER BORDER RULE

This macro demonstrates how you can change the graphics character presented in option 3 of the Line Draw menu to create other graphics effects in your text. It uses the double-angle foreign-language quotation mark (alternate IBM graphics character 175) to create a horizontal 65-character border in your documents. If you work with newsletters or brochures, you may want to enhance them with such borders and rules. You can select any graphics character your printer will print. See the next section, "Changing Graphics Characters," for a step-by-step explanation of how to change to other characters and symbols.

Begin macro	Macro name	Keystrokes	End macro
Ctrl-F10	**BORDER**	**BORDER Return** **Ctrl-F3 2 4 9** **175 Return Esc 65** **→ F7**	**Ctrl-F10**

Changing Graphics Characters

KEY SEQUENCE

Ctrl-F3 2 4 9 <number> **Return**

In addition to using the graphics symbols on the Line Draw menu, you can instruct WordPerfect to use any IBM graphics character your printer can print. You can also substitute any character on the keyboard for the character shown in option 3 of the Line Draw menu.

To change the graphic character of option 3,

1. Press Ctrl-F3 (Screen) and select option 2 (Line Draw).

2. Select option 4 (Change); then select option 9 (Other).

3. Enter the number corresponding to the graphics character you wish to use (see the following discussion) or press the key on the keyboard containing the character you wish to use. For example, to use the letter *q* as a graphics character, enter **q**.

4. Press Return. Option 3 will now display the character you have selected. Select that option to use the character in your graphics. To change back to the asterisk, the default character, follow steps 1–3 again, entering an asterisk.

To see the IBM graphics characters available to you, select option 3 (Ctrl/Alt Keys) from the Screen menu (Ctrl-F3). (This screen is illustrated in Figure 13.4 earlier in this chapter.) Read down the column and across the row to determine the number of any graphics characters you wish to use. For example, the double-angle quotation marks, which make interesting border characters, are 174 and 175.

Using Escape with Line Draw

To speed up drawing long lines, you can use the Esc key to specify how many times a command should be repeated. When you press Esc, the prompt

> **n = 8**

appears in the lower-left corner of the screen. You can change the number presented to another number, and any command you issue next will be repeated that number of times when you press Esc.

For example, to instruct WordPerfect to draw a 65-character line (the width of the printed text area),

1. Press Ctrl-F3 (Screen) and select option 2 (Line Draw).
2. Select option 1 (the single rule); then press Esc and enter **65**.
3. To tell the program to draw the single rule across the page and repeat the command 65 times, press →.

If you write macros for graphics shapes, you will use this feature often.

Revising Graphics

KEY SEQUENCE

To erase when Line Draw is on (Ctrl-F3 2):
   5
To erase when Line Draw is off:
   Ins Space bar or **Ins Del** or **Ins Backspace**
To cut (move) graphics:
   Alt-F4 (highlight area) **Ctrl-F4 5 1** (position cursor) **Ctrl-F4 6**
To copy graphics:
   Alt-F4 (highlight area) **Ctrl-F4 5 2** (position cursor)   **Ctrl-F4 6**
To delete all or part of a graphic image:
   Alt-F4 (highlight area) **Ctrl-F4 5 3**

You copy and cut graphics or portions of graphics by marking the graphic image as a block (Alt-F4), pressing Ctrl-F4 (Move), and selecting option 5 (Cut/

Copy Rectangle). The following menu appears:

1 Cut; 2 Copy; 3 Delete: 0

Select option 1 (Cut) or 2 (Copy) from the menu. Option 3 deletes the graphic image.

If you are copying the image, position the cursor where you want the graphic to appear; then press Ctrl-F4 (Move) again. Select option 6 (Retrieve Rectangle) to retrieve the image into your text. You can copy images between documents in this way.

To move an image from one document or window to another, select the Cut option (option 1); then position the cursor where you want the image to appear, press Ctrl-F4 (Move), and select option 6 (Retrieve Rectangle).

SUMMARY

This chapter has covered the techniques you use to create graphics in WordPerfect. Although it has presented only the basic techniques, you can combine them with other WordPerfect features, such as mathematics and merge printing, to create fairly sophisticated forms applications within WordPerfect. You can also use WordPerfect's graphics feature to generate borders and rules within your documents and to create bar charts illustrating spreadsheet data that you have imported.

Material of related interest is presented in the following chapters:

- Chapter 8, "Page Composition: Working with Columns," presents techniques to use when setting up text columns in newsletters, brochures, manuals, and other documents.

- Chapter 9, "Merge Printing," presents information about how to use special codes to insert material from other documents into forms.

- Chapter 11, "Mathematics, Equations, and Special Symbols," presents information about WordPerfect's mathematics features, which allow the program to make simple calculations on columns of numbers.

- Chapter 15, "Importing and Exporting Documents," presents information about bringing spreadsheet and database data into WordPerfect documents.

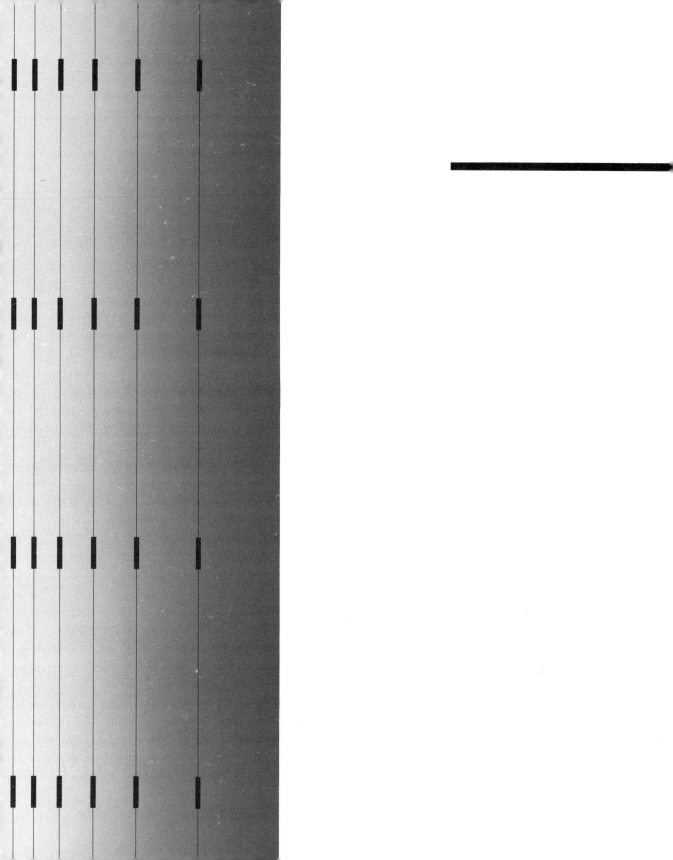

CHAPTER 14

CREATING AND USING MACROS

CREATING AND USING MACROS

This chapter discusses the creation and use of macros. WordPerfect macros can be used to customize word processing command sequences or enter repetitively typed text or perform a combination of the two. Because WordPerfect macros are so versatile, there are almost no applications or areas of the program in which they cannot be utilized.

Throughout this book, you will find example macros that you may want to use in your work. If you are new to WordPerfect macros, you should first read the material in this chapter. Afterward, you can consult the index to locate specific macros that occur throughout the text. By following the steps outlined for each macro, and with proper testing, you will soon be able to incorporate those macros of interest into your everyday work.

DEFINING AND EXECUTING MACROS

A macro is simply a sequence of keystrokes that are recorded and saved under a particular name. When you invoke the macro command and enter the macro name, WordPerfect replays all of the keystrokes exactly as they were originally entered. The keystrokes can consist solely of text entry, solely of WordPerfect command sequences, or a combination of text entry and word processing commands.

To create a macro, you press Ctrl-F10 (Macro Def). WordPerfect displays the prompt

Define Macro:

You then enter the name you wish to assign to the macro and press Return. You may enter a name up to eight characters long (the maximum allowed for any file name), so long as there are no spaces between the characters. The macro name must consist of at least two characters to have WordPerfect save it in its own file (see the section "Temporary Macros" that follows). Usually, you will want to keep your macro names short, perhaps restricted to two or three characters. What you want is a name that readily reminds you of the macro's function and is quick and easy to enter.

After you enter the macro name, WordPerfect displays the macro definition prompt

Macro Def

which flashes on and off continuously. This tells you that WordPerfect is now recording each keystroke that you make. This prompt continues to be displayed until you terminate the macro definition. While the prompt is flashing, enter the keystrokes exactly as you want them saved. When you have finished entering all of the keystrokes you want in the macro, press Ctrl-F10 to terminate keystroke entry.

As soon as you press Ctrl-F10 the second time, the Macro Def prompt disappears, and WordPerfect automatically saves the macro keystrokes you just entered under the name you assigned to the macro. WordPerfect gives all macro files the extension .MAC to distinguish them from regular document files.

To execute a macro, you press Alt-F10 (Macro), enter the name of the macro, and press Return. WordPerfect then enters all of the keystrokes precisely as you entered them. If you make a mistake and enter the name of a macro that does not exist, WordPerfect displays the error message "ERROR: File not found," and you will have to reenter this command sequence. If you ever want to terminate the execution of a macro while it is underway, you simply press F1 (Cancel). This aborts the macro at whatever keystroke it was entering when you pressed Cancel.

If, when you execute a macro, you find that it does not work as you intended, you will have to redefine it. Macro files cannot be edited in WordPerfect. If you try to retrieve a macro file as you would any normal document file, you will receive the error message "ERROR: Invalid file name."

The only way that the contents of a macro can be edited is by using a special macro editor. One such editor is included in the WordPerfect Library, an add-on product available from WordPerfect Corporation (for information about using this macro editor, see "Editing Macros with the WordPerfect Library's Macro/Program Editor" later in this chapter).

To redefine a macro, repeat the definition procedure as though you were defining the macro for the first time. When WordPerfect finds that the macro file already exists, it will prompt you with

Replace *<macro>*.MAC? (Y/N) N

where *macro* is the actual name of the macro that you entered and want to redefine. To redefine the macro, you type **Y**. To cancel this procedure, you just press Return.

For WordPerfect to execute a particular macro, its file must be in the default drive or directory. If you are using WordPerfect on a computer with two floppy disk drives, your default drive will be drive B, where you save your documents. As a result, the macros you save on your data disk reduce the amount of free space you have for saving the documents you create. Also, you will have to copy macros that you regularly use onto new data disks to make them available to the program (unless you want to go to the trouble of redefining them each time you change to a new data disk).

If you are using a hard disk system, the default directory must contain the macros you wish to use. However, you can get around this limitation by retrieving the document you want to edit and then making the directory that contains your macros the new default directory while you edit the document. To do this, you retrieve the document and then press F5 (List Files), type = , and enter the name of the directory that contains your macro files before you press Return. Then press F1 (Cancel) to return to your document and perform your editing.

If you are creating a new document, you make the directory containing your macro files the default directory (as just described) and then enter your document text. When you save the document, enter the complete path name, including the name of the directory where you want the document saved, to prevent its being saved in the directory that contains your macro files (see Chapter 6 for more information about using directories and naming files).

To get a directory listing of all of the macro files on your data disk or in your default directory, press F5 (List Files), and enter

*.MAC

before you press Return. To obtain a hard copy of this file listing, press Shift-PrtSc.

Alt Macros

In addition to standard macros, which are executed by pressing Alt-F10, entering the macro name, and pressing Return, you can create special macros, which are executed simply by pressing the Alt key and entering a single letter of the alphabet. These special Alt macros can be created only with the letters A through Z. You cannot use numbers or punctuation with the Alt key. However, the 26 Alt macros that you can create are very useful because they can be invoked much more quickly than regular macros.

To create an Alt macro, you press Ctrl-F10 to start the macro definition just as you do when creating regular macros. However, when you enter the macro name in response to the Define Macro prompt, you press the Alt key and then type the letter you wish to use. You will not see the macro name on your screen after the Define Macro prompt as you do when you are creating a regular macro. Instead, WordPerfect begins flashing the Macro Def prompt to let you know that it is now recording your keystrokes. If you have already used the letter you entered in an Alt macro, WordPerfect asks you whether you want to redefine it.

After you enter the keystrokes you want saved in the Alt macro, you press Ctrl-F10 again to terminate keystroke entry, just as you do to terminate a regular macro definition. To execute the macro, you need only press Alt and the letter key.

Alt macros are very convenient to use. However, it is easy to invoke an Alt macro in error. Because the Alt key is located immediately below the left Shift key on many IBM and IBM-compatible keyboards, you could easily execute an Alt macro when you intended to capitalize a letter. For that reason, you should not assign Alt macros to particularly complex and powerful, or destructive, tasks.

For example, if you create a macro to mark citations in tables of authorities, you would not want to name it Alt-T for fear that someday you may execute it when trying to capitalize the letter *t*. It would be safer to use a multiple-character macro name such as TOA so that you must execute the macro by pressing Alt-F10 and entering its three-character name.

Temporary Macros

If you want to create a macro whose function is very specialized and is not likely to be reused, or if you do not want to allocate precious disk space to macro files, you can create temporary macros that are never saved on disk. A temporary macro remains in the computer's memory and is available for use only until you exit WordPerfect.

To create a temporary macro, you press Ctrl-F10 to start the macro definition, and then you enter just a single character as the macro name before you press Return. The Macro Def prompt flashes, and you enter the keystrokes for the macro just as you do for any type of macro. When you are finished, press Ctrl-F10 again to terminate the definition. To execute a temporary macro, you press Alt-F10, enter the character you assigned to the macro, and press Return.

WordPerfect also allows you to create a temporary macro using the Return (Enter) key. When you create this macro, you just press Return in response to the Define Macro prompt after starting the macro definition. Afterward, you proceed to define the macro as you do any other macro. To execute the Return temporary macro, you press Alt-F10 and then press Return.

Temporary macros allow you to create and use macros whose functions are highly specific to the document you are creating. For example, you may find yourself typing a phrase, term, or name that, while occurring frequently in the document you are creating, is not likely to be used elsewhere. In such a case, you can assign its text to a temporary macro to make it easy to enter as you work.

Because temporary macros are not saved on disk, you will not receive any prompt warning you that you are about to redefine one of them. If you reuse a character that you previously assigned in the same work session, its new macro definition will replace the character's earlier function.

Pausing a Macro for Input

WordPerfect allows you to insert a pause for input in the macros you create. During this pause for input, you can manually enter text that you do not want entered automatically by the macro. To enter this type of pause in a macro, you press Ctrl-PgUp and press Return twice. The first Return enters the pause, and the second Return resumes the macro definition.

After you enter the pause for input, you continue to enter the keystrokes for your macro as usual. When you press Ctrl-PgUp, the computer will beep to indicate the pause. Be sure to press Return two more times after you hear this beep before you continue entering the rest of your macro keystrokes.

When you execute a macro that contains a pause for user input, WordPerfect will execute all of the keystrokes prior to the time when you pressed Ctrl-PgUp and Return the first time. When it reaches the pause, it will beep again, indicating that it is pausing. During the pause, you can enter whatever text or WordPerfect commands you wish. To resume macro execution, you press Return.

> *Note:* During a macro pause, you can enter any keystroke or command except a hard return. There is no way to manually enter a hard return during the pause because pressing the Return key always resumes the execution of the macro. If you need to enter hard returns, you must enter them after the pause or as part of the macro definition.

Many of your macros will alternate between keystrokes automatically entered during execution and pauses for input from the keyboard.

Often you will find it more efficient to enter pauses for input in merge operations because doing so allows you both to enter text from the keyboard and to enter required hard returns (merge operations are resumed by pressing F9). This kind of flexibility is not possible when you use a macro pause for input.

A macro can also be used to initiate a merge operation and then be executed upon completion of the merge operation. For information about combining macros and merge operations, refer to Chapter 9.

Entering Keystroke Delays and Making Macros Visible

When WordPerfect executes a macro, it does so invisibly and at top speed so that it is impossible for you to track its progress. In fact, when you execute a macro that contains few keystrokes and commands, its execution may seem almost instantaneous. To slow a macro's execution to a speed where you can follow its progress and to make it visible on your screen, you can enter a timed delay when defining it.

To enter a timed delay, you press Ctrl-PgUp followed by a whole number between 1 and 254 (you cannot enter fractions.) The number you enter becomes the timed-delay value, measured in tenths of a second. The program then delays each keystroke in the macro the number of seconds indicated by this value. For example, typing **10** after pressing Ctrl-PgUp enters a 1-second delay between each keystroke, typing **20** enters a 2-second delay, and so on.

Entering **2** as the timed-delay value makes the text appear on the screen at a rate that is quite legible. Be careful that you do not enter too large a value for the timed delay. Any value greater than 10 will make the text appear on the screen painfully slowly. However, if you are using a timed delay to track each step in the macro, you may want to enter a value between 10 and 20. This will give you plenty of time to abort the macro at any step by pressing F1 (Cancel).

If you press Ctrl-PgUp and enter a timed-delay value of **0**, WordPerfect will make the macro visible on the screen, although it will execute the keystrokes in the macro at top speed. To make a macro invisible at any point during its execution after you have entered a value that makes it visible, you press Ctrl-PgUp again and enter 255 before pressing Return. When you enter this timed-delay value, WordPerfect again executes the remaining keystrokes invisibly and at top speed.

You can combine the commands to make the macro visible, to delay its execution with the pause for input, and to make it invisible. For instance, you can construct a macro that begins by writing the standard text of a memorandum to the screen at a readable pace (Ctrl-PgUp 2 Return). The macro can then move the cursor to all of the places where you need to insert text, pausing to allow you to enter all of the nonstandard text from the keyboard (Ctrl-PgUp Return Return). As soon as you reach the last pause for input and press Return to resume macro execution, the macro can enter the command to save the document and enter the first part of its file name as MEMO. It can then pause again to allow you to append a unique ending, such as 821, to the file name so that the memo is saved under the name MEMO821 (Ctrl-PgUp Return Return). As soon as you press Return to save this new file, the macro resumes, once again becoming invisible as it executes the keystrokes to print a copy of the memo at top speed (Ctrl-PgUp 255 Return Shift-F7 1).

Repeating a Macro

You can repeat a macro by using the repeat function that WordPerfect assigns to the Esc key. You press Esc followed by the number of times you want to repeat the macro; then you press Alt-F10, enter the macro's name, and press Return. If the macro you want repeated is an Alt macro, you vary this procedure by pressing Alt and the appropriate letter instead of pressing Alt-F10, entering the macro name, and pressing Return.

For instance, you could use this technique with a macro that converts a single character from uppercase to lowercase to convert multiple characters to lowercase. You enter the macro to convert a single character from uppercase to lowercase according to this pattern:

Begin macro	*Macro name*	*Keystrokes*	*End macro*
Ctrl-F10	**LC**	**Alt-F4 →** **Shift-F3 2 F1**	**Ctrl-F10**

To begin the macro definition, you press Ctrl-F10, enter the macro name as **LC**, and press Return. Then you enter the keystrokes exactly as they are shown in the Keystrokes column. When you have finished, you terminate the definition by pressing Ctrl-F10 again.

To convert a letter from uppercase to lowercase, you position the cursor on the letter, press Alt-F10, enter **LC**, and press Return. To repeat this macro to convert a series of letters to lowercase, you press Esc, enter the number of characters to be converted, press Alt-F10, enter **LC**, and press Return.

For example, if you had entered the word *Memorandum* in all capital letters, as

MEMORANDUM

you would position the cursor on the *E* in *MEMORANDUM*, press Esc, enter **9** as the number of times to repeat the macro, and then press Alt-F10, type **LC**, and press Return to produce

Memorandum

using a single key sequence.

Chaining Macros

In addition to repeating a macro a set number of times using the Esc repeat function, you can have a macro continuously repeat its keystrokes until either you press F1 (Cancel) or the macro reaches the end of its search assignment. To do this, you enter a continuous loop that calls for the macro's reexecution as the last step in its definition. A macro that employs this technique is referred to as a self-chaining macro. You use it with WordPerfect's Search feature to avoid having it endlessly repeat until you manually abort it by pressing F1.

For example, in Chapter 3, in the section "Macros to Search and Replace Formatting Codes," a macro named ITAL is introduced whose function is to locate all underlined text in a document and replace it with the font change that would print the text in italic type when an Epson FX printer is used. The macro, reproduced here, locates the first occurrence of the [U] format code, enters the font change to shift into italics, then searches for the first occurrence of the [u] code, deletes the underlining, and enters the font change to shift back into regular type before it terminates.

Begin macro	*Macro name*	*Keystrokes*	*End macro*
Ctrl-F10	**ITAL**	**F2 Del F8 F2**	**Ctrl-F10**
		Ctrl-F8 1 ↓	
		4 Return 0	
		F2 F8 F8	

(continued)

← ← **Del F2**
Backspace Y
Ctrl-F8 1 ↓
1 Return 0

As the macro is currently defined, it must be invoked each time you want to change underlined text to italics. If you have a document that requires converting all underlining to italics, you can modify this basic macro so that it repeats itself until it can locate no more occurrences of the underlining format codes in the text. To do this, you enter all of the keystrokes as they are shown. However, before you terminate the definition with the second **Ctrl-F10**, you add the keystrokes **Alt-F10 ITAL Return**. The entire macro is then entered as follows:

Begin macro	*Macro name*	*Keystrokes*	*End Macro*
Ctrl-F10	**ITAL**	**F2 Del F8 F2**	**Ctrl-F10**
		Ctrl-F8 1 ↓	
		4 Return 0	
		F2 F8 F8	
		← ← **Del F2**	
		Backspace Y	
		Ctrl-F8 1 ↓	
		1 Return 0	
		Alt-F10 ITAL Return	

When you execute the modified ITAL macro, you will see the * Please Wait * prompt on the status line as the macro continuously reexecutes itself, removing all instances of underlining and replacing them with italics. When the Search feature can no longer locate any occurrences of the underlining format codes, the macro will terminate, and the * Please Wait * prompt will disappear from the screen.

If you want to make the ITAL macro visible in order to see each conversion as it takes place, you can modify its keystrokes further by adding a timed delay as the first keystrokes. To do this, you enter **Ctrl-PgUp**, the number of tenths of a second to delay between each keystroke (probably no more than 5), and **Return**.

It is important to understand the part the Search feature plays in automatically terminating this type of chained macro. If you chain a macro that does not use the Search feature, you will create an endless loop. The only way to get out of such a loop is to manually press F1. You should never create a self-chaining macro (one that calls for its own execution) that does not use the Search feature without adding a timed delay to make it visible on your screen. Without a timed delay, you will see only the * Please Wait * prompt on your screen as the macro continues to make whatever changes or additions its keystrokes call for over and over again in your document. Without making the macro visible, you will never know when the proper time is reached for you to terminate it by pressing F1.

For instance, suppose that you create a self-chaining macro that first retrieves a file containing a blank form that you plan to fill in manually, then enters a hard page break, and finally, calls for its own reexecution. If you do not enter a timed-delay value at the macro's inception, WordPerfect will continuously read in page after page of the blank forms without your knowing how many times this procedure has been repeated. However, if you enter the keystrokes

Ctrl-PgUp 20 Return

as the first step in the macro, you will see each form being retrieved and each hard page break being entered. Also, the delay will give you time to press F1 to stop the process when you see that you have a sufficient number of blank forms in the file.

Chaining Several Macros Together

This same chaining technique can be used to join two or more different macros. If you enter the name of a second macro as the last step in your macro definition of the first, the first macro will execute the second one right before it terminates. Then the second macro will execute its keystrokes exactly as they were defined.

You can use this technique to chain as many separate macros together as you wish. Each individual macro executes the next one in line before it terminates, creating a new, more complex macro made up of simpler ones.

This technique is quite useful when you are trying to create a really complex macro made up of many keystrokes. You can follow these steps in creating this type of chained macro:

1. Begin by deciding where the best places are to break the macro into separate macros.

2. Record the keystrokes required for each macro on paper.

3. Define each macro individually.

4. Test the macros in sequence by manually executing them one after the other in the same order you want them executed when they are chained together.

5. Redefine each macro, using your recorded keystrokes as a guide. This time, add the keystrokes that call for the execution of the next macro in the series after you have entered all of the other keystrokes exactly as you did before. (Only the last macro in the chain will not require this kind of redefinition.)

6. Test the final macro by executing the first macro in the series.

If all goes as planned, the macro will complete all of the keystrokes contained in each separate macro file, terminating only when it has executed all of the keystrokes in the very last macro in the series.

> *Note:* Because you have to redefine each macro in order to add the keystrokes that chain the next macro to it, this technique is of limited appeal. However, if you have the WordPerfect Library, you can use its macro editor to add the chaining keystrokes without having to redefine each macro from scratch (see "Editing Macros with the WordPerfect Library's Macro/Program Editor" that follows for details regarding its use).

Conditional Macro Chaining

When you define a chaining macro that executes either itself or another macro immediately before it terminates, it will perform this execution without fail each time you run the macro. However, you can also call for one macro to be executed only when a particular search string is not located within the document and for another macro to be executed only when the search string is located. Such macros make up what is referred to as a conditional macro chain because it contains macros that are executed only when a particular condition exists (in this case, when a particular search string is or is not found).

When you create this type of macro, you enter the call to execute the macro you want to use when the search string *cannot* be found at the very beginning of the macro, before you enter the search keystrokes. Then, after you have entered the Search command and all of the other commands that you want performed when the search string *is* located, you enter the call to have the macro reexecute itself. The first macro call is not executed until the search fails to locate the search string, whereas the last macro call (that calls itself) is executed repeatedly, so long as the search string is found.

To see how this technique works, we can apply it to the ITAL macro as it was modified earlier in the discussion about creating a self-chaining macro (see "Chaining Macros"). This macro searches for all underlining format codes, deletes them, and replaces them with the codes to shift in and out of italic type (for the Epson FX printer). Because the keystrokes **Alt-F10 ITAL Return** were added at the end of this macro, it continues this search and replace procedure continuously until WordPerfect can no longer locate any more occurrences of the underlining format codes.

To have the document automatically printed as soon as all of the underlining has been replaced with italics, you can add a call in the redefinition of the ITAL macro that executes a print macro as soon as the search for underlining in the document fails. To accomplish this, you redefine the ITAL macro as follows:

Begin macro	Macro name	Keystrokes	End macro
Ctrl-F10	**ITAL**	**Alt-F10 PRINT Return**	**Ctrl-F10**
		F2 Del F8 F2	
		Ctrl-F8 1 ↓	
		4 Return 0	
		F2 F8 F8	
		← ← **Del F2**	
		Backspace Y	
		Ctrl-F8 1 ↓	
		1 Return 0	
		Alt-F10 ITAL Return	

The first keystrokes you enter (Alt-F10 PRINT Return) execute the PRINT macro (which contains the keystrokes to print a copy of any document in memory). However, WordPerfect does not execute this macro when it reads these keystrokes. Instead, it executes the keystrokes that are entered after them, including those that reexecute the same macro (Alt-F10 ITAL Return). Each time WordPerfect reexecutes the ITAL macro and is still able to locate underlining format codes, it notes the call to execute the PRINT macro, but it does not act upon it. However, when Word-Perfect can find no further occurrences of underlining and the search terminates, the ITAL macro executes the PRINT macro and terminates.

Conditional chaining is often used with macros that chain a series of macros together. With a little planning, you can use these techniques to create complex procedures that flawlessly automate tedious editing tasks that might take you hours to accomplish manually in WordPerfect.

Planning Macros

You create WordPerfect macros with the program on line. Each keystroke you type is both recorded in the macro and entered into the document window where you are working. Before you enter a new macro, you may want to switch to an unused document window (Shift-F3). You can then use this window as a scratch pad where you can enter your standard text and format changes without affecting any of your existing documents.

However, it is not always possible to create a macro in a blank editing screen. Many macros require text to process during definition. For example, to create a macro that cuts a block of text, you must have some text on the screen that has previously been marked as a block that can be cut when defining the macro's keystrokes. Before you test any macro that you have created, you should always save the document that you will test it on. That way, you will not introduce changes that you have to edit manually.

Macros that require text to process during definition always assume that the conditions under which they were created will exist in the document when they are executed. For instance, if you execute the macro that cuts a marked block without first marking the block, or if you execute it in a new document window where no text yet exists, you will receive the message, * Macro Complete - Unknown display state *.

When planning your macro, before you actually begin to define it, you must also decide how much of a procedure should be automated. If you plan to manually move the cursor into the proper position each time you execute a particular macro, you will not include the keystrokes to reach the sample text you use in the macro's definition as part of the macro. However, if you always begin a procedure by moving the cursor to the very beginning or end of the document, you will want to include these cursor movement keystrokes in the first step of the macro.

Sometimes you must resist the temptation to automate too much of a procedure. If you make the macro too specific to the particular document you are working with, you may find it of limited, or no, value when you work on a new document. If you find yourself redefining a favorite macro each time you begin work on a new document, you may want to find ways to make it more versatile. Often this can be accomplished by retaining only those keystrokes that never vary in the macro.

Another way to make a macro more versatile and less application specific is to enter pauses for input whenever possible. For instance, if you often change the spacing in a document from single to double spacing and back, you can use a single macro that enters the commands to change the line spacing (Shift-F8 4), enters a pause for input (Ctrl-PgUp Return Return) that allows you to enter the line-spacing number, and then enters a final Return to enter the new value. You can then use this one macro whenever you want to change line spacing, regardless of whether you want to change to single spacing, double spacing, line-and-a-half spacing, or any other spacing.

When you make a typing mistake or press the wrong function key, these keystrokes, too, are added to your macro. To help reduce mistakes and the time spent redefining the macro, you can use the WordPerfect command key sequences included throughout this book as a guide. To locate the reference entry that contains the key sequence to which you wish to refer, you can look up the command by name in the "Command Index" at the end of the book. The page numbers in boldface type indicate where the key sequences occur. The key sequences for each command are clearly marked by a bold vertical bar on the page.

> *Note:* If you are uncertain about a convention used in the "Key Sequence" sections, refer to "Interpreting Key Sequences" in the Preface.

Editing Macros with the WordPerfect Library's Macro/Program Editor

The WordPerfect Library provides a collection of programs that supplement WordPerfect and help integrate it with other programs by WordPerfect Corporation. The library includes a shell program, a calculator, an appointment calendar and scheduler, a program called *Notebook* (a file manager that allows you to enter and save data for a secondary merge file on electronic note cards), a file manager (almost identical to the one in the WordPerfect program), a macro/program editor, and a game called *Beast*.

The shell program in the WordPerfect Library can partition your computer's RAM, allowing you to keep different WordPerfect programs resident in memory. This enables you to quickly and easily switch back and forth among the different programs that you have loaded.

This feature is particularly helpful when you edit macros with the library's macro editor, M-Edit, for it permits you to modify keystrokes within the macro and then immediately switch to a WordPerfect document window where you can test your changes. If the macro requires further modification, you can switch back to the M-Edit document window, perform your edit, and then return again to WordPerfect for further macro testing.

The WordPerfect Library is recommended for hard disk systems. Although you can use it on a floppy disk system, to do so requires you to perform frequent disk swapping. Figure 14.1 shows the opening screen of the WordPerfect Library program. To start the WordPerfect Library, you make the directory containing its programs the default directory, type **SHELL** at the DOS prompt, and press Return.

To run an application listed on the WordPerfect Library menu, you simply type its letter. For example, to run WordPerfect, you enter **A**, and to run the Macro Editor, M-Edit, you enter **I**. You can change the letter designations to associate each program with a more appropriate letter, such as W for WordPerfect and M for M-Edit.

Initially, you must tell the shell in which directory each application resides. To do this, you select 4 (Setup), the application, and enter the default directory and Startup command. When you are defining the setup for WordPerfect, you can also designate the startup options to be used when WordPerfect is started.

After you have started an application, such as WordPerfect, from the shell, you can return to the shell and start another program by pressing Ctrl-F1 and selecting option 1 (Go to Shell). The number of programs that you can run from the shell is limited only by the amount of RAM available.

The WordPerfect Library also provides a key combination that allows you to switch directly to a new application. For example, if you have started WordPerfect and then want to switch to the M-Edit program, you can press Shift-Alt and type **I** (the M-Edit program startup letter on the menu). If M-Edit is already loaded into RAM, the shell will switch to its window immediately. If it has not yet

```
┌─────────────────────────────────────────────────────────────┐
│ ▐WordPerfect Library          Friday, March 6, 1987, 11:54am▌│
│  A - WordPerfect 4.2                                         │
│                                                              │
│  B - MathPlan 2.1                                            │
│                                                              │
│  C - Calculator                                              │
│                                                              │
│  D - DOS Command                                             │
│                                                              │
│  E - Calendar                                                │
│                                                              │
│  F - File Manager                                            │
│                                                              │
│  G - NoteBook                                                │
│                                                              │
│  H - Program Editor                                          │
│                                                              │
│  I - Macro Editor                                            │
│                                                              │
│  J - Beast (Game)                                            │
│                                                              │
│ 1 Go to DOS; 2 Clipboard; 3 Change Dir; 4 Setup; 5 Memory Map: _    (F7 = Exit)│
└─────────────────────────────────────────────────────────────┘
```

FIGURE 14.1: The opening screen of the WordPerfect Library. To run an application from the shell program, you simply enter the letter that is listed immediately before the application. The shell also allows you to switch between application programs by pressing Shift-Alt and the letter associated with the program. This makes it extremely easy to switch from the macro editor directly to WordPerfect, where you can test the modifications that you just made to your macro, and then switch back to the editor if you need to make further changes.

been loaded, the shell will load it. To then switch back to the current document window in WordPerfect, you press Shift-Alt and type **A** (WordPerfect's startup letter on the menu).

> *Note:* You can also run M-Edit directly from DOS without using the shell program, just as you can WordPerfect. To do this, you make the directory or drive containing the M-Edit program current, enter the startup command **ME**, and press Return. However, starting with ME, M-Edit, will not allow you to toggle between programs, for example, between WordPerfect and the macro editor.

When you start M-Edit, you are presented with a blank editing screen much like WordPerfect's except that the status line contains

Mac 1 Ln 1 Pos 1

on the last line of the screen. You can use the macro editor to create or edit macros for any WordPerfect Corporation product (including the WordPerfect Library, MathPlan, and WordPerfect itself).

To retrieve a WordPerfect macro for editing, you press Shift-F10 (Retrieve, just as in WordPerfect) and enter the name of the macro. When you enter the file name, include the complete path name (most often, \WP) if the macro file is not in the library default directory. In addition, you must include the .MAC file-name extension, or you will receive the error message "ERROR: File not found," even if you otherwise entered the file name correctly.

The editor requires the .MAC extension because macro files created in other WordPerfect Corporation programs do not use this extension. For example, macros that you create in the WordPerfect Library are given the extension .SHM. Also, M-Edit uses the file-name extension to set the correct environment for interpreting the macro codes in the file. The program indicates the environment by displaying the extension letters in the lower-left corner of the M-Edit status line. When you retrieve a WordPerfect macro, you will see the letters MAC in this position on your screen.

To illustrate how you can use M-Edit to edit a WordPerfect macro, the steps for inserting the necessary keystrokes to add conditional chaining to the ITAL macro are outlined in the following discussion. This example macro was introduced in two earlier sections, "Chaining Macros" and "Conditional Macro Chaining." This macro changes each occurrence of underlining in a document to italics by locating and deleting the underlining format codes and then entering the font-change codes to shift in and out of the font that creates italic type for the Epson FX printer.

To automate this macro more fully, it can be redefined, as discussed in the text, so that it changes all occurrences of underlining to italics and then executes a macro that prints it. By using the M-Edit program, you can enter these modifications without having to reenter all of the basic keystrokes that change underlining to italics.

Figure 14.2 shows the ITAL macro loaded into M-Edit with no modifications. Notice that the keystroke commands it contains appear in the editor as English words enclosed in a pair of angle brackets. The first keystroke entered was F2. It appears in the editor as <Search>. Essentially, you are looking at Word-Perfect's name for this key enclosed in angle brackets. The first keystrokes that you actually press when you define the ITAL macro are

F2 Del F8 F2 Ctrl-F8 1 ↓ 4 Return 0

In the M-Edit screen, these keystrokes are translated to

<Search><Delete><Underline><Search End><Print Format>1<Down>4 0

Notice that the Return keypress after the 4 in the macro is not visible in the M-Edit screen. Instead of a transcription for pressing the Return key, an actual carriage return is entered in the macro. This is the reason that the 0 is entered on its own line.

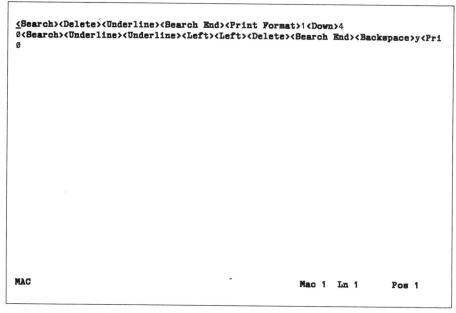

FIGURE 14.2: ITAL.MAC loaded into M-Edit, the macro program editor. Notice how the M-Edit program represents each keystroke command as an English word enclosed in angle brackets. These names are the same as the key names that WordPerfect gives to all of its command key sequences.

Because M-Edit is an editor rather than a word processor like WordPerfect, it does not automatically employ word wrap to keep the macro commands within the confines of the editing screen. Notice in Figure 14.2 that the second line of commands extends beyond the right edge of the screen. To see all of the commands in a single screen, you must use a special command, Ctrl-F2 (Wrap), to wrap the command line so that it conforms to the width of the screen (column position 78 in this case). When you press Ctrl-F2, M-Edit displays

Wrap with Confirm? (Y/N) N

If you type **Y**, M-Edit asks you to mark the position where each line should break, just as it does when you use WordPerfect's Hyphenation feature. Usually you can just press Return, and M-Edit will break each statement correctly. The wrap function is necessary only to break command statements; the macro editor automatically word wraps text that you enter in the macro.

Figure 14.3 shows you the contents of the ITAL macro after the Wrap command was used. You can see that the keystroke commands <Print Format>1 <Down>1, which were not visible on the screen when the macro was originally retrieved, now appear on their own line. Notice the small underscored box at the end of the second line. This mark is entered by the macro editor as a comment

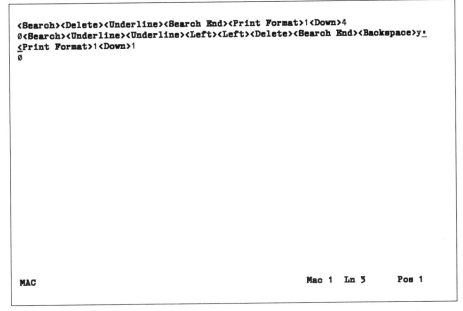

```
<Search><Delete><Underline><Search End><Print Format>1<Down>4
0<Search><Underline><Underline><Left><Left><Delete><Search End><Backspace>y_
<Print Format>1<Down>1
0



























MAC                                              Mac 1  Ln 3      Pos 1
```

FIGURE 14.3: ITAL.MAC after using the Wrap feature (Ctrl-F2) to word wrap the macro keystrokes. The Wrap feature adds a comment marker that causes keystroke commands extending beyond column 78 to wrap to the next line. Using the Wrap command in the ITAL macro allows you to read the four keystroke commands (now in line 3) that were not visible on the screen when the macro was originally retrieved (see Figure 14.2).

marker. It is this marker that causes the commands that extended beyond column 78 to be wrapped to the following line.

You can edit a macro with M-Edit pretty much as you do any WordPerfect document. The cursor movement functions are the same when you edit a macro as they are when you edit any regular WordPerfect document. Also, to delete a particular command, you can position the cursor under it and press Del, or you can press Backspace to delete a command to the left of the cursor.

However, there are some WordPerfect editing commands that do not work. Because the macro keystrokes are not separated by spaces as are individual words, pressing Ctrl-Backspace, which normally deletes the word at the cursor, has no effect in M-Edit. However, if you do delete a macro command in error, pressing F1 and typing **1** will restore it, just as it does text you delete in WordPerfect.

The macro editor's default setting is Insert mode, just as it is in WordPerfect (to change to Typeover mode, press Ins). This means that you can insert new text into the macro just as you do in any WordPerfect document. Also, you have to press Return only when you want to insert a blank line (with a hard return) into the macro.

To modify the ITAL macro so that it automatically executes the PRINT macro after it has changed all occurrences of underlining to italics requires not only that you add text (the name of the macros to chain to), but also that you add new command keystrokes. In this case, you need to add the keystrokes **Alt-F10** before you enter the name of the macro.

To add new keystroke commands, you must change to the Functions mode by pressing Ctrl-F10. Then when you press a key, M-Edit will insert the key name enclosed in angle brackets (that is, the macro keystrokes) rather than performing a function as it does in normal editing mode. When the Functions mode is on, M-Edit displays the word *Functions* immediately after the word *MAC* on the status line at the bottom of the screen. When the Functions mode is on, you must not press a cursor movement key to move to a new position in the macro where you want to insert the macro keystrokes. Doing so will enter the cursor movement as a macro keystroke rather than actually moving the cursor to the desired position.

In addition to using the Functions mode to enter macro keystrokes, you can insert macro keystrokes in normal editing mode by pressing Ctrl-V followed by the key or key sequence that you wish to enter. When you want to insert only a few macro keystrokes in various places in the macro, using Ctrl-V is often the safest way to do so.

To insert the first keystrokes in the macro, you position the cursor at the very beginning of the macro (Home Home ↑), press Ctrl-F10 to activate Functions mode, and press Alt-F10; this inserts the first keystroke as <Macro> in double intensity. Next, you enter **PRINT** as the name of the macro you want executed when the search for underlining codes fails. The name of the file you have just entered appears in single intensity on your screen. Then you press Return.

Next, you must move the cursor to the end of the macro, immediately after the 0, and add the keystrokes that reexecute the ITAL macro. To move the cursor, you must be in normal editing mode again. Press Ctrl-F10, and the word *Functions* disappears from the status line. Then move to the end of the macro (Home Home ↓) and press Ctrl-V. When you press Ctrl-V, M-Edit displays

Key: (MAC)

on the status line. When you press Alt-F10, it inserts the keystrokes as <Macro>. Then you type **ITAL** and press Return.

To save the macro as edited, you use the same key sequence as you do when saving a WordPerfect document. Press F7 (Exit) and respond to the same prompts to save the macro under the same name.

In addition to modifying an existing macro without having to completely redefine it, you can use M-Edit to document the macro's function. To add comments in a macro, you press Shift-F1 (when in normal editing mode). M-Edit inserts a comment marker (the underlined square) and a hard return at the cursor's position and positions the cursor between the square and the hard return. When you enter the text of your comment, it will automatically be underlined.

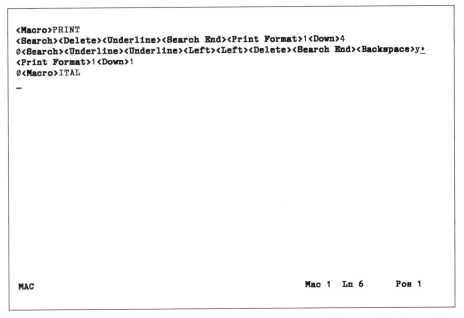

```
<Macro>PRINT
<Search><Delete><Underline><Search End><Print Format>1<Down>4
0<Search><Underline><Underline><Left><Left><Delete><Search End><Backspace>y.
<Print Format>1<Down>1
0<Macro>ITAL
_
```

MAC   Mac 1   Ln 6   Pos 1

FIGURE 14.4: ITAL.MAC after adding the keystrokes to perform conditional chaining. The additional keystrokes necessary to make this macro chain conditionally have been added without reentry of the entire macro.

When you are finished entering the text of your comment, you press the → key to move the cursor beyond the underlining format code. You do not enter Return. If you press Return, this adds a blank line in your macro (press Del to remove it).

Note that comments do not wrap at column position 78 as does regular text that you enter into a macro. To enter a long comment, break it into segments that will each fit within the columns and enter these segments on several lines as several comments.

COMMANDS TO DEFINE AND EXECUTE MACROS

KEY SEQUENCE

To create an Alt macro (invoked with Alt and a letter key):

Ctrl-F10 Alt<*letter*> <*macro keystrokes*> **Ctrl-F10**

To create all other macros:

Ctrl-F10 <*macro name consisting of two or more characters*> **Return**
<*macro keystrokes*> **Ctrl-F10**

To create a temporary macro:
> **Ctrl-F10** <*macro name consisting of one character*> **Return**
> <*macro keystrokes*> **Ctrl-F10**

To create a temporary macro invoked by Alt-F10 and the Return key:
> **Ctrl-F10 Return** <*macro keystrokes*> **Ctrl-F10**

To enter a pause for input in a macro:
> **Ctrl-PgUp Return Return**

To make a macro visible and execute it at normal speed:
> **Ctrl-PgUp 0 Return**

To enter a timed delay in the macro's execution:
> **Ctrl-PgUp** <*number between 1 and 254*> **Return**

To make a macro invisible after entering a timed delay:
> **Ctrl-PgUp 255 Return**

To execute an Alt macro:
> **Alt** <*letter*>

To execute any non-Alt macro:
> **Alt-F10** <*macro name*> **Return**

A macro is a recorded sequence of keystrokes that are saved in a file to allow you to use them repeatedly. They can be used to customize command sequences, enter repetitively used text, or perform a combination of these two tasks.

To create a macro, you follow these steps:

- Press Ctrl-F10 to begin the macro definition. WordPerfect will display the prompt Define Macro:. Enter a macro name from two to eight characters long, with no spaces between characters. Press Return after you enter the name.

- WordPerfect displays the prompt Macro Def, which flashes on and off continuously until you terminate the macro definition. Enter all of the keystrokes that you want included in the macro.

- Press Ctrl-F10 to terminate the macro definition. WordPerfect automatically saves the definition in a file. The program appends the extension .MAC to the end of the file name you assigned to the macro.

To execute a macro, you press Alt-F10. WordPerfect displays the prompt Macro:. Enter the name of the macro and press Return. WordPerfect replays all of the keystrokes it recorded when you originally defined the macro. If you want to terminate the macro before it is finished, press F1 (Cancel).

You can also define a special type of macro that is executed by pressing Alt and a letter key. To define this type of Alt macro, you follow these steps:

- Press Ctrl-F10 to begin the macro definition. WordPerfect displays the prompt Define Macro:. Press Alt and the letter you wish to assign to the macro you are about to create.
- WordPerfect displays the prompt Macro Def, which flashes on and off continuously until you terminate the macro definition. Enter all of the keystrokes that you want included in the macro.
- Press Ctrl-F10 to terminate the macro definition. WordPerfect automatically saves the Alt macro in a file called ALT<*l*>.MAC, where <*l*> is the letter of the alphabet you assigned to the macro.

To execute an Alt macro, you simply press Alt and the letter key you assigned to the macro. This type of macro is much easier to invoke and can be used to automate simple editing tasks that you use frequently in document creation.

If a macro that you have defined does not work as you intended, you will have to redefine it. To do this, repeat the procedure you used to start the definition process and enter the same name you used when you originally defined the macro. WordPerfect will display the message Replace <*macro name*>.MAC? (Y/N) N, where <*macro name*> is the actual macro name you entered. To redefine the macro, type **Y**. If you enter the macro name incorrectly, press Return.

Because these macros are saved in files, they must be on the disk in the default drive or in the default directory. If you try to execute a macro that is not on your data disk or in the default directory, WordPerfect will display the error message "ERROR: File not found."

If you are short on disk space or want to create a macro that you will not need again, you can create a temporary macro. To do this, you alter the macro definition procedure only slightly. After you press Ctrl-F10 to begin the definition, you enter a one-character macro name. You then enter your keystrokes as you would when defining a permanent macro, pressing Ctrl-F10 again when you are finished. To execute a temporary macro, you press Alt-F10, type the character assigned to the macro, and press Return.

You can also create a temporary macro that uses the Return key. To do this, press Ctrl-F10 and press Return at the Macro Define prompt. Then enter your keystrokes as you would when defining a permanent macro, pressing Ctrl-F10 again when you are finished. To execute a temporary Return macro, you simply press Alt-F10 and press Return.

Although many macros are used to automate a complete command sequence, some macros can be made more versatile by introducing a pause in them that allows you to enter text manually. To enter a pause for input, you press Ctrl-PgUp and then press the Return key twice. When you press Ctrl-PgUp,

WordPerfect sounds an audible beep. When you execute a macro that contains a pause (or pauses) for input, the macro will execute all keystrokes up to the place where you entered the pause and then beep to signal that it has paused. To resume macro execution after you have entered your text, press Return. (If you press Return to enter a hard return, the macro will resume execution instead.)

When macros are executed, they process the keystrokes in them so fast that you cannot follow their progress. To slow down the keystrokes and make them visible on your screen, you can add a timed delay in them. To do this, you press Ctrl-PgUp and then enter a value between 1 and 254. This value represents the number of seconds, in tenths of a second, that the macro will pause between each keystroke. For example, entering a value of **3** causes the macro to pause .3 second between each keystroke, and entering a value of 30 causes it to pause 3 seconds between each keystroke.

To make a macro visible on the screen (albeit at very high speed) and not enter a delay between the execution of each keystroke, you press Ctrl-PgUp and enter **0** as the timed-delay value. To make the remainder of a macro in which you previously entered a delay factor once again invisible and running at top speed, you press Ctrl-PgUp and enter 255 as the timed-delay value.

A macro can be started from within another macro, or a macro can be made to loop continuously by referencing itself. By including a search procedure that locates text that you want the macro to process, you can make a macro automatically repeat until it has operated on all occurrences of the search string. In addition, you can introduce conditional processing in a macro, whereby a second macro is not executed until the first one has operated on all occurrences of the text located by the search procedure. For more information and examples using these advanced macro techniques, refer to "Chaining Macros," "Chaining Several Macros Together," and "Conditional Macro Chaining" earlier in this chapter.

SUMMARY

This chapter has presented the basic information necessary for creating and using your own macros. Many example macros that may be of value in your work appear throughout this book. To locate specific macros that you want to incorporate into your work, refer to the index entry *Macro applications* in the topical index. Under this entry, you will find short functional descriptions of the sample macros as well as the numbers of the pages on which they appear.

Macros can also be used to execute merge operations or can be executed from within a merge operation upon its termination (using a pair of ^G merge codes). For information about using macros in merge operations, see Chapter 9, "Merge Operations."

PART

4

TECHNICAL REFERENCE

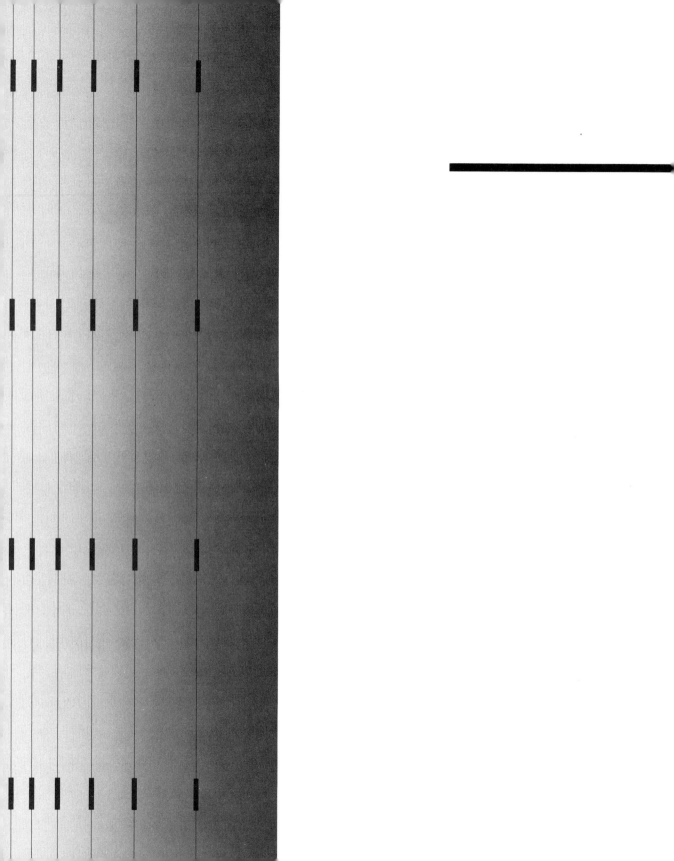

Importing and Exporting Documents

IMPORTING AND EXPORTING DOCUMENTS

As you work with WordPerfect, you may often want to set up documents you create so they can be used with other programs. You may, for example, want to give a document on disk to another department in your company that does not use WordPerfect but instead uses WordStar or some other word processing program. Likewise, you may sometimes want to import text from other word processing programs as well as data from spreadsheet or database management programs such as Lotus 1-2-3 or dBASE III. You may, for example, want to include spreadsheet data in a table in a report you are writing, or you may want to bring data into WordPerfect to use in graphics you create using the Line Draw feature. In addition, if you use WordPerfect's mail-merge facility, you will often want to import database data for use in a WordPerfect secondary merge file.

WordPerfect contains a built-in Text In/Out menu for converting WordPerfect text to DOS text file format (also called ASCII format). A separate Convert program, provided on the Learning disk, converts WordPerfect text directly to several formats used by other popular word processing programs, such as WordStar and MultiMate. It also allows you to import spreadsheet data saved in DIF (data interchange format) and accept data from dBASE and WordStar mail-merge files. In addition, you can send text to a DOS text file so that you can print it using the DOS Print command.

This chapter discusses how to import text and data into WordPerfect and prepare WordPerfect text for exportation to other programs.

EXPORTING DOS TEXT FILES

Converting a file to a DOS text file (a file in ASCII format) allows text created by one program to be used in other programs. When text is converted to DOS text file format, it loses the special formatting codes that the original word processing program inserted. When a WordPerfect document is converted to a DOS text file, soft returns ([SRt]) and soft page breaks are converted to hard returns ([HRt]), and hard returns become carriage return–line feeds.

You can use the Convert utility, a special program run outside of WordPerfect, to convert WordPerfect documents directly to certain other specific formats. For example, if you want to convert a WordPerfect document to IBM DisplayWrite III, you can convert it directly to IBM DCA (document content architecture), which WordPerfect also calls *Revisable-Form-Text.*

Within WordPerfect's Text In/Out menu there is also an option called *generic word processor format* that preserves much more of the original formatting than does the Convert utility. If you are converting a WordPerfect document for use by another word processing program not supported by the Convert utility, you should try using this format. Before you decide to convert a document to a DOS text file or to the generic word processor format, check whether one of the direct conversions on the Convert menu is suitable for the programs you are using. (See "Using the Convert Program" later in this chapter for instructions about how to use the utility to convert documents to other formats.)

IMPORTING DOS TEXT FILES (ASCII DOCUMENTS)

Normally, when you retrieve a document that is in DOS text file format, the end of each line contains a hard return ([HRt]). This is fine if you are importing lines of programming code or data that is in columns and rows. However, if you are importing text, the [HRt] at the end of each line makes the text difficult to reformat. Version 4.2 of WordPerfect allows you to use either of two options: one that places hard returns at the ends of lines or one that places soft returns at the ends of lines if they occur within the hyphenation zone.

If the WordPerfect document into which you are importing a DOS text file has margins narrower than the incoming DOS text file, the program will insert soft returns at the points where the WordPerfect margins are, and your lines may not be formatted as you prefer. For this reason, be sure to set margins in WordPerfect at 0 and 80 before importing the file if you want the text to appear line for line as it was in the other program.

Because DOS text files contain tabs that are set every eight spaces, you may also want to set similar tabs in your WordPerfect document before you import the file. This step is usually not necessary, but if you have any difficulty with the format of the incoming file once it is in WordPerfect, exit the document, set tabs at every eight spaces in a new document, and retrieve the DOS text file again.

WORDPERFECT'S CONVERT PROGRAM

WordPerfect also gives you a special Convert program that converts documents in selected formats directly to WordPerfect format and vice versa. When you use the Convert program, which is on the Learning disk, most formatting and text attributes, such as boldfacing, are converted into the appropriate codes for the new document. If the program you wish to convert the WordPerfect document to can use any of the formats supported by the Convert program, you should usually convert using those formats instead of the DOS (ASCII) text file format because you lose most text formatting attributes when you convert a file to a DOS text file.

In addition, you may often want to use a format on the Convert program as an intermediate step in converting a document to WordPerfect format. For example, as you will see later, converting a Lotus 1-2-3 database directly to a DIF file does not allow you to use the database as a WordPerfect secondary merge file. However, if you first convert the Lotus 1-2-3 database to dBASE (as a .DBF file), you can then import the dBASE file directly into WordPerfect and use it as a secondary merge file in mail-merge applications.

The Convert program allows you to bring in two types of files: files containing text, such as documents from other word processing programs and tables of data from other spreadsheet programs, and files containing data, such as data from a database program that you wish to use in mail-merge applications.

You can convert a WordPerfect document into the following formats:

- Revisable-Form-Text or Final-Form-Text, also called document content architecture (DCA), which is used by IBM mainframes for transferring documents created on microcomputers. Conversion to this format preserves many formatting commands. Many popular word processing programs have added DCA to their own conversion programs, so you may be able to convert a document in another program first to DCA and then directly to WordPerfect, retaining much of its formatting. Check the documentation of the program from which you are importing a document.

- Navy document interchange format (DIF), which is a form of DIF used for exchanging documents, not spreadsheet data.

- WordStar. Most popular word processing programs can convert their documents directly to this format. However, some format codes, such as tab codes, are not translated. If you are converting a WordStar document to WordPerfect, this is the option to use. You may also be able to use WordStar format as an intermediate format; try it and see. If tabs are not important in the incoming document, this format may work for you.

- MultiMate. Use this option to import MultiMate documents.

- Seven-bit transfer format, which is used for transferring WordPerfect documents (which contain 8-bit control codes) via modems that lack an 8-bit transfer protocol. Most communications programs provide their own 8-bit transfer protocols, but if the one you are using does not, you can use this option to transfer WordPerfect files. When you use this option, the receiver at the other end uses option 6 on the menu, 7-bit transfer format, to translate the file back into WordPerfect format.

In addition, you can convert documents in the preceding formats directly to WordPerfect format.

You can also convert documents as follows:

- You can convert dBASE, WordStar, or other mail-merge files into Word-Perfect secondary merge files.
- You can convert WordPerfect secondary merge files into DIF (spread-sheet) format.
- You can convert spreadsheet DIF files into WordPerfect secondary merge files.

See the section "Converting Database and Spreadsheet Files" later in this chapter for considerations you should keep in mind when working with these types of file.

CONVERTING DATABASE AND SPREADSHEET FILES

You can bring data into a WordPerfect document as text, which means that you cannot use it in mail-merge applications; as a delimited file, which means that each field and record is separated by a special character so that WordPerfect can convert it to its secondary merge format; or as a DIF file. The following sections discuss considerations you should keep in mind when importing data.

Importing Data as Text

Importing spreadsheet or database data to be used as text—most often, as tables—in WordPerfect may produce unsatisfactory results if you have not taken a few necessary steps before converting the document. For example, when you export a wide Lotus 1-2-3 file in ASCII format (by printing it to a disk using the /Print File command), you will first need to reset your margins in WordPerfect if you do not want the table broken at the existing margins. Spreadsheet data often comprises monthly figures, which means that you will have 12 columns of numbers, plus perhaps 1 column of labels and 1 column of totals. If each column contains four-digit numbers as well as a period and two digits for cents, you are obviously going to need a wider margin than the one you normally use. When your margins are not set wide enough to hold the incoming data, WordPerfect deletes any data that extends beyond the right margin. For this reason you should split wide spreadsheets into smaller segments within the spreadsheet program before you bring them into WordPerfect. You should also set any margins that you have specified in the other program to zero so that the table of data will appear at the cursor position in WordPerfect.

Likewise, if you are importing tables of data from a database program, you should create a report and sort or extract data so that it is arranged as you want it before you bring it into WordPerfect.

You may also wish to turn on condensed printing (see Chapter 5) when you print wide columns of data and turn it off again when you return to the text portion of your document.

Figure 15.1 shows tabular data that has been brought into WordPerfect from Lotus 1-2-3. The range of data was first printed to a .PRN file in Lotus 1-2-3; in WordPerfect, option 2 on the Document Conversion menu (Ctrl-F5) was used to insert hard returns and so preserve the ends of lines.

If you were to examine the Reveal Codes, you would see that instead of tabs between the columns, there are simply spaces. If you are planning to edit large tables of data in WordPerfect, you will not be able to manipulate them easily. For this reason, you should format tables of data in the program you are taking the data from before you bring the data into WordPerfect.

Importing Data for Use in Mail-Merge Operations

Before you can merge database data into a document such as a form letter in WordPerfect, you need to convert the data into WordPerfect secondary merge

```
Memo to: Planning Department
From: R. S. O'Donnell
Subject: Internal budgeting

The following figures for the first quarter should provide us a
good basis on which to project in-house allocations for the
coming year:

-

    DEPARTMENT TOTALS
    -----------------------------------------------
    Salaries              14292    14292    15917
    Expenses              23273    23273    24230
    ===============================================
    Monthly total         37565    37565    40146
    Year to date          37565    75129   115276




C:\123\DEPTBUD.PRN                       Doc 1  Pg 1  Ln 9      Pos 10
```

FIGURE 15.1: Lotus 1-2-3 data imported into WordPerfect. Option 2 on the Document Conversion menu (Ctrl-F5) inserts hard returns at the end of each line so that row and column data remains in its original format when it is imported into WordPerfect to be used as a table.

format. In this format, each field is terminated by a ^R (Merge Return) code, and the end of each record is indicated by a ^E (Merge End) code on a line by itself (see Chapter 9 for additional information about merge codes). In database files used for mail-merge operations, fields and records are arranged by using *delimiters,* which are special characters that indicate the ends of fields and records.

When you use the Version 4.2 Convert program with this type of file (option 7 on the Convert menu), it will prompt you for the character that separates fields, the character that separates records, and any characters that should be removed from the incoming file. You will need to type the character or enter its ASCII code equivalent in curly braces. For example, if a space is used to separate fields in the incoming data, you can press the space bar or enter {**32**}. If a carriage return and line feed separates records, you enter {**13**}{**10**}, which is the ASCII code for <CR><LF>. In addition, most delimited files use quotation marks (") around labels to distinguish them from values. You should mark these as characters to be removed by typing " when you are prompted for characters to delete.

Options 7 and 9 on the Convert menu convert mail-merge and spreadsheet DIF files, respectively, from other programs directly into WordPerfect secondary merge files. Option 8 converts WordPerfect secondary merge files into spreadsheet DIF format. You can use option 8 when you need to export WordPerfect mail-merge files to another program format.

In dBASE II or III, you can convert (copy) files to type DELIMITED, which is mail-merge format. If you are using dBASE III PLUS, you can convert (copy) files to type DIF. In dBASE III, you use the command

.COPY TO <*file name*> **DELIMITED**

The program automatically adds the .TXT extension for you. You will need to specify the file name with the .TXT extension when you use the Convert program. You will also need to respond to the prompts to indicate the field and record delimiters and to remove quotation marks, as previously mentioned.

When you bring a delimited (mail-merge) file into WordPerfect from dBASE II or III, you must reposition the codes that separate records (see "DELIM: A Macro to Reformat Delimited Files" later in this chapter).

If you are translating a file to DIF, the program will translate the whole file. If all you want is a few records, you must first prepare a report containing only those records. When you convert a DIF file, the field names are also converted, and you must manually remove them before you use the file as a WordPerfect secondary merge file. They will be listed at the beginning of the file.

In dBASE III PLUS, you can convert files directly to DIF and bring them in as WordPerfect secondary merge files. All the WordPerfect codes required will be in their correct places, and all you will have to do is remove the field names at the beginning of the file.

The command for translating a file to DIF is

.COPY TO *<file name>* **TYPE DIF**

The program automatically adds a .DIF extension for you; you will need to specify the file name with that extension when you use the Convert program.

DELIM: A MACRO TO REFORMAT DELIMITED FILES

Fields in files that are brought into WordPerfect's secondary merge format must be separated by ^R codes, and a ^E code must appear on a separate line at the end of each record to indicate the ends of the records. When you convert delimited files, the ^E code indicating the end of the record may not be on a separate line. The following macro searches for each ^E code and inserts a hard return before it, thus moving it to a separate line. The macro repeats itself until no more ^E codes are found.

Begin macro	*Macro name*	*Keystrokes*	*End macro*
Ctrl-F10	**DELIM**	**F2 Shift-F9 F2**	**Ctrl-F10**
		← F9 →	
		Alt-F10 DELIM	
		Return	

Converting Lotus 1-2-3 Databases to WordPerfect Secondary Merge Files

You can convert Lotus 1-2-3 databases for use in WordPerfect mail-merge operations, but you will need to take an intermediate step if the database contains numeric or date fields. The DIF format was designed for spreadsheet-to-spreadsheet conversions, and values are translated in the format in which the program stores them internally.

Normally, the receiving program, which is usually another spreadsheet, reformats values back into its own format. Because Lotus 1-2-3 stores data to a precision of 15 places, the data you import directly in a DIF file is largely useless for mail-merge applications. It is formatted in scientific notation. In addition, dates, which are stored as serial numbers, lose their formatting when imported in a DIF file. Figure 15.2 illustrates a Lotus 1-2-3 database; Figure 15.3 illustrates what happens when this database is brought directly into WordPerfect as a DIF file.

If you have access to dBASE III or dBASE III PLUS, you can solve this problem without having to manually reenter each number and date. Instead, you can first translate your Lotus 1-2-3 database to a dBASE database file, using the Lotus 1-2-3 Translate utility. You can then copy the resulting dBASE (.DBF) file

```
A1: [W16] 'COMPANY                                              READY

            A           B         C       D        E         F       G
 1   COMPANY         DATE      ITEM     QTY      COST    ORDERED  PAID
 2   FORTUNE PUBL    02-Jun-86 CH120      13     32.50    422.50     2
 3   ABC PRINTING    14-Jun-86 DK135       5    112.50    564.50     2
 4   FLEET LEASING   20-Jun-86 CB120       8     19.50    156.00     1
 5   AUTO CARE SHOP  24-Jun-86 DK130       4     90.00    360.00     1
 6
 7
 8
 9
10
11
12
13
14
15
16
17
18
19
20
   11-Feb-87  10:38 AM
```

FIGURE 15.2: The original Lotus 1-2-3 database. If such files are converted to DIF (by using the Lotus 1-2-3 Translate utility) for further conversion to WordPerfect secondary merge format, dates and values that are stored using up to 15 decimal places are not converted into a format that has any meaning in most merge documents.

to either a DIF (dBASE III PLUS) file or a delimited file format (dBASE II and III) and bring it into WordPerfect using the appropriate option on the Convert utility. Figure 15.4 illustrates the results of this three-step translation process (Lotus 1-2-3 to dBASE III PLUS, dBASE III PLUS to DIF, DIF to WordPerfect secondary merge file).

If you do not have access to dBASE, you should check whether the database management program you do have access to supports importation of Lotus 1-2-3 worksheets (most do) and can also create ASCII delimited files from the program's database format. For example, Paradox's ExportImport option allows you to import a Lotus 1-2-3 worksheet and to create an ASCII delimited file from the resulting database. You can also do the same thing using the R:BASE 5000 or R:BASE System V FileGateway program.

If you do not have access to an intermediate program that can perform these types of translations, you will have to manually reenter the numbers and dates in the WordPerfect secondary merge files in order to use them. Using the Lotus 1-2-3 /Print File command to create an ASCII file and then the MailMerge to WordPerfect secondary file command will not accomplish the desired results.

This is because the resulting .PRN file, though in ASCII code, is not delimited by any characters except spaces. Because of the way values are formatted in

```
FORTUNE PUBL^R
3.156500000000000E+04^R
CH120^R
13^R
3.250000000000000E+01^R
4.225000000000000E+02^R
2^R
^E
ABC PRINTING^R
3.157700000000000E+04^R
DK135^R
5^R
1.125000000000000E+02^R
5.645000000000000E+02^R
2^R
^E
FLEET LEASING^R
3.158300000000000E+04^R
CB120^R
8^R
1.950000000000000E+01^R
156^R
1^R
^E
C:\WP\BOOK\CLIENTS                         Doc 2  Pg 1  Ln 1      Pos 10
```

FIGURE 15.3: The Lotus database imported as a DIF file into WordPerfect. This file was first converted to DIF by using 1-2-3's Translate utility and then imported by selecting option 9 on the Convert menu. Date and value fields are not formatted correctly.

the Lotus 1-2-3 worksheet, the number of spaces between individual fields in the Print file varies. A MailMerge to WordPerfect secondary merge file conversion will work only if each field is separated by a single space and no field contains any internal spaces within its text. In such a case, you can tell WordPerfect to use the space ({32}) as the field delimiter, and a successful translation will result.

CONVERTING DOCUMENTS TO DOS TEXT FILES

KEY SEQUENCE

To save a document as a DOS text file:

Ctrl-F5 1 <*file name*> **Return**

To save a document in generic word processing format:

Ctrl-F5 6 <*file name*> **Return**

To save a document in WordPerfect 4.1 format:

Ctrl-F5 7 <*file name*> **Return**

```
COMPANY^R
DATE^R
ITEM^R
QTY^R
COST^R
ORDERED^R
PAID^R
^E
FORTUNE PUBL^R
19860602  ^R
CH120^R
13.00^R
32.50^R
422.50^R
2.00^R
^E
ABC PRINTING^R
19860614  ^R
DK135^R
5.00^R
112.50^R
564.50^R
2.00^R
^E
C:\WP\BOOK\CLIENT                    Doc 2  Pg 1  Ln 1      Pos 10
```

FIGURE 15.4: Successfully translating a Lotus 1-2-3 database. The file was first translated to dBASE III PLUS by using the Lotus Translate utility; the resulting .DBF file was then converted to a DIF file by using the COPY TO <*file name*> TYPE DIF command. The resulting DIF file was then converted to a WordPerfect secondary merge file by using the Spreadsheet DIF to Secondary Merge option (9) on the Convert utility. If you are using dBASE II or III, you can create an ASCII delimited file by using the dBASE COPY TO <*file name*> DELIMITED command. The resulting ASCII file format will then be converted to a WordPerfect secondary merge file using the MailMerge to Secondary merge file option (7) on the Convert utility.

To convert text to DOS text file format (ASCII format) within the WordPerfect program, you use the Ctrl-F5 (Text In/Out) key sequence. When you press Ctrl-F5, the screen shown in Figure 15.5 appears.

If you select option 1 on the Text In/Out menu, your WordPerfect document is converted to a DOS text file. In this format, most of the codes that WordPerfect inserted to control formatting are removed. Some WordPerfect codes that control indenting, centering, paragraph numbering, and the Date function are converted to ASCII codes, however. All of your document except its footnotes and endnotes will be converted.

To view your document in DOS text file format, you can exit to DOS (by pressing Ctrl-F1 and selecting option 1) and issue the DOS TYPE command with the name of your file. For example, to view a DOS text file named REPORT, you type **TYPE REPORT** at the A> or C> prompt. Using the TYPE command is a good way to see whether your document has been converted successfully to DOS text file format.

```
Document Conversion, Summary and Comments

     DOS Text File Format
          1 - Save
          2 - Retrieve  (CR/LF becomes [HRt])
          3 - Retrieve  (CR/LF in H-Zone becomes [SRt])

     Locked Document Format
          4 - Save
          5 - Retrieve

     Other Word Processor Formats
          6 - Save in a generic word processor format
          7 - Save in WordPerfect 4.1 format

     Document Summary and Comments
          A - Create/Edit Summary
          B - Create Comment
          C - Edit Comment
          D - Display Summary and Comments




Selection: 0
```

FIGURE 15.5: The Text In/Out screen. The options on this screen allow you to save and retrieve files in ASCII format, called *DOS text file format* by WordPerfect. You can also choose to save WordPerfect files in a generic word processing format to use with other programs.

You can also convert your WordPerfect document to a generic word processor format by using option 6 on the Text In/Out menu. In this format, special Word-Perfect format codes are not saved, but the overall text format is maintained. Footnotes and endnotes are not converted, however. In place of the codes that indicate centering, indenting, flush-right text, and soft returns, spaces are inserted, and <CR><LF> (carriage return–line feed) codes are inserted in place of hard returns. Consult the documentation of the other program you plan to use the document with to see which format it will accept.

In addition, you will notice on this menu that you can convert documents you create in WordPerfect 4.2 into WordPerfect 4.1 format. If you are working in a company in which one department has not upgraded to WordPerfect 4.2, for example, you may wish to use option 7 to prepare documents for that department.

Whenever you convert documents, you should save them with an optional extension that identifies the format they are in. If you save a document in another format with the same name under which you saved it in WordPerfect format, the WordPerfect-formatted document will be overwritten, and you will have to convert it back in order to use it again within WordPerfect. For example, you may want to save documents you have converted to DOS text file format with the extension .TXT or .ASC or save documents converted to WordStar with the extension .WSD.

If you are planning to convert a document for use in WordStar or MultiMate, you should use WordPerfect's Convert program. See the section "Using the Convert Program" that follows.

RETRIEVING A DOS TEXT FILE

> **KEY SEQUENCE**
>
> **Ctrl-F5 2** or *3* *<file name>* **Return**
> **F5** (highlight file name) **5 Return**

When you retrieve documents saved as DOS text files, you have two options: Option 2 on the Text In/Out menu converts carriage return and line feed entries into hard returns in WordPerfect; option 3 converts <CR><LF> entries into soft returns if they occur within the hyphenation zone. If you are bringing data into WordPerfect in columns and rows (for instance, data from Lotus 1-2-3 or dBASE III or lines of programming code), you should use option 2, which preserves the column and row format. You should also use this option to bring in DOS batch files to revise them. If you are bringing in text that has been word wrapped, you should use option 3.

If the file you are importing uses wide margins (as files in 80-column format do, for instance), you may want to set your margins in WordPerfect to be wider than the incoming file so that the format of the incoming document is preserved.

You can also use option 5 (Text In) on the List Files menu (F5) to retrieve DOS text files. To do so, highlight the name of the DOS text file, select option 5, and press Return. WordPerfect converts the file into WordPerfect format and inserts it at the position of the cursor on the editing screen.

USING THE CONVERT PROGRAM

> **KEY SEQUENCE**
>
> C>**CONVERT Return** *<input file name>* **Return** *<output file name>* **Return**
> *<input file format>* **Return** *<output file format>*

To use the Convert program, you must copy it into the directory where the files you wish to convert are stored.

1. At the DOS prompt (A> or C>), enter **CONVERT** and press Return (you can run this utility by using WordPerfect's DOS shell command, Ctrl-F1 1). The menu shown in Figure 15.6 appears.

2. Enter the name of the file you want to convert (the input file); then press Return.

3. Enter the name of the output file you wish the input file to be converted to; then press Return. The names must be different; you can add a three-letter extension, such as WSD for WordStar, to indicate the format to which the file has been converted. You can also indicate a drive letter to output the converted file to a disk in drive B, for example.

4. WordPerfect then displays the menu shown in Figure 15.7. Enter the number corresponding to the current format of the input file; then press Return. For example, if you are converting a WordPerfect document to another format, enter **1** and press Return.

5. Enter the number corresponding to the format you want the converted file to use and press Return. For example, to convert a document to WordStar format, enter **4** and press Return.

```
Name of Input File? \wp\book\preface
Name of Output File? b:pref


1 WordPerfect to another format
2 Revisable-Form-Text (IBM DCA Format) to WordPerfect
3 Navy DIF Standard to WordPerfect
4 WordStar 3.3 to WordPerfect
5 MultiMate 3.22 to WordPerfect
6 Seven-bit transfer format to WordPerfect
7 Mail Merge to WordPerfect Secondary Merge
8 WordPerfect Secondary Merge to Spreadsheet DIF
9 Spreadsheet DIF to WordPerfect Secondary Merge

Enter number of Conversion desired _
```

FIGURE 15.6: The Convert utility menu. This is a special, external program, located on the Learning disk that comes with WordPerfect. It allows you to convert files directly into many popular formats.

```
Name of Input File? \wp\book\preface
Name of Output File? b:pref


1 WordPerfect to another format
2 Revisable-Form-Text (IBM DCA Format) to WordPerfect
3 Navy DIF Standard to WordPerfect
4 WordStar 3.3 to WordPerfect
5 MultiMate 3.22 to WordPerfect
6 Seven-bit transfer format to WordPerfect
7 Mail Merge to WordPerfect Secondary Merge
8 WordPerfect Secondary Merge to Spreadsheet DIF
9 Spreadsheet DIF to WordPerfect Secondary Merge

Enter number of Conversion desired 1

1 Revisable-Form-Text (IBM DCA Format)
2 Final-Form-Text (IBM DCA Format)
3 Navy DIF Standard
4 WordStar 3.3
5 MultiMate 3.22
6 Seven-bit transfer format

Enter number of output file format desired _
```

FIGURE 15.7: Converting documents to different formats. Unlike when you convert to ASCII format, when you select formats from this menu, formatting codes and text attributes are preserved when the documents are converted.

SUMMARY

This chapter has reviewed the techniques you use to convert documents into various formats so that they can be used by WordPerfect or by other programs. It has also explored several considerations you should keep in mind when converting data from popular spreadsheet and database management programs such as Lotus 1-2-3 and dBASE.

For related information, you may wish to refer to Chapter 5, "Printing," which discusses printing to disk. Printing to disk preserves your document's formatting characteristics but allows you to print the document by using the DOS PRINT command.

If you are converting documents for use with mail merge programs, you may want to review the material in Chapter 9, "Merge Printing."

For more information about creating and using macros, see Chapter 14, "Creating and Using Macros."

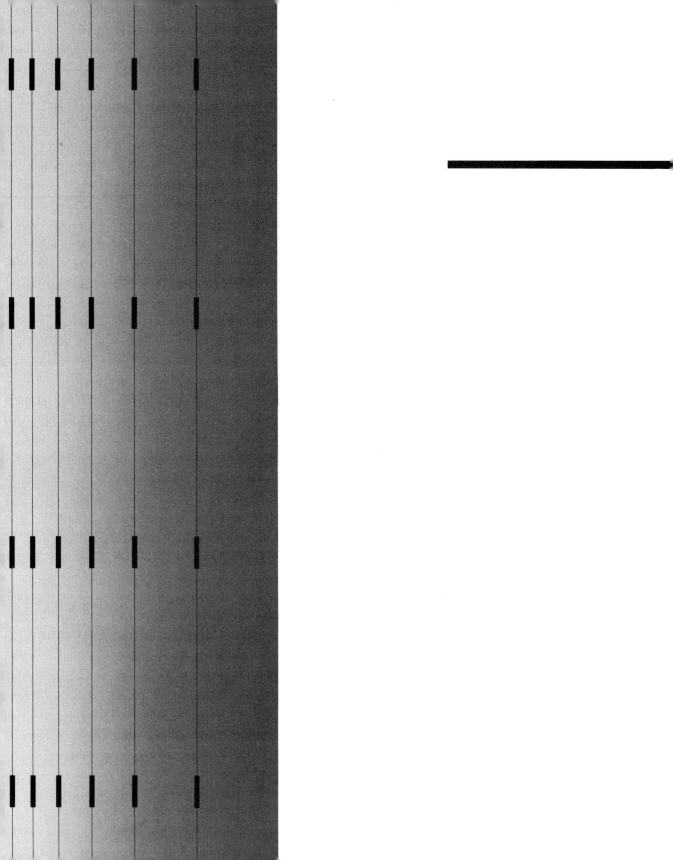

CHAPTER 16

INSTALLATION, SETUP, AND STARTUP OPTIONS

INSTALLATION, SETUP, AND STARTUP OPTIONS

T his chapter contains the information you need to install WordPerfect on both a floppy disk and a hard disk system. In addition, it discusses the default settings that you can change so that your customized settings are used each time you start WordPerfect. The WordPerfect program also contains options that you can specify each time you issue the startup command; these are discussed in this chapter as well.

INSTALLING WORDPERFECT

WordPerfect runs on IBM and IBM-compatible computers, as well as on other computers. This chapter discusses installation procedures for IBM and IBM-compatible computers that operate under PC-DOS and MS-DOS.

Installation on a Floppy Disk System

To install WordPerfect on a floppy disk system, you take the following steps:

1. Format five disks to be used as the working copies of your program disks plus a data disk—six disks in all. With your DOS disk in drive A and a blank disk in drive B, at the A> prompt enter the command

   FORMAT B:

   Follow the on-screen prompts. Format five disks in this way.

2. Use the command

   FORMAT B:/S

   to format the sixth disk. This is the disk you will use as your WordPerfect System disk. Label it *WordPerfect System* and return it to drive B.

3. Place the original WordPerfect System disk in drive A and enter

   COPY A:*.* B:

4. Repeat the process, copying each original disk to a blank formatted disk in drive B. Label each disk so that you can keep track of them. Also label the blank formatted disk that you will be using as a data disk.

5. Place your new WordPerfect System disk in drive A and the data disk in drive B.

You can now run WordPerfect by entering the command **WP.** (For instructions about how to specify the printer you are going to use, see Chapter 5.)

You may also want to change a few of the program's default settings or use some of the startup options. Refer to the sections later in this chapter for details about how to do so.

Installation on a Hard Disk System

To install WordPerfect on a hard disk, you will need to make a directory for your WordPerfect files and copy the WordPerfect System disk, Speller disk, and Thesaurus disk to that directory. In addition, you will probably want to copy the Help files from the Learning disk so that you can access on-line help at any time while using the program.

For example, to install WordPerfect in a directory named WP, take the following steps:

1. At the C > prompt, enter **MD\WP**.

2. Change to the WP directory by entering **CD\WP**.

3. Insert your WordPerfect System disk in drive A and enter **COPY A:*.***.

4. Repeat this process for your Speller and Thesaurus disks.

5. Copy the Help files from the Learning disk by inserting the Learning disk into drive A and entering **COPY A:WPHELP.FIL**.

You can now run WordPerfect by entering the command **WP.** (For instructions about how to specify the printer you are going to use, see Chapter 5.)

You may also want to change a few of the program's default settings, create a batch file to use with WordPerfect, or use some of the startup options. Refer to the sections later in this chapter for details about how to do so.

CHANGING DEFAULT SETTINGS

You may have personal preferences about how a word processing program operates. For example, WordPerfect's default setting is right-justified margins. If you prefer ragged-right margins, you can change this—and other default settings—by using WordPerfect's Setup menu.

To use the Setup menu, you start WordPerfect with the /S option. At the DOS prompt, enter **WP/S**. The Setup menu illustrated in Figure 16.1 appears.

When the Setup menu is displayed on the screen, you are presented with five selections:

   0 End Setup and enter WP
   1 Set Directories or Drives for Dictionary and Thesaurus Files
   2 Set Initial Settings
   3 Set Screen Size and Beep Options
   4 Set Backup Options

Choose any of the options you wish to modify by typing its number. After using all of the options you wish on this menu, type **0** to start the WordPerfect program.

Changing the Directory or Drive for the Dictionary and Thesaurus

WordPerfect normally looks for the Dictionary and Thesaurus files on the default drive and in the default directory. If you want to store these files elsewhere, you can specify another location by using option 1 on the Setup menu. If

```
                              Set-up Menu

        0 - End Set-up and enter WP

        1 - Set Directories or Drives for Dictionary and Thesaurus Files
        2 - Set Initial Settings
        3 - Set Screen and Beep Options
        4 - Set Backup Options

        Selection: _

        Press Cancel to ignore changes and return to DOS
```

FIGURE 16.1: WordPerfect's Setup menu. WordPerfect allows you to change default format settings as well as alter the screen size and set the program to make automatic timed backups. You can also turn off the beep feature that normally sounds when an error occurs.

you are using a floppy disk system, the files will normally be on a disk in drive B, so you should change the drive specification to B.

On a hard disk system, you may choose to store the files in a subdirectory under your main WordPerfect directory. If so, you need to enter the full path name of the directory.

Changing Default Format Options

Option 2 on the Setup menu allows you to change default format settings. The menu that appears when you select option 2 (Figure 16.2) allows you to set new default values for some of the options on the Line Format (Shift-F8), Page Format (Alt-F8), Print Format (Ctrl-F8), Print (Shift-F7), Date (Shift-F5), Mark Text (Alt-F5), Footnote (Ctrl-F7), and Screen (Ctrl-F3) menus. In addition, you can change the default entry mode from Insert to Typeover and change the number of times the Esc key repeats an operation. If you wish to display a document summary each time you save a document or exit WordPerfect, select the Text In/Out option.

```
Change Initial Settings

Press any of the keys listed below to change initial settings

Key              Initial Settings

Line Format      Tabs, Margins, Spacing, Hyphenation, Align Character
Page Format      Page # Pos, Page Length, Top Margin, Page # Col Pos, W/0
Print Format     Pitch, Font, Lines/Inch, Right Just, Underlining, SF Bin #
Print            Printer, Copies, Binding Width
Date             Date Format
Insert/Typeover  Insert/Typeover Mode
Mark Text        Paragraph Number Definition, Table of Authorities Definition
Footnote         Footnote/Endnote Options
Escape           Set N
Screen           Set Auto-rewrite
Text In/Out      Set Insert Document Summary on Save/Exit

Selection: _

Press Enter to return to the Set-up Menu
```

FIGURE 16.2: Default format options that can be changed. Option 2 on the Setup menu allows you to change many of WordPerfect's formatting options to the ones you prefer to use in most of your documents.

Changing the Default Screen Size

Option 3 on the Setup menu allows you to change the screen size from the normal 80 columns by 25 rows. You can use this option if you have a monitor or card that supports a larger screen size.

Setting Backup Options

Option 4 on the Setup menu allows you to specify whether to use the program's Automatic Backup feature and, if so, set the time between automatic backup operations. You can also specify whether you want to use the Original Backup feature. If you use this option, WordPerfect will use the old version of your document to make a backup file with the extension .BK! each time you save the document. You will then have a record of the last version of your document under the name <*file name*>.BK! as well as a copy of the latest version of the document saved under <*file name*>.

Figure 16.3 illustrates the backup options available to you.

```
Set Timed Backup

To safeguard against losing large amounts of text in the event of a power or
machine failure, WordPerfect can automatically backup the document on your
screen at a chosen time interval and to a chosen drive/directory (see Set-up
in the WordPerfect Installation pamphlet).  REMEMBER--THIS IS ONLY IN CASE OF
POWER OR MACHINE FAILURE.  WORDPERFECT DELETES THE TIMED BACKUP FILES WHEN YOU
EXIT NORMALLY FROM WORDPERFECT.  If you want the document saved as a file you
need to say 'yes' when you exit WordPerfect normally.

Number of minutes between each backup: 0


Set Original Backup

WordPerfect can rename the last copy of a document when a new version of the
document is saved.  The old copy has the same file name with an extension of
".BK!".  Take note that the files named "letter.1" and "letter.2" have the
same original backup file name of "letter.bk!".  In this case the latest
file saved will be backed up.

Backup the original document? (Y/N) N
```

FIGURE 16.3: Setting automatic backup options. WordPerfect is one of the few word processing programs that provides an Automatic Backup feature. If you live in an area that is prone to power failures, by all means take advantage of this option.

Changing the Default Beep Option

Option 5 on the Setup menu allows you to shut off the beep that normally sounds when a search fails or when you make a keyboard error. If you are working in an office environment, you may wish to eliminate the beep to avoid distracting others.

SPECIAL STARTUP OPTIONS

WordPerfect also provides other options that you can use with the basic Word-Perfect Startup command. You append these options to the command, separating the command and the option with a slash. Basically, these options are designed to help you customize WordPerfect before you begin to work with the program. Depending on your computer system, they can allow you to do such things as retrieve a particular document file for editing, invoke a macro, set the Timed Backup feature, and speed up and enhance the working of the program.

Combining Startup Options

Many of the various startup options discussed in the following sections can be combined, even though they are described separately. For instance, if you want to speed up the program operation using the /R option and also want to invoke a macro named CD at startup, you set the timed backup interval to 15 minutes and enter the command **WP/R/B-15/M-CD**. Remember not to enter spaces between the slashes and to enter a hyphen between the option letter and any particular required entry such as the macro name, file name, or number of minutes. (Chapter 1 discusses how to set up the CD macro referred to here.)

There are, however, two startup options that cannot be successfully combined with any of the others: specifying a particular file to be retrieved as part of the Startup command and entering WordPerfect through the Setup menu using the WP/S Startup command.

Creating an AUTOEXEC.BAT File
Containing Your WordPerfect Startup Options

If you have a series of startup options that you wish to invoke each time you use WordPerfect, you can include these in the batch files that you develop to automate the startup process.

You can also add these options to a special batch file called AUTOEXEC-.BAT that is automatically used each time you start the computer. You would use this method instead of including the files in the batch files described earlier if

WordPerfect is the program that you routinely work with each time you start the computer, and if you use the program on a hard disk system.

You can use WordPerfect to create the commands to be used in this file rather than using the DOS text editor. To do so, make the WordPerfect directory current and then follow these steps:

1. On the first line of the document, type **DATE** and press Return. (If your computer is equipped with a clock/calendar card, you omit this DATE command and the TIME command that follows.)

2. On the second line of the document, type **TIME** and press Return.

3. On the third line of the document, type **PATH C:\;C:\WP** (substitute the name of the directory that contains your WordPerfect program files if it is something other than WP). Using the PATH command allows you to start WordPerfect without having to use the CD (Change Directory) command to make the WordPerfect directory current.

4. On the fourth line of the document, you can type **PROMPT $P $G** and press Return. This is an optional command that instructs DOS to display the current directory (including the full path name) before the greater-than symbol (>) used as the standard DOS prompt. For instance, if you include this line in your AUTOEXEC.BAT file, WordPerfect displays the prompt

   C:\WP>

   instead of simply

   C>

   when you exit WordPerfect with the WP directory current. In other words, this command displays the name of the current directory, keeping you informed of where you are in the hard disk.

5. On the fifth line of the document, type the Startup command, including all of the options that you wish to use each time you start WordPerfect. For instance, you can enter **WP/R/B-15/M-CD** if you wish to use the RAM option to speed up the program, set timed backup operations at 15-minute intervals, and start the CD macro mentioned previously. After entering the WP command followed by all of the startup options you wish to use, press Return.

6. Save this file as a DOS text file rather than in WordPerfect's file format. To do this, you press Ctrl-F5 (Text In/Out), type **1**, enter the file name as **C:\AUTOEXEC.BAT**, and press Return. This saves this file in ASCII format in the root directory of the hard disk. Both of these conditions are required for this file to function properly.

7. Exit WordPerfect by pressing F7 and typing **N** and then **Y**. Test your AUTOEXEC.BAT file by holding down Ctrl-Alt and pressing Del and then releasing all three keys. The computer will automatically go through the startup sequence. It will then prompt you to enter the date and the time. After you enter this information, WordPerfect will be loaded into the computer's memory using the startup options you specified.

To determine which startup options you might wish to include in your AUTOEXEC.BAT file, read the following sections that describe each of their functions. Remember, you cannot combine accessing the Setup menu or loading a particular document file on startup with the other available options.

Starting WordPerfect from the Setup Menu

To permanently customize WordPerfect, you need to use the Setup menu. This menu includes options for defining the directories that contain your Dictionary and Thesaurus files and modifying the program's default format settings, screen size, backup options, and beep options (see "Changing Default Settings" earlier in this chapter). You change the basic Startup command to

C>WP/S

and press Return. As soon as the Setup menu is displayed on the screen, you are presented with five selections:

0 End Setup and enter WP
1 Set Directories or Drives for Dictionary and Thesaurus Files
2 Set Initial Settings
3 Set Screen Size and Beep Options
4 Set Backup Options

Choose any of the options you wish to modify by typing its number. After using all of the options you wish on this menu, type **0** to start the WordPerfect program. You will find detailed information about each of these menu options earlier in this chapter.

Starting WordPerfect and Setting a Timed Backup

In addition to permanently setting the Timed Backup feature using option 4 (Set Backup Options) on the Setup menu, you can also specify the number of minutes between backup operations while starting WordPerfect. For example, to start WordPerfect and set timed backup operations at 10-minute intervals, you enter

C>WP/B-10

and press Return. You can substitute any number of minutes for the 10 in this example. Just be aware that you must type **WP/B-** and follow it with the number corresponding to the interval you wish to use.

How often backup copies should be made depends upon the quality of the utilities in your area. If you experience frequent power interruptions or overloads in your building, you may want to set a very small interval between backup operations. The slight inconvenience you experience when WordPerfect interrupts your editing during its save operation can be trivial in comparison to the inconvenience of reentering a particularly tricky section of text.

Unlike the interval set from the Setup menu, the timed backup interval entered as part of the WordPerfect Startup command is in effect only for the duration of your work session. Once you exit WordPerfect to the operating system, the Timed Backup feature will return to its default setting. If you do not activate the feature using the Setup menu option, it will not be in effect at all when you use the program in a subsequent work session. This startup option is primarily intended for use when you want to temporarily override the timed backup interval defined with the Setup menu option.

Starting WordPerfect and Retrieving a Document to Edit

If you want to edit a particular document as soon as you load WordPerfect into the computer, you can include its file name as part of the Startup command. For example, if you wish to edit a document named SEC6 located on a data disk in drive A as soon as you start WordPerfect, you can enter the startup command as

C>WP A:SEC6

and then press Return. As soon as WordPerfect is loaded into memory, the document SEC6 on the disk in drive A will be retrieved and displayed on your screen, and you can begin your work. If the file name SEC6 is not located on the data disk in drive A when WordPerfect is loaded, you will receive the error message "Error—file not found."

Starting WordPerfect and Invoking a Macro

You can also start WordPerfect and have it invoke a macro as soon as the program is loaded into memory. For example, if you know that the first thing you need to do when WordPerfect is loaded is to change the directory, and if you have created a change-directory macro named CD (see Chapter 1), you can enter the Startup command as

C>WP/M-CD

and then press Return. As soon as the WordPerfect program files are loaded into your computer's memory, the CD macro will be started. As soon as the computer beeps, you just type the name of the new directory or edit the path name and press Return to make that directory current. Once the File Listing screen is displayed, you can retrieve the desired file for editing or press Esc to begin creating a new document to be saved in the file.

You can start any macro so long as it has been saved in the directory that WordPerfect uses on startup. In other words, if you start WordPerfect on a two-disk-drive system and make the data disk in drive B the current directory by entering, for example,

A>B: <Return>
B>A:WP/M-CD <Return>

the macro named CD must be located on the data disk in drive B. If it is not, WordPerfect will display the error message "Error—file not found" when it tries to invoke this macro.

If your macro is invoked using the Alt key and a letter key, you enter the macro name exactly as it is saved on your data directory. For example, if you want to invoke a macro named Alt-W upon program startup, you enter the Startup command as

C>WP/M-ALTW

and press Return.

Starting WordPerfect
and Redirecting Overflow Files to a New Directory

As you work on a document in WordPerfect, data is moved between RAM (the temporary memory that exists only while there is power) and your data disk. How frequently data is swapped out of RAM and stored on disk depends upon the total amount of memory in your computer. Parts of the document currently being created or edited are saved in different temporary files when this swap occurs. This movement of text out of RAM and into such files frees necessary computer memory so that you can continue to edit or add new text to your document. (This is the reason the size of your document files is limited by the amount of storage space available rather than the amount of memory in your computer.)

These files, called *overflow files,* are given different names, depending upon whether the text is located before or after the position of the cursor when this swapping occurs. Text located before the cursor's position is saved in a file named {WP}.TV1, and text located after the cursor's position is saved in a file named {WP}.BV1. (If you are creating or editing a document in the second window, overflow files {WP}.TV2 and {WP}.BV2 are created as well.)

When you exit WordPerfect by pressing F7 (Exit), these overflow files are closed, and the text is assembled as one document when you issue the Save command. If you do not use F7 to quit a work session in WordPerfect, these overflow files will still contain text when you next use the program. If WordPerfect detects that these files are not empty when you next use the program, it presents this prompt at the initial startup screen:

Are other copies of WordPerfect currently running? (Y/N)

When you type **N,** WordPerfect erases the contents of the overflow files and displays the standard editing screen.

> *Note:* You will still see the file names {WP}.TV1 and {WP}.BV1 listed when you obtain a directory listing, though the byte count will be set to 0. Early releases of Version 4.1 of WordPerfect presented you with three options after displaying the message "Overflow files exist." If you are using one of these releases, you type **3** and press Return to erase the contents of these files and to continue to the editing screen.

Normally, overflow files are saved in the drive or directory that WordPerfect uses at startup (WordPerfect always lists the directory that it is using at startup on the initial screen that it displays while the program files are being loaded into memory). You can change this so that the files are saved in a new drive or directory by appending **/D-** followed by the drive letter (and directory path name, if applicable) to the regular WordPerfect Startup command. For example, if you want the overflow files saved in the directory where you will be saving the document itself and this directory is named MARY, you start WordPerfect with this command:

C>/WP/D-C:\WP\MARY

Not only the overflow files but also buffers and temporary macros (see Chapter 14) are redirected to this new drive or directory. This means that if you are using WordPerfect on a two-disk-drive system and start it using both the /D- and /R options (see the section that follows), you can remove the WordPerfect System disk from drive A during program operation and replace it with a second data disk. In such a case, you would specify the startup command as

B>A:WP/D-B/R

The overflow files would then be saved on the data disk in drive B along with the documents you are creating and editing. The disk in drive A could then contain macros that you wish to use during the work session or a copy of the Learning disk that contains the WordPerfect help files that you might need to consult.

Starting WordPerfect and Making It Run Faster

WordPerfect requires at least 256K of RAM to run. If your computer has at least 512K or 640K of memory, you can use a /R option to make it run faster. When you use this startup option, WordPerfect loads the menus, error messages, and overlay files from the WordPerfect System disk into RAM. For example, you could start the program on a hard disk system using this option as follows:

C>WP/R

Once these files are loaded into memory, the program can access them more quickly than it can when it simply reads the data from the System disk.

As explained in the previous discussion of the /D- startup option, if you use these options together on a two-disk-drive system, you can remove the Word-Perfect System disk during operation. This allows you to use drive A to hold either the help files located on the Learning disk or a file containing macros you use in creating and editing your documents.

Starting WordPerfect with an Uninstalled Copy

If you start WordPerfect from a RAM drive rather than from one of your regular disk drives, you should use the WP/I startup option. You should also use this option if you have not copied WordPerfect onto a hard disk, and you start the program from a system disk in drive A.

Starting WordPerfect with the Nonflash Option

Some IBM-compatible computers require you to use the nonflash startup option to prevent the screen from going blank from time to time. This option is also required if you load WordPerfect from one of the window programs, such as TopView or Microsoft Windows. You specify the nonflash option in a startup command like this:

B>A:WP/NF

If you are using WordPerfect from a window program and experience a screen problem, you should modify the Startup command that the program uses to load WordPerfect for you in a similar manner.

Starting WordPerfect with the Nonsynch Option

You should use the nonsynch startup option if you are running WordPerfect on a Hyperion computer. It can also be used if your computer has a color monitor to make WordPerfect run a little faster. However, be aware that using this option with some color monitors causes "snow" when the screen is rewritten and program messages are updated. To use this option, you enter the Startup command as

B>A:WP/NS

and press Return.

Redefining the Cursor

The WordPerfect Learning disk contains a program called CURSOR.COM that you can use to change the flashing cursor indicator to a pattern other than an underline. There are 57 other patterns to select from, but your monitor may not be able to display some of them.

When you run the CURSOR program (by typing **CURSOR** while you are in the directory where CURSOR.COM resides), the screen shown in Figure 16.4 appears. The current cursor pattern is illustrated, and its two-letter designation appears at the bottom of the screen. Press the arrow keys to move the cursor to different locations on the grid and see how the cursor appears. (The differences are subtle; look carefully. As you approach the top right of the grid, the cursor gets larger.) You can press the space bar to see how each pattern looks in a line of text.

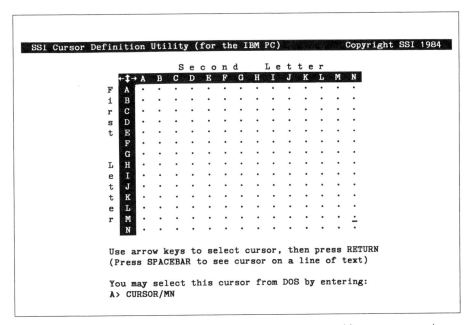

FIGURE 16.4: Changing the cursor pattern. You can change the pattern used for your cursor to a larger, much bolder block.

To use a different cursor pattern as the default cursor, select a pattern from the grid (note which pattern you have selected by copying the two-letter designation that appears at the bottom of the grid). Then press Return when the grid cursor displays the cursor you want to use. To use that pattern permanently, rewrite your AUTOEXEC.BAT file (see "Creating an AUTOEXEC.BAT File Containing Your WordPerfect Startup Options" earlier in this chapter) by adding the line

path name > **CURSOR/*nn***

where *nn* is the pattern you have chosen, and <*path name*> is the full path name of the directory in which the CURSOR program is located.

You cannot change the flashing cursor to a nonblinking cursor; however, if you prefer a larger, smaller, or dimmer cursor, you can select one by using this program.

Setting Screen Colors

KEY SEQUENCE

Ctrl-F3 4 <*monitor number*> **Y or N** <*colors*> **Shift-F3** <*colors*> **F7**

If you are using a color monitor, you may want to change the screen colors from the default setting of white on black. Option 4 of WordPerfect's Screen menu (Ctrl-F3) allows you to set screen colors. You can use different colors in the Document 1 and Document 2 windows.

To select different colors,

1. Press Ctrl-F3 (Screen) and select option 4 (Colors).
2. Enter the number corresponding to the type of monitor you are using.
3. Press Return to accept the default setting of slower text updating or enter **Y** for fast display.
4. Select the colors you would like as the background, foreground, underlining, boldfacing, and boldfacing/underlining colors. Enter the letter corresponding to each color. You can experiment to find the combinations you like by checking the text displayed at the side of the screen.
5. If you would like the Document 2 screen to use different colors than the Document 1 screen, press Shift-F3 and repeat step 4.
6. Press F7 when you have selected the colors you want to use. They will now be used as the default settings each time you start WordPerfect.

SUMMARY

This chapter has discussed how to install WordPerfect on your IBM or IBM-compatible system and change its options to meet your own needs. If you need additional information about installing your printer, refer to Chapter 5, "Printing." For more information about creating and using the macros discussed in this chapter, see Chapter 14, "Creating and Using Macros."

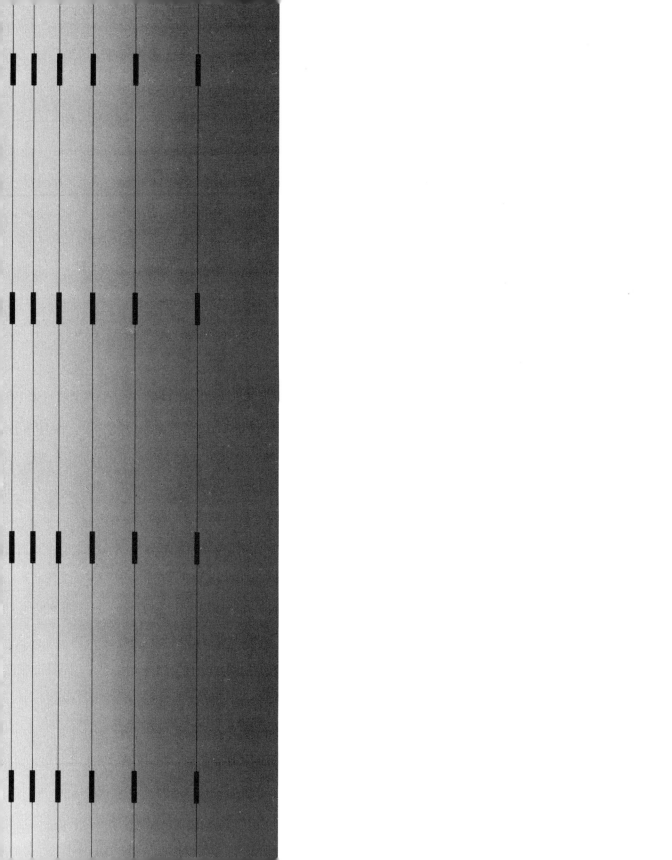

ASCII TABLE

ASCII Value	Character	Control Character	ASCII Value	Character
000	(null)	NUL	032	(space)
001	☺	SOH	033	!
002	●	STX	034	''
003	♥	ETX	035	#
004	♦	EOT	036	$
005	♣	ENQ	037	%
006	♠	ACK	038	&
007	(beep)	BEL	039	'
008	◘	BS	040	(
009	(tab)	HT	041	)
010	(line feed)	LF	042	*
011	(home)	VT	043	+
012	(form feed)	FF	044	,
013	(carriage return)	CR	045	-
014	♫	SO	046	.
015	☼	SI	047	/
016	►	DLE	048	0
017	◄	DC1	049	1
018	↕	DC2	050	2
019	!!	DC3	051	3
020	¶	DC4	052	4
021	§	NAK	053	5
022	▬	SYN	054	6
023	↨	ETB	055	7
024	↑	CAN	056	8
025	↓	EM	057	9
026	→	SUB	058	:
027	←	ESC	059	;
028	(cursor right)	FS	060	<
029	(cursor left)	GS	061	=
030	(cursor up)	RS	062	>
031	(cursor down)	US	063	?

APPENDIX A: ASCII Table (*IBM PC BASIC Manual*, pp. D-2 to D-5, ©1984 International Business Machines Corporation)

ASCII Value	Character	ASCII Value	Character
064	@	096	`
065	A	097	a
066	B	098	b
067	C	099	c
068	D	100	d
069	E	101	e
070	F	102	f
071	G	103	g
072	H	104	h
073	I	105	i
074	J	106	j
075	K	107	k
076	L	108	l
077	M	109	m
078	N	110	n
079	O	111	o
080	P	112	p
081	Q	113	q
082	R	114	r
083	S	115	s
084	T	116	t
085	U	117	u
086	V	118	v
087	W	119	w
088	X	120	x
089	Y	121	y
090	Z	122	z
091	[	123	{
092	\	124		
093	]	125	}
094	∧	126	~
095	—	127	⌂

APPENDIX A: ASCII Table (*IBM PC BASIC Manual*, pp. D-2 to D-5, ©1984 International Business Machines Corporation)

ASCII Value	Character	ASCII Value	Character
128	Ç	160	á
129	ü	161	í
130	é	162	ó
131	â	163	ú
132	ä	164	ñ
133	à	165	Ñ
134	å	166	ª
135	ç	167	º
136	ê	168	¿
137	ë	169	⌐
138	è	170	¬
139	ï	171	½
140	î	172	¼
141	ì	173	¡
142	Ä	174	«
143	Å	175	»
144	É	176	▒
145	æ	177	▒
146	Æ	178	▓
147	ô	179	│
148	ö	180	┤
149	ò	181	╡
150	û	182	╢
151	ù	183	╖
152	ÿ	184	╕
153	Ö	185	╣
154	Ü	186	║
155	¢	187	╗
156	£	188	╝
157	¥	189	╜
158	Pt	190	╛
159	ƒ	191	┐

APPENDIX A: ASCII Table (*IBM PC BASIC Manual*, pp. D-2 to D-5, ©1984 International Business Machines Corporation)

ASCII Value	Character	ASCII Value	Character
192	└	224	α
193	┴	225	β
194	┬	226	Γ
195	├	227	π
196	─	228	Σ
197	┼	229	σ
198	╞	230	μ
199	╟	231	τ
200	╚	232	Φ
201	╔	233	Θ
202	╩	234	Ω
203	╦	235	δ
204	╠	236	∞
205	═	237	$\varnothing$
206	╬	238	ϵ
207	╧	239	$\cap$
208	╨	240	$\equiv$
209	╤	241	$\pm$
210	╥	242	$\geq$
211	╙	243	$\leq$
212	╘	244	$\lceil$
213	╒	245	$\rfloor$
214	╓	246	$\div$
215	╫	247	$\approx$
216	╪	248	$\circ$
217	┘	249	$\bullet$
218	┌	250	·
219	■	251	$\sqrt{}$
220	▬	252	n
221	▌	253	²
222	▐	254	■
223	▀	255	(blank 'FF')

APPENDIX A: ASCII Table (*IBM PC BASIC Manual*, pp. D-2 to D-5, ©1984 International Business Machines Corporation)

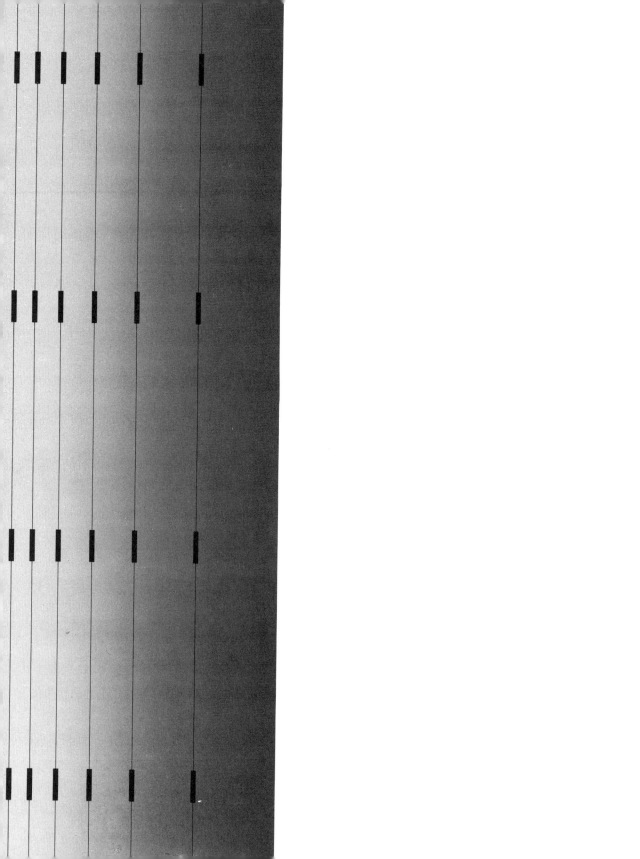

FORMATTING CODES

CODE	MEANING
[^](blinking)	Cursor Position
[ ]	Hard Space
[-]	Hyphen
-	Soft Hyphen
/	Cancel Hyphenation
[A][a]	Tab Align or Flush Right (begin and end)
[Adv▲]	Advance Up ½ Line
[Adv▼]	Advance Down ½ Line
[AdvLn:n]	Advance to Specified Line Number (n = line number)
[Align Char:]	Alignment Character
[B][b]	Bold (begin and end)
[Bin#:n]	Sheet Feeder Bin Number (n = bin number)
[Block]	Beginning of Block
[BlockPro:Off]	Block Protection off
[BlockPro:On]	Block Protection on
[C][c]	Centering (begin and end)
[Center Pg]	Center Current Page Top to Bottom
[Cmnd:]	Embedded Printer Command
[CndlEOP:n]	Conditional End of Page (n = number of lines)
[Col Def:]	Column Definition
[Col Off]	End of Text Columns
[Col On]	Beginning of Text Columns
[Date:n]	Date/Time Function (n = format)
[DefMark:Index, n]	Index Definition (n = format)
[DefMark:List, n]	List Definition (n = list number)
[DefMark:ToA, n]	Table of Authorities (n = section number)
[DefMark:ToC, n]	Table of Contents Definition (n = ToC level)
[EInd]	End of –> Indent or –> Indent <–
[EndDef]	End of Index, List, or Table of Contents
[EndMark:List, n]	End Marked Text (n = list number)
[EndMark:ToC, n]	End Marked Text (n = ToC level)
[E-Tabs:n, n]	Extended Tabs (begin with n, every n spaces)

APPENDIX B: Formatting Codes

CODE	MEANING
[Font Change:*n, n*]	Specify New Font or Print Wheel (*n* = pitch, font)
[FtnOpt]	Footnote/Endnote Options
[Hdr/Ftr:*n, n;*text]	Header or Footer Definition (*n* = type, occurrence)
[HPg]	Hard Page Break
[HRt]	Hard Return
[Hyph on]	Hyphenation On
[Hyph off]	Hyphenation Off
[HZone Set:*n, n*]	Reset Size of Hyphenation Zone (*n* = left, right)
[–> Indent]	Beginning of Indent
[–> Indent <–]	Beginning of Left/Right Indent
[Index:*heading; subheading*]	*Index Mark*
[LnNum:On]	Line Numbering On
[LnNum:Off]	Line Numbering Off
[LPI:*n*]	Lines per Inch (*n* = number of lines)
[← Mar Rel:*n*]	Left Margin Release (*n* = positions moved)
[Margin Set:*n, n*]	Left and Right Margin Reset (*n* = left, right margin setting)
[Mark:List, *n*]	Begin Marked Text for List (*n* = list number)
[Mark:ToC, *n*]	Begin Marked Text for ToC (*n* = ToC level)
[Math Def]	Definition of Math Columns
[Math Off]	End of Math
[Math On]	Beginning of Math
!	Formula Calculation
†	Subtotal Entry
+	Calculate Subtotal
T	Total Entry
=	Calculate Total
*	Calculate Grand Total
[Note:End, *n; [note#]text*]	*Endnote (n = endnote number)*
[Note:Foot, *n; [note#]text*]	Footnote (*n* = footnote number)
[Ovrstk]	Overstrike preceding Character

APPENDIX B: Formatting Codes (continued)

CODE	MEANING
[Par#:Auto]	Automatic Paragraph/Outline Number
[Par#:*n*]	Permanent Paragraph Number (*n* = level number)
[Par#Def]	Paragraph Numbering Definition
[Pg#:*n*]	New Page Number (*n* = page number)
[Pg# Col:*n, n, n*]	Column Position for Page Numbers (*n* = left, center, right)
[Pg Lnth:*n, n*]	Set Page Length (*n* = form lines, text lines)
[Pos Pg#:*n*]	Set Position for Page Numbers
[RedLn][r]	Redline (begin and end)
[Rt Just Off]	Right Justification Off
[Rt Just On]	Right Justification On
[Set Ftn#:*n*]	New Footnote Number (*n* = note number)
[Spacing Set:*n*]	Spacing Set (*n* = spacing increment)
[SPg]	Soft Page Break
[SRt]	Soft Return
[StrkOut][s]	Strikeout (begin and end)
[SubScrpt]	Subscript
[Sumry/Cmnt:*text*]	Document Summary or Comment
[SuprScrpt]	Superscript
[Suppress:*n*]	Suppress Page Format Options (*n* = format(s))
[TAB]	Move to Next Tab Stop
[Tab Set]	Tab Reset
[ToA:*n; [short form]*;]	Short Form for Table of Authorities (*n* = section number)
[ToA:*n;[short form]*; <*full form*>]	Full Form for Table of Authorities (*n* = section number)
[Top Mar:*n*]	Set Top Margin in Half Lines (*n* = margin setting)
[U][u]	Underlining (begin and end)
[Undrl Style:*n*]	Underlining Style (*n* = underlining style option number)
[W/O Off]	Widow/Orphan Protection Off
[W/O On]	Widow/Orphan Protection On

APPENDIX B: Formatting Codes (continued)

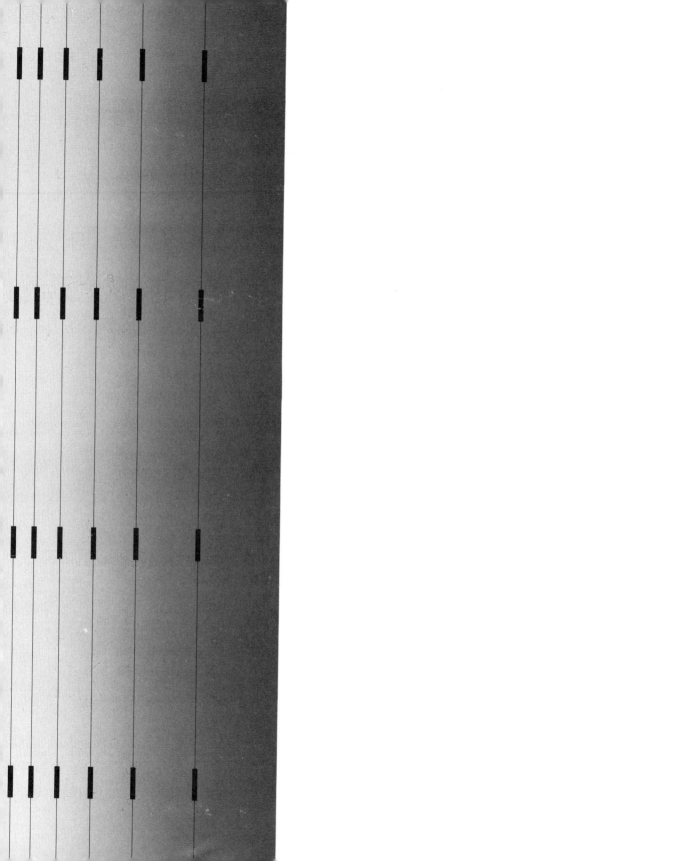

Using WordPerfect
with the HP LaserJet Printer

I f you are using WordPerfect with an HP LaserJet, HP LaserJet Plus, or HP LaserJet Series II printer, you have access to more type faces and printing enhancements than are available with traditional impact printers. However, in order to harness the potential of your laser printer, you must be thoroughly familiar with how it works with WordPerfect.

Installing the HP LaserJet

When you install the HP LaserJet, HP LaserJet Plus, or HP LaserJet Series II printer in WordPerfect, you must choose the appropriate printer definition not only for the type of printer (LaserJet, LaserJet +, or LaserJet 500 +), but also for the type of fonts you are using.

LaserJet printers have an internal font referred to as *font A*. Font A uses fixed 10-pitch (10 characters per inch) Courier type. In addition, LaserJet Plus and LaserJet II printers can produce this font in fixed 16.66 pitch (nearly 17 characters per inch). This font does not support italic type or, in the case of the LaserJet, boldface type.

All LaserJet printers will accept cartridges that increase your choice of typefaces, printing enhancements, and in some cases, even the characters that you can use. Once the cartridge is inserted into the port in the front of the printer, the LaserJet uses the fonts on that cartridge instead of the built-in Courier font.

Some cartridges not only alter the printing style and pitch, but also extend the character set to include special symbols and graphics characters. For example, Cartridge G (Prestige Elite Legal) gives you all of the basic keyboard characters in 12 pitch type plus symbols, such as copyright, paragraph, and section symbols, and line- and box-drawing characters.

In addition to supporting the use of font cartridges, HP LaserJet Plus and HP LaserJet Series II printers support the use of soft fonts (also referred to as *downloaded fonts*). Soft fonts are packaged in a set of disks. Soft fonts offer you an even wider choice of printing styles, enhancements, and character sets than are available on font cartridges. They not only give you more fonts than you get on a cartridge, but they are not subject to the wear and tear that a cartridge is. Font cartridges are guaranteed for only 500 insertions; soft fonts can last indefinitely (you can always make a new working copy of disks from your originals).

Most soft-font packages offer you a choice typefaces (for instance, Times Roman and Helvetica) in various point sizes (8, 10, 12, and so on), weights (light, medium, or bold), and styles (upright or italic). Also, each font in the set is proportionally spaced.

For example, when you purchase the AC set of soft fonts from Hewlett-Packard, you have a choice of 6, 8, 10, 12, 14, 18, 24, and 30 point Times Roman and Helvetica typefaces. In addition, you can print the 6, 8, 10, 12, and 14 point sizes in upright medium (regular) or bold or in italic medium type style. The 18, 24, and 30 point sizes in this set can be printed only in upright bold.

> *Note:* Strictly speaking, point size refers to only the vertical size of a typeface, with one point equal to 1/72 of an inch. Therefore, a change in point size affects the line spacing (lines per inch) that you use on a page. However, as you change point size, the width of the typeface also changes. This means that often you must also adjust the pitch (characters per inch) when you change point size. See Table C.1 later in this chapter for a list of suggested pitches to use with various point sizes.

Selecting the Appropriate Printer Definition

Before you can use any of the fonts that you have for HP LaserJet, HP LaserJet Plus, or HP LaserJet Series II (including the internal font A), you must copy the printer definition the font uses from the Printer 1 disk into your WPRINTER.FIL and WPFONT.FIL files. This is done by using the Select Printers option from the Printer Control screen (press Shift-F7 and type **4** and **3**). Then select the number of the printer you want to use, press the PgDn key, and indicate the letter of the drive that contains your Printer 1 disk (for more details, see "Installing a New Printer" in Chapter 5).

To reach the first printer definitions for the HP LaserJet printers, you need to press the PgDn key at least twice. In Version 4.2, the printer definitions for the LaserJet printers are numbered 80 through 114. Figure C.1 shows you the first screen containing LaserJet definitions (numbers 80 through 96). More LaserJet definitions (numbers 97 through 114) appear on the next screen.

Notice in this figure that the first seven definitions are only for the LaserJet; the rest apply to the LaserJet, LaserJet Plus (indicated by +), and LaserJet 500+. For example, to use the internal font A with any of these models, you select printer definition 87, A: Courier.

Normally, you will want to assign the font A printer definition to Printer 1. That way, you can use 10-pitch Courier for printing drafts of your documents. You can then assign other printer definitions to printers 2 through 6.

```
Printer Definitions in B:WPRINT1.ALL

    65  HP ThinkJet                  66  IBM Color Jetprinter
    67  IBM Color Printer            68  IBM Graphics Printer
    69  IBM Pageprinter Courier      70  IBM Pageprinter Essay PS
    71  IBM Pageprinter Gothic-text  72  IBM Pageprinter Landscape
    73  IBM Pageprinter Prestige     74  IBM Pageprinter Serif-text
    75  IBM Pageprinter Sonoran PS   76  IBM ProPrinter
    77  IBM Quietwriter              78  IBM Wheelprinter
    79  IBM Wheelprinter E           80  LaserJet B: Tms Rmn 1
    81  LaserJet F: Tms Rmn 2        82  LaserJet K: Tms Rmn Math
    83  LaserJet P: Tms Rmn P&L      84  LaserJet T: Helv Tax
    85  LaserJet U: Forms Port       86  LaserJet V: Forms Land
    87  LaserJt Reg,+,500+ A: Courier  88  LaserJt Reg,+,500+ C: Intl 1
    89  LaserJt Reg,+,500+ D: P Elite  90  LaserJt Reg,+,500+ E: Gothic
    91  LaserJt Reg,+,500+ G: Legal E  92  LaserJt Reg,+,500+ H: Legal C
    93  LaserJt Reg,+,500+ J: Math E   94  LaserJt Reg,+,500+ L: Cou P&L
    95  LaserJt Reg,+,500+ M: P E P&L  96  LaserJt Reg,+,500+ N: L G P&L


                                 PgDn for Additional Printer Definitions
                                 Exit when Done
    Printer 1                    Cancel to Ignore Changes
    Using Definition: _          Arrow Keys to Change Printer Number
```

FIGURE C.1: WordPerfect HP LaserJet printer definitions. This is the first printer definition screen that includes definitions for the LaserJet and LaserJet Plus printers (indicated by + and 500 +). The type of LaserJet printer is indicated, followed by the cartridge that the printer supports (A is the internal default font). The P&L at the end of some descriptions stands for *portrait and landscape*. If a definition does not contain this abbreviation, the printer is set up for only portrait mode. If you have a LaserJet II, you use the definitions for the LaserJet Plus.

If you use either of the soft fonts in the AA or AC set with your LaserJet Plus or LaserJet Series II printer, you will want to choose among printer definitions 105 through 111 (shown in Figure C.2) and assign the proper definitions to available printer numbers. Notice that WordPerfect currently offers five definitions for the AA set and two for the AC set.

When you select the number of the font you wish to use, WordPerfect asks you to indicate the port number. Most LaserJet printers come with a serial interface, although the LaserJet Plus and LaserJet II also can be configured with a Centronics parallel interface. If your LaserJet printer has a serial interface, you select the correct COM port number from the menu. If your LaserJet Plus or Series II printer uses a parallel interface, you select the proper LPT port number.

When you indicate a COM port, WordPerfect also prompts you for the baud rate, parity setting, number of stop bits, and number of character bits. The correct settings are as follows:

Baud Select	7 – 9600
Parity	0 – None

Stop Bits 1
Character Length 8

After you specify these settings, you will be prompted to indicate the type of paper feed. If you are using the LaserJet Plus or Series II, select the Continuous feed option (1). If you are using the LaserJet or LaserJet 500 + , select the Sheet Feeder option (3). After you indicate the number of lines between pages and the column position of the left edge of the paper (use the default settings) and the number of bins, select feeder number 17 for the LaserJet or 19 for the LaserJet 500 + .

After you have installed all of the printer definitions you wish to use, select the Display Printers and Fonts option (2) from the Printer Control screen and study the numbers assigned to the eight fonts available under each definition. You should probably obtain a hard copy of these two screens for use as you assign font changes in your documents. (To do this, press Shift-PrtSc, place the laser printer off line, and press Form Feed. After printing, press the on-line button again.) The fonts displayed in the printer definition are the only ones you can use without resorting to printer escape sequences to redefine the available fonts (see "Creating a New Soft Fonts Printer Definition" later in this appendix).

```
Printer Definitions in B:WPRINT1.ALL

 97  LaserJt Reg,+,500+ Q: Cour,LG    98  LaserJt Reg,+,500+ R: Present
 99  LaserJt Reg,+,500+ W: BarCode   100  LaserJt Reg,+,500+ Y: PC Cour
101  LaserJt+,500+ B: Tms Rmn 1      102  LaserJt+,500+ F: Tms Rmn 2
103  LaserJt+,500+ K: Tms Rmn Math   104  LaserJt+,500+ P: Tms Rmn P&L
105  LaserJt+,500+ Soft AA: Helv L   106  LaserJt+,500+ Soft AA: Helv P
107  LaserJt+,500+ Soft AA: Tm/Hel   108  LaserJt+,500+ Soft AA: Tms L
109  LaserJt+,500+ Soft AA: Tms P    110  LaserJt+,500+ Soft AC: Helv P
111  LaserJt+,500+ Soft AC: Tms P    112  LaserJt+,500+ T: Helv Tax
113. LaserJt+,500+ U: Forms Port     114  LaserJt+,500+ V: Forms Land
115  LaserWriter Helv Landscape      116  LaserWriter Helv Portrait
117  LaserWriter Times Landscape     118  LaserWriter Times Portrait
119  MPI Printmate 150               120  Mannesmann Tally MT180
121  Mannesmann Tally MT290 w/IBM    122  NEC 2050
123  NEC 3510/3530/7710/7730         124  NEC 3515/5515/7715/3525/7725
125  NEC 3550                        126  NEC 8830 (*NEC 8810)
127  NEC 8850                        128  NEC Elf 360


                                     PgDn for Additional Printer Definitions
                                     Exit when Done
Printer 1                            Cancel to Ignore Changes
Using Definition: _                  Arrow Keys to Change Printer Number
```

FIGURE C.2: More WordPerfect HP LaserJet printer definitions. This second printer definition screen for LaserJet printers shows both definitions for cartridges (97 through 104) for the AA and AC soft font sets. Notice that some of these definitions specify only portrait mode (P), and others specify only landscape mode (L).

Using Soft Fonts

When you use soft fonts with your LaserJet Plus or Series II printer, you must download the fonts before you can print with them. Downloading involves copying the definition of each font you wish to use from the appropriate disk to the printer memory. This procedure must be performed from within DOS using the DOWNLOAD.BAT program that comes on disk 1 of the soft-font set. You can perform this operation safely by using WordPerfect's DOS Shell feature to return to the DOS operating prompt (press Ctrl-F1 and type **1**).

The number of fonts in the soft-font set outnumber those currently defined by WordPerfect in the printer definition files for soft fonts. For instance, the AC set contains 72 different fonts (counting both portrait and landscape modes), although WordPerfect supports only 16 of these, all in portrait mode. Usually, you will want to download only the fonts supported by the printer definitions you have installed.

Downloading Fonts

Running the DOWNLOAD program is a simple process. However, you must be sure that you have a copy of your BASIC.COM file either on your soft font working disk or on a disk available to the \FONTS directory that contains the DOWNLOAD program (use the command PATH C:\;C:\DOS if necessary). Before you begin downloading soft fonts, make sure that any font cartridge has been removed. To do this, set the printer off line, remove the cartridge, and press the on-line button.

> *Note:* If you are using an IBM-compatible computer (other than a Compaq), your BASIC program may not be named BASIC.COM. If this is the case, you must change this name in the DOWNLOAD.BAS file to the name of your BASIC program before you run the DOWNLOAD program. You do this in WordPerfect by using the Text In/Out feature (press Ctrl-F5 and type **2**). Be sure to save the file as an ASCII file after making these changes by pressing Ctrl-F5 and typing **1**. The file DOWNLOAD.BAS may not, however, be included on disk 1 if you are using one of the newer soft fonts sets. If you do not find this file on the first disk of your set, you need not worry about the version of BASIC you are using.

If you are downloading the fonts from a floppy disk, copy on a new floppy disk the downloading programs (DOWNLOAD.BAT; DOWNLOAD.BAS, if it is included; PERMTEMP.EXE; PERMTEMP.BAS; IDFONT.EXE; and IDFONT.BAS) from disk 1 along with BASIC.COM and all of the files containing the fonts you want to use. If you are downloading the fonts from a hard disk, create a \FONTS directory, make it current, and then copy into this directory the downloading programs from disk 1 along with all of the files containing the fonts you want to use.

The file name given to each soft font identifies the font precisely. For instance, on disk 1 of the AC set, the font that gives you proportionally spaced 10-point italic Times Roman type in portrait mode is named

TR100IPN.USP

The first two letters of the file name stand for the typeface. In this case, TR stands for Times Roman. AC disks also include files that begin with HV, which stands for Helvetica type. The three digits that follow the typeface letters indicate the point size. The number 080 indicates 8 points, 100 indicates 10 points, 240 indicates 24 points, and so on. The letter that immediately follows the point size identifies the weight and style of the type: R indicates regular (or medium weight), B indicates boldface, and I indicates italics. The two characters that follow the weight designator indicate the pitch of the font or whether the font is proportionally spaced. Here, PN indicates that the font is proportionally spaced; the number 12 in this position would indicate 12 pitch.

The file-name extension indicates the symbol set. Soft fonts use three different symbol sets: the USASCII set, the Roman 8 Set, and the Roman 8 extended set. The USASCII set includes only standard letters, numbers, and punctuation symbols. Roman 8 and Roman 8 extended sets include these characters plus various foreign language, math and science, and graphics characters. If the font uses the USASCII symbol set, the extension begins with US. If the font uses one of the Roman 8 sets, the extension begins with either R8 or RE.

The very last character of the font file-name extension is P if the font prints in portrait mode, or L if the font prints in landscape mode. Portrait and landscape modes indicate the orientation of type on the page. In portrait mode the type extends across the width of the page (the normal orientation used for letters), and in landscape mode the type is turned 90 degrees and runs down the length of the page. Landscape mode is used whenever you are printing tables too wide to fit across the standard page width.

DOWNLOAD.BAT assumes that your LaserJet printer is connected to LPT1. In most cases, it will be connected to one of the COM ports. If your LaserJet printer has a serial interface, before you enter the download command, you must use the DOS MODE command to redirect all output to the appropriate COM port. For you to use the MODE command, your computer must load it from the DOS disk or DOS directory. If you are using a floppy disk system, put your DOS disk in the default drive. If you are using a hard disk, make sure that the path is set to your DOS directory. Then enter the following command:

MODE LPT1: = COM*x*

For *x*, substitute the number of the COM port that your LaserJet uses. For example, if your printer is connected to COM1, you would enter

MODE LPT1: = COM1

Note: Usually your AUTOEXEC.BAT file will contain this MODE command as well as the MODE command that sets the baud rate, parity, number of stop bits, and character length (MODE COM*x:* 9600,N,8,1,P). If this is the case, you do not need to redirect the output a second time. However, if you have not issued this MODE command to set the port's parameters, you must issue it as well as the MODE command to redirect output to the appropriate COM port before you print your documents in WordPerfect.

After you have taken these steps, you are ready to run the DOWNLOAD batch file. Make sure that the LaserJet printer is on and that the copied fonts and downloading programs are in the default drive or directory. Then, at the DOS prompt, type **DOWNLOAD** followed by the complete file name of the font you wish to use. For instance, to load the proportionally spaced 10-point italic Times Roman font in portrait mode, you enter

DOWNLOAD TR100IPN.USP

and press Return. You will then be prompted to give the font an ID number between 0 and 32767. The ID number you assign the font can be used instead of the escape sequence in a WordPerfect printer control code (Ctrl-F8 A). This is *not* the number you use to select the font for a particular document (Ctrl-F8 1). After you enter the ID number and press Return, the font will be downloaded to the LaserJet printer (this may take a few minutes, especially for large point sizes).

After the font has been downloaded, the program will ask if you want to make the font temporary or permanent. Making a font permanent means that it will not be erased from the printer's memory until you turn the power off. This allows you to reset the LaserJet printer without losing the font. You will almost always want to make the font permanent by typing **P.** However, even fonts that you designate as permanent will be lost as soon as you turn off the printer. This means that you must repeat this downloading procedure during each new work session in which you wish to use the font.

Before the DOWNLOAD program returns you to the operating system, you will be asked if you want the LaserJet printer to print a sample of the font. This sample will contain the ID number that you assigned to the font and a sample of all of the characters it contains. It is generally a good idea to have the printer produce this sample, especially if you are using the font for the first time. To get a sample page, type **Y** and either **P** to print in portrait mode or **L** to print in landscape mode.

After you are returned to the DOS prompt, repeat this entire downloading procedure for each of the fonts you want to use in your WordPerfect document. After you have finished, remember to type **EXIT** to return to WordPerfect if you used the DOS Shell feature to run the downloading program.

Using Downloaded Fonts in Your Document

Once you have configured the appropriate printer definitions for the soft fonts you have (either AA or AC) and have downloaded the particular fonts you wish to use, you can use the fonts. To do so, you have only to issue the appropriate font changes in your document and select the correct printer number before you print.

When selecting the font, you may also have to enter a new pitch (Ctrl-F8 1) or new line spacing (Shift-F8 4). Table C.1 lists suggested pitches to use with fonts of various point sizes. Notice that each pitch is followed by an asterisk (*) to indicate to WordPerfect that the font is proportionally spaced. Remember that you will also have to adjust the margin settings (Shift-F8 3) when you select a new pitch setting.

TYPE SIZE	PITCH SETTING
8 point	18*
10 point	15*
12 point	11*
18 point	8*
24 point	5*
30 point	5*
Note: Use the * (asterisk) after the pitch number only if the font is proportionally spaced.	

TABLE C.1: Suggested Pitches for Various Point Sizes

Often, you will want to mix fonts of different point sizes in a document. For example, you may want to set the basic text of a document in one point size and the headings in a slightly larger size. For most text, 10-point type is a good size. When selecting the point size for the headings, you should increase the point size by at least two points. For some applications, you may find it effective to increase the difference between the two point sizes even more.

Figures C.3 through C.6 illustrate the dramatic effect that changing type styles and point sizes can have on the printed result. Figure C.3 shows a sample page from an employee's handbook printed in 10-pitch Courier type (using Font 1 of the A: Courier printer definition). Figure C.4 shows the same page, this time printed in 10-point Times Roman type (using Font 1 of the AC: Tms P printer definition).

To accomplish this change, a font change was issued at the beginning of the document. The pitch was changed from 10 to 15*, and the font was left at 1. Also, immediately before sending the document to the LaserJet printer, the

WELCOME

Welcome to MagnaCorp. We hope this employee handbook will help to guide you through your first few days here. In addition, it contains valuable information about employee services and benefits available to you. Ask your manager or call the personnel office if you have any questions for which you cannot find the answers in this handbook.

Work Day

The official work day at MagnaCorp is 8:30 a.m. to 5:00 p.m. Flexible hours can be arranged with your manager.

Parking

As parking is limited, please apply to the personnel office for a parking slot assignment.

Hours

Noon to 1 p.m. has been reserved as lunch hour for all employees. Some departments have chosen to take lunch from 11:30 to 12:30 or from 12:30 to 1:30; check with your manager.

Cafeteria

The company cafeteria, located on the third floor, is open from 7 a.m. until 2 p.m. daily. Breakfast is available for your convenience until 9:00. After 2 p.m., vending machines with cold sandwiches and salads are available.

Recreational Facilities

MagnaCorp participates in the city recreational plan and therefore its employees have access to the municipal gym located at First and Brannan Streets. The jogging track and par course in Grant Park are also nearby. Showers and lockers for company employees are located near the south entrance of the main lobby.

Vacation

Full-time permanent employees are eligible for two weeks of paid vacation after six months of continuous employment. During the first five years of service, you earn three weeks of vacation per year. After five years of service, you receive four weeks of vacation.

FIGURE C.3: A sample page from an employee handbook printed with the LaserJet Plus using its internal font (A). This font (Font 1 in the A: Courier printer definition) gives the document a fixed spacing of 10 pitch in the Courier font designed to imitate the type of a standard typewriter.

WELCOME

Welcome to MagnaCorp. We hope this employee handbook will help to guide you through your first few days here. In addition, it contains valuable information about employee services and benefits available to you. Ask your manager or call the personnel office if you have any questions for which you cannot find the answers in this handbook.

Work Day

The official work day at MagnaCorp is 8:30 a.m. to 5:00 p.m. Flexible hours can be arranged with your manager.

Parking

As parking is limited, please apply to the personnel office for a parking slot assignment.

Hours

Noon to 1 p.m. has been reserved as lunch hour for all employees. Some departments have chosen to take lunch from 11:30 to 12:30 or from 12:30 to 1:30; check with your manager.

Cafeteria

The company cafeteria, located on the third floor, is open from 7 a.m. until 2 p.m. daily. Breakfast is available for your convenience until 9:00. After 2 p.m., vending machines with cold sandwiches and salads are available.

Recreational Facilities

MagnaCorp participates in the city recreational plan and therefore its employees have access to the municipal gym located at First and Brannan Streets. The jogging track and par course in Grant Park are also nearby. Showers and lockers for company employees are located near the south entrance of the main lobby.

Vacation

Full-time permanent employees are eligible for two weeks of paid vacation after six months of continuous employment. During the first five years of service, you earn three weeks of vacation per year. After five years of service, you receive four weeks of vacation.

Credit Union

MagnaCorp's credit union is located on the third floor. Hours are 9 to 6 p.m. daily. The credit union observes all national and bank holidays, whereas the company may or may not follow the same schedule.

FIGURE C.4: The same sample page as shown in Figure C.3, this time printed with the LaserJet Plus using one of the soft fonts in the AC set. This particular font (Font 1 in the AC: Tms P printer definition file) gives the document proportional spacing in 10-point Times Roman type. Contrast the typeset look of this printout with the typewritten look of that shown in Figure C.3.

printer number was changed using the Printer Options menu (Shift-F7 3) from 1 (the A: Courier definition) to 2 (the AC: Tms P definition). Notice the effect that proportional spacing has on the document—it gives it a typeset look.

Figure C.5 shows the page again, this time with the headings increased to 18 points. This was accomplished by issuing a font change before and after each heading in the document. To shift to 18-point type, the pitch was changed from 15* to 8*, and the font was changed from 1 (HP AD TmsRmn10R) to 7 (HP AD TmsRmn18B). At the end of each heading, another font change was issued to shift from 18 points back to 10 points (see Figure C.6). Prior to printing, the printer number was once again changed from 1 to 2 (changes made to the printer on the Options menu are temporary).

Figure C.7 shows the same page from the handbook, again using 10 points for the body of the text and 18 points for the headings. This time, however, the typeface has been changed from Times Roman to Helvetica. Making this printout simply required changing the printer number from 2 (Soft AC: Tms P) to 3 (the Soft AC: Helv P) just before sending the document to the LaserJet printer. Remember, however, that for this procedure to work, the files containing the 10- and 18-point Helvetica fonts must have already been downloaded to the printer.

Creating a New Soft-Fonts Printer Definition

As mentioned earlier, WordPerfect does not have predefined printer definitions for all of the fonts that you get in a soft-font set. However, you can create your own printer definitions to allow you to use additional point sizes and type styles.

To create a printer definition that supports new soft fonts, you need to use WordPerfect's PRINTER program (see "Creating and Modifying Printer Definitions" in Chapter 5 for more details about how to use this program). You will also need to refer to the documentation that comes with your soft-font disks.

Before you attempt to create a new printer definition file, copy the WPRINTER-.FIL and WPFONT.FIL files from your WordPerfect System disk or WordPerfect directory to a new floppy disk. Then copy the PRINTER.EXE file from the Printer 1 disk (if you are using Version 4.2) or the Learning disk (if you are using Version 4.1) to the disk that contains these two files.

After starting the PRINTER program, select option 3, Printer Definitions, from the main menu. Choose option A, Create, and enter the name of one of the currently defined printer definitions to use as a pattern. Select the printer definition that contains a range of fonts most similar to those that you are about to define. For example, if you want to define a new range of point sizes for a Times Roman font in portrait mode, you should use an existing Times Roman definition that specifies portrait mode and contains the font (in different sizes) that you want to use.

WELCOME

Welcome to MagnaCorp. We hope this employee handbook will help to guide you through your first few days here. In addition, it contains valuable information about employee services and benefits available to you. Ask your manager or call the personnel office if you have any questions for which you cannot find the answers in this handbook.

Work Day

The official work day at MagnaCorp is 8:30 a.m. to 5:00 p.m. Flexible hours can be arranged with your manager.

Parking

As parking is limited, please apply to the personnel office for a parking slot assignment.

Hours

Noon to 1 p.m. has been reserved as lunch hour for all employees. Some departments have chosen to take lunch from 11:30 to 12:30 or from 12:30 to 1:30; check with your manager.

Cafeteria

The company cafeteria, located on the third floor, is open from 7 a.m. until 2 p.m. daily. Breakfast is available for your convenience until 9:00. After 2 p.m., vending machines with cold sandwiches and salads are available.

Recreational Facilities

MagnaCorp participates in the city recreational plan and therefore its employees have access to the municipal gym located at First and Brannan Streets. The jogging track and par course in Grant Park are also nearby. Showers and lockers for company employees are located near the south entrance of the main lobby.

Vacation

Full-time permanent employees are eligible for two weeks of paid vacation after six months of continuous employment. During the first five years of service, you earn three weeks of vacation per year. After five years of service, you receive four weeks of vacation.

FIGURE C.5: The sample page from the handbook, this time mixing different point sizes but still using Times Roman type. To give the headings more impact and to set them off dramatically from the body of the text, they have been reset in 18 points (available only in bold in the AC soft font set). Notice the strong visual impact created just by increasing the point size and weight of the headings. Contrast this printout with that shown in Figure C.4.

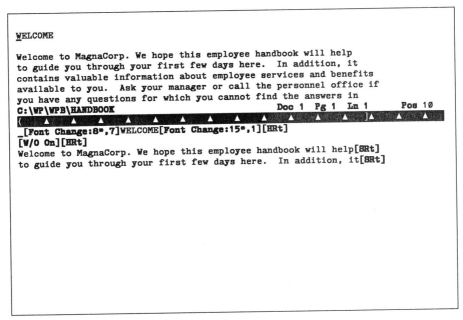

FIGURE C.6: The Reveal codes screen showing the font changes required to increase the headings in the handbook from 10-point to 18-point type. The first font change, which changes the pitch to 8* (the asterisk denotes proportional spacing) and implements Font 7 (HP AD TmsRmn18B), is placed before the heading WELCOME. The second font change, which changes the pitch to 15* and implements Font 1 (HP AD TmsRmn10R), shifts back into the regular 10-point type used in the body of the text and is placed at the end of the heading WELCOME. This combination of font-change codes is repeated for each heading in the employee handbook.

To illustrate the definition process, the following discussion walks you through the creation of a new printer definition for eight new fonts in the Times Roman typeface available in Hewlett-Packard's AE soft font set (this set supplements the fonts in the AC set). To keep the process as simple as possible, the point sizes and styles are matched as much as possible to the original AC: Tms P printer definition.

When prompted for the name for the new definition, LaserJet + Soft AE: Tms P is given. Figure C.8 shows you the printers currently defined. When prompted for the printer definition to use as a pattern, 5, LaserJet +,500 + Soft AC: Tms P, is selected.

After you select the pattern definition, WordPerfect displays a new set of menu selections. To create this definition, you use option 8 (which allows you to define fonts 1–4) and option 9 (which allows you to define fonts 5–8). Figure C.9 shows you the screen that appears when you select option 8.

The screen shown in Figure C.8 contains the escape sequences that are used to shift into each of the four fonts listed (notice that the LaserJet Plus printer does not require escape sequences to shift out of each font). Notice that the first part of these long escape sequences, <27>&10, is the same for each font change. This

WELCOME

Welcome to MagnaCorp. We hope this employee handbook will help to guide you through your first few days here. In addition, it contains valuable information about employee services and benefits available to you. Ask your manager or call the personnel office if you have any questions for which you cannot find the answers in this handbook.

Work Day

The official work day at MagnaCorp is 8:30 a.m. to 5:00 p.m. Flexible hours can be arranged with your manager.

Parking

As parking is limited, please apply to the personnel office for a parking slot assignment.

Hours

Noon to 1 p.m. has been reserved as lunch hour for all employees. Some departments have chosen to take lunch from 11:30 to 12:30 or from 12:30 to 1:30; check with your manager.

Cafeteria

The company cafeteria, located on the third floor, is open from 7 a.m. until 2 p.m. daily. Breakfast is available for your convenience until 9:00. After 2 p.m., vending machines with cold sandwiches and salads are available.

Recreational Facilities

MagnaCorp participates in the city recreational plan and therefore its employees have access to the municipal gym located at First and Brannan Streets. The jogging track and par course in Grant Park are also nearby. Showers and lockers for company employees are located near the south entrance of the main lobby.

Vacation

Full-time permanent employees are eligible for two weeks of paid vacation after six months of continuous employment. During the first five years of service, you earn three weeks of vacation per year. After five years of service, you receive four weeks of vacation.

FIGURE C.7: The sample page from the handbook, this time using the same point sizes as in Figure C.5 but printing in Helvetica instead of Times Roman type. To do this simply required changing the printer number from 2 (the Soft AC: Tms P) to 3 (the Soft AC: Helv P) just before sending the document to the LaserJet printer.

```
                    Printers Currently Defined
 1  Standard Printer                2  DOS Text Printer
 3  LaserJt Reg,+,500+ Q: Cour,LG   4  LaserJt Reg,+,500+ A: Courier
 5  LaserJt+,500+ Soft AC: Tms P    6  LaserJt+,500+ Soft AC: Helv P




Current Printer to Use as a Pattern: 5_
```

FIGURE C.8: Selecting a printer definition to use as a pattern in the PRINTER program. When you create a new printer definition, you always want to choose the current definition that most closely resembles the one you are about to create. In this example, printer definition 5, LaserJet + ,500 + Soft AC: Tms P, is used because it is set up for the same typeface (Times Roman) as the one we are creating and uses similar styles.

sequence is used to shift into portrait mode. To change these fonts to landscape mode, you change this code to <27>&l1O (lowercase L, 1, and uppercase O) for each sequence. Because we want all of the new fonts to be printed in portrait mode, there is no need to modify this part of the escape sequence.

Font 1 is currently defined to shift into 10-point medium Times Roman type. In the new definition, font 1 will be 11 point medium in the same typeface. In the AE soft-font documentation, the escape sequence for this font is listed as

^{E}c(0U^{E}c(s1p11v0s0b5T

The ^{E}c in the font documentation stands for Escape. Remember that when you enter printer control codes in WordPerfect, you must enter the escape character in its ASCII decimal code form, 27, enclosed in angle brackets (notice that this is the case in the escape sequences shown in Figure C.8). Thus, you enter the escape sequence for the new font as

<27>(0U<27>(s1p11vsb5T

Notice that the zeros after the *v* and *s* in the escape sequence have been omitted. They are not necessary when the *v* or *s* attribute is set to 0 (turned off). This is why they are not present in Font 1 in Figure C.8.

To change Font 1 from 10-point to 11-point Times Roman, you select item 1. This places the cursor on the current escape sequence, where it can be edited just like any text in WordPerfect (the editor is in Insert mode). The only modification of this font required is changing the *p* attribute (point size) from 10 to 11. To do this, you move the cursor to the 0 in *p10,* press Del, and type **1.** Then you press Return to return to the Select Item Number prompt.

When editing escape sequences, be careful not to change any more of the code than you have to. Before you begin editing, make a hard copy of the screen with Shift-PrtSc. That way, you can check your changes against the original escape sequence. Do not delete the <M> at the end of each escape sequence. This is a special code that WordPerfect uses to turn on proportional spacing. If you ever inadvertently delete this code, you must replace it by pressing Alt-M (you cannot reenter it by typing the letter *M* enclosed in angle brackets). Also, if you delete one of the <27> codes, you can replace it simply by pressing Esc (you do not have to type 27 and enclose it in angle brackets).

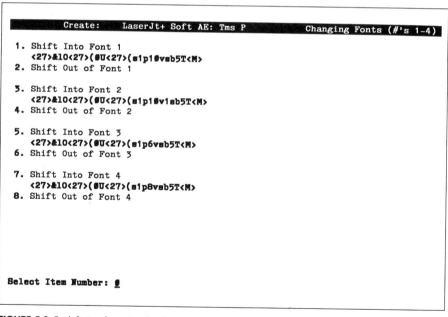

FIGURE C.9: Redefining fonts 1–4 for the new printer definition. Currently, the escape sequences shown in this figure are those used to shift into 10-point medium (1), 10-point italic (3), 6-point medium (5), and 8-point medium (7) type. By slightly editing these control codes, you can make them produce a new group of fonts (see Figure C.10).

Figure C.10 shows you all of the escape sequences for the new fonts after the original codes have been edited. Font 2 for this printer definition now shifts the print to 11-point italic Times Roman (when *v* is set to 1, you get italic type). Font 3 now produces 7-point medium Times Roman type, and Font 4 produces 9-point medium Times Roman type.

After you are finished modifying the font codes and have checked the escape sequences to make sure that they are correct, you press Return to select item 0. This returns you to the previous menu, where you can select option 9 to modify fonts 5–8. Figure C.11 shows these fonts after their escape sequences have been modified to use other point and type styles in the AE font set.

Font 5 has been changed from 8-point italic to 9-point italic type. Font 6 has been changed from 12-point medium type to 18-point medium type (remember that only 18-point bold is available in the AC soft-font set). Font 7 has been changed from 18-point bold type to 24-point medium type. Font 8 has been changed from 30-point bold to 30-point medium type. After all of these changes have been made, you press F7 (Exit) to exit and save the changes. If you want to return to previous menus and use other options, you press Return. However, be sure that you ultimately exit by using F7. If you use F1 (Cancel) or the 0 options to back out of the menus, your changes will not be saved.

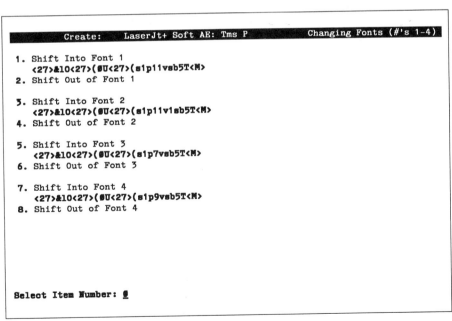

FIGURE C.10: Fonts 1–4 after their escape sequences have been modified for the new Soft AE: Tms P printer definition. Font 1 is now set for 11-point medium (1), Font 2 for 11-point italic (3), Font 3 for 7-point medium (5), and Font 4 for 9-point medium Times Roman type.

The new Soft AE: Tms P printer definition is now ready for use with Word-Perfect. The added fonts complement those already available from the Soft AC: Tms P definition. After exiting the PRINTER program, you can copy the WPRINTER.FIL and WPFONT.FIL files back to your WordPerfect System disk or into your WordPerfect directory on a hard disk.

To use the new Soft AE: Tms P printer definition, you must assign it a printer number. To do this, start WordPerfect, press Shift-F7, type **4,** and select option 3 (Select Printers) from the Printer Control screen. You will see the Soft AE: Tms P printer definition listed among those at the top of the screen. Select a printer number, enter the number given to the Soft AE: Tms P printer definition, and press Return. You will be prompted to define the port, baud rate, and so on. All of these settings should be correct, so you can press Return at each prompt.

When you examine the eight fonts for the Soft AE: Tms P printer definition (select option 2 from the Printer Control screen), you will see that the font descriptions are still those for the Soft AC: Tms P printer definition. Even though you have changed the escape sequences, the names of the character tables (which give each font its description) are not updated. You should make a hard

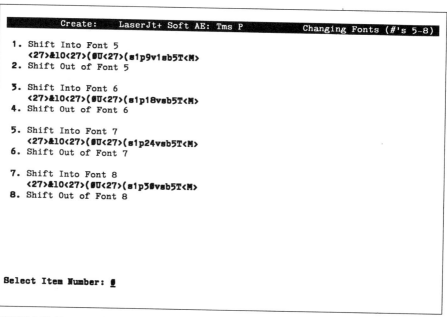

FIGURE C.11: Fonts 5–8 after their escape sequences have been modified for the new Soft AE: Tms P printer definition. Previously, Font 5 produced 8-point italic type. Now it is set for 9-point italic type (1). Font 6 has been changed from 12-point medium type to 18-point medium type (3). Font 7 has been changed from 18-point bold type to 24-point medium type (5). Font 8 has been changed from 30-point bold type to 30-point medium type (7).

copy of these descriptions (use Shift-PrtSc) and mark the new point sizes and styles for each of the fonts that you redefine.

When you want to use one of the new AE fonts in your document, you enter the appropriate font change. Remember to adjust the pitch for the point size used and to append an asterisk (*) to indicate that the font is proportionally spaced. Before you print your document, be sure that you have downloaded all of the fonts that you have used and that you change the number of the printer to be used before you send the document to the LaserJet printer.

By using this technique to create new printer definitions, you can produce many more type styles and print enhancements than are currently available in WordPerfect's font definitions, thus greatly increasing the versatility of your LaserJet printer and the quality of the documents you print in WordPerfect.

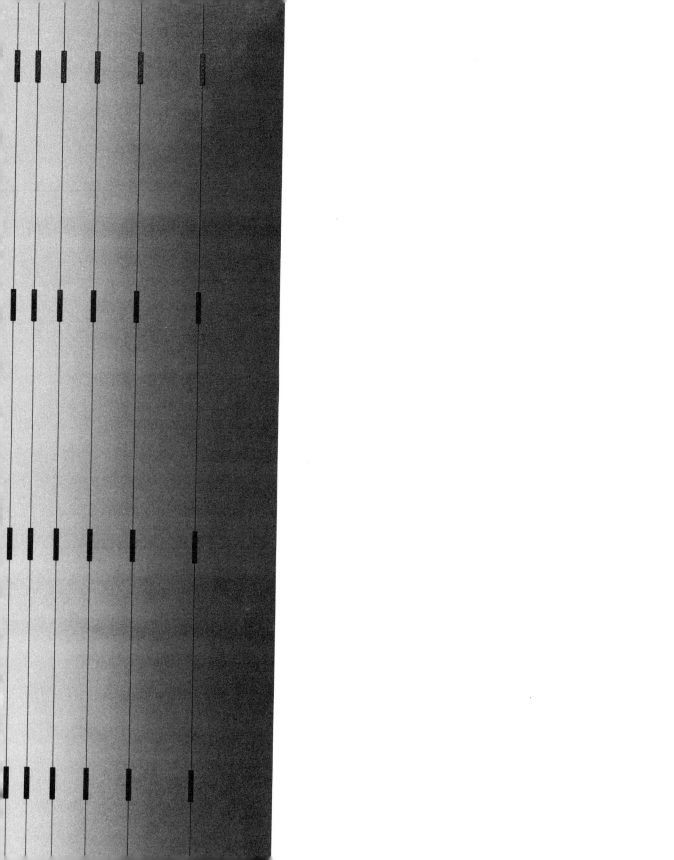

ALTERNATIVE KEYBOARDS

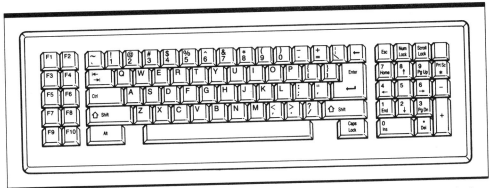

FIGURE D-1: IBM PC AT keyboard. Keys with similar labels work the same way in WordPerfect as described in the text. Note that only keys with specific functions in WordPerfect are labeled here.

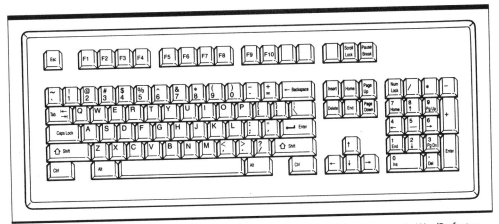

FIGURE D-2: IBM XT/AT enhanced keyboard. Keys with similar labels work the same way in WordPerfect as described in the text. Alternate cursor-control keys such as the duplicate arrow keys and Home and End keys may be used when the Num Lock key is pressed and the numeric keypad is being used for data entry. Note that only keys with specific functions in WordPerfect are labeled here.

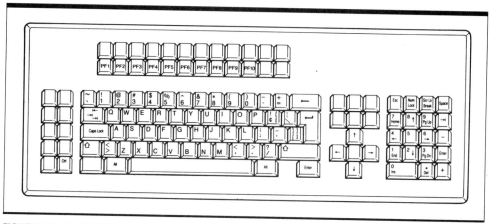

FIGURE D-3: IBM 3270-PC, PC/G, and PC/GX keyboard. Keys with similar labels work the same way in Word-Perfect as described in the text. Function keys PF1 through PF10 substitute for function keys F1 through F10. Alternate cursor movement arrow keys may be used when the Num Lock key is pressed and the numeric keypad is being used for data entry. The numeric keypad also contains duplicate Tab, space, and Enter keys for ease of data entry. Note that only keys with specific functions in WordPerfect are labeled here.

INDEX

COMMAND INDEX

This index lists WordPerfect commands and their key sequences. Page numbers in boldface show where to find the formal reference entry describing the use of the command. For index information on other subjects, refer to the Topical Index (page 652).

A

Advance,
  to specified line [Shift-F1 6], **249–250**, 538, 540
  up or down half line [Shift-F1 (4 *or* 5)], 467,
    469–470, **489–490**
Alignment character definition [Shift-F8 6], 60, **83**
Alt/Ctrl key reassign [Ctrl-F3 3], 472–473,
  494–496
Append marked block to end of disk file [Alt-F4
  Ctrl-F4 3], **116**
Auto rewrite [Ctrl-F3 5], **40–41**

B

Binding width [Shift-F7 3 3], **233, 236**
Block,
  append marked, to end of disk file [Alt-F4 Ctrl-F4
    3], **116**
  cut/copy [Alt-F4 Ctrl-F4], 53–54, 113, 116,
    137–139
  Key [Alt-F4], 111, **136**
  print [Alt-F4 Shift-F7], **241**
  protection [Alt-F4 Alt-F8], **205–206**
Bold Key [F6], 40, **85–86**, 117

C

Calculate [Alt-F7 2], **479**
Cancel Key [F1], **13**, 24–25, 385, 520, 526, 572
Cancel print job [Shift-F7 4 C], **238**
Case,
  lowercase conversion [Shift-F3 2 (block on)], **118**
  uppercase conversion [Shift-F3 1 (block on)], **118**
Centering,
  Key for [Shift-F6], 39, **81–82**
  page between top and bottom margins
    [Alt-F8 3], 58, **202–203**
Character,
  at cursor, delete [Del], 14, 50, **51**, 55, 470
  left of cursor, delete [Backspace], 50, **51**, 55
Characters,
  left of cursor within word, delete [Home
    Backspace], 52
  right of cursor within word, delete [Home Del],
    52
  per inch [Ctrl-F8], 226–227, **246**
  special (extended IBM character set) [Ctrl-V
    ASCII code], 131
Colors [Ctrl-F3 4], **612**
Column,
  cut/copy [Alt-F4 Ctrl-F4 4], **486–487**
  definition, newspaper/parallel [Alt-F7 4],
    353–366, **367–369**

display side by side [Alt-F7 5], **371–372**
math,
  on/off toggle [Alt-F7 1], 459, 474, **477–482**
  definition [Alt-F7 2], 466, **476–477**, 482–486
  retrieve [Ctrl-F4 (4, 5, *or* 6)], 27, **139–140**, 364
  text, on/off toggle [Alt-F7 3], 363, **369–370**
Command, repeat *n* times [Esc *n command*], **13**, 51,
  90
Comment,
  add [Ctrl-F5 (B *or* C)], 41, **43–47**
  edit [Ctrl-F5 C], 46
Conditional end of page [Alt-F8 9], 60, **167–168**
Convert case [Alt-F4 Shift-F3], **118**
Copy, files [F5 Return 8], **276–278**
Ctrl/Alt key reassign [Ctrl-F3 3], 472–473,
  494–496
Cut/copy,
  column [Alt-F4 Ctrl-F4 4], **486–487**
  rectangle [Alt-F4 Ctrl-F4 5], **547–548**
  sentence/paragraph/page [Ctrl-F4 (1, 2, *or* 3)],
    139–140

D

Date key [Shift-F5], **195–198**
Define,
  columns [Alt-F7 4], 353–366, **367–369**
  list/index/table [Alt-F5 6], **311–313**, 318–319,
    327–328, **336–337**, 346–348
  macro [Ctrl-F10], 553, **571–574**
Delete,
  character at cursor [Del], 14, 50, **51**, 55, 470
  character left of cursor [Backspace], 50, **51**, 55
  characters to left of cursor within word [Home
    Backspace], 52
  characters to right of cursor within word [Home
    Del], 52
  files [F5 Return 2], **278**
  to end of line [Ctrl-End], 50, **52–53**
  to end of page [Ctrl-PgDn], 50, **54**
  and Undelete [F1], 38, 53, **58**, 115
  word [Ctrl-Backspace], 50, **51–52**
Disk,
  directory, change [F5 Return 7], **267–271**
  file,
    look at contents of [F5 Return 6], 260,
      272–273
    retrieve [Shift-F10 (*or* F5 Return 1)], **27**
  print from [Shift-F7 4 P (*or* F5 Return 4)], 214,
    234–235, 237–238
  space, display [F5], **280–281**

TOPICAL INDEX

This index lists the general topics covered in the book. For command key sequences, refer to the COM-MAND INDEX. Formatting Codes are shown in Appendix B, pages 621 to 623. Tables of data presented in the text have been listed in their own section, in the front of the book.

Merging (cont.)
  importing data for use in, 585–587
  with keyboard data entry, 387–389
  key sequence commands for, 411–419
  macros in, 406–408
  menus for, creating, 408–411
  option codes for, 386–390, 397–411, 414–419
  pauses during, macros with, 557
  performing, 383–385
  primary/secondary files for, 377, 412
  with printing direct, 386–387
  screen messages during, 389–390
  and sorting, 438–441, 448, 451
Microsoft Windows program, 610
Microspacing, 248
Mil spec (legal style of paragraph numbering), 321, 328
Minus sign (–),
  as indicator of negative numbers, 462, 476
  as nonbreaking hyphen, 122–123, 145
Minus sign (–) for negative numbers, 145
MODE (DOS Command), 630
Moving, text, 113–114
MultiMate program, 2–3, 581, 583

N

Naming, files, 255–257
Negative numbers, designating, 462, 476
Neibauer, Alan R., 411
Nonbreak (hard) space, 123, 144–145
Nonflash option, 610
Nonsynch option, 610–611
Notes. *See* Footnotes/Endnotes
N prefix, 462–464, 479
Numbering,
  footnotes/endnotes, 303–304
  lines, 339–341
  outlines, 326–329
  pages, 159–162, 181–187
  paragraphs, 323–329
Numeric columns, 462, 474
Numeric keypad, 16, 20

O

Orphans/Widows, 37, 157, 166–167, 206–207
Other Mark Text Options screen, 313
Outlines,
  creating, 320–323
  numbering, 326–329
Overstrike, 150–153, 467

P

Page breaks,
  creating and deleting, 9, 80–81, 202–206
  hard, 21, 80, 160, 168, 204, 384
  soft, 21, 160, 166
  unwanted, 167

Page Format menu, 58–59
Page indicator, 8–9
Pages,
  beginning new, 80
  blank, adding/deleting, 161
  centering top to bottom, 202–203
  conditional end of, 60, 167–168
  copying and moving, 113–114
  cutting and copying, 139–141
  deleting to end of, 54
  deleting and undeleting, 114–115
  formatting considerations for, 157–169, 177–178
  keeping lines together at ends of, 204–207
  length of, 34, 36, 67–69, 247
  locating by page number, 21–22, 102
  numbering, 8, 34, 159–162, 165, 181–187
  number, position of, 182–186
  previewing layout of, 179–181
  printing selected, 217, 237–238
  spell checking of, 509, 519
  suppressing numbers on, 200–202
  see also Columns; Documents; Lines; Paragraphs; Tables; Text; Words
Paper,
  sheet-feeder bin for, 36, 221–222, 248
  size considerations for graphics, 535–536
  size of, 33–34, 68, 248
  using legal size, 37–38
  see also Graphics; Pages; Paragraphs; Printers
Paradox program, 588
Paragraph Numbering Definition screen, 328
Paragraphs,
  copying and moving, 113–114
  cutting and copying, 139–141
  deleting, 53–54
  deleting and undeleting, 114–115
  indenting, 77–80
  marking end of, 12
  numbering, 323–329
  sorting, 434–436, 448
Parentheses (as indicator of negative numbers), 462, 466, 476
Parity, 221, 223, 627
Password protection, 257–259, 281–283
Path names, 269
PERMTEMP.BAS/.EXE programs, 629
Pica type, 64–66, 157
Pitch, 34, 217, 226, 246, 626, 632
Plus sign (+), 443, 479
Portrait and landscape fonts, 627, 630
Ports,
  COM1/COM2, 221, 223
  printer, 221
  serial/parallel, 221, 223
  see also Printers
Position indicator, 9, 38

COMMANDS AND FUNCTIONS—LISTED ALPHABETICALLY

COMMAND	KEY SEQUENCE	COMMAND	KEY SEQUENCE
Advance to specified line	Shift-F1 6	Document summary (display)	Ctrl-F5 D
Advance up (or down) half line	Shift-F1 4 (or 5)	Edit a comment	Ctrl-F5 C
Alignment character definition	Shift-F8 6	Edit two documents (switch)	Shift-F3
Append marked block to end of disk file	Alt-F4 Ctrl-F4 3	End of field	F9
		End of record	Shift-F9
Auto rewrite	Ctrl-F3 5	Endnote (create)	Ctrl-F7 5
Binding width	Shift-F7 3 3	Endnote (edit)	Ctrl-F7 6
Block cut/copy	Alt-F4 Ctrl-F4	Execute merge	Ctrl-F9
Block Key	Alt-F4	Exit to DOS temporarily	Ctrl-F1 1
Block protection	Alt-F4 Alt-F8	Exit Key (exit from WordPerfect)	F7
Bold Key	F6	Extended characters	Ctrl-V <ASCII code> Return
Calculate (with Math on)	Alt-F7 2		
Cancel a print job	Shift-F7 4 C	Extended search	Home-F2
Cancel Key	F1	File management	F5
Case conversion	Alt-F4 Shift-F3	Flush Right Key	Alt-F6
Center Key	Shift-F6	Fonts (change)	Ctrl-F8 1
Center page between top and bottom margins	Alt-F8 3	Footnote Key	Ctrl-F7
		Forward Search Key	F2
Change default drive	F5 =	Generate list, index, and tables	Alt-F5 6 8
Characters per inch	Ctrl-F8 1	Go To Key	Ctrl-Home
Colors	Ctrl-F3 4	Hard page break	Ctrl-Return
Column cut or copy	Alt-F4 Ctrl-F4 4	Hard space	Home-Spacebar
Columns (define as newspaper or parallel)	Alt-F7 4	Headers or footers	Alt-F8 6
		Help Key	F3
Comment	Ctrl-F5 B (or C)	Hyphen character (hard)	Home-(hyphen)
Conditional end of page	Alt-F8 9	Hyphenation on/off	Shift-F8 5
Copy files	F5 Return 8	Hyphenation zone (set)	Shift-F8 5 3
Ctrl/Alt key reassign	Ctrl-F3 3	Import DOS text file	Ctrl-F5 2 (or F5 Return 5)
Cut, copy, append a marked block	Alt-F4 Ctrl-F4		
		Indent Key	F4
Cut or copy rectangle	Alt-F4 Ctrl-F4 5	Index (mark word for)	Alt-F5 5
Cut or copy sentence, paragraph, or page	Ctrl-F4 1 (or 2 or 3)	Justification off (on)	Ctrl-F8 3 (or 4)
Date Key	Shift-F5	Left/Right Indent Key	Shift-F4
Define lists, index, table of authorities, table of contents, paragraph/outline numbering	Alt-F5 6	Line drawing	Ctrl-F3 2
		Line Format Key	Shift-F8
		Line numbering	Ctrl-F8 B 2
Define macro	Ctrl-F10	Line spacing	Shift-F8 4
Delete character at cursor	Del	Lines per inch	Ctrl-F8 2
Delete character left of cursor	Backspace	List Files Key	F5
Delete characters to left of cursor within word	Home Backspace	List (mark text for list)	Alt-F4 Alt-F5 2
		Lock a file	Ctrl-F5 4
Delete characters to right of cursor within word	Home Del	Look at contents of a disk file	F5 Return 6
		Lowercase conversion	Shift-F3 2 (Block on)
Delete file(s)	F5 Return 2	Macro Define Key	Ctrl-F10
Delete to end of line	Ctrl-End	Macro Key (invoke)	Alt-F10
Delete to end of page	Ctrl-PgDn	Margin release	Shift-Tab
Delete word	Ctrl-Backspace	Margins (set)	Shift-F8 3
Disk directory (change)	F5 Return 7	Mark Text Key	Alt-F5
Display all print jobs	Shift-F7 4 D	Math column definition	Alt-F7 2
Display columns side by side	Alt-F7 5	Math columns on	Alt-F7 1
Display disk space	F5 Return	Math/Columns Key	Alt-F7
Display printers and fonts	Shift-F7 4 2	Merge Codes Key (insert codes)	Alt-F9
Document summary (create)	Ctrl-F5 A		